Integrating Language Arts and Social Studies for Kindergarten and Primary Children

Integrating Language Arts and Social Studies for Kindergarten and Primary Children

Patricia L. Roberts
California State University, Sacramento

John Jarolimek and Walter C. Parker
Donna E. Norton and Saundra E. Norton
Carol Seefeldt and Nita Barbour
Gail E. Tompkins and Kenneth Hoskisson

Merrill,
an imprint of Prentice Hall
Englewood Cliffs, New Jersey   Columbus, Ohio

Library of Congress Cataloging-in-Publication Data

Roberts, Patricia
    Integrating language arts and social studies for kindergarten and
primary children / Patricia L. Roberts ; John Jarolimek . . . [et
al.].
      p. cm.
    Includes bibliographical references and index.
    ISBN 0-02-408460-3 (pbk.)
    1. Language arts (Preschool)   2. Language arts (Primary)
3. Social sciences—Study and teaching (Early childhood)
4. Curriculum planning.   5. Language arts—Correlation with content
subjects.   6. Learning, Psychology of.   I. Title.
LB1140.5.L3R63   1996
372.6—dc20   95-33302
                                            CIP

Cover art: ©Manual Morales/The Image Bank
Editor: Bradley J. Potthoff
Production Editor: Louise N. Sette
Photo Editor: Anne Vega
Design Coordinator: Jill E. Bonar
Text Designer: Elm Street Publishing Services, Inc.
Cover Designer: Proof Positive/Farrowlyne Associates
Production Manager: Deidra M. Schwartz

This book was set in Times Roman by Carlisle Communications, Ltd., and was printed and bound by
The Banta Company. The cover was printed by The Banta Company.

Photo credits: Scott Cunningham, Merrill/Prentice Hall (pp. 2, 396, 450); Anne Vega, Merrill/Prentice
Hall (p. 184)

Printed in the United States of America

10 9 8 7 6 5 4 3 2 1

ISBN: 0-02-408460-3

Prentice-Hall International (UK) Limited, *London*
Prentice-Hall of Australia Pty. Limited, *Sydney*
Prentice-Hall of Canada, Inc., *Toronto*
Prentice-Hall Hispanoamericana, S. A., *Mexico*
Prentice-Hall of India Private Limited, *New Delhi*
Prentice-Hall of Japan, Inc., *Tokyo*
Simon & Schuster Asia Pte. Ltd., *Singapore*
Editora Prentice-Hall do Brasil, Ltda., *Rio de Janeiro*

PREFACE

*I*ntegrating Language Arts and Social Studies for Kindergarten and Primary Children sets forth an integated approach to curriculum in which social studies content, literature, and language arts skills are central. Language arts skills—listening, speaking, reading, writing, and thinking—are integrated into social studies and literature experiences that are based on meaningful content and children's experience. Children are invited to get involved in a variety of creative activities and learning situations that range from individual inquiry to group interactions.

ORGANIZATION AND FEATURES OF THE BOOK

Integrating Language Arts and Social Studies for Kindergarten and Primary Children is divided into four parts. Part I offers six chapters that describe the fundamentals important to teachers of children in kindergarten through grade 4. These chapters serve as an educational underpinning for the chapters that follow.

Part II contains six chapters. Chapter 7 introduces early language arts learning in the elementary school (kindergarten through grade 4) and offers guidelines for the curriculum. From Chapters 8 through 12, readers discover specific components relevant to teaching language arts from kindergarten through grade 4.

Part III illustrates how the fundamentals of teaching and learning described in Part I and the curriculum guidelines outlined in Part II can be implemented to meet children's needs while teaching social studies in kindergarten through grade 4. Chapter 13 thus focuses on early skills associated with social studies learning, and Chapter 14 focuses on ways to integrate social studies as the primary emphasis in an integrated curriculum for children, K–4. In these chapters, readers will discover ways to engage children in problems and issues and help them make links between social studies, language arts, and the world around them. Chapter 15 emphasizes student-centered instruction to reach the diverse cultural backgrounds and learning abilities of children with special needs.

Part IV offers instructional activites that engage children in collaborative learning, integrate language arts and social studies, and encourage cooperation and interaction. Chapter 16 presents activities designed to integrate language arts and social studies in interesting and meaningful ways and to encourage collaborative learning and cooperation among the children.

Integrating Language Arts and Social Studies for Kindergarten and Primary Children has several unique features designed to make the material as relevant as possible.

Spectrum of Integrated Curriculum

Part I begins with the Spectrum of Integrated Curriculum. This Spectrum provides a view of what an integrated curriculum and learning are really like from the teacher's point of view. The various steps in the spectrum show how teachers organize curriculum in various ways for integrated learning.

Advance Organizers

Each chapter begins with advance organizers that help readers preview the aspect of integrating language arts and social studies that is discussed on the subsequent pages.

End-of-Chapter Material

Each chapter ends with questions and activities suitable for either individual inquiry or group study and discussion. The activities are designed to help readers develop and polish their teaching skills related to teaching an integrated curriculum. Readers are guided to further reading by the references and resources.

ACKNOWLEDGMENTS

We, as editors, authors, and contributors, extend our appreciation to those who provided evaluative material for this book at various steps in its development. Particular thanks go to Brad Potthoff, Editor; Linda Scharp, Developmental Editor; Richard D. Kellough, Series Editor; and to the many teachers who tried activities in their classrooms and discussed their ideas for the manuscript. We hope that you, the reader, will find the book useful. We value your feedback about it.

Patricia Roberts

BRIEF CONTENTS

CONTENTS

PART II
Methods and Activities for Teaching Language Arts   184

7   Early Language Arts Learning   187

8   Listening   211

PART III
Methods and Activities for Social Studies 396

13 Early Social Studies Learning 399

14 Integrating Social Studies Across the Curriculum 419

Integrating Children's Learning: Rationale and Methods

In recent years, many educators have realized that, to be most effective in teaching the culturally and linguistically diverse children in today's classrooms, much of the learning in each discipline should be integrated with the whole curriculum and made meaningful to the lives of the children rather than simply taught as unrelated and separate disciplines at the same time each day (Watson & Konicek, 1990). In this book, we will describe the integrated curriculum related to the language arts and the social studies—especially for children in kindergarten through grade 4.

This book offers an approach in which social studies (content such as history, geography, economics, political science, anthropology, and sociology) and language arts (speaking, listening, reading, and writing) are integrated. Language skills, knowledge, and attitudes related to the social studies are taught in meaningful contexts as children study content areas and literature. In this integrated approach, children read to gather information from literature and social sciences. They read, reflect, and talk about what they read and hear, and they discuss before writing. They work together to compose, revise, and use the mechanical aspects of writing—punctuation and capitalization. They present their findings in various ways—reporting, demonstrating, dramatizing.

THE SPECTRUM OF *INTEGRATED CURRICULUM**

When learning about *integrated curriculum,* it is easy to be confused by the plethora of terms that are used, such as *thematic instruction, transdisciplinary instruction, multidisciplinary teaching, integrated studies, interdisciplinary curriculum, interdisciplinary thematic instruction,* and *integrated curriculum.* In essence, today, all of these terms mean the same thing. Further, because it is not always easy to tell where curriculum leaves off and instruction begins, let's assume for now that there is no difference between *curriculum* and *instruction.* We will use the terms *integrated curriculum* and *integrated instruction* interchangeably in this text.

Definition of *Integrated Curriculum*

The term *integrated curriculum* (or any of its synonyms) refers to both a way of teaching and a way of planning and organizing the instructional program so the discrete disciplines of subject matter are related to one another in a design that matches the developmental needs of the learners and that helps to connect their learning in ways that are meaningful to their current and past experiences. Integrated curriculum is the antithesis of traditional, disparate subject matter-oriented teaching and curriculum designations.

The concept of integrated curriculum is not new. It has gone in and out of favor throughout most of the history of education in this country. Thus efforts to integrate student learning have had varying labels.

---

*Developed by Richard D. Kellough.

The most recent popularity of integrated curriculum stems from the following movements:

1. Some of the National Science Foundation-supported, discovery-oriented, student-centered projects of the late 1950s, such as *Elementary School Science* (ESS), an integrated science program for grades K–6; *Man: A Course of Study* (MACOS), a hands-on, anthropology-based program for fifth graders; and *Environmental Studies* (name later changed to *ESSENCE*), an interdisciplinary program for use at all grades, K–12, regardless of subject-matter orientation.
2. The "middle school movement," which had its beginning in the 1960s.
3. The whole-language movement in language arts, which had its beginning in the 1980s.

Today's renewed interest in the development and implementation of integrated curriculum and instruction has risen from at least three sources: (1) the successful curriculum integration enjoyed by exemplary middle-level schools, (2) the literature-based movement in reading and language arts, and (3) recent research in cognitive science and neuroscience about how children learn (discussed in Chapter 1).

As is true for traditional curriculum and instruction, an integrated curriculum approach is not without critics. As stated by Jarolimek and Foster (1993),

> Parents and teachers who find conventional schools too highly structured, too regimented, and too adult-dominated find the child-centered activities of the integrated curriculum mode attractive [but] with its apparent lack of organization, its informality, and the permissiveness allowed [and] at a time when the nation seems to be calling for more fundamental approaches to education [and because school budgets are tighter], the integrated curriculum mode faces an uncertain future. (p. 149)

An integrated curriculum approach may not necessarily be the best approach for every school, nor the best for all learning for every child, nor is it necessarily the manner by which every teacher should or must always plan and teach.

Levels of Curriculum Integration

Efforts to connect children's learning with their experiences fall at various places on a spectrum or continuum, as illustrated in the accompanying table, from the least integrated instruction (level 1) to the most integrated (level 5).

This illustration should not be interpreted as going from "worst case scenario" (far left) to "best case scenario" (far right), although some experts may interpret it in exactly that way. It is meant solely to show how efforts to integrate fall on a continuum of sophistication and complexity. As a generalization, and for reasons that should become evident as you read this book, many teachers' personal preference is for an integrated curriculum somewhere at or between levels 3 and 4. Descriptions of each level of the continuum follow.

Level 1 is the traditional organization of curriculum and classroom instruction, in which teachers plan and arrange the subject-specific scope and sequence using topic outlines. Any attempts to help students connect their learning and their experiences are up to individual classroom teachers. A fourth-grade student in a school and classroom that have subject-specific instruction at varying times of the day (reading and language arts at 8:00, mathematics at 9:00, social studies at 10:30, and so on), is probably learning in a level 1 instructional environment, especially when what is being learned in one subject has little or no connection with content in another. This lack of integration also holds true for students who move during the school day from classroom to classroom, teacher to teacher, subject to subject, from one topic to another. A topic in science, for example, might be "earthquakes." A related topic in social studies might be "the social consequences of natural disasters." However, these two topics may not be studied by a student at the same time.

| LEAST INTEGRATED | | | | MOST INTEGRATED |
LEVEL 1	LEVEL 2	LEVEL 3	LEVEL 4	LEVEL 5
Subject-specific topic outline	Subject-specific thematic approach	Multidisciplinary thematic approach	Interdisciplinary thematic approach	Integrated thematic approach
No student collaboration in planning	Minimal student input	Some student input	Considerable student input in selecting themes and in planning	Maximum student and teacher collaboration
Teacher solo	Solo or teams	Solo or teams	Solo or teams	Solo or teams
Student input into decision making—low		Student input into decision making—high		Student input into decision making very high

If the same students are learning English/language arts, social studies/history, mathematics, or science using a thematic approach rather than a topic outline, then they are learning at **level 2** integration. At this level, themes for one discipline are not necessarily planned to correspond with themes of another or to be taught simultaneously. The difference between what is a topic and what is a theme is not always clear. But, for example, whereas "earthquakes" and "social consequences of natural disasters" are topics, "natural disasters" could be the theme or umbrella under which these two topics could fall. At this level, students may have some input into the decision making involved in planning themes and content.

When the same students are learning two or more of their core subjects (English/language arts, social studies/history, mathematics, and science) around a common theme, such as the theme "natural disasters," from one or more teachers, they are learning at **level 3** integration. At this level, teachers agree on a common theme and then *separately* cover that theme in their individual subject areas, usually at the same time during the school year. So, what students are learning from a teacher in one class is related to what they are concurrently learning in another or several others. Students may have some input into the decision making involved in selecting and planning themes and content. This is a commonly used approach and is the minimum level of expected participation for which this book is designed. (For primary-level teachers in self-contained classrooms, the logistics of integration are less complicated than when two or more teachers must collaborate for the integration to be successful.)

Level 4 integration occurs when teachers and students collaborate on a common theme and its content and when discipline boundaries begin to disappear as teachers teach about this common theme, either solo (as in a self-contained classroom) or as an interdisciplinary teaching team (comprised of several teachers working with a common group of students, such as in a school-within-a-school configuration).

When teachers and students have collaborated on a common theme and its content, when discipline boundaries are truly blurred during instruction, and when teachers of several grade levels (e.g., grades 2, 3, and 4) and of various subjects teach toward student understanding of aspects of the common theme, then this is **level 5,** an integrated thematic approach. (For detailed accounts of teaching at this level of integration, see Stevenson and Carr, 1993.)

Major Purposes in an Integrated Curriculum*

A major purpose of the integrated curriculum is to teach children to become self-reliant and independent problem solvers. Thus, integrated curriculum involves children directly and purposefully in learning. Another purpose is to help children to understand and appreciate the extent to which school learning is interrelated rather than separated into a variety of discrete subjects and skills, as is the case in traditional curriculum. An integrated curriculum is designed to create a high level of interest in learning that will become personalized and individualized. It seeks to construct situations in which children can learn what they want and need to know rather than what the curriculum specifies. As in inquiry, the purpose of integrated curriculum is to emphasize the process of learning as opposed to specific subject matter and skills. Further, this curriculum capitalizes on the social values of learning. Children are encouraged to work with others in collaborative and cooperative learning endeavors.

Assumptions in an Integrated Curriculum

According to Jarolimek and Parker (1993), several assumptions are made in the integrated curriculum approach:

- It is assumed that children have certain natural drives, urges, and interests that they bring to school with them.
- The teacher explores the backgrounds and interests of the children and converts these interests into learning activities.
- The teacher serves as a guide, adviser, and facilitator rather than as only a director of learning. To do this, the teacher is skilled, resourceful, and imaginative and sees possibilities for school-related learnings that interest the children. For example, the teacher can stimulate children's learning and provide learning materials for them to handle, to use in construction, to manipulate, to experiment with, to explore, and to puzzle over.
- The children are centrally involved in the learning process. It is expected that the students will initiate some activities and will assume responsibility for their own learning.
- A rich and stimulating learning environment with a wide variety of assorted learning materials provides children with many opportunities to explore their interests and to learn from direct experiences. The environment is warm, friendly, and stress-free, enabling the teacher to structure and guide the explorations of the children without stifling their initiative.
- Learning best takes place in settings that encourage social interaction and collaboration—students working with each other. Cross-age grouping is encouraged because children learn from each other.
- Evaluation of learning in the integrated curriculum is related to the purposes of this approach where the teacher observes and documents the extent to which students are involving themselves in their own learning—how well they are sharing, collaborating, cooperating, and assuming responsibility. The teacher will also evaluate behaviors such as these: how well students confront and work through problems; how well they use reading, writing, speaking, and listening as tools of learning; the extent to which their work shows improvement; and the extent to which they overcome their learning deficiencies. Emphasis is on individual progress rather than on comparing a student's achievement with that of class peers or with national test norms.

---

*Material in this section is drawn from Jarolimek and Foster (1993), (pp. 149–152). By permission of Prentice Hall Publishing Company.

In Part I, you will review important historical and recent work of cognitive psychologists, work that has led to a modern view of teaching for meaningful understanding, and a presentation of the relevant instructional methodology. As a classroom teacher, your instructional task is two-fold: (1) to plan for and provide developmentally appropriate hands-on experiences, with useful materials and the supportive environment necessary for children's meaningful exploration and discovery; (2) to know how to facilitate the most meaningful and longest lasting learning possible once the child's mind has been activated by the hands-on experience. This book is designed to help you complete those tasks. Although using examples that are mostly from language arts and social studies, Part I provides fundamentals that are important to all teachers of children from kindergarten through grade 4. ■

REFERENCES

Jarolimek, J., & Foster, C. D. (1993). *Teaching and learning in the elementary school,* 5th ed. Englewood Cliffs, NJ: Merrill/Prentice Hall.

Jarolimek, J., & Parker, W. C. (1993). *Social studies in elementary education* (9th ed.). Englewood Cliffs, NJ: Merrill/Prentice Hall.

Stevenson, C., & Carr, J. F. (Eds.). (1993). *Integrated studies in the middle grades.* New York: Teachers College Press.

Watson, B., & Konicek, R. (1990, May). Teaching for conceptual change: Confronting children's experience. *Phi Delta Kappan, 71* (9), 680–685.

CHAPTER 1

Learning and the Intellectual Development of Children

A n understanding of children—how they develop intellectually, how they think, what they think about, and how they learn and process information—is essential to being an effective classroom teacher. Much of what is known about how children learn and process information is knowledge that has been gained from cognitive research of recent years.

This chapter focuses on how children learn and process information. Specifically, this chapter is designed to help you understand the following points:

1. What is meant by *meaningful learning*.
2. The characteristics and developmental needs of children of grades K–4.
3. How learning is constructed.
4. The contributions of learning theorists Jean Piaget, Lev Vygotsky, Robert Gagné, Jerome Bruner, and David Ausubel.
5. The importance of learning as a cyclic process.
6. The value of using multilevel of instruction.
7. The rate of cognitive development and factors that effect it.
8. How conceptual understanding develops.
9. The process and benefits of learning by discovery.
10. The value of concept mapping as a cognitive tool.
11. The significance of decision making and the thought-process phases of instruction.
12. The value and variety of styles in teaching and learning.
13. The significance of the concept of learning modalities and intelligence.

A. MEANINGFUL LEARNING: THE CONSTRUCTION OF UNDERSTANDING

We know that the mere accumulation of pieces of information is at the lowest end of a spectrum of types of learning. To develop higher levels of thinking and meaningful learning, recent research supports the use of integrated instructional strategies that help children to make connections to what is being learned—strategies such as the whole language approach to reading and interdisciplinary thematic teaching.

Let's begin with a review of important historical and recent work of cognitive psychologists. In opposition to the traditional view that sees teaching as merely covering the prescribed material, a more modern view stresses the importance of learning being a personal process by which each learner builds on the personal knowledge and experiences that he or she brings to the learning experience. *Meaningful learning is learning that results when the learner makes connections between a new experience and prior knowledge and experiences that were stored in long-term memory.* For meaningful learning to occur, the concept of correct instruction, then, is to begin where the children are, with what they have experienced and know, or think they know, and correct their misconceptions while building on and connecting their understandings and experiences.

Like the construction of any large building, meaningful learning is a gradual and sometimes painstakingly slow process. As emphasized by Watson and Konicek (1990, p. 685), when compared with traditional instruction, teaching in this constructivist mode is slower, involving more discussion, debate, and the re-creation of ideas. Rather than following clearly defined and previously established steps, the curriculum evolves. It depends heavily on materials, and to a great extent, it is determined by the children's interests and questions. Less content is covered, fewer facts are memorized and tested for, and progress is sometimes very slow.

The methodology uses what is referred to as a *hands-on doing* (i.e., the learner is learning by doing) and *minds-on learning* (i.e., the learner is thinking about what she or he is learning and doing) approach to constructing, and often reconstructing, the child's perceptions. Hands-on learning engages the learner's mind, causing questioning. Hands-on and minds-on learning encourages students to question and then to devise ways of investigating tentative but temporarily satisfactory answers to questions. As a classroom teacher, your instructional task, then, is essentially two-fold: (1) to plan for and provide the hands-on experiences, providing the materials and the supportive environment necessary for children's meaningful exploration and discovery; and (2) to facilitate the most meaningful and longest lasting learning possible once the child's mind has been activated by the hands-on experience.

B. CHARACTERISTICS OF CHILDREN

From experience and research, specialists have come to accept certain precepts about children regardless of their individual genetic or cultural differences. A conscientious teacher will want to know that:

Universal Qualities

Children are adventurous. Children love to explore. When given an object with which to play, younger children try to take it apart and then put it together again. They love to touch and feel objects. Children are always wondering "what will happen if . . .?" and suggesting ideas for finding out. Children are natural questioners. The words *what, why,* and *how* are common in their vocabulary. While investigating, children work and learn best when they experience firsthand. Therefore, you should provide a wide variety of experiences that involve hands-on learning. Hands-on learning, questioning, and exploring engage the learner's mind. You should encourage rather than discourage their questions.

Children are energetic. Children would rather not sit for a long time; for some, it is nearly impossible. They would rather do than to listen, and even while listening, they may move their bodies restlessly. This difficulty in sitting quietly has a direct bearing on the child's attention span. As a result, teaching should provide for kinesthetic learning by providing many activities that give children the opportunity to be physically active.

Children are egocentric. Most children are egocentric: things are important to them insofar as they relate to themselves. In primary-grade children, this egocentricity is quite natural, because children find themselves in a strange yet wonderful world, filled with phenomena that are constantly effecting them. They tend to interpret the phenomena based on how the events affect them personally and to use everything they learn for the express purpose of adjusting to the world in which they live. As a teacher, you can help children understand this world and adjust to it in positive ways. As children develop psychologically, emotionally, and intellectually, they overcome this egocentricity.

An important skill needed for overcoming egocentricity is listening with understanding and empathy. Many children, however, and some adults, are not very good listeners. To help children develop this skill, you might ask a child to paraphrase what another has said and then ask the first child if, in fact, that is what he or she said. If it isn't, then have the child repeat what he or she said, and again ask another child to paraphrase that statement. Repeat this activity until the original child's statement is correctly understood.

Children are interpretive. Children are constantly interpreting their environment even though their interpretations are often incomplete, or even incorrect (and are referred to variously in the literature as *naive theories,* misconceptions, conceptual misunderstandings, or incongruent schemata). Children will, however, continue to arrive at interpretations that satisfy them and that allow them to function adequately in their daily lives.

Learners try to attach meaning to their experiences by referring to a body of related information from past experiences and knowledge stored in long-term memory. These experiences and knowledge are called networks or *schema*. A schema (plural, *schemata*) is a mental construct by which a learner organizes his or her perceptions of the environment. Learning continues as the learner assimilates new information into a schema and modifies or forms a new schema (a process known as *accommodation*), thus allowing the learner to function adequately.

Children's interpretations of phenomena change with their increasing maturity. Consequently, students are engaged in a constant process of revising interpretations as they grow in ability to understand and to think abstractly. A technique called concept mapping, discussed later, is a learning strategy useful in helping children integrate their knowledge and understandings that result in useful schemata (Novak, 1993).

Children come to your classroom with existing schemata about almost everything, which from an adult's point of view may or may not always be congruent with accepted views but, nevertheless, are valid. As a teacher, one of your more important tasks is to correct children's misconceptions. Not unlike many adults, children naturally resist changes to their interpretations, so correcting their misconceptions and building their understandings is no easy task. Even after children have had corrective instruction, they will often persist in their misconceptions. As Martin Haberman (1991) has pointed out, "Whenever children are asked to think about an idea in a way that questions common sense or a widely accepted assumption, that relates new ideas to ones previously learned, or that applies an idea to the problems of living, then there is a chance that good teaching is going on " (p. 294).

Regardless of the subject and grade level, children come to your classroom with misconceptions, and correcting their misconceptions is often a long and arduous task that demands your understanding, patience, and creative instruction. Children are much more likely to modify data from their experiences to accommodate their schemata than they are to change their beliefs as a result of new experiences (Watson & Konicek, 1990, p. 683). Perhaps this isn't so difficult to understand when we recall stories of reputable scientists, politicians, and attorneys who, stubbornly, were tempted to modify data to support their beliefs. Being stubbornly persistent, yet remaining open to change, are virtuous, although conflicting, human attributes. In the words of Brooks and Brooks (1993),

> Children of all ages develop and refine ideas about phenomena and then tenaciously hold onto these ideas as eternal truths. Even in the face of "authoritative" intervention and "hard" data that challenge their views, children typically adhere staunchly to their original notions. Through experiences that might engender contradictions, the frameworks for these notions weaken, causing children to rethink their perspectives and form new understandings. (p. 113)

Children are curious. Children are naturally inquisitive. While a young child's world is filled with wonder and excitement, an older child's curiosity will vary, depending on what catches his or her interest. Generally speaking, children are more interested in things that move than things that don't. They are more interested in objects that make things happen than those to which things are happening. Their curiosity is peaked by things that appear mysterious and magical. Good instruction takes advantage of this natural curiosity. That is why, for example, the use of "history mysteries or history ghost stories" and discrepant events (i.e., events that cause cognitive dissonance) are so popular and successful in developing children's interest in social studies. In the words of Brooks and Brooks (1993), "The line between cognitive dissonance, which can provoke a child's desire to persevere, and intrapersonal frustration, which interferes with the child's desire to resolve dissonance, is a fine one that is often difficult to recognize. To foster the development of children's abilities to organize and understand their individual worlds, teachers need to encourage children to find their own problems" (p. 29).

Children are persistent. As implied in the preceding discussion, children are tenacious. They like to achieve their objectives and will spend much time and effort at activities that are important and interesting to them. With those efforts comes a feeling of personal satisfaction and a sense of accomplishment. You must take advantage of this persistence and desire to achieve by helping children to acquire ownership of what is to be learned and by providing interesting and meaningful learning activities.

Children are social. Children like to be with their peers and to be accepted by them. They like to work together in planning and carrying out their activities. They work well together when given proper encouragement, when they understand the procedures, and when they are given clear direction and a worthwhile task. Each child develops a self-concept through these social interactions in school. The child will develop a satisfactory self-esteem when given an opportunity to work with others, to offer ideas, and to work out peer relationships. Your teaching can help foster not only the learning but also the development of each child's self-esteem by incorporating social-interaction teaching strategies, such as cooperative learning, peer tutoring, and cross-age teaching.

Children have a variety of psychological needs. Abraham Maslow (1970) presented a continuum of psychological needs ranging from the most basic—*physiological* (food, clothing, and shelter) and *security* needs (feeling of safety)—to *social* (sense of love and belonging) and *self-esteem* needs to the highest—*self-actualization* needs (full use of talents, capacities, and abilities, and acceptance of self and others). When children are frustrated because of lack of satisfaction of one or more of these needs, their classroom behavior is affected, and their learning is stifled (Reed & Sautter, 1990, pp. K1–K12). As a result, some children become aggressive and disrupt normal classroom procedures, hoping in this way to satisfy a basic need for recognition. Others become antisocial, apathetic, and fail to participate in class activities. Perhaps it is best explained by D. S. Eitzen (1992):

> Everyone needs a dream. Without a dream, we become apathetic. Without a dream, we become fatalistic. Without a dream and the hope of attaining it, society becomes our enemy. We educators must realize that some young people act in antisocial ways because they have lost their dreams. And we must realize that we as a society are partly responsible for that loss. Teaching is a noble profession whose goal is to increase the success rate for *all* children. We must do everything we can to achieve this goal. If not, we—society, schools, teachers, and children—will all fail. (p. 590)

The wise teacher is alert to any child whose basic psychological needs are not being satisfied. Perhaps it is the student who comes to school hungry. Perhaps it is the one who comes to school feeling insecure because of problems at home. Maybe it is the one who comes to school tired from spending each night sleeping and living out of an automobile or from being abused by a parent, friend, or relative. Although as a classroom teacher you cannot solve all the ailments of society, you do have an opportunity and responsibility to make all children feel welcome, respected, and wanted, at least while in your classroom.

Understanding the characteristics of children and their basic needs is the foundation for studying how they learn and think and how you can use that knowledge in your teaching.

C. INTELLECTUAL DEVELOPMENT AND HOW CHILDREN LEARN

Jean Piaget, Lev Vygotsky, Robert Gagné, Jerome Bruner, and David Ausubel are five learning theorists who have played major roles in developing today's theory of effective instruction. (See Figure 1.1.) Of the several psychologists whose theories of learning had an impact during the last half of the twentieth century, perhaps no other had such a wide-ranging influence on education as Swiss psychologist Jean Piaget (1896–1980). Although Piaget began to publish his insights in the 1920s, his work was not popularized in this country until the 1960s.

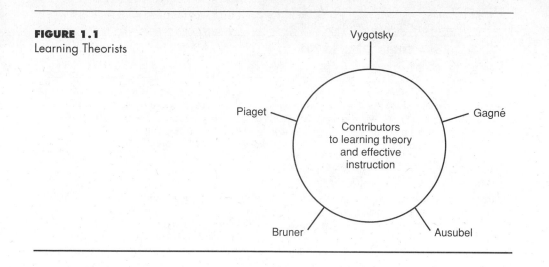

FIGURE 1.1
Learning Theorists

Piaget's Theory of Cognitive Development

Related to the intellectual development of the child, we now know the importance of the richness of a child's learning experiences (especially from birth to about age 11). The importance of the learning experiences that are afforded in the critical school years of kindergarten through grade 4 cannot be overstated.

Maintaining that knowledge is created as children interact with their social and physical environment, Piaget postulated four stages (or periods) of cognitive development from birth to post-adolescence (see Figure 1.2). Mental development begins with the first stage and, without skipping a stage, progresses developmentally through each succeeding stage.

Age ranges in Piaget's stages of cognitive development. You must be cautious about relying too much on the age ranges assigned to Piaget's periods of cognitive development because, these ages can vary widely depending on a number of factors, including the assessment procedures used. Furthermore, when confronted with perplexing situations, many learners, including adults, tend to revert to an earlier developmental stage.

Multilevel Instruction

Your students will likely be at different stages (and substages) of mental development, particularly by the fourth grade. It is important to try to attend to each child's developmental level. To do that, many teachers use *multilevel instruction* (known also as multitasking). Multilevel instruction is when different children are working at different tasks to accomplish the same objective or are working at different tasks to accomplish different objectives. When integrating disciplines, multitasking is an important and useful, perhaps even necessary, strategy.

Rate of Cognitive Development and Factors That Affect It

Piaget's four stages are general descriptions of the psychological processes in cognitive development, but the rate of development varies widely among children. The rate of cognitive development is affected by the individual's maturation, which is controlled by inherited biological factors and by the child's health, by the richness of the child's experiences and social interactions, and by the child's *equilibration*.

Concept Development

Equilibration is the learner's ability to regulate the processes of *assimilation* (input of new information into existing schemata) and *accommodation* (development of new or modification of old schemata). *Equilibrium* is the balance between assimilation and accommodation, a balance for which the brain is always internally striving. Disequilibrium is the state of imbalance. When disequilibrium occurs, the brain is motivated to assimilate and to accommodate. With or without a teacher's guidance, learners *will* assimilate information. The teacher's task is to facilitate the learner's continuing accurate construction of old and new

FIGURE 1.2
Piaget's Stages of Cognitive Development

Sensorimotor Stage (Birth to Age 2)

This is the stage from birth until about age 2. At this stage, children are bound to the moment and to their immediate environment. Learning and behaviors at this stage stem from the direct interaction with stimuli that the child can see or feel. Objects that are not seen are found only by random searching. Through direct interaction, the child begins to build mental concepts, associating actions and reactions, and later in the stage will begin to label people and objects and to show imagining. For example, seeing a parent preparing the child's food tells the child that he or she will soon be eating. The child, then, is developing a practical base of knowledge that forms the foundation for learning in the next stage.

Preoperational Stage (Ages 2–7)

From about ages 2 to 7, children at the preoperational stage can imagine and think before acting, rather than only respond to external stimuli. This stage is called *preoperational* because children do not use logical operations in thinking. In this stage, children are egocentric. Their worldview is subjective rather than objective. Because of egocentrism, it is difficult for them to consider and accept another person's point of view. They are perceptually oriented, that is, they make judgments based on how things look to them. These children do not think logically, and therefore do not reason by implication. Instead, they use an intuitive approach. At this stage, when confronted with new and discrepant information about a phenomenon, they adjust the new information to accommodate their existing beliefs about it.

At this stage, children can observe and describe variables (properties of an object or aspects of a phenomenon), but they concentrate on just one variable at a time, usually a variable that stands out visually. Children cannot coordinate variables, so they have difficulty in realizing that an object has several properties. Consequently, it is difficult for them to combine parts into a whole. Children at this stage can make simple classifications according to one or two properties but find it difficult to realize that multiple classifications are possible. Also, they can arrange objects in simple series but have trouble arranging them in a long series or inserting a new object in its proper place within a series. To these children, space is restricted to their neighborhood, and time is restricted to hours, days, and seasons.

Children in this stage have not yet developed the concept of conservation. This means that they do not understand that several objects can be rearranged and that the size, shape, or volume of a solid or liquid can be changed, yet the number of objects and the amount of solid or liquid will be unchanged or conserved. For example, if two rows of 10 objects are arranged so they take up the same area, children at this stage will state that the two rows are the same and there are the same number of objects in each row. If the objects in one row are spread out so the row is longer, children are likely to maintain that the longer row now has more objects in it. Similarly, if they are shown two identical balls of clay, they will agree that both balls contain the same amount of material. When, in full view, one of the balls is stretched out into the shape of a sausage, children at this stage are likely to say the sausage has more clay because it is larger, or less clay because it is thinner. Either way, these children are "centering" their attention on just one particular property (here, length or thickness) to the neglect of the other properties.

In both of the preceding examples, the reason for the children's thinking is that they do not yet understand reversibility. Their thinking cannot yet reverse itself back to the point of origin. As a result, these children do not understand that, since nothing has been removed or added, the extended row of objects can be rearranged to its original length, and the clay sausage can be made back into the original ball. They do not yet comprehend that action and thought processes are reversible.

---

schemata. Concept mapping (discussed later) has been shown to be an excellent tool for facilitating the learner's assimilation and accommodation.

Concept Attainment: A Continuing Cyclic Process

We can think of the learner's developing understanding of concepts (concept attainment) as being a cyclical (continuing) three-stage process. The first stage is an increasing awareness that is stimulated by the quality and richness of the child's learning environment; the second stage is disequilibrium; the third stage is reformulation of the concept, which is brought on by the learner's process of equilibration.

From neuroscience, new principles are emerging that may have profound effects on teaching and on how schools are organized. For example, as stated by Caine and Caine (1990), "Because there can be a five-year difference in maturation between any two 'average' children, gauging achievement on the basis of chronological age is inappropriate" (p. 66). Research by Sylwester, Chall, Wittrock, and Hart (1991) indicates brain growth spurts

FIGURE 1.2 cont'd

Not yet able to use abstract reasoning and only beginning to think conceptually, children at this stage of development learn best by manipulating objects in concrete situations rather than by abstract, verbal learning alone. For children at this stage, conceptual change comes very gradually.

Concrete Operations Stage (Ages 7–11)

The age span of this stage is from approximately 7 to 11. In this stage, learners can now perform logical operations. They can observe, judge, and evaluate in less egocentric terms than in the preoperational stage and can formulate more objective explanations. As a result, learners know how to solve physical problems. Because their thinking is still concrete and not abstract, they are limited to problems dealing with actual concrete situations. Early in this stage, learners cannot generalize, deal with hypothetical situations, or weigh possibilities.

Children at this stage can make multiple classifications, arrange objects in long series, and place new objects in their proper place in the series. Children can begin to comprehend geographical space and historical time. They develop the concepts of conservation according to their ease of learning: first, number of objects (age 6–7), then matter, length, area (age 7), weight (age 9–12), and volume (age 11 or more), in that order. They also develop the concept of reversibility and can now reverse the physical and mental processes when numbers of objects are rearranged or when the size and shape of matter are changed.

Later in this stage, children can hypothesize and do higher-level thinking. Not yet able to use abstract reasoning, and only beginning to be able to think conceptually children at this stage of development still learn best by manipulating objects in concrete situations rather than by verbal learning alone. At this stage, hands-on, active learning is most effective.

Formal Operations Stage (Age 11 and up)

Piaget initially believed that by age 15 most adolescents reach formal operational thinking, but now it is quite clear that many high school children—and even some adults—do not yet function at this level. Essentially, children who are quick to understand abstract ideas are formal thinkers. However, most middle-grade students are not at this stage. For them, *metacognition* (planning, monitoring, and evaluating one's own thinking) may be very difficult. In essence, metacognition is today's term for what Piaget referred to as *reflective abstraction,* or the reflection on one's own thinking, without which continued development cannot occur (Braten, 1991).

In this stage, learners' method of thinking shifts from the concrete to the more formal and abstract. They can now relate one abstraction to another and grow in ability to think conceptually. Learners can develop hypotheses, deduce possible consequences from them, then test these hypotheses with controlled experiments in which all of the variables are identical except the one being tested. When approaching a new problem, learners begin by formulating all of the possibilities and then determining which ones are substantiated through experimentation and logical analysis. After solving the problem, the learner can reflect on or rethink the thought processes that were used.

Piaget's Three-Phase Learning Cycle

To understand conceptual development and change, Piaget developed a theory of learning that involves children in a three-phase learning cycle. The three phases are (1) an exploratory hands-on phase, (2) a concept development phase, and (3) a concept application phase. When a learner is applying a concept (the third phase), the learner is involved in a hands-on activity. During application of a concept, the learner may discover new information that causes a change in his or her understanding of the concept being applied. Thus, the process of learning is cyclic. For a further discussion of the learning cycle model in a constructivist classroom, see Brooks and Brooks, 1993, pp. 116–118.

---

for children in grades 1, 2, 3, 6, 9, and 10. If schools were organized solely on this criterion, they would be configured in grade clusters K, 1–4, 5–8, and 9–12. In fact, increases in the use of the 5–8 grade span—the middle school—indicate that this configuration is becoming more widely accepted. From 1981 to 1992, the number of middle-level schools using a 5–8 grade span tripled, and when compared with 1981, only about one-third of middle-level schools in 1992 used the 7–9 grade span (Valentine et al., 1993, p. 19).

Lev Vygotsky: Cooperative Learning in a Supportive Environment

Soviet psychologist Lev Vygotsky (1896–1934), a contemporary of Piaget, studied and agreed with Piaget on most points, but differed with him on the importance of a child's social interactions. Vygotsky argued that learning is most effective when children cooperate with one another in a supportive learning environment under the careful guidance of a teacher. Cooperative learning, group problem solving, and cross-age tutoring are instructional strategies used today that have grown in popularity as a result of research evolving from the work of Vygotsky.

Robert Gagné and a General Learning Hierarchy

Well known for his hierarchy of learning levels, Robert Gagné views learning as the establishing of a capability to do something that the learner was not capable of doing previously. The emphasis is on the learner "doing" something. Related to this, Gagné postulates a hierarchy of learning capabilities. Learning one particular capability usually depends on having previously learned one or more simpler capabilities.

For Gagné, observable changes in behavior comprise the *only* criteria for inferring that learning has occurred. It follows, then, that the beginning, or lowest, level of a learning hierarchy would include very simple behaviors. These behaviors form the basis for learning more complex behaviors in the next level of the hierarchy. At each higher level, learning requires that the appropriate simpler, or less complex, behaviors have been acquired in the lower learning levels.

Gagné identifies eight levels of learning in this hierarchy. Beginning with the simplest and progressing to the most complex, these levels are described briefly in Table 1.1.

Signal learning. The individual learns to make a general conditioned response to a given signal. Examples are a child's pleasure produced by the sight of the child's pet animal or the child's expression of fright at the sound of a loud noise.

Stimulus-response learning. The individual acquires a precise physical or vocal response to a discriminated stimulus. An example is a child's initial learning of words by repeating the sounds and words of adults.

Chaining. Sometimes called skill learning, chaining is the linking of two or more units of simple stimulus-response learning. Chaining is limited to physical, nonverbal sequences. Examples include winding up of a toy, writing, running, and opening a door. The accuracy of the learning at this level depends on practice, prior experience, and reinforcement.

Verbal association. This is a form of chaining, but the links are verbal units. Naming an object is the simplest verbal association. In this case, the first stimulus-response link is involved in observing the object, and the second is involved in enabling the child to name the object. A more complex example of verbal chaining would be the rote memorization of a sequence of numbers, a formula, or the letters of the alphabet in sequence. Considered alone, these learned behaviors are not usually seen as important goals of teaching. However, viewed as a level in a hierarchy, they may be important first steps in certain higher levels of learning.

Multiple discrimination. Individually learned chains are linked to form multiple discriminations. Examples of learning at this level include the identification of the names of children in a classroom in which the learner associates each child with his or her distinctive appearance and correct name and, in science, learning the distinction between solids, liquids, and gases.

Concept learning. Learning a concept means learning to respond to stimuli by their abstract characteristics (such as position, shape, color, and number), as opposed to concrete physical properties. For example, a child may learn to call a two-inch cube a "block" and to apply this name to other objects that differ from it in size and shape. Later, the child learns the concept "cube" and, by so doing, can identify a class of objects that differ physically in many ways (e.g., by material, color, texture, and size). Rather than learning concepts in a trial-and-error accidental fashion, under the careful guidance of the teacher a child's learning is sequenced in a way that leads to the child's improved conceptual understanding.

Principle learning. In simplest terms, a principle is a chain of two or more concepts. In principle learning, the individual must relate two or more concepts. An example is the relation of a circle's circumference to its diameter. Three separate concepts (circumference, pi, and diameter) are linked or chained together.

Problem solving. According to Gagné, and as most learning theorists will agree, problem solving is the most sophisticated type of learning. In problem solving, the individual applies learned principles to achieve a goal. While achieving this goal, however, the learner becomes capable of new performances by using the new knowledge. When a problem is solved, new knowledge has been acquired, and the individual's capacity increases. The individual is now able to handle a wide class of problems similar to the one solved. What has been learned, according to Gagné, is a higher-order principle, which is the combined product of two or more lower-order principles.

Thus, when a child has acquired the capabilities and behaviors of a certain level of learning, we assume that the child has also acquired the capabilities and behaviors of all the learning levels below this level. Furthermore, if the child were having difficulty in demonstrating the capabilities and behaviors for a certain level, the teacher could simply test the child on the capabilities and behaviors of the lower levels to determine which one or ones were causing the difficulty.

Jerome Bruner and Discovery Learning

While a leading interpreter and promoter of Piaget's ideas, Bruner also made his own significant contributions on how children learn. Some of his thinking was influenced by the work of Vygotsky (Bruner, 1985). Like Piaget, Bruner maintains that each child passes through stages that are age-related and biologically determined, and that learning will depend primarily on the developmental level that the child has attained.

Bruner's theory also encompasses three major sequential stages that he refers to as representations. They can be thought of as ways of knowing. These are *enactive representation* (knowing that is related to movement, such as through direct experiencing or concrete activities); *iconic representation* (knowing that is related to visual and spatial, or graphic, representations, such as films and still visuals); and *symbolic representation* (knowing that is related to reason and logic, or that depends on the use of words and abstract symbolization). These stages correspond to the sensorimotor, concrete operations, and formal operations stages of Piaget.

According to Bruner, when a child learns concepts, the child can learn them only within the framework of the stage of intellectual development the child is in at the time. In teaching children, it is essential then that each child be helped to pass progressively from one stage of intellectual development to the next. Schools can do this by providing challenging but purposeful opportunities and problems for children that tempt them to forge ahead into the next stages of development. As a result, the children acquire a higher level of understanding.

Bruner and the Act of Learning

Bruner describes the act of learning as involving three almost simultaneous processes. The first is the process of acquiring new knowledge. The second is the process of manipulating this knowledge to make it fit new tasks or situations. The third is the process of evaluating the acquisition and manipulation of this knowledge. A major objective of learning is to introduce children at an early age to the ideas and styles that will help them become literate. Consequently, the school curriculum should be built around major conceptual schemes, skills, and values that society considers to be important. These should be taught as early as possible in a manner that is consistent with the child's stages of development and forms of thought, and then revisited many times throughout the school years to increase and deepen the learner's understanding.

Bruner has been an articulate advocate for discovery learning. He urges that, whenever possible, teaching and learning should be conducted in such a manner that children be given the opportunity to discover concepts for themselves.

Benefits of Discovery Learning

Bruner cites four major benefits of learning by discovery. First, there is an increase in intellectual potency. This means that discovery learning helps children learn how to learn. It helps learners develop skills in problem-solving, enabling them to arrange and apply what has been learned to new situations, and thus learn new concepts.

Second, discovery learning shifts motives for learning away from extrinsic rewards—that of satisfying others—to intrinsic rewards—internal self-rewarding satisfaction, that is, satisfying oneself.

Third, there is an opportunity to learn the working heuristics of discovery. By *heuristics,* Bruner means the methods in which students are educated to find out things independently. Only through problem-solving exercises and by the effort of discovery can learners find out things independently. The more adept learners become in the working heuristics of discovery, the more effective and the faster they will be in problem solving.

Fourth, discovery learning aids memory processing. Knowledge resulting from discovery learning is more easily remembered, and it is more readily recalled when needed. Bruner's work, strongly supported by recent brain research, provides a rationale for using discovery and hands-on learning activities.

David Ausubel and Meaningful Verbal Learning

David Ausubel (1963) is an advocate of *reception learning,* the receipt of ideas through transmission. He agrees with other psychologists that the development of problem-solving skills is a primary objective in teaching. However, similar to Gagné, he feels that effective problem solving and discovery are more likely to take place after children have learned key and supporting concepts, primarily through reception learning, that is, through direct instruction (expository teaching).

Ausubel strongly urges teachers to use learning situations and examples that are familiar to the children, which helps children to assimilate what is being learned with what they already know, making their learning more meaningful. Differing from Bruner, Ausubel believes that discovery learning is too time consuming to enable children to learn all they should know within the short time allotted to learning. Like Bruner and Gagné, he suggests that children in the primary grades should work on as many "hands-on" learning activities as possible, but for children beyond the primary grades, he recommends the increased use of learning by transmission, using teacher explanations, concept mapping, demonstrations, diagrams, and illustrations. Further, Ausubel cautions against learning by rote memorization, but he points out it is not always avoidable.

An example of learning by rote is when we memorize our telephone number or social security number. Learners must use rote memorization to learn information that is not connected to any prior knowledge. Learning by rote is easier if the new information can be connected to some prior knowledge. Often used to bridge the gap between rote learning and meaningful learning is the strategy known as *mnemonics,* which is any strategy that will assist memory. To avoid rote memorization, Ausubel encourages teachers to make the learning meaningful and longer lasting by using *advance organizers,* ideas that are presented to students before the new material and that mentally prepare them to integrate the new material into previously built cognitive structures. Many teachers' manuals address this technique.

There is no doubt that the most effective teaching occurs when students see meaning in what is being taught. A danger in expository teaching (i.e., in which students listen to the teacher, read, and memorize) is the tendency to rely too heavily on spoken communication, which for many learners is highly abstract and thus unlikely to be effective. This is especially true in classrooms with students with diverse cultural backgrounds and varied levels of language proficiency skill.

Concept Mapping

Based on Ausubel's theory of meaningful learning, a technique called concept mapping has been found useful for helping students change their misconceptions. Simply put, *concepts* can be thought of as classifications that attempt to organize the world of objects and events into a smaller number of categories. Or, as stated by Jarolimek and Parker (1993), "concepts are ideas. Social studies concepts often embody an elaborate meaning that evolves with experience and learning over a period of years" (p. 32). Additionally, there are language arts concepts, such as the concept of story, that have meaning that evolves over time. As pointed out by Tompkins and Hoskisson (1993), "children acquire this concept of story gradually, through listening to stories read to them, by reading stories themselves, and by telling and writing stories" (p. 311). Concepts hold meanings for students that develop in complexity with experience and learning over time. As an example from a content area study, a unit about life in New England and the activity of maple sugaring might include words in a word cluster that are critical to understanding the concept of sugaring, a feature of life in the region. For social studies, other examples of concepts from history are time, change, continuity of human life, the past, and the methods of the historian (p. 98).

A concept map (or a word cluster map) typically refers to a visual or graphic representation of concepts with connections (bridges) to show their relationships. Word cluster maps are used often in the primary grades. For an example, see Figure 1.3, a word cluster map that shows children's connections of relationships while studying concepts related to maple sugar.

The general procedure for concept mapping is to have students (1) identify important concepts in materials being studied, often by circling those concepts, (2) rank the concepts from the most general to the most specific, and then (3) arrange the concepts on a sheet of paper, connecting related ideas with lines and defining the connections between the related ideas. Concept mapping has been found to help children to organize and to represent their thoughts and to connect new knowledge to their past experiences and schemata. (For further information about concept mapping, see Novak, 1990.)

The purpose of word cluster mapping is to focus students' attention on the theme-related words that teachers want them to learn. Whenever possible, students should be involved in choosing some of the words for study, because the more they feel the need for individual words, the more likely they are to learn them. Words that are critical to understanding a concept can be taught directly or introduced through the various activities in which students are involved. Such activities can include field trips, hands-on activities, viewing films and videos, reading books, and listening to oral presentations.

Differences Among Theorists

At this point, it will be beneficial to review some of the differences among the theorists. For instance, while Bruner's description of his three representations of learning corresponds to Piaget's stages, he differs from Piaget in his interpretation of the role language plays in intellectual development.

Piaget believes that although thought and language are related, they are different systems. He posits that the child's thinking is based on a system of inner logic that evolves as

FIGURE 1.3
Word Cluster Map for Maple Sugar

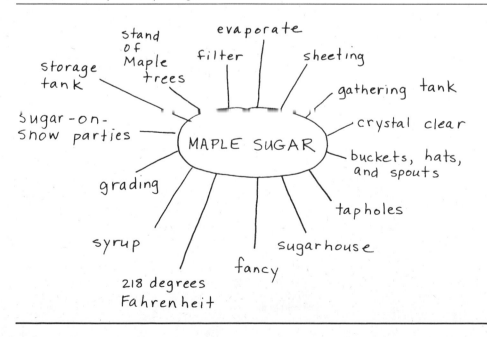

the child organizes and adapts to experiences. Bruner, however, maintains that thought is internalized language. In his view, the child translates experience into language and then uses language as an instrument of thinking. Table 1.2 highlights some of the major differences.

Bruner and Piaget differ also in their attitude toward the child's readiness for learning. Piaget concluded that the child's readiness for learning depends on maturation and intellectual development. Bruner, however, and some other researchers believe that a child is always ready to learn a concept at some level of sophistication. Bruner states that any subject can be taught effectively in some intellectually honest form to any child in any stage of development. He supports this concept, for example, by noting that only when the basic ideas of a subject are out of the context of the child's life experiences and are formalized by complex verbal statements do they become incomprehensible to children (and to adults). Gagné suggests that readiness depends on the successful development of lower-level skills and prior understandings.

Bruner differs from Gagné in his emphasis on learning. While Gagné emphasizes primarily the product of learning (the knowledge), Bruner's emphasis is on the process of learning (the skills). While for Gagné the key question is "*What* do you want the child to know?" for Bruner it is "*How* do you want the child to know?" For Gagné, the emphasis is on learning itself, whether by discovery, review, or practice. For Bruner, the emphasis is on learning by discovery; it is the method of learning that is important.

Bruner emphasizes problem solving as the place to start, which in turn leads to the development of necessary skills. The teacher can pose a question to be solved and then use it to motivate children to develop the necessary skills. On the other hand, Gagné sees problem solving as the *highest* level of learning, with the lower learning levels as prerequisites. For Gagné, the appropriate sequence in learning (and teaching) is from these lower levels toward problem solving. The teacher begins with simple ideas, relates all of them, builds on them, and works toward more complex levels of learning.

D. THE TEACHER AS DECISION MAKER

As you undoubtedly are aware, during any school day you will make hundreds of decisions, many of which must be made instantaneously. In addition, to prepare for the teaching day,

TABLE 1.2
Differences Among Learning Theorists

	BRUNER	**GAGNÉ**	**AUSUBEL**	**PIAGET**
Readiness for Learning	Child is always ready to learn.	Readiness depends on lower-level skills and prior understanding.	Use situations and examples familiar to children.	Readiness depends on child's maturation and intellectual development.
Learning	Hands-on learning. Emphasis on the process of learning (skills). Asks *how* do you want the child to know? Learning by discovery. Problem solving is the place to start.	Hands-on learning. Emphasizes the product of learning (knowledge). Asks *what* do you want the child to know? Features knowing through review, practice, and discovery. Problem solving is the highest level of learning. Lower-level learnings are prerequisites to higher levels.	Hands-on learning in primary grades. Increase in learning through teacher explanations, demonstrations, concept mapping, diagrams, and illustrations in higher grades.	Knowledge is created and learning takes place as children sequentially interact with their social and physical environment in an exploratory hands-on phase, a concept development phase, and a concept application phase.

you will have already made many decisions. During one school year, you will make thousands of decisions, many of which can and will affect the lives of children for years to come. For you this should seem an awesome responsibility, and it is.

To be an effective teacher, you must become adept both at making decisions that are carefully reasoned over time and at making decisions on the spot. To make decisions that affect students in the most positive ways, you need (1) common sense, (2) intelligence, (3) a background of theory in curriculum and instruction with extended practical experience in working with children, and (4) a willingness to think about and to reflect on your teaching and to continue learning all that is necessary to become an exemplary teacher.

Initially, of course, you will make errors in judgment, but you will also learn that children are fairly resilient and that there are specialists who will guide you, aid you, and help ensure that you learn from your errors. Keep in mind that the sheer number of decisions you make each day means that not all of them will be the best ones that could have been made had you had more time to think and better resources for planning.

Although effective teaching is based on research-based principles, good classroom teaching is also an art, and few rules apply to every teaching situation. In fact, decisions about your response to a child's inappropriate behavior or the selection of content, instructional objectives, materials for instruction, teaching strategies, and the techniques for assessing student achievement, are all the result of subjective judgments. Although you will make many decisions at a somewhat unhurried pace during planning, many others will be made intuitively on the spur of the moment. Once the school day has begun, you may lack time for making carefully thought-out judgments. At your best, you will base decisions on your knowledge of school policies, your teaching style, pedagogical research, the curriculum, and the nature of the students in your classroom. You will also base your decisions on instinct, common sense, and reflective judgment. The better your understanding and experience with schools, the content of the curriculum, and the students and how they develop intellectually, and the more time you give for thinking and careful reflection, the more likely it will be that your decisions will result in the student learning that you had planned. You will reflect on, conceptualize, and apply understandings from one teaching experience to the next. As your understandings about your classroom experiences accumulate, your teaching will become more routinized, predictable, and refined.

Decision-Making and the Thought-Processing Phases of Instruction

Madeline Hunter (1994) has defined teaching as "the process of making and implementing decisions before, during, and after instruction—decisions that, when implemented, increase the probability of learning" (p. 6). Instruction can be divided into four decision-making and thought-processing phases. These are the *preactive* (planning) phase, the *interactive* (teaching) phase, the *reflective* (analyzing and evaluating the teaching), and the *projective* (application of that reflection) (Costa, 1991). The preactive phase consists of all those intellectual functions and decisions you will make prior to actual instruction. The interactive phase includes all the decisions made during the act of teaching. As said earlier, decisions made during this phase are likely to be more intuitive, unconscious, and routine, than are those made during the planning phase. The reflective phase is the time you will make to reflect on, analyze, and judge the decisions and behaviors that occurred during the interactive phase. As a result of this reflection, decisions are made to use what was learned in subsequent teaching actions. At this point, you are in the projective phase, abstracting from your reflection and projecting your analysis into subsequent teaching actions.

Reflection and the Locus of Control

During the reflective phase, you have a choice of whether to assume full responsibility for the instructional outcomes or whether to assume responsibility for only the positive outcomes of the planned instruction while placing the blame for negative outcomes on outside forces (such as parents and guardians, child peer pressure, other teachers, administrators, or textbooks). Where you place responsibility for outcomes is referred to as *locus of control*. It seems axiomatic that teachers who are professional and competent tend to assume full responsibility for the instructional outcomes, regardless of whether those outcomes are the ones intended from the planning phase.

Personal Style of Teaching

Every teacher has a personal style of teaching that develops from a combination of personal traits and the expertise the teacher has in methodology, subject matter, and instructional theory. The most effective teachers can vary their styles—that is, their styles are flexible enough to encompass a variety of strategies and are therefore readily available to the different sorts of situations that may develop. *Teaching style is the way teachers teach, their distinctive mannerisms complemented by their choices of teaching behaviors and strategies.*

Effective teachers can modify their styles by selecting and using the strategy that is most appropriate, thus securing active child involvement and the greatest amount of child achievement. Highly effective teaching of this sort requires both expertise in a wide variety of methods and a sense of what method is appropriate for which situation. It also requires a command of the subject matter and an understanding of the students being taught. This may sound like a large order, but many beginning teachers become adept at this surprisingly quickly.

Thus, to be an effective teacher you should (1) develop a large repertoire of instructional strategies; (2) learn as much as you can about your students and their individual styles of learning; and (3) develop an eclectic style of teaching, one that is flexible and adaptable and can function at many locations along the spectrum of integrated learning that was presented in the beginning of Part I.

E. STYLES OF LEARNING

The most effective teachers adapt their teaching styles and methods to their students, using approaches that interest the children, that are neither too easy nor too difficult, that match the students' learning styles, and that are relevant to their lives. This adaptation process is further complicated because each child is different from every other. All do not have the same interests, abilities, backgrounds, or learning styles. As a matter of fact, children not only differ from one another but each child can change to some extent from day to day. What appeals to a child today may not have the same appeal tomorrow. Therefore, you need to consider both the nature of children in general (for example, methods appropriate for a particular first-grade class are unlikely to be the same as those that work best for most fourth graders) and each child in particular. What follows is a synopsis of what has been learned about aspects of student learning styles.

Brain Laterality

Research has shown that how a person learns is related to differences in the left and right hemispheres of the brain. This theory is sometimes referred to as *brain laterality* or brain hemisphericity. Verbal learning, logical and convergent thinking, and the academic cognitive processes are dominated by the left cerebral hemisphere, whereas affective, intuitive, spatial, emotional, and divergent thinking and visual elements are dominated by the right cerebral hemisphere. Some children are oriented toward right cerebral hemisphere learning and others toward the left. This means that some children learn better through verbal interactions while others learn through visual, kinesthetic, and tactile involvement.

Brain laterality and its implications for teaching. When integrating the disciplines and helping children connect what is being learned with real-life situations, the teacher is more likely to be teaching to both hemispheres. Caine and Caine (1990) underscore this by reminding us, "in a healthy person the two hemispheres are inextricably interactive, irrespective of whether a person is dealing with words, mathematics, music, or art" (p. 67).

Learning Modalities

Learning modality refers to the sensory portal means by which a child prefers to receive sensory reception (modality preference), or the actual way a child learns best (modality adeptness). Some children prefer learning by seeing, a visual modality; others prefer learning through instruction from others (through talk), an auditory modality; while still others prefer learning by doing and being physically involved, referred to as kinesthetic modality, and by touching objects, the tactile modality. Sometimes a child's modality preference is not that child's modality strength. While primary modality strength can be determined by observing children, it can also be mixed and it can change as the result of experience and intellectual maturity. As you might suspect, modality integration (using several modalities at once) has been found to contribute to better achievement in child learning.

Learning modalities and their implications for teaching. As a general rule, children prefer to learn by touching objects, by feeling shapes and textures, by interacting with each other, and by moving things around. In contrast, sitting and listening are difficult for many of them. Dependence on the tactile and kinesthetic modalities decreases with maturity. Some children are visual learners who can read easily and rapidly and can visualize what they are reading about.

Because most children neither have a preference nor a strength for auditory reception, teachers should limit their use of the lecture method of instruction. Furthermore, instruction that uses a singular approach, such as auditory (lecturing), limits children who learn better another way. This difference can affect student achievement. Finally, if a teacher's verbal communication conflicts with his or her nonverbal messages, children can become confused, and this too can affect their learning. (When there is a discrepancy between what the teacher says and what that teacher does, the teacher's nonverbal signal will win every time.)

You are advised to use strategies that integrate the modalities. Combining reception learning and cognitive mapping is an example of modality integration. When well designed, thematic units incorporate modality integration, too. In conclusion, then, when teaching a group of children who have mixed learning abilities, modality strengths, language proficiencies, and cultural backgrounds, the most successful teaching integrates learning modalities.

Learning Styles

Related to learning modality is a child's *learning style*, which can be defined as *independent forms of knowing and processing information.* While some children are comfortable with beginning their learning of a new idea in the abstract (such as through visual or verbal symbolization), others feel the need to begin with the concrete (learning by actually doing). Some children prosper while working in groups, and some prefer to work alone. Some are quick in their learning, whereas others are slow, methodical, cautious, and meticulous. Some can sustain attention on a single topic for a long time, becoming more absorbed in their study as time passes. Others are slower starters and more casual in their pursuits but are capable of shifting with ease from subject to subject. Some students can study in the midst of music, noise, or movement, whereas others need quiet, solitude, and a desk or table. The point is that students vary in not only their skills and preferences for receiving knowledge, but also in how they mentally process that information once it has been received. According to Keefe and Ferrell (1990), this mental processing is a person's style of learning, "a gestalt combining internal and external operations derived from the individual's neurobiology, personality, and development and reflected in learner behavior" (p. 59). There is a teaching aid, The Learning Style Inventory, that can assist in identifying a student's learning style. Two major differences in how people learn have been described by David Kolb (1985) and incorporated into the inventory, which focuses on ways situations are perceived and ways information is processed. In new situations, for example, people exhibit their perceptions—some will be watchers and others will be doers. It is important to note that learning style is not an indicator of intelligence, but rather an indicator of how a person learns.

Classification of Learning Styles

Although there are probably as many types of learning styles as there are individuals, most learning style classifications center around the recognition of four general types and are based on the early work of Carl Jung (1923). Two other studies—Dunn and Dunn (1978) and Gregorc (1985)—are also helpful in describing learning styles.

Anthony Gregorc (1979) classifies learning styles according to whether children prefer to begin with the concrete or the abstract and according to whether they prefer random or sequential ordering of information. As a result, the learning style classification has four categories:

- The *concrete sequential learner* prefers direct, hands-on experiences presented in a logical sequence.
- The *concrete random learner* prefers more wide-open, exploratory activities, such as games, role playing, simulations, and independent study.
- The *abstract sequential learner* is skilled in decoding verbal and symbolic messages, especially when presented in logical sequence.
- The *abstract random learner* can interpret meaning from nonverbal communications and consequently do well in discussions, debates, and media presentations (Heinich, Molenda, & Russell, 1993). Most children are better at one of the two categories of concrete learning than at either category of abstract learning.

Bernice McCarthy (1990) has described major learning styles and used different terminology, such as the imaginative learner, the analytic learner, the common sense learner, and the dynamic learner:

- The *imaginative learner* perceives information concretely and processes it reflectively. Imaginative learners learn well by listening and sharing with others, integrating the ideas of others with their own experiences. Imaginative learners often have difficulty adjusting to traditional teaching, which depends less on classroom interactions and children's sharing and connecting of their prior experiences. In a traditional classroom, the imaginative learner is likely to be an at-risk child.
- The *analytic learner* perceives information abstractly and processes it reflectively. The analytic learner prefers sequential thinking, needs details, and values what experts have to offer. Analytic learners do well in traditional classrooms.
- The *common sense learner* perceives information abstractly and processes it actively. The common sense learner is pragmatic and enjoys hands-on learning. Common sense learners sometimes find school frustrating unless they can see immediate use to what is being learned. In the traditional classroom, the common sense learner is likely to be a learner who is at risk of not completing school, of dropping out.
- The *dynamic learner* perceives information concretely and processes it actively. The dynamic learner also prefers hands-on learning and is excited by anything new. Dynamic learners are risk takers and are frustrated by learning if they see it as being tedious and sequential. In a traditional classroom, the dynamic learner also is likely to be an at-risk child.

With a system developed by McCarthy (1987) (called the 4MAT System), teachers employ a cycle of instructional strategies that reaches each child's learning style. As stated by McCarthy (1990), in the cycle learners "sense and feel, they experience, then they watch, they reflect, then they think, they develop theories, then they try out theories, they experiment. Finally, they evaluate and synthesize what they have learned in order to apply it to their next similar experience. They get smarter. They apply experience to experiences" (p. 33). And, in this process they are likely to be using all four learning modalities. (Compare the learning cycle described here with the learning cycle concepts of Piaget and Karplus discussed earlier in this chapter; see Figure 1.2.)

Related to intelligence, Howard Gardner has introduced seven learning styles or types of intelligence that affect learning styles: (1) *verbal-linguistic* (a sensitivity to the meaning and order of words); (2) *logical-mathematical* (the ability to handle chains of reasoning, to recognize patterns and order); (3) *intrapersonal* (sensitivity to one's emotional life as a means to understand oneself and others); (4) *visual-spatial* (the ability to manipulate the nature of space, such as through architecture, mime, or sculpture); (5) *musical-rhythmic* (sensitivity to pitch, melody, rhythm, and tone); (6) *body-kinesthetic* (the ability to use the body skillfully and to handle objects with dexterity); and (7) *interpersonal* (the ability to understand people and relationships) (Blythe & Gardner, 1990; Gardner, 1987).

Learning style and its implications for teaching. As implied previously, in the presentation of McCarthy's four types of learners, many educators believe that children who are at risk of not completing school are those who may be dominant in a cognitive learning style that is not a match with traditional teaching methods. Traditional methods are largely of McCarthy's analytic style, where information is presented in a logical, linear, sequential fashion, and of the first three Gardner types of intelligence: verbal-linguistic, logical-mathematical, and intrapersonal (Armstrong, 1988). Consequently, to better match methods of instruction with learning styles, some teachers (see Ellison, 1992) and schools (see Hoerr, 1992; Kranz, 1994) have structured the curriculum and instruction around Gardner's seven ways of knowing.

The importance to teachers of the preceding information about learning styles and types of intelligence is two-fold:

1. Intelligence is not a fixed or static reality, but can be learned, taught, and developed (Bracey, 1992; Lazear, 1992). This is important for students to understand, too. When students understand that intelligence is incremental, something that is developed through use over time, they tend to be more motivated to work at learning than when they believe intelligence is a fixed entity (Resnick & Klopfer, 1989).

2. Not all children learn and respond to learning situations in the same way. A child may learn differently according to the situation or according to the child's ethnicity, cultural background, or socioeconomic status. (For relevant discussions about students' cultural differences and learning styles, see Gallegos, 1993; Willis, 1993, p. 7.)

In a culture such as ours that values quantity, speed, and measurement, it is easy to make the mistake that being a slow learner is the same as being a poor learner. The perceptive teacher, however, understands that slowness may be simply another style of learning, with potential strengths of its own. Slowness can reflect many things—caution, a desire to be thorough or a meticulous style, a great interest in the matter being studied. To ignore the slow child or to treat all children who seem slow as though they were victims of some deficiency is to risk discouraging those who have deliberately opted for slowness and thus limiting their learning opportunities.

SUMMARY

As a teacher, you must recognize that children have different ways of receiving information and different ways of processing that information—different ways of knowing and of constructing their knowledge. These differences are unique and important, and they are what you must address in your teaching. You should try to learn as much as you can about how each child learns and processes information. The more you vary your teaching strategies and assist children in integrating their learning, the more likely you are to reach more of the children more of the time. To continue your effectiveness, you should

- learn as much about your students and their preferred styles of learning as you can;
- develop an eclectic style of teaching, one that is flexible and adaptable; and
- integrate the learning, thereby assisting children in their conceptual understandings by helping them to make bridges or connections between what they already know and what is being learned.

QUESTIONS AND ACTIVITIES FOR DISCUSSION

1. Give an example of multilevel teaching that you would use in your classroom. Of what benefit is the use of multilevel teaching?

2. In what ways is knowledge of teaching styles and child learning styles important for a teacher?

3. Describe the relationship between awareness, disequilibrium, and reformulation in learning.

4. Why do you agree/not agree that integration of the curriculum is important for learning?

5. Explain the concept of spectrum of curriculum integration. What relevance does this concept have for you?

6. For a concept usually taught in social studies at a grade level K–4, describe how you help children bridge their learning of that concept with what is going on in their lives.

7. Could the technique of concept mapping be used as an advance organizer? Explain your answer.

8. What recommendations for teaching do you have for a teacher in the following classroom situation? A teacher has a class of 33 fourth graders, who, during her lectures, teacher-led discussions, and recitation lessons, are restless, inattentive, and causing a major problem in classroom management. At the teacher's invitation, the school psychologist tests the children for learning modality and finds that 29 of the 33 children are predominately kinesthetic learners. Of what use is this information to the teacher? Describe what teaching strategies, if any, the teacher should try as a result of having this information.

9. Identify a topic of a social studies lesson for a grade level of your choice, grade K–4. Describe how you would teach that lesson from a behaviorist viewpoint; then describe how you would teach the same lesson from a constructivist viewpoint. Explain the differences.

10. Could you accept the view that learning is the product of creative inquiry through social interaction, with the children as active participants in that inquiry? Explain why you would or would not agree.

11. Can you recall or invent mnemonics that would be useful in your teaching? Share them with those of your colleagues.

12. Describe any prior concepts you held that changed as a result of your reading this chapter. Describe the changes.

REFERENCES AND SUGGESTED READINGS

Armstrong, T. (1988, September). Learning differences—Not disabilities. *Principal, 68*(1), 34–36.

Ausubel, D. P. (1963). *The psychology of meaningful verbal learning.* New York: Grune & Stratton.

Banks, C. B. (1991, May). Harmonizing child-teacher interactions: A case for learning styles. *Synthesis, 2*(2), 1–5.

Beilin, H. (1992, March). Piaget's enduring contribution to developmental psychology. *Developmental Psychology, 28*(2), 191–204.

Blythe, T., & Gardner, H. (1990, April). A school for all intelligences. *Educational Leadership, 47*(7), 33–37.

Bracey, G. W. (1991, October). Why can't they be like we were? *Phi Delta Kappan, 73*(2), 105–117.

Bracey, G. W. (1992, January). Getting smart(er) in school. *Phi Delta Kappan, 73*(5), 414–416.

Braten, I. (1991). Vygotsky as precursor to metacognitive theory: I. The concept of metacognition and its roots. *Scandinavian Journal of Educational Research, 35*(3), 179–192.

Brooks, J. G., & Brooks, M. G. (1993). *In search of understanding: The case for constructivist classrooms.* Alexandria, VA: Association for Supervision and Curriculum Development.

Bruner, J. S. (1960). *The process of education.* Cambridge, MA: Harvard University Press.

Bruner, J. S. (1966). *Toward a theory of instruction.* Cambridge, MA: Harvard University Press.

Bruner, J. S. (1985). Vygotsky: A historical and conceptual perspective. In J. Wertsch (Ed.), *Culture, communication and cognition: Vygotskian perspectives.* Cambridge, England: Cambridge University Press.

Bruner, J. S. (1990). *Acts of meaning.* Cambridge, MA: Harvard University Press.

Caine, R. N., & Caine, G. (1990, October). Understanding a brain-based approach to learning and teaching. *Educational Leadership, 48*(2), 66–70.

Caine, R. N., & Caine, G. (1991). *Making connections: Teaching and the human brain.* Alexandria, VA: Association for Supervision and Curriculum Development.

Carns, A. W., & Carns, M. R. (1991, May). Teaching study skills, cognitive strategies, and metacognitive skills through self-diagnosed learning styles. *School Counselor, 38*(5), 341–346.

Cooper, J. D. (1993). *Literacy: Helping children construct meaning.* (2nd ed.). Burlington, MA: Houghton Mifflin.

Costa, A. L. (1991). *The school as a home for the mind.* Palatine, IL: Skylight Publishing.

Cronin, J. F. (1993, April). Four misconceptions about authentic learning. *Educational Leadership, 50*(7), 78–80.

Curry, L. (1990, October). A critique of the research on learning styles. *Educational Leadership, 48*(2), 50–56.

Disability Resources. *Disability information at your fingertips.* Disability Resources, Four Glatter Lane, Centereach, NY 11720-1032.

Dunn, R., & Dunn, K. (1978). *Teaching children through their individual learning styles.* Reston, VA: Reston Publications.

Eitzen, D. Stanley. (1992, April). Problem children: The sociocultural roots. *Phi Delta Kappan, 73*(8), 584–590.

Ellison, L. (1992, October). Using multiple intelligences to set goals. *Educational Leadership, 50*(2), 69–72.

Erikson, E. (1950). *Childhood and society.* New York: Norton.

Fantuzzo, J. W., et al. (1992, September). Effects of reciprocal peer tutoring on mathematics and school adjustment: A component analysis. *Journal of Educational Psychology, 84*(3), 331–339.

Forman, G., & Kuschner, D. (1983). *The child's construction of knowledge: Piaget for teaching children.* Washington, DC: National Association for the Education of Young Children.

Fourgurean, J. M., et al. (1990, Spring). The link between learning style and Jungian psychological type: A finding of two bipolar preference dimensions. *Journal of Experimental Education, 58*(3), 225–237.

Gallegos, G. (1993, Fall). Learning styles in culturally diverse classrooms. *California Catalyst, 36*–41.

Gardner, H. (1982). *Art, mind and brain.* New York: Basic Books.

Gardner, H. (1985). *Frames of mind: The theory of multiple intelligence.* New York: Basic Books.

Gardner, H. (1987). The theory of multiple intelligences. *Annals of Dyslexia 37,* 19–35.

Gardner, H. (1991). *The unschooled mind: How children think and how schools should teach.* New York: Basic Books.

Gardner, H. (1993). *Creating minds.* New York: Basic Books.

Gardner, H., & Boix-Mansilla, V. (1994, February). Teaching for understanding—Within and across the disciplines. *Educational Leadership, 51*(5), 14–18.

Glasson, G. E., & Lalik, R. V. (1993, February). Reinterpreting the learning cycle from a social constructivist perspective: A qualitative study of teachers' beliefs and practices. *Journal of Research in Science Teaching, 30*(2), 187–207.

Grady, M. P. (1990). *Whole brain education.* Fastback 301. Bloomington, IN: Phi Delta Kappa Educational Foundation.

Gregorc, A. (1979, January). Learning and teaching styles—Potent forces behind them. *Educational Leadership,* 234–236.

Gregorc, A. (1985). *Gregorc style delineator.* Maynard, MA: Gabriel Systems.

Haberman, M. (1991, December). The pedagogy of poverty versus good teaching. *Phi Delta Kappan, 73*(4), 290–294.

Heinich, R., Molenda, M., & Russell, J. D. (1993). *Instructional media* (4th ed). New York: Macmillan.

Hoerr, T. R. (1992, October). How our school applied multiple intelligences theory. *Educational Leadership, 50*(2), 67–68.

Hunter, M. (1994). *Enhancing teaching.* New York: Macmillan.

Jarolimek, J., & Parker, W. C. (1993). *Social studies in elementary education* (9th ed.). Englewood Cliffs, NJ: Merrill/Prentice Hall.

Jones, B. F., & Fennimore, T. (1990). *The new definition of learning.* Oakbrook, IL: North Central Regional Educational Laboratory.

Jung, C. G. (1923). *Psychological types.* New York: Harcourt Brace.

Keefe, J. W. (1990, February). Learning style: Where are we going? *Momentum, 21*(1), 44–48.

Keefe, J. W., & Ferrell, B. G. (1990, October). Developing a defensible learning style paradigm. *Educational Leadership, 48*(2), 57–61.

Kolb, D. (1985). *The learning style inventory.* Boston, MA: McBer and Co.

Kranz, B. (1994). *Identifying talents among multicultural children.* Fastback 364. Bloomington, IN: Phi Delta Kappa Educational Foundation.

Lay-Dopyera, M., & Dopyera, J. (1986). Strategies for teaching. In C. Seefeldt (Ed.), *Early childhood curriculum: A review of current research.* New York: Teachers College Press, Columbia University.

Lazear, D. G. (1992). *Teaching for multiple intelligences.* Fastback 342. Bloomington, IN: Phi Delta Kappa Educational Foundation.

Lockhead, J. (1992, October). Knocking down the building blocks of learning: Constructivism and the ventures program. *Educational Studies in Mathematics, 23*(5), 543–552.

Lombardi, T. P. (1992). *Learning strategies for problem learners.* Fastback 345. Bloomington, IN: Phi Delta Kappa Educational Foundation.

McCarthy, B. (1987). *The FourMat system: Teaching to learning styles with right-left mode techniques.* Barrington, IL: Excel.

McCarthy, B. (1990, October). Using the 4MAT system to bring learning styles to schools. *Educational Leadership, 48*(2), 31–37.

McElroy, K. B. (1989, Winter). A taste of cooperativeness within an elementary school. *Pointer, 33*(2), 34–38.

Maslow, A. H. (1970). *Motivation and personality.* New York: Harper & Row.

Meador, K. (1993, March/April). Surviving a creative child's early years. *Gifted Child Today,* 16(2), 57–59.

National Association for the Education of Young Children. (1990). *Good teaching practices for older preschoolers and kindergartners.* Washington, DC: Author.

Novak, J. D. (1990). Concept maps and Venn diagrams: Two metacognitive tools to facilitate meaningful learning. *Instructional Science, 19*(1), 29–52.

Novak, J. D. (1993, March). How do we learn our lesson? *The Science Teacher, 60*(3), 50–55.

Perkins, D., & Blythe, T. (1994, February). Putting understanding up front. *Educational Leadership, 51*(5), 4–7.

Piaget, J. (1950). *The psychology of intelligence.* London: Routledge & Kegan Paul.

Piaget, J. (1972). *Science of education and the psychology of the child* (rev. ed.). New York: Viking. (Original work published 1965)

Piaget, J. (1977). *The development of thought: Elaboration of cognitive structures.* New York: Viking.

Prawat, R. S. (1992, May). Teachers' beliefs about teaching and learning: A constructivist perspective. *American Journal of Education, 100*(3), 354–395.

Raines, S. C., & Canady, R. J. (1992). *Story stretchers for the primary grades: Activities to expand children's favorite books.* Mt. Ranier, MD: Gryphon House.

Reed, S., & Sautter, R. Craig. (1990, June). Children of poverty: The status of 12 million young Americans. *Phi Delta Kappan, 71,* 10.

Resnick, L. B., & Klopfer, L. E. (1989). *Toward the thinking curriculum: Current cognitive research.* 1989 ASCD Yearbook. Alexandria, VA: Association for Supervision and Curriculum Development.

Samples, B. (1992, October). Using learning modalities to celebrate intelligence. *Educational Leadership, 50*(2), 62–66.

Shaughnessy, M. F. (1990). Cognitive structures of the gifted: Theoretical perspectives, factor analysis, triarchic theories of intelligence, and insight issues. *Gifted Education International, 6*(3), 149–151.

Sigel, I. E., & Cocking, R. R. (1977). *Cognitive development from childhood to adolescence: A constructivist perspective.* New York: Holt, Rinehart & Winston.

Sylwester, R. (1993, December/1994, January). What the biology of the brain tells us about learning. *Educational Leadership, 51*(4), 46–51.

Sylwester, R., Chall, J. S., Wittrock, M. C., & Hart, L. A. (1991, October). The educational implications of brain research. *Educational Leadership, 39*(1), 6–17.

Tompkins, G., & Hoskisson, K. (1993). *Language arts, content, and teaching strategies* (2nd ed.). Englewood Cliffs, NJ: Merrill/Prentice Hall.

Valentine, J. W., et al. (1993). *Leadership in middle level education.* Reston, VA: National Association of Secondary School Principals.

Vygotsky, L. (1926). *Thought and language*. Cambridge, MA: The M.I.T. Press.

Wang, M. C., Haertel, G. D., & Walberg, H. J. (1993, December/1994, January). What helps children learn? *Educational Leadership, 51*(4), 74–79.

Watson, B., & Konicek, R. (1990, May). Teaching for conceptual change: Confronting child's experience. *Phi Delta Kappan, 71* (9), 680–685.

Wertsch, J. (1985). *Vygotsky and the social formation of mind*. Cambridge, MA: Harvard University Press.

Willis, S. (1993, September). Multicultural teaching strategies. *ASCD Curriculum Update*. Alexandria, VA: Association for Supervision and Curriculum Development.

Willis, S. (1993, November). Teaching young children. *ASCD Curriculum Update*. Alexandria, VA: Association for Supervision and Curriculum Development.

Yarusso, L. (1992, April). Constructivism vs. objectivism. *Performance and Instruction, 31*(4), 7–9.

CHAPTER 2

Planning and Implementing a Supportive Environment for Learning

No matter how well prepared your instructional plans, they will likely go untaught or only partially taught if presented to children in a classroom environment that is nonsupportive and poorly managed. Thoughtful and thorough planning of your procedures for managing the classroom is as important a part of your preactive phase decision making as the preparation of units and daily lessons, and that is the reason the topic of planning and implementing is included here before the chapter on instructional planning. Just as you plan and write scheduled units and lessons, you should plan and write your management system long before you first meet your children. In this chapter, you will be given suggestions about how to do that. You will learn what is meant by a "supportive classroom environment," how to provide it, and how to effectively manage it to produce the most efficient instruction and the highest child achievement.

Specifically, this chapter is designed to help you understand:

1. The role of the teacher's and children's perceptions in effective teaching and successful learning.
2. The importance of getting the school year off to a good start and how to do it.
3. Ways to provide a supportive environment for learning.
4. Ways to manage the classroom effectively.
5. Ways to establish classroom procedures and rules of acceptable behavior.
6. Ways to avoid mistakes commonly made by beginning teachers.
7. Ways to provide a safe learning environment.

A. PERCEPTIONS

We all know teachers who get the very best from their students, even from those who are the most difficult to teach. It seems that these successful teachers embody an informal maxim:

> If you believe that children can learn, they will.
> If you believe that you can teach them, you will.
> If children believe that they can learn and want to learn, they will.

Regardless of individual circumstances and individual teaching styles, successful teachers (1) know that all children can learn; (2) expect the very best from each child; (3) establish a classroom climate that is conducive to child learning, that motivates children to do their very best; and, (4) effectively manage their classrooms so class time is most efficiently used with the least amount of disturbance to the learning process.

It has long been known that the effort that children are willing to spend on a learning task is a product of two factors: (1) the degree to which they believe they can successfully complete the task and achieve the rewards of that completion, and (2) the degree of value the children place on that reward. This is sometimes referred to as the *expectancy × value theory* (Feather, 1982). The importance of this concept is that for learning to occur, both aspects must be present—that is, the children must see meaning or value in the experience and perceive that they can achieve the intended outcome of the experience. Children are less likely to try to learn when they perceive no meaning or value in the material, and they are unlikely to try to learn when they feel incapable of learning it. In other words, before children *do,* they must feel they *can do,* and they must perceive an importance for doing it.

Therefore, regardless of how well you plan instruction, children must have certain perceptions to support the successful implementation of those plans:

1. Children must feel that the classroom environment is supportive of their efforts.
2. Children must feel welcome in your classroom.
3. Children must perceive the expected learning as being challenging but not impossible.
4. Children must perceive the expected learning outcomes as being worthy of their time and effort to try and achieve.

This chapter provides you with strategies for setting up and managing your classroom in a way that demonstrates to children that they can learn.

B. PROVIDING A SUPPORTIVE LEARNING ENVIRONMENT

It is probably no surprise to you when we tell you that teachers whose classrooms are pleasant, positive, and stimulating find that their children learn and behave better than do the children in classrooms where the atmospheres are harsh, negative, and unchallenging. In a negative classroom environment, teachers seem to "spend a great deal of time enforcing rules, punishing unacceptable behavior, demeaning children who misbehave, making children sit and be quiet, or refereeing disagreements." On the other hand, in positive classrooms, "teachers facilitate the development of self-control in children by using positive guidance techniques such as modeling and encouraging expected behavior, redirecting children to a more acceptable activity, and setting clear limits." In such classrooms, "teachers' expectations match and respect children's developing capabilities" (National Association for the Education of Young Children, 1990, pp. 8–9). Some specific suggestions follow for establishing a positive classroom atmosphere and providing a supportive environment for the development of meaningful understandings.

Get to Know the Children in Your Class

For classes to move forward smoothly and efficiently, they should fit the children's abilities, needs, interests, and goals. For meaningful and long-lasting learning, you must build instruction around their interests, perceptions, and perspectives. Therefore, you need to know the children well enough to be able to provide learning activities that they will find interesting, valuable, motivating, challenging, and rewarding. You can get to know your students as people in a number of different ways both inside and outside the classroom:

Inside the classroom
1. *Classroom sharing during the first week of school.* During the first week of school, many teachers have each child present information about himself or herself. For instance, each child answers questions such as: "What name would you like to be called by?" (When the pronunciation of the name is unique, take time to have the group repeat the name.) "How did you spend the summer vacation or where did you attend school last?" "Tell us

about your special interests." You might have children share information of this sort with each other in groups of three or four while you visit each group in turn. Yet another approach, for older children, is to include everyone in a game, having children answer the question on paper and then, as you read their answers, asking them to guess which child wrote each one.

2. *Observations of children in the classroom.* During classroom learning activities, effective teachers are constantly alert to the individual behavior (nonverbal as well as verbal) of each child in the class, whether the child is on task or gazing off and perhaps thinking about other things. Be cautious, however; gazing out the window does not necessarily mean that the child is not thinking about the learning task. During small-group work is a particularly good time to observe children and get to know more about each one's skills and interests.

3. *Conferences and interviews with children.* Conferences with children, and sometimes with their parents or guardians, afford yet another opportunity to show genuine interest in each child as a person as well as a student. Such conferences and interviews are managed by the use of open-ended questions. The teacher indicates by the questions and by nonjudgmental and empathic responses a genuine interest in the children.

4. *Writing.* Much can be learned about children by what they write and draw. It is important to encourage writing and drawing in your classroom, and you will want to read everything that children write and draw and to ask them for clarification when needed.

Outside the classroom

5. *Observations of children outside the classroom.* Another way to learn more about children is to observe them outside the classroom, for example, at lunchtime, recess, on the playground, and during other school activities.

6. *Conversations with children.* To learn more about your children you can spend time casually talking with individuals or small groups during lunchtime, on the playground, and during other activities.

7. *Cumulative record.* Held in the school office is the cumulative record for each child containing information recorded from year to year by teachers and other school professionals. Although you must use discretion in drawing any conclusions about information in the file, such information may help you get to know a particular child and his or her home circumstances better.

8. *Discussions with other professionals.* To better understand a child, it is often helpful to talk with that child's other or former teachers to learn of their perceptions and experiences with the child.

Learning Styles

Learning styles, a topic presented in Chapter 1, is discussed here as another important way of getting to know your children so that you can make your instruction most effective. Children who are exceptional or culturally different from you, in particular, may prefer to learn in ways that differ from your own preferred way of learning. As stated by Grant and Sleeter (1989),

> Learning styles overlap somewhat with cultural background and gender. Although not all members of a cultural or gender group learn in the same way, patterns exist in how members of different groups tend to approach tasks. . . . [However,] rather than generalizing about your own children based on the research on group differences, it is much more useful to investigate directly your own children's learning style preferences." (pp. 12–13)

To do this, you can develop a Learning Styles Record Sheet for recording data. A sample of a record sheet, based on the work of Bernice McCarthy (1990) has four major learning styles and is shown in Figure 2.1.

After analyzing data collected on the children in your class, you may notice certain learning style patterns based on gender and ethnic background; however, you should avoid stereotyping certain groups as learning a certain way. Instead, use the patterns you discover in the children's learning style preferences as guides for planning the lessons and selecting teaching strategies (Seefeldt, 1993, pp. 292–296).

FIGURE 2.1
Learning Styles Record Sheet
SOURCE: From "Using 4MAT System to Bring Learning Styles to Schools" by B. McCarthy, October 1990, *Educational Leadership*, 48(2), 32. Used by permission.

Student's Name			Date	
THE LEARNER		ALWAYS	SOMETIMES	SELDOM
Imaginative category				
1. Perceives information correctly				
2. Processes information reflectively				
3. Listens well				
4. Shares with others				
5. Integrates ideas of others				
Analytical category				
6. Perceives information abstractly				
7. Processes information reflectively				
8. Prefers sequential thinking				
9. Needs details				
10. Values what specialists offer				
Common sense category				
11. Perceives information abstractly				
12. Processes information actively				
13. Likes hands-on learning				
14. Is pragmatic				
15. Likes to see immediate use for what is learned				
Dynamic category				
16. Perceives information concretely				
17. Processes information actively				
18. Like hands-on learning				
19. Is excited by something new				
20. Is a risk taker				
21. Prefers nonsequential learning				

Comment here about student's method of working individually or with others; about content of people or things preferred; about need for high or low structure in class; about time spent watching and listening versus discussing and touching or about reading and writing versus moving.

Children's Experiential Background

Another way of getting to know the children in your class is to spend time in the neighborhoods in which they live. Observe and listen, finding things that you can use as examples or as lessons to help teach concepts. Record your observations in a table such as the one shown in Table 2.2.

C. CLASSROOM MANAGEMENT

What is a well-managed, effectively controlled classroom? Effective teaching requires a well-organized, businesslike classroom in which children work diligently at their learning tasks, free from distractions and disruptions caused by inappropriate behavior. Providing such a setting for learning is called effective classroom management.

Essential for effective classroom management is the maintenance of classroom control, that is, the process of controlling child behavior in the classroom. Classroom control involves both steps for preventing inappropriate child behavior and ideas for responding to a student whose behavior is inappropriate.

The aspect of control is frequently the most worrisome to beginning teachers, and they have good cause to be concerned. Even experienced teachers sometimes find control difficult, particularly where so many children come to school with so much psychological baggage and have already been alienated by bad experiences in their lives.

TABLE 2.2
Neighborhood Observation Sheet

OBSERVATIONS	IDEAS FOR USING OBSERVATIONS	RELATED ACADEMIC CONCEPTS*
1.		
2.		
3.		
4.		
5.		
6.		
7.		
8.		
9.		
10.		

*History: time, change, continuity of human life, the past, and the methods of a historian; Geography: concept of place, direction, location, relationships within places, spatial interactions, and regions; Economics: concepts of scarcity, decisions about resources, production, and the use of money and barter; Environmental Education: observations, aesthetic awareness, social consciousness, and interdependency; and Current Events: news and understanding it.
SOURCE: Based on Social Studies for the Preschool-Primary Child (4th ed.) by Carol Seefeldt, 1993, Englewood Cliffs, NJ: Merrill/Prentice Hall. pp. 111–181; and an observational sheet developed by Grant and Sleeter (1989, p. 19). By permission of Macmillan Publishing Company.

Another part of effective classroom management is good organization and administration of activities and materials. In a well-managed classroom, children know what to do, have the materials that are necessary to do it well, and stay on task while doing it; the classroom atmosphere is supportive, the assignments and procedures for doing those assignments are clear, the materials of instruction current, interesting, and readily available, and the classroom proceedings are businesslike. At all times, the teacher is in control, seeing that children are spending their time on appropriate tasks. For your teaching to be effective, you will want to continue to develop your skills in managing the classroom.

A well-managed classroom is one in which the teacher clearly is in charge and the children learn. *Effective classroom management* is the process of organizing and conducting a classroom so that it results in maximum learning. To manage your classroom successfully, you need to plan your lessons thoughtfully and thoroughly; provide children with a pleasant, supportive atmosphere; instill a desire and the confidence to learn and to achieve; establish control procedures; provide clearly understood routines; prevent distractions and disturbances; deal quickly and quietly with unavoidable distractions and disturbances; and, in general, promote effective child learning. If this sounds like a tall order, don't fret: if you adhere to the guidelines set forth in this chapter you will be successful.

D. PREPARATION PROVIDES CONFIDENCE AND SUCCESS

To be successful in classroom management, you will find that starting the school year in a positive way is essential for setting the tone for the rest of the year. Therefore, you should appear on the first day of school, and every day thereafter, as prepared and as confident as possible. Perhaps you will feel nervous and apprehensive, but being ready and well prepared will probably help you at least to appear to be confident. Then, if you proceed in a businesslike, matter-of-fact way, the impetus of your well-prepared beginning will cause the day to proceed as desired. You undoubtedly have heard it before, and now it is reiterated: we can't overemphasize the importance of getting the school year off to a good beginning, so let's begin this section by discussing how to do that.

Getting the School Year Off to a Good Beginning

Part of your preparation before the first day of school should be the determination of your classroom procedures and expectations for the children's behavior while they are in your classroom. These expectations and procedures must seem reasonable to your children and in enforcing them you must be consistent. Sometimes expectations and procedures can cause trouble, especially if there are too many. To avoid difficulty, it is best at first to present only the minimum number of procedures and expectations necessary to get off to an orderly beginning. Too many expectations and procedures at the beginning will only confuse children and make the classroom atmosphere seem repressive. By establishing and sticking to only a few explained expectations and procedures, you can leave yourself some room for judgments and maneuvering. The expectations and procedures should be quite specific so that children know exactly what is expected and what the consequences are for not following procedures. To encourage a constructive and supportive classroom environment, when responding to inappropriate behavior, we encourage you and your children to practice thinking in terms of "consequences" rather than of "punishment."

Once you have decided your initial expectations and procedures, you are ready to explain them to the children and to begin rehearsing some of the procedures on the very first day of class. You will want to do this in a positive way (see Figure 2.2). Children work best when teacher expectations are clear to them and when procedures are clearly understood and have become routine. Clear, consistent routines are the foundation for effective classroom management. As stated by Seefeldt and Barbour (1994), "routines help children know what behaviors will be expected and what behaviors are acceptable in different situations. Routines help make limits clear and ease life for the group" (p. 282).

E. COMMON TEACHER MISTAKES THAT CAUSE CHILD MISBEHAVIOR*

Often the inappropriate behavior of children in the classroom is a direct result of something that the teacher did or did not do. The following mistakes are commonly made by beginning teachers. Read and understand the relevancy of each one for your teaching.

Professional preparation
1. *Lack of or inadequate long-range planning.* Long-range, detailed planning is important for reasons discussed in the next chapter. A beginning teacher who makes inadequate plans is heading for trouble.
2. *Lack of or inadequate daily planning.* Sketchy, inadequate daily planning leads to ineffective teaching, classroom management problems, and eventual teaching failure.

---

*Adapted from 1994 copyright material by Richard D. Kellough.

FIGURE 2.2
Establishing Classroom Behavior, Expectations, Routines, and Procedures

When establishing classroom behavior expectations, routines, and procedures, remember that learning time needs to run efficiently (with no "dead spots"), smoothly (with routine procedures and smooth transitions between activities), and with minimum disruption. Try to state your expectations for children's classroom behavior, in a positive manner, emphasizing procedures and desired behaviors, stressing what children should *do*, rather than what they should *not do*.

As you prepare your expectations and procedures for classroom behavior, you need to consider what children need to know from the start. Then review and rehearse these with the children several times during the first week of school and then follow them consistently throughout the school year. Things that children need to know from the start include:

- *How to obtain your attention and help.* Most teachers who are effective classroom managers expect children to raise their hands and for only as long as necessary, until the teacher acknowledges (usually by a nod) that the child's hand has been seen. With that acknowledgment, the child should lower his or her hand. To prevent the child from becoming bored and restless from waiting, you should attend to them as quickly as possible. Expecting children to raise their hands before speaking allows you to control the noise and confusion level and to be proactive in deciding who speaks. The latter is important if you are to manage a classroom with equality—that is, with equal attention to individuals regardless of their gender, ethnicity, proximity to the teacher, or any other personal characteristic.
- *How to enter and leave the classroom.* From the beginning of the daily session to its end, teachers who are effective classroom managers expect children to be in their assigned seats or learning stations and to be attentive to the teacher or learning activity.

Sometimes, beginning teachers plan their lessons somewhat carefully early in the semester and are initially accepted by their children. However, after finding a few strategies that seem to work well for them, their lesson planning becomes increasingly sketchy, they fall into a rut of doing pretty much the same thing day after day (often, too much teacher talk, discussion, videos, and worksheets). They fail to consider and plan for individual child differences. By mid-semester they have stopped growing professionally and are experiencing an increasing number of problems with children and with parents.

3. *Using teacher time inefficiently.* Think carefully about what you are going to be doing every minute, planning for the most efficient and therefore the most effective use of *your* time in the classroom. Consider the following example. During a lesson, Angelica is recording child contributions on a large sheet of butcher paper taped to the writing board. Soliciting child responses, acknowledging those responses, holding and manipulating a writing pen, and writing on the paper each requires decisions and actions that consume valuable time and can distract Angelica from her children. An effective alternative is to have a reliable child helper do the writing while Angelica handles the solicitation and acknowledgment of child responses. That way Angelica has fewer decisions, fewer actions to distract her, and does not lose eye contact and proximity with the children in the classroom.

4. *Too much reliance on teacher talk for instruction and for classroom control.* Beginning teachers tend to rely too much on teacher talk. Unable to distinguish between important and unimportant verbiage, children will quickly tune the teacher out. In addition, useless verbalism, such as frequent global praise and verbal fill-ins (such as "okay"), cause children to pay less attention when the teacher has something to say that is truly important.

5. *Emphasizing the negative.* Too many verbal warnings to children for their inappropriate behavior and too little recognition for their positive behaviors does not help to establish the positive climate needed for the most effective learning to take place. As said earlier, reminding children of procedures is more positive and less repressive than is reprimanding them when they do not follow procedures.

6. *Using "Shh—" to obtain child attention or to quiet them.* Teachers who do this sound like a balloon with a slow leak. "Shh—" and the overuse of verbal fill-ins such as "okay" and "alright" should be eliminated from a teacher's professional vocabulary.

7. *Overusing verbal efforts to halt inappropriate child behavior.* Beginning teachers seem to rely too much on verbal interaction and not enough on nonverbal intervention techniques. To reprimand a child verbally for interrupting class activities is a use of the very

behavior you are trying to discourage, thereby reinforcing the behavior you are trying to stop. Instead, develop indirect, silent intervention techniques. Rather than reprimand, try to redirect the child's attention.

8. *Positioning body poorly in the classroom.* Always position your body so you can visually monitor the entire class.

9. *Using threats.* For example, one teacher told her children that, if they continued their inappropriate and disruptive talking, they would lose their break time. If you establish that consequence as part of the understood procedures, then don't *threaten* to take away their break time; *do* it. Follow through with procedures, but avoid threats of any kind. However, it is useful to remind children of procedures. Reminding them of procedures is different and more positive than is threatening them with punishment. In addition, be very cautious about ever punishing the entire group for the misbehavior of only a few. Although we understand the rationale behind it (to try to get group pressure to work for you), often the result is the opposite: children who have been behaving well become alienated from the teacher because they feel they have been punished unfairly for the misbehavior of others. Those children (as do their parents) expect the teacher to be able to handle behavior problems without punishing those whose behavior is appropriate; they are right in their expectation.

10. *Verbally reprimanding a child from the opposite side of the classroom.* Because of peer pressure, this distraction simply increases the "you versus them" syndrome. Redirect a child's behavior, when necessary, but do it quietly and privately.

11. *Trying to talk over child noise.* All that you will gain from trying to talk over a high noise level is a sore throat by the end of the school day. Trying to talk over such noise only reinforces the unwanted behavior.

12. *Intervening slowly during inappropriate child behavior.* Unless you nip it in the bud, inappropriate child behavior usually only gets worse, not better. It won't go away by itself. It's best to stop it quickly and resolutely. A teacher who ignores inappropriate behavior is, in effect, approving it. In turn, that approval reinforces the continuation of those inappropriate behaviors.

13. *Using ineffective facial expressions and body language.* Your gestures and body language say more to children than do your words. For example, a teacher didn't understand why his fourth-grade children would not respond to his repeated expression of, "I need your attention." In one instance, in less than 15 minutes he used that verbal expression eight times. Viewing his teaching that day on video helped him to understand the problem. He had been dressing very casually and standing most of the time with one hand in his pocket. At five foot eight, with a slight build and rather deadpan facial expression and nonexpressive voice, he did not have a commanding presence in the classroom. He returned to his classroom wearing a tie and using his hands, face, and voice more expressively. Rather than saying, "I need your attention," he waited in silence for the children to become attentive. It worked.

14. *Spending too much time with one child or one group while failing to monitor the entire classroom of children.* Spending too much time with any one child or a small group of children is, in effect, ignoring the rest of the class. For the best classroom management, you must continually monitor the entire classroom. How much time is too much? As a general rule, anything over 30 seconds with any one child or group is probably approaching too much time.

15. *Failing to keep children's attention on an educationally useful video or movie.* This usually happens because the teacher failed to give the children a written handout of questions or guidelines to focus their attention as they watch the audiovisual. Furthermore, an audiovisual is exactly that—audio and visual. To reinforce the learning, add a kinesthetic aspect (in this instance, the writing) to help to organize child learning and encourage hands-on and minds-on learning.

16. *Resorting too quickly to punishment for classroom misbehavior.* Too many beginning teachers mistakenly try either to ignore inappropriate behavior (but if ignored it will not go away) or they skip steps, resorting too quickly to punishment, such as taking away PATs (preferred activity time) or break time, or by assigning isolation. In-between steps include the use of alternative activities in the classroom. Too many teach-

ers unrealistically expect success having all 30 children doing the same thing at the same time rather than having several alternative activities simultaneously occurring in the classroom (multilevel teaching). For example, a child who is not responding well (i.e., being disruptive) to a class discussion (perhaps the child is an immature kinesthetic learner) might behave better when given the choice of moving to a quiet reading center in the classroom or to a learning activity center to work alone or with one other child. If, after trying an alternate activity, a child continues to be disruptive, then you may have to try another alternate activity or you may have to send the child to another supervised location (out of the classroom and that has been arranged by you prior to the incident) until you have time after class or after school to talk with the child about the problem.

17. *Using negative language.* Too many beginning teachers try to control children with negative language, such as "There should be *no* talking," or "*No* gum or candy in class or else you will get detention" (double mistake—negative language *and* threat), or "*No* getting out of your seats without my permission." Negative language is repressive and does not help instill a positive classroom environment. Children need to know what is expected of them and to understand classroom procedures. Therefore, to encourage a positive classroom atmosphere you should use concise positive language, reminding children exactly what they are expected to do rather than what they are *not* to do.

18. *Beginning a new activity before getting child attention.* A teacher who fails to consistently insist that children follow procedures and who does not wait until all children are in compliance before starting a new activity is destined for major problems in classroom control. You must establish and maintain classroom procedures. Starting an activity before all children are in compliance is, in effect, telling them that it is not necessary to follow expected procedures. You cannot tell children one thing and then do another. That is poor modeling behavior. Remember, what you do has a greater impact on child behavior than what you say (see Williams, 1993).

Professional classroom interactions

19. *Failing to learn and use names.* Teachers who do not know or use child names when addressing them are seen by the children as being impersonal and uncaring. You will want to quickly learn their names and then refer to them by their names when calling on them. (For several practical suggestions on how to learn student names, see Kelly, 1994.)

20. *Keeping children's hands raised too long.* Allowing children to have their hands raised too long before recognizing them and attending to their questions or responses provides them with time to fool around. Although you don't have to call on every child as soon as he or she raises a hand, you should acknowledge them quickly, with a nod or a wave of your hand, so they can lower their hand and return to their work, and then you should get to the child as quickly as possible. Procedures for this should be clearly understood by the children and consistently implemented by you.

21. *Interacting only with a "chosen few," rather than interacting with all children.* It can be easy to fall into a habit of interacting with only a few children, especially those who are vocal and who have "intelligent" contributions. However, your job is to teach all children and to do that you must be proactive in your interactions, not reactive.

22. *Talking to and interacting with only a portion of the classroom of children.* When leading a class discussion, too many beginning teachers favor (by their eye contact, proximity, and verbal interaction) only 40 to 65 percent of the children sometimes completely ignoring the others for an entire class period. Feeling ignored, those children will, in time, become uninterested and unruly. Remember to spread your interactions and to try and establish eye contact with every child at least once each minute.

23. *Pacing is too fast.* Children need time to mentally engage and understand the words a teacher uses. They need time to mentally and physically disengage from one activity and to engage in the next. You must remember that these transitions will always take more time for a classroom of 30 children than they do for just one person.

24. *Speaking level is either too loud or too soft.* A teacher's voice that is too loud can become irritating to some children, just as is a voice that cannot be heard nor understood.

Children will tune out a teacher who they cannot understand or whose voice is too soft or always loud.

25. *Standing too long in one place.* In the classroom, you must be mobile, as often said by experienced teachers, "to work the crowd."

26. *Sitting while teaching.* Unless reading a story to your children, there is seldom time to sit while teaching. You cannot adequately monitor the class while seated, nor can you afford to appear casual and uninterested in what children are doing.

27. *Being too serious, no fun.* No one would argue with the statement that good teaching is serious business. However, children respond best to teachers who obviously enjoy and have fun working with them and helping them learn.

28. *Failing to give children a pleasant daily greeting or to remind them to have a pleasant evening, weekend, or holiday.* Children are likely to perceive such a teacher as uncaring or impersonal.

29. *Sounding egocentric.* Try to avoid sounding egocentric. Sometimes it is subtle, such as when a teacher says, "What *I* am going to do now is . . ." rather than saying, "What *we* are going to do now is . . ." If you want to strive for group cohesiveness, that is, a sense of *we*-ness, than teach not as if you are the leader and your children are the followers, but rather in a manner that empowers the children in their learning.

30. *Wanting to be liked by the children.* Of course, every teacher wants to be liked, but for now don't worry about their liking you. If you are a teacher, then teach. Respect will be earned as a result of your good teaching and your caring about the learning of the children. Their liking for you will develop over time. Otherwise, in the beginning they may "like" you, but will lose respect (and like) for you later.

31. *Being uptight and anxious.* Children are quick at sensing when a teacher is anxious, and for that teacher, events in the classroom will probably not go well. Anxiety is highly contagious; if you are anxious, your children will sense it and become the same. To prevent this situation, you must prepare lessons carefully, thoughtfully, and thoroughly, and then focus on their implementation. Unless something personal in your life is making you anxious, you are likely to be in control and confident in the classroom when you have lessons that are well prepared. If you have a personal problem, you will need to concentrate on assuring that your anger, hostility, fear, or other negative emotions do not negatively affect your teaching and your interactions with the children. Regardless of your own personal life, your children will face you each day expecting to be taught.

Instruction

32. *Assigning a journal entry without first giving the topic careful thought.* Many fourth-grade teachers often begin each class meeting by assigning children to write an entry into their journals. If the question or topic is ambiguous and hurriedly prepared, without the teacher's having given thought to how children might interpret and respond to it, children will view such tasks as mere busy work. If they do it at all, it is only with a great deal of disruptive commotion and much less enthusiasm than if they were writing on a topic or doing another activity that has meaning and interest to them.

33. *Using the same teaching strategy or combination of strategies day after day.* Because of their differences, children respond best to a variety of well-planned and meaningful classroom activities.

34. *Using silence (wait time) inappropriately after asking a subject content question.* When expected to think deeply about a question, children need time. (This is discussed further in Chapter 4.)

35. *Using the overhead projector, bulletin board, and the writing board inefficiently.* A poorly prepared transparency and the ineffective use of the overhead projector, bulletin board, and writing board says to children that you are not a competent or caring teacher. Like a competent surgeon or automobile mechanic, a competent teacher selects and effectively uses the best professional tools available for the jobs to be done.

36. *Allowing children to shout out responses.* You cannot be proactive and in control of your classroom interactions if you allow children to shout out responses and questions

whenever they feel like it. Emphasize that they should raise their hands and be acknowledged before responding. Caving in to their natural impulsivity is not fostering their intellectual maturity.

37. *Collecting and returning papers before assigning something to do.* Children will become restless and inattentive if they have nothing to do while waiting to turn in or receive papers. Avoid any time in which children have nothing to do.

38. *Interrupting children verbally or nonverbally once they are on task.* Avoid doing or saying anything once children are working on their learning tasks. If you must make an important point, write it on the board. If you want to return some papers while they are working, do it in a way and when they are least likely to be distracted from their learning tasks.

39. *Settling for less when you should be trying for more; not getting the most from child responses to content discussion.* Don't hurry a discussion; squeeze child responses for all you can, especially when discussing a topic they are obviously interested in. Ask them for clarification or reasons for a response, ask for verification or data, have another child paraphrase what one has said, clarifying and elaborating for deeper thought and meaning. Too often, a teacher will ask a question, get an abbreviated (often one-word) response, and then move on to new content. Instead, follow a child's responses to your questions with additional questions that prompt them to think at higher levels.

40. *Giving global nonspecific praise.* For instance, the comment "Your rough drafts were really wonderful" says nothing and is simply another instance of useless verbalism. Instead, cite specific strengths in their drafts.

41. *Using color but without meaning.* Varying your use of color pens to write on overhead transparencies or using colored chalk or dry markers for board writing is attractive but will quickly lose its effectiveness unless the colors have meaning. If you color code as much as you can in the classroom so children understand the meaning of the colors, it will help facilitate their learning.

42. *Reading child work only for correct answers and not for process thinking.* Reading work only for "correct" responses reinforces the misconception that thinking, the process of arriving at answers or solutions, and alternative solutions or answers are unimportant or impossible.

43. *Forgetting to write time plans on the board.* Rather than yelling out how much time is left for an activity (and thereby interrupting thinking), before the activity begins you should write on the board how much time is allowed for it. Write the time the activity is to end. If during the activity a decision is made to change that then write the changed time on the board. Avoid distracting children once they are on task.

44. *Asking global questions that nobody will likely answer or rhetorical questions for which you do not expect a response.* Example: "Does everyone understand how that was done?" or "Are there any questions?" or "How do you all feel about . . . ?" If you want to check for understanding or opinions, then do a spot check by asking specific questions, allowing some time to think, and then calling on children or perhaps by asking for a show of hands of those who do understand. Avoid rhetorical questions. Otherwise children will not be able to tell when you expect them to think and respond.

45. *Failing to do frequent comprehension checks.* Too often, teachers simply plow through their lesson without checking for child comprehension. During direct instruction do a comprehension check every few minutes. Comprehension checks may be verbal (where you ask a question) or nonverbal (such as your observation of child body language and facial expressions).

46. *Using poorly worded, ambiguous questions.* Plan your questions, write them out; ask them to yourself; try to predict whether children will understand and how they will respond to a particular question.

47. *Failing to balance interactions with children according to gender.* Many teachers (experienced as well as beginning and female as well as male) interact more often with male than with female children. Avoid that inequity.

48. *Using false or stutter-start instruction.* A false or stutter start occurs when a teacher begins an activity, is distracted, begins again, is again distracted, tries again to start, and so on. During stutter starts, children become increasingly restless and inattentive,

making the final start almost impossible for the teacher to achieve. Avoid false starts. Begin each activity clearly and decisively.

49. *Taking too much time to give verbal directions for a new activity.* Children get impatient and restless during long verbal instructions. Give brief instructions (no more than 60 seconds should do it) to get the children started on their tasks. For more complicated activities, you can teach three or four children the instructions and then have those children do "workshops" with five or six other children in each workshop group, thereby freeing you to monitor the progress of each group.

50. *Taking too much time for an activity.* Whatever the activity, think carefully about how much time children can effectively attend to it. A general rule of thumb is that for most groups of children, when only one or two learning modalities are involved (e.g., auditory and visual), the activity should not extend beyond about 10 minutes; when more than two senses are involved (e.g., add tactile and kinesthetic), then the activity might extend longer, say for 20 or 30 minutes.

F. PRACTICING SAFETY IN THE CLASSROOM

All teachers must be constantly alert to potential safety hazards for their children while participating in activities in the classroom and on school-sponsored excursions outside the classroom. An unavoidable result of increased child involvement in active learning is the increased risk of injury due to the exposure to potentially harmful apparatus and materials. This fact should not prevent you, however, from planning and implementing the most meaningful lessons for your children, including lessons that involve them in meaningful activities, experiments, and investigations. Knowledge of safety procedures, awareness of potential hazardous situations, and implementation of the procedures will help you prepare yourself, your children, and the classroom environment to prevent accidents and to respond quickly to an emergency situation.

"Safety First" should be the motto for all learning activities. Many teachers have developed and used special lessons on safety in the classroom. Whether or not you use such a special lesson, you should remind the children of the rules and procedures and the reasons for them before beginning any lesson with a potential safety hazard.

Guidelines for Classroom Safety

Although your school district or state department of education may provide specific guidelines on safety in your school, and professional journals frequently have articles dealing with safety in the classroom, general safety guidelines about emergencies and natural disasters, use of equipment, the supervision of the children, and the general classroom environment are included here for your consideration.

Information

1. Post safety rules and classroom procedures for emergencies and natural disasters in the classroom. Be sure you model them yourself at all times. Review and rehearse the rules and procedures with children until they become routine. For example, the children can role-play extinguishing a small flame caused by a frayed electrical cord or role-play dialing 911 and giving the needed information.

2. You and your children should know what to do in case of emergencies. Emergency procedures—including the location of the nurse's office or the principal's office or the nearest telephone—should be posted conspicuously in the classroom, read aloud, discussed, and response procedures acted out.

3. Animal pets should not be handled by children. It is probably best that they not even be brought into the classroom.

4. Be alert to any child who has the potential for an allergic reaction to plants, animal fur, dust, and so on.

5. Because of potential diseases or allergic reactions, dead animals and decaying plant material should never be handled by children or brought to the classroom.

6. For absolutely no reason should blood or any other body fluid be extracted from children in the classroom.

Equipment

1. Sharp objects should be used with teacher approval and proper supervision. For example, some teachers demonstrate a safe way of carrying scissors—carrying them with the points of the blades down.
2. Heavy or otherwise dangerous items (such as glass items) should never be stored above the heads of children.
3. Items that could shatter when broken should not be in the classroom without teacher approval and proper supervision.
4. Every classroom should be equipped with a fully charged ABC-type fire extinguisher, and you as well as one or two reliable children should learn how to use it.
5. Avoid using extension cords that children can trip over; never overload an electrical circuit.
6. Periodically inspect all electrical equipment for frayed cords. If frayed, do not use them.
7. Avoid using flammable materials and alcohol burners. Rather than alcohol burners, use lighted candles or hot plates with caution. As an example, when children are sitting around the edge of a sheet, table cloth, or blanket and are watching popping popcorn from an electric popper, remind them to not only observe the distance the kernels travel from the force of heat but also to maintain a safe distance from the hot appliance and to note the safety procedure of placing a heat resistant pad, aluminum foil, or trivet under the popper.
8. Plants, animals, chemicals, and apparatus that are poisonous or otherwise dangerous should never be allowed in the classroom for any reason, even if brought and intended to be used for a demonstration by the teacher or a guest speaker.
9. If your classroom is equipped with natural gas, the master control for the gas outlets should be kept turned off.
10. Children should wear laboratory safety goggles when appropriate.

Child supervision

1. No child should ever be left unattended or unsupervised in the classroom or while on an outing. Every child should be within sight of the teacher or another supervising adult. All activities must be carefully monitored by the teacher or other supervising adult. Children must be discouraged and prohibited from doing any unauthorized activity.
2. Never allow a child to climb or to be in potentially dangerous body positions.
3. Never permit children to taste unknown substances. When appropriate, caution them about the possible ill effects of tasting the crayons, markers, paints, paste, play dough, baker's dough, and clay.
4. Children should not be permitted to overheat or to overexert themselves in the name of activities or experiments.
5. Use caution whenever using mechanical equipment with moving parts.
6. When working with molds, mushrooms, or bacteria, children should be provided with face masks and disposable gloves.
7. Use proper methods for the disposal of waste materials. Contact your school district to learn the local regulations for the disposal of various kinds of waste.

General classroom environment

1. Maintain a neat and orderly classroom, with aisles kept clear and books, backpacks, and other personal belongings kept in designated storage areas.
2. Maintain accurate labels on all drawers, cupboards, and containers.
3. Before taking children on a field trip, solicit reliable adult help, even if only for a short distance from the school. A reasonable ratio—a rule in many schools—is one adult for every 10 children.
4. A useful safety rule is that if you have doubts about the appropriateness of an activity for a particular group of children then it probably is not an appropriate activity. In any case, when in doubt discuss it with other teachers and the school principal. In some cases, permission of the parents or the guardians may be required.

SUMMARY

Children are more likely to learn when they feel that learning is important, interesting, and worth the time. In this chapter we described factors important for learning to occur. Just as important as specific attempts to motivate your children is how you manage your classroom—the strategies that you select and how those strategies—including safety procedures—are implemented.

As a classroom teacher you should not be expected to solve all the societal woes that can spill over into the classroom. But, on the other hand, as a professional you have certain responsibilities:

- to thoughtfully and thoroughly prepare for your classes;
- to professionally manage and control your classes;
- to maintain a safe learning environment; and
- to be able to diagnose, prescribe, and remedy those learning difficulties, disturbances, and minor misbehaviors that are the norm for classrooms and for the age group with whom you are working.

If you follow the guidelines provided in this book, you will be well on your way to developing a teaching style and management system that should help you teach smoothly, effectively, and without serious problems. It is important that you select the most appropriate strategies to accompany your teaching plans and complement your management system. The chapters that follow present guidelines for doing that.

QUESTIONS AND ACTIVITIES FOR DISCUSSION

1. Identify three suggestions you could give a colleague for using praise to reinforce a child's appropriate behavior.

2. Explain why it is important to prevent behavior problems before they occur. What are three preventative steps you will take to reduce the number of management problems you will encounter?

3. Describe two recommendations you would give a colleague if he or she had a problem with the classroom behavior of a specific child.

4. Explain the rationale for the phrase "catch them being good."

5. Explain why you think that some learning psychologists (e.g., Piaget) oppose the teacher's use of extrinsic reinforcement for managing child behavior.

6. Explain how your classroom management procedures and expectations might differ depending on the nature of the children, the grade level you are teaching, and on the activities in your classroom.

7. Why do you think that supervisors of teachers expect preservice teachers to prepare written classroom management plans?

8. Explain the difference between reprimanding a child for inappropriate classroom behavior and reminding that child of classroom procedures.

9. Explain why interrupting the discussion of a topic of study to verbally reprimand a child for inappropriate behavior would be considered inappropriate teacher behavior.

10. It has been said that 90 percent of control problems in the classroom are teacher-caused. Do you agree or disagree? Why or why not?

11. From your current observations and field work as related to this teacher preparation program, describe one specific example of educational practice that seems contradictory to exemplary practice or theory as presented in this chapter. What is your explanation for the discrepancy?

12. What is one prior concept you held that changed as a result of your experiences with this chapter? Describe the change.

REFERENCES AND SUGGESTED READINGS

Archambault, F. X., Jr., et al. (1993, Winter). Classroom practices used with gifted third and fourth grade children. *Journal for the Education of the Gifted, 16*(2), 103–119.

Baron, E. B. (1992). *Discipline strategies for teachers.* Fastback 344. Bloomington, IN: Phi Delta Kappa Educational Foundation.

Black, S. (1992, October). In praise of judicious praise. *Executive Editor, 14*(10), 24–27.

Blendinger, J., et al. (1993). *Win-win discipline.* Fastback 353. Bloomington, IN: Phi Delta Kappa Educational Foundation.

Chance, P. (1992, November). The rewards of learning. *Phi Delta Kappan, 74*(3), 200–207.

Chance, P. (1993, June). Sticking up for rewards. *Phi Delta Kappan, 74*(10), 787–790.

Feather, N. T. (Ed.) (1982). *Expectations and actions.* Hillsdale, NJ: Erlbaum.

Ferguson, E., & Houghton, S. (1992). The effects of contingent teacher praise, as specified by Canter's assertive discipline programme, on children's on-task behavior. *Educational Studies, 18*(1), 83–93.

Froyen, L. A. (1993). *Classroom management: The reflective teacher-leader* (2nd ed.). Englewood Cliffs, NJ: Merrill/Prentice Hall.

Grant, C. A., & Sleeter, C. E. (1989) *Turning on learning.* Englewood Cliffs, NJ: Merrill/Prentice Hall.

Harmin, M. (1994) *Inspiring active learning: A handbook for teachers.* Alexandria, VA: Association for Supervision and Curriculum Development.

Hunter, G. (1993, Winter) Existentialism: Practical classroom applications. *Educational Forum, 57*(2), 191–196.

Hunter, M. (1987). *Enhancing teaching.* New York: Macmillan.

Jones, F. (1987). *Positive classroom discipline.* New York: McGraw-Hill.

Kelly, E. B. (1994) *Memory enhancement for educators.* Fastback 365. Bloomington, IN: Phi Delta Kappa Educational Foundation.

Kounin, J. (1977). *Discipline and group management in classrooms.* New York: Holt, Rinehart & Winston.

McCarthy, B. (1990, October). Using 4MAT system to bring learning styles to schools. *Educational Leadership, 48*(2), 31–37.

Meador, K. (1993, March/April). Surviving a creative child's early years. *Gifted Child Today*, 16(2), 57–59.

Meier, J. H. (1992). *Behavior management for young children.* San Bernardino, CA: San Bernardino County Preschool Services Department.

Merrett, R., & Wheldall, K. (1992, September). Teachers' use of praise and reprimands to boys and girls. *Educational Review, 44*(1), 73–79.

National Association for the Education of Young Children. (1990). *Good teaching practices for older preschoolers and kindergartners.* Washington, DC: Author.

O'Brien, S. J. (1990, Summer). For parents particularly: Praising children—Five myths. *Childhood Education, 66*(4), 248–249.

Painter, G., & Corsini, R. J. (1990). *Effective discipline in the home and school.* Muncie, IN: Accelerated Development Incorporated.

Phillips, D. R., et al. (1994, February). Beans, blocks, and buttons: Developing thinking. *Educational Leadership 51*(5), 50–53.

Sanders, P. (1991, Fall). Helpful hints for teaching mathematics for children. *Rural Educator, 13*(1), 13–15.

Seefeldt, C. (1993). *Social studies for the preschool-primary child* (4th ed.). Englewood Cliffs, NJ: Merrill/Prentice Hall.

Seefeldt, C., & Barbour, N. (1994). *Early childhood education* (3rd ed.). Englewood Cliffs, NJ: Merrill/Prentice Hall.

Tauber, R. T. (1990, October). Criticism and deception: The pitfalls of praise. *NASSP Bulletin, 74*(528), 95–99.

Thomas, J. (1991, September). You're the greatest! *Principal, 71*(1), 32–33.

Tingley, S. (1992, September). Negative rewards. *Educational Leadership, 50*(1), 80.

Williams, M. M. (1993, November). Actions speak louder than words: What children think. *Educational Leadership, 51*(3), 22–23.

Wiske, M. S. (1994, February). How teaching for understanding changes the rules in the classroom. *Educational Leadership, 51*(5), 19–21.

CHAPTER 3

Curriculum Planning

Curriculum planning is a very large and important part of a teacher's job. Responsible for planning at three levels, you will participate in long-range planning (planning your instructional program for the school year and units of instruction) and short-term planning (daily lessons). Throughout your career you will be engaged almost continually in planning at each of these three levels; planning for instruction is a steady and cyclic process that involves the preactive and reflective thought-processing phases discussed in Chapter 1. The importance of mastering the process at the beginning of your career cannot be overemphasized.

Planning the curriculum for kindergarten and primary grades is the focus of this chapter; Chapter 4 prepares you for additional specifics of daily planning, especially for the older children in grade 4.

Specifically, on completion of this chapter, you should be able to respond to the following questions:

1. What goals will you establish for your students' growth and learning?
2. How will students achieve these goals and objectives?
3. How will you design a daily schedule to meet your goals and objectives?
4. What knowledge of children, their community, and cultural values do you need to plan a curriculum that will enable you to achieve your goals and objectives?
5. What will you consider when selecting content to teach?
6. Why do effective teachers plan for thematic, project, or unit learning?
7. Describe how you would plan a project or unit for young children.
8. How does a lesson plan differ from a unit plan?
9. Describe the importance of assessment of instruction and student learning. What are the strengths and weaknesses of tools used for assessment?

A. PLANNING TO TEACH

It seems impossible. How can you make plans and follow them when teaching young children? Children are too spontaneous, too absorbed in living in the here and now, and their interests are too fleeting to permit teachers to make plans days, weeks, or months ahead of time and then expect to follow them.

Planning to teach anyone of any age is a complicated and involved process. Philosophy and theory, however, guide teachers through the complexities of planning. A teacher who endorses the philosophy of behaviorism plans very differently from one who believes learning and teaching depend on the interactions of children and their physical, social, and intellectual environments.

Behaviorist Plans

If you endorse the theories of behaviorism, planning may not be all that complicated. Believing that teachers control and initiate children's learning, *behaviorists* feel secure about being clearly in charge. Even before meeting the children they will teach, behaviorists feel comfortable deciding what they will teach and when. They analyze what they want children to learn and then identify the specific skills, tasks, or concepts that are necessary to learning these things. They design a schedule of direct instruction, including drill and practice, along with a schedule of reinforcement and rewards they will give for correct responses.

Assessment is integral to the teaching/learning process and begins prior to instruction. Before presenting a lesson, a teacher would assess the children's knowledge of the content of the lesson. Based on the results of the assessment, plans may be revised. After the lesson is presented, children's learning is again assessed. If children have not attained the skill or knowledge presented, then the teacher begins again. The teacher may repeat the lesson or back up and present a prerequisite to success. When children demonstrate success, the teacher would move on and present the next skill or concept identified in the plan.

It is a time-consuming process to identify what children are to learn, break the learning down into small steps or stages, and then design a way to assess this learning. So a lot of planning may be completed by someone other than the teacher. The developers of scope and sequence charts and the authors of curriculum kits, programmed learning materials, and computer-assisted instruction are often the ones who identify what will be learned, the steps or stages, and the assessment. All the teacher has to do is to follow these prepared plans meticulously.

Constructionist Plans

On the other hand, if you believe that children learn as they live, that they construct their own knowledge, that learning is whole and integrated, then planning is a great deal more complicated. Those endorsing *interactionist* or *constructionist* theories believe that children must initiate a great deal of their own learning because learning is a do-it-yourself project. No one can teach another anything or learn by being told or through rote drill, recitation, or practice. Each individual constructs his or her own understanding and knowledge.

Constructionists do not believe that children should be left alone to construct their own knowledge and make sense of their buzzing, confusing world. As Froebel conceptualized, teachers identify goals for children's learning. Then, internalizing these goals, they structure the learning environment, scheduling abundant time for children to explore and experiment within the environment, and they plan learning experiences designed to enable children to achieve the goals.

The learning experiences are planned around children's interests and needs as well as the goals of the program. They may stem from any discipline—language, literature, music, mathematics, science, social studies, the visual arts—but all are designed to involve children in social, physical, and mental activity.

Instead of testing children, teachers observe them and enter into a dialogue with them to better understand what children are thinking and learning. Based on these interactions, teachers may structure additional experiences, offer information, or instruct a child or group of children as they guide them to achievement.

The constructionists place a lot of responsibility on the teacher. The teacher is the decision maker, the one who decides the goals and objectives for children's learning. It is the teacher who decides what and how children will learn, based on knowledge of the children, the community in which they live, and the subject matter.

B. SETTING GOALS AND OBJECTIVES

In many ways those who endorse the constructionist approach to teaching and learning are right. Absorbed in life and living, children do learn.

Yet, if we want children to live fully today and at the same time be prepared to live fully throughout their entire life, then their learning cannot be left up to chance encounters with the environment. The adults who care for, guide, and teach children will want to have clear goals and objectives for children's learning. Teachers need to consider the following:

- What do I really want the children to learn?
- How do I want them to grow?
- How will they learn, grow, and achieve?
- What experiences will extend and expand their innate, personal ideas of the world?
- How can I tell when a child has learned something?

What Are Your Goals?

The song "Happy Talk" from *South Pacific* says it well. To paraphrase: If you don't have a dream, how will you ever make a dream come true? The goals and objectives you set for children embody your dreams for them. What are your dreams for the children you teach? What do you want them to be like? How do you want them to change, learn, and grow? What do you want them to learn?

Identifying goals and objectives for your teaching and their learning does not constrain you or restrain children's spontaneity or their instantaneous and ever-changing interests. Rather, goals and objectives act like a compass and free teachers. Goals and objectives guide you, provide direction for selecting activities, determine your interactions with each child, and enable you to work with clarity of purpose and communicate this purpose to others.

General Goals

The term *goals* is used to describe the broad, overall aims of your program. Goals are usually stated generally and serve as a framework for more specific objectives. The goals you select will be based on the nature of the children you teach, the values and goals of the community in which the children live, and your own values. Some general goals for children are

To enable them to experience intellectual growth and educational stimulation, by aiding them in
- Developing a positive attitude toward learning
- Making discoveries and solving problems
- Sharpening sensory awareness by learning about the environment: exploring, observing, listening, touching, tasting, and smelling
- Expressing themselves verbally: communicating with others; increasing speaking, listening, and reading vocabulary; gaining skill in enunciation and pronunciation; developing auditory discrimination
- Developing concepts and understanding of the world through mathematics, science, social science, language arts, and other curriculum areas.

To help them to become emotionally sound, by aiding them in
- Building a positive self-concept; valuing themselves as unique individuals
- Becoming independent and self-reliant
- Developing confidence in others
- Persisting in their efforts and experiencing success
- Accepting and adjusting to opposition and lack of success
- Expressing emotions in positive ways.

To help them become socially well-adjusted, by aiding them in
- Building positive relationships with other children and adults
- Understanding and accepting the life-styles of others
- Experiencing recognition of their own rights as humans in a democratic society
- Participating as a leader as well as follower
- Accepting the responsibilities and limits involved in living in a democracy.

To enable each child to acquire physical well-being, by aiding them in

- Developing muscular control and coordination
- Establishing desirable health habits
- Developing wholesome attitudes toward the body and bodily functions
- Practicing safety procedures
- Experiencing a balanced program of rest, activity, and relaxation
- Accepting and understanding disabilities in self and others.

Specific Objectives

Goals are general, broad statements that provide an overall description of your program's major purposes. They are not specific enough to guide your daily interactions with the children, however, and do not permit you to determine when the children have reached them. More specific statements, *instructional objectives,* are often used, especially by those endorsing behavioral theories.

Instructional objectives are so specific that they name the behavior you want the children to exhibit. In writing these objectives, you avoid general terms like *know, understand, appreciate, enjoy, gain,* and *increase* and focus instead on exactly what behavior children will exhibit. Some examples of the terms you will use are *name, identify, construct, solve, select,* and *compare.*

An example of a broad goal statement is "Following a visit to a farm, children will have gained an understanding that there are many kinds of animals." An instructional objective for the same visit might be "After visiting the farm, children will be able to name four animals that live on a farm." Because the instructional objective specifies the behavior the children will exhibit, evaluation follows naturally. You will be able to determine when children have achieved the objective by observing their behaviors. Specific objectives are discussed in more detail in the next chapter.

Working With Mandated Goals and Objectives

Today, teachers are often given programs, plans, and goals and objectives that they must follow. Your school system might have a prepared curriculum guide that you are mandated to follow. Or you may be given a list of competencies that students are expected to achieve. Some school systems may expect you to use preselected reading, mathematics, or other content textbooks or to follow a curriculum kit purchased for the program.

The key to incorporating these mandated programs into your program lies in your ability to state your own goals and objectives for the children's learning and to articulate them to others. When you are clear about your own goals and objectives, you have the means to incorporate any mandate into your program (Seefeldt & Barbour, 1988). Consider the following example:

> ✦ Mr. B. was given a commercial curriculum kit to use in his class of 5-year-olds. This kit requires that the teacher use a puppet to shake hands and say "good morning" to each child in the group. Realizing that the children would never sit still long enough for the puppet to shake hands with each of them, he used songs and games to call each child's name and say good morning in a way that actively involved each of the children. When his supervisor challenged him, asking, "Where is the puppet, and why aren't you following the kit?" Mr. B. was able to describe and then demonstrate how the same goals (those of having the children say good morning and learn one another's names) were being met. He was just using a different method that was more suited to his own enthusiastic personality and the nature of the children. ✦

Presented with a list of competencies and the activities that were mandated to enable each child to achieve them, another teacher took her own list of goals and objectives and matched them to the stated competencies. Thus she was able to document how her goals and objectives were congruent with those of the system. From the mandated activities, she selected ones that she knew were appropriate for the children and substituted some other experiences and activities for those that were inappropriate. She, too, was able to articulate and demonstrate how the experiences and activities she planned were similar to the mandates, and that she was successful in accomplishing the same ends.

One first-grade teacher was required to have two reading groups. She had tested the children and found that there were actually three distinct levels rather than the mandated two. She worked with three reading groups for most lessons but put the children into two groups for other activities. She was able to demonstrate how her class functioned with three as well as two groups.

Teachers may have to make hard choices when faced with other mandates.

❖ Ms. S. was mandated to have every child in her kindergarten on a specified page of a workbook by a given date. Aware of her own value system and the needs of the children, many of whom were immigrants and just learning English as a second language, she discussed the mandate with her principal. He refused to bend, on the grounds that parents, community, and the school board demanded accountability. Ms. S. could not accept this position and asked for a transfer to another school where the principal held values more like hers. ❖

Like Ms. S., all teachers must feel satisfied, content, and secure to work effectively with children.

Achieving Goals and Objectives Through the Daily Schedule

Now that you have decided on the general goals for learning, growth, and development of the children in your class and on some specific instructional objectives, you can plan for ways for children to attain these ends. You can achieve both broad and general goals and very specific objectives through the general routines of the day, week, month, and year; the planned activities; specific lessons; and the projects and themes for children's learning.

Planning Routines and Schedules

The daily schedule. The daily schedule reflects your goals and objectives as well as the needs of all children. Daily schedules differ depending on the program, the ages of the children involved, whether the program is full or half day, and whether it continues year-round. All daily schedules include the components described below.

Arrival. Set aside time to greet the children and their parents and to give children time to settle in. It is an informal yet important time that sets the tone for the rest of the school day. Have your daily materials ready so that you will be free to talk with children in a relaxed, attentive manner.

Kindergarten and primary-grade children all need to be greeted individually. Have some quiet games and activities ready. As children enter the room, they can talk informally with one another, assume responsibility for pets, or care for plants. Some children might select games or another individual or group activity as they begin their day. One primary teacher used this time for committees of children to collect milk money, take the lunchroom count, and do other bookkeeping activities that teachers sometimes spend much of the morning completing.

Planning. Involve the children in some form of planning. Children can meet together as a group to discuss the plans for the day. This gives them a sense of unity and security as the group is informed of the choices available; they can receive guidance in making individual plans. This time might also include group activities such as reading stories, poems, or singing together.

In the primary grades, children feel secure when the daily schedule is posted. Children need to know when they will be working as a total group, when their specific small-group skill lessons will take place, and when they will be free for individual projects or work.

Activity time. The heart of any early childhood program is the large block of time in the middle of the morning (and in full-day programs, again in the afternoon) that is reserved for work and play activities. This is when children engage in individual activities or work in small groups. It is the time when you can circulate among the children, working with individuals or groups, interacting and relating in ways that promote growth and learning.

In the primary grades, this time is usually reserved for reading and mathematics instruction. While the teacher works with small groups on reading, mathematics, or other skill development, the other children may be engaged in projects. Projects are designed to correlate with the mathematics, reading, and other skill activities and might involve such activities as building bridges in the sandbox or using mathematics and reading skills to construct a playhouse or block building.

During this activity time, children are responsible for their own toileting needs, rest, and food. Some teachers use this for snack time as well. During open snack time, small pitchers of juice or milk and a basket of crackers or a plate of snack foods are set on a table. When children feel hungry, they go to the table, pour a glass of juice, select a snack and napkin, and go to a quiet area of the room to eat.

At the end of the activity period, everyone participates in cleanup. Giving specific directions, such as "Vanessa, put the blocks on this shelf," permits children to take an active part in cleaning up and helps them to gain a sense of accomplishment. A song might help speed the time. Using any tune, you might sing, "picking up blocks, putting them on the shelf, now it's cleanup time."

Children in kindergarten and primary grades need little direction in cleaning up. A reminder that in a minute or two it will be cleanup time and perhaps suggestions for how to begin cleaning up are all that is required.

Group sharing. Following the active morning work, children need a time to relax, reflect, and come together as a group. This time may be used to discuss the morning activities, share experiences of the past day, listen to a story, or sing songs. It is a time for children to receive recognition for accomplishments and build feelings of togetherness through group activities.

Outdoor activity. All children need time outdoors. Some programs are able to combine outdoor and indoor activity times by opening sliding doors. Other programs are unable to do this and must schedule a time for active play outdoors.

Lunch or dismissal. If your program is half day, you'll next prepare the children for dismissal. They'll collect their work and wrap things up. A discussion of the morning's events, preliminary planning for the next day, and singing, storytelling, or special activities may take place.

In full-day programs, this time is devoted to group activity as well as preparation for lunch. As some children prepare themselves for lunch by washing their hands and faces, others will be setting tables and helping to prepare food. At the same time, group activities may be taking place, with children singing, listening to stories, or putting on a puppet show.

Ideally lunch will be family style. When meals are served in the classroom with small groups of children eating together and serving themselves under the guidance of an adult, lunch is a pleasant time for nourishing the body as well as learning. In kindergarten and primary grades, children may find that a quiet time following lunch is good for completing projects, doing individual or small-group work, or engaging in another relaxing activity.

Afternoon activity time. After children rest for a period, afternoon activity time takes place. Activities could include another period of outdoor play, a trip to a place of interest, or a special event like cooking or science. Children in the primary grades use this time as another work period. A light snack may be served.

Evaluation and dismissal. Following this large block of time for activity and work, the day ends with evaluation and dismissal. As in half-day programs, children gather their work together, meet for reflection on the day, or sing, tell stories, or play games. Then they prepare to go home.

Including the spontaneous. Teaching young children is never predictable. Even the best of daily schedules can be derailed by the spontaneity of young children. Although you want to have clear goals and objectives and a routine that children are able to depend on day after day, you still will need to consider the spontaneous nature of young children.

As children work and play together, their interests and needs will change. Be ready to change plans and routines and make new ones to follow these interests. If children are absorbed in sociodramatic play when it is time for their snack, make the snack a part of their play. One group of children became involved in building a large fort on the play yard.

Rather than stopping their play to return to the classroom, the primary teacher arranged an open snack on a picnic table in the yard.

This teacher recognized the potential for using math knowledge in building the fort. She also canceled her scheduled math time and permitted the children to continue outdoor fort building all morning. When the principal questioned her judgment, she detailed all of the math concepts and skills the children used as they measured materials for the fort and solved problems. At times, you will want to follow children's spontaneous interests by changing your own plans. Many teachers keep plans ready for events that they know will happen and that will be of high and immediate interest to the children. These can be computer lesson or unit plans or a plan for some activity. For instance, you know that at one time or another young children will probably argue over the use of equipment, materials, and toys. Before the start of the school year, you can identify a book, poem, or game that pertains to the topic of sharing and keep it ready to use when an argument occurs.

Keep plans ready for other things that you know will happen. These might include the following:

- The first snowfall and other seasonal changes
- Mathematics counting in one-to-one correspondence, such as counting the number of napkins needed at snack time
- The study of insects, plants, and animals common to the area
- The diversity of jobs within the school.

You can keep many other plans ready to build on the spontaneous or incidental. One teacher prepared "concept boxes." In shoe boxes, she stored note cards with goals and objectives, materials, suggested activities, and even copies of poems and the titles of books that focused on a given concept. She had boxes on insects, birds, sharing and cooperating, clothing, rain, snow, wind, water, magnets, and many other topics. When she observed children's interest in a topic or event, she had boxes of materials ready on a variety of topics that she knew would spontaneously grab children's interests.

Achieving Goals and Objectives Through Curriculum

Years ago Lucy Sprague Mitchell said that each teacher was responsible for creating the curriculum. She wrote in *Young Geographers* (1934) that teachers create the curriculum anew for each group of young children taught. The tasks of the teacher, Mitchell claimed, were to study children, to understand their interests and abilities, and to study the environment in which they were born, "to watch the children's behavior in their environment, to note when they first discover relations and what they are. On the basis of these findings each school will make its own curriculum for small children" (p. 12).

Today, it is recognized that teachers do have a great deal of responsibility for creating curriculum. To create curriculum anew for each group of young children, teachers

- Must be familiar with the nature of the total group of children and each individual child within that group
- Have knowledge of the community in which each child lives
- Be competent in every subject-matter discipline and knowledgeable of the content from every field
- Understand the strategies for introducing this content to young children
- Be able to plan for thematic, integrated learning.

Knowledge of Children. With the publication of *Developmentally Appropriate Practice in Early Childhood Programs Serving Children from Birth Through Age 8* (Bredekamp, 1987), the National Association for the Education of Young Children, which published it, challenged the field of early childhood education to base curriculum and programs for young children on knowledge of children's growth, development, and learning. This means that curriculum is planned to be both age appropriate and appropriate for each individual.

1. *Age appropriateness*. Knowledge of the predictable changes that occur in all domains of development—physical, emotional, social, and cognitive—is the framework from which teachers prepare the learning environment and plan appropriate experiences.
2. *Individual appropriateness*. Each child is a unique individual with an individual pattern and time of growth and an individual personality, learning style, and family background. Both the curriculum and adults' interactions with children should be responsive to these individual differences (Bredekamp, 1987, p. 2).

Planning begins with knowledge of children's growth and development as well as of their abilities and capabilities. Basing plans on both the universal characteristics—those that make all young children alike—and on those characteristics that make each an individual is one way teachers can contribute toward helping children live their lives fully each day and preparing them to take their place as citizens of a democratic society.

So alike—so different. Children, so alike, are also so different. Each child grows and learns according to an individual internal plan. Each brings different experiences, interests, abilities, and needs to school.

Experiences. Most children enter school with a full, rich background of experiences. Many children have had opportunities to explore their immediate neighborhoods, to become familiar with others who are younger and older than they, and have discovered relationships of things in their environment. Teachers who are knowledgeable about children's experiences can better plan learning experiences that will enable them to achieve goals and objectives. Teachers could

- Visit children's homes and talk with their parents about the things the children have done and experienced
- Walk around children's neighborhoods to see what experiences the community offers children
- Interview the children, asking them to tell about the things they have done, like to do, and would like to do.

With some understanding of children's experiences at home and in the community, you will have a better sense of how to build on them and support them with experiences at school. New activities can be planned to clarify and expand on children's experiences, and new goals and objectives for children's learning may be determined.

Interests. Research suggests that when children, as all humans, are interested in something, learning not only has more meaning, but also is more efficient. "Interest-based activities (whether playing with a toy or reading on a topic of interest) are seen as highly motivating and involve attention, concentration, persistence, increased knowledge, and value" (Hidi, 1990, p. 554).

Fortunately children are interested in learning about everything. They enter school interested in "ants, worms, cars, boats, water, air, space, foreign countries, letters, machines, cosmic forces, good and evil" (Martin, 1985, p. 396). To plan a curriculum, you will need some idea of what interests the group and each child within the group. You might begin by

- Talking with children informally, as they work and play, asking them what they would like to know more about, what they would like to do, or what they already know a lot about
- Observing children as they play, noting the things they play with, how they use materials, what they play, talk about, and whom they select to play with
- Noting the books they choose, the songs they like best, and the materials and toys they select
- Discussing children's interests with their parents, asking what the children like to do at home.

Abilities. Not only do children bring a wide range of experiences and interests to the classroom, but they also bring great differences in social, emotional, physical, and intellectual abilities. These differences in abilities form the basis of other goals and objectives for the group and individual children. To determine the abilities of children, you might do the following:

- Review past records of health and physical growth
- Observe them at play and note social skills and the nature of their interactions with others
- Structure some task for them to complete, observing how successful each child is
- Review results of standardized measures or plan to administer a standardized assessment of abilities.

Special needs. All children are special, with individual needs, strengths, and weaknesses. Some children, however, have needs and individual characteristics that require special planning and care. Planning involves meeting the special needs of these children. You might

- Ask the parents, who are most knowledgeable of the needs of their child, how you can best plan to meet these needs in school
- Listen to the parents' agendas and wishes for their child
- Plan with professionals and others who have expertise in meeting the special needs of children
- Take time to observe special needs children as they interact with others, work, and play.

Knowledge of the community. Knowledge of child growth and development is not the only foundation on which plans are made (Bredekamp, 1991). First, as Lucy Sprague Mitchell (1934) suggested, teachers must become aware of the nature of the "here and now" world in which children live. Then they must develop knowledge of the culture and values of this world.

The child's physical world. Years ago teachers were a part of children's communities. Living in the same neighborhood, shopping in the same stores, and attending the same church or synagogue as the children, teachers had intimate knowledge of the children's world. Today, however, teachers and the children they teach are separated. Because they live in communities that may be very different from those of the children they teach, teachers will need to become knowledgeable of the nature of their students' community. Effective teachers study the physical nature of the children's community. Some teachers drive or walk around the children's neighborhood. One teacher asked a parent to guide her through the neighborhood of the school. As they walked and talked together, they noted the following:

- The physical nature of the area
- Places children enjoyed going
- Places for children's play
- Historical aspects of the neighborhood
- Neighbors with special skills or resources
- Places of business
- Other resources for children's learning.

One day after school, the teacher walked through the neighborhood again. This time she noted where children played, the pathways they took on their way home, and the way they interacted with peers, parents, and other adults. She also noted how people functioned in the neighborhood, gaining insights into the nature of the children's world that affected her plans for the coming school year.

Cultural knowledge and values. Less concrete, but perhaps even more important than understanding the nature of children's physical environment, is knowledge of the culture and values of the community. Teachers try to become acquainted with each child's ethnic and cultural backgrounds as well as the culture and values of the community as a whole. This can be done through various sources.

1. *Informal Conversations.* Early in the school year, teachers can talk informally with parents and children. They can ask them what they do on weekends, in the evenings, before school starts, or on vacations. They can note the traditions, customs, language, special foods, items of dress, and types of celebrations mentioned by the children or their parents during these conversations.
2. *Resource Persons.* A resource person might be able to inform teachers about the traditions, history, and meaning of a group's practices. When teachers are committed to learning about other cultures and are sincere in their interest, parents are generally open to describing their cultural values.
3. *Formal In-Service Activities.* Teachers and administrators can initiate a variety of activities and programs designed to acquaint other teachers with different cultures and values. One school enrolled a large number of children from Cambodia. A resource person who knew about the Cambodian culture and its roles for children and their families was invited to talk with the teachers. In a short period of time, the resource person was able to provide the teachers and administrators with a base of knowledge that they could use in understanding and teaching the Cambodian American children in their school.

Other meetings might be sponsored by community organizations or local businesses and could involve parents and other community residents. Slides, videos, and photographs of the community are helpful in illustrating the culture of a community.

Knowledge of content. What knowledge of content do teachers of young children need? Ruth Stanton reportedly answered this question in the early 1990s by saying teachers first needed a doctorate in psychology and medicine and then four years of study of astronomy, biology, economics, geography, mathematics, and so on through to zoology. By the time she is 83, she said, she'll be ready to teach young children (Beyer, 1968).

Obviously, it is laughable to think that any one person could become knowledgeable of all content from every discipline. Yet teachers of young children do need a basic familiarity with content from every discipline in order to make it accessible to young children. For example:

> ✤ A child was examining seashells left on the science table in a kindergarten. She asked the teacher, "Where did the animal go?" The teacher replied, "Oh, the animal that once lived in that shell went off to find another home, a prettier one than this shell." When the teacher was asked why she elected to tell this to the child she said, "Well, that's how snails find homes, they crawl around on the ocean floor until they find a shell home." ✤

The answer may seem laughable to us, but it is not laughable to think of a teacher who doesn't have knowledge of a subject responding inaccurately to children's spontaneous questions, interests, and ideas.

To make the vast and overwhelming amount of knowledge accessible to both teacher and child, authorities in content areas have identified key concepts, overriding principles, generalizations, or ideas from every subject matter to help the teacher organize discrete subject matter. Mitchell (1934) described how key concepts from the field of geography could unify geography curriculum and enable teachers to make it accessible to young children.

Starting with infancy and ending with the 12-year-old, Mitchell specified the interests, drives, orientation, and tools of children and matched them with key content from geography. She observed how the infant, long before walking and talking, attends to and experiences the qualities of things and how the understanding of the relationship of self to not-self develops. The tools of the infant were the use of the senses and muscles in direct exploration of the environment. The content of geography was that of directly experiencing the immediate environment (Mitchell, 1934, pp. 18–21).

Bruner further articulated the idea. In *The Process of Education* (1960), he pointed out that each subject in every discipline has its own structure. This structure, illustrated with key concepts, can be used by teachers to organize and direct interactions with children.

Bredekamp and Rosegrant (1992) conceptualize the use of key concepts as a cycle of learning and teaching, as shown in Table 3.1. They conceive of learning as a "process of movement from the more concrete, personalized understandings of very young children to the conventional understandings of society" (p. 32). They write:

The cycle of learning begins in awareness. *Awareness* is broad recognition of the parameters of the learning—events, objects, people, or concepts; *awareness* comes from exposure, from experience. The next step in the process is exploration.

Exploration is the process of figuring out the components or attributes of events, objects, people, or concepts by whatever means available; young children activate all of their senses during exploration. While *exploring,* children construct their own personal meaning of their experiences.

Inquiry is the term we apply to the adaptation process during which children examine their conceptual understandings and compare them to those of other people or to objective reality. At this point in the cycle, the learner develops understanding of commonalities across events, objects, people, or concepts. Children begin to generalize personal concepts and adapt them to more adult ways of thinking and behaving.

Utilization is the functional level of learning, at which children can apply or make use of their understanding of events, objects, people, and concepts.

TABLE 3.1
Cycle of Learning and Teaching

	WHAT CHILDREN DO	**WHAT TEACHERS DO**
AWARENESS	Experience Acquire an interest Recognize broad parameters Attend Perceive	Create the environment Provide opportunities by introducing new objects, events, people Invite interest by posing problem or question Respond to child's interest or shared experience Show interest, enthusiasm
EXPLORATION	Observe Explore materials Collect information Discover Create Figure out components Construct own understanding Apply own rules Create personal meaning Represent own meaning	Facilitate Support and enhance exploration Provide opportunities for active exploration Extend play Describe child's activity Ask open-ended questions—"What else could you do?" Respect child's thinking and rule systems Allow for constructive error
INQUIRY	Examine Investigate Propose explanations Focus Compare own thinking with that of others Generalize Relate to prior learning Adjust to conventional rule systems	Help children refine understanding Guide children, focus attention Ask more focused questions—"What else works like this?" "What happens if . . . ?" Provide information when requested—"How do you spell . . . ?" Help children make connections
UTILIZATION	Use the learning in many ways; learning becomes functional Represent learning in various ways Apply learning to new situations Formulate new hypotheses and repeat cycle	Create vehicles for application in real world Help children apply learning to new situations Provide meaningful situations in which to use learning

SOURCE: S. Bredekamp and T. Rosegrant (eds.), *Reaching Potentials* (Washington, DC: National Association for the Education of Young Children, 1992), p. 33. Reprinted with permission.

The learning cycle repeats because when the learner utilizes knowledge, skills, or dispositions, new awareness is created about what is not known or understood.

But what content will I teach? For teachers who support the interactionist theory, or constructionism, that children construct their own knowledge, Lucy Sprague Mitchell (1934) was correct: Teachers must plan their own curriculum. As discussed in Chapter 4, there will be guidelines from school systems, state departments of education, and curriculum planners, but it will be the teacher—with the knowledge of the children, their community, and their lives within the community—who will make the final decision. To undertake the planning, teachers might ask themselves the following:

1. From this body of knowledge and subject matter, what holds meaning for this group of children and for each individual child? The key concepts of any subject matter are developed gradually. With measurement, for example, preschoolers might sift sand and pour it from one container to another, while a group of second graders gets involved in weighing containers of sand to determine which holds the most.
2. What aspects of this concept or content can be introduced to children through their own firsthand experiences in the classroom or in the community? Many events in the classroom will allow children to expand their knowledge of a subject, and field trips can extend this understanding.
3. What ideas or understanding do children already have of this content or concept? Even though young children cannot define or describe a concept, they still may have an understanding or knowledge of it. For example, children know about cooperation because they do cooperate, but few of them would be able to give a definition of the term. Six- or 7-year-olds draw maps and can use them to find a hidden treasure at a birthday party, but they will not be able to use and understand the abstract concepts involved in mapping, such as a scale dimension or key for map interpretation, until after 11 or 12 years.
4. How could this concept or content be integrated with what children have already experienced or learned in the kindergarten, or a primary grade? Children in one school in a port city visited the harbor each year. Preschoolers watched the boats dock and went on a short ride around the harbor. In successive years, their teachers would ask what they remembered of the harbor and set up specific things to investigate. By third grade, these children had investigated such things as types of ships using the harbor, products brought into the harbor, and jobs related to the harbor.
5. What elements of this specific concept does a novice learner need to learn now? In other words, teachers make decisions between what a child can know, understand, or discover about a subject compared to an older more competent or proficient learner.

C. LONG-TERM PLANNING

Just as children cannot be separated into segments for social, emotional, physical, or intellectual development, so too content cannot be presented as separate and discrete subject matter. Identifying themes or units of study that emphasize key or major concepts has long been suggested as a means of unifying the curriculum. Planning around a theme or a unit is congruent with the belief that children are active and learn through their interactions with the social and physical environment. "The learning experiences in a unit of study allow children the opportunity to learn concepts as parts of an integrated whole, rather than isolated bits and pieces of information under a particular content area" (Raines & Canady, 1990, p. 12).

Units and projects organized around a theme accomplish a number of things, including the following:

1. They offer opportunities for a group of children to build a sense of community by working together around a common interest over time. When children work together, they have the opportunity to learn more about each other and to develop relationships. They teach and check one another by spontaneously offering criticism and information as they exchange ideas and knowledge in a cooperative effort. Vygotsky saw this type of social activity as the generator of thought. He believed that individual consciousness is built

from outside through relations with others: "The mechanism of social behavior and consciousness are the same" (Vygotsky, 1986, p. ii).

2. When content is a part of an organized whole, children see it as useful and relevant to their daily lives. "Conceptual organizers such as themes, units, or projects, give children something meaningful and substantive to engage their minds. It is difficult for children to make sense of abstract concepts such as colors, mathematical symbols, or letter sounds when they are presented at random and devoid of any meaningful context" (National Association for the Education of Young Children [NAEYC], 1991, p. 30).

3. The projects and units provide for flexibility of teaching and learning by building on children's interests and experiences. Children's informal and spontaneous interactions with materials, blocks, toys, and books can take place, but there is also an active role for the teacher who guides and supports children's experiences. Katz and Chard (1989) believe that purposeful project work may even include some direct instruction if needed to guide and facilitate children's work.

   Because units and projects are flexible, they can be planned for varying lengths of time. Some seem to end as quickly as they begin if children's interests are satisfied immediately. Others extend for several weeks or even months. As children's interests expand, new ideas are generated and new information sought.

4. The units and projects can meet individual children's needs through a variety of learning experiences and opportunities offered over time. Children can pace themselves, staying with a specific activity for a long period of time to satisfy their interests or needs, or they can select tasks that permit them to practice skills or gain mastery over new ones.

In one kindergarten, a visit from a police officer turned into a semester-long project, which illustrates how units or thematic learning can offer children an opportunity to work together and build a sense of community, opportunities for meaningful learning, and flexibility. The police officer permitted children to sit in her police car. Following the visit, the children began building a police car out of large blocks. A sign was made to let others know the block structure represented a police car and was not to be disturbed. The teacher added a steering wheel, a piece that looked like an instrument panel, and some boards for the children to use however they wanted. The block structure expanded and became a more permanent "car" with seats, dashboard, horn, and gear shift.

As the children's interest continued to revolve around making the car more and more realistic, the teacher provided booklets so children could keep a record of their work on the car. She added books and read the children stories about cars. With a prop, the teacher demonstrated how an engine works. Videos of police cars in action were shown. With the aid of charts depicting a variety of cars and trucks, the teacher asked children to make comparisons on the basis of size, shape, and function. Finally, she added wires, bulbs, and batteries to the children's block structure. With the help of a volunteer, the children were able to connect the wires and turn the lights on and off.

Throughout the project, the teacher varied her involvement from that of direct instructor to unobtrusive observer. And although this unit lasted several months, not all of the children participated in the activities all of the time. One group of girls quickly lost interest in building the police car although they often "rode" in it. Noticing the girls' interest in an apple that had begun to rot and was covered with mold, the teacher directed their attention to molds. These girls focused their time on looking for moldy things, finding pictures of mold in an encyclopedia, and drawing their own "mold" pictures.

Planning for Unit, Project, or Thematic Learning

You will concentrate on the following as you write your plans for unit, project, or thematic learning: selecting a topic, specifying goals and objectives, identifying content, and deciding on procedures for introducing the unit, learning experiences, specific lessons, and a summary activity, and choosing a means for evaluating the unit or project.

Topic. The theme or topic of the unit or project can stem from a number of sources. The selection of a project topic is a complex process, and the genesis can take a number of forms such as

1. The teacher may observe something of interest and importance to the children and introduce this for a topic.
2. A topic may stem from the teacher's interest or professional curiosity.
3. The topic might stem from some serendipity that redirects the attention of the children and the teacher to another focus (New, 1993).
4. Some topics may also be selected by the parents or some need of the community.

Specifying goals and objectives. Objectives direct the unit or project. They tell what the unit is to accomplish and how the children will change, and they lead to an evaluation of the unit. Objectives are flexible, however. At all times, teachers remain alert to children's interests and look for new objectives and ways to extend children's enthusiasm and curiosity for the theme or topic.

Content. You should list the content the unit or theme will cover. You will want to organize and specify the facts, information, and knowledge that will be presented. A list of available materials and possible field trips should be included.

Here, too, flexibility is key. Guided by the overall goals and objectives of the program, teachers select additional content to meet children's changing developmental and learning needs.

Procedures. The procedures consist of an introduction, a variety of learning experiences, and a summary or concluding activity.

Introduction. Almost anything that motivates and stimulates children's interest can be used to introduce the unit or project. The purpose of the introduction is to arouse children's curiosity by stimulating their interest in the topic. This could be

- *A teacher-initiated discussion.* You might ask the children some questions or make a statement to stimulate their thinking or interest. For example, a unit or theme on birds could begin with your saying, "On your way to school you see many things. As you walk home, see how many different birds you can observe."
- *Incidental experiences.* Sometimes a unit arises from unplanned experiences. The birth of a baby to one of the families might begin a unit on growth. Some event in the community—an election, fire-safety week, new construction—might initiate a unit.
- *Audiovisual resources.* A television show, filmstrip, record, or slides could stimulate interest in a topic. You can use other media as well, such as newspapers, news magazines, or segments of TV news.
- *Ongoing activities.* Units can lead to other units. A study of the grocery store might lead to a unit on food, purchasers, consumers, or transportation. In one kindergarten, a unit on seashells led directly into a study of life in the sea, and then life on land.
- *An arranged environment.* To call children's attention to a topic and then stimulate questions and interest, you could display objects from another country, place, or time or a poster or an open book, or you could prepare a bulletin board. For example, you could place a branding iron on the library table along with a few books opened to pictures of cowhands at branding time to introduce a unit on this type of work.

Learning experiences. Learning experiences are the heart of a unit or project. Rather than a listing of isolated activities, these experiences are planned to foster the goals and objectives of the unit. You can plan some activities for individual children, others for small groups, and still others for the total group.

Because the purpose of a unit is to build a strong relationship between learning experiences and content, you will want to design the learning experiences so they work together to form a whole. You can plan a sequential presentation of learning experiences around the objectives of the unit. Analysis of each objective will suggest activities that would foster children's attainment of the objective. Ask yourself these questions: "What experiences will foster this goal? Which should come first and provide a base for further experiences? What will extend and clarify children's understanding?"

Learning experiences may come from any of the following content areas:

1. *Language arts.* Some examples of activities in language arts that can be planned as part of the unit are oral discussions; listening to records; recording ideas in writing; dictating to a teacher or tape recorder; reporting to a group; and writing or dictating letters, booklets, or stories.
2. *Social studies.* Field trips through the school, neighborhood, or community are considered a part of a unit plan. Or visitors from the school and community can be invited to the class. Films, filmstrips, slides, models, and pictures can supplement and complement field trips.
3. *Visual arts.* Painting, constructing, drawing, modeling with clay, paper weaving, and many other arts-and-crafts activities can be coordinated throughout the unit.
4. *Mathematics.* Any unit presents opportunities to use math concepts. Children might measure, weigh, count, add, or classify objects as a part of the unit. One unit, stimulated by the discovery of parsley caterpillars on the play yard, led to the children's determining how many days the caterpillars spent eating, how long they were, how many days it took for the chrysalides to form, and the number of days it took for butterflies to emerge.
5. *Science.* Both the biological and physical sciences can be promoted through unit activities. By building a "police car," the children came into contact with the function of engines, wheels, and the concept of electricity.

Not all learning experiences are educational. "Experiences and education cannot be directly equated to each other" (Dewey, 1938, p. 14). Learning experiences that are educational are the following:

- Firsthand
- Child initiated
- Meaningful
- Continuous
- Covered with language
- Those that involve others.

Firsthand. Children must be able to touch, handle, move, taste, pound, see, hear, and do something in order to learn from an experience. "When we experience something, we act upon it, we do something with it" (Dewey, 1944, p. 139). You can provide for firsthand experiences through the activity centers arranged throughout the room and by allowing time for children to explore them fully. With the time and freedom to explore, experiment, and engage in hands-on activity, children, alone or with others, will be able to find something to act on and something to do.

Child initiated. If children are to learn from their experiences, they must be able to initiate their own experiences. By letting children select whether to build with blocks and how to do so or to paint at the easel, teachers at least partially solve the problem of matching the circumstances of children's learning to their current intellectual growth (Hunt, 1961). When children select their own activities and experiences, they are in control and they gravitate toward that which fits their intellectual needs. They may choose to put the same puzzle together over and over to satisfy their need for mastery, or they may try to build an arch with blocks, challenging their current ways of knowing.

Children initiate their own learning by being involved in the planning process. Often child-initiated plans are informal and take place when 3- and 4-year-olds are asked to plan what they will do next or for the morning. Five-year-olds are able to make plans for a party the next week or for some event at the end of the month. Primary-age children are able to make more extensive and long-range plans.

More formal child-initiated planning can also take place. At the Center for Young Children at the University of Maryland, the kindergarten teacher sent letters of welcome to each child who would be in kindergarten in the fall. Included in the mailing was a postcard she had addressed to herself on which the children were to tell her the things they wanted to learn in kindergarten. The children were to send the postcard back to her. On the first day of school, the teacher categorized children's postcards by topics. The class then discussed, and later voted on, the topic they wished to begin studying.

Other teachers ask children what they know of a given topic, what they want to learn about the topic, and after they have had learning experiences, what they have learned. Children's responses are recorded and referred to as plans evolve. Some teachers ask children to make predictions before planning a lesson or unit. In New York City, a teacher asked a group to predict how many people would run in the New York marathon, how far the runners would run, how much time it would take the runners, and who would win. By recording their answers, and based on their predictions, she made decisions about specific topics that would be included in the unit and learning experiences.

All children should be asked to take part in making plans. Some may be too shy to speak in front of a group or not quick enough to take their turn; they will need opportunities other than group discussions to contribute their ideas. Some planning can take place by talking with individuals or small groups of children while they work and play.

Meaningful. Children learn best when the content has meaning to them. Meaningful content is age appropriate. In one group, several of the families of the children had new babies. Two mothers brought their babies to visit the class, and the teacher read books on birth and growth. The children were fascinated and expressed interest in the books and in describing how the real babies were like those in the stories. Then the teacher used a strategy she had heard about from a friend who taught high school. Following the visit of the babies, the teacher presented each child with a raw egg; half of them had a blue dot, and the others a pink dot. She explained to the children that they were to take care of their eggs all day. She said, "Babies need a lot of care. It's a big responsibility to care for a baby. The egg is like your baby. Take care of it. If you desert it, your baby may be hurt."

The children went off to work in centers carrying their eggs. A group building with blocks soon tired of the eggs and put them in their cubbies. Later, when they put some of their work in the cubbies, they accidentally broke their eggs, which they had forgotten about. After the mess was cleaned up, the other teachers and the principal asked her why she had selected this particular activity. She explained that she wanted children to learn how much responsibility it takes to care for babies. Clearly, these young children, who needed to be cared for themselves instead of learning to be responsible for another, found no meaning in the activity. Without meaning, it was not a learning experience (Barbour & Seefeldt, 1993).

Continuous. Experiences are not isolated. A thread of meaning should run through children's experiences, with one experience building on another. In one primary classroom, children's interest in a stray kitten on the play yard led the teacher to reading a story about kittens. Next, a veterinarian visited the class. She described how kittens grew and discussed her occupation. The class sorted and classified pictures of cats living in the wild, zoos, and homes, and took a trip to the zoo so the children could observe the big cats.

The children compared sizes and weights of cats, and they observed, discussed, and charted the likenesses and differences between cats and other animals. As the children's interest expanded, they consulted reference books and viewed filmstrips. They painted pictures of cats and other animals and created books. These experiences, presented as a continuous whole, gave children the opportunity to develop conceptual relationships between the separate subjects of biology, mathematics, language, and science.

Language. Shared experiences and activities give children something to talk about. Given the freedom to talk, children's informal conversations and interactions "contribute substantially to intellectual development in general, and literacy growth in particular" (Dyson, 1987). Children converse informally as they work together on a puzzle, rotate the eggs in the incubator, or build with blocks.

More formal conversations take place during group times. Teachers encourage children to tell how they completed a project, found their way to the nurse's office, or why they think the fish died. They discuss plans for the day or the party next week.

Experiences demand expression. Langer (1942) believed humans were born with an urgent physiological need to express the meaning of their experiences in symbolic form—a need no other living creature has. As children think about their experiences, they develop ideas about them and feel the need to express them in some way. Expression of their ideas can take many forms. Children may draw or paint a picture about their experience or they may dance about it, or describe it in speech or writing.

Little by little, children take responsibility for their own writing. They begin by copying letters, words, and sentences, or by writing, figuring out and inventing their own spelling as they go.

Involve others. Children need to share an experience with others in order to learn from it. First, by sharing the same experience, children have a base for social activity and their play. In one classroom, a behind-the-counter trip to a fast-food restaurant resulted in sociodramatic play, with children taking on the roles of cooks, servers, and customers.

Summary activity or conclusion. An experience is not educational unless there is time to reflect on it. After having an experience, children need some way to organize, present, or summarize their perceptions and ideas about it. In the British Infant Schools, children created displays that represented and summarized their experiences. One display, a table covered with a colorful cloth, consisted of seashells grouped by type, and mounted pictures and stories about seashells hung above the table. A few books were open to pictures of shells.

Primary children may use graphs to organize an experience. The number of cardinals, blue jays, and other birds observed feeding at the windowsill bird feeder were charted as a graph in one classroom.

Individuals or groups may present their ideas or findings to the class. They may put on a play, acting out a story they've read or one they've created, or show and tell the group about their experiences. Other ways children can organize an experience are to draw or paint about it, dance, or write about the experience.

Assessment. No unit is complete without an evaluation. The summary activities will provide an opportunity to evaluate the theme or project. Both the process and products that result from summary activities can be analyzed to determine whether or not children are achieving the goals of the program. How did the children work together? Do their activities show growth of knowledge from awareness to utilization? Are children moving to more sophisticated understandings, relating current experiences to previous activities?

You can get children to evaluate their own experiences by asking them to tell what they liked the best, what they know now that they didn't know before the project or unit, or what skills they gained. What knowledge or skills do they still want to know about?

D. SHORT-TERM PLANNING: LESSON PLANS

There will be times, perhaps during a unit or period, when you will want to achieve a goal or objective of the program through a specific lesson. Planned lessons differ from unit or project plans in length of time and in purpose. The planned lessons are part of a unit or project and may last 10 or 20 minutes or for a morning or day. As discussed in Chapter 4, a lesson has very specific goals and objectives directing specific learning activities.

Beginning teachers find that writing lesson plans helps guide their thinking about what they will do. Even experienced teachers continue to write lesson plans and use them to help inform parents, administrators, and other teachers about what they are teaching and children are learning. Once you start writing a lesson plan for every lesson, planning becomes a habit or task that is done easily and facilitates your teaching.

Every lesson plan includes a statement of goals and objectives, a statement of procedures, and an evaluation.

Goals, Objectives, and Procedures of a Lesson Plan

Go back to the general, broad goals of the program. Select one of them. Then plan one or two very specific instructional objectives for the lesson. An instructional objective, such as, "after listening to a story of the three bears, the children will be able to identify the biggest and smallest chairs in the room," describes the activity as well as very specifically what the children will be able to do after the learning activity.

Procedures are the activities you and the children will do to achieve goals and instructional objectives. They include your own preparation, some way of initiating the lesson, and the activities you will follow.

Always prepare yourself before a lesson by refreshing your knowledge of the topic. If you want to introduce children to the concept of shadows, you may read something about the rotation of the Earth or attend a lecture at a local college on the solar system. This ensures that you will present children with accurate information, gives you the knowledge necessary to answer questions, and allows you to arrange activities and experiences in the correct sequence.

Next, find out what the children know and understand about the topic. As you work with children, ask them what they know about shadows, the sun, and the Earth. Try to uncover their knowledge of the topic. This permits you to present children with experiences that build on their knowledge and provide a challenge without overwhelming them.

Locate resources and materials for the lesson. Identify possible resource people, library books, audiovisual aids, and any other materials you might need for art activities, dramatic play, and any other experiences you are planning.

Think of a way to initiate the lesson. You do not necessarily have to entertain children, but you should think of a way to interest them. You might introduce them to the game of shadow tag, put pictures of shadows around the room, or read Blaise Cender's *Shadows* (1982).

Now select the activities. In selecting activities, ask yourself, "How will this enable children to achieve the specified goals and objectives?" One teacher selected the activity of pasting cotton balls on cardboard to develop children's concepts of snow. When asked how this related to her goal of increasing children's knowledge of snow, she replied, "but it's so cute, and the children just love it." Obviously this activity did not aid in achieving her goal.

Select learning activities that

- Permit children to have an intense personal involvement in the experience. It should be of interest to them and relevant to their lives.
- Offer emotional satisfaction. The experience should offer a challenge but also be one that children can successfully achieve.
- Give children an opportunity to think. The experience will demand that they think. There should be consequences that children will have to relate to their experiences or future events, and they'll have to think about and reflect on the experience.

Assessment

The final stage of lesson planning is deciding whether the goals and objectives for the lesson have been fulfilled. If you've stated instructional objectives, you have built *evaluation* into the lesson.

At this point, you want to evaluate only a specific lesson, not the entire program. Evaluation can include observations of the children during work and play and over a period of time. The teacher who developed the lesson on shadows observed children playing with their own shadows over a number of weeks. She noted how each one used vocabulary and how each one demonstrated knowledge of and interest in shadows.

Other lessons can be evaluated by asking children to draw, dance, or act something out. A learning station, game, or specific task can be designed to help you determine children's understanding of the goals and objectives of a specific lesson.

Figures 3.1 and 3.2 provide an example of a unit plan and a sample lesson plan, respectively. Section M of Chapter 4 includes a complete integrated unit with daily lessons.

E. THE FINAL STEP—ASSESSMENT

You determine the worth or value of your teaching during the assessment process. It is then that you judge whether the children have learned what you set out to teach. Careful planning is useless if you have no way of determining whether you have reached your goals.

You need to know how far you have come in achieving the goals of the daily schedule, lessons, and units. Are you going to repeat these programs next year simply because you wrote them and they seemed to go reasonably well regardless of the children's achievement, growth, or learning?

FIGURE 3.1

An Example of a Unit Plan

Topic

Select a topic that reflects the interests, needs, and background experiences of the children and fits the goals and objectives of the program. Ask children about the things they're interested in, or interview the parents to gain insights into children's interests. Observe children at play to determine their interests and thinking.

Goals and Objectives

Determine the general goal for the unit as well as specific objectives. Select one or two broad, general goals and a few specific objectives.

Content or Scope

Even though you're planning for the unit to be presented over a number of weeks, limit the scope of the unit. Select the points you want to cover and identify the facts and concepts you will present.

Materials and Resources

Identify available materials, possible field trips, and other resources you will use.

Initiating the Unit

The purpose of the initial activity is to arouse the children's curiosity by stimulating their interest. Some suggested activities might be audiovisual materials, an arranged environment—such as a branding iron and books on cowhands left on the library table for a unit on jobs of cowhands—or it may be teacher-directed, "Today we're going to learn about. . . ."

Learning Experiences

The learning experiences are the heart of the unit. Rather than a listing of isolated activities, these experiences are planned to foster the unit's goals and objectives and to support the content and theme. All learning experiences should work together to form a unified whole because the purpose of the unit is to build a strong relationship between experiences and content. A sequential presentation of learning experiences can be planned around the objectives. Ask yourself, "What experiences will foster this goal? Which should come first and provide a base for further experiences? What will extend and clarify children's learning?" Experiences will include those from the language arts, mathematics, science, music, or social studies.

Summary

A culminating activity provides time for review, closure, and reflection. It gives children an opportunity to tie concepts together. Units could end with children singing songs, acting out stories, dictating experience charts or thank-you letters, completing booklets, or sharing with others through a celebration. A "cowhand" day ended the unit on jobs of a cowhand, and the children made chili and took their "bedrolls" to the play yard for rest. They invited parents and siblings to join them in "cowhand" day and listen to them sing songs of cowhands, eat the chili, and describe the jobs of cowhands past and present.

Assessment

Did the unit fulfill the goals and objectives? How successful was the total experience? Observe children and ask them to complete specific tasks. You might also ask children to evaluate their own experiences by asking them "What did you like the best?" "What do you know about cowhands that you didn't know before?" Or children could draw pictures of cowhands, dictate stories, or write about cowhands.

Assessment lets you judge the worth of your teaching, the program, and the children's learning. All assessment should be authentic, that is, related to the ongoing activities and curriculum of the program. Authentic assessment is a part of the program, adding or complementing what is already going on; it does not detract from the daily program, and it is not divorced from the daily activities of the center or school.

Authentic assessment can be informal and ongoing; formative; or summative.

Informal and ongoing assessment is common. All good teachers automatically judge the value of their teaching and program as well as the growth of the children at the moment of their teaching.

Teachers should informally reflect about the activities and experiences of the past day, week, or month. "Today went really well, didn't it?" "Alberto listened to the story today

FIGURE 3.2
A Sample Lesson Plan

A Visit Around the School and Retelling of the Events (Kindergarten)

Generalizations:
1. Events can be retold in sequence.
2. Printed words are symbols for speech.

Learning environment:
The principal's office, library, cafeteria, music room, the first-grade room, the kindergarten room, and/or other rooms the children select. Chart paper, felt-tip pen, and pointer for the teacher at circle time.

Behavioral objectives:
1. Children will be able to retell in order the events of the visit around the school.
2. Children will identify the room visited—"reading" from the chart made by the teacher and children.

Procedure:
1. At the beginning of the day, the teacher announces that the children, in groups of five, will visit several other rooms in the school today.
2. The teacher elicits from the children names of different rooms and lets the children select five to visit.
3. The children and teacher take the trip, stopping at each room, and the teacher elicits from children what room it is, its function, and the order of visiting.
4. At circle time children retell the events of the trip in sequential order, while the teacher writes on the chart the rooms visited as children name them.
5. After the list is complete, the teacher uses the pointer and asks the children to name the rooms as he or she moves pointer from left to right under each room to be named.

Adjustments for skill levels:
1. The teacher asks children with fewer concepts first, accepting less advanced sentence structure or one-word answers.
2. The teacher asks the more advanced child afterward, requiring more complete sentences.

Assessment:
1. Later, in an interview with each child, the teacher checks to see if the child can retell the visit in sequence.
2. By noting the ability of children to pick out room names from the chart, the teacher checks, by observation, the development of the generalization that printed words stand for speech.

---

and answered two very involved questions." "Li is making progress; did you hear her playing with Emily?"

Feedback, given to children as they work, is one form of ongoing, continual assessment. Children need to know how well they are doing in socializing, developing skills, and acquiring knowledge. Immediate feedback lets them know the progress they are making and gives information that enables them to continue working. Feedback isn't just praise; it offers children specific information about their current work and progress. "You can climb to the third rung." "You painted with three colors today." "You know all of the vowels." Some feedback helps children clarify their tasks. "Put this here, then try it this way." Other feedback permits them to analyze and evaluate their own work: "How did you think it went?" "What would happen if you. . . ?" When feedback is based on the child's individual work and progress, it helps the child feel worthy, respected, and valued.

Your program is also the focus of ongoing evaluation. Parents, other teachers, or supervisors may comment on the success of the total program. "The children seem to be doing very well." "Everyone is growing steadily in the program."

The term *formative assessment* was first used to refer to curriculum improvement: "It involves the collection of appropriate evidence during the construction and trying out of a new curriculum in such a way that revisions of the curriculum can be based on evidence" (Bloom, Hastings, & Madaus, 1971, p. 117). Now the term is used for any assessment of the teaching-learning process that leads to improving the curriculum, teaching, and children's growth and learning.

Formative assessment, which helps you to formulate goals and objectives for your program and children's learning, is also ongoing and continual, but it is more formal. In formative assessment, you systematically collect evidence that will be used to assess the worth of your teaching, the program, and the children's growth and learning. Then you use this evidence to make changes in the program, curriculum, goals and objectives, content, and teaching to improve the quality of children's experiences in the early childhood program.

Summative assessment usually takes place at the end of a lesson, unit, or school year. It is often conducted by an unbiased outsider to provide an objective evaluation and judgment about the success of your teaching, curriculum, or program. Standardized tests are the most frequently used tool for summative assessment. These tests determine how children stand in relation to children of the same age or level throughout the nation. Thus a judgment can be reached as to the program's value, the effectiveness of your teaching and the curriculum, and the nature of children's growth, development, and learning.

Because summative assessment is frequently mandated by the funding agency, the school system, or the legislature, you probably will have little input into the decision to be a part of summative assessment procedures. You can, however, familiarize yourself with the assessment tools in order to be in a position to recommend appropriate measurement procedures.

Tools for Assessment

By becoming acquainted with a variety of assessment methods, including the use of standardized tests, you may be able to influence selection of measurement tools and procedures suitable to evaluating the growth of the children you teach and your program. A variety of measurement procedures can be used in both formative and summative assessments. These include *systematic* observations of children's behaviors, structured interviews, records of children's work, checklists and rating scales, and standardized tests. (See also Chapter 5.)

Observations. From the day the early kindergarten teachers heard G. Stanley Hall discussing the value of observing children, early childhood educators have used systematic observation of children as a means of evaluating their growth and achievement as well as a way to judge programs and teaching.

Scientific observations of children, unlike standardized testing, are authentic and unobtrusive; they do not interrupt the child or the activities of the day. They are natural and do not consist of contrived tasks, but instead they use children's natural environment and ongoing activities.

Observations that are collected and analyzed over time also yield a great deal of information about children. Some educators believe that behaviors that deviate from the norm can be accurately identified when children, especially those with handicapping conditions, are observed under similar conditions over time or while completing similar tasks.

It takes some time and training to learn to observe children objectively. Observations, unlike standardized tests, have the weakness of being open to different interpretations and the biases of the observer. If, however, you learn to focus on the behavior of the children you are observing and you describe it without drawing inferences, you'll have an accurate and objective evaluation method.

Structured interviews. You can combine observational techniques with structured interviews. You might model these after Piaget's techniques as you interview children and record their responses. This will give you an objective perception of their developmental levels as well as of the progress they are making.

A specific task might be designed based on a program goal or objective. For instance, if you want children to learn to count using one-to-one correspondence, you might use a flannel board and cut-out trees and ask children to count the number of trees by placing them one at a time on the flannel board. Or you might arrange some cutouts, perhaps pumpkins, in groups on the flannel board and ask children to tell you which group has the most or least.

If your goal is to foster children's use of descriptive language, you could find a picture book and ask them to tell you about the pictures. Or you might show individuals a picture and have them tell you all they can about it.

Begin by establishing rapport with the children and by building security. Ask questions designed to probe the children's thinking, such as "Why does the sun come up?" Design the questions to relate to your goals and objectives.

When a child has answered, don't indicate whether the response is correct but probe for a deeper understanding of the child's thinking. Ask why, or say, "Tell me more. . . ," "Show me," "Another girl told me. . . . What do you think of that?" In this way, you'll be able to uncover more of children's thinking and ideas.

Give children plenty of time to respond. When giving standardized tests, time is limited; when administering an individual interview, you'll want to give children all the time they need to think and respond.

Interviews can be conducted during activity time or any time you and a child can get together for a few moments. As you interview children, look for the following:

1. *Consistency.* Does the child have a stable set of responses? Does the child reply in the same way to the same type of questions?
2. *Accuracy.* Are the child's answers correct? Is the response accurate even if it does not include all of the possibilities?
3. *Clarity.* Is the response clear and acceptable?
4. *Fullness.* How complete was the response? How many aspects of the concept were not covered by the response? How many illustrations of the concept were given?

Children may not be able to verbalize some of their concepts or understandings. Ask them to show you, draw, find an example of the concept, or act it out. They can also use pictures and manipulable objects (Darrow, 1964).

Work records and portfolios. Interviews and observations are wonderful sources of information about children's progress, their strengths and weaknesses, and the concepts or skills they have or have not yet mastered. Another excellent and authentic way of illustrating children's progress is by collecting samples of their work over time (Grace & Shores, 1992). Teachers collect all types of work as examples of children's achievement (Meisels & Steele, 1991). In many classrooms children have their own math folders, reading folders, and science and social studies portfolios of projects.

Examples of samples that are included in portfolios are

- Children's drawings, paintings, scribbles, or other work
- Logs of books read to or by children
- Photos of children working, or of a special product
- Notes and comments from interviews with the child
- Copies of pages of journals with invented spelling preserved
- Tape recordings of children telling or reading a story, reciting a poem, or recording some special event
- Videos of children
- Dictated or written stories.

Children, teachers, and parents all contribute to a portfolio. The child, as well as teachers and parents, should have the opportunity to select work samples to place in the portfolio. Meisels and Steele (1991) suggest that teachers guide the process of asking a child to contribute work samples to the portfolio. The teacher might ask the child to select something that was difficult to do, that illustrates a special accomplishment, or has special merit and meaning.

All materials should be dated and something should be recorded about when, how, and under what conditions that work was completed. Growth charts, checklists, standardized test scores, and observation information can be included.

When work in the portfolios is an accurate representation of children's growth and achievement, teachers can use the portfolio to assess their progress. The work is not to be compared with the work of other children, but rather each child's work should be analyzed and assessed for progress toward a standard of performance. The standard is consistent with the teacher's curriculum and with appropriate developmental expectations (Grace & Shores, 1992).

Some teachers assess the portfolio with the child. Going through samples of work, the child or teacher enters into a dialogue about the work samples. The teacher can gain insights into the child's perceptions as well as the total worth of the program by learning the child's perspective of his or her work and progress.

In the primary grades, teachers, parents, and children can confer together over the portfolio. In one school, teachers ask the child to show and discuss the work samples in his or her portfolio with the parent before all of them meet. Then all of them have a conference to discuss the portfolio.

However the portfolio is used, the idea is to use samples of the work in order to reach conclusions about children's achievement, abilities, strengths, weaknesses, and needs. These conclusions can be the basis for planning to meet each child's needs and strengthening the total program.

Checklists and rating scales. Some teachers find checklists or rating scales convenient ways to evaluate children's progress. You can design and construct checklists to assess attainment of specific goals, skills, or concepts. Other checklists are based on more general goals of early childhood education and are provided by school systems or state departments of education. Figure 3.3 gives examples of a checklist and a rating scale. (See also Chapter 5.)

Self-assessment. Self-assessment is not only useful for you, but it also enables children to begin to monitor their own thinking and learning. Asking children to assess their growth gives you insights into the agreement between your goals and the children's expectations for themselves. The children also are given an opportunity to make decisions about their own learning.

You might ask children to describe their progress in a specific curriculum area. "What did you like best and why?" "What materials did you enjoy painting with?" "What did you learn today?" "What do you want to learn next?" "What is your hardest subject?" "How do you think you can learn to do that?" "How many things do you know now that you didn't know at the beginning of school?"

Older children can make booklets recording answers to these questions, dictating, writing, and illustrating what they've learned. Some teachers have found that checklists children complete for themselves foster self-assessment.

FIGURE 3.3
Checklist and Rating Scale

A Checklist
General Response to Language
A check (√) is placed in the "Yes" column when the child is able to demonstrate each item.

	Yes	No
Expresses self spontaneously		
Uses sentences to express ideas		
Likes to be read to		
Remembers stories read aloud		
Sequence of events		
Names of characters		
Can turn pages of a book		
Begins at front of book		
Begins at left of page		

A Rating Scale
Auditory Skills Rating Scale
A check (√) is placed in the appropriate column.

	Always	Sometimes	Never
The child can follow one oral direction.			
Can follow two oral directions			
Can repeat two sounds the same			
The child remembers the tune or words to a song.			
The child remembers the main ideas of a story read aloud.			
The child can repeat 1,5; 6,9,3; 4,8,1,7.			

In one third-grade classroom, children kept cards listing the books they were reading at school or home. At various times they wrote different information on the card, for example, characters (list major/minor ones, describe your favorite/least favorite one), setting (does it change), story events, and feelings about the book. By using their cards, the teacher could quickly see what books (level, type, number) the children were reading and how they were interpreting the stories (Barbour & Seefeldt, 1993).

After completing the social studies and science units, a first-grade teacher made lists with the children of the concepts they felt they had learned, and he posted these lists. At different times, he also asked children to write in their journals what they remember about a certain topic, as well as any skills they felt they had improved on. The lists jogged children's memories and aided them in spelling difficult words. Their responses were used by the teacher in planning follow-up lessons and as references for parent conferences.

Standardized tests. *Standardized tests* are given under specific conditions and involve following a manual for exact directions and timing. Two kinds of standardized tests are available: norm-referenced and criterion-referenced. Standardized tests are not always appropriate; Figure 3.4 indicates purposes for which they must not be used.

Norm-referenced tests. A *norm-referenced standardized test* gives you a score that tells you how the child's performance on that test compares to that of other children of the same age and grade. Norm-referenced tests are used to assess a child's general readiness for a curriculum; to predict success; or to evaluate the success of a program, the curriculum, or your teaching. That they are standardized means you can take a child's test score and compare it to those of children across the nation. The raw score is also believed to be reliable and stable because of the standardization and norming procedures. This means that if you give the test several times to the same child, the child will probably perform at about the same level.

There are problems with using standardized tests with young children. First, young children are not good test takers (National Association for the Education of Young Children, 1988). Five-year-old Andrea delightedly informed her mother, "I'm the smartest kid in the class!" When asked why she thought this, Andrea replied, "We had a test today that would tell how smart we were, and I marked every answer even before the teacher handed the test out to the other kids!"

Other children mark only items in the middle or to one side. Still others refuse to respond at all. Christie Marie told her mother, "I didn't tell the teacher anything. She's dumb. I answered all those questions when I was in kindergarten."

Then too, young children are growing rapidly. Developmental spurts and lags are common. What a child learned one day may not be revealed for weeks, as the child focuses on gaining some other skill. A single test given on one day may be a poor indicator of the child's growth, development, and potential.

Further, test bias is well documented. Some standardized tests are normed on groups of children that differ from those you are teaching. For instance, if a test has been normed on middle-class white children living in the suburbs, then it is unfair to use it to judge the growth of children who are bilingual or from a different cultural background by comparing their test scores to these children's.

Because norm-referenced tests tell you only how the child does in relation to others of the same age across the nation, they are often not very useful to you as a teacher. These tests

FIGURE 3.4
Tests Can Be Dangerous

DANGER

Tests and young children
    No Test Score Can Be Used To:
        Deny children access to an early childhood program
        Fail children
        Place children in remedial, developmental, or special classes

---

do not offer you information on children's specific strengths and weaknesses and may just confirm what you already know about the child and his or her progress in your program. Before administering a standardized test to young children, NAEYC (1988) suggests you ask yourself: "What new information about the child will be gained by giving this test?" and "How else could I find out more about the child?" Figure 3.5 offers guidelines for test use.

Criterion-referenced tests. *Criterion-referenced tests* are designed to assess how well a child has mastered a set of instructional goals and objectives, with the criteria specified. Usually this is a teacher-made test. It can be designed to assess anything that determines whether a child has achieved the teacher's specific goals and objectives. Such tests are useful because you can determine criteria that are appropriate to your goals and objectives. The tests tell you how well the child has mastered material, not necessarily how well the child is doing in comparison to others of the same age. The design of criterion-referenced assessment is discussed in Chapter 5.

Deciding on Tests

Standardized tests are often used in summative assessment, in which an outsider evaluates your program and judges its worth or value. Because many standardized tests are not appropriate to use with young children and others do not reflect the goals and objectives of your program, be certain you can have some input into the selection of tests that will be used to evaluate you and the children.

1. *Be certain you can specify your goals and objectives.* When you have taken time and care to specify your goals and objectives, communicate them to the decision makers and make certain that the selected test is congruent with your goals. You cannot permit yourself, the children, or your program to be judged by a measure that bears no relation to your goals and objectives (Perrone, 1991).
2. *Ask how efficient the test is.* Examine the test to see how much time it takes to administer, the energy required from you and the children, and the amount of information the test will yield. With the increasing stress on accountability in most school systems, many programs require children to be subjected to a large number of tests. Many diagnostic tests require a great deal of your time and the children's energies, and they detract from your

FIGURE 3.5
Types of Tests and Appropriate Use
Adapted from *Testing of Young Children: Concerns and Cautions* by National Association for the Education of Young Children (NAEYC), 1988.

Achievement Tests
Measure what children have learned. They are not intelligence tests.
If you want to find out what children have learned in the program, you might use an achievement test.

Intelligence Tests
Assess children's abilities.
When you want to know a child's capacity or ability, an intelligence test may be given.

Readiness Tests
"Assess the skills children have acquired so teachers can plan instruction accordingly" (NAEYC, 1988)
These tests, like achievement tests, can be used to help teachers plan instruction.

Developmental Screening Tests
Assess children's ability to acquire skills, rather than which skills they already have.
Screening can be used to identify children who need more diagnostic testing to help plan for remediation strategies.

Diagnostic Tests
Like screening tests, diagnostic tests may be used to uncover areas of growth or development in need of remediation.
They can be useful in determining the nature of a child's problem.

program. If tests demand too much time, show how you're able to obtain the same type of information through systematic observations of children, records of their work, or a structured interview or task (National Association of State Boards of Education, 1988).

3. *Look at the validity of the test.* Find out how valid the test is. Does it measure what the publishers claim it does? Look the test up in a reference book, perhaps Buros's *Eighth Mental Measurements Yearbook (1980),* to see what the experts think of the test and to find out about its validity.

4. *Is the test reliable?* As you find out about the validity of the test, check to see if it's stable. Find out if children will score about the same way each time they take it.

5. *The norming population.* It is important that any standardized test selected is developed and normed on children with backgrounds similar to those of the children you are teaching, and that special needs children can also respond to the test (Anastasi, 1976).

6. *How will the test scores be used?* More and more frequently, standardized tests scores are being used to keep children from entering kindergarten or to place them in pre- or developmental kindergarten programs. The use of test scores to deny children access to an early childhood program or to fail children once they are in the program, is unethical and immoral (NAEYC, 1988).

SUMMARY

In summary, planning to teach young children is complex. It begins, perhaps, with deciding on whether you believe young children learn through direct instruction or are guided in constructing their own knowledge. If you accept the theories of the constructionists, then you will need to

- Determine the broad goals of your program and the specific learning objectives.
- Plan a daily schedule that will foster the children's attainment of these goals.
- Plan curriculum experiences around the idea that children construct their own knowledge.
- Increase your own professional knowledge—of the child, the community in which the child lives, and the subject-matter content.
- Use your knowledge to plan for unit, thematic, or project learning as well as for specific lessons.
- Finally, you will need to be able to assess children's learning, your teaching, and the program. Understanding how to use authentic assessment and evaluation methods completes the planning process and is discussed further in Chapter 5. In Chapter 4, we focus on additional details of lesson planning.

QUESTIONS AND ACTIVITIES FOR DISCUSSION

1. Collect daily schedules and lesson and unit plans from teachers in K–4 classrooms. Look at state department of education curriculum guidebooks or other curriculum books for lesson plans. Analyze and compare them, asking yourself:
   a. How are the needs of individual children considered in these plans?
   b. Is there a balance in the plans?
   c. How do the plans reflect the values of the teacher, the school, or the system?
   d. Which of these plans would you use, and why?

2. Suppose you wanted children to learn to distinguish between poisonous and nonpoisonous plants found in your community. Write a general goal, specific objective, and learning activity suited to 2-, 4-, and 7-year-olds.

3. Observe an early childhood setting. Note each time a child encounters a learning situation not previously planned by the teacher. Were these encounters used for learning?

4. Ask a teacher if you can see copies of the types of achievement tests used in your community to assess the achievement of young children. What do these tests measure? Are they valid? How and when are they used?

5. Observe as a teacher or staff member interviews children to assess their growth, development, and learning. How is the information used?

6. Describe any prior concepts you held that changed as a result of your experiences with this chapter. Describe the changes.

REFERENCES AND SUGGESTED READINGS

Anastasi, A. (1976). *Psychological testing* (4th ed.). New York: Macmillan.

Barbour, N., & Seefeldt, C. (1993). *Developmental continuity across the preschool and primary grades.* Wheaton, MD: Association for Childhood Education International.

Beyer, E. (1968). *Teaching young children.* New York: Pegasus.

Bloom, B. S., Hastings, J. T., & Madaus, G. F. (1971). *Handbook on formative and summative evaluation of student learning.* New York: McGraw-Hill.

Bredekamp, S. (1987). *Developmentally appropriate practice in early childhood programs serving children from birth through age 8: Expanded edition.* Washington, DC: National Association for the Education of Young Children.

Bredekamp, S. (1991). Redeveloping early childhood education: A response to Kendler. *Early Childhood Research Quarterly, 6,* 199–211.

Bredekamp, S., & Rosegrant, T. (1992). *Reaching potentials: Appropriate curriculum and assessment for young children.* Washington, DC: National Association for the Education of Young Children.

Bruner, J. (1960). *The process of education.* Cambridge, MA: Harvard University Press.

Bruner, J. (1968). *Man: A course of study.* Cambridge, MA: Educational Development Center.

Buros, O. K. (1980). *Eighth mental measurements yearbook.* Highland Park, NJ: Gryphon.

Caine, G., & Caine, R. N. (1993, Fall). The critical need for a mental model of meaningful learning. *California Catalyst,* 18–21.

Cender, B. (1982). *Shadows.* New York: Macmillan.

Darrow, H. (1964). *Research: Children's concepts.* Washington, DC: Association for Childhood Education International.

Dempster, F. N. (1993, February). Exposing our students to less should help them learn more. *Phi Delta Kappan, 74*(6), 433–437.

Dewey, J. (1938). *Experience and education.* New York: Macmillan.

Dewey, J. (1944). *Democracy and education.* New York: Free Press.

Dyson, A. (1987). The value of time off-task. *Harvard Educational Review, 57,* 112–124.

Grace, F., & Shores, E. F. (1992). *The portfolio and its use: Developmental appropriate assessment of young children.* Little Rock, AR: Southern Association for the Education of Young Children.

Hidi, S. (1990). Interest and its contribution as a mental resource for learning. *Review of Educational Research, 60,* 549–573.

Hunt, J. M. (1961). *Intelligence and experience.* New York: Ronald.

Jacobs, H. H. (1989). *Interdisciplinary curriculum: Design and implementation.* Alexandria, VA: Association for Supervision and Curriculum Development.

Katz, L. G., & Chard, S. C. (1989). *Engaging children's mind.* Norwood, NJ: Ablex.

Langer, S. (1942). *Philosophy in a new key.* Cambridge, MA: Harvard University Press.

Lewis, B., et al. (1993, April). Fostering communication in mathematics using children's literature. *Arithmetic Teacher, 40*(8), 470–473.

Martin, A. (1985). Back to basics. *Harvard Educational Review, 55,* 318–321.

Meisels, S., & Steele, D. (1991). *The early childhood portfolio collection process.* Ann Arbor, MI: Center for Human Growth and Development, University of Michigan.

Mitchell, L. S. (1934). *Young geographers.* New York: Bank Street.

National Association for the Education of Young Children. (1988). *Testing of young children: Concerns and cautions.* Washington, DC: Author.

National Association for the Education of Young Children. (1991). *Guidelines for appropriate curriculum control and assessment in programs serving children ages 3–8.* Washington, DC: Author.

National Association of State Boards of Education. (1988). *Right from the start.* Alexandria, VA: National State Boards of Education.

New, B. (1993). The integrated early childhood curriculum: New interpretations based on research and practice. In C. Seefeldt (Ed.), *The early childhood curriculum: A review of current research* (pp. 286–325). New York: Teachers College Press.

Perrone, V. (1991). On standardized testing. A position paper. *Childhood Education, 67,* 131–143.

Raines, S. C., & Canady, R. J. (1990). *The whole language kindergarten.* New York: Teachers College Press.

Vygotsky, L. S. (1978). *Mind in society: The development of psychological process.* Cambridge, MA: Harvard University Press.

CHAPTER 4

Lesson Planning

The emphasis in this chapter is on the importance and the details of planning for your daily instruction. You will be guided through the process of selecting content to preparing the specific learning outcomes expected as children learn that content. Then, from a content outline and the related and specific learning outcomes, in the sections that follow, you learn how to prepare daily lessons.

Specifically, this chapter will help you understand:

1. Reasons for and components of careful instructional planning
2. The variety of documents that provide guidance for content selection
3. National curriculum standards
4. How student textbooks can be useful
5. How to incorporate cooperation and collaboration in instructional planning
6. More about aims, goals, and objectives
7. How to prepare and classify instructional objectives
8. How to assess learning through a response journal
9. The contemporary emphasis on character education
10. Questioning techniques
11. The process of instructional planning
12. How to prepare daily lessons.

Although careful planning is a critical skill for a teacher, a well-developed plan for teaching will not guarantee the success of a lesson or unit or even the overall effectiveness of a course. The *lack* of a well developed plan, however, will almost certainly result in poor teaching. Like a good map, a good plan facilitates reaching the planned destination with more confidence and with fewer wrong turns.

The heart of good planning is good decision making. For every plan, you must decide what your goals and objectives are, what specific subject matter should be taught, what materials of instruction are available and appropriate, and what methods and techniques should be employed to accomplish the objectives. Making these decisions is complicated because there are so many choices. Therefore, you must be knowledgeable about the principles that provide the foundation for effective year-long, unit, and lesson planning. The principles of all levels of educational planning are similar, which makes mastering the necessary skills easier than you might think.

A. REASONS FOR PLANNING

Thoughtful and thorough planning is vital if effective teaching is to occur. It helps produce a well-organized and a purposeful classroom atmosphere and reduces the likelihood of problems in classroom control. Teachers who have not planned or who have not planned well will have more problems than is imaginable. During planning it is useful to keep in mind these two important teaching goals: (1) to not waste anyone's time and (2) to select strategies that keep students physically and mentally engaged on task and that assure student learning.

Planning well also helps guarantee that you know the subject, for in planning carefully you will more likely become expert with the subject-matter content and the methods of teaching it. You cannot know all there is to know about the subject matter, but careful planning is likely to prevent you from fumbling through half-digested, poorly understood content and making too many errors along the way. Thoughtful and thorough planning is likely to make your classes more lively, more interesting, more accurate, and more relevant, and your teaching more successful. Although good planning assures that you know the material, have thought through the methods of instruction, and are less likely to have problems in classroom control, there are other reasons for planning carefully.

Careful planning helps to ensure program coherence. Daily plans are an integral part of a larger plan represented by course goals and objectives. Students' learning experiences are thoughtfully planned in sequence and then orchestrated by a teacher who understands the rationale for their respective positions in the curriculum—not precluding, of course, an occasional diversion from planned activities.

Unless the subject content you are preparing to teach stands alone, follows nothing, and leads to nothing (which is unlikely), there are prerequisites to what you want your students to learn, and there are learning objectives that follow and build on this learning. Good planning provides a mechanism for *scope* (the content that is studied) and *sequence* (the order by which content is studied) articulation.

The diversity of children in today's classrooms demands that you give planning considerations to those individual differences—whether they are cultural experiences, different learning styles, various levels of proficiency in the use of the English language, special needs, or any other concerns.

Another reason for careful planning is to ensure program continuation. In your absence, a substitute teacher or other members of the teaching team can fill in, continuing your program.

Thorough and thoughtful planning is important for a teacher's self-assessment. After an activity, a lesson, a unit, and at the end of a semester and the school year, you will assess what you did and what effect it had on student achievement. As discussed in Chapter 1, this is the reflective phase of the thought-processing phases of instruction.

Finally, administrators expect you to plan thoroughly and thoughtfully. Your plans represent a criterion recognized and evaluated by administrators, because with those experienced in such matters, it is aphoristic that poor planning is a precursor to incompetent teaching.

B. COMPONENTS OF PLANNING

Eight components should be considered in instructional planning.

1. *Statement of philosophy.* This is a general statement about why the plan is important and how children will learn its content.
2. *Needs assessment.* By its wording, the statement of philosophy should reflect an appreciation for the cultural plurality of the nation and of the school, with a corresponding perception of the needs of society, its children, and of the functions served by the school. The statement of philosophy and needs of the students should be consistent with the school's mission or philosophy statement. (Every school or school district has such a statement, which usually can be found posted in the office, in classrooms, and in the student and parent handbook.)
3. *Aims, goals, and objectives.* The plan's stated aims, goals, and objectives should be consistent with the school's mission or philosophy statement. (The difference in these terms—aims, goals, and objectives—is discussed later in this chapter.)

4. *Sequence.* Sometimes referred to as vertical articulation, sequence refers to the plan's relationship or connection to the content learning that preceded and that follows, in the kindergarten through 12th-grade curriculum.
5. *Integration.* Sometimes referred to as horizontal articulation, integration refers to the plan's connection with other curriculum and co-curriculum activities across the grade level. For example, the fourth-grade language arts program may be articulated with the social studies program.
6. *Sequentially Planned Learning Activities.* This is the presentation of organized and sequential units and lessons appropriate for the subject, grade level, and age and diversity of the children.
7. *Resources Needed.* This is a listing of resources, such as books, speakers, field trips, and media materials.
8. *Assessment Strategies.* Consistent with the objectives, assessment strategies include procedures for (a) diagnosing what students know or think they know (their misconceptions) *prior* to the instruction (diagnostic assessment or preassessment), (b) the evaluation of student achievement *during* instruction to find out what students are learning (formative assessment), and (c) *after* the instruction to find out what they have learned (summative assessment).

C. PLANNING A PROGRAM OF INSTRUCTION

When planning a program of instruction, you need to decide what is to be accomplished during the time in which students are assigned to your classroom, whether for an academic year, a semester, or some lesser time period. To help in deciding what is to be accomplished, you will

- Probe, analyze, and translate your own convictions, knowledge, and skills into behaviors that foster the intellectual development of your students.
- Review school and other public resource documents for mandates and guidelines.
- Talk with colleagues and learn of common expectations.

In addition, and as discussed later in this chapter, you will want to determine what exactly is to be accomplished and how many teachers collaboratively plan with their students.

Documents That Provide Guidance for Content Selection

Documents produced at the national level, state department of education curriculum publications, district courses of study, and school-adopted printed and nonprinted materials are the sources you will examine. Your nearest college or university library may be a source for such documents. Others may be reviewed at local schools and district offices. You can also request a list of curriculum publications from your state department of education.

National Curriculum Standards

The National Council on Education Standards and Testing has recommended that national standards for subject-matter content in education be developed for all core subjects—the arts, civics/social studies, English/language arts/reading, geography, history, mathematics, and science. Standards are a definition of what students should know and be able to do. For the subjects and grade level of interest to you, you will want to follow the development of national curriculum standards.

In 1989, the National Commission on Social Studies in the Schools (NCSSS) prepared the goals and vision of the social studies for young people for citizenship and leadership in the next century (for grades K–4, see Part II). Subsequently, several states, usually through state curriculum frameworks, were following those standards or developing similar ones to guide what and how social studies were taught and how student progress was assessed. (For an account of a K–12 program that does *not* follow NCSSS guidelines, see Hill, 1993.) Addresses for information or ordering information related to the NCSSS report and others on social studies curriculum follow:

National Commission on Social Studies in the Schools. To order *Charting a Course: Social Studies for the 21st Century,* write to The National Association for the Education of Young Children Order Processing, 1834 Connecticut Ave., NW, Washington, DC 20009.

National Council for the Social Studies. To order *Social Studies for Early Childhood and Elementary Schoolchildren: Preparing for the 21st Century,* contact National Council for the Social Studies, 3501 Newark St., NW, Washington, DC 20016.

California State Department of Education. To order the *History-Social Science Framework,* write to California State Department of Education, Order Department, Sacramento, CA 95819 (no. 59, 60, 61, 129, 573).

Two organizations dedicated to improving the quality of instruction of reading and the other language arts are the International Reading Association (IRA) and the National Council of Teachers of English (NCTE). The two groups help keep preservice and inservice educators in touch with new trends in the field through their published journals—*Language Arts* and *The Reading Teacher*—which include suggestions for teaching, research studies, and reviews of children's literature, professional books, and classroom materials. Selected addresses for information or ordering information related to these two organizations and their publications are:

Language Arts. National Council of Teachers of English, 1111 Kenyon Road, Urbana, IL 61801.

The Reading Teacher. International Reading Association, P.O. Box 8139, Newark, DE 19711.

Guided by the recommendations of these dedicated organizations and the content of state frameworks, especially those of the larger states such as California, Florida, and Texas, publishers of student textbooks and other instructional materials will develop their new or revised printed and nonprinted instructional materials. By the year 2000, all new standards will likely be in place and having a positive effect on student achievement in classroom learning.

Another organization, the National Writing Project (NWP), can help you learn more about teaching writing when you attend a sponsored and affiliated workshop in your area. For additional information, contact the National Writing Project, School of Education, University of California, Berkeley, CA 94720.

Student Textbooks

Traditionally, a considerable amount of class time is devoted to the use of social studies and language arts textbooks and other printed materials. There has often been a gap between what is needed in textbooks and what is available for student use. In recent years, considerable national attention has been given to finding ways to improve the quality of student textbooks, with particular attention given to the need to develop student skills in critical thinking and higher-order problem solving.

For several reasons—the recognition of different individual learning styles of students, the increasing costs of textbooks, the decreasing availability of funds, and the availability of nonprint learning materials—textbook appearance, content, and use has changed considerably in recent years. Still, "ninety percent of all classroom activity is regulated by textbooks" (Starr, 1989, p. 106).

School districts have textbook adoption cycles (usually every five or so years), that is, the period in which books are used, until the next adoption cycle. If you are a preservice or first-year teacher, most likely you will be told what books you will be using. Starting now, you will want to become familiar with textbooks you may be using and how you may be using them.

How a textbook can be helpful to students.   Textbooks can help children in their learning by providing

- An instructional base that builds higher-order thinking activities (inquiry discussions, problem recognition, and problem solving) that help develop critical thinking skills

- A basis for selecting the subject matter that can guide educational decisions about content in the classroom
- An organization of basic or important content with models and examples
- Information about other readings and resources to enhance the learning experiences of students
- Previously tested practice activities and suggestions for learning experiences (Jarolimek & Parker, 1993).

Problems with reliance on a single textbook. Despite its many uses, the student textbook should not be considered the "be-all and end-all" of instruction. The textbook is only one of many teaching tools and should not be cherished as the ultimate word. Of the many ways to use student textbooks, perhaps the least acceptable is to depend completely on a single book and require students to simply memorize content from it. That is the lowest level of learning; furthermore, it implies that you are unaware of other sources of instructional materials and have nothing more to contribute to student learning.

Another potential problem brought about by reliance on a single textbook is that textbook publishers prepare books for use in a larger market, that is, for national or statewide use, and your state and district-adopted textbook may not, in the view of some members of the school community, adequately address issues of special interest and importance to your community. That is another reason that some teachers and schools, as well as many textbook publishers, provide supplementary printed and nonprint materials for student use. (At least 24 states use statewide textbook adoption review committees to review books and to then provide public school districts with lists of recommended books from which a district may select its books and purchase them with funds provided by the state.)

Another reason to provide supplementary reading materials is to ensure multicultural balance. A single textbook may not provide the balance needed to correct the cultural and ethnic biases that have been traditional in our schools and in our teaching, such as linguistic bias (the use of masculine terms and pronouns); stereotyping; invisibility of women, minorities, and disabled persons on printed pages; and imbalance (the avoidance of controversial topics and the discussion of reality, discrimination, and prejudice) (Sadker, Sadker, & Long, 1989). See Banks and Banks (1989) for excellent ideas and resources on bringing multicultural balance to your curriculum.

Still another problem brought about by reliance on a single source is that, too often, the adopted textbook may not be at the appropriate reading level. In today's heterogeneous (mixed-ability grouping) classrooms, the reading range can vary by as much as two-thirds of the chronological age of the students in the classroom. That means that if the chronological age is 9 years (as is typical for fourth-grade students) then the reading-level range would be 6 years; that is to say, the class may have some children reading only at a preschool level while others may be reading at a high school level. All teachers need to know about the kinds of problem readers and share in the responsibility of seeing that those children get help in developing their reading skills.

General guidelines for textbook use. Now that you have reviewed the problems that reliance on a single textbook can bring to your instruction, consider the following general guidelines for using a textbook as a learning tool.

For social studies and language arts in grades K–4, children can benefit from having their own textbooks, especially when the textbooks are current and realistically illustrated. Because of a school's budget constraints, however, the textbooks may *not* be the latest editions, and in some schools only classroom sets may be available for children to use only during the school day. When that is the case, students may not be allowed to take the books home or may be allowed only occasionally to check them out overnight. In other classrooms, there may be no textbooks at all. To avoid such problems, you will want to maintain supplementary reading materials for student use in the classroom. School and community librarians usually are delighted to cooperate with teachers in selecting and providing such materials.

Some students benefit from drill, practice, and reinforcement afforded by accompanying workbooks, but not all students necessarily do. As a matter of fact, the traditional workbook, now nearly extinct, is being replaced by modern technology afforded by computer software, videodiscs, and compact discs. For the most effective teaching, student workbooks, ditto work sheets, flashcards, and other similarly structured abstract materials should *not* dominate your instruction (National Association for the Education of Young Children, 1990, p. 7). As the costs of hardware and software programs decrease, the use of programs by individual students is also becoming more common. Computers provide students with a psychologically safer learning environment. With computer programs and interactive media, students have greater control over the pace of the instruction, can repeat instruction if necessary, or ask for further clarification, without fear of having to publicly ask for help.

You should provide vocabulary lists related to topics in the text to help students learn meanings of important words and phrases. Teach students how to study from their textbook. There are several similar methods for doing this, such as the SQ4R method, the SQ3R method and the PQRST method:

- *SQ4R method: Survey* the chapter, ask *questions* about what was read, *read* to answer the questions, *recite* the answers, *record* important items from the chapter into notebooks, and then *review* it all.
- *SQ3R method: Survey* the chapter, ask *questions* about what was read, *read, recite,* and *review.*
- *PQRST method: Preview* to identify the main idea, ask *questions* you expect to find answers to, *read* the material, *state* the main idea of the material, and *test* yourself by answering the questions you posed earlier (Kelly, 1994).

Encourage students to search other sources for content that will update that found in their textbook, especially the social studies book and when that book is several years old. A 1994 survey by Quality Education Data, Inc., found that 23.8 percent or 19,967 schools were using the Internet services. In contrast, 5,000 schools use *Prodigy* and 4,000 use *America Online.* This is especially important in an area such as the social studies, where there is such a tremendous growth in the amount of new information, and, as discussed in the preceding section, it is important whenever a multicultural balance is needed.

Encourage students to be alert for errors in their books—content errors, printing errors, and discrepancies or imbalance in the treatment of minorities, women, and persons with special needs—and perhaps give students some sort of reward, such as points, when they bring an error to your attention. Encouraging students to be alert for errors in the textbook encourages critical reading, critical thinking, and healthy skepticism.

Progressing from one cover of the textbook to the other in one school year is not necessarily an indicator of good teaching. The emphasis in instruction should be on *mastery* of content rather than simply on the *coverage* of content. The textbook is one resource; to enhance their learning, children should be encouraged to use a variety of resources.

Individualize the learning for students according to their reading and learning abilities. Consider differentiated assignments, in the textbook and supplementary materials. When using supplementary materials, consider using several rather than just one. Except to make life a bit simpler for the teacher, it makes no sense for the typical classroom today, with its diversity of students, to have all students doing the same assignments. When students are to use materials not designed to accompany their text, however, edit the materials so they relate well to your instructional objectives.

During your teaching career, it is likely that you will witness and be a part of a revolution in the design of school textbooks. Already some school districts and states allow teachers in certain disciplines (where the technology is available) to choose between student textbooks as we have known them and interactive videodisc programs. As an example of a school-business partnership in Great Falls, Virginia, the Computertots company sends instructors and CD-ROMs to kindergartens to introduce children to the media, and one Computertot instructor teaches students the following words to sing to the tune of *Frere Jacques* (Are You Sleeping?): "Disc is loading, Disc is loading, Drive to Ram, Drive to Ram. Busy light is burning. Busy light is burning. When it's gone, Then we're on" (Wilson, 1994, p. 35). In the state of Maine's southern public and private schools—some located on rocky islands and peninsulas—electronic links will be established between schools in two districts, local libraries, and nearby Bowdoin College, all funded by a grant from the

National Infrastructure in Education. Also available for elementary school research are library systems (e.g., *Athena* from Nichols Advanced Technologies, Inc.), with graphics that have been designed to be operated in Microsoft Windows and Macintosh environments.

With the revolution in computer chip technology, it has been predicted that student textbooks may soon take on a whole new appearance. With that will come dramatic changes in the importance and use of student texts, as well as new problems for the teacher, some of which are predictable. Student "texts" may become credit-card size, increasing the chance of students losing their books. On the positive side, the classroom teacher will probably have available a variety of "textbooks" to better address the reading levels, interests, learning styles, and abilities of individual students. Distribution and maintenance of reading materials could create an even greater demand on the teacher's time. Regardless, dramatic and exciting events have begun to transform a teaching tool that has not changed much throughout the history of education in this country. As an electronic multimedia tool, the textbook of the twenty-first century (Textbook 2000) may be "an interactive device that offers text, sound, and video" (Gifford, 1991, pp. 15–16). "Textbooks 2000" may be housed in Education Villages, as is being done in Charlotte, North Carolina, with the assistance of a grant from IBM as part of their "Reinventing Education" reform plan. Charlotte's Education Village (two elementary schools, one middle school, one high school with instruction by performance group not grade levels) will extend to media centers that will be used by the students during the day and open to the public in the afternoons and evenings. The media centers/libraries will have a museum atmosphere, a variety of new technology and a multidisciplinary curriculum. Learning alcoves with computer terminals will be built in the schools' corridors so students can access information anywhere on their campuses. Future plans will be designed for linking the schools to the North Carolina Information Highway, for connecting the schools to students' homes, and for broadcasting educational and cultural programs into the home (Greenfield, 1993; "News" 1994).

D. COLLABORATIVE AND COOPERATIVE TEAM PLANNING

As you have learned, you need not do all your planning from scratch, and neither do you need to do all your planning alone. Planning for teaching can be thought of as rehearsing what will be done in the classroom, rehearsing it mentally and on paper (Murray, 1980). In classrooms today, which tend to be more project oriented and student and group centered than traditional classrooms where the teacher was the primary provider of information, students more actively participate in their learning. The teacher provides some structure and assistance, but the collaborative approach requires students to inquire and interact, to generate ideas, to seriously listen and talk with one another, and to recognize that their thoughts and experiences are valuable and essential to meaningful learning.

Team Planning

Many teachers plan together in teams. Planning procedures are the same as discussed earlier, except that team members plan together or split the responsibilities and then share their individual planning, cooperatively working on a final plan. Team planning works best when members of the teaching team share a common planning time.

Collaborative Teacher-Student Planning

As discussed in Chapter 3, teachers should encourage children to participate in planning some phase of their learning, from planning an entire course of study or units within that course of study to planning specific learning activities within a unit of study. Such participation tends to give students a proprietary interest in the activities, thereby increasing their motivation for learning. Students' contributions to the plan often seem more meaningful to them than what others have planned for them. And they like to see their own plans succeed. Thus, teacher-student collaboration in planning can be an effective motivational tool.

Preparing for the Year

While some authors believe that the first step in preparing to teach is to write the objectives, others believe that a more logical first step is to prepare a sequential topic outline, and that is the procedure followed here. The sequential outline might be prepared by one teacher, by a teaching team, or collaboratively with the children. Whatever is the case, from that outline, you can then prepare some of the important expected learning outcomes. Once you have decided the content and anticipated outcomes, you are ready to divide that into subdivisions or units of instruction and then prepare those units with the daily lessons.

Most beginning teachers are presented with the topic outlines and the instructional objectives (in the course of study or in the teacher's edition of the student textbook) with the often unspoken expectation that they will teach from them. And, for you, this may be the case, but someone had to have written those, and that someone was one or several teachers. So, as a beginning teacher, you should know how it is done, for someday you will be concentrating on it in earnest.

A Caution About Selecting and Sequencing Content

Be aware that beginning teachers sometimes have unrealistic expectations about the amount of content that a heterogeneous group of children can study, comprehend, and learn over a given period of time, especially as learning by those students is influenced by their special needs and diverse cultural and language backgrounds. Reviewing school and other public documents and talking with experienced teachers in your school are very helpful in selecting and sequencing realistic content, and later developing a time frame for teaching that content. Citing the work of Duckworth (1986), Eisner (1985), and Katz (1985), Brooks and Brooks (1993) conclude,

> Constructivist teachers have discovered that the prescribed scope, sequence, and timeline often interfere with their ability to help students understand complex concepts. Rigid timelines are also at odds with research on how human beings form meaningful theories about the ways the world works, how students and teachers develop an appreciation of knowledge and understanding, and how one creates the disposition to inquire about phenomena not fully understood. Most curriculums simply pack too much information into too little time—at a significant cost to the learner. (p. 29)

Once you have analyzed various curriculum documents and have prepared a content outline, you are ready to prepare the anticipated learning outcomes and write the specific instructional objectives, known also as behavioral (or performance) objectives—statements that describe what students will be able to do after completing the instructional experience.

E. EXAMPLES OF AIMS, GOALS, AND OBJECTIVES

As you read in the previous chapter, you will often encounter the compound structure that reads "goals and objectives." A distinction needs to be understood. The easiest way to understand the difference between the words *goals* and *objectives* is to look at your intent.

Goals are ideal states that you intend to reach, that is, ideals that you would like to have accomplished. Goals may be stated as teacher goals, as student goals, or, collaboratively, as class or course goals. Ideally, all three goals should be the same. If, for example, the goal is to improve students' ability to solve simple addition problems, the teacher or course goal could be stated as follows:

- *Teacher or course goal:* To help students improve their ability to identify and to solve addition problems.

If the goal is written with student input, the student goal could be stated as follows:

- *Student goal:* To improve my ability to identify and solve addition problems.

Goals are general statements of intent prepared early in course planning. Goals are useful when planned cooperatively with students or when shared with them as advance mental organizers. The students then know what to expect and will begin to prepare mentally to learn that material. Whereas goals are general, the objectives based on them are specific. The value of stating learning objectives in behavioral terms and in providing advance organizers is well documented by research (Good & Brophy, 1994, p. 244). Objectives are *not* intentions. They are the actual behaviors teachers intend to cause students to display. In short, objectives are what children *do*.

The terminology used for designating the various types of objectives is not standardized. In the literature, the most general educational objectives are often called *aims;* the general objectives of schools, curricula, and courses are called *goals;* the objectives of units and lessons are called *instructional objectives*. Whereas some authors distinguish between "instructional objectives" (objectives that are *not* behavior specific) and "behavioral or performance objectives" (objectives that *are* behavior specific), the terms are used here interchangeably to stress the importance of writing objectives for instruction in terms that are measurable. Aims are more general than goals; goals are more general than objectives; and instructional (behavioral) objectives are quite specific.

As implied in the preceding paragraphs, goals guide the instructional methods; objectives drive student performance. Assessment of student achievement in learning should assess that performance. Assessment procedures that match the instructional objectives are sometimes referred to as aligned or authentic assessment (discussed in the next chapter).

Goals are general statements, usually not even complete sentences, often beginning with the infinitive "to," which identify what the teacher intends the students to learn. Objectives, stated in performance (behavioral) terms, are specific actions and should be written as complete sentences that include the verb "will" to indicate what each student is expected to be able to do as a result of the instructional experience.

While instructional goals may not always be quantifiable, that is, readily measurable, instructional objectives should be measurable. Furthermore, those objectives are, in essence, what is measured for by instruments designed to assess student learning authentically. Consider the following examples of goals and objectives:

Goal   To provide reading opportunities for students.
Objective   The student will read two books at home within a two-month period.

F. INSTRUCTIONAL OBJECTIVES AND THEIR RELATIONSHIP TO INSTRUCTION AND ASSESSMENT

One purpose for writing objectives in specific (i.e., behavioral) terms is to be able to assess with precision whether the instruction has resulted in the desired behavior. In many school districts, educational goals are established as competencies that students are expected to achieve. This is known variously as *competency-based, performance-based,* or *outcome-based education*. (For informative articles about outcome-based education, see the March 1994 issue of *Educational Leadership*.) These goals are then divided into specific performance objectives, sometimes referred to as *goal indicators*. When children perform the competencies called for by these objectives, their education is considered successful. Expecting children to achieve one set of competencies before moving on to the next set is called *mastery learning*. The success of school curricula, teacher performance, and student achievement may each be assessed according to these criteria.

Assessment is not difficult to accomplish when the desired performance is overt, that is, when it can be observed directly. The sample objective in the preceding section is an example of an overt objective.

Assessment is more difficult to accomplish when the desired behavior is covert, that is, when it is not directly observable. Although certainly no less important, behaviors that call for "appreciation," "discovery," or "understanding," for example, are not directly observable because they occur within a person, and so are covert behaviors. Since covert behavior cannot be observed directly, the only way to tell whether the objective has been achieved is to observe behavior that may indicate that achievement. The objective, then, must be written in overt language, and evaluators can only assume or trust that the observed behavior is, in fact, reasonably indicative of the expected learning outcome.

Behaviorism and Constructivism: Are They Compatible?

While behaviorists (behaviorism) assume a definition of learning that deals only with changes in observable behavior (overt), constructivists (and cognitivism), as discussed in

Chapter 1, hold that learning entails the construction or reshaping of mental schemata and that mental processes mediate learning, and so are concerned with both overt and covert behaviors (Perkins & Blythe, 1994).

Furthermore, when assessing whether an objective has been achieved, the assessment device must be consistent with the desired learning outcome; otherwise the assessment is invalid. When the measuring device and the learning objective are compatible, the assessment is referred to as being authentic. For example, a person's competency to teach social studies to third-grade children is best (i.e., with highest reliability) measured by directly observing that person *doing* that very thing—teaching social studies to third-grade children. That is assessment that is authentic (and, it is also an example of *performance assessment,* discussed in the next chapter). Using a standardized paper-and-pencil test to determine a person's ability to teach social studies to third graders is not.

Does the previous discussion mean that you must be one or the other, a behaviorist or a constructivist? Probably not. For now, the point is that when writing instructional objectives you should write most or all of your basic expectations (minimal competency expectations) in overt terms (the topic of the next section). On the other hand, you cannot be expected to foresee all learning that occurs or to translate all that is learned into behavioral terms. We agree with those who argue that any effort to write all learning objectives in behavioral terms in effect neglects the individual learner; such an approach does not give the greatest consideration for the diversity among learners. Learning that is most meaningful to children is not so neatly or easily predicted and isolated. Rather than teaching one objective at a time, much of the time your teaching will be directed toward the simultaneous learning of multiple objectives, understandings, and appreciations. When you assess for learning, however, assessment is cleaner and certainly easier when objectives are assessed one at a time.

G. PREPARING INSTRUCTIONAL OBJECTIVES

When preparing instructional objectives, you will want to ask yourself: "How will the student demonstrate that the objective has been reached?" The objective must include an action that demonstrates that the objective has been achieved. That portion of the objective is sometimes referred to as the *terminal behavior,* or the *anticipated measurable performance,* and is important in an outcome-based educational (OBE) program (Kudlas, 1994).

Four Key Components to Writing Objectives

When completely written, an instructional objective has four key components. To aid in your understanding and remembering, you can refer to this as the ABCDs of writing objectives.

> *First Component: Audience.* The *A* of the ABCDs—*audience*—is the student for whom the objective is intended. To address the audience, teachers sometimes begin their objectives with the phrase "The student will be able to . . . ," or personalize the objective as "You will be able to . . . ."
>
> *Second Component: Behavior.* The next component of an objective is the expected *behavior*—the *B* of the ABCDs. The expected behavior (or performance) should be written with verbs that are measurable, that is, with action verbs so that it is directly observable that an objective has been reached. As discussed previously, some verbs describe covert behaviors that are vague, ambiguous, and not clearly measurable. When writing objectives, avoid verbs that are not clearly measurable, such as *appreciate, believe, comprehend, enjoy, know, learn, like,* and *understand* (see Figure 4.1).
>
> *Third Component: Conditions.* The *C* of the ABCDs—*conditions*—is the setting in which the behavior will be demonstrated by the student and observed by the teacher. In our earlier sample objective beginning "the student will read . . .," the conditions are: "at home within a two-month period."
>
> *Fourth Component: Degree of Expected Performance.* The last characteristic, one not always included in objectives written by teachers, is the *degree of expected performance*—the *D* of the ABCDs. This is the feature that allows for assessment of student

FIGURE 4.1

Verbs to Avoid When Writing Objectives

appreciate	enjoy	indicate	like
believe	familiarize	know	realize
comprehend	grasp	learn	understand

FIGURE 4.2

Recognizing Measurable Objectives

Assess your skill in recognizing measurable objectives, or those that are stated in behavioral terms. Place an X before each of the following that is a student-centered behavioral objective that is clearly measurable. Although "audience," "conditions," and "performance levels" may be absent, ask yourself, "As stated, is it a student-centered objective that is measurable?" If it is, then place an X in the blank. An answer key follows. After checking your answers, discuss your responses with your classmates and instructor.

_____   1. To develop an appreciation for working in small groups.

_____   2. To identify four types of structures people use for homes.

_____   3. To provide meaningful experiences for the children.

_____   4. To recognize main ideas in social studies text.

_____   5. To boot up a writing program on the computer.

_____   6. To correctly locate a specific reference in the library.

_____   7. To develop skills in inquiry.

_____   8. To prepare an argument for or against the use of clear cutting of timber areas.

_____   9. To show how to use the index to find factual material in a textbook.

_____   10. To know examples of consumer fraud.

Answer key: 2, 4, 5, 6, 8, 9.

Items 1, 3, 7, and 10 are inadequate because of their ambiguity. Item 3 is not even a student learning objective; it is a teacher goal. "To develop" and "to know" can have too many interpretations.

Although the conditions are not always given, items 2, 4, 5, 6, and 8 are clearly measurable. The teacher would have no difficulty recognizing when a learner had reached those objectives.

learning. When mastery learning is expected (achievement of 85 to 100 percent) the level of expected performance is usually omitted because it is understood. (In teaching for mastery learning, the performance-level expectation is 100 percent. In reality, however, the performance level will most likely be between 85 and 95 percent, particularly when working with a group of students rather than an individual student. The 5 to 15 percent difference allows for human error, as can occur with written and oral communication.)

Performance level is used to evaluate student achievement, and sometimes it is used to evaluate the effectiveness of the teaching. Student grades or achievement marks might be based on performance levels; evaluation of teacher effectiveness might be based on the level of student performance. Now, using Figure 4.2, turn your attention and skill toward recognizing objectives that are measurable.

H. CLASSIFICATION OF LEARNING OBJECTIVES

Three domains for classifying instructional objectives are useful for planning and assessing student learning. These are

- *Cognitive domain.* This is the domain of learning that involves mental operations, from the lowest level of simple recall of information to high-level and complex evaluative processes.

- *Affective domain.* This domain of learning involves feelings, attitudes, and values, from lower levels of acquisition to the highest level of internalization and action.
- *Psychomotor domain.* This is the domain of learning that involves simple manipulation of materials on up to the higher level of communication of ideas, and finally, the highest level of creative performance.

Schools attempt to provide learning experiences designed to meet the needs of the total child. Specifically, five areas of developmental needs are identified: (1) intellectual, (2) physical, (3) psychological, (4) social, and (5) moral and ethical. You should include learning objectives that address each of these developmental needs. While the intellectual instructional objectives are primarily within the cognitive domain and physical instructional objectives are within the psychomotor, the others mostly are within the affective domain. Too often, especially when teaching social studies and language arts skills, teachers direct their attention to the cognitive and affective domains, assuming that the psychomotor developmental needs will take care of themselves. Effective teachers direct their planning and sequence their instruction to guide students from the lowest to highest levels of operation within and across each of the domains of learning.

In the following section, three developmental hierarchies will guide your understanding of how you can address each of the areas of needs. Notice the illustrative verbs within each hierarchy of each domain. These verbs help you to design objectives for your lesson plans.

Cognitive Domain Hierarchy/Taxonomy

In the taxonomy of objectives that is most widely accepted, Benjamin Bloom and his associates (1984) arranged cognitive objectives into classifications according to the complexity of the skills and abilities embodied in the objectives. The resulting taxonomy portrays a ladder ranging from the simplest to the most complex intellectual processes.

Rather than an orderly progression from simple to complex mental operations as illustrated by Bloom's taxonomy, other researchers prefer an identification of cognitive abilities that range from simple information storage and retrieval, through a higher level of discrimination and concept attainment, and to the highest cognitive ability to recognize and solve problems (Gagné, Briggs, & Wager, 1988). *It is important to understand that, regardless of the domain and within each, prerequisite to a student's ability to function at one level of the hierarchy is the student's ability to function at the preceding level or levels.* In other words, when a child is functioning at the third level of the cognitive domain, that child is also automatically and simultaneously functioning at the first and second levels. For example, we cannot apply knowledge that we do not have or that we cannot recall or understand.

The six major categories (or levels) in Bloom's taxonomy of cognitive objectives are

1. *Knowledge.* Recognizing and recalling information.
2. *Comprehension.* Basic understanding of the meaning of information.
3. *Application.* Using information in new situations.
4. *Analysis.* Ability to dissect information into component parts and see relationships.
5. *Synthesis.* Putting components together to form new ideas.
6. *Evaluation.* Judging the worth of an idea, notion, theory, thesis, proposition, information, or opinion.

The last three—analysis, synthesis, and evaluation—are the *higher-order thinking skills.*

Although space here does not allow elaboration, Bloom's taxonomy includes various subcategories within each of these six major categories. It is less important that an objective be absolutely classified than it is that you are cognizant of hierarchies of thinking and doing and understand the importance of attending to student cognitive development and intellectual behavior from lower to higher levels of operation in all three domains. A discussion of each of Bloom's six categories follows.

Knowledge.   The basic element in Bloom's taxonomy concerns the acquisition of knowledge—the ability to recognize and recall information. Although this is the lowest level of the six categories, the information to be learned may not itself be at a low level. In fact, the information may be at an extremely high level. Bloom includes at this level knowledge of principles, generalizations, theories, structures, and methodology, as well as knowledge of facts and ways of dealing with facts.

Action verbs appropriate for this category include *choose, complete, define, describe, identify, indicate, list, locate, match, name, outline, recall, recognize, select,* and *state.* (Note that because of imperfections in the English language, some verbs may be appropriately used at more than one cognitive level. For example, students may be asked to *describe* what they recall—knowledge—about the types of structures people use for homes, or students might be asked to *describe* their understanding—comprehension—of examples of consumer fraud.)

The following are examples of objectives at this cognitive level. Note especially the verb used in each example.

- The student *will state* at least three essential characteristics of the concept "region."
- Given a passage of social studies text, the student *will list* the main idea(s).

Beyond the first category, knowledge, the remaining five categories of Bloom's taxonomy of the cognitive domain deal with the *use* of knowledge.

Comprehension. Comprehension includes the ability to translate or explain knowledge, to interpret that knowledge, and to extrapolate from it to address new situations.

Action verbs appropriate for this category include *change, classify, convert, defend, derive, describe, estimate, expand, explain, generalize, infer, interpret, paraphrase, predict, recognize, summarize,* and *translate.*

Examples of objectives in this category are

- The student *will explain* at least three characteristics of the concept "region."
- The student *will summarize* the main idea(s) in a passage of social studies text.

Application. Once students understand information, they should be able to apply it. This is the category of operation above comprehension.

Action verbs include *apply, compute, demonstrate, develop, discover, discuss, modify, operate, participate, perform, plan, predict, relate, show, solve,* and *use.*

Examples of objectives in this category are

- The student *will discuss* one or more essential characteristics of the concept "region," demonstrating his or her comprehension of how the region differs from another.
- Given a passage of social studies text, the student *will discuss* the main idea(s), demonstrating his or her comprehension of how some details in the text are related to the selected idea.

Analysis. This category includes objectives that require students to use the skills of analysis.

Action verbs appropriate for this category include *analyze, break down, categorize, classify, compare, contrast, debate, deduce, diagram, differentiate, discriminate, identify, illustrate, infer, outline, relate, separate,* and *subdivide.*

Examples of objectives in this category include

- The student *will contrast* how a selected region differs from another region.
- The student *will make a diagram* of a geographic region showing one or two essential characteristics of the region.

Synthesis. This category includes objectives that involve such skills as designing a plan, proposing a set of operations, and deriving a series of abstract relations.

Action verbs appropriate for this category include *arrange, categorize, classify, combine, compile, constitute, create, design, develop, devise, document, explain, formulate, generate, modify, organize, originate, plan, produce, rearrange, reconstruct, revise, rewrite, summarize, synthesize, tell, transmit,* and *write.*

Examples of objectives in this category are

- Using what is known about characteristics of regions, the student *will explain* two or three essential characteristics of the region in which the student lives.
- Related to the concept of "region," the student *will devise* a presentation about a selected geographic area and summarize why it is (or is not) a region.

Evaluation. The highest cognitive category of Bloom's taxonomy is evaluation. This includes offering opinions and making value judgments. Action verbs appropriate for this category include *appraise, argue, assess, compare, conclude, consider, contrast, criticize, decide, discriminate, evaluate, explain, interpret, judge, justify, rank, rate, relate, standardize, support,* and *validate.*

Examples of objectives in this category are

- Using the region in which the student lives and another selected geographic area, the student will *compare and contrast* the areas to decide which area has the essential characteristics of the concept of "region."
- The student *will argue* for or against the main idea(s) in a selection of social studies text.

It is important to remember that in this domain, analysis, synthesis, and evaluation are the higher-order thinking skills on which you will focus a great deal of your teaching.

Now, by referring to Figure 4.3, check your understanding.

Affective Domain Hierarchy/Taxonomy

Krathwohl, Bloom, and Masia (1964) developed a taxonomy for the affective domain. The following are their major levels (or categories), from least internalized to most internalized:

FIGURE 4.3
Classifying Cognitive Objectives

Assess your ability to recognize the level of cognitive objectives. For each of the following cognitive objectives, identify by appropriate letter the *highest* level of operation that is called for: (K) knowledge; (C) comprehension; (AP) application; (AN) analysis; (S) synthesis; or (E) evaluation. Check your answers with the answer key and discuss the results with your classmates and instructor. Your understanding of the concept involved here is more important than whether you score 100 percent against the answer key.

_____ 1. In a few sentences the student will summarize the difference between the two concepts of "justice" and "laws."

_____ 2. The student will name what responsibility means to him or her (doing your part).

_____ 3. The student will explain what is needed to cooperate—to work with others.

_____ 4. The student will collect data and make a graph to determine the average length of their sentences in a paragraph.

_____ 5. If you were to repeat the social studies presentation, explain how you might do it better.

_____ 6. The student will record information about an example of a country with democratic government.

_____ 7. The student will tell which country's government does not represent the concept of democracy: United States, Canada, Mexico, or Iraq.

_____ 8. The student will locate the name of a country whose government fits the concept of democracy.

_____ 9. The student will describe the changes the state capital would have to undergo to become a village.

_____ 10. Given a collection of pictures of villages, cities, and suburbs, the student will separate the pictures into three groups, those that are villages, those that are cities, and those that are suburbs.

Answer Key: 1 = C; 2 = K; 3 = AP; 4 = S; 5 = E; 6 = K; 7 = E; 8 = AN; 9 = S; 10 = K.

1. *Receiving.* Awareness of the affective stimulus and the beginning of favorable feelings toward it.
2. *Responding.* Taking an interest in the stimulus and viewing it favorably.
3. *Valuing.* Showing a tentative belief in the value of the affective stimulus and becoming committed to it.
4. *Organizing.* Organization of values into a system of dominant and supporting values.
5. *Internalizing values.* Beliefs and behavior are consistent—a way of life.

The following paragraphs provide an understanding of the types of objectives that fit the categories of the affective domain. Although there is considerable overlap from one category to another, the categories give a basis by which to judge the quality of objectives and the level of learning within this domain.

Receiving. At this level, the least internalized, the student exhibits willingness to give attention to particular phenomena or stimuli, and the teacher is able to arouse, sustain, and direct that attention.

Action verbs appropriate for this category include *ask, choose, describe, differentiate, distinguish, hold, identify, locate, name, point to, recall, recognize, reply, select,* and *use.*

Examples of objectives in this category are:

- The student pays close attention to the directions for the social studies or language arts activity.
- During class discussions the student listens attentively to the ideas being expressed by others.
- During instructional activities the student demonstrates sensitivity to the property of others.

Responding. Students respond to the stimulus they have received. They may do so because of some external pressure (an extrinsic source of motivation), or they may do so voluntarily because they find it interesting or because responding gives them satisfaction (intrinsic motivation).

Action verbs appropriate for this category include *answer, applaud, approve, assist, comply, command, discuss, greet, help, label, perform, play, practice, present, read, recite, report, select, spend (leisure time in), tell,* and *write.*

Examples of objectives at this level are

- The student voluntarily selects books on topics related to social studies from the library for pleasurable reading.
- The student discusses what others have said.
- The student willingly cooperates with others during collaborative group learning activities.

Valuing. Objectives at the valuing level concern children's beliefs, attitudes, and appreciations. The simplest objectives concern a student's acceptance of beliefs and values. Higher objectives concern a child's learning to prefer certain values and finally becoming committed to them.

Action verbs appropriate for this level include *argue, assist, complete, describe, differentiate, explain, follow, form, initiate, invite, join, justify, propose, protest, read, report, select, share, study, support,* and *work.*

Examples of objectives in this category include

- The student initiates a movement against an action that could have a negative impact on the school campus environment.
- The student supports actions against gender, racial, and ethnic discrimination.
- The student argues in favor of or against the use of a former nuclear power plant for nuclear waste storage.

Organizing. This level in the affective domain concerns the building of a personal value system. At this level, the student is conceptualizing values and arranging them in a value system that recognizes priorities and the relative importance of various values faced in life.

Action verbs appropriate for this level include *adhere, alter, arrange, balance, combine, compare, defend, define, discuss, explain, form, generalize, identify, integrate, modify, order, organize, prepare, relate,* and *synthesize.*

Examples of objectives at this level are

- The student modifies his or her own behavior to conform with acceptable social behavior in the classroom, school, and community.
- The student forms and adheres to a personal standard of social ethics.
- The student defines and integrates with the larger culture the important values of his or her own culture.

Personal value system. This is the last and highest level within the affective domain. At this level, the student's behaviors are consistent with his or her beliefs.

Action verbs appropriate for this level include *act, complete, display, influence, listen, modify, perform, practice, propose, qualify, question, revise, serve, solve,* and *verify.*

Examples of objectives appropriate for this level are

- The student behaves according to a well-defined and ethical code of behavior.
- The student practices accuracy in his or her verbal communication.
- The student works independently and diligently.

Psychomotor Domain Hierarchy/Taxonomy

Whereas identification and classification within the cognitive and affective domains are generally agreed upon, there has been less agreement on the classification within the psychomotor domain. Originally of interest primarily to physical education teachers and teachers of young children, the goal of this domain was simply that of developing and categorizing proficiency in skills dealing with gross and fine muscle control. However, today's classification of that domain, and as presented here, follows that lead but includes at its highest level the most creative and inventive behaviors, thus coordinating skills and knowledge from all three domains. Consequently, the objectives are arranged in a hierarchy from simple gross locomotor control to the most creative and complex, requiring originality and fine locomotor control.

Harrow (1977) developed the following taxonomy of the psychomotor domain. Included are sample objectives as well as a list of possible action verbs for each level of the psychomotor domain. The levels are

1. *Movement.* This involves gross motor coordination.
   Action verbs appropriate for this level include *adjust, carry, clean, locate, obtain,* and *walk.*
   Sample objectives for this level are
   - The student correctly operates a hand-held tape recorder.
   - The student correctly grasps and carries the magnifying glass and map atlas to the workstation.
2. *Manipulating.* This level involves fine motor coordination.
   Action verbs appropriate for this level include *assemble, build, calibrate, connect,* and *thread.*
   Sample objectives for this level are
   - The student will rehearse a specified oral interview using the tape recorder.
   - The student will use the computer and software program correctly.
3. *Communicating.* This level involves the communication of ideas and feelings.
   Action verbs appropriate for this level include *analyze, ask, describe, draw, explain,* and *write.*
   Sample objectives for this level are
   - The student will draw a map of the school campus.
   - The student will analyze his or her oral interview rehearsal and describe what will be changed before the actual interview.

4. *Creating*. This is the highest level of this domain, and *of all domains,* and represents the student's coordination of thinking, learning, and behaving in all three domains.
   Action verbs appropriate for this level include *create, design,* and *invent.*
   Sample objectives for this level are
   - From his or her own data collecting about governments that are democracies, the student will design a futuristic democracy in an imagined country.
   - From materials that have been discarded in the environment, the student will design (a) a machine for collecting discarded materials in a specific environment or (b) an environment for an imaginary animal that he or she has mentally created.

I. USING THE TAXONOMIES

Theoretically, as noted earlier, the taxonomies are so constructed that students achieve each lower level before being ready to move to the next higher levels. But because categories overlap, this theory does not always hold in practice. The taxonomies are important in that they emphasize the various levels to which instruction must aspire. For learning to be worthwhile, you must formulate and teach to objectives from the higher levels of the taxonomies (the higher-order thinking skills) as well as from the lower ones. Student thinking and behaving must be moved from the lowest to the highest levels of thinking and behavior.

In using the taxonomies, remember that the point is to formulate the best objectives for the job to be done. The taxonomies provide the mechanism for assuring that you do not spend a disproportionate amount of time on simple recall of facts and low-order learning, that is, learning that is relatively trivial. Writing objectives is essential to the preparation of good items for the assessment of student learning. Clearly communicating your behavioral expectations to students and then specifically assessing student learning against those expectations make the teaching most efficient and effective, and they make the assessment of the learning more authentic. This does not mean to imply that you will *always* write behavioral objectives for everything taught, nor will you always be highly accurate in measuring what students have learned. Learning that is meaningful to students is not as easily compartmentalized as the taxonomies of educational objectives would imply.

Using a Response Journal to Assess for Meaningful Learning

With learning that is most important and that has the most meaning to students, the domains are inextricably interconnected, that is "we 'think' with our feelings and 'feel' with our thoughts" (Caine & Caine, 1993, p. 19). Consequently, when assessing for student learning, you must look for those connections. One way of doing that is to have students maintain a journal in which they reflect on and respond to their learning.

Journal writing extends children's expressive language by letting them experiment in explaining what they have done, how they feel about it, and what new ideas they have. You may want to respond to what they write about. It is important, though, that you take the time to read the journals and respond to their experiences. Your responses should be positive, and you should pose questions or reflect on their thoughts. You should not, however, comment on the mechanics of their writing, as children must feel free in journal writing (Seefeldt & Barbour, 1994).

Using journals, children may reflect on and respond to their learning using the following categories, adapted with permission (Fersh, 1993, ppl. 23–24).

1. "I never knew that." In this category, student responses are primarily to factual information, responses to their new knowledge, to the bits and pieces of raw information, often expected to be memorized, regardless of how meaningful to students it might be. However, because this is only fragmented knowledge, and merely scratches the surface of meaningful learning, it must not be the end-all of student learning. Learning that is meaningful goes beyond the "I never knew that" category, expands on the bits and pieces, connects them, allowing learners to make sense out of what they are learning. Learning that does not extend beyond the "I never knew that" category is dysfunctional.

2. "I never thought of that." Here, student responses reveal an additional way of perceiving. Their responses may include elements of "I never knew that" but also contain higher-level thinking as a result of their reflection on that knowledge.

3. "I never felt that." In this category, student responses are connected to the affective, eliciting more of an emotional response than a cognitive one. Meaningful learning is much more than intellectual understanding, it includes a "felt" meaning (Caine & Caine, 1993, p. 19).

4. "I never appreciated that." Responses in this category reflect a sense of recognition that one's own life can be enriched by what others have created or done, or that something already known can be valued from an additional perspective.

5. "I never realized that." In this fifth category, student responses indicate an awareness of overall patterns and dynamic ways in which behavior is holistic, establishing meaningful and potentially useful connections among knowledge, values, and purposes.

Character Education

Related especially to the affective domain, although not exclusive of the cognitive and psychomotor domains, is a resurgence in a national interest in the development of children's values, especially those of honesty, kindness, respect, and responsibility—that is called character education (Massey, 1993). For example, Wynne and Ryan (1993) state that "transmitting character, academics, and discipline—essentially, 'traditional' moral values—to pupils is a vital educational responsibility" (p. 3). Thus, if one agrees with that interpretation, then the teaching of moral values is the transmission of character, academics, and discipline and clearly implies learning that transcends the three domains of learning presented in this chapter.

Whether defined as ethics, citizenship, moral values, or personal development, character education has long been part of public education in this country (Burrett & Rusnak, 1993). Today, stimulated by a perceived need to reduce student antisocial behaviors (such as drug abuse and violence) and to produce more respectful and responsible citizens, with a primary focus on the affective domain, many schools and districts are developing curricula in character education and instruction in conflict resolution, with the ultimate goal of "developing mature adults capable of responsible citizenship and moral action" (Burrett & Rusnak, 1993, p. 15). Some specific techniques are to sensitize students to value issues through role playing and creative drama, have students take the opposite point of view in discussions, promote higher-order thinking about value issues through appropriate questioning techniques, arrange action-oriented projects, use parents and community members to assist in projects, highlight examples of class and individual cooperation in serving the school and community, and make student service projects visible in the school and community (p. 29).

J. QUESTIONING TECHNIQUES

Properly following the discussion of instructional objectives and the discussion about character education is this discussion of an instructional strategy and behavior of fundamental importance to teaching—the use of questioning. You will use questioning for so many purposes that you must be highly skilled in its use to teach most effectively.

Purposes for Using Questioning

You will adapt the type and form of each question that you ask to the purpose for which it is asked. The purposes that questions can serve can be separated into five categories:

1. *To give instructions courteously.* For example, "Lucy, would you please turn out the lights so we can show the slides?"

2. *To review and remind students of classroom procedures.* For example, if students continue to talk without first raising their hands and being recognized by you, you can stop the lesson and ask, "Class, I think we need to review the procedure for answering my questions. For talking, what is the procedure that we agreed on?"

3. *To gather information.* For example, "How many of you have finished the problems?" or to find out whether a student knows or can do something, such as, "Carol, would you please read for us the temperature of the aquarium?"

4. *To discover student interests or experiences.* For example, "How many of you have already been to the marine aquarium?"
5. *To guide student thinking and learning.* This category of questioning is the focus of our attention now. Questions in this category are used to not only encourage students, establish rapport, and give students opportunities for expressing themselves, but also to
   - Clarify a student response
   - Elicit specific responses through convergent thinking
   - Cue students
   - Elicit open-ended responses through divergent thinking
   - Ask students to place a value on something
   - Focus student attention
   - Probe for further information
   - Recall and review information
   - Draw relationships (comparing, contrasting, classifying, interpreting, summarizing)
   - Help children think about their own thinking (metacognition).

Types of Cognitive Questioning

Before going further let us define, describe, and provide examples for each of the types of cognitive questions that you will use in teaching. Then, in the section that follows, we focus your attention on the levels of cognitive questions.

Clarifying question. The clarifying question is used to gain more information from a student to help the teacher better understand a child's ideas, feelings, and thought processes. Asking the child to elaborate on an initial response will often encourage the child to think deeper, restructure her or his thinking, and while doing so, discover a fallacy in the original response. Examples of clarifying questions are: "What I hear you saying is that you would rather work alone than in your group. Is that correct?" Research has shown a strong positive correlation between student learning and development of metacognitive skills and the teacher's use of questions that ask children for clarification (Costa, 1991, p. 63). In addition, by seeking clarification, the teacher is likely to be demonstrating an interest in the child and her or his thinking.

Convergent thinking question. Convergent thinking questions (also called "narrow" questions) are low-order thinking questions that have a singular answer (such as recall questions discussed and exemplified in the next section). Examples of convergent questions are: "If the sides of the figure are 4 feet, 4 feet, 5 feet, and 5 feet, what is its perimeter?" "What is the name of the planet that is nearest to our sun?"

Cueing question. If you ask a question to which, after sufficient wait-time (longer than 2 seconds and as long as 9), no students respond or where their responses indicate they need more information, then you can ask a question that cues the answer or response you are seeking. In essence, you are going backward in your questioning sequence to cue the students. For example, if a teacher asks students, "How many legs do ants and bees have?" and there is no accurate response, then she might cue the answer with the following information and question, "The class to which those animals belong is sometimes called Hexapoda. Does that name give anyone a clue about the number of legs they have?"

Divergent thinking question. Divergent thinking questions (also known as "broad," "reflective," or "thought" questions) are open-ended (having no singularly correct answer), high-order thinking questions (requiring analysis, synthesis, or evaluation), that force students to think creatively, to leave the comfortable confines of the known and reach out into the unknown. An example of a question that requires divergent thinking is "What might we be able to do to improve the environment at Jefferson School?"

Evaluative question. Some types of questions, whether convergent or divergent, require students to place a value on something. Those are referred to as evaluative questions. If the teacher and the students all agree on certain premises, then the evaluative question would also be a convergent question. If original assumptions differ, then the response to the evaluative question would be more subjective, and therefore that evaluative question would be divergent. An example of an evaluative question is "Should the United States allow clear cutting in its National Forests?"

Focus question. This is any question designed to focus student thinking. For example, the question of the preceding paragraph is a focus question when the teacher is attempting to focus student attention on the social and scientific issues involved in clear cutting.

Probing question. Similar to a clarifying question, the probing question requires student thinking to go beyond superficial "first-answer" or single-word responses. Examples of probing questions are "Why, Sean, do you think that every person has the right to say what he or she believes?" Or "Could you give us an example?"

Levels of Cognitive Questions and Student Thinking

Questions posed by you are cues to your students to the level of thinking expected of them, ranging from the lowest level of mental operation, requiring simple recall of knowledge (convergent thinking), to the highest, requiring divergent thought and application of that thought. It is important that you (1) are aware of the levels of thinking, (2) understand the importance of attending to student thinking from low to higher levels of operation, and (3) that you understand that what may be a matter of simple recall of information for one child may require a higher-order mental activity, such as figuring something out by deduction for another.

You should structure and sequence your questions in ways that guide children to higher levels of thinking. To help your understanding, three levels of questioning and thinking are described below (Costa, 1989, 1991; Eisner, 1979). You should recognize the similarity between these three levels of questions and the six levels of thinking from Bloom's taxonomy of cognitive objectives. For your daily use of questioning, it is just as useful but more practical to think and behave in terms of these three levels, rather than of six.

1. *Lowest level (the data input phase): gathering and recalling information.* At this level, questions are designed to solicit from students concepts, information, feelings, or experiences that were gained in the past and stored in memory. Sample key words and desired behaviors are *complete, count, define, describe, identify, list, match, name, observe, recall, recite,* and *select.*
2. *Intermediate level (the data processing phase): processing information.* At this level, questions are designed to draw relationships of cause and effect, to synthesize, analyze, summarize, compare, contrast, or to classify data. Sample key words and desired behaviors are *analyze, classify, compare, contrast, distinguish, explain, group, infer, make an analogy, organize, plan,* and *synthesize.*
3. *Highest level (the data output phase): applying and evaluating in new situations.* Questions at this level encourage students to think intuitively, creatively, and hypothetically, to use their imaginations, to expose a value system, or to make a judgment. Sample key words and desired behaviors are *apply a principle, build a model, evaluate, extrapolate, forecast, generalize, hypothesize, imagine, judge, predict,* and *speculate.*

You should use the type of question that is best suited for the purpose, use a variety of different levels of questions, and structure questions to move student thinking to higher levels. When their teachers use higher-level questions, students tend to score higher on tests of critical thinking and on standardized tests of achievement (Newton, 1978; Redfield & Rousseau, 1981).

Developing your skill in the use of questioning needs your attention to detail and practice. The guidelines that follow will provide that detail.

Guidelines for Using Questioning

As is emphasized many times in several ways throughout this book, your goals are to help your students learn how to solve problems, to make decisions and value judgments, to think creatively and critically, and to feel good about themselves and their learning rather than to simply fill their minds with bits and pieces of information. How you construe your questions and how you carry out your questioning strategy is important to the realization of these goals.

Preparing questions. When preparing questions, consider the following guidelines:

1. *Cognitive questions* should be planned, thoughtfully worded, and written into your lesson plan. Thoughtful preparation of questions helps to ensure that they are clear and specific, not ambiguous, that the vocabulary is appropriate, and that each question matches its purpose. Incorporate questions into your lessons as instructional devices, welcomed pauses, attention grabbers, and as checks for student comprehension. Thoughtful teachers even plan questions that they intend to ask specific students.
2. *Match questions with their purposes*. Carefully planned questions allows them to be sequenced and worded to match the levels of cognitive thinking expected of students.

Demonstrate to students how to develop their higher-order thinking skills. To demonstrate, you must use specific terminology that provides students with examples of experiences consonant with the meanings of the cognitive words. You should demonstrate this everyday so students learn the cognitive terminology (Costa, 1991, p. 110). As stated by Brooks and Brooks (1993), "framing tasks around cognitive activities such as analysis, interpretation, and prediction—and explicitly using those terms with students—fosters the construction of new understandings" (p. 105). Here are three examples:

Instead of	*Say*
"How else might it be done?"	"How could you *apply*. . . ?"
"Are you going to get quiet?"	"If we are going to hear what Joan has to say, what do you need to do?"
"How do you know that is so?"	"What evidence do you have?"

Implementing questions. Careful preparation of questions is one part of the skill in questioning; implementation is the other part. Here are some suggestions for effective implementation.

1. *Avoid too much teacher talk*. Avoid bombarding students with too much teacher talk. This could be especially true for teachers who are nervous, such as might be the case for many during initial weeks of their student teaching. Knowledge of the guidelines being presented here will be helpful in avoiding that syndrome. Remind yourself to be quiet after you ask a question that you have carefully formulated. Sometimes, due to lack of confidence, especially when a question hasn't been carefully planned by the teacher, the teacher asks the question, then, with a slight change in wording, asks it again, or asks several questions, one after another. That is too much verbiage, and "shotgun" questioning only confuses students, while allowing too little time for them to think.
2. *Allow time to think*. After asking a question, provide students with adequate time to think. Knowing the subject better than the students know it and having given prior thought to the subject, too many teachers fail to allow students sufficient time to think after asking a question. After asking a well-worded question, you should remain quiet for awhile, allowing students time to think and to respond. And, if you wait long enough, they usually will.

   After asking a question, how long should you wait before you do something? You should wait at least 2 seconds, and as long as 9. Stop reading now, and look at your watch or a clock to get a feeling for how long 2 seconds is. Then, observe how long 9 seconds is. Did 9 seconds seem a long time? Because most of us are not used to silence in the classroom, 2 seconds of silence can seem quite long, while 9 seconds can seem eternal. If, for some reason, students have not responded after a period of 2 to 9 seconds of wait time, then you can ask the question again (but don't reword an already carefully worded question, or else students are likely to think it is a new question), pause for several seconds, then if you still haven't received a response you can call on a student, then another, if necessary, after sufficient wait time. Soon you will get a response that can be built upon. Never answer your own question! For a further discussion of the importance of wait time in a constructivist classroom, see Brooks and Brooks (1993, pp. 114–115).

3. *Call on all students.* Practice calling on all students, not just the bright or the slow, not just the boys or the girls, not only those in the front of the room, but all of them. To do these things takes concentrated effort on your part, but it is important, especially when teaching language arts and social studies. (For useful tips, see Feder-Feitel, 1994, pp. 56–60, 64–66, and 1994, pp. 54–59.)

4. *Allow equal wait time.* Give the same amount of wait time (think time) for all students. This, too, will require concentrated effort on your part, but it also is important to do. A teacher who waits for less time when calling on a slow student or students of one gender more than the other is showing a prejudice or a lack of confidence in certain students, both of which are detrimental to establishing for all students a positive, equal, and safe environment for classroom learning. Show confidence in all students and never discriminate by expecting less or more from some than from others.

5. *Be courteous in your interactions.* When you ask questions, don't let students randomly shout out their answers, but instead, require them to raise their hands and to be called on before they respond. Establish that procedure and stick with it. This helps to assure that you call on all students equally, equally distributing your interactions with the students and that girls are not interacted with less because boys tend to be more obstreperous. Even at the college level, male students tend to be more vociferous than female students, and when allowed by the instructor, tend to outtalk and to interrupt their female peers. Every teacher has the responsibility to guarantee a nonbiased and equal distribution of interaction time in the classroom.

6. *Use strong praise sparingly.* Use of strong praise is sometimes okay, especially when working with students who are different and when asking questions of simple low-level recall. But, when you want students to think divergently and creatively, you should be stingy with your use of strong praise to student responses. Strong praise from a teacher tends to terminate divergent and creative thinking.

   One of your goals is to help students find intrinsic sources for motivation, that is, an inner drive of intent or desire that causes them to want to learn. Use of strong praise tends to build conformity, causing students to depend on outside forces, that is, the giver of praise for their worth, rather than on themselves. An example of a strong praise response is when a teacher responds to a student answer with, "That's right! Very good." On the other hand, passive acceptance responses, such as "Okay, that seems to be one possibility," keep the door open for further thinking, particularly for higher level, divergent thinking.

   Another example of a passive acceptance response is one used in brainstorming sessions, when the teacher says, "After asking the question, and giving you time to think about it, I will hear your ideas and record them on the board." Only after all student responses have been heard and recorded does the class begin to consider each. In the classroom, that kind of nonjudgmental acceptance of all ideas will generate a great deal of expression of high-level thought. (For further discussion of research findings about the use of praise and rewards in teaching, see Joyce & Showers, 1988, and Lepper & Green, 1978.)

7. *Encourage students to ask questions about content and process.* There is no such thing as a "dumb" question from a child. Sometimes students, like everyone else, ask questions that they could just as easily look up. Those questions can consume precious class time. For a teacher, this can be frustrating. A teacher's initial reaction might be to quickly and mistakenly brush that type of question off with sarcasm, while assuming that the student is too lazy to look up an answer. In such instances, you are advised to think before responding and to respond kindly and professionally, although in the busy life of a classroom teacher, that may not always be so easy to do. However, be assured, there is a reason for a student's question. Perhaps the student is signaling a need for recognition.

   It is sometimes easy for a child to feel alone and insignificant in school, and a student's making an effort to interact with you can be a positive sign. So, carefully gauge your responses to those efforts. If a student question is really off track, off the wall, out of order, and out of context with the content of the lesson, as a possible response, consider this: "That is an interesting question (or comment) and I would very much like to talk with you more about it. Later, when we have some time, could you and I talk more about it?"

Children's questions can and should be used as springboards for further questions, discussion, and investigations. Children should be encouraged to ask questions that challenge the textbook, the process, or other person's statements, and they should be encouraged to seek the facts or evidence behind a statement.

Being able to ask questions may be more important than having right answers. Knowledge is derived from asking questions. Being able to recognize problems and to formulate questions is a skill and the key to problem solving and critical thinking skill development. While teaching social studies or language arts, you have a responsibility to encourage students to formulate questions and to help them word their questions in ways that enable them to seek tentative answers. This process is necessary to build a base of knowledge that students can call on over and over to link, interpret, and explain new information in new situations (Resnick & Klopfer, 1989, p. 5).

8. *Remember that questioning is the cornerstone of critical thinking and real-world problem solving.* With real-world problem solving, there are usually no absolute right answers. Rather than "correct" answers, some are better than others. The person with a problem (a) recognizes the problem, (b) formulates a question about that problem (Should I buy a house or rent? Should I date this person or not? Should I take this job or not? Which car should I buy? Should I abuse drugs or not?), (c) collects data, and (d) arrives at a temporarily acceptable answer to the problem, while realizing that at some time later new data may dictate a review of the former conclusion. For example, if an astronomer believes she has discovered a new galaxy, there is no textbook (or teacher) to which she may refer to find out if she is right. Rather, on the basis of her self-confidence in problem identification, asking questions, collecting enough data, and arriving at a tentative conclusion based on those data, she assumes that for now her conclusion is safe.

9. *Avoid bluffing an answer to a question for which you do not have an answer.* There is nothing wrong with admitting that you do not know. It helps students realize that you are human. It helps them maintain an adequate self-esteem, realizing that they are okay. What *is* important is that you know where and how to find possible answers, and that you help students develop that same knowledge and those same skills.

Examining the level of questions in course materials. In a recent analysis of eight science textbooks and their end-of-chapter questions, 87.5 percent of those questions were at the input level, and 78.8 percent of all textbook questions were at the input level (Gall, 1984; Hunkins, 1989; Steinbrink, 1985). Using the questions in Figure 4.4, examine course materials used by a school where you might soon be teaching and compare the results of your analysis with those data.

K. PROCESSES IN INSTRUCTIONAL PLANNING

Complete planning for instruction is an eight-step process. Certain of the steps with guidelines that follow have previously been addressed and are included here so you will understand where they fit in the planning process. Here are the steps and guidelines for what is referred to as the "eight-step planning process."

1. *Course and school goals.* Consider and understand your course goals and their relationship to the goals and the mission of the school. Content taught in your classroom is not isolated but is an integral part of the total school curriculum, both vertically (in grades K–12) and horizontally (across grade level).
2. *Expectations.* Consider topics and skills that you are "expected" to teach, such as ones that may be found in the course of study.
3. *Academic year-long calendar plan.* You must consider where you want the class of students to be months from now. So, working from your tentative topic outline and with the school calendar in hand, begin by deciding approximately how much class time should be devoted to each topic, penciling those times onto the subject outline.

FIGURE 4.4
Examining Course Materials for Level of Questioning

Examine course materials for the levels of questions presented to students. Examine a student science textbook (or other instructional material) for a grade level you intend to teach, specifically examining questions posed for the students, perhaps found at the ends of chapters. Also examine workbooks, examinations, instructional packages, and any other printed or electronic (i.e., computer software programs) materials used by students. Share your findings with other members of your class. Include this information in your review:

1. Materials examined (include date of publication and target students).
2. Examples of level one (input recall level) questions found.
3. Examples of level two (processing level) questions found.
4. Examples of level three (application level) questions found.
5. Approximate percentages of questions at each level.
     Level 1 = _____%   Level 2 = _____%   Level 3 = _____%
6. Did you find evidence of question-level sequencing? If so, describe it.
7. From your analysis, what can you conclude about the level of student thinking expected of students using the materials analyzed?

---

4. *Course or class schedule*. This schedule becomes a part of the course syllabus that is presented to parents at Back-to-School Night or to fourth-grade students during the first week of school. The schedule should remain flexible to allow for the unexpected, such as cancellation or interruption of a class meeting or an unpredictable extended study of a particular topic.

5. *Daily lessons*. Working from the course schedule, you are then ready to prepare daily lessons, keeping in mind the abilities and interests of your students while making decisions about appropriate strategies and learning experiences. Preparation of daily lessons takes considerable time, and continues throughout the year and throughout your career. You will arrange and prepare instructional notes, demonstrations, discussion topics and questions, classroom exercises, appearances of guest speakers, use of media and materials, field trips, and tools for the assessment of student learning.

   Because one class meeting is often determined by accomplishments of the preceding meeting (especially if you are teaching toward mastery or using a constructivist approach), your lessons are never "set in stone" and, regardless of your approach, will need steady revising and evaluation by you.

6. *Instructional objectives*. With the finalized subject schedule, and as you prepare the daily lessons, you will complete your preparation of the instructional objectives. These instructional objectives are critical for the accomplishment of step 7.

7. *Assessment*. This important step deals with how you will preassess student understandings and assess student achievement. Included in this component are your decisions about assignments, diagnostic tools such as tests, and the procedure by which evaluative marks or grades will be determined. Assessment is the topic of the next chapter.

8. *Classroom management*. This final and important step in planning involves your decisions and planning for a safe and effective classroom environment so that the most efficient learning of your units and lessons will occur, and was the topic of Chapter 2.

L. THE DAILY LESSON PLAN

Effective teachers are always planning for their classes. For the long range, they plan the scope and sequence of content. They develop units, and within units they design the activities to be used and the assessments of learning to be done. They familiarize themselves with textbooks, materials, media, and new innovations in subject content. Yet—despite all this planning—the daily lesson plan remains pivotal to the planning process.

Assumptions About Lesson Planning

Not all teachers need elaborate written plans for every lesson. Sometimes effective and skilled teachers need only a sketchy outline. Sometimes they may not need written plans at all. Experienced teachers who have taught the topic many times in the past may need only the presence of students to stimulate a pattern of presentation that has often been successful (though frequent use of old patterns may lead one into the rut of unimaginative teaching), and you probably do not need to be reminded that the obsolescence of many past classroom practices have been substantiated repeatedly by researchers. For example, the National Association for the Education of Young Children (1990, pp. 6–7, used with permission) advocates that the following inappropriate instructional strategies be replaced by their more appropriate counterparts:

Inappropriate Practice

Teachers use highly structured, teacher-directed lessons almost exclusively.

The teacher directs all the activity, deciding what students will do and when. The teacher does most of the activity for the children, such as performing steps in an experiment. Children are expected to sit down, watch, be quiet, and listen, or do paper-and-pencil tasks for inappropriately long periods of time. A major portion of time is spent passively sitting, listening, and waiting.

Large group, teacher-directed instruction is used most of the time.

Appropriate Practice

Teachers prepare the environment for students to learn through active exploration and interactions with adults, other children, and materials. Students select many of their own activities from among a variety of learning areas.

Students are expected to be physically and mentally active. Students choose from among activities the teacher has set up or they spontaneously initiate activities.

Students work individually or in small, informal groups most of the time.

Considering the diversity among teachers, their instructional styles, their students, and what research has shown, certain assumptions can be made about lesson planning:

1. Not all teachers need elaborate written plans for all lessons.
2. Beginning teachers need to prepare detailed written lesson plans.
3. Some topics require more detailed planning than others do.
4. Some experienced teachers have clearly defined goals and objectives in mind even though they have not written them into lesson plans.
5. The depth of knowledge a teacher has about a topic influences the amount of planning necessary for the lessons.
6. The skill a teacher has in following a train of thought in the presence of distraction will influence the amount of detail necessary when planning activities.
7. A plan is more likely to be carefully plotted when it is written out.
8. The diversity of students within today's classroom necessitates careful and thoughtful consideration about individualizing the instruction; these considerations are best implemented when they have been thoughtfully written into lesson plans.
9. There is no particular pattern or format that all teachers need to follow when writing out plans. (Some teacher-preparation programs have agreed on certain lesson-plan formats for their student teachers; you need to know if this is the case for your program.)
10. All effective teachers have a planned pattern of instruction for every lesson, whether that plan is written out or not.

Written Lesson Plans

Well-written lesson plans have many uses. They give a teacher an agenda or outline to follow in teaching a lesson. They give a substitute teacher a basis for presenting appropriate lessons to a class. They are certainly very useful when a teacher is planning to use the same lesson again in the future. They provide the teacher with something to fall back on in case of a memory lapse, an interruption, or some distraction, such as a call from the office or a fire drill. Above all, they provide beginners with security, because with a carefully prepared plan, a beginning teacher can walk into a classroom with confidence gained from having developed a sensible framework for that day's instruction.

Thus, as a beginning teacher, you should make considerably detailed lesson plans. Naturally, this will require a great deal of work for at least the first year or two, but the reward of knowing that you have prepared and presented effective lessons will compensate for that effort. Since most teachers plan their daily lessons only a day or two ahead, you can expect a busy first year of teaching.

Some prospective teachers are concerned with being seen using a written plan in class, thinking it may suggest that the teacher has not mastered the subject. On the contrary, a lesson plan is a visible sign of preparation on the part of the teacher. A written lesson plan shows that thinking and planning have taken place and that the teacher has a road map to work through the lesson no matter what the distractions. Most experienced teachers agree that there is no excuse for appearing before a class without evidence of careful preparation.

A Continual Process

Experienced teachers may not require plans as detailed as those necessary for beginning teachers—after all, experienced teachers often can develop shortcuts to lesson planning without sacrificing effectiveness. Yet lesson planning is a continual process even for them, for there is always a need to keep materials and plans current and relevant. Because no two groups of students are ever exactly the same, today's lesson plan will probably need to be tailored to the specific needs of next year's group of students. Also, because the content of a topic changes as new developments occur or new theories are introduced, your objectives and the objectives of the students, school, and teaching faculty will change.

For these reasons, lesson plans should be in a constant state of revision. Once the basic framework is developed, however, the task of updating and modifying becomes minimal. If you maintain your plans on a computer, making necessary changes from time to time becomes even easier.

The daily lesson plan should provide a tentative outline but should always remain flexible. A carefully worked-out plan may have to be set aside because of the unpredictable, serendipitous effect of a "teachable moment" or because of unforeseen circumstances, such as a delayed school bus, an impromptu school assembly program, or a fire drill. A daily lesson planned to cover six aspects of a given topic may end with only three of the points having been considered. These occurrences are natural in a school setting, and the teacher and the plans must be flexible enough to accommodate this reality.

The Problem of Time

Since planning is a skill that takes years of experience to master, a beginning teacher should overplan rather than run the risk of having too few activities to occupy the time the students are in the classroom. One way to ensure that you overplan is to include alternate activities in your lesson plan. (Sample lesson plans are shown at the ends of Chapters 8–12).

The Daily Plan Book

A distinction needs to be made between actual lesson plans and the book of daily plans that many schools require teachers to maintain and even submit to their supervisors a week in advance. A daily-plan book is most assuredly not a daily lesson plan. Rather, it is a layout sheet on which the teacher shows what lessons will be taught during the week, month, or term. Usually the book provides only a small lined box for each class period for each day of the week. These books are useful for outlining the topics, activities, and assignments projected for the week or term, and supervisors sometimes use them to check the adequacy of teachers' course plans. They can also be useful for substitute teachers, who must try to fill in for you when you are absent. But they are not daily plans. Teachers who believe that the notations in the daily plan book are lesson plans are fooling themselves. Student teachers should not use these in place of authentic lesson plans.

Constructing a Daily Lesson Plan

Each teacher should develop a personal system of lesson planning—the system that works best for that teacher. But a beginning teacher probably needs a more substantial framework from which to work. For that reason, this section provides a "preferred" lesson plan format. In addition, you will find alternative formats in this and later chapters. Nothing is sacred about any of these formats, however. Each has worked for some teachers in the past. As you review the preferred format and the others throughout the book, determine which appeals to your style of presentation and use it with your own modifications until you find or develop a better model.

Whatever the format, however, all plans should be written out in an intelligible style. There is good reason to question teachers who say they have no need for a written plan because they have their lessons planned "in their heads." The hours in a school day are many, as are the numbers of students in each classroom. When multiplied by the number of school days in a week, a semester, or a year, the task of keeping so many things in one's head becomes mind-boggling. Until you have considerable experience behind you, you will need to write and keep detailed daily plans for guidance and reference.

Components of a Daily Lesson Plan

As a rule, your written lesson plan should contain the following basic elements: (1) descriptive data, (2) materials, (3) goals and objectives, (4) rationale, (5) body of the lesson plan, and (6) assessment and revision plans. These components need not be present in every written lesson plan, nor must they be presented in any particular format nor are they inclusive or exclusive. You might choose to include additional components or subsections. You may not want to spend time developing a formal rationale, although you probably should. Figure 4.5 illustrates a format that includes the six components and sample subsections of those components.

Following are descriptions and several examples of the six major components with explanations of why each is essential.

Descriptive data. This is the demographic and logistical information that identifies details about the class. Anyone reading this information should be able to identify when and where the class meets, who is teaching it, and what is being taught. Although as the teacher you know this information, someone else may not. Administrators, members of the teaching team, and substitute teachers—and, if you are the student teacher, your university supervisor and cooperating teacher—appreciate this information, especially when asked to fill in for you, even if only for a few minutes during a class session. Most teachers find out which items of descriptive data are most beneficial in their situation and then develop their own identifiers.

Remember: *The mark of a well-prepared, clearly written lesson plan is the ease with which someone else (such as a substitute teacher) could implement it.*

The descriptive data include:

1. *Classroom and grade level.* These serve as headings for the plan and facilitate orderly filing of plans.
2. *Name of the unit.* Inclusion of this facilitates the orderly control of the hundreds of lesson plans a teacher constructs. For example:
    Social Studies (History)   Unit: Settlement of Plymouth Colony
3. *Topic to be considered within the unit.* This is also useful for control and identification. For example:
    Social Studies (History)   Unit: Settlement of Plymouth Colony
                    Topic: Jobs in Plymouth Colony

Goals and objectives. In a lesson plan, the instructional goals are general statements of what students will learn from that lesson. Teachers and students need to know what the lesson is designed to accomplish. In clear, understandable language, the general goal statement provides that information.

Examples of goals are:

- To develop student's understanding of the concept of region
- To understand the concepts of main idea and related details

FIGURE 4.5
Sample Lesson Plan Format with Six Components

1. **Descriptive Data**
   Teacher _____ Date_____
   Grade level _____ Room number_____
   Unit _____ Lesson topic_____
2. **Lesson Goals and Objectives**
   Instructional Goals (general objectives):

   Specific (performance) objectives:
   Cognitive:

   Affective:

   Psychomotor:

3. **Rationale**
4. **Plan**
   Content:

   Procedure with time plan:
   Set (introduction):

   Modeling:

   Guided (coached) practice:

   Assignments:

   Closure:

5. **Materials Needed**
   Audiovisual:

   Other:

6. **Assessment and Revision**
   Assessment of learning:

   Plan for revision:

The objectives of the lesson are included as specific statements detailing precisely what students will be able to do as a result of the learning of the lesson. Teachers and students need to know that. Behavioral objectives provide clear statements of what learning is to occur. In addition, from clearly written behavioral objectives, assessment items can be written to measure whether students have accomplished the objectives. The type of assessment item used (discussed in the next chapter) should not only *measure for* the instructional objective but should also *be compatible with* the objective being assessed. As discussed earlier, your specific objectives might be covert or overt or a combination of both. Examples include

- The student will be able to list the main ideas in a selected passage of social studies prose. (overt, cognitive)
- The student will be able to rehearse an oral interview using a tape recorder. (overt, cognitive, and psychomotor)

Setting specific objectives is a crucial step in developing any lesson plan. Many lessons go wrong at this point. In writing specific objectives, teachers sometimes mistakenly list what they intend to do—such as "cover the next five pages" or "do the next 10 problems"—and fail to focus on what the learning objective in these activities truly is. When you approach this step in your lesson planning, ask yourself, "What do I want my students to be able to demonstrate from this lesson?" Your answers to that question are your objectives!

Rationale. The rationale is an explanation of why the lesson is important and why the instructional methods chosen will achieve the objectives. Parents, students, teachers, administrators, and others have the right to know why specific content is being taught and why the methods are being used. Teachers become reflective decision makers when they challenge themselves to think about what they are teaching, how they are teaching it, and why it must be taught. Sometimes teachers include the rationale statement in the beginning of the unit plan, but not in each daily lesson. See the "Sample Integrated Unit Plan With Daily Lessons," section M, for a sample rationale statement.

Body of the lesson. The plan is the sequence of the lesson. For reasons discussed earlier, teachers must plan their lessons carefully. The body of the lesson plan consists of the following elements:

Content. Content is the substance of the lesson, the information to be presented, obtained, and learned. The teacher selects appropriate information to meet the learning objectives, the level of competence of the students, and content requirements at that grade level.

To make sure your lesson actually covers what it should, you should write down exactly what content you intend to cover. This material may be placed in a separate section or combined with the procedure section. The important thing is to be sure that your information is written down so you can refer to it quickly and easily when you need to. If, for instance, you are going to introduce new material using a 5-minute lecture, you will want to outline the content of that lecture. The word *outline* is not used casually—you need not have pages of notes to sift through; nor should you ever read declarative statements to your students. You should be familiar enough with the content so that an outline (in detail, if necessary) will be sufficient to carry on the lesson.

If you intend to conduct the lesson using discussion, you should write out the key discussion questions.

Instruction. The procedure or procedures to be used, sometimes referred to as the *instructional components,* is instruction. Appropriate instructional methods are chosen to meet the objectives, to match the students' learning styles, and to ensure that all children have equal opportunity to learn.

In this section, you establish what you and your students will do during the lesson. Ordinarily, you should plan this section of your lesson as an organized entity having a beginning (an introduction or set), a middle, and an end (called the closure) to be completed during the lesson. This structure is not always needed, because some lessons are simply parts of units or long-term plans and merely carry on activities spelled out in those long-term plans. Still, most daily lessons need to include the following elements in their procedure:

1. *An introduction.* The process used to prepare the students mentally for the lesson
2. *Lesson development.* The detailing of activities that occur between the beginning and the end of the lesson
3. *Plans for guided (or coached) practice.* Ways that you intend to have children interact in the classroom, receiving guidance or coaching from each other and from you
4. *The lesson conclusion (or closure).* The planned process of bringing the lesson to an end, thereby providing students with a sense of completeness and, with effective teaching, accomplishment and comprehension by helping students to synthesize the information learned from the lesson
5. *A timetable.* This serves simply as a planning and implementation guide
6. *Assignments.* What students are instructed to do as follow up to the lesson, either as homework or as in-class work, providing students an opportunity to learn further and to practice what is being learned.

Let's now consider each of these procedural elements in further detail.

Introduction to the lesson. Like any good performance, a lesson needs an effective beginning. In many respects, the introduction sets the tone for the rest of the lesson by alerting students that the business of learning is to begin. The introduction should be an attention-getter. If it is exciting, interesting, or innovative, it can create a favorable mood for the lesson. In any case, a thoughtful introduction serves as a solid indicator that you are well prepared.

Although it is difficult to develop an exciting introduction to every lesson taught each day, there are always a variety of options to spice up the launching of a lesson. You might, for instance, begin the lesson by briefly reviewing the previous lesson, thereby helping children connect the learning. Another possibility is to review vocabulary words from previous lessons and to introduce new ones. Still another possibility is to use the key point of the day's lesson as an introduction and then again as the conclusion. Sometimes teachers begin a lesson by demonstrating a discrepant event—an event that is contrary to what one might expect. Yet another possibility is to begin the lesson with a writing activity on some controversial aspect of the ensuing lesson.

In short, you can use the introduction of the lesson to review past learning, tie the new lesson to the previous lesson, introduce new material, point out the objectives of the new lesson, help students connect their learning with other disciplines or with real life, or—by showing what will be learned and why the learning is important—induce in children a mindset favorable to the new lesson.

Lesson development. The developmental activities, which, as shown in the sample lesson plan, comprise the bulk of the lesson plan, are the specifics by which you intend to achieve your lesson objectives. They include activities that present information, demonstrate skills, provide reinforcement of previously learned material, and provide other opportunities to develop understanding and skill. In addition, by actions and words, during lesson development the teacher models the behaviors expected of the students. Children in grades K–4 need such modeling. By effective modeling, the teacher can exemplify the anticipated learning outcomes. Activities of this section of the lesson plan should be described in some detail so you will know exactly what you plan to do and, during the stress of the class, you will not forget details of your plan and the subject content. For this reason, you should note the answers to the questions you intend to ask and the solutions to problems you intend to have your students solve.

Benefits of coached practice. Allowing time in class for children to begin work on homework assignments and long-term projects is highly recommended because it provides opportunity for the teacher to give students individual attention (guided or coached practice). Being able to coach students is the reason for in-class time to begin assignments. The benefits of coached practice include being able to (1) monitor students work so they don't go too far in the wrong direction, (2) help children to reflect on their thinking, (3) assess the progress of individual students, and (4) discover or create a "teachable moment." For the latter, for example, while observing and monitoring student practice, the teacher might discover a commonly shared student misconception. The teacher could then talk about and attempt to clarify that misconception or, collaboratively with students, plan a subsequent lesson centered around that misconception.

Lesson conclusion. Having a clear-cut closure to the lesson is as important as having a strong introduction. The closure complements the introduction. The concluding activity should summarize and bind together what has ensued in the developmental stage and should reinforce the principal points of the lesson. One way to accomplish these ends is to restate the key points of the lesson. Another is to briefly outline the major points. Still another is to repeat the major concept. No matter what approach you take, the concluding activity is usually brief and to the point.

The timetable. To estimate the time factors in any lesson can be very difficult. A good procedure is to gauge the amount of time needed for each learning activity and note that alongside the activity and strategy in your plan, as shown in the sample lesson plans. Placing too much faith in your time estimate may be foolish—an estimate is more for your guidance in planning than for anything else. Beginning teachers frequently find that their discussions and presentations do not last as long as expected. Another important reason for including a time plan in your lesson is to give information to students about how much time they have for a particular activity, such as a laboratory activity or cooperative learning group activity.

Materials and equipment. Materials of instruction include the textbook, supplementary readings, media, and other supplies necessary to accomplish the lesson objectives. Teachers must be sure that the proper and necessary materials are available for the lesson, which takes planning. Students cannot use what they do not have available in the classroom.

Assessment and revision. You must include in your lesson plan details of how you will assess how well children *are* learning (formative assessment) and how well they *have* learned (summative assessment). Comprehension checks for formative assessment can be in the form of questions you and the children ask during the lesson. Questions you intend to ask (and possible answers) should be built into the developmental section of your lesson plan.

For summative assessment, teachers typically use review questions at the end of a lesson (as a closure) or the beginning of the next lesson (as a review or transfer introduction), independent practice at the completion of a lesson, and tests. Again, questions for checking for comprehension should be detailed in your lesson plan.

In most lesson plan formats, a section is reserved for making notes or comments about the lesson, which can be particularly useful if you plan to use the lesson again at some later date.

Components Related to the Daily Lesson Plan

Assignments. When an assignment is to be given, it should be noted in your lesson plan. When to present it to students is optional—except that it should never be yelled as an afterthought as the students are exiting the classroom at the end of the day. Whether begun and completed during classtime or done out of school, assignments are best written on the chalkboard or in a special place on the bulletin board, on a handout, or in the syllabus. Take extra care to ensure that assignment specifications are clear to the students. It is also important to remember that assignments and procedures are not the same thing. An assignment tells students *what* is to be done; procedures explain *how* to do it. Although an assignment may include specific procedures, merely spelling out procedures is not the same thing as making an academic assignment. When students are given an assignment, they need to understand the reasons for doing it as well as have some notion about ways the assignment might be done.

Many teachers give weekly assignments to students, requiring that they maintain an assignment schedule in their portfolios. When given periodically, rather than daily, assignments should still appear in your daily lesson plans so you can remind students of them. Once assignment specifications are given, it is a good idea not to make major modifications to them, and it is especially important not to change assignment specifications several days after an assignment has been given. Last-minute changes in specifications can be very frustrating to students who have already begun or completed the assignment and show little respect for those students.

Special notes and reminders. Many teachers provide a place in their lesson plan format for special notes and reminders. Most of the time you will not need such reminders, but when you do, it helps to have them in a regular location in your lesson plan so you can refer to them quickly. In this special section, you can place reminders concerning such things as announcements to be made, school programs, makeup work for certain students, and so on. These things may or may not be important, but they do need to be remembered.

M. SAMPLE INTEGRATED UNIT PLAN WITH DAILY LESSONS

The following is a sample unit plan with daily lessons that can be adjusted for use for specific grade levels. As you read through this sample unit, you will notice the use of an abbreviated format for presenting the lessons, but sometimes the narrative is extended to review how a teacher might actually conduct each lesson. Notice also how the students' responses are varied from day to day. At the beginning of the unit are suggestions for unit extension and additional resources. These can provide ideas for daily variation to meet individual student needs, as well as assist you in preparing a similar unit. After reviewing this sample, complete the analysis of it for a discussion with your classmates.

SAMPLE UNIT PLAN

Descriptive Data:

Teacher _____   Date _____

Grade Level _____   Room _____

Unit   People in Early Plymouth in North America

Topic   People Related to Early Plymouth in North America*

Summary for Integrated Unit About People in Plymouth in North America

Time line

This unit was designed as part of the social studies program about the development of the United States of America.

Unit evaluation

Assessment of individual student learning was made through teacher observation and student participation in the unit activities. Daily ongoing assessment of the students' progress and a cumulative evaluation at the completion of all of the lessons were also made.

Field-testing and analysis

Field testing was conducted in the classroom with an inservice teacher in attendance. It appeared that the students were interested and that they transferred their reading skills to this content area.

Materials

Needed materials are included in each lesson.

Rationale and adaptability for different grade levels

Though designed for grade 4, this ITU about People in Early Plymouth in North America can be adapted for students in different grades. It is part of the social studies program about the development of the United States and is related to the scope and sequence model in a document by the National Council for the Social Studies (NCSS). For example, in the NCSS document, it is recommended that grade 1 develop an understanding of the individual in social groups, such as family life (family life at Plymouth); that grade 2 understand basic needs of social groups, such as neighborhood (Plymouth can be compared with students' neighborhoods); that grade 3 understand sharing earth and space with others, such as the community (available services now in students' community and at Plymouth can be compared); and that grade 4 understand human life in varied environments (Plymouth colony is a varied environment in a different historical setting).

Through selected learning materials, students will develop a better understanding of our country as they study people with different backgrounds, ideas, and ways of life. In this unit, students become better acquainted with the early settlement of Plymouth Colony, the people who lived there, and some of the reasons they came to North America. As students learn about this historical period of U.S. history, the teacher can guide them to compare that time period with present-day events and develop new insights about newcomers in history and newcomers in the United States today.

Special notes concerning grade level, special needs students, and a multicultural component

In many of the activities, students selected partners in groups with whom to complete the activities. ESL students were assigned to work with students who had strong oral skills. When appropriate, selections of children's literature that present children of different ethnic and cultural groups were read aloud.

Individual differences

The following provisions were made for individual differences related to reading assignments:

- Blind and visually impaired students were given brailled materials, talking books, raised relief maps, projection magnifiers, and large-type printed materials. Write for information about products, reports, films, and publications to the American Foundation for the Blind, Consumer Products Department, 15 West 16th Street, New York, NY 10011.
- Deaf and hearing impaired students were assisted by a parent interpreter as needed, and visuals and the overhead projector were used for writing questions and responses. Write for information and catalog of products to Gallaudet University.
- Gifted students were given extensive reading from a unit bibliography that led to class reports, independent inquiry, and biographical research about such persons as Sir George Carteret, Pocahontas, Squanto, Peter Stuyvesant, and John Winthrop.

Sample of Unit Bibliography

African heritage

Petry, A. (1964). *Tituba of Salem Village*. New York: Crowell. Tituba, an intelligent black slave is vulnerable to suspicion and attack from the witch-hunters in Salem. Historical fiction. (grades 6 and up)

Asian heritage

Namioka, L. (1992). *The Coming of the Bear*. New York: HarperCollins. Tells about two samurai in the 1600s, Zenta and Matsuzo, who escape to Ezo (now Hokkaido) and realize the warlike tension between the Aimu who live there and Japanese colonists who are trying to settle on the island. The two solve the mystery of the bear who keeps attacking the settlers during the winter and ease the tensions of war. Historical fiction. (grades 5–9)

*Adapted from Jarolimek & Parker (1993) and Kellough & Roberts (1994, pp. 238–243).

European heritage

Anderson, J. (1984). *The First Thanksgiving Feast.* Illustrated by G. Ancona. New York: Clarion. First-person accounts of life at Plymouth in the 1620s. The photographs are taken at Plimouth Plantation, a Living History Museum. Nonfiction. (grades 3–6)

Bulla, C. R. (1956). *John Billington, Friend of Squanto.* Illustrated by P. Burchard. New York: Crowell. Presents a brief picture of the Pilgrims at Plymouth Colony. Biography. (grades 2–4)

Bulla, C. R. (1981). *A Lion to Guard Us.* New York: Crowell. Three motherless London children sail to Jamestown to find their father in the new colony. When the ship is wrecked in a storm near Bermuda, the children save their lion's head door knocker. They survive on the island until another ship is built to take them to Virginia. There, they find their father, one of the few who survives the Starving Time in 1609. Young Jenny hangs the lion's head on a peg above the door latch, a symbol of their former home. Fiction. (grades 2–3)

Dalgliesh. A. (1954). *The Thanksgiving Story.* New York: Scribner's. Fictional account of the voyage of the Mayflower is followed by the first year at Plymouth, culminating with the Thanksgiving feast with the Indians. The story focuses on the children of the Hopkins family, the hardships of the voyage, and the first winter. Spring brings the arrival of a new baby in their new home, planting, harvesting, and giving thanks. Fiction. (grades 2–3)

Hunter, M. (1981). *You Never Knew Her as I Did!* New York: Harper. Will, a young page at Lochleven Castle, writes his memoirs of 1542–1587 about Mary, Queen of Scots. Fiction. (grade 4 and up)

Kagan, M. (1989). *Vision in the sky: New Haven's Early Years, 1638–1783.* Hamden, CT: Linnet Press. Presents aspects of colonial life with a focus on the strict Puritan values they lived by and their relations with original Native Americans. They give up security and comfort for their hopes. The book ends with the defeat of the British Redcoats in the Revolutionary War. Nonfiction. (grade 3 and up)

Marvin, I. R. (1993). *Shipwrecked on Padre Island.* Illustrated by L. Miller. New York: Hendrick-Long. Marooned in 1554, 13-year-old Catalina loses her bracelet which is found 400 years later by 13-year-old Jilliane. Fiction. (grades 5–7)

Monjo, F. (1972). *The Secret of Sachem's Tree.* Illustrated by M. Tomes. New York: Coward, McCann & Geoghan. Story of the people who hid the Connecticut charter in an oak tree in 1667 to keep the charter from being returned to England. Based on historical facts. Fiction. (grades 2–4)

Quackenbush, R. (1986). *Old Silver Legs Takes Over: A Story of Peter Stuyvesant.* Englewood Cliffs, NJ: Prentice Hall. Portrays the life of Stuyvesant, a colorful leader of New Amsterdam. Latino/Hispanic Heritage. (grade 3 and up)

Rohmer, H., O. Chow, & M. Vidauke. (1987). *The Invisible Hunters.* Chicago: Children's Book Pr. Portrays the impact of the first European traders on the life of the Miskiot Indians in 17th-century Nicaragua. Historical fiction. (grades 4–6)

Stone, M. (1989). *Rebellion's Song.* Austin, TX: Steck-Vaughn. This has six biographies about people of the colonial period. (grades 3–4)

Walters, K. (1993). *Samuel Eaton's Day: A Day in the Life of a Pilgrim Boy.* New York: Scholastic. Set in 1627 at Plimouth Plantation (note authentic historical spelling), the book portrays a hard day in the life of 7-year-old Samuel as he gets dressed, checks his animal snare, and gathers wood before he eats his breakfast of curds, mussels, and parsley. During the day, he helps the men harvest rye despite the pain of his blisters. Historical fiction. (grades 2–4)

Original Native American heritage

Brebeuf, Father Jean de. (1993). *The Huron Carol.* Dutton. This is the story of the birth of Christ as set in the Huron world, written by a missionary, Father Jean de Brebeuf, in the 1600s. Folk literature. (grade 4)

Bulla, C. R. (1988). *Squanto, Friend of the Pilgrims.* New York: Scholastic. The story of the life of the Native American who helped the European Pilgrims survive in the New World. Portrays the assistance given by Squanto (Tisqugntum, ?–1662) to the pilgrims at Plymouth Colony. He teaches the Pilgrims the Indian way of planting corn and helps them survive their first winter in Plymouth. Biography. (grades 2–4)

Fritz, J. (1982). *The Double Life of Pocahontas.* (1982). Illustrated by E. Young. New York: Putnam. Details life of a Native American princess and her journey to England as the wife of John Rolfe. Biography. (grades 4–6)

Kessel, J. K. (1983). *Squanto and the First Thanksgiving.* Illustrated by L. Donze. New York: Carolrhoda. Squanto, the last of the Patuxet Indians, teaches the Pilgrims ways to survive the harsh winter in Massachusetts. Biography. (grades 1–3)

Differently abled heritage

De Trevino, E. B. (1963). *Nacar, The White Deer.* New York: Farrar, Straus & Giroux. A mute Mexican shepherd boy protects a white deer and presents it to the King of Spain in 1630. Historical fiction. (grade 4)

Female image heritage

Christian, M. B. (1990). *Goody Sherman's Pig.* New York: Macmillan. Based on historical facts, Goody Sherman in 1636 took up a legal battle over her runaway pig with church elders and the courts. It was said that her battle caused the colony to create two legislative branches of government. Fiction. (grades 3–4)

Fradin, D. B. (1990). *Anne Hutchinson.* New York: Enslow. Discusses life of Hutchinson (1591–1643), who holds meetings in which she preaches that true religion is the following of God's guidance through an "Inner Light" without regard to the preachings of a church or minister. Later in Massachusetts in 1638, Anne is put on trial for "traducing" the ministers, is found guilty, and ordered to leave the colony. Anne's family moves and starts a settlement at Portsmouth that offers complete religious freedom for all, where she lives until a move to Pelham Bay, New York, where she is killed by Indians in 1643. Biography. (grades 3–4)

Fritz, E. I. (1991). *Anne Hutchinson.* New York: Chelsea. Details Anne's early life and gives a historical context for her banishment from the New England colony. Biography. (grade 4)

Nichols, J. K. (1993). *A Matter of Conscience: The Trial of Anne Hutchinson.* Illustrated by D. Krovatin. Austin, TX: Steck-Vaughn. Describes religious climate in which Anne lived and mentions the difference between a "Covenant of Works" and a "Covenant of Grace," two views that help readers understand her words and actions before and after her trial. Biography. (grade 4)

Religious minority heritage

Aliki. (1984). *The Story of William Penn.* Englewood Cliffs, NJ: Prentice Hall. William Penn (1644–1718), a Quaker, establishes the colony of Pennsylvania as a refuge for religious nonconformers, and he treats fairly the Indians who named him Onas, which meant quill or pen. Biography. (grade 4)

Ammon, R. (1989). *Growing Up Amish.* New York: Atheneum. Portrays the history of the Amish movement and shows the Amish lifestyle in a Pennsylvania Dutch area. Nonfiction. (grade 4)

Costabel, E. D. (1988). *The Jews of New Amsterdam.* New York: Atheneum. Recounts the struggles of the Jews who journeyed to America from Brazil during the colonial period and discovered that the United States did not hold equality for all its people. Nonfiction. (grade 4)

- Language minority students were provided with bilingual materials as needed and, when desired, bicultural material. Write to National Clearinghouse for Bilingual Education, 1300 Wilson Boulevard, Suite B2–11, Rosslyn, VA 22209 and Gryphon House, 3706 Otis House, P.O. Box 217, Mount Ranier, MD 20822 (multiethnic books).
- Less able students were provided with easy-to-read books, filmstrips to view partnerships, brief assignments, and cooperative learning groups. Write to inquire about materials for persons with learning disabilities and those who are educable mentally retarded to C.C. Publications, Inc., P.O. Box 23699, Tigard, OR 97223.
- Students with physical impairments were provided with a buddy system to assist them in using reference materials and other equipment and resources. Write to inquire about reading programs to the National Library Service for the Blind and Physically Handicapped, Library of Congress, Washington DC 20542 and to Telesonsory Systems, Inc., 3408 Hillview Avenue, P.O. Box 10099, Palo Alto, CA 94304.
- Regular education students were provided with textbooks and supplemental books to read to respond to questions in a unit study guide.

LESSON #1

Descriptive Data:

Teacher _____   Date _____

Grade Level _____   Room _____

Unit   People Related to Early Plymouth in North America

Lesson #1 Topic Pilgrims at Plimoth (Plymouth)

Lesson goal and objective:

Students will:

1. Study examples of early Pilgrims and then compare and contrast them with a data chart.

Rationale and guiding question(s):

Content is related to the scope and sequence model in a document by the National Council for the Social Studies (NCSS) and in local school district and state curricula. *Q:* Who were some of the early Pilgrims at Plymouth? What were some of their reasons for coming to North America?

Plan and procedures:

1. The teacher asks questions to determine the students' concept of Pilgrims: What is a colonist? a Pilgrim? Were there Pilgrims from other countries in Early America? Why? What person do you think of when you think of Pilgrims/settlers in early America? The teacher learns that the students' information about Pilgrims is scanty and proceeds with a concept-formation lesson on Pilgrims in early America.
2. The teacher guides students to some examples of people associated with Plymouth and decides to use Squanto, John Billington, Govenor William Bradford, along with a fictionalized boy of the times, Samuel Eaton. The teacher engages the students in building up their understanding of the concept "explorers" by studying each of the examples and then comparing and contrasting them on a data chart. The teacher designs the data chart in the following manner after asking students to brainstorm questions about family life, social groups, available services, and other topics they want to find out about related to the people of Plymouth. The teacher asks and encourages the students to take the chart home to complete as homework.

EXAMPLES OF PEOPLE ASSOCIATED WITH PLYMOUTH	IN CHARGE?	FOOD?	ACTIVITIES?	SHELTER?	OTHER?
DATA CHART QUESTIONS					
1. Squanto					
2. John Billington					
3. Govenor Bradford					
4. Samuel Eaton					
5. Others					

Materials:

Library books, bulletin board and illustrations of settlers, globe, map, and chalk.

Assessment and revision:

The teacher observes students' ability to use a data chart to record information they find about historical personages.

LESSON #2

Descriptive Data:

Teacher _____ Date _____

Grade Level _____ Room _____

Unit   Native Americans in Plymouth Colony Region

Lesson #2 Topic People of the Breaking Day

Lesson goals and objectives:

Students will:

1. Observe a filmstrip of People of the Breaking Day.
2. List as many things as they can remember having seen in the filmstrip.
3. Examine the list to see if certain pieces of information on the list seem to go together or to be related in groups.
4. Suggest labels for the groups of information and refer to them to respond to discussion questions.

Rationale and guiding question(s):

Content is related to the scope and sequence model in a document by the National Council for the Social Studies (NCSS) and in local school district and state curricula. *Q:* Related to Plymouth Colony, who were some of the Native Americans in the Massachusetts region and what did they do?

Plan and procedures:

1. The teacher invites the students to observe a filmstrip based on the book, *People of the Breaking Day* (1990, New York: Atheneum, Grades 4–5) by Marcia Sewall. The material portrays the Wampanoag people as a proud industrious nation in southeastern Massachusetts before the settlers arrived. It describes the life in the tribe, the place of each member in the society, and details about hunting, farming, survival skills, and the value of a harmonious relationship with nature. It includes recreational and spiritual activities.
2. After the filmstrip, the teacher asks students to list as many things as they can remember having seen in the filmstrip. As students name what they observed, the teacher writes their responses on the board—for instance, responses about ways the people hunted, farmed, and their respect for nature. After listing what the students observed, the teacher asks them to examine the list to see if certain pieces of information on the list seem to go together or to be related. The teacher guides them in grouping together information that has something in common, as, for instance, activities reserved for the women, what the children did, and what responsibilities the men had. The groups are shown on the board.
3. After placing related items in the same group, the teacher asks students to think of names or labels for the groups. The labels are written on the board by the appropriate groups.
4. The teacher asks students to refer to the groups on the board and respond to these questions:
   a. What are things human beings can do that no other creatures can do?
   b. What natural resources did Native Americans depend on in their everyday life?
   c. Suppose a visitor from another country spent a day with the People of the Breaking Day—what would the person see?
   d. What did you see in the filmstrip about the children?
   e. What surprised you most in the filmstrip?

Materials:

Filmstrip, library books, writing board, and chalk.

Assessment and revision:

The teacher observes students' ability to list as many things as they can remember having seen in the filmstrip; to examine the list for related information; to suggest names or labels for the related groups; and to refer to the groups on the board to respond to discussion questions. The lesson will be retaught as a mini-lesson to selected students who had difficulty recalling items, examining items, determining relationships, and using groups as referents for a discussion.

LESSON #3

Descriptive Data:

Teacher _____ Date _____

Grade Level _____ Room _____

Unit   People Related to Early Plymouth in North America

Lesson #3 Topic Group Memberships of Pilgrims and Native Americans

Lesson goals and objectives:

Students will:

1. Identify human groups.
2. Become aware of reasons people band together.

Rationale and guiding question(s):

Content is related to the scope and sequence model in a document by the National Council for the Social Studies (NCSS) and in local school district and state curricula. *Q:* What human groups were there among the Pilgrims and Native American of the period? What are some of the reasons people band together?

Plan and procedures:
1. The teacher asks students to look at five illustrations of groups and suggest a title for each one (for example, a baseball team, family eating dinner together, and so on). The teacher asks students to think of a word/words that could describe *all* of the illustrations (*human groups*) and writes the heading "Human Groups" on the board.
2. Students are asked to contribute names of additional groups they know, and the teacher adds their suggestions to the board. The teacher asks students to provide reasons each human group is grouped together and adds the students' comments to the board.

HUMAN GROUPS	
NAMES	*WHY THEY ARE TOGETHER*
hunting group	to search for food in a cooperative way
play group	to be entertained
family group eating together	to show they care and love one another

3. The teacher reviews illustrations of groups with the students and asks for their ideas about ways that the groups can be identified (for example, a tribe might be identified by a tribal sign or symbol; a family might be identified by distinguishing looks).
4. Students are given discarded magazines and asked to locate and cut out illustrations of human groups. In the whole group, each student is asked to show the selected illustrations with the sentence frame, "I think this is a picture of a group because. . . ." Each picture is affixed to mural paper in the classroom under the heading "Human Groups."

Materials:
Magazines, scissors, mural paper, data chart, writing board, and chalk.

Assessment and revision:
The teacher observes and uses anecdotal records to document students' participation in providing reasons why each human group has banded together and in responding to "I think this is a picture of a group because. . . ."

LESSON #4

Descriptive Data:
Teacher _____   Date _____
Grade Level _____   Room _____
Unit   People in Early Plymouth in North America
Lesson #4 Topic Pilgrims and Problem Solving at Plymouth

Lesson goals and objectives:
Students will:
1. Discuss problem solving.
2. Work cooperatively and collaboratively in small groups.
3. Discuss the question about the safety of eating unfamiliar plants by the Pilgrims; discuss what decisions would have to be made by the Pilgrims.

Rationale and guiding question(s):
What were some Pilgrims' problems in gathering food from unfamiliar plants?

Plan and procedures:
1. The teacher asks the class to divide into small groups of three or four and gives each group an unfamiliar food (for example, bok choy, rosemary leaves and branches, cilantro, jicama, kiwi, leek, elephant garlic, and so on).
2. The teacher asks students to imagine that they are members of a food-gathering group at Plymouth. Their group has just found one of these foods during their daily search. They do not know what it is since this is the first time they have seen this food. Their group is not sure if the food is safe to eat. Pose this question to the groups: Discuss what you will do about this "food." What might happen based on your decision?
3. After the groups have time to discuss the food, their decisions, and the consequences, the teacher asks the whole group to report its decisions and consequences to the class. The teacher writes each group's decisions (and their consequences) on the board:
   Group 1's decision   consequences
   Group 2's decision   consequences
   Group 3's decision   consequences
4. The teacher reviews the groups' decisions and invites students to consider the consequences of each decision:
   a. Ignore the food and look for something else that might be familiar (the group may lose out on finding a tasty new food for the colony).
   b. Test the food by eating a small bite of it (the group might become ill if the food was toxic to humans).
   c. Test the food in a way other than eating it (the group would have to take the time to figure out how to do this).
5. The teacher asks the groups to consider decision c and design a plan to test the safety of eating a newly found plant food. In the whole group, students then report on their discussion and plans for testing the unfamiliar food.

Materials:
Library books, data chart, writing board and illustrations of Pilgrims/Native Americans, globe, map, and chalk.

Assessment and revision:

Teacher assessment will be based on the students' participation in group work. The teacher meets with groups, observes, and makes notes on adhesive-backed note paper to later affix to the assessment checklist the teacher has for each student. The teacher will transfer the information from the note paper to the checklist form. A sample checklist can look like the following:

Assessment Checklist for Group Work

Student _____   Date _____

Teacher _____   Period _____

	OFTEN	SOMETIMES	SELDOM

The student participated in:
the task of the group
helping others
decision making
discussing information
organizing information
drawing conclusion(s)
preparing materials to present findings
discussing positive contributions of others
making a positive contribution to the group

LESSON #5

Descriptive Data:

Teacher _____   Date _____

Grade Level _____   Room _____

Unit   People in Early Plymouth in North America

Lesson #5 Topic Jobs in Plymouth Colony

Lesson goals and objectives:

Students will:

1. Each select a different job from Plymouth Colony life: blacksmith, candlemaker, farmer, homemaker, hunter, minister, and others.
2. Discover what skills and responsibilities each worker had in Plymouth Colony.
3. Share information by showing a sketch of something the worker might have created or used.
4. Work cooperatively and collaboratively in groups.

Rationale and guiding question(s):

What different jobs were needed in Plymouth Colony?

Plan and procedures:

1. The teacher reviews the activity with students. The students are engaged in their various research tasks related to jobs in Plymouth Colony. The teacher assists and moves from one group to another.
2. The teacher asks students as a whole group to discuss what was done, what help is still needed, and what is planned for the next day's work.
3. When the various reports about jobs are done, the teacher schedules time for students to plan the presentation of their reports (using murals, posters, puppets, drama, bulletin board, diorama, or other means) and then share the information they found with the class.

Materials:

Library books, writing board, chalk, paper, and pencils.

Assessment and revision:

The teacher will assess students using anecdotal records about their cooperative and collaborative group work, participation in discussion, and presentations of the reports about jobs in the colony.

LESSON #6

Descriptive Data:

Teacher _____   Date _____

Grade Level _____   Room _____

Unit   People in Early Plymouth in North America

Lesson #6 Topic Other Problems at Plymouth

Lesson goals and objectives:

Students will:

1. Read selected materials and respond to the guiding question about problems in Plymouth Colony.
2. Rank the problems with the greatest hardship (from the students' point of view) as number one and so on.
3. Justify their choices for their rankings.

Rationale and guiding question(s):
What can we learn about other problems the colonists faced?

Plan and procedures:
1. Students read selected materials and respond to the guiding question. A student volunteer records the problems in the colonies on the board.
2. With the students, the teacher reviews the list of problems and groups similar problems together under student-selected headings such as "Shelter Problems," "Food Problems," and so on. The teacher asks students to rank the problems with the greatest hardship (from the students' point of view) as number one and so on. The teacher asks students to justify their choices for their rankings. A discussion of the ranking closes the lesson.
3. Additional Interdisciplinary Feature: Mathematics. Related to mathematics, the students' rankings can be written on the board.

Materials:
Library books, data chart, and writing board.

Assessment and revision:
The teacher observes students' participation in discussion and the ranking procedure.

LESSON #7

Descriptive Data:

Teacher _____ Date _____
Grade Level _____ Room_____
Unit   Native Americans in Plymouth Colony Region
Lesson #7 Topic Successful and Unsuccessful Times in Plymouth

Lesson goals and objectives:
Students will:
1. Provide reasons why these early Pilgrims traveled to North America.
2. Examine four ways that a word or term can be defined (such as with a dictionary, demonstrating, describing, and displaying an illustration).
3. Give opinions about the success or lack of success in activities at Plymouth Colony and support their opinions with evidence from their reading.

Rationale and guiding question(s):
In what ways was the colony of Plymouth successful? Unsuccessful?

Plan and procedures:
1. With the students, the teacher asks, "What can we say are the reasons these early Pilgrims traveled to North America?" The students respond and the reasons are written on the board. They discuss which activities in Plymouth were successful and which were not from their points of view.
   The teacher listens for the use of specific terms that need to be clarified. "Gretchen, you mentioned that William Randolph was a *governor*. How does your textbook or dictionary define *governor*?" Gretchen is asked to read the definition. The teacher points out that students can always define a term by reading the definition in a dictionary, a glossary, or in the context of sentences in the text. "But there are other ways to define a term. For example, we can define a term by demonstrating something about it. Who wants to define *governor* by demonstrating something a governor of a colony might do?" Student responses are elicited. "We can also define something by describing it. Who wants to define *governor* by describing something about a governor?" The students respond. "And then, we can define a word or term by displaying an illustration. Who will find a picture to help us define *governor*?" There is a discussion of the pictures the students locate and the contribution of the pictures to the definition of the word.
2. The teacher elicits from students the four major ways that a word or term can be defined and records their responses as a summary on the board:

Defining a Word or Term

| Dictionary | Demonstrating |
| Describing | Displaying an illustration |

3. The teacher asks the whole group to consider their reasons that early colonists journeyed to North America and generalize, "Considering your reasons and our reading about the colonists, would you say the Pilgrims were successful or unsuccessful in starting the colony of Plymouth in North America?" In the discussion, the teacher asks students to clarify and define some of the terms they use and to support their opinions about the success or lack of success in activities at Plymouth Colony with evidence from their reading.
4. Additional Interdisciplinary Feature: Literacy. See above procedures related to defining words and terms.

Materials:
Dictionary, board, chalk, student textbooks, and library books.

Assessment and revision:
The teacher monitors the students' participation in the discussion and in defining words and terms.

LESSON #8

Descriptive Data:
Teacher _____ Date _____
Grade Level _____ Room _____
Unit   People in Early Plymouth in North America
Lesson #8 Topic Pilgrims and Native Americans at Plymouth

Lesson goals and objectives:
Students will:
1. Study examples of Pilgrims/Native Americans and then compare and contrast them with information on a data chart.
2. Write/dictate summary sentences about the similarities and differences of the people.
3. Listen to and read information about two or three other historical personalities and decide which of them, if any, could be classified as a Pilgrim (early colonist, Native American of the period).
4. Work cooperatively and collaboratively in small groups.
5. Create a fictional character from data sheets and summary sentences to be sure the character they create has some of the characteristics mentioned that Pilgrims (early colonists, Native Americans of the period) had.

Rationale and guiding question(s):
Who were some of the Pilgrims/Native Americans at Plymouth? What did they do? What were some of the Pilgrims' reasons for coming to North America?

Plan and procedures:
1. The teacher distributes an exercise to the students to help them organize and summarize the information about historical personalities at Plymouth. The students are engaged in responding to a worksheet similar to the following one:

I Can Organize and Summarize
Student _____ Date _____
Teacher _____ Period _____

Instructions: To organize the material on this worksheet, scan your reading material, review your notes about any media you reviewed, and recall what you learned from the group reports. Write the missing information in the blanks that are provided.

Personality	*Known for*
_____	_____
_____	_____
_____	_____
_____	_____

To help you summarize, consider the following: Explain why Plymouth Colony was started. What main idea or statement can you make from this information?
2. The teacher writes students' comments on the board and asks them to contribute a summary sentence of the similarities of the people (for example, these are the ways the people were alike—they. . . . The teacher repeats the activity for contrasting and having students write a summary sentence of the differences of the people. When the information has been gathered and written on the chart, the teacher asks questions to guide students toward contrasting and comparing the people and their contributions: In what way could you say some of these people are alike? (Pilgrims, early colonists). In what way could you say these people were different? (individuals, different backgrounds).
3. The teacher reads aloud information about two or three other historical personalities and asks students to decide which of them, if any, could be classified as a Pilgrim (early colonist, Native American of the period).
4. The teacher asks students to get into teams of three or four and create a fictional character and a day's activities of a Pilgrim (early colonist, Native American of the period). The teacher sets the stage by saying, each group should create a fictional character from data sheets and summary sentences to be sure the character they create has some of the characteristics mentioned that Pilgrims (early colonists, Native Americans of the period) had.
5. The teacher asks two groups to share what they created for the fictional character of the time period.

Materials:
Library books, data chart, writing board and illustrations of Pilgrims/Native Americans, globe, map, and chalk.

Assessment and revision:
Teacher evaluation will be based on (1) students' responses to the worksheet and the way(s) they organize and summarize information; (2) observation of the student teams as they create a fictional character and a day's activities of a Pilgrim; (3) evaluation of the fictional characters who should have some of the characteristics mentioned that Pilgrims (early colonists, Native Americans of the period) had.

LESSON #9

Descriptive Data:
Teacher _____ Date _____
Grade Level _____ Room _____
Unit   People in Early Plymouth in North America
Lesson #9 Topic Examples of Non-Colonists

Lesson goal and objective:
Students will:
1. Listen to examples read aloud of historical figures other than Pilgrims/early colonists/Native Americans and then describe some changes that would be needed to make the historical figure an example of a Pilgrim, an early colonist, or a Native American of the time period.

Rationale and guiding question(s):
What needs to be changed to make each of several historical personalities a Pilgrim, an early colonist, or a Native American of the period?

Plan and procedures:
1. The teacher reads aloud *brief* biographical sketches of several historical figures, all of which were not in the time period of the Pilgrims at Plymouth. The teacher announces that the students' challenge will be to describe some of the changes that would be needed to make the historical figure an example of being a Pilgrim, an early colonist, or a Native American of the period.
2. First, the teacher reads aloud selections from *Good Queen Bess: The Story of Elizabeth I of England* (1991, New York: Four Winds. Grades 4–5) by Diane Stanley and Peter Vennema. The biography portrays the life of Elizabeth (1533–1603) and her influence on religion, politics, and exploration of the New World. After reading the selection, the teacher asks students to suggest the changes that would have to be made in Queen Elizabeth's life to be able to classify her as a Pilgrim, an early colonist, or a Native American of the period.
3. After students have made their suggestions, the teacher describes another figure, Henry Hudson—a British sea captain—by reading selections from *Henry Hudson: Arctic Explorer and North American Adventurer* (1991, New York: Gareth Stevens, Grades 2–4) by I. Asimov & E. Kaplan. Hudson first was sent in the *Hopewell* by the English Muscovy Company to find a passage to the east around North America in 1607. On a similar voyage in 1611, the crew mutinies and places Hudson, his son, and loyal sailors adrift in a small boat and they are never heard from again. The students are asked and helped to make the needed changes.

Materials:
Biographical sketches, writing board, and chalk.

Assessment and revision:
The teacher observes students and uses anecdotal records to document their participation in the discussion and the ways they described some of the changes that would be needed to make the historical figure an example of being a Pilgrim, an early colonist, or a Native American of the period.

LESSON #10

Descriptive Data:
Teacher _____ Date _____
Grade Level _____ Room _____
Unit   People in Early Plymouth in North America
Lesson #10 Topic More Examples of Colonists

Lesson goal and objective:
Students will:
1. Work cooperatively and collaboratively in small groups to write biographies on the founders of Plymouth Colony or on Native Americans of the period or to gather information about this first colony and use the information to advise others on how best to organize a colony.

Rationale and guiding question(s):
Who were some of the other historical personalities related to Plymouth Colony and what did they contribute?

Plan and procedures:
1. The teacher asks students to work in small groups to write brief biographies about selected Pilgrims and Native Americans related to Plymouth Colony. One of the groups gathers information about the colony and uses the information to describe to others how the colony was organized.
2. The students read aloud their biographies and report on their methods of gathering information.
3. The teacher guides a discussion with this question: "Some people believe that people change the earth. How might we go about finding out if this was true of the people who lived in Plymouth and the Native Americans in the region?" At this point, the biographies and gathered information are used to search for documentation of the teacher's announced generalization.

4. Additional Interdisciplinary Feature: Music.
- Introduce the flute and invite the students to sing several songs related to the time period. Display the long maple fife banded with brass ferrules that comes with the book *Amy, Ben and Catalpa the Cat* (1990, Colonial Williamsburg Press, Grades 1–2) by Alice S. Owens. It is the story of children's adventures in eighteenth-century Williamsburg, and several tunes of the times are included along with flute instructions.
- Engage students in independent reading with A. Blackwood's *Beethoven*, M. B. Goffstein's *A Little Schubert,* and D. Lasker's *The Boy Who Loved Music.* To connect the composer with events in this period, use a time line on a transparency to show the era in which each lived. Ask students to prepare drawings of a composer, play samples of musical scores, and write background facts on transparencies to introduce a favorite composer of the period.
- Have students sing the Shaker abecedarium from *A Peaceful Kingdom* (1976, New York: Viking. All grades) by the Provensons to the tune of "The Alphabet Song" and sing the story-songs that have historical significance from *Pop! Goes the Weasel and Yankee Doodle: New York in 1776 and Today with Songs and Pictures* (1976, New York: Harper) by Robert Quackenbush.

Materials:
Biography books, writing board and chalk, paper, and pencils.

Assessment and revision:
The teacher observes and keeps anecdotal records of students' participation in small groups and in reporting. The teacher also reads brief biographies written by the students.

LESSON #11

Descriptive Data:
Teacher _____ Date _____
Grade Level _____ Room _____
Unit   People Related to Early Plymouth in North America
Lesson #11 Topic Quiz Show About What Was Learned

Lesson goals and objectives:
Students will:
1. Retrieve information for a quiz show about the Pilgrims and Native Americans related to the Plymouth Colony.
2. Work cooperatively and collaboratively in three groups.
3. Take turns describing or giving clues about a person, place, thing, activity, or event related to Plymouth Colony.

Rationale and guiding question(s):
What did we learn about Pilgrims and Native Americans related to Plymouth Colony?

Plan and procedures:
1. The teacher introduces a quiz show format for a final review: "Today, we are going to use our worksheets and your notes to get information for a quiz show about the Pilgrims and Native Americans related to the Plymouth Colony. In the quiz show, one group describes a person, place, thing, or activity related to Plymouth Colony. The group's members give some clues. The other two groups try to identify the person, place, or thing."
2. With the teacher facilitating the quiz show to review the information the students have gained, students can organize into three groups and take turns describing or giving clues about a person, place, thing, activity, or event related to Plymouth Colony.

Materials:
Index cards to prepare questions for quiz show.

Assessment and Revision:
The teacher assesses students' responses to the quiz show format and the way(s) they demonstrate that they can share information about a person, place, thing, event, or activity related to Plymouth Colony. Examples of the questions prepared by each student can be placed in his or her portfolio.

Assessment Strategies for Unit
Checklist for assessment
A unit checklist can be developed from information gained from the unit. It can be a record of a student's participation, skills, and knowledge. If a checklist is used from unit to unit, the teacher may observe different behaviors and skills contributed by a student and will have a record of each student's individual differences.

Unit checklist: Date _____   Student _____

OBJECTIVES	ACHIEVED
1. Identifies explorers, reasons for exploration, and initial contributions to colony development.	_____
2. Identifies settlements and problems.	_____
3. Recognizes how early English colonies developed.	_____

4. Develops skills:
   Discussing _____
   Locating information _____
   Reading at different speeds _____
   Studying _____
   Evaluating _____
   Making decisions and justifying choices _____
   Independent work _____
   Group work _____
   Classifying and categorizing _____
   Gathering information _____
   Reporting to class _____
   Organizing information _____
   Summarizing _____
   Reading and understanding maps _____
   Applying information _____
   Testing situations _____
   Other _____

Additional teacher comments_____

_____

_____

_____

_____

_____

_____

_____

_____

Studying the Sample Unit Plan

Instructions: The purpose of this exercise is to study the sample unit plan for its inclusions. Use the following questions as a guide to that study. Share and compare your responses with those of your classmates.

1. What is the central theme of this unit?
2. What is the intended duration of this unit?
3. What are the educational goals of this unit?
4. Are the learning objectives for this unit clearly stated?
5. Do the objectives appear to contribute to the learning goals of the unit? Explain.
6. Are the instructional procedures clearly spelled out?
7. Do the learning activities appear feasible? Explain.
8. Does the unit have an introductory activity that will accomplish the purposes as spelled out in the earlier discussion of the six steps for unit planning? Explain.
9. Does the plan include developmental activities? If so, identify them.
10. Does the plan include culminating activities? If so, identify them.
11. Describe the unit's learning assessment strategies.
12. Does the unit clearly identify the materials needed for implementation of the unit? And does it appear that the materials are readily available?
13. Could this unit plan be adaptable and used as an interdisciplinary unit? If so, explain several changes that could be made to make it an interdisciplinary thematic unit.
14. Are there multiethnic components to this unit plan? If so, identify them.
15. Does this plan take into account student differences in learning styles and learning modalities? If so, explain how.

16. Identify by day the various teaching strategies used in the narrative discussion of implementation of this unit. For example: Day 1—teacher-led discussion; visuals; silent reading; teacher use of questioning (and so on).
17. Specifically how does this unit plan address student
    Reading skills?
    Study skills?
    Thinking skills?
18. Consider the questions used by the teacher in the sample unit plan and identify several that are at the
    Recall (input) level
    Processing level
    Application (output) level
19. Does this unit make any attempt to help students make connections in their learning? If so, explain where and how.
20. Would you label the suggested assessment procedures for this unit "authentic"? (See Chapter 3 or 5 if you need help on this question.) Explain.
21. Complete the following activity web for this unit. In the boxes for each of the content areas of the curriculum, place content-related activities that are studied in this unit.

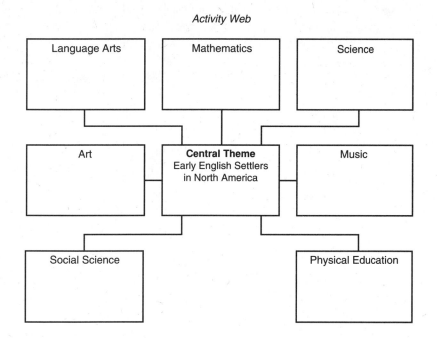

Activity Web

22. Now analyze the activity web. How many content areas were touched on in this unit? Which ones were? Which were not?

SUMMARY

This chapter focused on the importance and details of planning for daily instruction. You read about the process of selecting content, preparing specific learning outcomes, and preparing daily lessons. To recap, consider these major points:

- Process of selecting content. Your final decisions about what content to teach will be guided by articles in professional journals; discussions with other teachers; local courses of study; state curriculum documents; the differences, interests, and abilities of your students; and your own personal convictions, knowledge, and skills.
- Preparing specific learning outcomes. When teachers prepare specific objectives (by writing them themselves or by borrowing them from other sources) and teach toward those objectives, student learning is improved. It is expected that you will plan well and specifically what you intend your

students to learn, to convey your expectations to your students, and to assess their learning against that specificity.

- Preparing daily plans. Developing units of instruction and accompanying daily plans that integrate student learning and provide a sense of meaning for the children requires coordination throughout the curriculum—which is defined in this book as consisting of all the planned experiences students encounter while at school. Hence, for students, learning is a process of discovering how information, knowledge, and ideas are interrelated and learning to make sense out of self, of school, and of life. Shaping chunks of information into units, and units into daily lessons, helps students to process and to make sense out of knowledge.

There is no single best way to organize a daily lesson plan, no fool-proof formula that will guarantee an effective lesson. With experience and the increased competence that comes from reflecting on that experience, you will develop your own style, your own methods of implementing that style, and your own formula for preparing a lesson plan. Like a map, your lesson plan charts the course, places markers along the trails, pinpoints danger areas, highlights areas of interest and importance along the way, and ultimately brings the traveler to the objective.

QUESTIONS AND ACTIVITIES FOR DISCUSSION

1. Explain how a textbook can facilitate a student's learning in social studies and language arts.

2. From your current observations and field work in your teacher preparation program, clearly identify one specific example of educational practice that seems contradictory to exemplary practice or theory as presented in this chapter. Explain the discrepancy.

3. Describe three reasons a student teacher and a first-year teacher need to prepare detailed lesson and unit plans.

4. Explain why you should know how to prepare detailed plans even when the textbook program you are using provides them.

5. When, if ever, during instruction, should you divert from the written plan?

6. Explain the importance of preassessing student learning. When do you do a preassessment? How can it be done?

7. Explain why lesson planning should be a continual process.

8. Explain interdisciplinary thematic unit planning.

9. Explain the concept of "student-negotiated curriculum." Is it used today? Why or why not?

10. Explain the relationship of planning to the preactive and reflective thought-processing phases of instruction.

11. Explain your point of view about having national standards for each subject discipline taught in public schools. Who should prepare these standards? Who should decide how the standards are to be implemented and student learning assessed?

12. Using the format presented in the sample unit plan of Section M, prepare one integrated social studies and language arts daily lesson plan for a specific grade level, K–4, and then share your lesson plan with your colleagues for their feedback.

13. Describe any prior concepts you held that changed as a result of your experiences with this chapter. Describe the changes.

REFERENCES AND SUGGESTED READINGS

Ahlgren, A., & Rutherford, F. J. (1993, May). Where is project 2061 today? *Educational Leadership, 50*(8), 19–22.

Barba, R. H., et al. (1993, May). User-friendly text: Keys to readability and comprehension. *The Science Teacher, 60*(5), 15–17.

Bellamy, N. (1994, March). Bias in the classroom: Are we guilty? *Science Scope, 17*(6), 60–63.

Bloom, B. S. (1984). *Taxonomy of educational objectives, book I: Cognitive domain.* White Plains, NY: Longman.

Brandt, R. S. (1992–1993, December–January). On outcome-based education: A conversation with Bill Spady. *Educational Leadership, 50*(4), 66–70.

Brandt, R. S. (Ed.). (1988). *Content of the curriculum. 1988 ASCD Yearbook.* Alexandria, VA: Association for Supervision and Curriculum Development.

Brooks, J. G., & Brooks, M. G. (1993). *In search of understanding: The case for constructivist classrooms.* Alexandria, VA: Association for Supervision and Curriculum Development.

Brutlag, D., & Maples, C. (1992, March). Making connections: Beyond the surface. *Mathematics Teacher, 85*(3), 230–235.

Burrett, K., & Rusnak, T. (1993). *Integrated character education.* Fastback 351. Bloomington, IN: Phi Delta Kappan Educational Foundation.

Caine, G., & Caine, R. N. (1993, Fall). The critical need for a mental model of meaningful learning. *California Catalyst,* 18–21.

Costa, A. L. (1989). *The enabling behaviors.* Orangevale, CA: Search Models Unlimited.

Costa, A. L. (1991). *The school as a home for the mind.* Palatine, IL: Skylight Publishing.

Dempster, F. N. (1993, February). Exposing our students to less should help them learn more. *Phi Delta Kappan, 74*(6), 433–437.

Duckworth, E. (1986, November). Teaching as research. *Harvard Educational Review, 56*(4), 481–495.

Eisner, E. (1979). *The educational imagination.* New York: Macmillan.

Eisner, E. (Ed.). (1985). Aesthetic modes of knowing. *Learning and teaching the ways of knowing, 84th yearbook of the National Society for the Study of Education.* Chicago: University of Chicago Press.

Eisner, E. (1993, February). Why standards may not improve schools. *Educational Leadership, 50*(5), 22–23.

Elmore, R. F., & Fuhrman, S. H. (Eds.). (1994). *The governance of curriculum.* Alexandria, VA: The 1994 Yearbook of the Association for Supervision and Curriculum Development, Association for Supervision and Curriculum Development.

Evans, K. M., & King, J. A. (March, 1994). Research on OBE: What we know and don't know. *Educational Leadership, 51*(6), 12–17.

Feder-Feitel, L. (1993, March). How to avoid gender bias. *Creative Classroom, 7*(5), 56–63.

Feder-Feitel, L. (1994, March). How to avoid gender bias: Part II. *Creative Classroom, 8*(5), 56–60, 64–66.

Fersh, S. (1993). *Integrating the trans-national/cultural dimension.* Fastback 361. Bloomington, IN: Phi Delta Kappa Educational Foundation.

Gagné, R. M., Briggs, L., & Wager, W. (1988). *Principles of instructional design* (3rd ed.). New York: Holt, Rinehart & Winston.

Gall, M. (1984, November). Synthesis of research on teachers' questioning. *Educational Leadership, 42,* 40–47.

Gifford, B. R. (1991, October/November). The textbook of the 21st century. *Syllabus, 19,* 15–16.

Gollnick, D. M., & Chinn, P. C. (1994). *Multicultural education in a pluralistic society* (4th ed.). New York: Macmillan.

Good, T. L., & Brophy, J. E. (1994). *Looking in classrooms* (6th ed.). New York: HarperCollins.

Gray, I. L., & Hymel, G. M. (Eds.). (1992). *Successful schooling for all: A primer on outcome-based education and mastery learning.* Johnson City, NY: Network for Outcome-Based Schools.

Greenfield, E. (1993, May). Evolution of the textbook: From print to multimedia. *T.H.E. Journal, 20*(10), 12, 14, 16, and 19.

Harrow, A. J. (1977). *Taxonomy of the psychomotor domain.* White Plains, NY: Longman.

Hill, D. (1993, September). Math's angry man. *Teacher Magazine, 5*(1), 24–28.

Hinton, N. K. (1994). The pyramid approach to reading, writing, and asking questions. *Science Scope, 17*(5), 44–49.

Hunkins, F. P. (1989). *Teaching thinking through effective questioning.* Boston: Christopher-Gordon.

Jarolimek, J., & Parker, W. C. (1993). *Social studies in elementary education* (9th ed.). Englewood Cliffs, NJ: Merrill/Prentice Hall.

Joyce, B., & Showers, B. (1988). *Student achievement through staff development.* New York: Longman.

Katz, L. G. (1985). Dispositions in early childhood education. *ERIC/EECE Bulletin, 18*(2). Urbana, IL: ERIC Clearinghouse on Elementary and Early Childhood Education.

Kellough, R. D., & Roberts, P. L. (1994). *A resource guide for elementary school teaching: Planning for competence* (3rd ed.). Englewood Cliffs, NJ: Merrill/Prentice Hall.

Kelly, E. B. (1994). *Memory enhancement for educators.* Fastback 365. Bloomington, IN: Phi Delta Kappa Educational Foundation.

Krathwohl, D. R., Bloom, B. S., & Masia, B. B. (1964). *Taxonomy of educational goals, handbook II: Affective domain.* New York: David McKay.

Kudlas, J. M. (1994, May). Implications of OBE: What you should know about outcome-based education. *The Science Teacher, 61*(5), 32–35.

Leach, L. S. (1994, March). Sexism in the classroom: A self-quiz for teachers. *Science Scope, 17*(6), 54–59.

Lepper, M., & Green, D. (Eds.). (1978). *The hidden cost of rewards: New perspectives on the psychology of human motivation.* New York: Erlbaum.

Martin, B. L., & Briggs, L. J. (1986). *The affective and cognitive domains.* Englewood Cliffs, NJ: Educational Technology Publications.

Massey, M. (1993, May). Interest in character education seen growing. *ASCD Update, 35*(4), 4–5.

Murray, D. M. (1980). Writing as process: How writing finds its own meaning. In T. R. Donovan & B. W. McClelland (Eds.), *Eight approaches to teaching composition.* Urbana, IL: National Council of Teachers of English.

National Association for the Education of Young Children. (1990). *Good teaching practices for older preschoolers and kindergartners.* Washington, DC: Author.

Nelson, J. R., & Frederick, L. (1994, February). Can children design curriculum? *Educational Leadership, 51*(5), 71–74.

News. (1994, December). *School Library Journal, 40*(12), 16.

Newton, B. (1978, March–April). Theoretical basis for higher cognitive questioning—An avenue to critical thinking. *Education, 98*(3), 286–290.

Olson, R. (1994, December). Fasten your seatbelts. *School Library Journal, 40*(12), 35.

O'Neil, J. (1993, February). Can national standards make a difference? *Educational Leadership, 50*(5) 4–8.

Perkins, D., & Blythe, T. (1994, February). Putting understanding up front. *Educational Leadership, 51*(5), 4–7.

Ravitch, D. (1993, June). Launching a revolution in standards and assessments. *Phi Delta Kappan, 70*(10), 767–772.

Redfield, D., & Rousseau, E. (1981, Summer). A meta-analysis of experimental research on teacher questioning behavior. *Review of Educational Research, 51*(2), 237–245.

Resnick, L. B., & Klopfer, L. E. (Eds.). (1989). *Toward the thinking curriculum: Current cognitive research.* 1989 ASCD Yearbook. Alexandria, VA: Association for Supervision and Curriculum Development.

Sadker, M., Sadker, D., & Long, L. (1989). Gender and educational equality. In J. A. Banks & C. A. McGee Banks (Eds.), *Multicultural education: Issues and perspectives* (Chapter 6). Boston: Allyn & Bacon.

Seefeldt, C., & Barbour, N. (1994). *Early childhood education* (3rd ed.). Englewood Cliffs, NJ: Merrill/Prentice Hall.

Singer, H., & Donlan, D. (1990). *Reading and learning from text.* Hillsdale, NJ: Lawrence Erlbaum.

Slaughter, J. P. (1993). *Beyond storybooks: Young children and the shared book experience.* Newark, DE: International Reading Association.

Smith, M. S., et al. (1994). National curriculum standards: Are they desirable and feasible? Chapter 2 of R. F. Elmore and S. H. Fuhrman (Eds.), *The governance of curriculum.* Alexandria, VA: The 1994 Yearbook of the Association for Supervision and Curriculum Development, Association for Supervision and Curriculum Development.

Sosniak, L. A., & Stodolsky, S. S. (1993, January). Teachers and textbooks: Materials used in four fourth-grade classrooms. *Elementary School Journal, 93*(3), 249–275.

Starr, J. (1989). The great textbook war. In H. Holtz, I. Marcus, J. Dougherty, J. Michaels, & R. Peduzzi (Eds.). *Education and the American dream: Conservatives, liberals, and radicals debate the future of education.* Grandy, MA: Bergin & Garvey.

Steinbrink, J. E. (1985, January/February). The social studies learner as questioner. *The Social Studies, 76,* 38–40.

Towers, J. M. (1992, Spring). Outcome-based education: Another educational bandwagon? *Educational Forum, 56*(3), 291–305.

Wynne, E. A., & Ryan, K. (1993). *Reclaiming our schools: A handbook on teaching character, academics, and discipline.* New York: Macmillan.

CHAPTER 5

Assessment of Learning

Assessment (i.e., evaluation) is an integral part of and an ongoing process within the educational scene. Curricula, buildings, materials, specific courses, teachers, supervisors, administrators, equipment—all must be periodically assessed in relation to student learning, the purpose of any school. When gaps between anticipated results and student achievement exist, efforts are made to eliminate those factors that seem to be limiting the educational output or to improve the situation in some other way. Thus, educational progress occurs.

To learn effectively, children need to know how they are doing. Similarly, to be an effective teacher, you must be informed about what each child knows, feels, and can do, so that you can help students build on their skills, knowledge, and attitudes. Therefore you and your students need continuous feedback on their progress and problems in order to plan appropriate learning activities and to make adjustments to those already planned. If this feedback says that progress is slow, you can provide alternative activities; if it indicates that some or all of the children have already mastered the desired learning, you can eliminate unnecessary activities and practice for some or for all of the children. In short, assessment provides a key for both effective teaching and learning.

The importance of continuous assessment mandates that you know the principles and techniques of assessment. Building on the discussion in Chapter 3, this chapter explains some assessment techniques and shows you how to construct and use criterion-referenced assessment instruments and make sense of data obtained. We define the terms related to assessment, consider what makes a good assessment instrument, relate the criteria to both standardized and nonstandardized instruments, suggest procedures to use in constructing assessment items, point out the advantages and disadvantages of different assessment items and procedures, and explain the construction and use of alternative assessment devices (see also Chapters 8 through 12 for examples of alternative assessment). Specifically, this chapter will help you better understand:

1. The purposes of assessment
2. Guidelines for assessing learning
3. Terms used in assessment
4. The meaning of *authentic assessment*
5. The role of assessment in cooperative learning
6. How to involve students in self-assessment

7. How to use portfolios and checklists for assessment
8. How to maintain records of student achievement
9. Grading, marking, and reporting
10. The difference between criterion-referenced and norm-referenced measurement
11. Testing for student learning
12. Problems related to testing
13. How to prepare different types of assessment items
14. How to report student achievement
15. How to meet and collaborate with parents and guardians.

A. PURPOSES OF ASSESSMENT

Assessment of achievement in student learning is designed to serve several purposes:

1. *To assess and improve student learning.* To assess and improve student learning is the function usually associated with assessment and is the topic of this chapter.
2. *To identify children's strengths and weaknesses.* Identification and assessment of children's strengths and weaknesses are necessary for two purposes: to structure and restructure the learning activities and to restructure the curriculum. Concerning the first purpose, data on student strengths and weaknesses regarding content and process skills are important in planning activities appropriate for both skill development and intellectual development. This is diagnostic assessment (also known as preassessment). For the second purpose, data on student strengths and weaknesses in content and skills are useful for making appropriate modifications to the curriculum.
3. *To assess the effectiveness of a particular instructional strategy.* It is important for you to know how well a particular strategy helped children accomplish a particular goal or objective. Competent teachers continually evaluate their strategy choices, using a number of sources: student achievement as measured by assessment instruments, their own intuition, informal feedback given by the children, and informal feedback given by colleagues, such as by members of a teaching team.
4. *To assess and improve the effectiveness of curriculum programs.* Components of the curriculum are continually assessed by committees of teachers and administrators. The assessment is done while students are learning (formative assessment), and after (summative assessment).
5. *To assess and improve teaching effectiveness.* Today's exemplary K–4 teachers are education specialists and are as unique as the clientele they serve. To improve student learning, teachers are periodically evaluated on the basis of their commitment to working with children at this level, their ability to cope with children at a particular age or grade level, and (3) their ability to show mastery of appropriate instructional techniques—techniques that are articulated throughout this text.
6. *To communicate to and involve parents and guardians in their children's learning.* Parents, communities, and school boards all share in accountability for the effectiveness of the learning of their children. Today's schools are reaching out and engaging parents, guardians, and the community in their children's education. All teachers play an important role in the process of communicating with, reaching out to, and involving parents.

B. GUIDELINES FOR ASSESSING LEARNING

Because the welfare and, indeed, the future of so many people depend on the outcomes of assessment, it is impossible to overemphasize its importance. For a learning endeavor to be successful, the learner must have answers to basic questions: Where am I going? Where am I now? How do I get where I am going? How will I know when I get there? Am I on the right track for getting there? These questions are integral to a good assessment program. Of course, in the process of teaching and learning, the answers may be ever-changing, and the teacher continues to assess and adjust plans as appropriate and necessary.

Principles That Guide the Assessment Program

Based on the preceding questions, the following principles are suggested as guides for the assessment program:

- Both teachers and students need to know how well they are doing.
- Evidence and data regarding how well the teacher and students are doing should come from a variety of sources.
- Assessment is an ongoing process. The selection and implementation of plans and activities require continuous monitoring and assessment to check on progress and to change or adopt strategies to promote desired behavior.
- Self-assessment is an important component of any successful assessment program. It also involves helping children develop the skills necessary for them to assume increasingly greater ownership of their own learning.
- The program of assessment should help teaching effectiveness and contribute to the intellectual and psychological growth of children.
- Assessment is a reciprocal process that includes assessment of teacher performance as well as student achievement.
- A teacher's responsibility is to facilitate student learning and to assess student progress, and for that, the teacher should be held accountable.

C. CLARIFICATION OF TERMS USED IN ASSESSMENT

When discussing the assessment component of teaching and learning, it is easy to be confused by the terminology. To assist your reading and understanding, we offer the following clarification.

Assessment and Evaluation

Although some authors distinguish between the terms *assessment* (the process of finding out what children are learning, a relatively neutral process) and *evaluation* (making sense of what was found out, a subjective process), the difference may be too slight to matter for the purposes of this text. Therefore, consider the terms to be synonymous.

Measurement and Assessment

Measurement refers to quantifiable data about specific behaviors. Tests and the statistical procedures used to analyze the results are examples. Measurement is a descriptive and objective process, that is, it is relatively free from human value judgments.

Assessment includes objective data from measurement but also other types of information, some of which are more subjective, such as information from anecdotal records and teacher observations and ratings of student performance. In addition to the use of objective data (data from measurement), assessment also includes arriving at value judgments made on the basis of subjective information.

An example of the use of these terms follows. A teacher may share the information that Sarah Jones received a score in the 90th percentile on the third-grade statewide test of basic skills (a statement of measurement), but may add that "according to my assessment of her work in my class, she has not been an outstanding student" (a statement of assessment).

Validity and Reliability

The degree to which a measuring instrument actually measures what it is intended to measure is called the instrument's *validity*. When we ask if an assessment instrument has validity, key questions concerning that instrument are

- Does the instrument adequately sample the intended content?
- Does it measure the cognitive, affective, and psychomotor skills that are important to the unit of content being tested?
- Does it sample all the instructional objectives of that unit?

As a specific example, if a social studies teacher wants to find out if students have learned how to use map symbols, the teacher can carefully select a test question (or performance situation) that will clearly indicate what is being measured. One way to determine this would be to make a map drawing with symbols and ask students to use the map to decide the correct answers to the given questions. The students would then be asked to identify the correct answers from a list of choices.

The accuracy with which a technique consistently measures what it does measure is called its *reliability*. If, for example, you know that you weigh 114 pounds and a scale consistently records 114 pounds when you stand on it, then that scale has reliability. However, if the same scale consistently records 100 pounds when you stand on it, we can still say the scale has reliability. This example demonstrates that an instrument can be reliable (it produces similar results when used again and again), yet not necessarily valid (in this second instance, the scale is not measuring what it is supposed to measure, so although it is reliable, it is not valid). Although a technique might be reliable but not valid, a technique must have reliability before it can have validity.

The need for reliability can be shown clearly with the previous example, that of the students' use of map symbols. If the teacher asks students to use a given map and map symbols to decide on a correct answer to a question (i.e., Is the land north of location A, mostly swamp, mostly desert, or mostly mountainous?), the answer will give the teacher no assurance that students can consistently use map symbols (Jarolimek & Parker, 1993, p. 178). It is necessary to have students determine what is happening using several questions requiring the use of map symbols to be confident that they know how to use a map and its symbols. Thus, the greater the number of test items or situations on this problem, the higher the reliability. The higher the reliability, the more consistency there will be in students' scores measuring their understanding of this particular concept.

D. ASSESSING STUDENT LEARNING

There are three general approaches for assessing a student's achievement: you can assess (1) what the student *says*—for example, a student's contributions to class discussions; (2) what the student *does*—for example, a student's performance, as in the preceding example involving using map symbols; and, (3) what the student *writes*—for example, as shown by items in the student's portfolio—for example, homework assignments, checklists, written tests, and the student's journal writing. Although your own situation and personal philosophy will dictate the levels of importance and weight you give to each avenue of assessment, you should have a strong rationale if you value and weigh the three categories differently than one-third each.

Authentic Assessment

When assessing for student achievement, it is important that you use procedures that are compatible with your instructional objectives. This compatibility is referred to as *authentic assessment*. It means that the teaching methods and the assessment procedures are in harmony with the desired outcomes (Jarolimek & Parker, 1993, pp. 453, 471). Other terms used for "authentic" assessment are *accurate, active, aligned, alternative,* and *direct*. Although the term *performance assessment* is sometimes used, performance assessment refers to the type of student response being assessed, whereas *authentic assessment* refers to the assessment situation. Although not all performance assessments are authentic, assessments that are authentic are most assuredly performance assessments (Meyer, 1992).

In essential learnings in social studies, for example, "teachers need to plan ways for children to exhibit or demonstrate their grasp of these learnings. Built into these exhibitions is the requirement that learners demonstrate their ability to *use* what they have learned to accomplish some task. Rather than merely reproducing knowledge, children analyze, manipulate, or interpret it in some way or ways required by the exhibition" (Jarolimek & Parker, 1993, p. 451). An authentic assessment technique would be a performance item that actually involves the students in classifying information to show their understanding of a particular idea (for example, the idea of democracy). Students who can classify and who understand the idea of democracy can distinguish between the governments of various countries, identify countries whose government is democratic and those whose government is not, and use their knowledge to create a fictional country with a democratic political system. Further, they can review any countries they identified as not examples of a democracy and specify changes that would be needed to make that country's political system democratic. Thus, for an authentic assessment of students' understanding of what they have been learning, it is suggested that you use a performance-based assessment procedure.

Assessment: A Three-Step Process

Assessing a student's achievement is a three-step process involving (1) diagnostic assessment, which is an assessment (sometimes called a preassessment) of the student's knowledge and skills *before* the new instruction; (2) formative assessment, the assessment of learning *during* the instruction; and (3) summative assessment, the assessment of learning *after* the instruction, and ultimately represented by the student's term, semester, or year's achievement grade. Grades shown on unit tests, progress reports, deficiency notices, and six-week, or quarter grades (in a semester-based program) are examples of formative evaluation reports. An end-of-the-chapter test or a unit test is summative when the test represents the absolute end of the student's learning of material of that instructional unit.

Assessing what a student says and does. When evaluating what a student says, you should (1) listen to the student's questions, responses, and interactions with others and (2) observe the student's attentiveness, involvement in class activities, and responses to challenges.

Notice that we say you should listen and observe. While listening to what the student is saying, you should also be observing the student's nonverbal behaviors. For this you can use checklists and rating scales, behavioral growth record forms, observations of the student's performance in classroom activities, and periodic conferences with the student. Figure 5.1 illustrates a sample form for recording and evaluating teacher observations of a student's verbal and nonverbal behaviors.

Please remember that, with each technique used, you proceed from your awareness of anticipated learning outcomes (the instructional objectives) to your evaluation of that student's progress toward meeting those objectives. This process is referred to as *criterion-referenced assessment*.

To evaluate what a student says and does, you will find these guidelines helpful:

1. Maintain an anecdotal record book or folder, with a separate section for your records of each student.
2. For a specific activity, list the desirable behaviors.

FIGURE 5.1
Evaluating and Recording Student Behaviors: Sample Form

| Student _____ Course_____ School_____ |
| Observer_____ Date_____ Period_____ |

Objective for Time Period	Desired Behavior	What Student Did, Said, or Wrote

Teacher's (observer's) comments

3. Check the list against the specific instructional objectives.
4. Record your observations as soon as possible following your observation. Audio or video recordings and, of course, computer software programs, can help you check the accuracy of your memory, but if this is inconvenient, you will want to schedule time during school, immediately after, or later that evening to record your observations while they are still fresh in your memory.
5. Record your professional judgment about the student's progress toward the desired behavior, but think it through before transferring it to a permanent record.
6. Write comments that are reminders to yourself, such as:

"Check validity of observation by further testing."

"Discuss observations with student's parent."

"Discuss observations with school counselor."

"Discuss observations with other teachers on the teaching team."

Assessing what a student writes. When assessing what a student writes you can consider spelling, stories they write, handwriting, journals, knowledge of grammar, letters, life stories, newspapers, poems, research reports, use of words, and participation in the writing process. In many schools, checklists, classroom observations, anecdotal records, conferences, interviews, and language samples are the tools usually used for the formative evaluation of each student's achievement. Tests, too, should be a part of this formative assessment process, but tests are also used for summative evaluation at the end of a unit and for diagnostic assessment.

Your summative assessment of a student's achievement, and any other final judgment made by you about a student, can affect the emotional and intellectual development of that student. Special attention is given to this later in this chapter under the section "Recording Teacher Observations and Judgments."

When assessing what a student writes, use the following guidelines.

1. Assessment criteria should correlate and be compatible with specific instructional objectives.
2. Read everything a student writes. When it is important for the student to do, it is equally important that you give your professional attention to the product of the student's efforts.
3. Provide positive written or verbal comments about the student's work. Rather than just writing "good" on a student's paper, briefly state what specifically made it "good." Try to avoid negative comments. Rather than simply saying or pointing out that the student didn't do it right, tell or show the student acceptable ways to improve the work. For reinforcement, use positive rewards as frequently as possible.
4. Think before writing a comment on a student's paper and ask yourself how you think the student (or a parent or guardian) will interpret the comment and if that is the interpretation you intend.
5. Write only positive comments or grades in student journals. The purpose of student journals is to encourage students to write, to reflect on their thinking, and to record their reflective and creative thoughts. In journal writing, students should be encouraged to write about their experiences in school and out of school, especially about their experiences related to what is being learned and about how they are learning it. Writing in journals gives them practice in expressing themselves in written form and in connecting their learning and should take place in a non-threatening environment. Negative comments and evaluations from teachers might discourage creative and spontaneous expression. When responding to a student's dialogue journal—in which students and teachers "talk" through writing—Staton (1987) suggests ways to respond and continue the dialogue:
   - Acknowledge students' ideas and encourage them to continue to write about their interests.
   - Support students by complimenting them about behavior and school work.
   - Provide new information about topics so that students will want to read your responses.
   - Write less than the students do.
   - Avoid unspecific comments like "good idea" or "very interesting."
   - Ask only a few questions; instead, encourage students to ask you questions. (pp. 47–63)

6. When reviewing student portfolios, speak with students individually about their progress in their learning as shown by the materials in their portfolio. As with student journals, the portfolio itself should *not* be graded or compared in any way with those of other students. Its purpose is for student self-assessment and to show progress in learning. For this to happen, students should keep in their portfolio all papers related to the course (Staton, 1987).

7. When reading student journals, talk individually with students to seek clarification about their expressions. Student journals are useful to the teacher (of any subject field) in understanding the student's thought processes and writing skills (diagnostic assessment), and journals should *not* be graded. It is normal for students to misspell words in their journal entries, and the emphasis should be on what they say, not on how correctly they write. For record keeping/grading purposes, teachers may simply record whether the student is maintaining a journal and, perhaps, make a judgment about the quantity of writing in it, but not of the quality.

Regardless of avenues chosen and the relative weights you give them, you must evaluate against the instructional objectives. Any given objective may be checked by using more than one method and by using more than one instrument. Subjectivity, inherent in the evaluation process, may be reduced as you check for validity, comparing results of one measuring technique against those of another.

While evaluation of cognitive objectives lends itself to traditional written tests of achievement, the evaluation of affective and psychomotor domains require the use of performance checklists based on observing student behaviors in action. However, as indicated in the earlier discussion, for assessing cognitive learning as well, educators today are encouraging the use of alternatives to traditional paper-and-pencil testing. Alternative assessment strategies include anecdotal records, checklists, conferences, diaries and logs, exhibits, experience summaries, group discussions, observations, portfolios, skits, oral presentations, performance tests, and work samples. Advantages claimed for the use of authentic assessment include their direct (performance-based, criterion-referenced, outcome-based) measurement of what students should know and can do and their emphasis on higher-order thinking. On the other hand, disadvantages of authentic assessment include a higher cost, difficulty in making results consistent and usable, and problems with validity, reliability, and comparability.

Unfortunately, the teacher who may never see a student again after a given school year may never observe the effects that teacher has had on a student's values and attitudes. On the other hand, in schools where groups or teams of teachers remain with the same cohort of students throughout several years of school (sometimes called "houses," or "villages"), those teachers often do have the opportunity to observe the positive changes in their students' values and attitudes.

E. COOPERATIVE LEARNING AND ASSESSMENT

The purpose of a cooperative learning group is for the group to learn, which means that individuals within the group must learn. Group achievement in learning, then, depends on the learning of individuals within the group. Rather than competing for rewards for achievement, members of the group cooperate by helping each other to learn so the group reward will be a good one. Theoretically, when small groups of students of mixed backgrounds, skills, and capabilities work together toward a common goal, their liking and respect for one another increases. As a result, there is an increase in each student's self-esteem *and* academic achievement.

When recognizing the achievement of a cooperative learning group, the group's achievement and individual achievement are rewarded. Remembering that the emphasis must be on peer support rather than peer pressure, you must be cautious about ever giving group grades. Some teachers give bonus points to all members of the group to add to their individual scores when everyone in the group has reached preset criteria. These preset standards can be different for individuals within a group, depending on each member's ability and past performance. It is important that each member of a group feel rewarded and successful. Some teachers also give subjective grades to individual students on their role performances within the group.

To determine students' report card marks or grades, the teacher measures individual student achievement through individual results on tests and other sources of data. The final grade or mark is based on those as well as on the child's performance in the group.

F. INVOLVING CHILDREN IN SELF-ASSESSMENT

In exemplary school programs, students' continuous self-assessment is an important component of evaluation. If students are to improve in understanding their own thinking (metacognition) and in their intellectual development, then they must receive instruction and guidance in how to become more responsible for their own learning (empowered). During that process they learn to think better of themselves and of their individual capabilities. This improved self-esteem is the result of educational successes, along with guidance in self-understanding.

Using Portfolios

To meet these goals, teachers should provide opportunities for students to think about what they are learning, how they are learning it, and how far they have progressed. One procedure is for students to maintain portfolios of their work, periodically using rating scales or checklists to assess their own progress. The student portfolio should be well organized and contain assignment sheets, class worksheets, completed homework, forms for student self-evaluation and reflection on their work, and other class materials thought important by the students and teacher.

Although portfolio assessment as an alternative to traditional methods of evaluating student progress has gained momentum in recent years, setting standards is very difficult. Thus far, research on the use of portfolios for assessment indicates that validity and reliability of teacher evaluation is quite low (O'Neil, 1993). Before using portfolios as an alternative to traditional testing, teachers must consider and clearly understand the reasons for doing it, carefully decide on portfolio content, consider parent and guardian reactions, and anticipate grading problems (Black, 1993). For other resources on the use of student portfolios, refer to the suggested readings at the end of this chapter, and for specific information about language arts and social studies portfolios, see Chapter 8. General information on portfolio assessment can be found in *Portfolio News,* Portfolio Assessment Clearinghouse, San Dieguito High School District, 710 Encinitas Blvd., Encinitas, CA 92024; and *Portfolio Assessment Newsletter,* Northwest Evaluation Association, 5 Centerpointe Drive, Suite 100, Lake Oswego, OR 97035.

While emphasizing the criteria for evaluation, rating scales and checklists provide students with means of expressing their feelings and give the teacher still another source of data for use in evaluation. To provide students with reinforcement and guidance to improve their learning and development, teachers meet with individual students to discuss their self-evaluations. Such conferences should provide students with understandable and achievable short-term goals and help them develop and maintain an adequate self-esteem.

Although almost any of the instruments used for evaluating student work can be used for student self-evaluation, in some cases it might be better to use those constructed with the student's understanding of the instrument in mind. Student self-evaluation and reflection should be done on a regular and continuing basis, so the student can make comparisons from one time to the next. You will need to help students learn how to analyze these comparisons. Comparisons should give a student information previously not recognized about his or her own progress and growth. One of the items maintained by students in their portfolios is a series of self-evaluation checklists. (See also Chapter 3.)

Using Checklists

Items on the student's self-evaluation checklist will vary depending on grade level. Generic items similar to those in Figure 5.2 can be easily used by a student to compare with previous self-evaluations, while open-ended questions allow the student to provide additional information and to do some expressive writing.

Here are some general guidelines for using student portfolios in your assessment of student learning.

FIGURE 5.2
Student Self-Evaluation: Sample Form

Student Self-Evaluation Form
(To be kept in student's portfolio)

Student: Date:
Teacher: Number:

Circle one response for each of the first six items.
1. Since my last self-evaluation my assignments have been turned in
   a. always on time.
   b. always late.
   c. sometimes late; sometimes on time.
   d. other
2. Most of my classmates
   a. like me.
   b. don't like me.
   c. ignore me.
   d. other
3. I think I am
   a. smart.
   b. the smartest in the class.
   c. the slowest in the class.
   d. other
4. Since my last self-evaluation, I think I am
   a. doing better.
   b. doing worse.
   c. doing about the same.
   d. other
5. In this class
   a. I am learning a lot.
   b. I am not learning very much.
   c. I am not learning anything.
   d. other
6. In this class, I think
   a. I am doing the best work I can.
   b. I am not doing as well as I can.
   c. other
7. This is something I have learned since my last self-evaluation and that I have used outside of school:

8. This is something I have learned about myself since my last self-evaluation:

- Contents of the portfolio should reflect your instructional aims and course objectives. The aims and objectives could be listed on a sheet and kept in the front or back of the portfolio.
- Date everything that goes into the portfolio and record when you review the enclosed material.
- For one-third of the materials, determine what materials should be kept in the portfolio and announce when, how, and by what criteria, the materials will be reviewed by you; for a second third of the materials, invite each student to select what materials should be placed in the portfolio and which ones should be reviewed by you; for a final third of the materials, invite the student's parents or guardian to select what materials seen in the home should be placed in the portfolio.
- Give all responsibility for maintaining the portfolio to the students. The teacher, however, is responsible for documenting children's oral and written language development and their progress in developing knowledge and skills related to social studies or language arts, all of which provide the complex "portfolio" of assessment.
- Portfolios should be kept in the classroom.

G. MAINTAINING RECORDS OF STUDENT ACHIEVEMENT

You will want to maintain well-organized and complete records of student achievement. You may do this in a written record book or on an electronic record book (that is, a commercially developed computer software program or one you develop yourself, perhaps by using a computer software program spreadsheet as the base). The record book should include tardies, absences, and all records of scores on tests, homework, projects, and other assignments.

Anecdotal records can be maintained in alphabetical order by the name of each student in a separate binder with a separate section for each student. Daily interactions and events occur in the classroom that may provide informative data about a student's intellectual, emotional, and physical development. Maintaining a dated record of your observations of these interactions and events can provide important information that might otherwise be forgotten if you do not write it down. At the end of a unit and again at the conclusion of a grading term, you will want to review your records. During the course of the school year, your anecdotal records (and those of other members of your teaching team) will provide important information about the intellectual, psychological, and physical development of each student and reveal ideas about attention that may need to be given to individual students.

Recording Teacher Observations and Judgments

As said before, you will want to carefully think through any written comments that you intend to make about a student. Students can be quite sensitive to what others say about them, particularly to negative comments made by a teacher. Additionally, we have seen anecdotal comments in students' permanent records that said more about the teachers who made the comments than about the students. Careless, hurried, and thoughtless comments can be detrimental to a student's welfare and progress in school.

Teacher comments must be professional; that is, they must be diagnostically useful to the continued intellectual and psychological development of the child. This is true for any comment you make or write, whether on a student's paper, on the student's permanent school record, or on a note sent home to a student's parent or guardian.

As an example, consider the following unprofessional comment observed in one student's permanent record. A teacher wrote, "John is lazy." Describing John as "lazy" could be done by anyone; it is nonproductive, and it is certainly not a professional diagnosis. How many times do you suppose John needs to receive such negative descriptions of his behavior before he begins to believe that he is just that—lazy—and, as a result, will act that way even more often? Written comments like that can also be damaging because they may be read by John's next teacher, who may simply perpetuate the same expectation of John. To say that John is lazy merely describes behavior as judged by the teacher who wrote the comment. More important, and more professional, would be for the teacher to try to analyze *why* John is behaving that way, then to prescribe activities that are likely to motivate John to assume a more constructive attitude and to take charge of his own learning behavior.

For students' continued intellectual and emotional development, your comments should be useful, productive, analytical, diagnostic, and prescriptive. The professional teacher makes diagnoses and prepares descriptions; a professional teacher does *not* label students as being "lazy," "vulgar," "slow," "stupid," "difficult," or "dumb." The professional teacher sees the behavior of a student as being goal-directed. Perhaps "lazy" John found that particular behavioral pattern won him attention. John's goal, then, was attention (don't we all need attention?), and John assumed negative, perhaps even self-destructive, behavioral patterns to reach that goal. The professional task of any teacher is to facilitate the learner's understanding (perception) of a goal, with the identification of acceptable behaviors positively designed to reach that goal. What separates the professional teacher from anyone off the street is the teacher's ability to go beyond mere description of behavior. Always keep that in mind when you write comments that will be read by students, by their parents or guardians, and by other teachers.

H. GRADING AND MARKING STUDENT ACHIEVEMENT

If conditions were ideal (which they are not), and if teachers did their job perfectly well (which many of us do not), then all students would receive top marks (the ultimate in mastery learning), and there would be less of a need here to talk about grading. Mastery learning implies that some end point of learning is attainable, but there probably isn't an end point. In any case, because conditions for teaching are never ideal, and we teachers are mere humans, let us continue with this topic (of grading) that is undoubtedly of special interest to you, to your students, to their parents or guardians, and to school counselors, administrators, school boards, and college admissions offices.

In this chapter we have frequently used the term *achievement,* which means accomplishment. But is it accomplishment of the instructional objectives against preset standards, or is it simply accomplishment? Most teachers probably choose the former, in which they subjectively establish a standard that must be met for a student to receive a certain grade for an assignment, a test, a quarter, a semester, or a course. Achievement, then, is decided by degrees of accomplishment.

Preset standards are usually expressed in percentages (degrees of accomplishment) needed for marks or *ABC* grades. If no student achieves the standard required for an *A* grade, for example, then no student receives an *A*. On the other hand, if all students meet the preset standard for the *A* grade, then all receive *A*s. Determining student grades on the basis of preset standards is referred to as criterion-referenced grading.

Criterion-Referenced Versus Norm-Referenced Grading

As stated in the preceding paragraph, criterion-referenced grading is based on preset standards. Norm-referenced grading, on the other hand, is based on the relative accomplishment of individuals in the group (say, one classroom of third-grade students), or in a larger group (perhaps all students enrolled in the third grade in a given school district). It compares and ranks students and is commonly known as "grading on a curve." Because it encourages competition and discourages cooperative learning, norm-referenced grading is not recommended. Norm-referenced grading is educationally dysfunctional. After all, each child is an individual and should not be converted to a statistic on a frequency-distribution curve. For your own information, after several years of teaching, you can produce frequency-distribution studies of grades you have given, but do *not* grade students on a curve. Grades for student achievement should be tied to performance levels and determined on the basis of each student's achievement toward preset standards.

In criterion-referenced grading, the aim is to communicate information about an individual student's progress in knowledge and work skills in comparison to that student's previous attainment or in the pursuit of an absolute, such as content mastery. Criterion-referenced grading is featured in continuous-progress curricula, competency-based (outcome-based education) curricula, and other programs that focus on individualized education.

Criterion-referenced or competency-based grading is based on the level at which each child meets the specified objectives (standards) for the course. The objectives must be clearly stated to represent important student learning outcomes. This approach implies that effective teaching and learning result in high grades (*A*s) for most students. In fact, when a mastery concept is used, the student must accomplish the objectives before being allowed to proceed to the next learning task. The philosophy of teachers who favor criterion-referenced procedures recognizes individual potential. Such teachers accept the challenge of finding teaching strategies to help students progress from where they are to the next designated level. Instead of wondering how Sally compares with Juanita, the comparison is between what Juanita could do yesterday and what she can do today, and how well these performances compare to the preset standard.

Most school systems use some sort of combination of both norm-referenced and criterion-referenced data. For example, a report card for a fourth-grade student might indicate how that student is meeting certain criteria, such as an *A* grade for addition of whole numbers. Another entry might show that this mastery is expected, however, at the third grade. Both criterion- and norm-referenced data may be communicated to the parents or guardians and students. Appropriate procedures should be used: a criterion-referenced approach to show whether the student can accomplish the task, and a norm-referenced approach to show how well that student performs compared to the larger group to which the student belongs. Sometimes, one or the other is needed; other times, both are required.

Determining Grades

Determining achievement grades for student performance is serious business, for which you must make several important and professional decisions. Although in some schools only marks such as *E, S,* and *I,* are used, for most upper primary grades and up, percentages of accomplishment and *ABC* grades are used. To help you determine your grading policy, you may want to consider the following guidelines:

1. At the start of the school term, explain your marking and grading policies *first to your-self,* then to your students and to their parents or guardians at "back-to-school night," by a written explanation that is sent home, or both.
2. When converting your interpretation of a student's accomplishments to a letter grade, be as objective as possible.
3. Build your grading policy around accomplishment rather than failure, where students proceed from one accomplishment to the next. This is continuous promotion, not necessarily from one grade to the next, but within the classroom. (Some schools have done away with grade-level designation and, in its place, use the concept of continuous promotion from the time of student entry into the school through graduation or exit.)
4. In setting criteria for *ABC* grades, select a percentage standard, such as 92 percent for an *A,* 85 percent for a *B,* 75 percent for a *C,* and 65 percent for a *D.* Cutoff percentages used are your decision, although the district, school, or program area may have established guidelines to which you are expected to adhere.
5. "Evaluation" and "grading" are *not* synonymous. As you learned earlier, evaluation implies the collection of information from a variety of sources, including measurement techniques and subjective observations. These data, then, become the basis for arriving at a final grade, which in effect is a final value judgment. Grades are one aspect of evaluation and are intended to communicate educational progress to students and to their parents or guardians. For final grades to be valid indicators of that progress, you *must* use a variety of sources of data for their determination.
6. For the determination of students' final grades, you might want to use a point system, where things that students write, say and do are given points (but not for journals or portfolios, unless simply based on whether the student completes one); then the possible point total is the factor for grade determination. For example, if 92 percent is the cutoff for an *A,* and 500 points are possible, then any student with 460 points or more (500 $\times$ .92) has achieved an *A.* Likewise, for a test or any other assignment, if the value is 100 points, the cutoff for an A is 92 (100 $\times$ .92). With a point system and preset standards, the teacher and students, at any time during the year, always know the current points possible and can easily calculate a student's current grade standing. Then, as far as a current grade is concerned, students know always where they stand in the course.
7. Because students will be absent and miss assignments and tests, you should decide beforehand your policy about makeup work. Your policies about late assignments and missed tests must be clearly communicated to students and their parents or guardians. For makeup work, please consider the following.

Homework assignments. For homework assignments, a recommendation is that, after due dates have been negotiated or set, you strictly adhere to them, giving no credit or reduced credit for work that is turned in late. You may think this is harsh and rigid, but experience has shown it to be a good policy to which students can and should adjust. Of course, students must be given their assignments, not at the last minute, but long before the due dates.

Tests. When students are absent when tests are given, you have several options. Some teachers allow students to miss or discount one test per grading period. Another technique is to allow each student to substitute a written homework assignment or project for one missed test. Still another option is to give the absent student the choice of either taking a makeup test or having the next test count double. When makeup tests are given, the makeup test should be taken within a week of the regular test unless there is a compelling reason (such as a medical problem, emergency, or family problem) this cannot happen.

If a student is absent during performance testing, for any reason, the logistics and possible diminished reliability of having to readminister the test for one student may necessitate giving the student a written test as an alternative.

I. TESTING FOR ACHIEVEMENT

One source of information used for determining grades are data obtained from testing for student achievement. Competent planning, preparing, administering, and scoring of tests is an important professional skill, for which you will gain valuable practical experience during your student teaching. The following sections offer helpful information that you will want to refer to while you are student teaching and again, occasionally, during your first few years as an inservice teacher.

Purposes for Testing

Although textbook publisher's tests, test item pools, and standardized tests are available from a variety of sources, because schools are different, teachers are different, and children are different, most of the time you will be designing and preparing your tests for your purposes for your distinct group of students.

Tests can be designed for several purposes, and a variety of kinds of tests and alternate test items will keep your testing program interesting, useful, and reliable. As a university student, you are probably most experienced with testing for measuring for achievement, but you will use tests for other reasons as well. Other purposes for which tests are used include

- To assess and aid in curriculum development
- To help determine teaching effectiveness
- To help students develop positive attitudes, appreciations, and values
- To help students increase their understanding and retention of facts, principles, skills, and concepts
- To motivate students
- To provide diagnostic information for planning for individualization of instruction
- To provide review and drill to enhance teaching and learning
- To serve as a source of information for students and parents.

When and How Often to Test for Achievement

It is difficult to generalize about how often to test for student achievement, but we believe that testing should be cumulative and frequent—that is, each assessment should measure the student's understanding of previously learned material as well as for the current unit of study, and testing should occur as often as once a week. Advantages of cumulative assessment include the review, reinforcement, and articulation of old material with the recent. The advantages of frequent assessment include a reduction in student anxiety over tests and an increase in the validity of final grades.

Test Construction

After determining the reasons for which you are designing and administering a test, you need to identify the specific instructional objectives the test is being designed to measure. (As you learned in the previous chapter, your written instructional objectives are specific so that you can write test items to measure against those objectives.) So, the first step in test construction is to identify the purpose(s) of the test. The second step is to identify the objectives to be measured, and the third step is to prepare the test items. The best time to prepare draft items is after you have prepared your instructional objectives, that is, while the objectives are fresh in your mind, which means before the lessons are taught. After you teach a lesson, you will want to rework your first draft of the test items for that lesson to modify it as a result of what was taught and learned.

Administering Tests

For many students, test taking causes high anxiety. To more accurately measure student achievement, you will want to take steps to reduce that anxiety. Students demonstrate test anxiety in various ways. Just before and during testing some are quiet and thoughtful, whereas others are noisy and disruptive. To control or reduce student anxieties, consider the following suggestions when administering tests.

1. Since students respond best to familiar routine, plan your program so tests are given at regular intervals (perhaps the same day each week) and administered at the same time and in the same way.
2. Avoid writing tests that are too long and that will take too much time. Sometimes beginning teachers have unreasonable expectations of students' attention spans during testing. Frequent testing with frequent sampling of student knowledge is preferred over infrequent and long tests that attempt to cover everything.
3. When giving paper-and-pencil tests, try to arrange the classroom so it is well ventilated, the temperature is comfortable, and the seats are well spaced. If spacing is a problem, consider using alternate forms of the test—giving students seated adjacent to one another different forms of the same test, for example, multiple-choice answer alternatives are arranged in different order.
4. Before test time be certain that you have a sufficient number of copies of the test. Although this may sound trite, we have known too many instances where the teacher started testing with an insufficient number of test copies. Perhaps the test was duplicated for the teacher by someone else and a mistake was made in the number run off. However it is done, to avoid a serious problem, ensure you have sufficient copies of the test.
5. Before distributing the test, explain to students what they are to do when finished (such as begin a homework assignment), because not all of the students will finish at the same time. Rather than expecting students to sit quietly after finishing a test, give them some task to complete.
6. When ready to test, don't drag it out. Distribute tests quickly and efficiently. Once testing has begun, avoid interrupting the students. Items of important information can be written on the board or saved until all are finished with the test. During testing, remain in the room and visually monitor the students. If it is not at the end of the school day or before a recess or lunch, plan a more relaxed activity after the test. Both, just prior to and immediately after a major test, it's improbable that any teacher can teach a lesson with a high degree of student interest in it.

Problems Related to Testing

Cheating. Cheating on tests does occur, but you can take steps to discourage it or to reduce the opportunity and pressure to cheat. For example:

1. Space students or, as mentioned before, use alternate forms of the test.
2. Schedule frequent tests and have the tests represent equivalent weights and values for grading and marking purposes. This strategy reduces some of the text anxiety and the pressure for good grades that students experience. This also increases student learning by "stimulating greater effort and providing intermittent feedback" to the student (Walberg, 1990).
3. Prepare test questions that are clear and are not ambiguous, thereby reducing any student frustration caused by a question or instructions that they do not understand.
4. As said before, avoid tests that are too long and that will take too much time. During long tests, some students get discouraged and restless, and that is when classroom management problems can occur.
5. By their very nature, performance tests can put even greater pressure on some students and provide more opportunity for cheating. To avoid this, have several monitors when administering performance tests to an entire class or, if that isn't possible, consider testing groups of students, such as cooperative learning groups, rather than individuals. Evaluation of test performance would be based on group rather than individual achievement.
6. Consider using open-text and open-notebook tests. When students can use their books and pages of notes, it not only reduces anxiety but it also helps them with the organization and retention of what has been learned.

If you suspect cheating *is* occurring, move to the area of the suspected student. Usually your presence will stop it. When you suspect cheating *has* occurred, you are faced with a dilemma. Unless your suspicion is backed by solid proof, you are advised to forget it, but keep a close watch on the student the next time to prevent cheating from happening. Your job is not to catch students doing something dishonest but to prevent it. If you have absolute proof that a student has cheated, then you are obligated to proceed with school policy on student cheating. The policy may call for a session with the principal or with the student and the student's parent or guardian, and perhaps an automatic *F* grade on the test.

Time needed to take a test. As mentioned previously, avoid giving tests that are too long and that will take too much time. Preparing and administering good tests is a skill that you will develop over time. In the meantime, it is best to test frequently and to use tests that sample student achievement rather than try for a comprehensive measure of that achievement.

Some students take more time on the same test than do others. You want to avoid giving too much time, or classroom management problems will result. On the other hand, you don't want to cut short the time needed by students who can do well but need more time to think and to write. As a guide for determining about how much time to allow students to complete a test, see Table 5.1. For example, for a test with 10 multiple-choice items, 5 arrangement items, and 2 short-explanation items, you would want to plan for about 30 minutes for the group of students to complete the test.

J. PREPARING ASSESSMENT ITEMS

Writing good assessment items is yet another professional skill, and to become proficient at it takes study, time, and practice. Because of the recognized importance of an assessment program, please assume this professional charge seriously and responsibly. Although poorly prepared items take no time at all to prepare, they will cause you more trouble than you can ever imagine. As a professional, you should take the time to study different types of assessment items and how best to write them; then practice writing them. When preparing assessment items, you should ensure that they match and sufficiently cover your instructional objectives. In addition, you should prepare each item carefully enough to be reasonably confident that it will be understood by the student in the manner that you anticipate its being understood.

Classification of Assessment Items

Assessment items can be classified as verbal (oral or written words), visual (pictures and diagrams), and manipulative or performance based (handling of materials and equipment). Written verbal items have traditionally been most frequently used in testing. However, visual tests are useful, for example, when working with students who lack fluency with the written word, or when testing for the knowledge of students who have limited proficiency in English.

Performance and Alternative Assessment

Performance items and tests are useful when measuring for psychomotor skill development, as is common in performance testing of locomotor skills, such as a student's ability

TABLE 5.1
Time to Allow for Testing as Determined by the Types of Assessment Items

TYPE OF TEST ITEM	TIME NEEDED PER ITEM
matching	1 minute per matching item
multiple choice	1 minute per item
completion and correction	1 minute per item
completion drawing	2–3 minutes
arrangement and grouping	2–3 minutes
identification	2–3 minutes
short explanation	2–3 minutes
essay and performance	10 or more minutes

to carry a globe (gross motor skill) or to establish a level of brightness suitable for eye comfort on a computer screen (fine motor skill). Performance testing can also be a part of a wider testing program that includes testing for higher-level skills and knowledge, as when a student or small group of children are given the task (objective) of creating from discarded materials a habitat for an imaginary animal, and then displaying and describing their product to the rest of the class.

As mentioned earlier, educators today have taken a renewed interest in performance testing as a more authentic means of assessing learning. In a program for teacher preparation, the field experience called student teaching is an example of performance assessment, that is, it is used to assess the teacher candidate's ability to teach. Most of us would probably agree that assessment of student teaching is a more authentic assessment of a candidate's ability to teach than would be a written (paper-and-pencil test) or verbal (oral test) assessment.

Performance testing is usually more expensive than is verbal, and verbal testing is more time consuming and expensive than is written testing. Regardless, a good assessment program will use alternate forms of assessment and not rely solely on one form (such as written) and only on one type of that form (such as the multiple-choice item). For hands-on/minds-on social studies and language arts instruction in grades K–4, assessment and performance form a natural alliance. Abby Barry Bergman (1993), principal of a New Jersey elementary school, gives the following example:

> Consider an activity in which young children sort a collection of objects based upon a criterion such as color, size, or shape. To assess whether or not a youngster internalized the process of sorting, you could ask her to sort a new set of materials and then describe the sorting criterion. At once, you observe whether or not the child can perform this task. What could be a simpler or more valid assessment? Yet some assessment programs ask children to choose the one object pictured among an array of others that does not belong with the group. Although there may be some relationship between selecting a picture of an object that does not belong with a given group and the operation of sorting, why stray so far from the original activity? (p. 20)

The type of test and items you use depends on your purpose and objectives. Carefully consider the alternatives within that framework. As noted, a good assessment program will likely include items from all three types to provide validity checks and to account for the individual differences of children. That is what writers of articles in professional journals are referring to when they talk about alternative assessment. They are encouraging the use of multiple assessment items, as opposed to the traditional heavy reliance on objective items such as multiple-choice questions.

General Guidelines for Assessment

Much of the assessment of learning in social studies and language arts is done informally by the teacher. Many times each day, you will observe learners and judge the quality of their work. You will notice what problems individual children are encountering and what kind of help they need to progress. The following are general guidelines for the assessment of children's learning in the early grades:

1. Observing children is essential. The teacher should observe what children do with materials before and after instruction. Observations of children, unlike formal testing, are authentic and unobtrusive; they do not interrupt the child or the activities of the moment. They are natural and do not consist of contrived tasks.
2. Interview the child, asking nonjudgmental questions to probe for a child's understanding. Interviews can be conducted during activity time or any time you and a child can get together for a few moments. As you interview, Seefeldt and Barbour (1994) suggest looking for
    a. *Consistency:* Does the child have a stable set of responses? Does the child reply in the same way to the same type of questions?
    b. *Accuracy:* Are the child's answers correct? Is the response accurate even if it does not include all of the possibilities?
    c. *Clarity:* Is the response clear and acceptable?
    d. *Fullness:* How complete was the response? How many aspects of the concept were not covered by the response? How many illustrations of the concept were given?

Children may not always be able to verbalize some of their concepts or understandings. Ask them to show you, draw, find an example of the concept, act it out, or use pictures and manipulatives to illustrate their ideas (pp. 207–208).

3. Record children's behavior and your observations over time. Observations that you collect and analyze over time yield a great deal of information about children. For this, teachers use behavior checklists, rating scales, work records, student self-evaluations, portfolios, and other alternative assessment techniques.

4. Assess the accuracy of the product of the child's learning. In the early grades, children often make something as a part of their learning, such as a sketch or drawing or another product related to a language arts or social studies activity.

Guidelines for Preparing Assessment Items

You can construct assessment items to assess the student's progress in the information and skills area of instruction in social studies and the language arts. Items can be designed to evaluate the student's ability to use reference material, to read social studies materials, to understand vocabulary, to evaluate news stories, to distinguish between fact and opinion, and other skills. In preparing assessment items, you should

1. Include several kinds of items (see list that follows under section K). As emphasized by Bergman (1993), "the accuracy of assessment increases when you apply more than one type of measure" (p. 22).
2. Assure that content coverage is complete, that is, that all objectives are being measured.
3. Assure that each item of the test is reliable, that it measures the intended objective. One way to check item reliability is to have more than one test item or device measuring for the same objective.
4. Assure that each item is clear and unambiguous.
5. Plan the item to be difficult enough for the poorly prepared student but easy enough for the student who is well prepared.
6. Maintain a bank of your items with each item coded according to its matching instructional objective and according to its domain (cognitive, affective, or psychomotor), perhaps according to its level within the hierarchy of that particular domain; and whether it requires low-level recall, processing, or application. Computer software programs are available for that. Ready-made test item banks are available on computer disks and accompany many programs or textbooks. If you use them, be certain that the items match your course objectives and that they are well written. It doesn't follow that because they were published they are necessarily well written. Some state departments of education have made efforts to develop test banks for teachers. For example, see Willis (1990). When preparing items for your own test bank, use your best creative writing skills—prepare items that match your objectives, put them aside, think about them, then work them again.

The short brief tests you administer to your students should represent your best professional effort—clean and without spelling and grammar errors. One that is obviously hurriedly prepared and wrought with spelling errors will quickly be frowned upon by discerning parents or guardians and, if you are a student teacher, will certainly bring about a strong admonishment from your university supervisor and, if the sloppiness continues, your speedy dismissal from the program.

Attaining Content Validity

To ensure that a test measures what it is supposed to measure, you can construct a table of specifications. This two-way grid indicates behavior in one dimension and content in the other (see Tables 5.2A and 5.2B).

In this grid, behavior relates to the three domains: cognitive, affective, and psychomotor. In Table 5.2A, the cognitive domain, involving mental processes, is divided, according to Bloom's taxonomy (Chapter 4), into six categories: (1) knowledge or simple recall, (2) comprehension, (3) application, (4) analysis, (5) synthesis (often involving an original product in oral or written form), and (6) evaluation. The specifications table of Table 5.2A does not specify levels within the affective and psychomotor domains.

TABLE 5.2A
Table of Specifications I

CONTENT	BEHAVIORS								TOTAL
	Cognitive						Affective	Psychomotor	
Science Grade 3	Knowledge	Comprehension	Application	Analysis	Synthesis	Evaluation			
Colonization									
I. Vocabulary Development		2 (1,2)	3 (2)						
II. Concepts		2 (3,4)	1 (4)						
III. Applications	1 (5)	1				1 (5)			
IV. Problem-solving		1 (6)							
TOTAL	1	6	4			1			12

TABLE 5.2B
Table of Specifications II

CONTENT	BEHAVIORS							TOTAL
	Cognitive			Affective		Psychomotor		
	Input	Processing	Application	Low	High	Low	High	
I.								
II.								
III.								
IV.								
TOTAL								

To use a table of specifications, the teacher examining objectives for the unit decides what emphasis should be given to the behavior and to the content. For instance, if vocabulary development is a concern for this class, then probably 20 percent of the test on vocabulary may be appropriate, but 50 percent would be unsuitable. This planning enables the teacher to design a test to fit the situation, rather than a haphazard test that does not correspond to the objectives either in content or behavior emphasis.

Since knowledge questions are easy to write, tests often fail to go beyond that level even though the objectives state that the student will analyze and evaluate. The sample table of specifications for a third-grade social studies unit on colonization indicates a distribution of questions on a test. Since this test is to be an objective test and it is so difficult to write objective type items to test syntheses and affective and psychomotor behavior, this table of specifications calls for no test items in these areas. If these categories are included in the unit objectives, some other additional assessment devices must be used to test learning in these categories. The teacher could also show the objectives tested, as indicated within parentheses in Table 5.2A. Then, a later check on inclusion of all objectives is easy.

Preferred by some teachers is the alternative table shown in Table 5.2B. Rather than differentiating among all six of Bloom's cognitive levels, this table separates cognitive objectives into just three levels—those that require simple low-level recall of knowledge, those that require information processing, and those that require application of the new knowledge. In addition, in this table the affective and psychomotor domains each are divided into low- and high-level behaviors.

K. SPECIFIC GUIDELINES FOR PREPARING ITEMS FOR USE IN ASSESSMENT

The following section presents the advantages, disadvantages, and guidelines for use of 12 types of items in what is referred to as alternative assessment. When reading the advantages and disadvantages of each type, you will notice that some types are appropriate for use in direct or performance assessment, while others are not.

Arrangement Type

Description: Terms or real objects (realia) are to be arranged in a specified order.

> *Example 1:* After seeing the steps performed in a simple folk dance from another culture, demonstrate them in order from the first dance step to the last.

> *Example 2:* The assortment of paper figures on the table represents the jobs people had in a colonial New England town. (Note: The jobs include candlemaker, homemaker, blacksmith, weaver, farmer, minister, doctor). Arrange the jobs in their order of importance from your point of view.

Advantages: This type of item tests for knowledge of sequence and order and is good for review, for starting discussions, and for performance assessment. Example 2 is an informal performance test item recommended for observing and assessing the intellectual development of students.

Disadvantage: Scoring may be difficult, so be cautious and meticulous when using this type for grading purposes.

Guideline for use: When it is a paper-and-pencil arrangement, as in example 1, include instructions to students to include the rationale for their arrangement, making it a combined arrangement and short-explanation type, allowing space for explanations on an answer sheet, which enhances reliability.

Completion-Drawing Type

Description: An incomplete drawing is presented, and the student is to complete it.

Example 1: Connect the following items with arrow lines to show the stages from planting of cotton to the distribution of wearing apparel to consumers.

Example 2: In the following food web, draw arrow lines showing which figures are consumers and which are producers.

Advantages: This type requires less time than is required for a complete drawing, as may be required in an essay item. Scoring is relatively easy.

Disadvantage: Care needs to be exercised in the instructions so students do not misinterpret the expectation.

Guidelines for use: Use occasionally for diversion, but take care in preparing. Examples 1 and 2 are typical of this type when used in integrated thematic teaching. This type can be instructive when assessing for student thinking. Consider making the item a combined completion-drawing, short-explanation type by having students include their rationales for their drawings. Be sure to allow space for their explanations.

Completion-Statement Type

Description: An incomplete sentence is presented, and the student is to complete it by filling in the blank space(s).

Example 1: Two objects of historical significance from the time period 1776 are _____ and _____.

Example 2: As the first part of a historian's method of study, historians _____.

Advantages: This type is easy to devise, to take, and to score.

Disadvantages: Although the first example is a performance type, when using completion-statement items, there can be a tendency to emphasize rote memory. It is difficult to write this type of item to measure higher levels of cognition. You must be alert for a correct response different from the expected. For example, in Example 2, although the teacher's key has "identify the problem" as the correct answer, a student might answer the question with "investigate (determine the situation, decide what's wrong, etc.) the problem," which is equally correct.

Guideline for use: Use occasionally for review. Except when it is a performance item, you are advised to avoid using this type for grading, or unless you can write quality items that extend student thinking beyond that of mere recall. In all instances, avoid copying items verbatim from the student book. As with all types, be sure to provide adequate space for students' answers.

Correction Type

Description: Similar to the completion type, except that sentences or paragraphs are complete but with italicized or underlined words that can be changed to make the sentence correct.

Example 1: New inventions lead to change in *trays* of living.

Example 2: Because the peoples of the world are interdependent, the behaviors of one group affect the *hives* of the other groups.

Example 3: Families are the primary *beans* of socialization in all cultures.

Advantages: Writing this type can be fun for the teacher for the purpose of review. Students may enjoy this type for the tension relief afforded by the incorrect absurdities.

Disadvantages: Like the completion type, the correction type tends to measure low-level recall and rote memory. The underlined or italicized incorrect items could be so whimsical that they might cause more classroom disturbance than you want.

Guidelines for use: Use occasionally for diversion. Try to write items that measure for higher-level cognition. Consider making it a combined correction, short-explanation type. Be sure to allow spacing for student explanations.

Essay Type

Description: A question or problem is presented, and the student is to compose a response in sustained prose, using the student's own words, phrases, and ideas, within the limits of the question or problem.

Example 1: Explain the actions of a person of prominence in 1776 that made him or her famous.

Example 2: Explain how your life might be different in the winter if you lived in Norway.

Advantages: Measures higher mental processes, such as ability to synthesize material and to express ideas in clear and precise written language. Especially useful in integrated thematic teaching. Provides practice in written expression.

Disadvantages: Essay items require a good deal of time to read and to score. They tend to provide an unreliable sampling of achievement and are vulnerable to teacher subjectivity and unreliable scoring. Furthermore, they tend to punish students who write slowly and laboriously, who have limited proficiency in written language, but who may have achieved as well as students who write faster and are more proficient in the language. Essay items tend to favor students who have fluency with words but whose achievement may not necessarily be better. In addition, unless the students have been given instruction in their meaning and in how to respond to them, the teacher should not assume that students understand key directive verbs such as *explain* and *discuss.*

Guidelines for use

1. When preparing an essay-only test, many questions, each requiring a relatively short prose response, are preferable to a smaller number of questions requiring long prose responses. Briefer answers tend to be more precise, and many items provide a more reliable sampling of student achievement. When preparing short prose response-type questions, be sure to avoid using words verbatim from the student textbook.
2. Prior to using this type of test item, give your students instruction and practice in responding to key directive verbs that will be used (Jenkinson, 1988):

   Compare asks for an analysis of similarity and difference, but with a greater emphasis on similarities or likenesses.

   Contrast asks more for differences than for similarities.

   Criticize asks for the good and bad aspects of an idea or situation.

   Define asks student to express clearly and concisely the meaning of a term, as in the dictionary or in the student's own words.

   Diagram asks student to put quantities or numerical values into the form of a chart, a graph, or a drawing.

   Discuss asks student to explain or argue, presenting various sides of events, ideas, or situations.

   Evaluate means to express worth, value, and judgment.

   Explain means to describe with an emphasis on cause and effect.

   Illustrate means to describe by means of examples, figures, pictures, or diagrams.

   Interpret means to describe or explain a given fact, theory, principle, or doctrine in a specific context.

   Justify asks student to show reasons, with an emphasis on correct, positive, and advantageous aspects.

List means just that, to simply name items in a category or to include them in a list, without much description.

Outline means to give a short summary with headings and subheadings.

Prove means to present materials as witnesses, proof, and evidence.

Relate means to tell how specified things are connected or brought into some kind of relationship.

Summarize asks student to recapitulate the main points without examples or illustrations.

Trace asks student to follow a history or series of events step by step by going backward over the evidence.

3. After preparing essay items, make a tentative scoring key, deciding the key ideas you expect students to identify and how many points will be allotted to each.

4. Students should be informed about the relative test value for each essay item. Point values, if different for each item, can be listed in the margin of the test next to each item.

5. Different qualities of achievement are more likely comparable when all students must answer the same questions, as opposed to providing a list of essay items from which students may select those they answer.

6. Allow students adequate test time for a full response.

7. To nullify the "halo effect," some teachers use a number code rather than having students write their names on essay papers. In this way, the teacher is unaware of whose paper is being read. If you do this, use caution not to misplace or become confused about the identification codes.

8. When reading student essay responses, read all student papers for one item at a time. While doing that, make notes to yourself, and then read all the answers again, scoring each student's paper for that item. Repeat the process for the next item. While scoring essay responses, keep in mind the nature of the objective being measured, which may or may not include the qualities of handwriting, grammar, spelling, and neatness.

9. While they have some understanding of a concept, many students in the early grades are not yet facile with written expression, so you must be patient, tolerant, positive, and helpful. Mark papers with positive and constructive comments, showing students ways they could have explained or responded better.

Grouping Type

Description: Several items are presented, and students select and group those that are related in some way.

> *Example 1:* Separate the following numbered historical figures from 1776 into two groups: place those who are people of prominence from America's colonies in group A and those who are not from America's colonies in group B.

> *Example 2:* Circle the one outline of a country that is least like the others in its government: (Canada, Iraq, America.)

Advantages: This type of item tests knowledge of grouping and can be used to measure for higher levels of cognition and to stimulate discussion. If students manipulate actual items, then it is closer to an authentic assessment type as well. You will note that Example 2 is similar to a multiple-choice item.

Disadvantage: Remain alert for student responses that offer a valid alternative rationale for grouping.

Guideline for use: To allow for an alternative correct response, consider making the item a combination grouping, short-explanation type, being certain to allow adequate space for student explanations.

Identification Type

Description: Unknown specimens are to be identified by name or some other criterion.

> *Example 1:* Identify each of the pictures of workers by name.

> *Example 2:* Identify by name and use each of the worker's tools on the table.

Advantages: Verbalization (that is, the use of abstract symbolization) is less significant, as the student is working with real objects. This type of item should measure higher-level learning rather than simple recall. The item can also be written to measure procedural understanding such as asking students to identify steps in booting up a computer program or to use a tape recorder for interviewing. This is another useful type for authentic assessment.

Disadvantages: To be fair, the examples used should be equally familiar or unfamiliar to all students. Adequate materials must be provided.

Guidelines for use: If photographs, drawings, photocopies and recordings are used, they must be clear to students.

Matching Type

Description: Match related items from a list of numbered items to a list of lettered choices, or in some way connect items that are the same or related. To eliminate the paper-and-pencil aspect and make the item more direct, use direction such as, "Of the items from the table, pair up those that are most alike."

Example 1: In the blank space next to each name in Column A put the letter of the best answer from Column B.

Stem Column	Answer Column
_____1. George	A. Franklin
_____2. Benjamin	B. Washington
	C. Revere

Example 2: Match items in Column A (stem column) to those of Column B (answer column) by drawing lines to match the pairs.

Column A	Column B
Christopher	Franklin
Benjamin	Tubman
Harriet	Columbus
Abraham	Booth
	Lincoln

Example 3: Match items in Column A (cause column) to those of Column B (answer column) by putting the letter of the best answer from the answer column to match cause and effect.

Cause	Effect
_____ 1. Expanding factories needed many workers.	A. Workers lived in crowded and congested conditions.
_____ 2. Workers needed to live close to their jobs.	B. Immigrant workers came to the United States in large numbers.
	C. Immigrant workers did not arrive in America in large numbers.

Advantages: This type can measure for ability to judge relationships and to differentiate between similar ideas, facts, definitions, and concepts. This type is easy to score, can test a broad range of content, and reduces guessing, especially if one group contains more items than the other. This type is interesting to students and adaptable for performance assessment.

Disadvantages: This type is not easily adapted to measuring for higher cognition. Because all parts of the item must be homogeneous, it is possible that clues will be given, thus reducing item validity. For example, a student might have a legitimate rationale for an "incorrect" response.

Guidelines for use: The number of items in the answer column should exceed the number in the stem column. The number of items to be matched should not exceed 12. Matching sets should have high homogeneity; that is, items in both columns (or groups) should be of the same general category. The directions should state if answers can be used more than once. Be prepared for students who can legitimately defend an "incorrect" response.

Multiple-Choice Type

Description: This type is similar to the completion item in that statements are presented, sometimes in incomplete form. This type requires recognition or even higher cognitive processes, rather than mere recall.

> *Example 1:* Of the following four heating fuels—coal, electricity, gas, oil—the one that is the cleanest to use in the home is: _____.
>
>   a. coal
>   b. gas
>   c. oil
>   d. electricity
>
> *Example 2:* From the following list of fuels, the one that has the *most* adverse effect on our environment is:
>
>   a. coal
>   b. electricity
>   c. gas
>   d. oil

Advantages: Items can be answered and scored quickly. A wide range of content and higher levels of cognition can be tested in a relatively short time. Excellent for all testing purposes—motivation, review, and assessment of learning.

Disadvantages: Unfortunately, because multiple-choice items are relatively easy to write, there is a tendency to write items measuring only low levels of cognition. Multiple-choice items are excellent for major testing, but it takes time to write quality questions that measure higher levels of learning.

Guidelines for use:

1. If the item is in the form of an incomplete statement, it should be meaningful in itself and imply a direct question rather than merely lead into a collection of unrelated true and false statements.
2. Use a level of language that is easy enough for even the poorest readers to understand and avoid unnecessary wordiness.
3. If there is much variation in the length of alternatives, arrange them in order from shortest to longest.
4. For single-word alternatives, use alphabetical arrangement of alternatives.
5. Incorrect responses (called distracters) should be plausible and related to the same concept as the correct alternative. Although an occasional humorous distracter helps to relieve text anxiety, they should be avoided since they offer no measuring value.
6. Arrangement of alternatives should be uniform throughout the test and listed in vertical (column) form rather than in horizontal (paragraph) form.
7. Every item should be grammatically consistent; for example, if the stem is in the form of an incomplete sentence, it should be possible to complete the sentence by attaching any of the alternatives to it.
8. It is not necessary to maintain a fixed number of alternatives for every item, but the use of less than three is not recommended. The use of four or five reduces chance responses and guessing, thereby increasing reliability for the item.
9. The item should be expressed in positive form. A negative form presents a psychological disadvantage to students. Negative items are those that ask what is *not* characteristic of something or what is the *least* useful. Discard the item if you cannot express it in positive terminology.
10. Responses such as "all of these" or "none of these" should be used only when they will contribute more than another plausible distracter. Take care that such responses answer or complete the item. "All of the above" is a poorer alternative than "none of the above" because items that use it as a correct response need to have four or five correct answers; also, if it is the right answer, knowledge of any two of the distracters will cue it.

11. There must be only one correct or best response. However, this is easier said than done.
12. The stem must mean the same thing to every student.
13. Measuring for understanding of definitions is better tested by furnishing the name or word and requiring a choice between alternative definitions than by presenting the definition and requiring a choice between alternative words.
14. The stem should state a single and specific point.
15. The stem must not clue the correct alternative.
16. Avoid using alternatives that include absolute terms such as *never* and *always*.
17. Multiple-choice items need not be entirely verbal. Consider the use of realia, charts, diagrams, and other visuals. They will make the test more interesting, especially to students with low verbal abilities or limited proficiency in English and, consequently, make the assessment more authentic.
18. Once you have composed a multiple-choice test, tally the position of answers to be sure they are evenly distributed, to avoid the common psychological mistake (when there are four alternatives) of consistently placing the correct alternative in the third position.
19. Consider providing space between test items for students to include their rationales for their response selections, thus making the test a combination multiple-choice and short-explanation item type. This provides feedback for students who can rationalize an alternative that you had not considered plausible. It also provides for the measurement of higher levels of cognition and encourages student writing.
20. While scoring, tally the incorrect responses for each item on a blank copy of the test. Analyze incorrect responses for each item to discover potential errors in your scoring key. If, for example, many students select "B" for an item and your key says "A" is the correct answer, you may have made a mistake on your scoring key or in teaching the lesson.

Performance Type

Description: Provided with certain conditions or materials, the student solves a problem or accomplishes some other action.

Example 1:

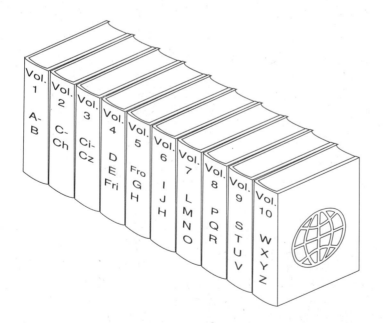

USING THE ENCYCLOPEDIA

Directions: Using the ten-volume *Our Own Encyclopedia* shown in this diagram, select the number of the volume in which you would find information about each of the items listed below. Write the number of the volume you select in the spaces on the left side of the sheet. Then list the volume number of *World Book* in which the same items are found in the spaces on the right side of the sheet.

Our Own		*World Book*
_____ 1.	Earthquakes in Guatemala	1. _____
_____ 2.	The French writer Crèvecoeur	2. _____
_____ 3.	The history of rocketry	3. _____
_____ 4.	The People's Republic of China	4. _____
_____ 5.	Russia	5. _____
_____ 6.	Apple-growing in Washington State	6. _____
_____ 7.	Jet aircraft	7. _____
_____ 8.	Countries that are members of the United Nations	8. _____
_____ 9.	Unidentified flying objects	9. _____
_____ 10.	The history of Czechoslovakia	10. _____

Advantages: Performance test item types come closer to direct measurement (authentic assessment) of certain expected outcomes than do most other types, although other types of questions can actually be prepared as performance-type items, that is, where the student actually does what he or she is being tested for. Learning that is difficult to verbalize can be assessed since little or no verbalization may be necessary. Students who do poorly on verbal tests may do well on performance tests. For example, this is often true for students who have learning disabilities.

Disadvantages: A performance item can be difficult and time consuming to administer to a group of students. Scoring may tend to be subjective, and it could be difficult to give make-up tests to students who were absent.

Guidelines for use: Use your creativity to design and use performance tests, as they tend to measure the most important objectives. To reduce subjectivity in scoring, prepare distinct scoring guidelines (rubrics), as was discussed in scoring essay-type questions. To set up a performance test situation you should:

1. Specify the performance objective.
2. Specify the test situation or conditions.
3. Establish the criteria (scoring rubric) for judging the excellence of the process or product.
4. Make a checklist for scoring the performance or product. (This checklist is simply a listing of the criteria you established in step 3. It would be impossible to use a rating scale because it ordinarily makes scoring too complicated.)
5. Prepare directions in writing, outlining the situation with instructions for the students to follow. For example, a checklist for student project work might be as follows:

Check each item if the project comes up to standard in this particular category.

_____ 1. Accurate in content.
_____ 2. Neat and attractive.
_____ 3. Attentive to detail.

Short-Explanation Type

Description: The short-explanation question is an essay-type but requires a shorter answer.

Example 1: Read the following paragraph carefully. Then write a sentence telling what the paragraph is describing.

It is the first Tuesday in November. On this day, your neighbor's garage has the flag of the United States flying outside its doors. All day long, people are coming and going in and out of the garage. A sign on the side of the garage reads "Polling Place." What is going on in your neighbor's garage?
Sentence:_____

Example 2: Explain what is incorrect or misleading about the following statement.

Colorado and Nevada were settled by people moving east.
Explanation:_____

Advantages: Like the essay type, the student's understanding is assessed, but this type takes less time for the teacher to read and to score. In example 2, for instance, the sentence represents a misconception about direction of the westward movement. As discussed in Chapter 1, teachers have an obligation and an opportunity to correct student misconceptions, providing they have a correct understanding of the concept. This type of test item can be useful in assessing conceptual understanding and critical thinking.

By using several questions of this type, a greater amount of content can be covered than with a fewer number of essay questions. This type of question is good practice for students to learn to express themselves in writing.

Disadvantages: Some students will have difficulty expressing themselves in a limited fashion or in writing. They need practice and time in doing so.

Guidelines for use: This type is useful for occasional reviews and as an option to other types of questions. For scoring, follow the same guidelines as for the essay-type item.

True-False Type

Description: A statement is presented that students are to judge as being accurate or not.

Example 1: The Plains Indians lived in villages called pueblos. T or F?

Example 2: The Mormons settled at Great Salt Lake in a region then owned by California. T or F?

Advantages: Many items can be answered in a relatively short time, making broad content coverage possible. Scoring is quick and simple. True-false items are good for starting discussions, for review, and for diagnostic evaluation (preassessment).

Disadvantages: As illustrated by the examples, it is difficult to write true-false items that are purely true or false, or without qualifying them in a way that clues the answer. Much of the content that most easily lends itself to this type of test item is trivial. Students have a 50 percent chance of guessing the correct answer, thus giving this item type poor validity and poor reliability. Scoring and grading give no clue about why the student missed an item. The disadvantages of true-false items far outweigh the advantages; pure true-false items should *never* be used for arriving at grades. For grading purposes, you may use modified true-false items, where space is provided between items for students to write in explanations, thus making the item a combined true-false, short-explanation type. Give the students a direction to rewrite any statement they consider false on a line below the original statement and make it true. Thus:

Example 1: The Plains Indians lived in villages called pueblos. T or F?

If False, rewrite to make true:_____

Guidelines for preparing true-false items:

First write the statement as a true statement; then make it false by changing a word or phrase. Additional suggestions follow:

1. Use positive statements. Negative statements tend to confuse students.
2. A true-false statement should include only one idea.
3. Try to use an equal number of true and false items.
4. Avoid specific determiners (such as *always, all,* or *none,* which may clue that the statement is false).
5. Use statements without clues. For example, words such as *often, probably,* and *sometimes* may clue students that the statement is true.
6. Avoid words that may have different meanings for different students.
7. Avoid using verbatim language from the student textbook.
8. Avoid trick items.
9. As stated earlier, for grading purposes, you may use modified true-false items that provide space between items for students to write in their explanations, thus making the item a combined true-false, short-explanation type. Another form of modified true-false item is the use of "sometimes-always-never," where a third alternative, "sometimes," is introduced to reduce the chance for guessing.

L. REPORTING CHILDREN'S ACHIEVEMENT

One of your major responsibilities as a classroom teacher is to report student progress in achievement to parents or guardians. In some schools the reporting is about student progress and effort as well as about achievement. Reporting is done in at least two, and sometimes three ways, and examples are described as follows.

The Grade Report

Every six to nine weeks a grade report (report card) is issued (from four to six times a year, depending on the school district). This grade report represents an achievement grade (formative evaluation), and the second or third one of the semester is also the semester grade. For courses that are only one semester long, it also is the final grade (summative evaluation). In essence, the first and sometimes second reports are progress notices, with the semester grade being the one that is transferred to the student's transcript of records. In some schools, the traditional report card is marked and sent home either with the student or by mail. In many schools, reporting is done by computer printouts, often sent by mail directly to the student's home address. (In some schools, as an effort to involve parents, the parents or guardians are expected to come to the school on a given day and pick up the grade report.)

Whichever reporting form is used, you must separate your assessments of a student's social behaviors (classroom conduct) from the student's academic achievement. Academic achievement (or accomplishment) is represented by a letter (sometimes a number) grade (*A* through *E* or *F,* or *E, S,* and *U,* or *1* to *5,* and sometimes with minuses and pluses), and the social behavior by a "satisfactory" or an "unsatisfactory" or by more specific items, sometimes supplemented by the teacher's written or computer-generated comments. In some instances, the reporting form may have a place for the teacher to check whether basic grade-level standards have been met in language arts, social studies, and other subject areas. (See Figure 5.3.)

Direct Contact With Parents

Although not always obligatory, some teachers contact parents or guardians by telephone, especially when a student has shown a sudden turn for either the worse or the better in academic achievement or in classroom behavior. That initiative and contact by the teacher is usually welcomed by parents and can lead to private and productive conferences with the teacher. A telephone conversation saves valuable time for both the teacher and the parent.

Another way of contacting parents is by letter. Contacting a parent by letter gives you time to think, to make clear your thoughts and concerns to that parent, and to invite the parent to respond at the parent's convenience by letter, by phone, or by arranging to have a conference with you.

Conferences and Meetings With Parents

You will meet many parents or guardians early in the school year during Back to School Night and throughout the year in parent conferences. For the beginning teacher, these meetings with parents can be anxious times. Here are guidelines to help you with those experiences.

Back-to-School Night is the evening early in the school year when parents can come to the school and meet their child's teachers. The parents arrive at the child's homebase and then proceed through a simulation of their son or daughter's school day, and as a group while meeting each class and each teacher for a few minutes. Later, there is an Open House, where parents may have more time to talk individually with teachers, but Open House is usually a time for the school and teachers to celebrate the work and progress of the students for that year. Throughout the school year there will be opportunities for you and parents to meet and to talk about the children.

At back-to-school night. On this evening parents are anxious to learn as much as they can about their child's new teachers. During that meeting you will make some straightforward remarks about yourself and then discuss your expectations of the students.

Although there will be precious little time for questions from the parents, during your introduction the parents will be delighted to learn that you have your program well planned;

Progress Report
Kindergarten

STUDENT'S NAME: _____ 19____ School year 19____

TEACHER: _____ GRADE: _____

SCHOOL: _____

EXPLANATION OF SYMBOLS: S – Satisfactory   N – Needs Improvement

PHYSICAL DEVELOPMENT

Shows large muscle control in such activities as:

	1	2	3
Hopping			
Jumping			
Skipping			
Walking on Toes			
Bouncing Ball			
Catching Ball			
Jumping Rope, Assisted			
Walking Balance Board			

Demonstrates small muscle control when:

Handling crayon, pencil, and scissors			
Tying a shoe			

SOCIAL DEVELOPMENT AND WORK HABITS

Displays enthusiasm			
Shows reasonable attention span			
Finishes assigned work			
Follows directions			
Shares willingly			
Gets along well with others			
Follows rules			
Works independently			
Listens to directions			

LANGUAGE DEVELOPMENT

Basic Knowledge:

Knows full name			
Knows address or bus stop			
Knows telephone number			
Knows days of week			

Knows basic colors			
Knows left from right			
Knows basic shapes			
Knows Pledge of Allegiance			
Knows body parts			
Knows simple nursery rhymes and poems			

Skills and Habits

Speaks in complete sentences			
Uses adequate vocabulary to express ideas			
Shows interest in books, stories, poetry, and pictures			
Writes letters with reasonable skill			
Prints name			
Draws basic shapes			

Letters and Sounds

Recognizes sound of letters			
Knows names of capital letters			
Knows names of lowercase letters			
Knows rhyming words			

COUNTING AND MEASURING

Recognizes numbers			
Counts by rote			
Writes numbers with reasonable skill			
Counts objects			
Counts backwards, 10–1			

ART

Demonstrates ability to work with a variety of art media			

MUSIC

Takes part in rhythmic activities			
Participates in singing			

Teacher Comments

1st Report _____

2nd Report _____

3rd Report _____

FIGURE 5.3
Sample Progress Report for Kindergarten

145

are a task master; and will communicate with them. The parents and guardians will be pleased to know that you are from the school of the three F's—firm, friendly, and fair.

Specifically, parents will expect to learn about your curriculum—goals and objectives, any long-term projects, and testing and grading procedures. They will need to know what you expect of them: will there be homework, and if so, should they help their children with it? How can they contact you? Try to anticipate other questions. Your principal and colleagues can help you anticipate and prepare for these questions. Of course, you can never prepare for the question that comes from left field. Just stay calm and don't get flustered. Ten minutes will fly by quickly, and parents will be reassured to know you are an in-control person.

As parents who have attended many back-to-school nights at the schools our children have attended and are attending, we continue to be both surprised and dismayed that so few teachers seem well-prepared for the few minutes they have with the parents. Considering how often we hear about teachers wanting more involvement of parents, few seem delighted that parents have indeed come, and few teachers take full advantage of this time with parents to truly celebrate their programs.

Parent-teacher conference. When meeting parents for conferences, you should be as specific as possible when explaining the progress of their child in your class. Help them understand, but don't saturate them with more information than they need. Resist any tendency to talk too much. Allow time for the parent to ask questions. Keep your answers succinct. Never compare one student with another or with the rest of the class. If parents ask a question for which you do not have an answer, tell them you will try to find an answer and will phone them as quickly as you can. And do it. Have the student's portfolio and other work with you during parent conferences so you can show them examples of what is being discussed. Also, have your grade book on hand, or a computer print out of it, but be prepared to protect from the parent the names and records of the other students.

Sometimes it is helpful to have a three-way conference, a conference with the parent, the student, and you, or a conference with the parent, the principal, and several or all of the student's teachers.

Ideas for Teacher and Parent/Guardian Collaboration

When parents ask how they can help in the child's learning, here are suggestions you might offer them:

- Encourage them to plan short family meetings after dinner, but while they are still seated at the table. Ask for a "tableside" report of "What's happening in the school?" Ask, "How can I help?" When their child expresses a concern, emphasize ways to solve problems that occur. Help the child develop his or her problem solving skills.
- Parents might ask their child to share with them each day one specific thing learned that day.
- They could remind their child to bring their portfolios home each Friday to share with them. They should look for a place in the portfolio where they will sign to show they have reviewed their child's work and then return the materials with the child on Monday. On the form for the parents' or guardian's signature, they should look for a column for teacher and parent comments or notes to each other. Writing comments will maintain this important line of communication between the parents and their child's teacher.
- Helping a child become a critical thinker is one of the aims of education and one that parents can help to reinforce by asking "what if" questions; thinking aloud as a model for their child's thinking development. Further, they can encourage their child's metacognition by asking questions such as, "How did you arrive at that conclusion?" or "How do you feel about your conclusion now?" They should ask these questions about the child's everyday social interactions and topics that are important to the child, ask the child to elaborate on his or her ideas, allowing the child to make mistakes, and encouraging the child to learn from them.

- Parents should limit and control their child's television pleasure viewing.
- Parents or guardians should set up a regular schedule of reviewing with the child his or her portfolio.
- They should set up a regular time each evening for a family discussion about school.
- Let parents and guardians know that several books are available for them to read and discuss at home. To help them choose books, the United States government has a variety of free or low-cost booklets available. For information parents can contact the Consumer Information Center, Department TH, Pueblo, CO 81109. Other useful resources are *Helping Your Child Use the Library* (item 465V); *Becoming a Nation of Readers: What Parents Can Do* (item 459V); and *Help Your Child Do Better at School* (item 412V). Additionally, you are encouraged to go to the neighborhood public library and ask for a librarian's help in locating helpful resources.
- If parents are interested in strategies for increasing home-school collaboration, suggest any or all of the following: *Beyond the Bake Sale: An Educator's Guide to Working with Parents* (Columbia, MD: National Committee for Citizens in Education, 1985) by Anne T. Henderson, Carl Marburger, and Theodora Ooms; "Parent Involvement," in *Phi Delta Kappan* (Volume 72, No. 5, January 1991); *Communicating with Parents* by Janet Chrispeels, Marcia Boruta, and Mary Daugherty (San Diego: San Diego County Office of Education, 1988); *The Evidence Continues to Grow: Parent Involvement Improves Student Achievement* (Columbia, MD: National Committee for Citizens in Education, 1987); and *Parenting for Education* by Paula Lowe and Carl Trendler (Seattle: U.S. West Education Foundation, 1989).

Tompkins and Hoskisson (1991) provide suggestions for encouraging and nurturing children's (ages 4–10) interest in writing, such as submitting writing to a children's magazine, making writing a natural part of family life, and linking language arts to real life as well as social studies topics in the issues. Other useful references for improving parent-teacher relations are D. J. Croft, *Parents and Teachers: A Resource Book for Home, School, and Community Relations* (Belmont, CA: Wadsworth, 1979), and A. Honig, "Parent Involvement in Early Childhood Education," in B. Spodek (Ed.), *Handbook of Research in Early Childhood Education* (New York: Free Press, 1982).

Dealing With an Angry Parent or Guardian

If a parent or guardian is angry or hostile toward you and the school, here are guidelines for dealing with that hostility:

- Remain calm in your discussion with parents or guardians allowing them to talk out their hostility while you say very little. Usually, the less you say the better off you will be. What you do say must be objective and to the point of the child's work in your classroom. Parents may just need to vent frustrations that might have very little to do with you, the school, or even the child.
- Consider all the points made by parents and guardians. Do *not* allow yourself to be intimidated or backed into a corner. If the parent tries to do so by attacking you personally, do not press your defense at this point. Perhaps the parent has made a point that you should take time to consider, and now is a good time to arrange for another conference with the parent for about a week later. In a follow-up conference, and agreed to by the parent, you may want to consider bringing in a mediator, such as another member of your teaching team, an administrator, or a school counselor.
- Keep the conversation focused on this parent's child and his or her progress. You must *not* talk about other students. The parent is *not* your rival and should not be viewed as such. Keep focused on the idea that both of you share a concern for the academic and emotional well-being of the child. Use your best skills in critical thinking and problem solving and try to keep the discussion focused by identifying the problem(s), defining it, and then arriving at some decision about how mutually to solve it. To this end, you may need to ask for help from a third party, such as the child's school counselor. If agreed to by the parent, please take that step.

- Present the image of the capable professional. Parents do *not* need to hear about how busy you are, about your personal problems, or about how many other students you are dealing with daily (unless, of course, a parent asks). Parents expect you to be the capable professional who knows what to do and is doing it.

SUMMARY

Since assessment is an integral factor in the teaching-learning process, you will want to include the following in your teaching performance:

- Use a variety of instruments to assess student learning. Keep children informed of their progress. Return papers promptly, review answers to all questions, and respond to inquiries about marks given.
- Use assessment procedures continuously so as to contribute to the positive development of the individual student. Such an emphasis requires that the assessment be important to the child and related to what the child considers important. Effective assessment is helping students to recognize their competencies and achievements. It encourages further learning and the selection of appropriate tasks. The goals of assessment instruments should serve as a challenge, but they should be attainable. Goals set too high or tests with questions that are too hard discourage children and diminish the motivational factor. Goals set too low, with questions that are too easy, encourage disregard of the subject content that is taught.
- Use objective and impartial assessment. Do not allow personal feelings to enter into a grade. The grade earned should reflect the student's level of achievement based on the same objective standard used for all.
- Involve students in assessment planning, which reinforces individual student development and provides an accepting, stimulating learning environment. Try to minimize arguments about grades, cheating, and teacher subjectivity by making students a part of assessment. Remain alert while students are taking a test. Do not occupy yourself with other tasks at your desk. Circulate around the room, observe the students, and present at least a psychological deterrent to cheating by your demeanor and presence; be sure not to distract.
- Involve students, whenever feasible, in setting up assessment criteria and establishing the relative importance of activities. Such cooperative planning is a learning experience for children and encourages self-assessment.
- Give clear directions on any assessments that you give. Before permitting students to begin, explain any ambiguities that result from the terminology used. Base your assessments on the material that has been taught. Your purpose in giving assessments, of course, is not to trap or confuse students but to evaluate how well they have assimilated the important aspects of learning.
- Think through your marking procedures carefully, planning them, and explaining your policies to the students. Explain the various factors to be considered in arriving at a grade and the weight accorded to such things as homework, written assignments, and oral contributions before study is begun.
- Adapt the grading system of the school or district to your situation. Establish your own standard and grade each student in relation to it. For example, consider as tentative the grade you arrive at after examining the objective data you have accumulated. Consider extenuating circumstances, such as sudden illness, prolonged absence for a serious matter, and so on before making the grades permanent. Adjusting a borderline mark into the higher alternative in the light of some classroom performance is indeed a professionally defensible decision. Almost never, though, is it prudent to award a lower grade to a student than that student has already earned on the basis of the objective data.
- Maintain accurate and clear records of assessment results so that you will have an adequate and varied supply of data on which to base your judgments about achievement. Sufficient data of this sort are especially helpful when final grades are called into question or when students or parents require information in depth.

Additional discussions of assessment, specific to language arts and social studies teaching, are presented in Parts II and III.

QUESTIONS AND ACTIVITIES FOR DISCUSSION

1. Other than a paper-and-pencil test, identify three alternative assessment techniques for assessing student learning during or at completion of an integrated language arts and social studies unit.

2. Investigate various ways that schools are experimenting today with assessing and reporting student achievement. Share with your colleagues what you find. Analyze the pros and cons of various systems of assessing and reporting.

3. When using a point system for determining student grades, is it educationally defensible to give a student a higher grade than that student's points call for? A lower grade? Give your rationale for your answers.

4. Explain one or two of the dangers in using true-false and completion-type items in assessing student learning in language arts and social studies and using the results for grade determination.

5. Explain the concept of "authentic assessment." Is it the same as "performance assessment"? Explain why or why not.

6. Describe any student learning activities or situations in language arts and social studies learning that should *not* be graded but should or could be used for assessment of student learning.

7. For a specified grade level that you intend to teach, describe the items and their relative weights that you would use for determining grades for social studies and language arts. Explain your rationale for the percentage weight distribution.

8. Explain the value of and give a specific example of a performance test item that you would use in teaching social studies to children in a specified grade, K–4.

9. Explain the value of and give a specific example of a performance test item that you would use in teaching language arts in a specified grade, K–4.

10. From your current observations and field work as related to this teacher preparation program, clearly identify one specific example of educational practice that seems contradictory to exemplary practice or theory as presented in this chapter. Present your explanation for the discrepancy.

11. Related to language arts assessment, locate, read, and report back to classmates on one of the following sources or another article of your choice:

Grammar: Pooley, R. C. (1974). *The Teaching of English Usage.* Urbana, IL: National Council of Teachers of English.

Handwriting: Barbe, W. B., Lucas, V. H., Wasylyk, T. M., Hackney, C. S., & Braun, L. A. (1984). *Zaner-Bloser Creative Growth in Handwriting* (Grades K–8). Columbus, OH: Zaner-Bloser.

Journals: Tway, E. (1984). *Time for Writing in the Elementary School.* Urbana, IL: ERIC Clearinghouse on Reading and Communication Skills and the National Council of Teachers of English.

Letter Writing: Tompkins, G., & Hoskisson, L. (1991) *Language Arts, Content and Teaching Strategies* (2nd ed.). New York: Merrill/Macmillan, pp. 379–380.

Life Stories: Tompkins & Hoskisson (1991, pp. 389–390). See also Bentley, R., & Butler, S. (1988). *LifeWriting: Self-Exploration through Writing and Life Review.* Dubuque, IA: Kendall/Hunt.

Listening: Tompkins & Hoskisson (1991, pp. 120, 127).

Newspapers: Tompkins & Hoskisson (1991, pp. 370–371).

Poems: Tompkins & Hoskisson (1991, p. 427).

Reading: Gillet, J. W., & Temple, C. (1982). *Understanding Reading Problems: Assessment and Instruction.* Boston: Little, Brown.

Research Reports: Tompkins & Hoskisson (1991, pp. 361–362).

Storywriting: Bosma, B. (1987). *Fairy Tales, Fables, Legends, and Myths: Using Folk Literature in Your Classroom.* New York: Teachers College Press.

Spelling: Graves, D. H. (1977). Research Update: Spelling Texts and Structural Analysis Methods. *Language Arts, 54,* 86–90. See also Gentry, J. R. (1981). Learning to Spell Developmentally. *The Reading Teacher, 34,:* 378–381; Horn, T. D. (1947). The Effect of the Corrected Test on Learning to Spell. *Elementary School Journal, 47,* 277–285; and Johnson, T. D., Langford, K. G., & Quorn, K. C. (1981). Characteristics of an Effective Spelling Program. *Language Arts, 58,* 581–588.

Use of Words: Tompkins & Hoskisson (1991, pp. 101–102). See also *The Primary Language Record: Handbook for Teachers* (1989). Portsmouth, NH: The Center for Language in Primary Education. Heinemann.

Writing. Kramer, C. J. (1990, December). Documenting Reading and Writing Growth in the Primary Grades Using Informal Methods of Evaluation. *The Reading Teacher, 44*(4), 356–357. See also *Manitoba Writing Assessment Program: A Report of the Measurement and Evaluation Branch.* (1979). Manitoba Province, Department of Education, 979; and Edelsky, C. (1986). *Writing in a Bilingual Program: Hable Una Vez.* Norwood, NJ: Ablex.

12. Related to social studies assessment, locate, read, and report back to classmates on one of the following sources or another article of your choice:

Anecdotal Records: Jarolimek, J., & Parker, W. C. (1993). *Social Studies in Elementary Education* (9th ed.). (p. 459). Englewood Cliffs, NJ: Merrill/Prentice Hall.

Authentic Assessment: Wiggins, G. (1989, April). Teaching to the Authentic Test. *Educational Leadership, 46,* 41–47.

Checklists: Jarolimek & Parker (1993, pp. 457–458).

Conferences: Jarolimek & Parker (1993, p. 458).

Diaries and Logs: Jarolimek & Parker (1993, p. 461).

Group Discussion: Jarolimek & Parker (1993, pp. 455–456).

Observations: Jarolimek & Parker (1993, pp. 456–457).

Portfolios and Work Samples: Valencia, S. (1990, January). A Portfolio Approach to Classroom Reading Assessment: The Whys, Whats, and Hows. *The Reading Teacher, 44,* 338–340. See also Wolf, D. P. (1989, April). Portfolio Assessment: Sampling Student Work. *Educational Leadership, 46,* 35–39; and Lamme, L. L., & Hysmith, D. (1991, February). One School's Adventure into Portfolio Assessment. *Language Arts, 68*(6), 17–23.

13. Describe any prior concepts you held that changed as a result of your experiences with this chapter. Describe the changes.

REFERENCES AND SUGGESTED READINGS

Abruscato, J. (1993, February). Early results and tentative implications from the Vermont Portfolio Project. *Phi Delta Kappan, 74*(6), 474–477.

Bergman, A. B. (1993, February). Performance assessment for early childhood. *Science and Children, 30*(5), 20–22.

Black, S. (1993, February). Portfolio assessment. *Executive Educator, 15*(1), 28–31.

Bracey, G. W. (1993, January). Assessing the new assessments. *Principal, 72*(3), 34–36.

Chambers, D. L. (1993, February) Standardized testing impedes reform. *Educational Leadership, 50*(5), 80–81.

Doran, R. L., et al. (1993, September). Authentic assessment: An instrument for consistency. *The Science Teacher, 60*(6), 37–41.

Ebel, R. L., & Frisbie, D. A. (1991). *Essentials of educational measurement* (5th ed.). Needham Heights, MA: Allyn & Bacon.

Evans, C. S. (1993, February). When teachers look at student work. *Educational Leadership, 50*(5), 71–72.

Feuer, M. J., & Fulton, K. (1993, February). The many faces of performance assessment. *Phi Delta Kappan, 74*(6), 478.

Goldman, J. P. (1989, December). Student portfolios already proven in some schools. *School Administrator, 46*(11), 11.

Hansen, J. (1992, Winter). Evaluation: My portfolio shows who I am. *Quarterly of the National Writing Project and the Center for the Study of Writing and Literacy, 14*(1), 5–6, 9.

Harmon, J. L., Aschbacher, P., & Winters, L. (1992). *A practical guide to alternative assessment.* Alexandria, VA: Association for Supervision and Curriculum Development.

Jarolimek, J., & Parker, W. C. (1993). *Social studies in elementary education* (9th ed.). Englewood Cliffs, NJ: Merrill/Prentice Hall.

Jenkinson, E. B. (1988, June). Practice helps with essay exams. *Phi Delta Kappan, 69,* 10.

Jongsma, K. S. (1991, December). Rethinking Grading Practices (Research to Practice). *The Reading Teacher, 45*(4), 318–320.

Kohn, A. (1991, February). Group grade grubbing versus cooperative learning. *Educational Leadership, 48*(5), 83–87.

Krechevsky, M. (1991, February). Project spectrum: An innovative assessment alternative. *Educational Leadership, 48*(5), 43–48.

LeBuffe, J. R. (1993, September). Performance assessment. *The Science Teacher, 60*(6), 46–48.

Madaus, G. F., & Tan, A. G. A. (1993). The growth of assessment. In Gordon Cawelti (Ed.), *1993 ASCD Yearbook. Challenges and achievements of American education.* Alexandria, VA: Association for Supervision and Curriculum Development.

Maeroff, G. I. (1991, December). Assessing alternative assessment. *Phi Delta Kappan, 73*(4), 272–282.

Meyer, C. A. (1992, May). What's the difference between "authentic" and "performance" assessment? *Educational Leadership, 49*(8), 39–40.

O'Neil, J. (1993, October). Portfolio assessment bears the burden of popularity. *ASCD Update, 35*(8), 3, 8.

Perrone, V. (Ed.). (1991). *Expanding student assessment.* Alexandria, VA: Association for Supervision and Curriculum Development.

Schulz, E. (1993, September). Putting portfolios to the test. *Teacher Magazine, 5*(1), 36–41.

Seefeldt, C., & Barbour, N. (1994). *Early childhood education* (3rd ed.). Englewood Cliffs, NJ: Merrill/Prentice Hall.

Simmons, J. (1990, March). Portfolio as large-scale assessment. *Language Arts, 67*(3), 262–268.

Simmons, R. (1994, February). The horse before the cart: Assessing for understanding. *Educational Leadership, 51*(5), 22–23.

Sperling, D. (1993, February). What's worth an A? *Educational Leadership, 50*(5) 73–75.

Staton, J. (1987). The power of responding in dialogue journals. In T. Fulwiler (Ed.), *The Journal Book*. Portsmouth, NH: Boynton-Cook.

Walberg, H. J. (1990, February). Productive teaching and instruction: Assessing the knowledge base. *Phi Delta Kappan, 71*(6), 470–478.

Wiggins, G. (1993, November). Assessment: Authenticity, context, and validity. *Phi Delta Kappan, 75*(3), 200–214.

Willis, J. A. (1990, Summer). Learning outcome testing program: Standardized classroom testing in West Virginia through item banking, test generation, and curricular management software. *Educational Measurement: Issues and Practices, 9*(2), 11–14.

Wolf, D. P. (1989, April). Portfolio assessment: Sampling student work. *Educational Leadership, 46*(7), 35–39.

Worthen, B. R. (1993, February). Critical issues that will determine the future of alternative assessment. *Phi Delta Kappan, 74*(6), 444–454.

CHAPTER 6

The Selection and Use of Aids and Resources

Cognitive tools are important in helping children construct their understandings. You will be pleased to know that there is a large variety of useful and effective educational materials, aids, and resources from which to draw as you plan your instructional experiences for language arts and social studies learning. It is sometimes possible, however, to become overwhelmed by the sheer quantity of different materials available for classroom use—textbooks, pamphlets, anthologies, encyclopedias, tests, supplementary texts, paperbacks, programmed instructional systems, dictionaries, reference books, classroom periodicals, newspapers, films, records, cassettes, computer software, transparencies, realia, games, filmstrips, audio- and videotapes, slides, globes, manipulatives, CD-ROMs, videodiscs, and graphics. You could and will spend much time reviewing, sorting, selecting, and practicing with these materials and tools. Although nobody can make the job easier for you, this chapter will expedite the process by providing guidelines for using nonprojected and projected aids and materials, and information about where to obtain additional resources. Specifically, this chapter will help you in:

1. Using nonprojected instructional materials, including a readability formula.
2. Finding sources of free and inexpensive printed and audiovisual materials.
3. Identifying the variety of professional journals, periodicals, and other sources relevant to teaching language arts and social studies in grades K–4.
4. Understanding copyright laws for copying printed materials, video, and software programs.
5. Using the classroom writing board.
6. Using the classroom bulletin board.
7. Using the story felt board.
8. Using charts, posters, and graphs.
9. Using the community as a rich instructional resource.
10. Using projected and recorded instructional materials.
11. Knowing what to do when equipment malfunctions.
12. Using the overhead projector.
13. Using slides, filmstrips, and 16-mm films.
14. Using instructional television.
15. Using videos, videodiscs, and CD-ROMs.
16. Using computers and multimedia programs.

A. NONPROJECTED INSTRUCTIONAL TOOLS

Whereas projected aids are those that require electricity to project images onto screens, we begin this chapter with a discussion about nonprojected materials—printed materials, three-dimensional objects, and flat materials on which to write or display—and about the community as a rich resource.

Printed Materials

Historically, of all the nonprojected materials for instruction, the printed textbook has had the greatest influence on teaching. When selecting textbooks and other printed materials, one item of concern to teachers should be the reading or readability level of the material. Sometimes the textbook publisher supplies the reading level. If not, you can apply selections to a readability formula or use a simpler method of merely having students read selections from the book aloud. If they can read the selections without stumbling over many of the words and can tell you the gist of what they have read, you can feel confident that the textbook is not too difficult.

Fry Readability Formula

To estimate the reading-grade level of a student textbook, you can use a readability formula such as the Fry technique. The procedure for the Fry technique is to:

1. Determine the average number of syllables in three 100-word selections, taking one from the beginning, one from the middle, and one from the ending parts of the book.
2. Determine the average number of sentences in the three 100-word selections.
3. Plot the two values on the readability graph (Figure 6.1). Their intersection will give you an approximation of the text's reading level at the 50 percent to 75 percent comprehension level.

Since readability formulas give only the technical reading level of a book, you will have to interpret the results by subjectively estimating the conceptual reading level of the work. To do so, consider your students' experience with the subject, the number of new ideas introduced, the abstraction of the ideas, and the author's external and internal cues. Then raise or lower the estimated level of difficulty.

   To tell how well your students can read the text, use the Cloze technique, or an informal reading inventory. The Cloze technique that was first described by Bormuth (1968) has since appeared in a number of versions (Fry, 1977). The procedure is as follows. From the textbook, select several typical passages so that you will have a total of 400 to 415 words. Delete every eighth word in the passage except for the words in the first and last sentences, proper names, numbers, and initialed words in sentences. It will be helpful if you eliminate 50 words. Duplicate the passages with 10 to 15 blank spaces replacing the eliminated words. Pass out these "mutilated" readings to the students. Ask them to fill in the blanks with the most appropriate words they can think of. Collect the papers. Score them by counting all the words that are the exact words in the original text and by dividing the number of correct responses by the number possible. McKenna (1976) suggests that you not count synonyms or verbs of different tense. (Having 50 blanks makes this division easy.)

$$\text{Score} = \frac{\text{Number of correct responses}}{\text{Number possible}}$$

   You can assume that students who score better than 50 percent can read the book quite well, students who score between 40 and 50 percent can read the book at the instructional level, and students who score below 40 percent will probably find the book difficult.

   To conduct an informal silent reading inventory, ask your students to read four or five pages of the book, and then give them a 10-item quiz on what they read. You can consider the text too difficult for any student who scores less than 70 percent on the quiz. Similarly, to conduct an informal oral reading inventory, have a student read a 100-word passage. The text is too difficult if the student stumbles over and misses more than 5 percent of the words (Johnson & Kress, 1965).

FIGURE 6.1
Fry Readability Graph
SOURCE: Edward Fry, "A Readability Formula That Saves Time," *Journal of Reading* (April 1968), 11:587.

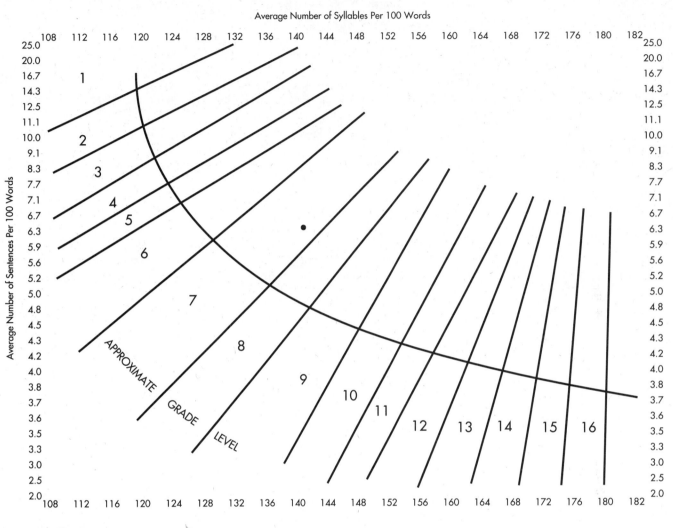

Average Number of Syllables Per 100 Words

Average Number of Sentences Per 100 Words

Directions:
Randomly select three 100-word passages from a book or an article. Plot average number of syllables and average number of sentences per 100 words on graph to determine the grade level of the material. Choose more passages per book if great variability is observed and conclude that the book has uneven readability. Few books will fall in gray area but when they do grade level scores are invalid.

Count proper nouns, numerals, and initializations as words. Count a syllable for each symbol. For example, "1945" is 1 word and 4 syllables and "IRA" is 1 word and 3 syllables.

Example:	Syllables	Sentences
1st Hundred Words	124	6.6
2nd Hundred Words	141	5.5
3rd Hundred Words	158	6.8
Average	141	6.3

Readability 7th Grade (see dot plotted on graph)

Multitext and Multireading Approaches

Expressing a dissatisfaction with the single-textbook approach to teaching, some teachers have substituted a multitext strategy, in which they use one set of books for one topic and another set for another topic. This strategy provides some flexibility, though it really is only a series of single texts.

Other teachers, especially those using an integrated thematic approach, use a strategy that incorporates many readings for a topic during the same unit. This multireading strategy gives students a certain amount of choice in what they read. The various readings allow for differences in reading ability and interest level. By using a study guide, all the students can be directed toward specific information and concepts, but they do not all have to read the same selections.

Beginning a Resources File

Besides the student textbook and perhaps an accompanying workbook, there is a vast array of other printed materials available for use in teaching social studies and language arts, many of which are available without cost. (See sources of free and inexpensive materials that follow.) It is a good idea to immediately begin a file of printed materials and other resources that you can use in your teaching. Figure 6.2 is offered to help you begin that process.

Printed materials include books, workbooks, pamphlets, magazines, brochures, newspapers, professional journals, periodicals, and duplicated materials. When reviewing these materials, you should be alert to the following factors:

- Appropriateness of the material in both content and in reading level.
- Articles in newspapers, magazines, and periodicals, related to the content that your students will be studying or to the skills they will be learning.
- Assorted materials that emphasize thinking and problem solving rather than rote memorization. With an assortment of materials, you can have students working on similar but different assignments depending on their interests and abilities—an example of multilevel teaching.
- Pamphlets, brochures, and other duplicated materials that students can read for specific information and viewpoints about particular topics.
- Relatively inexpensive paperback books that would provide multiple book readings for your class and that make it possible for students to read primary sources.

FIGURE 6.2

Beginning a Professional Materials Resource File

You should start now building your own personal file of aids and resources for teaching, a file that will continue throughout your professional career. Begin your file either on a computer database program or on 3" × 5" file cards (that are color coded) listing:

1. Name of resource
2. How to get and when available
3. How to use
4. Evaluative comments including grade level best for.

Organize the file in whatever way that makes most sense to you. Cross-reference or color-code your system to accommodate the following categories of aids and resources:

1. Articles from magazines, newspapers, journals, and periodicals
2. Assessment items
3. Compact disks sources
4. Computer software sources
5. Games and games sources
6. Guest speakers and other community resources
7. Integrated curriculum ideas
8. Media catalogs
9. Motivational ideas
10. Multimedia program sources
11. Pictures, posters, and other stills
12. Sources of free and inexpensive items
13. Student worksheets
14. Supply catalogs
15. Thematic unit ideas
16. Unit and lesson plan ideas
17. Unit and lesson plans completed
18. Videocassette titles and sources
19. Videodisc titles and sources
20. Other or Miscellaneous (i.e., manipulatives).

Sources of Free and Inexpensive Printed Materials

For free and inexpensive printed materials look for sources in your college or university, public library, or resource center at a local school district (see Figure 6.3).

Professional Journals and Periodicals for Language Arts and Social Studies Teachers of Grades K–4

Figure 6.4 lists many professional periodicals and journals that can provide useful ideas for teaching social studies and language arts and that carry information about instructional materials and how to get them. Check your university or college library for these and other titles of interest to you.

Student Magazines for Grades K–4

Shown in Figure 6.5 is a sample listing of the many magazines for children that can provide useful material for teaching social studies and language arts and that carry information for children. Most of these magazines are likely to be in your nearby public library branch. Many of them publish children's drawings, jokes, letters, poems, and riddles. Others have story contests and list free and inexpensive items for children to send for, including books, brochures, posters, recipes, and stamp kits. Locate and browse through

---

FIGURE 6.3
Resources for Free and Inexpensive Printed Materials

A Guide to Print and Nonprint Materials Available from Organizations, Industry, Governmental Agencies and Specialized Publishers. New York: Neal Schuman.
Civil Aeronautics Administration. *Sources of Free and Low-Cost Materials.* Washington, DC: U.S. Department of Commerce.
Educator's Guide to Free Health, Physical Education, and Recreation Materials. Randolph, WI: Educators Progress Service.
Educator's Guide to Free Materials. Randolph, WI: Educators Progress Service.
Educator's Guide to Free Social Studies Materials. Randolph, WI: Educators Progress Service.
Educator's Guide to Free Teaching Aids. Randolph, WI: Educators Progress Service.
Ewing, S. (1984). *A Guide to Over One Thousand Things You Can Get for Free.* Lynn, MA: Sunnyside Publishing Company.
Free and Inexpensive Learning Materials. Nashville, TN: Division of Surveys and Field Services, George Peabody College for Teachers.
Index to Multi-Ethnic Teaching Materials and Teaching Resources. Washington, DC: National Education Association.
NSTA Reports! Published six times each year by the National Social Studies Teachers Association and distributed to its membership, *Reports!* includes a section titled "Social Studies Teacher's Grab Bag," which provides a current listing of resources for free and inexpensive materials for social studies teachers. Arlington, VA: National Social Studies Teachers Association.

FIGURE 6.4
Professional Periodicals

American Teacher	Journal of Elementary Social Studies
Childhood Education	Education
Computing Teacher, The	Journal of Learning Disabilities
Early Childhood Research Quarterly	Language Arts Teacher, The
Educational Horizons	Learning
Educational Leadership	Phi Delta Kappan
Educational Researcher	School Social Studies and Language Arts
Elementary School Journal, The	Social Studies Scope
Instructor	Social Studies Teacher, The
Journal for Research in Language Arts	Teacher K–8
Education	Teacher Magazine
Journal of Computers in Language Arts and	Young Children
Social Studies Teaching	

FIGURE 6.5
Children's Magazines

Boys Life. 1325 Walnut Hill Lane, Irving, TX 75062. Features scouting, sports, hobbies, and famous personalities.

Cobblestone. 28 Main Street, Peterborough, NH 03458. Features historical themes in the issues.

Cricket. Box 100, LaSalle, IL 61301. Includes fiction and nonfiction as well as poetry, puzzles, and songs.

Dynamite/Arcade. 730 Broadway, New York, NY 10003. This is an interactive format with pull-out games and posters, articles about personalities, and computer and video news.

Electric Company. One Lincoln Plaza, New York, NY 10023. Features themes with jokes, cartoons, games, and puzzles.

Freebies. 407 State Street, Santa Barbara, CA 93120. Lists free and inexpensive items for children to send for such as books, brochures, and recipes.

Highlights. 803 Church Street, Honesdale, PA 18431. Covers moral values, reading, and thinking skills as well as word games and crafts with a reference guide for teachers and parents.

Jack and Jill. 1100 Waterway Blvd., Indianapolis, IN 46206. Features health and nutrition through stories, puzzles, and crafts.

National Geographic World. Dept. 00484, 17th and M Streets, NW Washington, DC 20036. Features children around the world through illustrations, articles, games and crafts.

National Wildlife. 1416 16th Street, NW, Washington, DC 20036. Features environment and wildlife issues.

Odyssey. 1027 N. 7th Street, Milwaukee, WI 53233. Features articles about astronomy and space.

Pack-o-Fun. 14 Main Street, Park Ridge, IL 60068. Features craft projects for discarded materials.

Penny Power. 256 Washington Street, Mount Vernon, NY 10553. Features articles to make children money-smart with an emphasis on economics and finance.

Ranger Rick. 1412 16th Street, NW, Washington, DC 20036. Features nature and people protecting nature through articles and illustrations.

Scienceland. 501 5th Avenue, Dept. SSL, New York, NY 10164. Emphasizes scientific thinking through monthly themes.

Sesame Street. One Lincoln Plaza, New York, NY 10023. Emphasizes activities to foster school preparation and includes parent's guide in each issue.

Sprint. 730 Broadway, New York, NY 10003. Emphasizes current news related to different subject areas.

Stone Soup. P.O. Box 83, Santa Cruz, CA 95063. Has stories, poems, artwork, and book reviews.

Your Big Backyard. 1412 16th Street, NW, Washington, DC 20036. Has brief articles, games, crafts, and stories.

3-2-1 Contact. One Lincoln Plaza, New York, NY 10023. Features science themes in issues along with contests, crafts, and games.

---

these and other magazines for young people that are of interest to you. Write to the editor for further information.

The ERIC Information Network

The Educational Resources Information Center (ERIC) system, established by the United States Office of Education, is a widely used network providing access to information and research in education. While there are 16 clearinghouses providing information on specific subjects, addresses for those of particular interest for teaching social studies and language arts follow:

Elementary and Early Childhood Education. University of Illinois, College of Education, 805 W. Pennsylvania Avenue, Urbana, IL 61601.

Handicapped and Gifted Children. Council for Exceptional Children, 1920 Association Drive, Reston, VA 22091.

Reading and Communication Skills. Indiana University, 2606 East 10th Street, Smith Research Center, Suite 150, Bloomington, IN 47408.

Social Studies, Language Arts, and Environmental Education. Ohio State University, 1200 Chambers Road, 3rd Floor, Columbus, OH 43212-1792.

Tests, Measurements, and Evaluation. American Institutes for Research, Washington Research Center, 1055 Thomas Jefferson Street, NW, Washington, DC 20007-3893.

Copying Printed Materials

You must know the laws about the use of copyrighted materials, printed and nonprinted. Although space here prohibits full inclusion of U.S. legal guidelines, your local school district should be able to provide a copy of current district policies for compliance with copyright laws.

When preparing to make a copy, you must find out whether the copying is permitted by law under the category of "permitted use." If not allowed under "permitted use," then you must get written permission to reproduce the material from the holder of the copyright. When using printed materials adhere to the guidelines shown in Figure 6.6.

B. THE WRITING BOARD

Your classroom may have either a board that is painted plywood (chalkboard); a magnetic chalkboard (plywood with a magnetic backing); or a white or colored (light green and light blue are common) multipurpose board on which you write with special marking pens. Multipurpose boards are important for classrooms where chalkdust would create problems—where it would aggravate allergies or interfere with computer maintenance. In addition to providing a surface on which you can write and draw, the multipurpose board can be used as a projection screen and as a surface to which figures cut from colored transparency film will stick. It may also have a magnetic backing that enables you to use objects attached to magnets and manipulate figures backed with small pieces of magnetic tape.

Electronic whiteboard extension. Extending the purposes of the multipurpose board is an electronic whiteboard that can transfer whatever information is written on it to a connected PC or Mac computer monitor, which in turn can save the material as a computer file. The board uses special dry-erase markers and erasers that have optically encoded sleeves that enable the device to track their position on the board. The data are then converted into a display for the computer monitor, which may then be printed, cut and pasted into other applications, sent as e-mail or fax message, or networked to other sites. For information,

FIGURE 6.6
Guidelines for Copying Copyrighted Printed Materials
SOURCE: Section 107 of the 1976 Federal Omnibus Copyright Revision Act.

Permitted uses: You may make

1. Single copies of:
   - A chapter of a book
   - An article from a periodical, magazine, or newspaper
   - A short story, short essay, or short poem whether or not from a collected work
   - A chart, graph, diagram, drawing, or cartoon
   - An illustration from a book, magazine, or newspaper.
2. Multiple copies for classroom use (not to exceed one copy per student in a course) of:
   - A complete poem if less than 250 words
   - An excerpt from a longer poem, but not to exceed 250 words
   - A complete article, story, or essay of less than 2,500 words
   - An excerpt from a larger printed work not to exceed 10 percent of the whole or 1,000 words
   - One chart, graph, diagram, cartoon, or picture per book or magazine issue.

Prohibited uses: You may *not*:

1. Copy more than one work or two excerpts from a single author during one class term (semester or year)
2. Copy more than three works from a collective work or periodical volume during one class term
3. Reproduce more than nine sets of multiple copies for distribution to students in one class term
4. Copy to create, replace, or substitute for anthologies or collective works
5. Copy "consumable" works, e.g., workbooks, standardized tests, or answer sheets
6. Copy the same work year after year.

contact Microfield Graphics, Inc., 9825 SW Sunshine Court, Beaverton, OR 97005. (503) 626-9393.

Board talk ideas. Except for announcements called "Board Talk" that you place on the board, each day, each class, and even each new idea should begin with a clean board. Each day and class should end with a clean board, too. More "Board Talk" ideas are:

1. Use colored chalk (or dry marking pens) to highlight your "board talk." Beginning at the top left of the board, print or write neatly and clearly, with the writing intentionally positioned to indicate content relationships—"causal, oppositional, numerical, comparative, categorical, and so on" (Hunter, 1994, p. 135).
2. Use the writing board to acknowledge acceptance and to record student contributions. Print instructions for an activity on the board rather than giving them orally. At the top of the board frame, you may find clips that are handy for hanging posters, maps, charts, and children's work.
3. Learn to write on the board without having to entirely turn your back to children or block their view of the board. When you have a lot of material to put on the board, do it before class and then cover it, or better yet, put the material on transparencies and use the overhead projector rather than the board, or use both. Be careful about not writing too much information. When using the writing board to complement your teacher talk, write only key words and simple diagrams, thereby making it possible for the student's right brain hemisphere to process what is seen, while the left hemisphere processes the elaboration provided by your words (Hunter, 1994, p. 133).

C. VISUAL DISPLAYS

Visual displays include bulletin boards, charts, graphs, flip charts, magnetic boards, realia (real objects), pictures, and posters. As a new or visiting member of a faculty, one of your first tasks is to find out what visual materials are available for your use and where they are kept. Here are guidelines for their use.

The Classroom Bulletin Board

Bulletin boards are found in nearly every classroom, and although sometimes poorly used or not used at all, they can be relatively inexpensively transformed into attractive and valuable instructional tools. When preparing a bulletin board, it is important to reflect gender and ethnic equity. Read the following suggestions for ideas for the effective use of the classroom bulletin board.

Making a C.A.S.E. for bulletin boards. How can you effectively use a classroom bulletin board? Your classroom bulletin board will be most effective if you consider the "CASE" (adapted with permission from Kellough & Roberts, 1994).

   C for colorful constructions and captions
   A for attractive arrangement
   S for simple and student prepared
   E for enrichment and extensions of learning.

C: Colorful constructions and captions. Take time to plan the colors you select for your board, and whenever possible, include different materials for the letters and for the background of the board. For letter variety, consider patterns on bright cloth such as denim, felt, and corduroy. Search for special letters: they might be magnetic or ceramic, or precut letters of different sizes. Or make unique letters by cutting them from magazines, newspapers, posters, or stencils, or by printing the letters with rubber stamps, sponges, or vegetable prints. You may print the shapes of letters by dabbing colors on ABC shapes with sponges, rubber stamps, or with vegetable slices that leave an imprint.

For the background of your board and the borders, consider gift-wrapping paper, wallpaper samples, shelf paper, remnants of fabric—flowers, polka dots, plaids, solids, or checks. Corrugated cardboard makes sturdy borders: cut out scallops, the shape of a picket fence, or make jagged points for an icicle effect. Other colorful borders can be made with wide braid, wide rickrack, or a contrasting fabric or paper. Constructions for the board may be simple ones made of yarn, ribbon, braid, cardboard pointers, maps, scrolls, banners, pennants, wheels that turn, cardboard doors that open, shuttered windows to peek through, or flaps that pull down or up and can be peered under or over.

If you need more bulletin board space, prepare large, lightweight screens from the cardboard sides of a tall refrigerator carton, available from an appliance store. One creative teacher asked for, and received without charge, several empty gallon ice-cream containers from a local ice-cream shop. The teacher then stacked five of the containers on top of one another, fastened them together with wide masking tape, painted them, and prepared her own bulletin board "totem pole" for display in the corner of the classroom. On that circular display space, the students placed their items about a current unit of study.

A: Attractive arrangement. Use your creative imagination to make the board attractive and encourage the children to suggest input in designing attractive bulletin boards. When the children make suggestions, ask them: In what ways is your arrangement interesting? Where did you use texture? In what ways did you consider the shapes of the items selected? Which colors are the most attractive? In what way(s) does the caption attract your attention?

S: Simple and student prepared. The bulletin board should be simple and emphasize one main idea, concept, topic, or theme; the captions should be short and concise.

Suggest that your students prepare a class bulletin board and schedule class meeting time to discuss this with them. Elicit the children's ideas and write them in a list on the board. Refer to the list to engage the children in one or more of the following:

- They can help plan. Why not let them diagram their ideas and share them with each other?
- They can discuss. Is there a more meaningful way to evaluate what they see, to discuss the internal criteria that each student brings to class, or to begin to talk about the different values that each student may have?
- They can arrange materials. Why not let them discover the concepts of balance and symmetry?
- They can construct and contribute. Will they feel they are more actively involved and are really participating if it is *their* bulletin board?

    When the bulletin board is finished, your students can get further involved by (1) reviewing the design of the board during a class meeting; (2) discussing the materials used; and (3) by discussing the information their bulletin board is emphasizing.

Additional class projects may be planned during this meeting. For instance, do the students want a bulletin board group or committee for their class? Do they want a permanent committee, or one in which the membership changes from month to month? Or, do they prefer that existing cooperative learning groups assume bulletin board responsibility, with periodic rotation of that responsibility? Do they want to meet regularly? Can they work quietly and not disturb other students who may still be completing their other learning tasks? Should they prepare the board, or should the committee ask everyone to contribute ideas and items for the weekly or monthly bulletin board? Does the committee want to keep a register, guest book, or guest file of students who contribute to the board? Should there be an honorary list of bulletin board illustrators? Should the authors of selected captions sign their names beneath each caption? Do they want to keep a file binder of all of the different diagrams of proposed bulletin boards? At each class meeting, should they discuss the proposed diagrams with the entire class? Should they ask the class to evaluate which idea would be an appropriate one for a particular study topic? What other records do they want to keep? Should there be a bulletin board medal or a classroom award?

E: Enrichment and extensions of learning. Illustrations on the bulletin board can accent learning topics; verbs can vitalize the captions; phrases can punctuate a student's thoughts; and alliteration can announce anything you wish on the board. The following are examples.

Animals can accent! Pandas, panthers, and parrots can help present punctuation symbols; a giant octopus can show students eight rules to remember, eight things to remember when preparing a book report, or eight activities to complete when academic work is finished early; a student can fish for anything—math facts, correctly spelled words, or the meanings of social studies words; a bear character helps students to "bear down" on errors of any kind; a large pair of shoes helps "stamp out" errors, incomplete work, forgotten school materials, or student misbehavior. Dinosaurs can begin a search for any topic, and pack rats can lead readers into phrases, prose, or poetry.

Verbs can vitalize! Someone or something (your choice) can "swing into" any curriculum area. Some of the verbs used often are *soar, win, buzz, rake, scurry, score, retell,* and *race.*

Phrases point out! Some of the short, concise phrases used as captions may include:

Roll into _____	All aboard for _____	Race into _____
Hop into _____	Peer into _____	Grow up with _____
Bone up on _____	Tune into _____	Monkey with_____
Looking good with _____	Fly high with _____	Get on track with _____

Alliteration announces! Some classroom bulletin boards show Viking Ships or Voyages that guide a student to vocabulary words; Monsters Monitor Math Madness; other boards present Surprises of Spring, Fantasies of Fall, Wonders of Winter, and Safety in Summer; still other boards send messages about Library Lingo, Dictionary Dynamite, and Thesaurus Treats.

The Story Felt Board*

Interacting with figures for a story felt board and retelling stories is an excellent activity for children. This is a language experience that should be encouraged. Specialists in children's literature emphasize that felt boards provide opportunity for children to practice telling stories more easily. Once they have seen their teacher tell a story with felt-board figures, they are eager to do it themselves. In addition to being an attention-getting strategy, another advantage in using a felt board is that the figures can be arranged in sequence and serve as cues for the story. Further, when a storyteller is finished, children can retell the story in their own words. Most children also like to make their own figures and tell their own stories. It is important to carefully select stories that have simple settings, few characters, and fairly uncomplicated plots. Norton emphasizes those stories that lend themselves to felt-board interpretations have only a few major characters and can be told by both adults and children. Norton suggests sharing folktales such as *The Three Billy Goats Gruff* and *The Donkey, the Table, and the Stick.* Traditional and literary folktales that have a sequential accumulation of characters and actions are especially adaptable for flannel-board or felt-board retellings.

The felt board: A felt board is T.O.P.S.   Indeed, a felt (or flannel) board may be considered T.O.P.S. in your classroom, since it has many uses and is a flexible teaching tool. With it, you can present lessons from any subject area or stories of any kind. Sometimes the students can follow your presentation on small, individual felt boards, and at other times they may assist you by manipulating the objects on the board. Consider the letters that spell TOPS:

T for teacher use
O for object variety
P for planning, presenting, and plotting
S for student use.

T: Teacher Use.   For primary students, teachers may use the felt board for (1) presenting stories; (2) presenting rhymes; (3) matching rhyming pictures; (4) presenting objects;

---

*Adapted from Richard D. Kellough and Patricia L. Roberts, *A Resource Guide for Elementary School Teaching: Planning for Competence,* 3d ed. (Englewood Cliffs, NJ: Prentice Hall, 1994), pp. 397–400. Reprinted with the permission of Simon & Schuster, Inc.

(5) listening to beginning sounds, matching them, and classifying object pictures; (6) recognizing colors and color words; (7) selecting pictures showing opposite concepts; (8) arranging objects or pictures in sequence; (9) comparing and contrasting sizes of objects; and (10) creating an individual story with unique combinations of animals, places, and objects.

There are felt cutouts for numerals, for arranging members in sets for math; for words, symbols, and punctuation marks for spelling, labeling, and showing quotations in conversations. Commercial bulletin board sets are easily adapted to the felt board and supply ready-made materials for such topics as traffic control symbols, insects, nutrition, the solar system, prehistoric animals, telling time, and the world of money. Primary students can plan balanced meals by selecting colorful food objects, and the life cycle of a plant or insect can be traced by intermediate-grade students; career choice can be a discussion for older students who may display people, props, and labels.

When considering story presentations, you may want to select one of the following:

Primary students:

Aardema, V. *Borrequita and the Coyote: A Tale from Ayutla, Mexico.* Illustrated by P. Mathers. New York: Knopf, 1991. A crafty little lamb fools a hungry coyote.

Kleven, E. *The Lion and the Little Red Bird.* Illustrated. New York: Dutton, 1992. Two animals don't understand one another's language.

Rounds, G. *Three Little Pigs and the Big Bad Wolf.* Illustrated. New York: Holiday House, 1992. Has capitalized words for reading-aloud activities.

Young, E. *Seven Blind Mice.* Illustrated. New York: Philomel, 1992. Each mouse investigates a strange object until they discover that wisdom is seeing the whole thing.

Grade 4 students:

Perrault, C. *Puss in Boots.* Retold by L. Kirstein. Illustrated by Alan Vaes. New York: Little, Brown. 1992. Alliterative prose for reading aloud.

San Souci, R. D. *Sukey and the Mermaid.* Illustrated by B. Pinkney. New York: Four Winds, 1992. An African-American girl develops a special friendship with a benevolent mermaid.

Yacowitz, C. *The Jade Stone.* Illustrated by Ju-Yong Chen. New York: Holiday House. 1992. A stone carver carves what he hears in a jade stone and creates three carp.

Your options for including the felt board in a particular lesson are quite varied: (1) you can take the total responsibility of presenting and moving the felt-board objects; (2) you can encourage the students to participate and move the objects; (3) you can present the lesson while students follow the story by placing objects from their individual sets on small felt boards at their desks or tables (during a previous activity time, the students would have received ditto copies of characters, cut out the characters, and glued or pasted small bits of flannel or felt to the backs of the characters to prepare their individual sets); (4) you may arrange the students into teams of two, and ask them to tell the lesson or story to one another by moving the board objects; or (5) you may assign one group to a larger board for a group presentation.

O: Object variety. The variety of objects you may use with a felt board is nearly unlimited. How can you prepare this wide collection of felt board objects?

1. *Consider Pellon objects.* With *permanent* coloring pens, draw directly on white Pellon. (Watercolor from pens will come off on your hands either today or at a future date.) Add facial features, clothing details, or other special items. One teacher adds sequins and small glittering stars. Another adds rickrack or gold glitter. Still another adds beads and tiny buttons to a character's costume. Your artwork as well as that of the students shows up quite well when you draw on Pellon. Pellon is often used for interfacing in clothing, so white Pellon is usually available in a fabric store.

2. *Consider felt, flannel, and sandpaper objects.* Objects may be cut directly from these materials, or the materials may be glued to the back of any object. Students enjoy seeing sandpaper letters, bright felt or flannel cutouts of holiday items—orange pumpkins, green pine trees, red valentine hearts, and shamrocks.

3. *Consider objects from published material.* Save catalogs, magazines, inexpensive books, posters, greeting cards, and discarded textbooks. Cut the objects you need from these materials and back the objects with any of the materials that will adhere to the felt board.

4. *Consider objects from commercial felt-board sets.* Visit your nearest teacher's exchange or write to a school supply company for a current catalog. Look for felt-board sets or bulletin board sets that you can adapt.

5. *Consider objects with a Velcro variation.* Some teachers add a border of Velcro across the top of their felt boards so they can place "real" objects on the board as they tell a story or give a presentation. Other teachers place small pieces of Velcro in strategic spots on the felt board, spots to hold a little bear's small chair, for example, or Mama Bear's bowl and spoon. Remember to back your realia with Velcro also.

6. *Consider objects with a magnet.* Some teachers prepare a felt-board slipcover to slide over a large metal board (such as a large cookie sheet or a piece of sheet metal) in order to use magnets. One teacher prepared a scene for the base of a green felt board to represent grass, flowers, rocks, and trees. Behind each gray felt "rock" was a circular cutout, exposing the metal sheet. This enabled the teacher to remove a felt "rock" at an appropriate time and place a small wooden animal, backed with a magnet, on the board to add interest and a three-dimensional quality to the presentation. Multipurpose writing boards, as discussed earlier in this chapter, usually have a metal backing so they can be used as magnet boards much in the same way as just discussed. Instead of felt materials, you can use various colors of thin plastic film, which will stick to the board when smoothed into place.

7. *Consider a looped-cloth variation.* One fabric, commonly known as looped-cloth, is very useful for a slipcover for your felt board. This cloth has loops in the fabric. Put self-adhesive picture-hanging hooks on the back of the heavier objects and hang these into the loops of the poodle-cloth.

P: Planning, presenting, and plotting. Planning, presenting, and plotting are three basics crucial to your felt-board story or lesson. Plan to use familiar objects if possible; present your story or lesson after preparing it thoroughly in a logical, sequential way. Plotting means that you carefully arrange your presentation. You may tell a story with a satisfying ending or share nonfictional information. The information can be facts that portray another point of view or facts about something the students might not have known before. It can be an interesting presentation of the life cycle of an insect, a review of cloud shapes, or a metamorphosis not often illustrated in student texts.

S: Student use. Get your students involved with felt boards. Individual felt boards are quickly and easily made by pasting $8\frac{1}{2}'' \times 11''$ pieces of felt to the outside of large manila mailing envelopes. (Students may place the objects inside the envelopes to keep them secure.) Students can brace the envelopes against a textbook, at their desks. Extra bits and pieces of felt or other materials that adhere to felt can be placed inside the envelope, and additional objects may be made as needed.

What can a student do with an individual felt board?

- Place objects, along with the teacher, as the story or lesson is told; assist the teacher after the lesson by removing the objects in sequence; help to retell the story or summarize the lesson.
- Tell the story to one another in teams of two.
- Place accompanying objects on the board as an audiotape of the story or lesson is heard.
- Create original stories or presentations.
- Create original objects for presentation of information gained from a story or a lesson.

How to avoid problems when using a felt board. *Problem: The cutouts get mixed up.* You may wish to number your cutouts in order of their use in the presentation. Number them on their backs and lay them face down on the table when you are ready to begin. Arrange them in numerical order.

Problem: The cutouts fall off the felt board. Check your board to see whether you need to add another backing of felt. Add more if needed. One teacher uses an old brush to brush up the nap on the back of the cutouts as well as to brush up the nap on the board before each story. Another teacher sprays a light mist of pattern adhesive spray on the felt-board surface before the story. (Pattern spray is available at your nearest fabric store.) Still another teacher periodically replaces the felt on the back of the cutouts. Consider backing your cutouts, not with felt, but with Pellon. If the cutouts fall, prepare to keep your story or lesson moving smoothly by placing a short row of straight pins into the back of your board. When a cutout falls, reach back quickly, select a pin, and again attach the loose character or object. Remember not to crowd your board with too many objects at any one time. Remove objects as your presentation sequence moves along.

Problem: You lose your place in the lesson or story. Rehearse your presentation. If possible, audiotape your presentation in advance, replay the tape, and self-evaluate. How long will the presentation take? Did you practice placing your cutouts on the board? Do you have room for them? Rehearsing with an audiotape will help your presentation flow smoothly as you develop your skill in doing more than one thing at a time. Perhaps you may want to write notes for yourself in large, legible writing and place these notes on the table near the cutouts. One teacher pins large note cards on the back of the board; another prepares a low cardboard screen, about six inches high, to stand in front of the table top. This low screen, cut from three sides of a cardboard box and gaily decorated, conceals the cutouts and the teacher's notes.

Charts, Posters, and Graphs

Charts, posters, and graphs can be used for displays just as bulletin boards are, but as a rule, they are better suited for explaining, illustrating, clarifying, and reinforcing specific points in lessons. Charts, posters, and graphs might also be included in a bulletin board display. The previous guidelines for use of the writing board and bulletin board also apply to the use of charts, posters, and graphs. Clarity, simplicity, and attractiveness are essential considerations. Here are additional suggestions for their preparation and use.

Most students enjoy making charts, posters, and graphs. Involve them in doing so, in finding information, planning how to represent it, and making the chart or poster. Have the author(s) of the chart or poster sign it, and then display it in the classroom. Students should credit their sources on the graphs and charts.

Students may need help in keeping their graphs proportional, and that provides an opportunity to help them develop language arts and thinking skills.

Students can also enjoy designing flip charts, a series of charts or posters (may include graphs) to illustrate certain points or a series of related points. To make a large flip chart, they can use the large pads used by artists for sketching; to make mini-flip charts to use in dyads, they can use small note pads.

D. THE COMMUNITY AS A RESOURCE

One of the richest resources is the local community and the people and places in it. You will want to build your own file of community resources—speakers, sources for free materials, and field trip locations. You may want to check to see if your school already has a community resource file available for your use. Note, however, that it may need updating.

A community resource file should contain information about possible field trip locations (see Figure 6.7), community resource people who could serve as guest speakers or mentors, and local agencies that can provide information and instructional materials.

E. PROJECTED AND RECORDED INSTRUCTIONAL TOOLS

Continuing with our discussion of instructional tools that are available for use in teaching, the focus next is on equipment that depends on electricity to project light and sound and to focus images on screens. Included are projectors of various sorts, computers, CD-ROMs, sound recorders, video recorders, and laser videodisc players. The aim is *not* to teach you how to operate modern equipment but to help you develop a philosophy for using it and to provide strategies for using these instructional tools in your teaching.

FIGURE 6.7
Community Resources for Speakers and Field Trips

Airports	Mail receiving and forwarding
Adobe buildings, workers	Map designers
Advertisers	Marble and granite companies
Aerospace industries	Marinas
Agents of government departments	Marine equipment and supplies
Airmail facilities	Markets
Ambulance service	Martial arts centers
Amphitheaters	Meat cutting services
Apiaries	Metal workers and stampers
Aquariums	Microfilm services
Automobile service stations	Newspapers
Backyards	Orchards
Banks	Parks
Bird and wildlife sanctuaries	Photography studios
Botanical gardens	Planetariums
Buildings under construction	Power plants
Canals and water projects	Publishers
Chemical plants	Quarries
Circus and theme parks	Radio stations
Dairies	Ranches
Earthquake and disaster centers	Real estate offices
Embassies	Recording services
Farms	Recycling centers
Fire departments	Research laboratories
Flower shows	Sanitation departments
Forests and forest preserves	Sawmills
Gardens	Scientific supply companies
Gas companies	Shorelines (streams, lakes, oceans)
Geological sites	Telecommunications centers
Gravel pits	Telephone companies
Greenhouses	Television stations
Health departments and hospitals	Universities and colleges
Highway construction sites	Waste disposal and recycling
Industrial plants	Water reservoir and treatment plants
Machine shops	Wildlife preserves
Machinery rental companies	Weather bureaus
Magicians	Zoos

Media Equipment

Certain teaching tools that rely on sight and sound fall into the category of media known as audiovisual aids. Included in this general category are such teaching tools as charts, models, pictures, graphs, maps, mock-ups, globes, flannel boards, writing boards, and all of the other tools previously discussed. Also included in the general category of audiovisual aids are devices that require electricity for their operation—projectors of various sorts, computers, sound recorders, video recorders, videodisc and compact disc players, and so forth. This section is about the selection and use of tools of this second group, the ones that require electricity to project sight and sound and that focus images onto screens.

These instructional tools are aids to your teaching. It is important to remember that their role is to aid you, not to teach for you. You must still select the objectives, orchestrate the instructional plan, assess the results, and follow up the lessons. If you use audiovisual aids prudently, your teaching and students' learning will benefit.

Uses of Audiovisual Aids

The main effort of any teacher in instruction is to make the learning clear—communicate the idea, capture the content, clarify the obscure for the students. Hence, teachers almost universally rely on the spoken word as their primary medium of communication. Most of the day is filled with explanation and discourse, to the point that the teaching profession has been accused of making words more important rant than reality—perpetuating a culture of verbalism in the schools. Teachers use definitions, recitations, and—perhaps too often—rote memory in the quest of the goals for the day.

The learning experiences ladder. To rely on learning through verbalism is to rely on communication through abstract symbolization. Audiovisual aids can facilitate communication and understanding by adding dimensions to the learning, thus making the learning less abstract. Symbols (in this case, letters and words) may not always communicate what is intended. To better understand this concept, which to this point has been presented entirely in one dimension (by words) let's add a dimension (a visual representation); see the Learning Experiences Ladder of Figure 6.8.

The Learning Experiences Ladder represents the range of learning experiences from most direct (bottom of ladder) to most abstract (top of ladder). When selecting learning experiences, it is important to select activities that are as direct as possible. *When students are involved in direct experiences, they are using more of their sensory input modalities (auditory, visual, tactile, kinesthetic), which leads to the most effective and longest-lasting learning.* As discussed in Chapter 1, this is hands-on/minds-on learning. This is learning at the bottom of the ladder. At the other end are abstract experiences, in which the learner is exposed only to symbolization (that is, words and numbers) using only one or two senses (auditory or visual). The teacher talks, while the students watch and listen. Visual and verbal symbolic experiences, although impossible to avoid when teaching, are less effective in assuring that planned learning occurs. This is especially true with younger children, children with special needs, slower learners, learners with limited proficiency in using the English language, and intellectually immature learners. It is even true for many adult learners.

As seen from the Learning Experiences Ladder, when teaching about tide pools, the most effective mode is to take the students to a tide pool (bottom of the ladder: the most direct experience) where students can see, hear, touch, smell, and perhaps even taste (if not toxic) the tide pool. The least effective mode is for the teacher merely to talk about a tide pool (top of the ladder; the most abstract symbolic experience), which engages only one sense—auditory.

Of course, for various reasons—safety, lack of resources for a field trip, location of your school—you may not be able to take the students to a tide pool. Because you cannot (and should not) always use the most direct experience, at times you must select an experience higher on the ladder, and audiovisual aids can provide the avenue for doing that. Self-discovery teaching is not always appropriate. Sometimes it is better to build on what others have discovered and learned. Although learners do not need to "reinvent the wheel," the most effective learning engages most or all of their senses. On the Learning Experiences Ladder, these are the experiences within the bottom three rungs—the direct, simulated, and vicarious categories. Simulated and vicarious learning experiences, such as can be provided with videos and computers, can be nearly as useful as direct experiences.

Another value of direct, simulated, and vicarious experiences is that they tend to be interdisciplinary, that is, they cross subject boundaries. This makes those experiences especially useful for teachers who want to help students connect the learning of one discipline with that of others and with their own life experiences. Direct, simulated, and vicarious experiences are more like real life.

General Guidelines for Using Audiovisual Aids

Like any other boon to progress, audiovisual aids must be worked with if they are to yield what is expected. A mediocre teacher who is content to get by without expending additional effort will in all likelihood remain just that, a mediocre teacher, despite the excellent quality of whatever aids he or she chances to use. Because mediocre teachers fail to rise to the occasion and hence present instruction poorly, their lessons are less effective and less impressive than they could have been. Effective teachers make the inquiry about available audiovisual aids and expend the effort needed to implement them well for the benefit of the students. Effective teachers will capitalize on the drama made possible by the shift in interaction strategy and enhance the quest for knowledge by using vivid material. Such teaching involves four steps:

1. Selecting the proper audiovisual material
2. Preparing for using the material
3. Guiding the audiovisual activity
4. Following up the audiovisual activity.

FIGURE 6.8
The Learning Experiences Ladder
SOURCE: From Richard D. Kellough, *A Resource Guide for Teaching: K–12* (Englewood Cliffs, NJ: Prentice Hall, 1994), pp. 289–291. For earlier versions of this concept, see Charles F. Hoban, Sr., et al., *Visualizing the Curriculum* (New York: Dryden, 1937), p. 39; Jerome S. Bruner, *Toward a Theory of Instruction* (Cambridge: Harvard University Press, 1966), p. 49; Edgar Dale, *Audio-Visual Methods in Teaching* (New York: Holt, Rinehart & Winston, 1969), p. 108; and Eugene C. Kim and Richard D. Kellough, *A Resource Guide for Secondary School Teaching: Planning for Competence*, 6th ed. (Englewood Cliffs, NJ: Prentice Hall, 1995), p. 136.

Verbal Experiences
Teacher talk, written words; engaging one sense; the most abstract symbolization; students are physically inactive.
Examples
1. Listening to the teacher talk about tide pools.
2. Listening to a student report on the Grand Canyon.

Visual Experiences
Still pictures, diagrams, charts; engaging one sense; typically symbolic; students are physically inactive.
Examples
1. Viewing slides of tide pools.
2. Viewing drawings and photographs of the Grand Canyon.

Vicarious Experiences
Laser video-disc programs, computer programs, video programs; engaging more than one sense; students are indirectly "doing," possibly some limited physical activity.
Examples
1. Interacting with a computer program about wave action and life in tide pools.
2. Viewing and listening to a video program on the Grand Canyon.

Simulated Experiences
Role-playing, experiments, simulations, mock-ups, working models; all or nearly all senses are engaged; activity often integrates disciplines and is closest to the real thing.
Examples
1. Building a working model of a tide pool.
2. Building a working model of the Grand Canyon.

Direct Experiences
Students are actually doing what is being learned; true inquiry; all senses are engaged; activity usually integrates disciplines.
Examples
1. Visiting a tide pool.
2. Visiting the Grand Canyon.

Abstract

Concrete

Selecting the proper audiovisual material. Care must be exercised in selecting an audiovisual aid for use in the classroom. A poor selection of inappropriate material can turn an excellent lesson plan into a disappointing fiasco. An audiovisual aid that projects garbled sound, outdated pictures, or obscure or shaky images will not be met with a delighted response from the students. Material that is too difficult or boring, takes too long to set up, or is not suitable for students in kindergarten through grade 4 will dampen the enthusiasm of students.

In selecting audiovisual materials, you should follow an inquiry routine similar to this:

1. Is the contemplated material suitable? Will it help to achieve the objective of the intended lesson? Will it present an accurate understanding of the facts in the case? Will it highlight the important points? Will it work with the equipment available at the school?
2. Is the material within the level of understanding of the students? Is it too mature? Too embarrassing? Too dated?
3. Is the material lucid in its presentation? Is it clear in its images and sounds?
4. Is the material readily available? Will it be available when needed?

The best response for most of these questions can come after a careful previewing of the material. Sometimes, because of existing conditions, this dry run is not possible. However, the best way to discover how inadequate the catalog descriptions are of films, filmstrips, videotapes, videodiscs, computer software, and compact discs—or the condition in which the product has been left by previous users—is to try them out yourself under practice conditions.

Preparing for using the audiovisual material. Using audiovisual aids with maximum effectiveness usually requires preparation of two types: psychological and physical. From the psychological standpoint, students have to be prepped for use of the material and coached on how best to profit from its presentation. You will need to set the scene, to make clear the purpose of the activity, suggest points to look for, present problems to solve, and in general, clue your students about potential dangers that may mislead them.

From the physical standpoint, preparation pertaining to the machine to be used, the equipment involved, and the arrangement of the classroom furniture will have to be attended to. Sometimes, as with the use of the writing board, preparation is minimal. All that may be necessary may be the identification of the aid, a brief recitation concerning the use you intend to make of it, and a satisfactory supply of chalk and erasers. At other times, however, as when the morning or afternoon sun affects classroom visibility, each section of the classroom will need to be checked, as well as the focusing dials of the apparatus for appropriate sharpness of images and the amplitude dials for clarity of voice sound. Without preparation, bedlam can ensue. The missing chalk, the borrowing and lending of board erasers among the students, or the absence of an extension cord can spell defeat for even the best audiovisual aid. Double-checking the readiness of the equipment to be used is vital to success.

Guiding the audiovisual activity. The purpose of audiovisual materials is not to replace teaching but to make teaching more effective. Therefore, you cannot always expect the tool to do all the work. You should, however, make it work for your purposes. You will have to highlight in advance the usage of those things that you want to be remembered most completely. You may have to enumerate the concepts that are developed or to illustrate relationships or conclusions that you wish to be drawn. You may have to prepare and distribute a study guide or a list of questions for students to respond to, to stop the presentation periodically for hints or questions, or maybe even to repeat the entire performance to ensure a more thorough grasp of particulars. Student learning using audiovisual materials can be enhanced by your coached guidance before, during, and after viewing or use of the materials.

Following up the audiovisual activity. Audiovisual presentations that are allowed to stand alone squander valuable learning opportunities. Some activity or discussion should provide a summary and closure. Such postmortems should have been a vital part of your lesson plan and preparation for the use of the material. Upon completion of the use of the aid, students should be expected to respond to the sets of questions proposed in the preview activity. Points that were fuzzily made should be clarified. Questions that were not answered should be pursued in depth. Responses that go beyond the present scope of the inquiry should be noted and earmarked for further probing at some later date. Quizzes, reviews, practice, and discussions all can be used to tie loose ends together, to highlight the major concepts, to connect and clinch the essential learnings. The planned, efficient use of the aid helps send the message to students that audiovisual presentations are learning opportunities rather than recreational time outs.

When Equipment Malfunctions

When using audiovisual equipment, it is nearly always best to set up the equipment and have it ready to go before children arrive in the classroom. That helps avoid problems in classroom management that can occur when there is a delay because the equipment was not ready. Of course, delays may be unavoidable when equipment breaks down or if a videotape breaks.

Remember the "law" that says if anything can go wrong it will? It is particularly relevant when using equipment discussed in this section. The professional teacher is prepared for such emergencies. Effectively planning for and responding to this eventuality is a part of your system of movement management. That preparation includes consideration of the following.

When equipment malfunctions, three principles should be kept in mind: (1) You want to avoid dead time in the classroom. (2) You want to avoid causing permanent damage to equipment. (3) You want to avoid losing content continuity of a lesson. So, what do you do when equipment breaks down? The answer is, *be prepared*.

If a projector bulb goes out, quickly insert another. That means that you should have an extra bulb on hand. If a tape breaks, you can do a quick temporary splice with cellophane tape. That means that tape should be readily available. And, if you must do a temporary splice, do it on the film or videotape that has already run through the machine, rather than on the end yet to go through, so as not to damage the machine or the film. Then, after class or after school, be sure to notify the person in charge of the tape that a temporary splice was made, so the tape can be permanently repaired before use again.

If a fuse blows, or for some other reason you lose power, or you can see that there is going to be too much dead time before the equipment is working again, that is the time to go to an alternate lesson plan. You have probably heard the expression, "go to Plan B." It is a useful phrase, and what is meant by it is, that, without missing a beat in the lesson, you immediately and smoothly switch to an alternate learning activity. For you, the beginning teacher, it doesn't mean that you must plan *two* lessons for every one, but, when planning a lesson that uses audiovisual equipment, you should plan in your lesson an alternative activity, just in case. Then, you can move your students into the planned alternative activity quickly and smoothly.

F. PROJECTORS

Projection machines today are lighter, more energy efficient, and easier to operate than they were a few years ago; they have been almost "defanged." Among the most common and useful to the classroom teacher are the overhead projector, the slide projector, the filmstrip projector, and, of course, the 16-mm film projector. Because limited space in this book disallows the luxury of presenting the operating procedures for every model of projector that you may come across in classrooms, this presentation is limited to guidelines for their use. Since operations from one projector to the next are quite similar, this should be no major problem for you. At any school there are teachers who will gladly answer questions you may have about a specific projector.

The Overhead Projector

The overhead projector is a versatile, effective, and reliable teaching tool. Except for the bulb burning out, not much else can go wrong with an overhead projector. There is no film to break or program to crash. And, along with a bulletin board and a writing board, nearly every classroom has one.

The overhead projector projects light through objects that are transparent (see Figure 6.9). An overhead projector usually works quite well in a fully lit room. Truly portable overhead projectors are available that can be carried easily from place to place in their compact cases.

Other types of overhead projectors include rear-projection systems that allow the teacher to stand to the side rather than between students and the screen, and overhead video projectors that use video cameras to send images that are projected by television monitors. Some schools use overhead video camera technology that focuses on an object, pages of a book, or a demonstration, while sending a clear image to a video monitor with a screen large enough for an entire class to clearly see.

In some respects, the overhead projector is more practical than the writing board, particularly for a beginning teacher who is nervous. Use of the overhead projector rather than the writing board can help avoid tension by decreasing the need to pace back and forth to the board. And, by using an overhead projector rather than a writing board, you can maintain both eye contact and physical proximity with students, both of which are important for maintaining classroom control.

Consider the following specific guidelines when using the overhead projector:

1. For writing using an overhead projector, ordinary felt-tip pens are not satisfactory. Select a transparency marking pen available at an office supply store. The ink of these pens is water soluble, so keep the palm of your hand from resting on the transparency or you will have ink smudges on your transparency and on your hand. Non-water soluble pens—permanent markers—can be used, but to reuse the transparency it must be cleaned with an alcohol solvent (ditto fluid works, but, for safety, be sure there is proper ventilation) or a plastic eraser. With a cleaning solvent, you can clean and dry with paper toweling or a soft rag. To highlight the writing on a transparency and to organize student learning, use pens in a variety of colors. Transparency pens tend to dry out quickly and are relatively expensive, so the caps must be taken on and off frequently, which can be a nuisance when working with several colors. Practice writing on a transparency and also practice making overlays.

2. You can use an acetate transparency roll or single sheets of flat transparencies. Flat sheets of transparency come in different colors—clear, red, blue, yellow, and green, which can be useful in making overlays.

3. Some teachers prefer to prepare an outline of a lesson in advance, on transparencies, which allows more careful preparation of the transparencies, and they are then ready for reuse at another time. Some teachers prefer to use an opaque material, such as 3″ × 5″ note cards, to block out prewritten material and then uncover it at the moment it is being discussed. For preparation of permanent transparencies, you will probably want to use "permanent marker" pens, rather than those that are water soluble and can be easily smudged. Heavy paper frames are available for permanent transparencies; marginal notes can be written on the frames.

4. Other transparent materials can be shown on an overhead projector, such as transparent rulers, protractors, Petri dishes, and even objects that are opaque if you want to simply show silhouette.

5. Find the best place in your classroom to place the projector. If there is no classroom projection screen, you can hang white paper or a sheet, use a white multipurpose board, or a white or near-white wall.

6. Have you ever attended a presentation by someone using an overhead projector, but who was not using it properly? It can be frustrating to members of an audience when the image is too small, out of focus, partially off the screen, or partially blocked from view by the presenter. To use this teaching tool in a professional manner: Turn on the projector (the switch is probably on the front), place the projector so that the projected white light covers the entire screen and hits the screen at a 90-degree angle, then focus the image to be projected. Face the students while using the projector. The fact that you do not lose eye contact with your students is a major advantage of using the overhead projector rather than a writing board. What you write, as you face your students, will

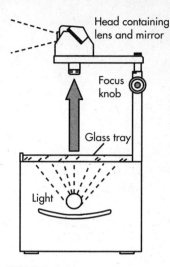

FIGURE 6.9
Overhead Projector, Cutaway View
SOURCE: Eugene C. Kim and Richard D. Kellough *A Resource Guide for Secondary School Teaching: Planning for Competence,* 6th ed. (Englewood Cliffs, NJ: Merrill/Prentice Hall, 1995). Reprinted with the permission of Simon & Schuster, Inc.

show up perfectly (unless out of focus, or off the screen). Rather than using your finger to point to detail, or pointing to the screen (thereby turning away from your students), use a pencil by laying the pencil directly on the transparency with the tip of the pencil pointing to the detail being emphasized.

7. To lessen distraction, you may want to turn the overhead projector off when you want student attention to be shifted back to you or when changing transparencies.

8. Personal computers with laser printers and thermal processing (copy) machines, probably located in the teacher's work room or in the school's main office, can be used to make permanent transparencies.

9. Calculators are available specifically for use on the overhead projector, as is a screen that fits onto the platform and is circuited to computers, so whatever is displayed on the computer monitor is also projected onto the classroom screen.

10. Tracing enlarged versions of transparent charts or drawings onto paper or onto the writing board is easily done with use of the overhead projector. The image projected onto the screen can be made smaller or larger by moving the projector closer or farther away, respectively, and then traced when you have the size you want.

11. An overhead projector or a filmstrip projector can be used as a light source (spotlight) to highlight demonstrations by you or by your students.

12. Commercial transparencies are available from a variety of school supply houses. For sources, check the catalogs available in your school office, or at the audiovisual and resources centers in your school district. See Figure 6.10 for sample sources.

Slides and Filmstrips

Slides and filmstrips are variations of the same medium, and most of what can be said about the use of one is true for the other. In fact, one projector may sometimes serve both functions. Filmstrips are, in effect, a series of slides connected on a roll of film. Slides can be made into filmstrips. Relatively inexpensive technology is now available that allows you to take slides or home movies and convert them into videocassettes. Because of their greater instructional flexibility, their low cost, and greater visual impact, videocassettes have literally replaced films and filmstrips for school use.

For teaching purposes, 35-mm slides are still quite useful and are available from school supply houses and, of course, from your own collection and from students and friends. Some schools have the equipment for making slides from computer programs.

16-mm Films

Because they are less expensive to make and because they offer more instructional flexibility, videocassettes and videodiscs have replaced many 16-mm films. In fact, laser videodiscs may eventually replace traditional textbooks as well. For example, in 1991, the State of Texas became the first state to allow its schools to use state textbook funds to purchase videodisc programs as an alternative to traditional textbooks in science, and in 1992,

FIGURE 6.10
Sources of Overhead Transparencies

BJ's School Supplies, 1807 19th Street, Bakersfield, CA 93301.
Carolina Biological Supply Company, 2700 York Road, Burlington, NC 27215.
Denoyer-Geppert Audiovisuals, 5235 Ravenswood Ave., Chicago, IL 60640.
E.M.E., P.O. Box 2805, Danbury, CT 06813-2805.
Hammond, Inc., 515 Valley Street, Maplewood, NJ 07040.
Lakeshore Curriculum Materials Co., 1144 Montague Ave., San Leandro, CA 94577.
Media Associates, Inc., 7322 Ohms Lane, Minneapolis, MN 55435.
MMI Corporation, 2950 Wyman Parkway, P.O. Box 19907, Baltimore, MD 21211.
Stasiuk Enterprises, 3150 NE 30th Ave., P.O. Box 12484, Portland, OR 97212.
3M Audio Visual, Building 225-3NE, 3M Center, St. Paul, MN 55144.
United Transparencies, P.O. Box 688, Binghamton, NY 13902.
Ward's Natural Social Studies, 5100 West Henrietta Rd., P.O. Box 92912, Rochester, NY 14692-9012.

the State of Utah adopted a multimedia system for teaching English as a second language. Other states will most certainly follow these precedents. Although there are still some effective and new 16-mm films available for instruction, many others are old and sometimes include dated or incorrect information. As with filmstrips, you need to view films carefully and critically before showing them to your class. Many classic films are now available on videocassette or on videodisc.

G. TELEVISION, VIDEOS, AND VIDEODISCS

Everyone knows that television, videos, and videodiscs represent a powerful medium. Their use as teaching aids, however, may present scheduling, curriculum, and physical problems that some elementary schools have not been able to adequately handle.

Television

For purposes of professional discussion, television programming can be divided into three categories: instructional television, educational television, and general commercial television. Instructional television refers to programs specifically designed as classroom instruction; educational television, to programs of cable television and of public broadcasting designed to educate in general, but not aimed at classroom instruction; and general commercial television programs include the entertainment and public service programs of the television networks and local stations.

Watch for announcements for special educational programs in professional journals, such as *Social Studies and Children* and in the monthly issue of *National Geographic* magazine. And, of course, television program listings can be obtained from your local commercial, educational, or cable companies or by writing directly to network stations. Addresses for the major national networks are:

American Broadcasting Company, Inc. (ABC), 1330 Avenue of the Americas, New York, NY 10019.
Columbia Broadcasting System, Inc. (CBS), 51 East 52nd Street, New York, NY 10019.
National Broadcasting Company (NBC), RCA Building, 30 Rockefeller Plaza, New York, NY 10020.

Videos and Videodiscs

Combined with a television monitor, the VCR (videocassette recorder) is one of the most popular and frequently used pieces of audiovisual equipment in today's classroom. In a teacher survey conducted by *Instructor* (Teachers Speak Out on Technology in the Classroom, April 1991), the videocassette recorder was reported to be the most popular technology device used by teachers. Videotaped programs can do nearly everything that 16-mm films can do. In addition, combined with a video camera, the VCR makes it possible to record student activities, practice, projects, demonstrations, and your own teaching. It gives children a marvelous opportunity to self-assess as they see and hear themselves in action.

Entire course packages and supplements are now available on videocassettes or on computer programs. The school where you student teach and where you eventually are employed may have a collection of such programs. Some teachers make their own.

Laser videodiscs and players for classroom use are reasonably priced, with an ever-increasing variety of disc topics for classroom use. There are two formats of laser videodisc: (1) freeze-frame format (CAV—constant angular velocity, or standard play) and (2) non-freeze-frame format (CLV—constant linear velocity, or extended play). Both will play on all laser disc players. Laser videodisc players are quite similar to VCRs and just as easy to operate. The discs are visual archives or visual databases that contain large amounts of information that can be easily retrieved, reorganized, filed, and controlled by the user with the remote control that accompanies the player. Each side of a double-sided disc stores 54,000 separate still-frames of information—whether pictures, printed text, diagrams, films, or any combination of these. Visuals, both still and motion sequences, can be stored and then selected for showing on a television monitor or programmed onto a computer disc for a special presentation. More than 2,000 videodisc titles are now available for educational use. By the time you read these words, there may be more than 3,000 titles. Your school, or district audiovisual or curriculum resource center probably has some titles already; for additional titles, refer to the latest annual edition of *Videodisc Compendium,* published and sold by Emerging Technology Consultants, Inc., 2819 Hamline Avenue North, St. Paul, MN 55113. Phone (612) 639-3973, Fax (612) 639-0110.

Carefully selected programs, tapes, discs, films, and slides enhance student learning. For example, laser videodiscs offer quick and efficient accessibility of thousands of visuals, thus providing an appreciated boost to teachers of students with limited language proficiency. In social studies, with the use of still-frame control, students can visually observe phenomena that previous children only read about.

Resources for Videodisc Titles

Check school supply catalogs for additional titles and sources for videodiscs. Here are addresses to which you can send for information.

Addison-Wesley Publishing Co., 2725 Sand Hill Rd., Menlo Park, CA 94025.
AIMS Media, 9710 De Soto Ave., Chatsworth, CA 91311.
Beacon Films, 1560 Sherman Ave., Ste. 100, Evanston, IL 60201.
Central Scientific Co., 3300 CENCO Pkwy., Franklin Park, IL 60131.
Churchill Media, 12210 Nebraska Avenue, Los Angeles, CA 90025-3600.
CLEARVUE/EAV, Inc., 6465 N. Avondale Ave., Chicago, IL 60631.
Coronet/MTI Film & Video, 108 Wilmot Road, Deerfield, IL 60015.
DEMCO, Inc., 4810 Forest Run Rd., P.O. Box 7488, Madison, WI 53707.
Educational Activities, Inc., P.O. Box 392, Freeport, NY 11520.
Edunetics Corporation, 1600 Wilson Blvd., Ste. 710, Arlington, VA 22209.
Emerging Technology Consultants, Inc., 2819 Hamline Ave., North, St. Paul, MN 55112.
Encyclopaedia Britannica Educational Corp., 310 S. Michigan Ave., 6th floor, Chicago, IL 60604-9839.
Films Incorporated, 5547 N. Ravenswood, Chicago, IL 60640.
Frey Scientific, 905 Hickory Lane., Mansfield, OH 44905.
GPN, P.O. Box 80669, Lincoln, NE 68501.
Hubbard Scientific, Inc., 3101 Iris Ave., Ste. 215, Boulder, CO 80301.
Information Access Company, 362 Lakeside Dr., Foster City, CA 94404.
Instructional Video, P.O. Box 21, Maumee, OH 43537.
Macmillan/McGraw-Hill School Division, 4635 Hilton Corporate Dr., Columbus, OH 43232-4163.
MECC, 6160 Summit Drive North, Minneapolis, MN 55430-4003.
Miramar Productions, 200 Second Ave., W., Seattle, WA 98119-4203.
MMI Corporation, 2950 Wyman Parkway, P.O. Box 19907, Baltimore, MD 21211.
Nasco, P.O. Box 901, Fort Atkinson, WI 53538-0901.
National Geographic Society Education Services Division, 1145 17th St., NW, Washington, DC 20036.
National Social Studies Programs, Inc., P.O. Box 41, W. Wilson St., Batavia, IL 60510.
Nystrom, 3333 N. Elston Ave., Chicago, IL 60618.
Optical Data Corporation, 30 Technology Drive, Warren, NJ 07059.
Optilearn, Inc., Park Ridge Dr., Ste. 200, Stevens Point, WI 54481.
Phoenix Learning Group, 2349 Chaffee Dr., St. Louis, MO 63146.
Prentice Hall School Group, 113 Sylvan Ave., Englewood Cliffs, NJ 07632.
Queue, Inc., 338 Commerce Dr., Fairfield, CT 06430.
Sargent-Welch Scientific Co., P.O. Box 1026, Skokie, IL 60076-8026.
Satellite Data Systems, Inc., P.O. Box 219, Cleveland, MN 56017.
Scholastic Software, 730 Broadway, New York, NY 10003.
Social Studies for Kids, 9950 Concord Church Rd., Lewisville, NC 27023.
Social Studies Kit and Boreal Laboratories, 777 E. Park Dr., Tonawanda, NY 14150.
Tom Snyder Productions, 80 Coolidge Hill Rd., Watertown, MA 02172.

Sunburst/Wings for Learning, 101 Castleton St., Pleasantville, NY 10570-0100.

SVE, 1345 W. Diversey Pkw., Chicago, IL 60614.

Tandy Corp./Radio Shack, 1600 One Tandy Center, Ft. Worth, TX 76102.

Videodiscovery, Inc., 1700 Westlake Ave., N, Suite 600, Seattle, WA 98109-3012.

Ztek Co., P.O. Box 1055, Louisville, KY 40201-1055.

H. COMPUTERS

As a teacher in the twenty-first century, you must understand and be able to use computers as well as you can read and write. To complete your teaching credential, your teacher education program and state teacher licensing commission probably require this at some level of competency, or will soon.

The computer can be valuable to you in several ways:

- The computer can be useful in managing the instruction, by obtaining information, storing and preparing test materials, maintaining attendance and grade records, and preparing programs to aid in the academic development of individual students. This category of uses of the computer is referred to as computer-managed instruction, or CMI.
- The computer can be used for instruction, with the use of various instructional software programs. In their analysis of research studies, Hancock and Betts (1994) report that "in some schools, computer-assisted instruction (CAI) using integrated learning systems (individualized academic tutorials) has shown impressive gains, especially in the early years and among under-achieving urban populations" (p. 25). At Benjamin Banneker Computers Elementary School (Kansas City, MO), where students are expected to spend 50 percent of their daily learning time on a computer (and where, in their classrooms, they have one computer for every two students), their fourth and fifth graders now test out on the Iowa Test of Basic Skills (ITBS) at grades 5.4 and 5.8, respectively. When these same fifth graders entered the program as third graders, many of them were more than a year behind. Today, some of those fifth graders work at a tenth-grade level (Richey, 1994).
- The computer can be used to teach about computers and to help students develop their skills in computer use.
- And, with the help of software programs about thinking, the computer can be used to teach about thinking and to help students develop their thinking skills.

For students, use of the computer is motivating, exciting, and effective as an instructional tool. Consider the following examples.

Computer programs can motivate. For example, one teacher motivated his students to write by sending their writing work to another class electronically. That was the beginning of the *kids2kids Writing Circle,* a national electronic writing project. (For information on necessary equipment, how to participate, and how to register with the network, see Pinney, 1991.)

Computer programs can activate. In Maine, a group of students prepares maps of local land and water resources from computer analyses of satellite images of the coastline, analyzes the maps, and then advises local authorities on development. Mixing technology and environmental awareness, the students have learned that they can exercise some control over their environment and their future (Wolcott, 1991).

Computer programs can excite. Especially exciting to students are computers with telecommunications systems that connect with other students from around the world, providing an exciting format for comparing data, sharing ideas, and encouraging students to challenge each other toward better understandings of global environmental problems. As an example, many classrooms have joined the World School for Adventure Learning, one goal of which is to establish and sustain a global telecommunications network of schools for ongoing, interactive environmental studies. For more information about World School, contact University of St. Thomas World School for Adventure Learning, 2115 Summit Avenue, St. Paul, MN 55105. Similarly, the National Association of Secondary School Principals has joined the Global Learning Corporation to produce World Classroom, a telecommunications network involving K–12 students and teachers in global educational activities. For information, contact NASSP Partnerships International at 800-253-7746.

The Placement and Use of Computers in Schools

Your use of the computer for instruction is determined by your knowledge and skills with its use, the number of computers that you have available, where computers are placed in the school, and the available software. Despite tight budgets, schools continue to purchase computers. Approximately 50 percent of the computers in schools are found in classrooms, and about 40 percent are in computer labs. The days of a computer in every classroom are far from having yet arrived, however (National School Boards Association, 1993). As of the 1992–1993 school year, nearly half of the computers in schools were still mid-1980s Apple IIe machines not capable of running newer educational software (Beckner & Barker, 1994).

Here are some possibilities for computer placement and how classroom teachers work within each.

Situation 1. Many schools have one or more *computer labs* in which a teacher may schedule an entire class or send a small group of students for computer work. In such labs, student computers may be networked to the teacher's computer in the lab so that the teacher can control and monitor each student's work. For a discussion on how to use cooperative learning groups on computers and using the computer to apply social studies skills such as map reading, graph reading, chart interpretation, thinking, and problem solving, see the periodicals *Social Education* and *Social Studies and the Young Learner* and Neal, 1994.

Situation 2. Some classrooms have one computer connected to a large screen video monitor. The teacher or a student works at the computer, and the monitor screen can be seen by the entire class. As they view the screen, children can verbally respond and interact to what is happening on the computer.

Situation 3. In your classroom, you may be fortunate to have one or more computers, a videodisc player, an overhead projector (one that has light projection from the base), and an LCD (liquid crystal display) projection system. Coupled with the overhead projector, the LCD projection system allows you to project onto your large wall screen (and TV monitor at the same time) any image from computer software or a videodisc. With this system, all students can see and verbally interact with the multimedia instruction.

Situation 4. Many classrooms have one or more computers. If this is the case in your classroom, then you will most likely have one or two students working at the computer while others are doing other learning activities (an example of multilevel teaching).

Computers can be an integral part of a learning activity center or an interest center within the classroom, and an important aid in your overall effort to individualize instruction in your classroom.

Learning Activity Centers and Interest Centers

Special techniques for both integrating learning of content and individualizing instruction are learning activity centers and interest centers. Interest centers are broad-based areas for learning organized around some theme and designed to foster the broad goals of the educational program (Seefeldt & Barbour, 1994). An interest center might be, for example, an art center, a language arts center, a social studies center, a computer center, a writing center, or a reading center. An interest center is *an area for learning organized around some theme and designed to foster the broad goals of the curriculum.*

A learning activity center (LAC) is more specific in what it is designed to teach, reinforce, clarify, and extend, in terms of its instructional objectives. The LAC is *a special station located in the classroom where an individual student (or a group of two, if student interaction is necessary) can quietly work and learn at his or her own pace.* All materials needed are provided at the learning center, including clear instructions for operation of the center. The value of learning centers and interest centers as instructional devices lies with at least two characteristics: while working at the center, the student (1) is giving time and quality attention to the learning task; and (2) is likely to be engaging her or his most effective learning modality, or integrating all learning modalities.

The following guidelines for setting up either type of center have been adapted with permission from Kellough and Roberts, 1994, pp. 367–368:

- The educational purpose of the center should be clearly understood by the children.
- A center should be attractive, purposeful, and uncluttered.
- A center should *never* be used for punishment.
- Materials at the center should be available, described, and their use easily understood by the child.
- Materials used in a center should be safe for a child to use alone.
- Specific instructional objectives (for the LAC) and the instructions for use of the center should be clearly posted and understood by the child. An audio- or videocassette is sometimes used for this purpose.
- The center should be easily supervised by you or an adult aide.
- The center should contain a variety of activities geared to the varying abilities and interest levels of the students. A choice of two or more activities at each center is one way to provide for this.
- Topics for the center should be related to the instructional program, as review, reinforcement, remediation, or enrichment.
- When designing a center, consider planning the center's theme in a way that integrates the child's learning by providing activities that cross subject boundaries.

Computer and Multimedia Programs

When selecting software programs you and your colleagues need, of course, choose those that are compatible with your brand of computer(s) and with your instructional objectives. According to a recent study of computers in U.S. schools (National Science Teachers Association, 1994, p. 3), about half are old computers for which software is no longer made and multimedia software and computer networks are not available. As budgets permit, schools will need to replace their old computers.

Like laser videodiscs and compact discs, computer software programs are continually being developed, and other than the sample listing in Table 6.1, are too many and varied to list here. For listings of computer programs for teaching mathematics, refer to the monthly computer software review from the Media Evaluation Center, Department of Public Instruction in Raleigh, North Carolina, in *School Library Journal* (249 West 17th Street, New York, NY 10011).

Selecting Computer Software

When selecting software programs you need, of course, choose those that are compatible with your brand of computer(s) and with your instructional objectives. For evaluating computer

TABLE 6.1

Sample Computer Software Programs

TOPIC	TITLE	COMPUTER*	COMPANY
LANGUAGE ARTS	EasyBook	MAC	Chickadee Software
	Picture a Story	AP II	MECC
	Charlotte's Web	APII	Humanities Software
	My Own Stories	IBM	MECC
SOCIAL STUDIES	The Learn About Collection	MAC	Sunburst
	Project Zoo	AP	National Geographic
	History Makers	APII	MECC
	Time Riders (history)	IBM	The Learning Co.

*Key to computer brand: AP = Apple; IBM = International Business Machines; MAC = Apple Macintosh.

software programs and testing them for their compatibility with your social studies or language arts objectives, there are many forms available. Evaluation forms are usually available from the local school district, the state department of education, and professional associations, such as the National Social Studies Teachers Association.

When reviewing computer software, you should *reject* any software that:

- Gives an audible response to student errors. No child should be forced to advertise mistakes to the whole class.
- Rewards failure. Some programs make it more fun to fail than to succeed.
- Has sound that cannot be controlled. The teacher should be able to easily turn sound on and off.
- Has technical problems. Is the software written so that it will not crash if the user accidentally types the wrong key? Incorrect responses should lead to software-initiated help comments.
- Has uncontrolled screen advance. Advancing to the next page should be under user control, not automatically timed.
- Gives inadequate on-screen instructions. All necessary instructions to run the program must be interactively displayed on the screen (in a continuously displayed instruction window if possible).
- Has factual errors. Information displayed must be accurate in content, spelling, and grammar.
- Contains insults, sarcasm, and derogatory remarks. Students' character should not be compromised.
- Has poor documentation. Demand a teacher's guide that compares in quality to a textbook teacher's guide or other teaching aid.
- Does not come with a backup copy. Publishers should recognize the unique vulnerability of magnetic disks and offer low-cost replacement. (Information from Media Evaluation Center, Department of Public Instruction in Raleigh, North Carolina. See also monthly computer software review in *School Library Journal,* 249 West 17th Street, New York, NY 10011.)

The CD-ROM

Computers have three types of storage disks—the floppy disk, the hard disk, and the CD-ROM, which is an abbreviation for "compact disc—read only memory." Use of a CD-ROM disc requires a CD-ROM drive. Newer computers may have built-in CD-ROM drives, while others and older ones must be connected to one. As with floppy and hard disks, CD-ROMs are used for storing characters in a digital format, while images on a videodisc are stored in an analog format. The CD-ROM is capable of storing approximately 250,000 pages of text, or the equivalent of 1,520 360K floppy disks or eight 70M hard disks, and therefore is ideal for storing large amounts of information such as encyclopedias and other reference books, whereas videodiscs are ideal for storing video stills and motion images. To aid in student research, the magazines with the highest subscriber volume in elementary school libraries are available on a CD-ROM product called *Primary Search* (EBSCO Pub., P.O. Box 2250, Peabody, MA 01960-7250). Additionally, the complete 26-volume printed version of Compton's Encyclopedia is available on CD-ROM. The disk, titled *Compton's Multimedia Encyclopedia,* contains about an hour of music plus animated sequences and *Merriam-Webster's Intermediate Dictionary.* The disk is recommended for ages 6 through adult, requires a Mac LC computer or higher (with 40 MB Hard Disk, a CD-ROM drive, and a 12-inch or larger color monitor), and has a suggested retail price of $795, although it can be purchased for considerably less. For example, in 1993 it was available from MacWarehouse (1720 Oak Street, P.O. Box 3013, Lakewood, NJ 08701-9917) for $595.

As with videodiscs, information stored on a CD-ROM disc cannot be erased or modified. Any information stored on a CD-ROM disk or a videodisc can be found and retrieved within a few seconds. CD-ROMs are available from the distributors of videodiscs. Sample CD-ROM multimedia programs appropriate for fourth-grade students include *"Cell"ebration, Forces & Motion,* and *Simple Machines,* available from Social Studies for Kids, 9950 Concord Church Rd., Lewisville, NC 27023; and *Space Shuttle,* from The Follette Software Company,

809 N. Front St., McHendry, IL 60050. Two publications that focus on CD-ROM products are *CD-ROM Professional*, available at newsstands, and the newsletter *Children's Software Revue*, available for $24 from 520 N. Adams St., Ypsilanti, MI 48197. Phone (313) 480-0040.

Sources of Free and Inexpensive Audiovisual Materials

Check your college or university library for the free and inexpensive audiovisual materials listed in Figure 6.11.

Using Copyrighted Video and Computer Programs

You must be knowledgeable about the laws on the use of copyrighted videos and computer software materials. Although space here prohibits full inclusion of U.S. legal guidelines, your local school district undoubtedly can provide a copy of current district policies to ensure compliance with all copyright laws. As said earlier in the discussion about the use of printed materials that are copyrighted, when preparing to make any copy you must find out whether the copying is permitted by law under the category of "permitted use." If not allowed under "permitted use," then you must get written permission to reproduce the material from the holder of the copyright. Figures 6.12 and 6.13 present guidelines for copying

FIGURE 6.11

Resources for Free and Inexpensive Audiovisual Materials

1. Professional periodicals and journals for teachers.
2. *An Annotated Bibliography of Audiovisual Materials Related to Understanding and Teaching the Culturally Disadvantaged.* Washington, DC: National Education Association.
3. *Catalog of Audiovisual Materials: A Guide to Government Sources* (ED 198 822). Arlington, VA: ERIC Documents Reproduction Service.
4. *Catalog of Free-Loan Educational Films/Video.* St. Petersburg, FL: Modern Talking Picture Service.
5. From Educator's Progress Service, Randolph, WI.
   Educator's Guide to Free Audio and Video Materials
   Educator's Guide to Free Films
   Educator's Guide to Free Filmstrips
   Guide to Free Computer Materials

FIGURE 6.12

Copyright Law for Off-Air Videotaping

SOURCE: From Robert Heinich, Michael Molenda, and James D. Russell, *Instructional Media*, 4th ed. (Englewood Cliffs, NJ: Prentice Hall, 1993), p. 431. Reprinted with the permission of Simon & Schuster, Inc.

Permitted Uses

You may:
1. Request your media center or audiovisual coordinator to record a program for you if you cannot or if you lack the equipment.
2. Keep a videotaped copy of a broadcast (including cable transmission) for 45 calendar days, after which the program must be erased.
3. Use the program in class once during the first 10 school days of the 45 calendar days, and a second time if instruction needs to be reinforced.
4. Have professional staff view the program several times for evaluation purposes during the full 45-day period.
5. Make a few copies to meet legitimate needs, but these copies must be erased when the original videotape is erased.
6. Use only a part of the program if instructional needs warrant (but see the next list).
7. Enter into a licensing agreement with the copyright holder to continue use of the program.

Prohibited Uses

You may *not*:
1. Videotape premium cable services such as HBO without express permission.
2. Alter the original content of the program.
3. Exclude the copyright notice on the program.
4. Videorecord before a request for use—the request to record must come from an instructor.
5. Keep the program, and any copies, after 45 days.

FIGURE 6.13
Copyright Law for Use of Computer Software
SOURCE: From the December, 1980, Congressional amendment to the 1976 Copyright Act.

COMPUTER SOFTWARE

Permitted Uses

You may:
1. Make a single back-up or archival copy of the computer program.
2. Adapt the computer program to another language if the program is unavailable in the target language.
3. Add features to make better use of the computer program.

Prohibited Uses

You may *not*:
1. Make multiple copies.
2. Make replacement copies from an archival or back-up copy.
3. Make copies of copyrighted programs to be sold, leased, loaned, transmitted, or given away.

videotapes and computer software. As of this writing, there are no guidelines for fair use of films, filmstrips, and slides.

I. CALCULATORS

The National Council of Teachers of English (NCTE) recommends that language arts programs at all levels take full advantage of calculators and computers in language arts instruction. The value in the use of calculators in the integration of instruction in social studies and language arts is well documented by numerous research studies (Shaver & Lukins, 1973; Travers, 1973). For example, research has shown a positive relationship between calculator use and higher scores on basic skills tests (Hancock & Betts, 1994). With calculators, students can concentrate on the problem-solving process rather than on the calculations associated with problems. The problem-solving performance of students, particularly girls, improves significantly with ready access to calculators because students are freed to concentrate on higher level aspects of the problem instead of routine calculations. Furthermore, some software programs have calculators built into the software. (See *Let's Go There: Beginning Map and Geography Skills* and *Graph Maker: Introduction to Graphs and Charts,* Troll Associates, 100 Corporate Drive, Mahwah, NJ 07430.) Specific advantages and techniques for using the calculator in instruction are demonstrated in Part II.

SUMMARY

In this chapter, you have reviewed information about the variety of tools available to supplement your instruction. When used widely, these tools will help you to reach more of your students more of the time. As you know, teachers must meet the needs of all of their students—many of whom are linguistically and culturally diverse. The material presented in this chapter should be of help in doing that. The future will undoubtedly bring technological innovations that will be even more helpful—compact discs, computers, and telecommunications equipment mark only the beginning of a teaching revolution. Within the next decade, new instructional delivery systems made possible by microcomputers and multimedia workstations will likely fundamentally alter the role of the classroom teacher.

You should remain alert to developing technologies for your teaching. Laser videodiscs and CD-ROMs interfaced with computers (that is, the use of multimedia) and telecommunications offer exciting technologies for teachers. New instructional technologies are advancing at an increasingly rapid rate. For example, in 1993, the states of California, Florida, and Texas jointly awarded a contract to a software developer and textbook publishing company to cooperate in developing a multimedia history and social science curriculum targeted for LPE students. Called Vital Links, the program will consist of an interrelated series of videodiscs, CD-ROMs, and print materials, and is planned for availability in 1995.

You must maintain vigilance over new developments, constantly looking for those that will not only help make student learning meaningful and interesting, and your teaching effective, but will also be cost effective as well.

QUESTIONS AND ACTIVITIES FOR DISCUSSION

1. Explain how your effective use of the writing board can help students see relationships among verbal concepts or information.

2. In selecting student reading materials, what should you look for?

3. Where could you turn to find out more about instructional materials that might be suitable for use in your teaching?

4. Describe what you should look for when deciding whether material that you have obtained free is suitable for use in teaching children in grades K–4.

5. Describe ways that you could use your school neighborhood and community as a rich resource for learning.

6. From your point of view, what is meant by the following: It has been said that the overhead projector can be one of the teacher's best friends.

7. Describe two ways that the laser videodisc can be used in teaching integrated curriculum.

8. Share with others in your class your knowledge, observations, and feelings about the use of multimedia and telecommunications for teaching. From your discussion, what more would you like to know about the use of multimedia and telecommunications for teaching integrated language arts and social studies? How might you learn more about these things?

9. Describe any prior concepts you held that changed as a result of the experiences of this chapter. Describe the changes.

REFERENCES AND SUGGESTED READINGS

Beardslee, E. C., & Davis, G. L. (1989). *Interactive videodisc and the teaching-learning process.* Fastback 294. Bloomington, IN: Phi Delta Kappa Educational Foundation.

Beckner, W., & Barker, Bruce O. (1994). *Technology in rural education.* Fastback 366. Bloomington, IN: Phi Delta Kappa Educational Foundation.

Bormuth, J. (1968, April). The cloze readability procedure. *Elementary English, 45,* 429–436.

Bruner, J. S. (1966). *Toward a theory of instruction.* Cambridge: Harvard University Press.

Clements, C. H., et al. (1993, January). Young children and computers: Crossroads and directions from research. Research in review. *Young Children, 48*(2), 56–64.

Dale, E. (1969). *Audio-visual methods in teaching.* New York: Holt, Rinehart & Winston.

Dalton, D. W. (1990, Winter). The effects of cooperative learning strategies on achievement and attitudes during interactive video. *Journal of Computer-Based Instruction, 17*(1), 8–16.

Dyer, D. C., et al. (1991, May). Changes in teachers' beliefs and practices in technology-rich classrooms. *Educational Leadership, 48*(8), 45–52.

Fry, E. (1977, December). Fry's readability graph: Clarifications, validity, and extension. *Journal of Reading,* 249.

Griest, G., & Loader, D. (1993, April). Constructivist environments. *Computing Teacher, 20*(7), 8, 10–12, 14–15.

Hancock, V., & Betts, F. (1994, April). From the lagging to the leading edge. *Educational Leadership, 51*(7), 24–29.

Heinich, R., Molenda, M., & Russell, J. D. (1993). *Instructional Media* (4th ed.). New York: Macmillan.

Hoban, C. F., Sr., et al. (1937). *Visualizing the curriculum.* New York: Dryden.

Hunter, M. (1994). *Enhancing teaching.* New York: Macmillan.

Is it okay for schools to copy software? (1991). Washington, DC: Software Publishers Association.

Johnson, L. N., & Tulley, S. (1989). *Interactive television: Progress and potential.* Fastback 289. Bloomington, IN: Phi Delta Kappa Educational Foundation.

Johnson, M. S., & Kress, R. A. (1965). *Informal reading inventories.* Newark, DE: International Reading Association.

Kanning, R. G. (1994, April). What multimedia can do in our classrooms. *Educational Leadership, 51*(7), 40–44.

Kaplan, N., et al. (1992, April). The classroom manager. Hands-on multimedia. *Instructor, 101*(8), 105.

Kellough, R. D., & Roberts, P. L. (1994). *A resource guide for elementary school teaching: Planning for competence* (3rd ed.). New York: Macmillan.

Kemeny, J. G. (1991, Winter). Software for the classroom. *Language Arts and Computer Education, 25*(1), 33–37.

Kernan, M., et al. (1991, September/October). Making and using audiovisuals. *Book Report, 10*(2), 16–17, 19–21, 23, 25–35.

Kim, E. C., & Kellough, R. D. (1995). *A resource guide for secondary school teaching: Planning for competency* (6th ed.). New York: Macmillan.

Malouf, D. B., et al. (1991, Spring). Integrating computer software into effective instruction. *Teaching Exceptional Children, 23*(3), 54–56.

McDermott, C., & Trimble, K. (1993, Fall). Neighborhoods as learning laboratories. *California Catalyst,* 28–34.

McKenna, N. (1976, November). Synonymic versus verbatim scoring of the Cloze Procedure. *Journal of Reading, 20,* 141–143.

Mead, J., et al. (1991, January). Teaching with technology. *Teacher Magazine, 2*(4), 29–57.

Muir, M. (1994, April). Putting computer projects at the heart of the curriculum. *Educational Leadership, 51*(7), 30–32.

Murray, K. T. (1994, March). Copyright and the educator. *Phi Delta Kappan, 75*(7), 552–555.

National School Boards Association. (1993, December). Education vital signs, *The American School Board Journal, 180*(12), A22.

Neal, J. S. (1994, January). The interpersonal computer. *Social Studies Scope, 17*(4), 24–27.

Norton, D. E. (1991). *Through the eyes of a child.* Englewood Cliffs, NJ: Merrill/Prentice Hall.

Oaks, M., & Pedras, M. J. (1992, February). Technology education: A catalyst for curriculum integration. *Technology Teacher, 51*(5), 11–14.

O'Neil, J. (1993, October). Using technology to support authentic learning. *ASCD Update, 35*(8), 1, 4–5.

Pattillo, J., & Vaughan, E. (1992). *Learning centers for child-centered classrooms.* NEA Early Childhood Education Series. Washington, DC: National Education Association.

Pinney, S. (1991, April). Long distance writing. *Instructor, 100*(8), 69–70.

Rakow, S. J., & Brandhorst, T. R. (1989). *Using microcomputers for teaching social studies.* Fastback 297. Bloomington, IN: Phi Delta Kappa Educational Foundation.

Richey, E. (1994, April). Urban success stories. *Educational Leadership, 51*(7), 55–57.

Rock, H. M., & Cummings, A. (1994, April). Can videodiscs improve student outcomes? *Educational Leadership, 51*(7), 46–50.

Seefeldt, C., & Barbour, N. (1994). *Early childhood education* (3d ed.). Englewood Cliffs, NJ: Merrill/Prentice Hall.

Shaver, J. P., & Lukins, A. G. (1973). Research on teaching social studies. In *Handbook on teaching* (pp. 1243–1262). Chicago: American Educational Research Association.

Snider, R. C. (1992, November). The machine in the classroom. *Phi Delta Kappan, 74*(4), 316–323.

Talab, R. S. (1989). *Copyright and instructional technologies: A guide to fair use and permissions* (2d ed.). Washington, DC: Association for Educational Communications and Technology.

Taylor, L., & Thompson, V. (1992, January). Teaching language arts with technology. How to win people and influence friends: Calculators in the primary grades. *Arithmetic Teacher, 39*(5), 42–44.

Tomecek, S. M. (1993, February). Make contact with a new medium. *Social Studies and Children, 30*(5), 47–48.

Travers, R. M. W. (1973). Educational technology and related research viewed as a political force. In *Handbook of research on teaching* (pp. 979–996). Chicago: American Educational Research Association.

Wishnietsky, D. H. (1993). *Using computer technology to create a global classroom.* Fastback 356. Bloomington, IN: Phi Delta Kappa Educational Foundation.

Wolcott, L. (1991, March). The new cartographers. In Maine, students are helping map the future. *Teacher Magazine, 2*(6), 30–31.

Woody, III, R. H., & Woody, II, R. H. (1994). *Music copyright law in education.* Fastback 368. Bloomington, IN: Phi Delta Kappa Educational Foundation.

PART

II

Methods and Activities for Teaching Language Arts

To many educators, it is clear that to be most effective in teaching children of diverse backgrounds in today's classrooms, the learning in each discipline must be integrated with the learning in other disciplines to be made more meaningful to the lives of the children.

For higher levels of thinking and for learning that is most meaningful, recent research supports the use of an integrated curriculum and instructional techniques for social interaction. As a classroom teacher, your instructional task is two-fold: (1) to plan for and provide developmentally appropriate hands-on experiences, with useful materials and the supportive environment necessary for children's meaningful exploration and discovery; and (2) to know how to facilitate the most meaningful and longest lasting learning possible once the child's mind has been activated by the hands-on experience. In Parts II through IV, we present techniques designed to help you complete those tasks, beginning with the integration of language arts.

Content presented in Chapters 7 through 12 are consistent with the approach recommended by the National Association for the Education of Young Children (NAEYC) in its 1987 publication, *Developmentally Appropriate Practice in Early Childhood Programs Serving Children from Birth through Age 8* and its 1991 publication, *Early Childhood Teacher Education Guidelines: Basic and Advanced.* The contents also relate to the guidelines for a language arts program published by the National Council of Teachers of English in *Guidelines to Evaluate the English Component in the Elementary School Program* (1976). The guidelines focus on individual and group differences, principles of language learning, and objectives and evaluation. Related to the guidelines, Chapter 7 focuses your attention on language arts learning, techniques, and some selected resources for kindergarten through grade four. Addressing a recommended approach relevant to the grades K–4 language arts curriculum are the topics of Chapters 8 through 12. In those chapters, you will find strategies and resources for using computers related to language arts and social studies content, topical lists of children's books, techniques for accommodating learners with special needs, and a discussion of useful assessment strategies. The publications cited earlier recommend broad language arts goals that center on increasing children's skills in listening, speaking, reading, and writing. These goals lend themselves to the teaching of social studies content discussed in later chapters. For grades K–4, these four goals are described as

Goal 1: Listening

In grades K–4, children will develop the ability to listen so they can make sense of their environment and be able to vary their listening strategies—marginal, appreciative, attentive, and analytical—appropriately (National Council of Teachers of English, 1954). When children listen while doing other tasks, they are marginally hearing what is happening around them or what is being said. Children who listen for pleasure or entertainment will develop their appreciation for sounds—sounds of language and sounds around them in their world. Additionally, children can listen

CHAPTER 7
Early Language Arts Learning
The introduction to Part II and this chapter are adapted from Carol Seefeldt & Nina Barbour, Early Childhood Education: An Introduction, 3rd ed. (Englewood Cliffs, NJ: Merrill/Prentice Hall), pp. 333–371. By permission of Carol Seefeldt, Nina Barbour, and Prentice Hall.

CHAPTER 8
Listening
Adapted from Gail Tompkins & Kenneth Hoskisson, Language Arts: Content and Teaching Strategies, 3rd ed. (Englewood Cliffs, NJ: Merrill/Prentice Hall, 1995). By permission of the authors and Prentice Hall.

CHAPTER 9
Speaking: Talk in the Classroom
Adapted from Gail Tompkins & Kenneth Hoskisson, Language Arts: Content and Teaching Strategies, 3rd ed. (Englewood Cliffs, NJ: Merrill/Prentice Hall, 1995). By permission of the authors and Prentice Hall.

CHAPTER 10
The Writing Process
Adapted from Gail Tompkins & Kenneth Hoskisson, Language Arts: Content and Teaching Strategies, 3rd ed. (Englewood Cliffs, NJ: Merrill/Prentice Hall, 1995). By permission of the authors and Prentice Hall.

CHAPTER 11
The Writer's Tools:
Spelling, Handwriting,
Grammar, Punctuation,
and Capitalization
*Adapted from Gail Tompkins
& Kenneth Hoskisson,
Language Arts: Content and
Teaching Strategies, 3rd ed.
(Englewood Cliffs, NJ:
Merrill/Prentice Hall, 1995).
By permission of the authors
and Prentice Hall.*

CHAPTER 12
Reading and Connections
With Writing
*Adapted from Richard D.
Kellough & Patricia L.
Roberts, A Resource Guide
for Elementary School
Teaching: Planning for
Competence, 3rd ed.
(Englewood Cliffs, NJ:
Merrill/Prentice Hall, 1994,
pp. 436–440; and from Gail
Tompkins & Kenneth
Hoskisson, Language Arts:
Content and Teaching
Strategies, 3rd ed.
(Englewood Cliffs, NJ:
Merrill/Prentice Hall, 1995).
By permission of the authors
and Prentice Hall.*

attentively—carefully—to get information or listen analytically to figure out what is being said or what is going on that will affect them and their responses.

Goal 2: Speaking

In grades K–4, children can develop the ability to speak clearly and distinctly so they can be understood at home, school, and in their world around them. In these situations, children will want to tell others what they need; they will want to tell stories that they hear from family members and school personnel, recite poems, and talk about characters in a puppet show or on television. They can learn ways to speak that are linked to the speaking situation; for example, family members and friends will talk informally with them, and the children can use informal speech in return. School personnel will use more formal speech with them, and children can learn what is needed to respond—to take the role of a character in a story or dramatic play situation or to present what is needed to give a summary, a report, or a book review.

Goal 3: Writing

In grades K–4, children can develop the ability to write to express themselves for their own amusement, for pleasure, to share information, and to show their appreciation. Young children can begin with marks, scribbles, letters, phonetic spellings of words, letters that spell their own names—and go on to discover different purposes for writing as well as the writing styles that reinforce each of the purposes.

Goal 4: Reading

In grades K–4, children can develop the ability to read a variety of materials for enjoyment and pleasure and to get the information they need, to locate topics, and to follow directions. Linked to writing, children learn that their scribbles on paper relate to reading, begin to recognize letters and words, and become cognizant of the relationships of letters to sounds and letters to words. When they learn strategies for figuring out parts of the reading material, they realize they are reading. As they develop their reading skills, they will learn that there are different types of texts to read and that there are different reasons for reading.

As the previously mentioned recommendations, guidelines, and goals indicate, children use a variety of methods to communicate with one another. Verbal and written language forms are their most effective tools of communication. By developing these skills, children gain a deeper understanding of the complexity of their world. Language provides them with the means of understanding their role and significance in society. It becomes the major vehicle for expressing their needs and wants, for giving and getting information, and for expressing feelings and understanding how others feel. The following chapters in this part enable you to focus on the importance of early language arts learning as you see how children of all cultures gradually acquire communications skills. ■

CHAPTER 7

Early Language Arts Learning

In this chapter, you will focus on the goals of language arts for young children and how to provide them with learning opportunities and integrate language arts into the curriculum. Specifically, this chapter is designed to help you in

1. Identifying the elements of language that children have.
2. Describing the explanations of different theorists about how children learn language.
3. Understanding the developmental factors that affect children's progress in the early grades in reading and writing.
4. Developing speaking and listening activities that you would implement in grades K–4.
5. Developing writing activities that promote literacy skills for children in grades K–4.
6. Being aware of some of the opposing views of how to teach children to read (Seefeldt & Barbour, 1994, p. 333).

A. BASIC LEVELS OF LANGUAGE LEARNING

With little or no formal teaching, children of all cultures gradually acquire the means of communicating with significant others in their environment. Infants' differentiated crying, cooing, and verbal play, together with responses from linguistically competent others, are the beginnings of an interactive process in which children learn the five basic levels of language learning: *phonology* (sound system); *morphology* (rules regarding words); *syntax* (grammatical structure); *semantics* (meaning of words); and *pragmatics* (appropriate usage). By age 5, children, unless they are suffering from physical or emotional impairments, have learned to use the rules of their language environment effectively. Whether they speak the dominant language of the school that they enter or a dialect or another language, they have acquired the basic skills of language acquisition on which to build further literacy skills.

Phonology (Sound System)

During the babbling stage, infants have the capacity to produce a wide range of sounds. The sounds babies produce gradually become closer to the sounds they hear in the adult language environment. As infants begin to put sounds together to make meaning, as in *mama, mik* (milk), or *baw* (ball), they are beginning to develop mastery over the phonetic system of their language.

By 5 years of age, many children have mastered most of the sounds of their language, although some children of 7 or 8 years of age are still struggling with the *r* or *l* sounds in clusters and say *pwease* for *please* or *cwy* for *cry* (Tompkins & Hoskisson, 1995, p. 21).

Morphology (Rules Governing Words)

As children begin to realize that combinations of sounds have meaning, they begin to learn new words. By 18 months, children may have a vocabulary of 20 to 50 words, and by age 4, they frequently are able to produce over 2,000 words. Even before entering school, children are beginning to understand morphemic rules. They can correctly make words plural and use the past tense of verbs. When children begin to over-generalize and say *sockez* for the plural of *socks* or *wented* instead of *went*, it is evident that they have become aware of a rule and are not thinking of words that are plural or in the past tense as new and different. Although many of the rules for changing words are learned early, some are not acquired until 6 to 10 years of age (Wood, 1976, p. 124).

Syntax (Grammatical Structure)

Children begin learning the *syntax*, or the grammar, of the language as soon as they begin to join words into sentences. They understand grammatical structure as soon as they understand multiple-word sentences. One toddler correctly brought his father's slippers when told to "go get Daddy's slippers." Another found her milk bottle in her crib when asked, "Where's your bottle?" The development of syntax proceeds through specific stages (Braine, 1963). As early as 12 to 18 months of age, children use words in different grammatical functions. For example, they may say *mama* with different intonations meaning, "Here is Mama," "This is Mama's hat," or "The dog hurt Mama" (Bloom, 1976). At 18 months, children speak in two-word sentences, and by 2 to 3 years of age, children can correctly use multiple words in different types of sentences: declarative ("Daddy's home"), negative ("Daddy's not there"), interrogative ("Where is Daddy?"), and imperative ("Don't do that, Daddy!") (Menyuk, 1971, p. 103).

By ages 5 to 7, children are mastering the correct use of pronouns, nouns and their modifiers (for example, this child, these children), and verb tenses. They use adverbial phrases, prepositional phrases, and conjunctions in correct sequence and form (Menyuk, 1969, p. 30). While this development seems impressive, complex structures of language may not be mastered until children are 10 years of age (Kessel, 1970). Chomsky (1969) discovered that children still have trouble using and responding correctly to grammatical structure when terms like *promise, ask,* and *easy to see* are used.

Semantics (Meaning of Words)

While children learn the sounds and patterns of their language, they must also learn that words convey meaning depending on the context in which they are used. Semantic development is a long and complicated process, and it relates closely to the Piagetian stages of intellectual development (See Chapter 1). Wood describes the four stages of semantic development as: sentence dictionary, word dictionary-abridged, word dictionary-unabridged, and semantic dictionary (Wood, 1976).

At the sensorimotor stage, children at first use single words as if they were entire sentences. They form a sentence dictionary in which "meanings [are] tied to functions that words perform" (Wood, 1976, p. 150). For example, Chan, a young toddler, ran around the house looking for his daddy. He first said "Daddy?" meaning "Where is Daddy?" Then, looking in the bathroom and shaking his head, he said, "Daddy," meaning "Daddy's not in the shower"; finally, he went to the back door, opened it, and with hands on hips, yelled "Daddy!" meaning "Daddy, come here!"

Between ages 2 and 7, during the preoperational stage, children are forming "word dictionaries-abridged." Children are separating the words from the sentence and are attaching meanings to the words; the meanings are tied to concrete actions. A house, for one 5-year-old, was "where Mommy, Daddy, my cat, and me live," and an apartment was "where Grandma lives with Pukey" (the canary). During this stage, children become aware that language is ambiguous in that terms may convey more than one meaning. They can deal with this ambiguity on the concrete level but not yet on the abstract. They can understand that a cold person could mean something other than that the person felt cold to the touch (Schickedanz, York, Stewart, & White, 1983).

From ages 7 to 11, children are at a concrete operational stage of thinking and are expanding their ability to discern meaning. Children are still tied to direct experiences and processes, but they are developing "word dictionaries-unabridged." A child at this stage understands the function of a house and may give it a definition as a place where you sleep, eat, and have your friends visit.

Pragmatics (Appropriate Usage)

Pragmatics is the ability to adapt one's speech patterns and word usage to differing social contexts (Bernstein, 1970; Sapir, 1929; Whorf, 1956). Children learn the rules of conversation from the communities in which they live (Heath, 1983; Labov, 1970; Tizard & Hughes, 1984; Vygotsky, 1962), but the specific rules of conversation and the way these rules are taught vary in different social and cultural milieus (Snow, 1989). The schools most children enter use the syntactic rules of Standard American English and the politeness rules of middle-class society.

Appropriate usage not only means that children must learn different word or grammatical usage but also that they must learn to whom they can speak, how they are to respond, under what circumstances they can speak and in what tone of voice, and which movements are appropriate (Ferrara, 1982). Learning the social conventions for proper usage starts early. Toddlers learn that certain intonation patterns, gestures, body movements, and persons involved in the conversation may signify different things even though the grammatical pattern may be the same. For example, when Josh wanted to be picked up, he raised his arms and demanded of his mother, "Mommy, up," placing an emphasis on the word *up*. But earlier in the day, wanting to know if his mother was out of bed yet, he had asked, "Mommy up?" with his head cocked slightly as if listening and using a rising inflection after the word *up*.

By age 4, children demonstrate amazing skill in using the proper conventions. Jalongo (1992) describes a group of children who changed roles frequently while at play. First one child was the teacher with an authoritative voice: "OK, children, . . . no gum chewing in school." Then she became the child in a submissive role: "Teacher, I have to go home now." Finally, she was a peer with equal status: "Let's pretend they are talking to each other." Body movement and tonal expressions rather accurately portrayed the "person" she was at any given moment in the play. The children in this brief play episode switched in and out of roles, at times in the same sentence.

Even fairly young children, as they move from one milieu to another, begin to learn that there are "proper" ways to say things depending on where they find themselves. One 5-year-old announced to her friend who had just said, "I ain't goin' to the circus," "You aren't 'spose to say 'ain't' at school. You say, I'm going, I'm goin', I am goin'."

The rules for social behavior can vary from one culture to another. Young children who have not had experiences changing milieus may have difficulty at first adjusting to the social rules of the school. In one classroom with children of many different ages, older children helped the teacher to communicate with new children not familiar with the school language and culture. Ms. D, the teacher, wasn't successful in getting Philip, a 5-year-old just entering school, to join the other children in a circle. She first used a polite invitation to call all the children. When Philip didn't move, she said a more stern and specific command to Philip. Then, Greg, a seasoned 8-year-old, raised his hand and asked quietly, "Do you want me to get him for you?" Upon receiving a polite "Yes, thank you, Greg," he yelled to Philip, "Boy, get yo'r butt over here, yu' hear!" When Philip came immediately to sit beside Greg, Greg bent to him and continued, "When she say 'Boys and girls join me in the circle,' she mean come here. And when she say, *Philip*, it's time for circle! she mean get yo'r butt *here* (pats a spot beside himself) NOW!" Greg had learned not only the correct language patterns of the school but also the politeness rules. He first raised his hand and then asked permission to call Philip. Given permission, he used language and tonal patterns familiar to Philip. Greg was even skillful at switching between the two patterns to explain to Philip what the teacher's words meant.

Children like Philip and Greg can adapt and learn new speech patterns and word usage, but when the school-language expectations are too different from the child's language learning patterns, respect for that child's language needs to be accompanied with help in learning new sets of rules for different contexts. Greg has learned to code-switch, or use two language patterns in appropriate ways and at appropriate times. In the supportive environment of Ms. D's classroom, he helps others to adapt to the language and culture patterns of the school.

In most schools today, there are children from a variety of linguistic and cultural backgrounds whose phonology, syntax, semantics, and pragmatics are different from those of Standard American English, but who have indeed mastered the language rules of their own communities. It is important in schools that children's home language be respected while they hear and gradually learn Standard English.

Language learning is an ongoing process. The oral aspect and rule formation of the phonology, morphology, syntax, semantics, and pragmatics are learned early as children interact with significant adults in their environment. Some refinements and changes may take place as they progress in school, but new learning and refinements will be built on the basic language structures that children have learned much earlier in their own community of speakers.

B. HOW CHILDREN LEARN LANGUAGE

A great deal of research in language acquisition, from various fields of inquiry, has been conducted over the century. The richness of this research is apparent from the amount of knowledge available about when children acquire particular language skills. However, there still is debate about how language is acquired (Ingraham, 1989). Researchers from such various fields as education, psychology, ethnography, sociology, and linguistics have advanced different explanations.

No single theory explains the complicated process of language development. Many theorists have contributed to our overall understanding. Knowledge of the many different points of view can help as you interact with children and design a program to foster language growth.

The Nativist View

The *nativist,* or maturational, view is that children are "prewired" for language and that language is a process of normal maturation. Chomsky (1965), Lenneberg (1967), and McNeill (1966) are strong proponents of this theory.

Lenneberg (1967) maintains that language development is biologically determined and that its onset is regular and consistent with all children in all cultures. Chomsky (1965) explains children's ability to produce and understand novel sentences as an innate capacity. Children do not just repeat expressions they've learned, but they also test the rules they've formulated about their language. Children refine and generate a wide range of expressions from the particular sentences or expressions they hear.

McNeill (1966) believes children instinctively understand that there are basic structures or kernel sentences from which all other sentence types are generated. Through early hypothesizing and trial and error, children formulate the rules for transforming the basic structures into all sentence types.

The Behaviorist View

Behavioral theorists believe that significant others in children's lives model language behavior and reinforce children's responses through various reinforcing strategies until the responses resemble the model. According to Skinner (1957), language is a collection of verbal operants acquired through stimulus-response-reward conditioning and emitted as a function of various sorts of stimuli (See also Chapters 1 and 3).

Habituated to the use of language, children recognize its use as a means of gaining control over their environment and of receiving constant reinforcement (Mowrer, 1960). The child's novel language behavior is "as though he had learned the rules" as a result of this generalized imitative repertoire (Peterson, 1971). Parents and teachers continually reinforce children by using language to control the environment, so children continue to become habituated to the language and learn its more complex structures (Staats, 1971).

The Interactionist/Constructivist View

In recent years, greater emphasis has been placed on an interactionist/constructivist view, stressing the social context of language development. The interactionist/constructivists acknowledge that certain functions of language are genetically determined, but maturational changes occur as children learn how to use language appropriately within their culture. Language and reasoning skills develop as children interact and respond to the language that is part of their environment. This interaction enables them to formulate rules for communicating in that environment. Vygotsky's (1962) and Piaget's (1955) views of language development reflect this theory. Both see language and thought as related developments that occur during different stages of development: sensorimotor, preoperational, concrete operations, and formal operations. (See Chapters 1 and 3.)

As discussed in Chapter 1, Piaget (1955) maintains that language develops along with the child's capacity for logical thought, judgment, and reasoning, and that language reflects these capacities. He notes that children have certain biological capacities for language learning, but as these internal structures grow and develop, children must interact with their environment and absorb these elements into their internal structure before the next stage takes place. Children need a language-rich environment to be able to construct the phonetic, morphemic, syntactic, and semantic rules of language. They also need to practice language in a variety of ways and for a variety of purposes.

According to Vygotsky (1962), children develop external speech, apart from thought, during the sensorimotor stage. Speech may accompany action, but it is not connected to an understanding of speech as communication. During the preoperational stage, this egocentric speech becomes inner speech, a sort of unconnected talk that one hears in one's head. At the same time, children become conscious that, through speech, they can communicate ideas and concepts. Vygotsky maintains that human consciousness develops through words. This awareness becomes apparent in children's language development as they become interested in learning the names of things and constantly ask to be informed.

Vygotsky places great emphasis on the adult role in this language development. He maintains that children develop their understanding of the rules and function of language from the adults who use that language in consistent and stable ways. In the beginning, children have vague notions of the meanings of adults' overt language even before they can say the words. These vague concepts or ideas come closer to adult meanings in a series of more complex ways (not unlike Piaget's stages) as the child interacts with the adult. During these stages, adults supply more context for concepts as children build and refine their own meaning. Although the children construct meaning, the adults determine the direction of their thinking process. "Verbal intercourse with adults becomes a powerful factor in the development of the child's concept" (Vygotsky, 1962, p. 69).

In the last two decades, ethnographic research on children's developing literacy (both oral and written) has added to our understanding of the sociocultural effect on language development. Some of the research has emphasized how the adult language environment can affect the more complex development of children's language and thus children's capacity for thought (Tizard, 1981).

Other researchers point out that children learn not only the structure of the language in a particular culture, but as they interact with parents and important people from their community, they also learn modes of communication and values related to differing literacy events (Heath, 1983; Teale, 1986). Different parental language styles, interactions, and values attached to reading and writing also affect children's literacy development (Bernstein, 1970; Elardo, Bradley, & Caldwell, 1977; Honig, 1982; Teale, 1986). Parental styles that include such characteristics as reading to children, mealtime conversations, role playing in pretend games, expanding children's language, engaging children in several verbal interchanges, responding to children's questions about reading and writing, and encouraging children's attempts at "pretend" writing and reading are related to children's more extensive use of oral and written language and problem-solving ability (Adams, 1990; Clay, 1991).

In addition, much research focuses on the interrelatedness of oral and written language development and on the importance of the social milieu—not only at home and in the community but also at school—in fostering that development (Hepler, 1991; Kantor, Miller, & Fernie, 1992).

C. PROVIDING LEARNING OPPORTUNITIES

Even though children seem to learn language as naturally as they grow, the adults around them can foster this growth. Specific experiences within a language-rich environment can be planned to foster language growth.

Infants

Babies hear and respond to sounds in their environment, but all communication with infants isn't verbal. A great deal of language play goes on as infants are picked up, stroked, and receive eye-to-eye and cheek-to-cheek contact. Babies in turn touch, stroke, and pull at you as you interact nonverbally or talk with them.

When you bathe, feed, change, or dress infants, talk with them about what you are doing and call them by name. If they coo or babble, imitate these sounds. Babies will then imitate the sounds you make. Vary the sound slightly to see if the baby will imitate the new sound. Hum, sing, and recite nursery rhymes when you're around the baby.

Speech with an infant should be natural for you. Nevertheless, this speech will be altered somewhat by the use of shorter sentences and by speaking somewhat slower and using simpler terms. Low and Moely (1988) have found that children whose mothers changed the complexity of their speech, yet used adult labels and not baby talk, developed vocabulary earlier than other children.

Even though you're not speaking baby talk to infants, altering speech may be necessary. "It may be that children cannot learn to talk without [this]" (Schachter & Stage, 1982, p. 70). As you feed the infant, talk about the food: "Oh, peas for lunch. . . ." "Open wide your little mouth, and *do* put it in." As you dress a baby, name and label the infant's actions and yours. "The head goes in first. Peek-a-boo!" "I can find your arm and then your other arm. Two arms."

Although the human voice is most important to the infant, babies also learn about their environment from other sounds they hear. As a baby stays awake longer, you can take the child to different rooms, outdoors, and even on trips. When the baby starts to become aware of the sounds from the environment, you can reinforce them. For example, an infant may turn toward the ticking clock, and you can remark, "The clock makes a pretty sound—tick, tock." The infant may be startled if someone bangs the door. You may need to comfort the child by saying, "That was an awful bang." The sound of your voice is soothing and reassuring, and at the same time you have imitated the sounds the child hears in the environment.

Infants can also be introduced to literature. Their experiences with literature are out of the oral tradition. What baby doesn't delight in "This is the Way the Lady Rides," while being jounced on someone's knee, or doesn't giggle while being swung up high to the tune of "Dickery Dickery Dare"? The rhythmic flow of the English nursery rhyme "Rock-a-Bye Baby" or the Puerto Rican nursery rhyme *"Que linda manito"* (What a pretty hand) (Delacre, 1989) is soothing and calming and introduces children to the sounds and patterns of their language.

Infants are not too young to be exposed to books. You can hold the baby in your lap and point to the pictures in a book. A 9- or 10-month-old may be able to point to the picture when you ask, "Where's the ball?" or "Where's the mommy?" If babies are exposed to books and pictures, by the time they are a year old they may be interested in turning the pages of the book themselves, even jabbering away in imitation of your reading.

There are excellent books made of sturdy cardboard with thick pages for the very young child. These usually portray everyday objects simply drawn and are very colorful. Examples are Tana Hoban's *What's That?* and a series of books by such authors as Dick Bruna, Helen Oxenburg, Jan Ormerod, and Rosemary Wells. Children enjoy looking at these books, patting them, and having an adult share the experiences with them.

Toddlers

Toddlers' curiosity about the world is boundless. To know about things is to name them, and children of this age demand words and labels for everything. Through this labeling, children are crystallizing their vague impressions of objects into firmer concepts (Cassirer,

1984; Taylor & Gelman, 1988). As toddlers' worlds expand, their vocabulary will increase rapidly. In an early childhood program, these children need many opportunities to solidify their concepts by engaging in listening, speaking, prereading, and prewriting activities with a concerned adult.

Speaking. Adult-child interactions include an adult who expands and elaborates on the language of the toddler and encourages speaking. Reinforcing the toddler's language and providing language models can extend vocabulary. When the toddler remarks, "Mommy gone," you might respond "Yes, mommy has gone, but she'll be back after your nap." Your reply extends the sentence the child has given. If the child notices the bunny in the classroom and says, "Bunny eat," you might respond, "Yes, the bunny is eating carrots. Do you eat carrots too?"

Children don't need to be with a constantly talking adult, but they do need interested people to notice what they are doing and to comment on it. You could comment on a picture a child has painted: "You used a lot of red paint," or "Let's see how many blocks you have on your tower," or "Your new shoes are the same color as mine."

Listening. As toddlers move about the environment, they can be encouraged to listen as well as talk. Beginning attending skills and critical listening skills are established by calling attention to and naming sounds both indoors and outdoors. The crunch of leaves, patter of rain, buzz of a bee, whistle of a teakettle, shout of a friend, or sound of footsteps on the stairs can all be used to foster listening skills.

Prereading. For toddlers, speaking, listening, reading, and writing are interrelated. Daily routines and activities provide them with "reading" opportunities. Pictures on cubbyholes can eventually help toddlers to find the place to put their belongings. As you play records, look at the title and read the name of the song. Some children may be able to pick out their favorite record by "reading" some distinctive mark on the cover. Covers of books become familiar if the story is read over and over, as do labels on food containers or other objects.

Books are enjoyed on a one-to-one basis or in small groups. You can plan at least one special story time each day. Introduce old favorites, folktales, and nursery rhymes as well as new books. Books selected for toddlers should have a simple text. Toddlers enjoy books that provide a feeling of security, such as Kay Chorao's *Baby's Lap Book,* Ruth Krauss's *The Bundle Book,* or Margot Zemach's *Hush Little Baby.*

Other books that can help toddlers understand about themselves are Pat Hutchins' *Titch,* Ruth Krauss's *The Carrot Seed,* and Anne Rockwell and Harlow Rockwell's *Can I Help?* Children's expanding language is stimulated by books such as Leo Lionni's *Little Blue and Little Yellow,* Nancy Carlstrom's *Jesse Bear, What Will You Wear?* and Bruno Munari's *Who's There? Open the Door.* The world is full of experiences, and the toddler enjoys hearing that others may have similar experiences or feelings. Robert McClosky's *Blueberries for Sal,* Ezra Jack Keats's *Peter's Chair,* and Charlotte Zolotow's *William's Doll* delight children as they identify with the feelings of wanting a mother near, jealousy of a new baby, or wanting a special toy.

Toddlers should have access to some of the books because they often enjoy hearing the same story read over and over again. From being read to, children develop their own understandings of literacy, such as: books have a beginning, even if one holds them differently from the adult's way of holding them; one turns pages, moves one's head, and talks, then turns more pages until the last page of the book, when the cover is closed and the book is put away. When books are familiar enough, some toddlers may even begin to notice if a page is skipped or words are left out. They may begin to *pretend read* by copying the adult's gestures, turning pages, and speaking with a different intonation.

Poetry for the toddler may be recited rather than read. From the nursery rhymes and Mother Goose tales, children hear the first of many stories that have a beginning, middle, and end. They delight in hearing what happened in "Humpty-Dumpty," "Little Jack Horner," "Hickory, Dickory, Dock," and "Jack and Jill." Daily experiences are enriched as poetry is recited while toddlers are involved in some activity. "One, two, buckle my shoe" or "There was a little girl who had a little curl," or "This is the way we brush our teeth" are introduced as children put on shoes, comb hair, or brush their teeth. Children may chime in or begin to repeat some of the phrases on their own, modifying the text.

Prewriting. *Prewriting* begins with fine-motor skill development. Providing children with many experiences to manipulate objects, touch and feel things, pick up beads, work switches, turn things, and operate locks is helpful in fostering small-muscle development. Pegboards, blocks, puzzles, and art materials offer children other means of developing fine-motor skills that will later be used for writing.

Toddlers are also interested in making marks on paper. Their scribbles with crayon, pencil, or magic markers are often accompanied by talk. These drawings are their first incursions into writing. The explanations they make or the labels they give these early marks are their beginning experiences with getting and giving meaning to symbols.

Although children may not become independent readers or writers until they are 7 or 8 years of age, informal and relaxed literacy experiences start early and lay the foundation for the enjoyment of reading and writing in later years.

Preschoolers and Kindergartners

Preschoolers' and kindergartners' language flourishes. They talk on and on about anything and everything, jumping from one topic to the next. Many will talk about an event saying "and then . . . and then . . . and then . . ." They delight in playing with language and will make up silly jingles, rhymes, and songs. Four- and especially 5-year-olds use language correctly—making only a few pronunciation errors or pronoun and verb tense errors. They are beginning to use pencils and crayons in a more controlled fashion. A few may be able to write the letters of their name, and some are aware of sound-letter relationships and may recognize that the marks on a page give a message. Very few 4- and 5-year-olds are able actually to read.

Speaking and listening to each other. Preschoolers and kindergartners are expanding vocabularies, using more elaborate sentence structure and refining the proper use of indefinite adjectives and pronouns. They are better able to participate in all four types of listening: marginal, appreciative, attentive, and analytical. The program for these children, therefore, permits opportunities for them to do a great deal of talking and listening.

Work in interest centers is conducive to conversations among small groups of children as they figure out how to build something, who will be the mother, or how they can work together. Adults continue to be resources for children's language and play by entering into the play at appropriate times or adding props if play is faltering.

Listening to and discussing literature. New and exciting worlds are opened to children through good literature. Kindergartners and preschoolers listen attentively to literature and are able to understand that other children have feelings similar to theirs. They are comforted to know that others can imagine the same or more horrible monsters than they do but that life is firmly planted in reality. They enjoy a wide range of books, but the books should be read more than once. New depths of understanding can be seen, and children can make the story truly their own after becoming familiar with it.

Choose a variety of books portraying people of all cultures and life-styles. Share with children the delightful books about African-American characters such as Lucille Clifton's *Everett Anderson's Nine Month Long,* Faith Ringgold's *The Tar Beach,* and John Steptoe's *Daddy Is a Monster . . . Sometimes.* Hispanic characters are portrayed in Marie Hall Ets and A. Labastida's *Nine Days to Christmas* and Leo Politi's *Three Stalks of Corn,* and Asian characters in Taro Yashima's *The Village Tree* or Yoshiko Uchida's *The Rooster Who Understood Japanese.* Books portraying Native Americans include Byrd Baylor's *Hawk, I'm Your Brother* and Paul Goble's *Death of the Iron Horse.*

Children also need exposure to books portraying imaginative, capable women, who can do any number of tasks, such as Margaret Mahy's *The Horrendous Hullabaloo,* Eve Merriam's *Boys and Girls. Girls and Boys,* and Natalie Babbitt's *Phoebe's Revolt.* "Ebonee," a delightful poem in Sharon Bell Mathis' *Red Dog. Football Poems. Blue Fly.,* extols the virtues of a female football player.

When reading to preschoolers and kindergartners, think about how you will present the story. You might read the title and ask them to guess what the story will be about. Or you could tell them the story is about someone like themselves who wants something very much. As you draw the children into the story, you are giving them a purpose for listening. After the story has been read, allow time for discussion. You could begin with one or two questions that recall parts of the story, but you also want to develop analytical, as well as attentive, listening skills. Help children translate the story into their own experiences and feelings with questions like "Which person did you like the best?" "How would you feel if you lost your tooth?" "What do you suppose Archie and Peter saw through the goggles?" If children have difficulty responding to your questions, model your own responses to the text. "I remember when I lost my first tooth, I put it right under my pillow" or "I don't know if I'd have been smart enough to wish on a feather if I lost my tooth, as Sal did."

Poetry continues in the lives of 4- and 5-year-olds, who enjoy and will recite a wide range of poetry. They like lyric poetry because of the special sounds or the imagery it brings to their everyday experiences. For example, Mother Goose tales and the humorous poetry of A. A. Milne, Edward Lear, Rachel Field, and Jack Prelutsky are all appropriate for children of this age. M. H. Arbuthnot and Shelton Root's *Time for Poetry* contains a collection of well-known poems for children of all ages.

Finger plays are a type of poetry. Some finger plays are of limited literary quality, but others are appropriate because they are useful in teaching children language patterns or counting. Many Mother Goose rhymes as well as poetry of high literary quality can be introduced as finger plays, with children creating their own motions to go with the poem.

Introducing folk rhymes or poetry of different cultures allows children to share the special quality and rhythm of differing language patterns and gestures. Marc Brown's *Finger Rhymes* and *Hand Rhymes,* Barbara Michels and Bettye White's *Apples on a Stick: The Folklore of Black Children,* Isabel Schon's *Doña Blanca and Other Hispanic Nursery Rhymes and Games,* and Demi's *In the Eyes of the Cat: Japanese Poetry for All Seasons* are examples of such collections. Inviting parents to come to class and share folk stories, finger plays, songs, and nursery rhymes or poetry that have been a part of their culture ensures more accurate rhythmic and tonal expressions and increases the range of language experiences for all children.

Reading and writing: Developmental factors. The answer to the question the 5-year-old asks in Miriam Cohen's story *When Will I Read?* depends on many factors.

Learning to read is not something that happens overnight. It takes place gradually in the context of total language experiences. Developmental factors may affect the learning process: physical, perceptual, cognitive, language, affective, and environmental/experiential. Having developed or not developed any one of these factors does not necessarily determine a child's ability to learn to read. Reading is a complex process, and the interrelatedness of the components seems to affect a child's progress in reading as much as anything.

Physical. A child who is in poor health and whose needs for proper nutrition and rest have not been met may have difficulty learning to read. Children who have hearing or visual impairments, or those with delayed speech or some other physical problem, may require special attention in learning to read and write.

Perceptual. To read, it is necessary to associate the printed language with the spoken language. To write, it is necessary to translate oral sounds into graphic representations. These associations require the child to discriminate among letters and sounds. Although children may be able to see and hear without difficulty, they may have problems distinguishing similarities and differences in sounds and words. Some children may need practice focusing attention, attending to details, and developing observation skills.

Cognitive. Reading and writing are cognitive processes, and such components as comprehension, problem solving, and reasoning require intellectual capacities. Severely retarded people do not learn to read. A high IQ, however, is not a prerequisite for the process. At one time, it was determined that children should have a mental age of $6\frac{1}{2}$ before being introduced to reading (Morphett & Washburne, 1931). Durkin (1966), summarizing other studies, suggests that the type of instruction is more important than the specific mental age.

Language. Preschoolers are usually skillful users of oral language. Many have had experiences in drawing and labeling and talking about their drawings. This skill is important because it serves as the basis for children to understand the printed word. Some children will have less advanced language fluency because they may not have had the opportunities for speaking, listening, and drawing that other children have had. As these children become involved in the reading process, they may need more opportunities for dialogue with adults and peers regarding their in- and out-of-school experiences.

Affective. Just as you consider children's physical well-being and cognitive development, you also should be concerned with their affective development. Children may be linguistically capable, intellectually ready, and physically capable—but still have difficulty adjusting to reading and writing. How children feel about themselves, school, and others can have an effect on their ability to learn to read.

Some children come to school believing that they can read and write because they know their favorite stories by heart or because their markings on paper have meaning for them. Teachers who prize and encourage these early attempts at literacy provide an important affective climate for children's progress toward reading and writing. Teachers who tell children by word or by deed that they are not reading the words correctly or not writing according to an adult's standard discourage too many children. Unfortunately these discouragements affect how children view their ability to master the steps toward literacy.

Environmental/experiential readiness. To give meaning to children's early reading and writing experiences, it is important to provide prereading materials and prewriting experiences that match children's concepts. All children come to school with a variety of experiences. Some may have broader and more varied experiences than others, but all children's concepts can be extended through trips within the community, through books, films, and pictures that provide different cultural experiences, through cooking and sampling known and unknown foods, and through playing with new and old friends in blocks, in the housekeeping or dramatic play area, with sand and water, and at the woodworking bench. Special art, music, science, or social studies projects provide additional content from which they will learn new concepts.

Developing literacy skills. Important literacy skills are being developed in these preschool/kindergarten years: interest in reading and writing; recognition of the relationship of print to the oral rendering of that print; knowledge of the conventions of print and a beginning awareness of the terms that describe those conventions; concept of story.

Interest in reading and writing. As children listen to stories and poems from the wide selection of good children's books, they begin to enjoy the special pleasure of sharing an experience with an imaginary character or discovering new information. Preschoolers' and kindergartners' developing interest in writing and reading is evident when they ask for special books to be reread, select a variety of books, experiment with writing, and are curious about the printed materials in their environment.

Recognition of the relationship of print to the oral rendering of that print. When children first hear stories, they do not realize that the print and the telling of the story go together. Often they believe that the story is from the pictures. Occasionally pointing to the text as you read and indicating where you start to read will help children grasp that the markings in the text are what you are reading, not the pictures. As children "pretend read" back to you and to each other, ask them to point to where they are reading. From stories read and reread, children become adept at "reading" the story, beginning at the top and turning the page at the correct words.

Knowledge of the conventions of print and a beginning awareness of the terms that describe those conventions. From experiences with books and from following along during the rereading of dictated stories or Big Books, children learn the convention of the directionality of print: Reading starts at the top of a page, the left page is read before the right page, and reading starts from the left of the page and goes to the right. When you reach the end of the line, you move down a line but back to the left side.

Further experiences in these conventions are provided as children watch you write their dictated stories. As you write, occasionally remark that a word needs a capital letter or a period is needed at the end of that thought. As you reread these stories with the children, move your hand along under the print to reinforce how the reading moves along.

Eventually children learn other conventions of print: that there is a relationship between sounds and letters, that several sounds make up a word, that spaces exist to separate words, that several words make up a thought or sentence, and that there are punctuation conventions to indicate different types of sentences. Kindergartners and preschoolers may become aware of only a few of these conventions, but in their various experiences with print, some of them will begin to sort out sound/letter relationships at the beginning and ending of words. Middle sounds are usually the last to be distinguished. Children will begin to point to words that begin with the same letters or sounds as their names. The difference between letter names and letter sounds can be confusing to children just learning the relationship between letters and sounds. It is important that you, as the teacher, are sure which you are talking about as you discuss letters with children.

As children dictate their special words or phrases to you, they should watch you write and spell the words. Have them trace the letters and talk with them about the parts of the words. For example, you might ask them if they recognize any letters or if the word has a beginning sound like one of their other key words. When they give a phrase, such as *pumpkin pie,* you might note that it is really two words and that there is a space between *pumpkin* and *pie.* They may note that the beginning of both words is the same or may be able to find all the *p*'s in the phrase. The discussion must be at each child's level of awareness and interest. From the discussion and from children's explorations in writing, be aware of the conventions that each child is discovering. Keeping notes on these discoveries will help you know how to proceed according to each child's interest and involvement. Children do not develop in the same way or at the same rate while learning these concepts. They need many experiences with the printed environment and many opportunities to ask questions, make hypotheses, and confirm their perceptions both with peers and with adults.

Concept of story. Applebee (1978, 1980) and Whaley (1981) have noted that many preschoolers and kindergartners have a sense of what makes a story. These children know that markers indicate the beginning and ending of a story, such as "once upon a time" and "the end." This concept is an important beginning in developing literacy, for children must come to understand that a written story has a different organization and structure than oral text (Halliday & Hasan, 1976).

Researchers have found that various ways of interacting with children increase their memory and concept of story. Several researchers maintain that children who have a sense of story are able to understand and remember details and events from the story much better than those who do not (Bower, Black, & Turner, 1979; Mandler & Johnson, 1977; Rumelhart, 1978). You can help children acquire this essential insight by reading aloud to them from a wide range of good children's literature (Teale, 1984; Wells, 1985). Morrow (1985) has found that helping children retell stories by prompting their memory with such questions as "What happened next?" or "Did that happen first or last?" extend their comprehension. Children's comprehension can be further developed as you encourage them to read the same story with you several times, answering questions about any confusion over the story as you share a reading and retelling experience (Pappas & Brown, 1987).

D. INTEGRATING THE LANGUAGE ARTS INTO THE CURRICULUM

During the preschool and kindergarten years, literacy events should be integrated into the entire curriculum. Children are laying important foundations for reading and writing as they are involved in the formal and informal activities of each day.

Formal *prereading* activities for 5-year-olds should be provided as you read stories and poetry to them. Time should be provided in the schedule to read to students individually or in small groups as well as in large groups. Children's favorite books should be read over and over again. Encourage them to read along with you. As they become familiar with the author's language and begin to say the words of the text as the pages are turned, they are taking the first steps toward literacy by pretending to read. Some of the stories and poetry may be copied onto large chart paper or selected from Big Books and read together as a class or privately, as in a "shared book experience" (Holdaway, 1979, 1984).

The best books to read for these shared experiences are the type known as *predictable stories.* These books offer clear, repetitive story patterns, have repetitions of lyrical language, or have familiar sequences, such as counting or the days of the week. The concepts and themes are those familiar to young children. Folktales like "The Three Bears" and "The House That Jack Built," storybooks like Pat Hutchins' *The Doorbell Rang* and Larry Brimmer's *Country Bear's Good Neighbor,* and counting books like Eric Carle's *The Very Hungry Caterpillar* and Molly Bang's *Ten, Nine, Eight* are examples of predictable books.

Informal prereading takes place throughout the curriculum in such activities as "reading" one's favorite story to a peer or to a favorite doll; "reading" along with a taped story; "reading" recipes for cooking, labels and signs in dramatic play activities, directions for an art or woodworking project; and "reading pictures or signs" to find out where to put things or whose job it is to clean up.

Formal or informal reading activities may also be conducted as children "read" their own or another's dictated key words or stories (Ashton-Warner, 1986; Veatch, 1979).

The writing process evolves during the preschool and kindergarten years as well. Researchers maintain that drawing is a part of the writing strategy (Baghban, 1984; Dyson, 1986; Graves, 1983). As children draw, they create imaginary worlds, often labeling and talking about their drawings as part of the creative process. Students' formal writing activities may be copying of labels or the story dictated from their drawings. Informal activities take place as they "pretend write" a grocery list for shopping, a note to leave for their mother, a letter to send by post, or the steps for making popcorn.

Children's early writings move through scribblings and attempts at making letters to attempts at matching letters to the sounds they hear in the words or phrases. They are also developing concepts about their own writings. Clay (1991) points out that children first make marks or scribbles for the enjoyment of seeing these marks on paper. Later children develop the concept that these marks have meaning even though they cannot decipher them. At this stage, it is not uncommon for a child to bring these scribblings to an adult and ask the adult to read it. If the adult responds by asking the child what he or she has written, the child is likely to say "I don't know, I can't read." In the final scribbling stage, children become aware that they can "write" a message and "read" it for a friend or an adult. These concepts are important steps before the child moves on to writing strings of letters and matching letters to sounds.

Then students should be given many opportunities to write using their own inventions for making letters and for spelling. As their fine-motor skills become better developed, their letters will be better formed. As they become more aware of conventional print, their spelling will come closer to conventional spelling (Bissex, 1980; Temple, Nathan, & Burris, 1982). In the process of writing, children reveal their awareness of sound/letter relationships as well as their understanding of the conventions of print.

Discussion is an integral part of both the reading and the writing processes. As students share a book or read each other's *invented spellings,* they challenge the assumptions that each has made about the print. Throne (1988) points out the intense involvement children sustain as they discover how the written language works.

Although some children may appear to learn the reading and writing process naturally and move smoothly through each of the stages, not all children will (Hayes, 1990). As you surround children with books and prints, you also are an active writer, reader, and discussant—modeling how letters are made, pointing out where the message is, and discussing how you make letters or make sense of a text. You must become observant of the children who are grasping the concepts about print and those who do not seem to be progressing as well. The children who are moving more slowly may need you to work with them more directly in talking and pointing out the elements of the written text.

Setting the Environment

Children in preschool and kindergarten settings need a print-rich environment. The books that are available should be selected from the excellent offerings in children's literature. Print that is functional and gives messages to children should be on the bulletin boards, chalkboards, and in play areas. Children's own messages, labels, lists, and beginning writings should be part of these postings. Writing and art centers should contain a variety of papers, pencils, crayons, paintbrushes, and magic markers. Five-year-olds do not need formal phonics lessons or formal lessons in writing letters, but they do need time and opportunity to discover what makes reading and writing work.

Listening and speaking become a part of the reading and writing process when schedules and space are organized to permit different kinds of interaction.

Schedules should be arranged so that there are several short periods of time in the day for such formal group activities as listening to stories; reading poems, stories, or directions for making things; discussing events; and writing experiences, stories, lists, or class letters. Large blocks of time should be scheduled for informal activities in which children can explore personal literacy activities that may have been prompted by a group activity or by dramatic play, science experiments, block play, cooking experiences, listening to tapes, or painting. Classroom space must be organized so that children can come together as a group, but there should be smaller spaces for sharing learning with one or more peers or with an adult and space to work quietly alone.

Listening and Speaking

Six-, 7-, and 8-year-olds have good control over their language. For the most part, they can articulate well and are able to give directions, be critical, and use language creatively. In these years, children are acquiring much larger vocabularies, new meanings for words, and more complex thought and language structure. As children develop and expand literacy skills, the language arts curriculum should provide purposeful and functional activities that reflect the interdependence of listening, speaking, writing, and reading skills.

In the primary years, children can develop their abilities to:

- Listen attentively for longer periods
- Follow a topic and contribute ideas to that topic
- Gain information and share understandings
- Be critical of what they hear and express reasons for their criticism
- Appreciate creative language expression

Opportunities for children to express themselves should be created in the classroom. A variety of strategies and questioning techniques can foster children's speaking and listening skills. It may be helpful to wait a few moments to allow children time to think of their responses. You can encourage children to expand on their responses. For example, if, during a discussion of a story, children respond "bad" to the question "How would you feel if someone did that to you?" you can extend their thinking, vocabulary, and language structure by asking "What other words can you use to express *bad?* Can you say how you would feel with two or three words?" or "How would you finish the sentence: I would feel so bad I . . . ?"

Group discussions. In group discussion, you can encourage children to listen to one another, to keep to the topic, and to ask each other questions. The topic for discussion should be clear, perhaps announced or decided upon ahead of time so children can "research" or think about the ideas they wish to share. You shouldn't expect children automatically to keep to the topic; adults do not. At first allow some diversions, and as children become better able to express themselves, work toward keeping the children on the subject. Encourage them to ask each other questions. These can be used to extend or clarify the original statement. Young children's questions can become repetitive. If this happens, model new types of questions and encourage children to use other types.

Full-group, as well as small-group, discussion times are possible. One first-grade teacher structured his science activities to include small-group discussions. He first did demonstrations with the whole class, for example, planting seeds and stating hypotheses about their growth. In groups of three or four, children were to carry out the procedure for planting, set up their experimental conditions, and make their recording charts.

Informal talk was required, and children were encouraged to keep this talk related to the task. When a group had finished setting up an experiment, the children in it were expected to examine books about seeds and growing things. The children were encouraged to share what they had discovered in their books and to ask each other questions. The teacher circulated, helping, listening, and joining in as appropriate. The small groups then reported to the total group the results of their experiments as well as discoveries from their reading.

Dramatics. Reading, writing, speaking, and listening are all language arts skills used and applied as primary-age children become involved in dramatic activities. Children will learn lines from predetermined stories, plays, or poems and will interpret dialogue and action. They may create their own dramas as productions to present to the class, to others in the school, and to parents.

Television. Because most children watch a great deal of television, you can use this medium for developing listening and speaking skills. Use children's home viewing as the focus of discussions. You could ask them to compare programs or discuss different television characters and how real they are. Characters on one show can be compared with those on another.

Older children might discuss how a character like Superman changes before one's eyes, which can lead into an exploration of television's techniques for creating fantasy. Or you could ask children to listen carefully to an advertisement for one of their favorite products and then have them compare the real product with the advertisement's claims.

Other children might note the adjectives or verbs used in a particular advertisement or some of the expressions of a television character. Both younger and older children can retell the events of a particular show or describe the setting of a program. If programs are taped, it is easier to control and schedule viewing so all children can have a common experience. Parts of a tape can be viewed to check initial conclusions.

Projects. Craft, cooking, social studies, and science projects all provide children with opportunities for extending their listening and speaking skills. As projects are completed, children can share them with a small group or the total class. You can show children how to make a presentation interesting and to the point. One first-grade team role played making pretzels. Children became bowls, ingredients, rolling pins, and twisted pretzels as a narrator told the story.

Writing

Writing in the primary grades is a continuation of the preschool and kindergarten experiences. From early writing experiences—drawing, list-making, labeling, experience stories, and compositions with invented spellings—children progress to writing more complex texts. Britton (1970) has identified three functional categories of writing: *expressive, poetic,* and *transactional:*

- Expressive writing is the way children usually begin their first experiments with writing. They write about themselves, their actions, their feelings, and their ideas.
- Poetic writing begins as children become aware of the conventions of stories and poetry. They begin to use some literary elements in their writing. They write about the princess or the wise man who occupied the castle. The castle might be in the forest or beside a lake. They will have become aware that there are three parts in storytelling: a clear opening statement, for example, "One time there was this big volcano"; a series of events; and a resolution, with an ending like "They all lived happily ever after," or even "They all sat down to lunch." Thus, children are beginning to recognize that stories have characters, a setting, and a plot. As they become more aware of the rhyme and rhythm of poetic language, their own attempts at writing will be to make their story sound more "like book words."
- Transactional writing is the expository writing of explanations, arguments, instructions, and persuasions. It can be quite a challenge for children to share in writing information about different breeds of dogs or to persuade others by means of the school newspaper that the schoolyard should be kept clean. Yet children in the primary years can learn the different types of writing, or these various "voices." Their first efforts may not be clearly in one category, but as they gain experience and share their writing with others, they will become more skilled in writing for different purposes (Salinger, 1988).

Writing should be an integral part of the total curriculum. You may have a writing center, but that should be the place where writing materials are stored for easy access.

Dictionaries, all kinds of paper and writing implements, and children's work folders may be kept there. You will want to plan writing as part of children's daily experiences, both informal and formal.

Informal Activities. A variety of writing materials should be available to children in various places in the classroom. Children should be encouraged to draw/write ideas even when they are involved in other work activities or in play. Messages can be written, lists can be made, labels can be attached to projects, newly discovered words can be jotted in notebooks. You need to model such writing and spontaneously respond to children's attempts at extending their writing competencies. Children should come to view writing as a natural means of communication.

During these informal times, you should not make any judgments about form or substance because children need some opportunities to practice and experiment with written language without the imposition of adult standards. As children gain confidence in their ability to use writing as a means of communication, you can devise more formal types of instruction to encourage them to attend to the mechanics of writing.

Messages. Questions on the writing board or at various work areas in the room can encourage children to write comments and responses. The message may be a question encouraging them to puzzle something out, for example, estimating: "How may blocks will fit along this line?" Children could write their guess with a signature beside it. Older children could write how they came to guess that number. As children gain confidence about spelling and simple punctuation, a message might be written with deliberate errors asking, "Who can correct THIS?" A note to complement group projects might read, "How did you get the light to turn on?" A reminder that classroom jobs need doing could say, "The fish need to be fed today. Write and tell me who fed them and how much was given to the fish."

A message center could be established in the classroom where children could leave notes for each other. If there is a parent bulletin board in your room, you could encourage children to leave a note for a parent or caregiver there. It might be important to establish how long a note should stay up.

Lists. As children plan special events, projects, or assignments, you can have them make lists to practice the mechanics of writing and to help them organize their ideas. The list of groceries to buy for the soup-making event will ensure that nothing is forgotten. Lists of people and their assignments for a project could keep the project moving. Ideas for building a rocket ship could serve as a reminder of what needs doing next. You could encourage children to make lists of things they need to bring from home the next day or questions to ask or important things to tell their parents. One second-grade teacher asked children to watch the moon rise each night for two weeks and draw what they saw, noting the position in the sky and the time when they looked. The drawings served as a graphic reminder of the changes that were occurring. Their informal jottings were the basis for informal and formal discussions during the two-week period.

Labels. As children draw, create, or make materials during work or recess time, different sizes and shapes of stiff paper need to be available for making labels. The post office needs letter boxes with names on them. The village will need street signs. Labels on the geographic representations in the sandbox will identify the rivers, the peninsula, and the harbor. Creative titles for painting or wood and clay sculptures can be attached to children's work for display or simply to be put on a shelf to be found again before taking home.

Newly discovered words. Encourage children to jot down words whose sounds they like. Each student may have to keep a small notebook handy. They may choose words that they read, hear people say, or see or hear on television. You may need some occasional reinforcing activities to encourage the habit. One teacher had a "stump the teacher" day. Third graders would write a word on the writing board from their list in hopes of having discovered a word the teacher did not know. The child writing the word had to spell it correctly and know its meaning and how to use it. Often a search in the dictionary was necessary to affirm the authenticity of the word. For more common words children can pantomime or draw and have others guess their special word.

During a more relaxed time, children can share a special word and explain where they found it and why they like it. The students' notebooks should be handy as they do their formal writing. By looking at it, they may get ideas or find a more descriptive word for their stories. Children should be encouraged to share lists.

Through such informal writing, children begin to develop a habit of extending their thoughts through writing.

Formal activities.   Students' experiences in formal writing allow them to learn that journals, stories, and expository writing use different styles. The mechanics of writing are important, but they should be taught in context and not as a separate subskill. You can help children develop their writing through individual teacher-child conferences and through peer conferences in which two children work together.

Journal writing.   Journal writing extends children's expressive language by letting them experiment in explaining what they have done, how they feel about it, and what new ideas they have. You may want to respond to what they write about. It is important, though, that you take the time to read the journals and respond to their experiences. Responses should be positive, and you should pose questions or reflect on their thoughts. Do not make comments on the mechanics of writing. Children should feel free in journal writing.

Writing stories.   Students' story writing gives opportunities for them to use their imagination. From their early experiences of hearing stories, children begin to develop an ear for the lyrical quality of language as well as a concept of story patterns. In many ways, you can help students' development.

It is important to read good literature to children several times a week. Hearing rich and vivid language will expand their knowledge of words. Some teachers have found that using story starters helps children break the barrier of writing the first sentence. Other teachers have found that, after reading several opening sentences from well-known children's books, students may use the opening of a favorite story to begin their story. As they gain confidence, however, they begin to use their own creations. When students write daily, you may want to encourage them to focus on a particular part of the story, such as characters, plot, or setting. After reading passages describing settings from several different authors, you might ask children to experiment with writing more detailed settings. As you read stories that have a similar plot structure, ask children to plan stories that follow that pattern. Children can also try to write character descriptions that clarify not only a physical appearance but also a personality.

Expository writing.   Children should write nonnarrative texts for many reasons. You might start by having them write a report of a trip or a special event and read it to you, the parents, the principal, or another teacher. As children progress, social studies and science can serve as the basis for a topic for which they become the expert. Remember that children need some guidance and choices in this type of study and reporting. Children can decide what they want to find out and how they want to represent what they have learned. You may need to help them sort through materials, discover the important points, and find ways to note the points they want to discuss. When children have their own ideas about how they want to proceed, it is wise to allow them to experiment with their strategies. Later, discuss with the entire group their successes and difficulties. Explore ways they might do things differently next time.

Mechanics of writing.   The first and most essential objectives for beginning any writing are getting ideas to flow and putting those ideas in writing. The mechanics of writing come later. Children master the mechanics of writing as they learn to revise and rewrite ideas and correct syntax. It is not always easy to convince primary-age children of the importance of rewriting and revision. As children recognize themselves as writers, they need to realize that writing is a process of planning, writing a draft, and revising, sometimes several times before the final version is ready for the public. Children can be helped in this process by the notion of publishing their final draft as a book, for the school bulletin board, or for the school newspaper. You can use both teacher-child conferences and peer conferences in helping children do these rewrites.

Teacher-child conferences. It is important that you establish a routine in the classroom so that each child has a private time with you for conferences. Daily conferences for each child are not necessary, but two or three a week can help to keep students' interest high. Conferences should follow some sort of routine and have a clear purpose; they should change as children develop greater skills (Graves, 1983).

In conferences, students share their writing with you, and you ask questions and make comments to extend their thoughts. In the early stages of writing, you should ask about any misspellings and incorrect grammar or punctuation only when the writing does not communicate students' meaning. As children practice writing and try out the phonetic spellings of words, their spelling and punctuation should improve. Some teachers have found that encouraging children to underline words they are not sure are spelled correctly permits them to reread their writing and do some critical assessment before the conference. As good rapport and enjoyment of writing develop, students can be challenged to improve spelling, punctuation, and handwriting skills for the purpose of presenting their writing for publication. (See more on this topic in Chapter 5.)

Peer conferences. In the primary grades, peer conferences must be handled with care. You may want the first peer groups to consist of two compatible students who share their ideas for stories or reports in "prewrite sessions." Later you can redirect these experiences by changing the focus from one in which children just share ideas to encouraging one child to share ideas and the other to question or challenge them. Use peers to extend thinking. In these dialogues, students are developing important negotiating skills that help them to think, reconsider, and defend their ideas. As the comfort level of sharing with a partner increases, students can be encouraged to share what they have written. For primary-age children, it may be wise for you to establish a beginning protocol of things to be checked by the partner, for example:

- One thing I liked in the story and why
- Something I didn't understand in the story
- Words I couldn't read
- Are all the punctuation marks in place?

It may be wise to model the procedure and questions to be asked by partners. Group discussions about things that are helpful and not helpful in the peer conferences can lead to changing the protocols. In productive peer conferences, children are learning to improve all language arts skills: listening, speaking, reading, and writing.

Reading

The primary purpose of learning to read is to be able to comprehend a variety of written messages. During the primary years, children's comprehension grows as they learn how and where to get different types of information, how to read texts that have a specialized vocabulary, how to read more complicated directions, and how to read in order to expand personal pleasure. In this process children also extend their knowledge and understanding of *cue systems: graphophonic cues* (letter/sound relationships), syntactic cues (order and patterns of words), and semantic cues (how words are used for meaning). During this century, there has been a lot of controversy about the best way to teach reading. Yet in spite of vast amounts of research, no definitive means has been found (Barbour, 1992). The present controversy presents two opposing views of how children learn to read. One perspective maintains that children must first learn the *subskills* of the linguistic system by progressing from letters and the sounds these letters make, to figuring out words from the sounds of the letters, to making sense of these words in sentences. As they learn these subskills, they are expected to develop comprehension skills. Phonic rules assist the children in acquiring these subskills.

The *whole language philosophy* (sometimes referred to as emergent literacy or literature-based approach) is a belief that children learn to read and write in the same natural way that they learn to walk and talk (Smith, 1992).

Goodman, Smith, Meredith, and Goodman (1987) point out that reading is a constructive process and that children get meaning from symbols in context by using inferring, predicting, confirming, and correcting strategies. Linguistic principles are not learned as isolated units but are learned as children use these strategies to figure out and construct the meaning of any given text. Adults and older children in a print-rich environment provide models and facilitate the process. Teachers at some point "hand each child over to authors" (Smith, 1992, p. 435). The child learns to read as more skilled readers read with the child and then children themselves begin to "read" familiar text. Authors incorporate meaning through pictures and context. By encouraging and facilitating the reading and rereading of favorite stories, adults help children recognize that authors convey their meaning in the text (Smith, 1992, pp. 435–436).

Subskills approach. Although some *basal readers* use a whole language approach to reading, most are based on a subskills approach. Most elementary classrooms use at least one basal reading series. Such series provide children a reading text with controlled vocabulary and syntactic structure. A teacher's manual gives ideas and suggestions for teaching the lesson as well as for independent activities children can complete to reinforce the lesson.

All reading series have books designated for a particular grade level. Within each grade level are subdivisions, so children can read texts of increasingly difficult content. Because basal texts are graded, they lend themselves to the formation of subgroups in the classroom. Often classroom teachers using these texts place children in groups based on reading level, and they select texts from a given series that seems to be at the most appropriate level for each group.

The basal text is a useful tool for instruction, particularly for new teachers. The vocabulary is controlled and has enough repetition of new words and phrases so children get practice and experience in reading these expressions. Skills are developed sequentially. The drawbacks to the approach are that lessons can be monotonous if they are always conducted in the same way. Also, the basal requires that all children in a particular group be at the same level of competence and be taught the skill in the same fashion. The usefulness of phonics rules and children's knowledge aren't always taken into account when using the basals. In spite of the research that indicates that only about 18 of the 45 phonic generalizations are useful (Clymer, 1963), most basal texts provide lessons for all 45 (Barbour, 1992). Taylor, Frye, and Goetz (1990) found that phonics lessons were taught successfully only to children who already knew the phonic skill, and those who didn't know it tended not to learn it. If teachers do use a basal series, then flexibility in its use, creative approaches, and individualizing the instruction for each child will enhance the learning-to-read process.

Whole language philosophy. Whole language is a philosophical view of how children learn both oral and written language. Learning to read, write, and speak is achieved by observing the process used by those who have acquired the skills, by experimenting, and finally by figuring out the cue systems to extract meaning and to communicate. This approach emphasizes the interrelatedness of the language arts skills—listening, speaking, writing, and reading—and the interrelatedness of learning to read in all curriculum areas.

In classrooms where teachers adhere to a whole language philosophy, there is a print-rich environment. Themes or special topics form the unit of study for the reading of literature and for reading in content areas. Teachers personalize and individualize the instruction. Skill lessons are taught as children need skills to figure out the meaning of a passage or the way to express themselves in writing. The physical and emotional environment of the classroom supports the notion that all children can learn to read, even if the rate of progress and the manner in which a child learns to read are different.

Print-rich environment. A print-rich environment offers children a wide selection of both fiction and nonfiction books and stories. With some teacher guidance, children are given the freedom to select their own texts. Having outstanding children's books in the classroom gives children both a taste of good literature and a chance to develop lifelong reading habits.

Themes or special topics. At times you may want to select a class topic, have children read different books, and discuss various concepts or points of view about the topic. One primary classroom teacher chose the life of Helen Keller to enrich children's interest in knowing more about different handicapping conditions. Another used mysteries as a topic, including different children's mystery stories while introducing the concept of using clues in science class to unravel some of science's mysteries. Writing stories, making oral or written reports, and designing an art project using these themes integrates the language arts program.

Personalized, individualized instruction. A personalized and individualized program enables students to build on prior knowledge and strengths as they improve their reading/writing skills. Teachers guide and facilitate the process, holding frequent conferences with each child and observing each child's strategies for getting meaning. Linguistic principles are discussed as children make discoveries about the rules of written language from both reading and writing.

Individual or group skills lessons. The teacher may present individual or group skills lessons from time to time, depending on students' needs. Assessment of such needs may be made in the formal reading time with the teacher or as students are reading in other areas of the classroom. In one first-grade classroom, a teacher discovered that one child had theorized that the letter *c* had only one sound—that of *k*. As he tried to make this reasoning work, he sounded out the word *cinnamon* that was in the recipe he was using as "kinaman." Up to this point his theory had worked, so he had not realized that the letter *c* had more than one sound. As he began comparing words beginning with *ci* and *ce* with those beginning with *ca, co,* and *cu,* he became aware that the letter had two sounds, and he quickly discovered the "rule."

An environment that prizes differences. Although children may be grouped from time to time for different instructional purposes, a teacher espousing a whole language philosophy would not group children in set reading groups. Rather, children would read in different types of groups for different purposes. Children might listen to stories being read or shared in a whole-class setting. They might read with or to a few friends who share an interest in a similar topic. They might practice oral or choral reading or work on particular skills with those who are at their skill level. They would spend much time in silent reading, gleaning information for science, social studies, math, or literature topics as well as finding new sources of pleasure.

In such a classroom, children aren't measured by the "grade level" at which they are reading, but rather on the progress they are making as they read and discuss different types of text. Reading is not viewed as an isolated subject but is facilitated as part of literacy development. Reading materials are discussed, listened to, and written about. The skills developed in one area of literacy reinforce and enhance the entire process.

Teachers using the whole language philosophy must be organized. They must also be adept at keeping records on children's progress, recognizing children's competence levels, and organizing a group of children to work independently. But more important, they must be knowledgeable about language and how it is learned. A teacher's viewpoint can affect how well a child learns to read. Strict adherence to a belief system that maintains that there is only one way to teach reading will result in many children not "joining the literacy club" (Clay, 1991; Smith 1992).

SUMMARY

Language is an important part of young children's lives. Without a facility in language, children are limited intellectually as well as socially and emotionally. Without the ability to manipulate and understand words, they are restricted in their ability to receive information from others, from books and other printed materials, or to develop ideas and communicate them to others. Consider these main points:

- Whether in a child care center, kindergarten, preschool, or primary grade, the entire day's program is directed at fostering children's ability to use and understand language in a manner that respects regional, cultural, and socioeconomic differences in family backgrounds.
- Language begins with experiences. When a program is based on experiences, children have feelings and ideas to express and communicate to others. Children gain a common base for learning and using language when they join together in wondering how a moth emerges from a cocoon, in building a police car out of boxes and blocks, or in listening to firefighters tell about their work. As children grow in their ability to speak and listen, their need for written language emerges and they begin to invent ways to use writing to record and communicate their ideas and experiences.
- From the base of listening, speaking, and prewriting experiences, children gain a readiness for reading. Each experience with language helps to foster children's ability to perceive the connection between the printed and spoken word, as well as decoding abilities necessary for learning to read.

QUESTIONS AND ACTIVITIES FOR DISCUSSION

1. Ask a 5-year-old to select a picture of a person or object from a book or magazine. Then you choose a picture. Using the two pictures, have the child talk about them while you record what the child is saying. Compare the number of words, the descriptive adjectives, and the complexity of sentence structure the child uses in describing each picture. Determine which picture elicited the more complex speech.

2. View the film *Foundations of Reading and Writing* (available from Campus Films, 20 East 46th Street, New York, NY 10017) or another film about teaching reading and writing to young children. List the activities shown and indicate whether they develop prereading, writing, listening, or speaking skills, or some or all of these skills. Compare these activities to those you observe in a preschool or kindergarten program.

3. Select a poem appropriate for choral recitation. With a group of third graders, rehearse and practice the poem for presentation to the entire class or to other children.

4. Walk the route a child would take to school. Record all the written words or letters you observe, such as those on signs, posters, and shop windows as well as words or letters on trucks that pass. Take that walk again with a 5- or 6-year-old, and as a game point out some of these words or letters to see if the child recognizes any. Later make flashcards of the words or letters that the child seemed to recognize to determine if any are recognizable without the object.

5. Create a card file of books and poems that you have read or shared with children. Note the age of the child and the child's reaction. Your collection should include books and poems that are appropriate for various ages and are representative of different cultures, both genders as positive role models, and developmentally different children.

6. Describe any prior concepts you had that changed as a result of your experiences with this chapter. Describe the changes.

CHILDREN'S BOOKS

Arbuthnot, M. H., & Root, S. (1968). *Time for poetry* (3rd ed.). Glenview, IL: Scott Foresman.

Babbitt, N. (1977). *Phoebe's revolt*. New York: Farrar, Straus & Giroux.

Bang, M. (1983). *Ten, nine, eight*. New York: Greenwillow.

Baylor, B. (1976). *Hawk, I'm your brother*. New York: Scribner's.

Brimmer, L. D. (1988). *Country bear's good neighbor*. New York: Orchard Books/Franklin Watts.

Brown, M. (1980). *Finger rhymes*. New York: Dutton.

Brown, M. (1985). *Hand rhymes*. New York: Dutton.

Bruna, D. (1978). *I can dress myself*. New York: Methuen.

Carle, E. (1969). *The very hungry caterpillar*. New York: Philomel.

Carlstrom, N. W. (1986). *Jesse Bear, what will you wear?* New York: Macmillan.

Cauley, L. B. (1981). *Goldilocks and the three bears*. New York: Putnam.

Chorao, K. (1977). *The baby's lap book*. New York: Dutton.

Clifton, L. (1978). *Everett Anderson's nine month long*. New York: Harper & Row.

Cohen, M. (1977). *When will I read?* New York: Greenwillow.

Delacre, L. (1989). *Arroz con leche: Popular rhymes from Latin America*. New York: Scholastic.

Demi. (1992). *In the eyes of the cat: Japanese poetry for all seasons*. New York: Holt, Rinehart & Winston.

Ets, M. H., & Labastida, A. (1959). *Nine days to Christmas*. New York: Viking.

Goble, P. (1987). *Death of the Iron Horse*. New York: Bradbury.

Greenfield, E. (1991). *Night on neighborhood streets*. New York: Dial.

Hague, M. (1984). *Mother Goose: A collection of classic nursery rhymes*. New York: Holt, Rinehart & Winston.

Hoban, T. (1985). *What's that?* New York: Greenwillow.

Hutchins, P. (1977). *Titch*. New York: Greenwillow.

Hutchins, P. (1986). *The doorbell rang*. New York: Greenwillow.

Keats, E. J. (1981). *Peter's chair*. New York: Harper & Row.

Krauss, R. (1945). *The carrot seed*. New York: Harper & Row.

Krauss, R. (1951). *The bundle book*. New York: Harper & Row.

Leaf, M. (1987). *Eyes of the dragon*. New York: Lothrop.

Lear, E. (1980). *A book of nonsense*. New York: Viking.

Lionni, L. (1959). *Little blue and little yellow*. New York: Astor-Honor.

Kennedy, X. J., & Kennedy, D. M. (1992). *Talking like the rain: A first book of poems*. Boston: Little Brown.

Mahy, M. (1992). *The horrendous hullabaloo*. New York: Viking.

Mathis, S. B. (1991). *Red dog. Football poems. Blue fly*. New York: Viking.

McClosky, R. (1948). *Blueberries for Sal*. New York: Viking.

Merriam, E. (1972). *Boys and girls. Girls and boys*. New York: Henry Holt.

Michels, B., & White, B. (1983). *Apples on a stick: The folklore of black children*. New York: Coward-McCann.

Milne, A. A. (1958). *The world of Christopher Robin*. New York: Dutton.

Munari, B. (1980). *Who's there? Open the door*. New York: Philomel.

Ormerod, J. (1985). *Messy baby*. New York: Lothrop.

Oxenburg, H. (1983). *The birthday party*. New York: Simon & Schuster.

Peppe, R. (1985). *The house that Jack built*. New York: Delacorte.

Politi, L. (1976). *Three stalks of corn*. New York: Scribner's.

Prelutsky, J. (1984). *The new kid on the block*. New York: Greenwillow.

Ra, C. F. (Comp.). (1987). *Trot, trot to Boston: Play rhymes for baby*. New York: Lothrop.

Ringgold, F. (1991). *Tar Beach*. New York: Crown.

Rockwell, A., & Rockwell, H. (1982). *Can I help?* New York: Macmillan.

Schon, I. (1983). *Dona Blanca and other Hispanic nursery rhymes and games*. New York: Denison.

Steptoe, J. (1980). *Daddy is a monster . . . sometimes*. New York: Lippincott.

Uchida, Y. (1976). *The rooster who understood Japanese*. New York: Scribner's.

Untermeyer, L. (1959). *The golden treasury of poetry*. New York: Golden Press.

Wells, R. (1985). *Max's breakfast*. New York: Dial.

Yashima, T. (1953). *The village tree*. New York: Viking.

Zemach, M. (1976). *Hush little baby*. New York: Dutton.

Zolotow, C. (1972). *William's doll*. New York: Harper & Row.

REFERENCES AND SUGGESTED READINGS

Adams, M. J. (1990). *Beginning to read: Thinking and learning about print*. Cambridge, MA: The MIT Press.

Applebee, A. N. (1978). *The child's concept of story: Ages two to seventeen*. Chicago: University of Chicago Press.

Applebee, A. N. (1980). Children's narratives. New Directions. *The Reading Teacher, 34,* 137–142.

Ashton-Warner, S. (1986). *Teacher*. New York: Simon & Schuster. (Original work pub. 1963)

Baghban, M. (1984). *Our daughter learns to read and write*. Newark, DE: International Reading Association.

Barbour, N. (1992). Reading. In C. Seefeldt (Ed.), *The early childhood curriculum. A review of current research* (pp. 118–151). New York: Teachers College Press.

Bernstein, B. (1970). A sociolinguistic approach to socialization with some reference to educability. In F. Williams (Ed.), *Language and poverty: Perspectives on a theme* (pp. 25–62). Chicago: Markham.

Bissex, G. L. (1980). *Gnys at wrk: A child learns to read and write*. Cambridge, MA: Harvard University Press.

Bloom, L. (1976). *Language development: Form and function in emerging grammars*. Hawthorne, NY: Mouton.

Bower, G. H., Black, J. B., & Turner, T. J. (1979). Scripts in memory for text. *Cognitive Psychology, 11,* 177–220.

Braine, M. (1963). On learning the grammatical order of words. *Psychological Review, 70,* 345–348.

Britton, J. (1970). *Language and learning*. New York: Penguin Books.

Cassirer, E. (1984). An essay on man. In A. Berthoff (Ed.), *Reclaiming the imagination* (pp. 107–113). Montclair, NJ: Boynton/Cook.

Chomsky, C. (1969). *The acquisition of syntax in children from five to ten*. Cambridge, MA: The MIT Press.

Chomsky, N. (1965). *Aspects of the theory of syntax*. Cambridge, MA: The MIT Press.

Clay, M. M. (1991). *Becoming literate: The construction of inner control*. Portsmouth, NH: Heinemann.

Clymer, T. (1963). The utility of phonic generalizations in primary years. *Reading Teacher, 16,* 252–258.

Delacre, L. (1989). *Arroz con leche: Popular rhythms from Latin America*. New York: Scholastic.

Durkin, D. (1966). *Children who read early*. New York: Teachers College Press.

Dyson, A. H. (1986). Transitions and tensions: Interrelationship between the drawing, talking and dictating of young children. *Research in the Teaching of English, 20*(4), 379–409.

Elardo, R., Bradley, R., & Caldwell, B. M. (1977). A longitudinal study of the relation of infants' home environments to language development at age three. *Child Development, 48,* 595–603.

Ferrara, A. (1982). Pragmatics. In T. A. van Dijk (Ed.), *Handbook of discourse analysis: Vol. 2. Dimensions of discourse* (pp. 137–159). Orlando, FL: Academic Press.

Goodman, K. S., Smith, E. B., Meredith, R., & Goodman, Y. M. (1987). *Language and thinking in school: A whole language curriculum*. New York: Richard C. Owen.

Graves, D. (1983). *Writing: Teachers and children at work.* Portsmouth, NH: Heinemann.

Halliday, M. A. K., & Hasan, R. (1976). *Cohesion in English.* New York: Longman.

Hayes, L. F. (1990). From scribbling to writing: Smoothing the way. *Young Children, 45*(3), 62–68.

Heath, S. B. (1983). *Ways with words: Language, life and work in communities, and classrooms.* New York: Cambridge University Press.

Hepler, S. (1991). Talking our way to literacy in the classroom community. *The New Advocate, 4*(3), 179–191.

Holdaway, D. (1979). *The foundations of literacy.* New York: Ashton Scholastic.

Holdaway, D. (1984). *Stability and change in literacy learning.* Portsmouth, NH: Heinemann.

Honig, A. S. (1982). Language environments for young children. *Young Children, 38,* 56–57.

Ingraham, D. (1989). *First language acquisition.* Cambridge, MA: Cambridge University Press.

Jalongo, M. R. (1992). *Early childhood language arts.* Boston: Allyn & Bacon.

Kantor, R., Miller, S. M., & Fernie, D. E. (1992). Diverse paths to literacy in a preschool classroom: A sociocultural perspective. *Reading Research Quarterly, 27*(3), 185–201.

Kessel, F. (1970). The role of syntax in children's comprehension from ages six to twelve. *Child Development, 35*(6), 48–58.

Labov, W. (1970). The logic of nonstandard English. In F. Williams (Ed.), *Language and poverty: Perspectives on a theme* (pp. 153–190). Chicago: Markham.

Lenneberg, E. (1967). *Biological foundations of language.* New York: John Wiley.

Low, J. M., & Moely, B. E. (1988). Early word acquisition: Relationships to syntactic and semantic aspects of maternal speech. *Child Study Journal, 18*(1), 47–54.

Mandler, J. M., & Johnson, N. S. (1977). Remembrance of things passed: Story structure and recall. *Cognitive Psychology, 9,* 111–151.

McNeill, D. (1966). Developmental psycholinguistics. In F. Smith & G. Miller (Eds.), *The genesis of language: A psycholinguistic approach* (pp. 15–82). Cambridge, MA: The MIT Press.

Menyuk, P. (1969). *Sentences children use.* Cambridge, MA: The MIT Press.

Menyuk, P. (1971). *The acquisition and development of language.* Englewood Cliffs, NJ: Prentice Hall.

Moffett, J., & Wagner, B. (1992). *Student-centered language arts, K–12.* Portsmouth, NH: Boynton/Cook Heinemann.

Morphett, M. V., & Washburne, C. (1931). When should children learn to read? *Elementary School Journal, 29,* 497–503.

Morrow, L. M. (1985). Retelling stories: A strategy for improving young children's comprehension, concept of story structure and oral language complexity. *The Elementary School Journal, 85,* 648–661.

Mowrer, O. H. (1960). *Learning theory and the symbolic process.* New York: John Wiley.

National Association for the Education of Young Children. (1987). *Developmentally appropriate practice in early childhood programs serving children from birth through age 8.* Washington, DC: NAEYC.

National Association for the Education of Young Children. (1991). *Early childhood teacher education guidelines: Basic and advanced.* Washington, DC: NAEYC.

National Council of Teachers of English. (1954). *Language arts for today's children.* New York: Appleton-Century-Crofts.

National Council of Teachers of English. (1976). *Guidelines to evaluate the English component in the elementary school program.* Urbana, IL: NCTE.

Ollila, L. O., & Mayfield, M. I. (Eds.). (1992). *Emerging literacy: Preschool, kindergarten, and primary grades.* Boston: Allyn & Bacon.

Pappas, C. C., & Brown, E. (1987). Learning to read by reading. Learning how to extend the functional potential of language. *Research in the Teaching of English, 2*(2), 160–177.

Pellegrini, A. D., & Galda, L. (1986). The role of theory in oral and written language curriculum. *The Elementary School Journal, 87*(2), 201–208.

Peterson, R. (1971). Imitation: A basic behavioral mechanism. *Journal of Applied Behavioral Analysis, 4,* 1–9.

Piaget, J. (1955). *The language and thought of the child.* New York: Noonday.

Rumelhart, D. E. (1978). Understanding and summarizing brief stories. In D. Laberge & J. Samuels (Eds.), *Basic processes in reading: Perception and comprehension* (pp. 265–305). Hillsdale, NJ: Erlbaum.

Salinger, T. (1988). *Language arts and literacy for young children.* New York: Macmillan.

Sapir, E. (1929). The status of linguistics as a science. *Language, 5,* 207–214.

Schachter, F. F., & Stage, A. A. (1982). Adults talk and children's language development. In S. G. Moore & C. R. Cooper (Eds.), *The young child: Reviews of research* (pp. 79–97). Washington, DC: National Association for the Education of Young Children.

Schickedanz, J., York, M., Stewart, L., & White, D. (1983). *Strategies for teaching young children.* Englewood Cliffs, NJ: Prentice Hall.

Seefeldt, C., & Barbour, N. (1994). *Early childhood education: An introduction* (3rd ed.). Englewood Cliffs, NJ: Merrill/Prentice Hall.

Skinner, B. F. (1957). *Verbal behavior.* New York: Appleton-Century-Crofts.

Slobin, D. (1966). The acquisition of Russian as a native language. In F. L. Smith & G. C. Miller (Eds.), *The genesis of language: A psycholinguistic approach* (pp. 129–149). Cambridge, MA: The MIT Press.

Smith, F. (1992). Learning to read: The neverending debate. *Phi Delta Kappan, 76*(6), 432–441.

Snow, C. E. (1989). Understanding social interaction and language acquisition: Sentences are not enough. In M. H. Bornstein & J. S. Bruner (Eds.), *Interaction in human development* (pp. 83–105). Hillsdale, NJ: Lawrence Erlbaum.

Staats, A. (1971). Linguistic-mentalistic theory versus an explanatory s-r learning theory of language development. In D. Slobin (Ed.), *The ontogenesis of grammar: A theoretical symposium* (pp. 103–153). New York: Academic Press.

Taylor, B. M., Frye, J. B., & Goetz, T. M. (1990). Reducing the number of reading skill activities in the elementary classroom. *Journal of Reading Behavior, 22*(2), 167–179.

Taylor, M., & Gelman, S. A. (1988). Adjectives and nouns. Children's strategies for learning new words. *Child Development, 59,* 411–419.

Teale, W. H. (1984). Reading to our children: Its significance for literary development. In H. Goelman, A. A. Oberg, & F. Smith (Eds.), *Awakening to literacy* (pp. 110–121). Portsmouth, NH: Heinemann.

Teale, W. H. (1986). Home background and young children's literacy development. In W. H. Teale & E. Sulzby (Eds.), *Emergent literacy: Writing and reading* (pp. 173–207). Norwood, NJ: Ablex.

Temple, C. A., Nathan, R. G., & Burris, N. A. (1982). *The beginning of writing.* Boston: Allyn & Bacon.

Throne, J. (1988). Becoming a kindergarten of readers? *Young Children, 43*(6), 10–16.

Tizard, B. (1981). Language at home and at school. In C. B. Cazden (Ed.), *Language in early childhood education* (pp. 17–28). Washington, DC: National Association for the Education of Young Children.

Tizard, B., & Hughes, M. (1984). *Young children learning.* Cambridge, MA: Harvard University Press.

Tompkins, G., & Hoskisson, K. (1995). *Language arts content and teaching strategies* (3rd ed.). Englewood Cliffs, NJ: Merrill/Prentice Hall.

Veatch, J. (1979). *Key words to reading: The language approach begins.* Columbus, OH: Merrill.

Vygotsky, L. S. (1962). *Thought and language.* New York: John Wiley.

Wells, G. (1981). *Learning through interaction: The study of language development.* New York: Cambridge University Press.

Wells, G. (1985). Preschool literacy-related activities and success in school. In D. R. Olson, N. Torrance, & A. Hildyard (Eds.), *Literacy, language and learning* (pp. 229–255). New York: Cambridge University Press.

Whaley, J. F. (1981). Reader's expectations for story structure. *Reading Research Quarterly, 17,* 90–114.

Whorf, B. L. (1956). Science and linguistics. In J. B. Carroll (Ed.), *Thought and reality: Selected writings of Benjamin Lee Whorf* (pp. 207–219). Cambridge, MA: The MIT Press.

Willinski, J. (1990). *The new literacy: Redefining reading and writing in the schools.* London: Routledge.

Wood, B. S. (1976). *Children and communication: Verbal and nonverbal language development.* Englewood Cliffs, NJ: Prentice Hall.

CHAPTER 8

Listening

Listening is the first language mode that children acquire, and it provides the basis for the other language arts (Lundsteen, 1979). Infants use listening to begin the process of learning to comprehend and produce language. From the beginning of their lives, they listen to sounds in their immediate environment, attend to speech sounds, and construct their knowledge of oral language. Listening is also important in learning to read. Children are introduced to reading by having stories read to them. When children are read to, they begin to see the connection between what they hear and what they see on the printed page. Reading and listening comprehension skills—main ideas, details, sequence, and so on—are similar in many ways (Sticht & James, 1984).

Listening also influences writing. Hansen explains, "A writing/reading program begins with listening, and listening holds the program together" (1987, p. 69). Writing begins as talk written down, and the stories students read become models for their writing. Listening is essential for students sharing their writing in conferences and receiving feedback on how to improve it. Inner listening, or "dialoguing" with oneself, also occurs as students write and revise their writing. Listening is "the most used and perhaps the most important of the language (and learning) arts" (Devine, 1982, p. 1).

Researchers have found that more of children's and adults' time is spent in listening than in the total time spent reading, writing, and talking. Figure 8.1 illustrates the amount of time we communicate in each language mode. Both children and adults spend approximately 50 percent of their communication time listening. Language researcher Walter Loban compares the four language modes this way: "We listen a book a day, we speak a book a week, we read a book a month, and we write a book a year" (cited in Erickson, 1985). Despite the importance of listening in our lives, listening has been called the "neglected" or "orphan" language art for 35 years or more (Anderson, 1949). Little time has been devoted to listening instruction in most classrooms; listening is not stressed in language arts textbooks; and teachers often complain that they do not know how to teach listening (Devine, 1978; Landry, 1969; Wolvin & Coakley, 1979).

Related to listening instruction, this chapter focuses your attention on the most-used language art, listening. Specifically, this chapter is designed to help you reflect on:

FIGURE 8.1
Percentage of Communication Time in Each Language Mode
Data from Rankin, 1928; Wilt, 1950; Werner, 1975.

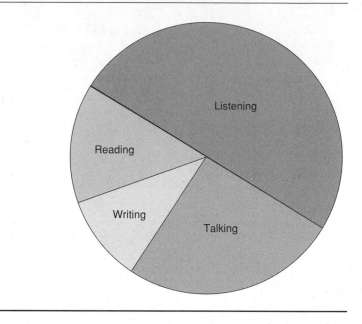

1. The listening process
2. Comprehensive listening
3. Critical listening
4. Appreciative listening
5. Classroom activities used to foster listening skills
6. Problem-solving activities
7. Assessment techniques for listening instruction.

A. WHAT IS LISTENING?

Listening is elusive because it occurs internally. Lundsteen (1979) describes listening as the "most mysterious" language process. In fact, teachers often do not know whether listening has occurred until they ask students to apply what they have listened to by answering questions, completing assignments, or taking tests. Even then, there is no guarantee that the students' responses indicate that they have listened, because they may have known the material before listening or learned it from someone else at about the same time.

The Listening Process

Listening is a highly complex, interactive process "by which spoken language is converted to meaning in the mind" (Lundsteen, 1979, p. 1). As this definition suggests, listening is more than just hearing, even though children and adults often use the two terms, *hearing* and *listening,* synonymously. Rather, hearing is an integral component, but only one component, of the listening process; it is thinking or converting to meaning what one hears that is the crucial part of the listening process.

Wolvin and Coakley (1979) describe three steps in the listening process: receiving, attending, and assigning meaning. In the first step, the listener receives the aural stimuli or the aural and visual stimuli presented by the speaker. Next, the listener focuses on selected stimuli while ignoring other distracting stimuli. Because so many stimuli surround students in the classroom, they must attend to the speaker's message, focusing on the most important information in that message. In the third step, the listener assigns meaning to, or understands, the speaker's message. Listeners assign meaning using assimilation and accommodation to fit the message into their existing cognitive structures or to create new structures if necessary. Responding or reacting to the message is not considered part of the listening process; the response occurs afterward, and it sets another communication process into action in which the listener becomes the message sender.

The second step of Wolvin and Coakley's listening process model may be called the "paying attention" component. Elementary teachers spend a great deal of instructional time reminding students to pay attention; unfortunately, however, children often do not understand the admonition. When asked to explain what "paying attention" means, some children equate it with physical behaviors such as not kicking their feet or cleaning off their desks. Learning to attend to the speaker's message is especially important because researchers have learned that students can listen to 250 words per minute, two to three times the normal rate of talking (Foulke, 1968). This differential allows one the time to tune in and out as well as to become distracted during listening.

Furthermore, the intensity of students' need to attend to the speaker's message varies with the purpose for listening. Some types of listening require more attentiveness than others. Effective listeners, for example, listen differently to directions on how to reach a friend's home than to a poem or story being read aloud.

Purposes for Listening

Why do we listen? Students often answer that question by explaining that they listen to learn or to avoid punishment (Tompkins, Friend, & Smith, 1984). It is unfortunate that some students have such a vague and limited view of the purposes for listening. Communication experts (Wolvin & Coakley, 1979) delineate five more specific purposes: discriminative listening, comprehensive listening, critical listening, appreciative listening, and therapeutic listening.

Discriminative listening. People listen to distinguish sounds and to develop a sensitivity to nonverbal communication. Teaching discriminative listening involves one sort of activity in the primary grades and a different activity for older students. Having kindergarten and first-grade students listen to tape-recorded animal sounds and common household noises is one discriminative listening activity. Most children are able to discriminate among sounds by the time they reach age 5 or 6. In contrast, developing a sensitivity to the messages that people communicate nonverbally is a lifelong learning task.

Comprehensive listening. People listen to understand a message, and this is the type of listening required in many instructional activities. Students need to determine the speaker's purpose and then organize the spoken information so as to remember it. Elementary students usually receive little instruction in comprehensive listening; rather, teachers assume that students simply know how to listen. Note-taking is typically the one comprehensive listening strategy taught in the elementary grades, although there are other strategies elementary students can learn and use.

Critical listening. People listen first to comprehend and then to evaluate a message. Critical listening is an extension of comprehensive listening. As in comprehensive listening, listeners seek to understand a message, but then they must filter the message to detect propaganda devices and persuasive language. People listen critically when they listen to debates, commercials, political speeches, and other arguments.

Appreciative listening. People listen to a speaker or reader for enjoyment. Listening to someone read literature or stories aloud or recite poems is a pleasurable activity. An important part of teaching listening in the elementary grades is to read aloud to students. Teachers can encourage and extend children's enjoyment of listening. Listening to classmates talk and share ideas is another component of appreciative listening. Students need to learn how to participate in conversations, discussions, and other talk activities, which we will discuss in Chapter 9.

Therapeutic listening. People listen to allow a speaker to talk through a problem. Children, as well as adults, serve as sympathetic listeners for friends and family members. Although this type of listening is important, it is less appropriate for elementary students, so we will not discuss it in this chapter.

Our focus will be on the three listening purposes that are most appropriate for elementary students: *comprehensive listening,* or the type of listening required in many instructional activities; *critical listening,* or learning to detect propaganda devices and persuasive language; and *appreciative listening,* or listening to conversation and to literature read aloud for pleasure.

The Need for Systematic Instruction

Activities involving listening go on in every elementary classroom. Students listen to the teacher give directions and instruction, to tape-recorded stories at listening centers, to classmates during discussions, and to someone reading stories and poetry aloud. Since listening plays a significant role in these and other classroom activities, listening is not neglected. But whereas these activities provide opportunities for students to practice listening skills, they do *not* teach them how to be more effective listeners.

Language arts educators have repeatedly cited the need for systematic instruction in listening (Devine, 1978; Lundsteen, 1979; Pearson & Fielding, 1982; Wolvin & Coakley, 1985). Most of what has traditionally been called "listening instruction" has been merely practice. When students listen to a story at a listening center and then answer questions about it, for example, teachers assume that the students know *how* to listen and will thus be able to answer the questions. But listening at a listening center is only a form of practice. Perhaps one reason listening has not been taught is simply that teachers do not know how to teach it. In a survey of elementary teachers enrolled in master's degree programs, only 17 percent recalled receiving any instruction in how to teach listening in their language arts methods class (Tompkins, Smith, & Friend, 1984). The teachers instead reported using practice activities instead of listening instruction.

In contrast to practice activities, listening instruction should teach students specific strategies to use when listening. Imagery, organization, and questions are examples of strategies that help students attend to the important information in a message and understand it more readily. Teachers have assumed that students acquire these strategies intuitively. Certainly some do; however, many students do not recognize that different listening purposes require different strategies. Many students have only one approach to listening, no matter what the purpose. They say they listen as hard as they can and try to remember everything. This strategy seems destined to fail for at least two reasons: (1) trying to remember everything places an impossible demand on short-term memory, and (2) many items in a message are not important enough to remember. Other students equate listening with intelligence, assuming that they "just aren't smart enough" if they are poor listeners.

B. COMPREHENSIVE LISTENING

Comprehensive listening is listening to understand a message, and it is the most common type of listening in school. For example, a fifth-grade teacher who discusses the causes of the American Revolution, a first-grade teacher who explains how to dial 911 in an emergency, and an eighth-grade teacher who discusses the greenhouse effect are providing information for students to relate to what they already know and remember.

Whether or not students comprehend and remember the message is determined by many factors. Some factors are operative before listening, others during and after. First, students need a background of prior knowledge about the content they are listening to. They must be able to relate what they are about to hear to what they already know, and speakers can help provide some of these links. Second, as they listen, students must use a strategy or other technique to help them remember. They need to organize and chunk the information they receive. They may want to take notes to help them remember. Then, after listening, students should somehow apply what they have heard so there is a reason to remember the information.

Strategies for Listening

Six listening strategies elementary students can learn and use are creating imagery, categorizing, asking questions, organizing, note-taking, and attention-directing (Tompkins, Friend, & Smith, 1987). These strategies are primarily aimed at comprehensive listening, but can also be used for other listening purposes. The purpose of each strategy is to help students organize and remember what they listen to.

Strategy 1: Forming a picture in your mind. Students can draw a mental picture while listening to help them remember. The imagery strategy is especially useful when a speaker's message has many visual images, details, or descriptive words, and when students are listening for enjoyment. Stories and pictures help teach students to create images, and students can draw or write about the mental pictures they create.

Strategy 2: Putting information into groups. Students can categorize so as to group or cluster information when the speaker's message contains many pieces of information, comparisons, or contrasts. Students could use this strategy, for example, as they listen to a comparison of reptiles and amphibians. The teacher can make a two-column chart on the writing board, labeling one column *reptiles* and the other *amphibians*. Then together, teacher and students make notes in the columns while they listen or immediately after. Similarly, students can divide a sheet of paper into two columns and make notes themselves.

When students are listening to presentations that contain information on more than two or three categories, such as a presentation on the five basic food groups, drawing a cluster diagram on the writing board helps students classify what they are listening to. Students can also draw a cluster diagram on a sheet of paper and take notes about each food group by drawing lines from each food group and adding details. An example of a cluster diagram appears in Figure 8.2.

Strategy 3: Asking questions. Students can ask questions to increase their understanding of a speaker's message. Two types of questions are helpful: students can ask the speaker to clarify information, or they can ask themselves questions to monitor their listening and understanding. Most students are familiar with asking questions of a speaker, but the idea of self-questions is usually new to them. Develop a list of self-questions similar to those that follow to help students understand the self-questioning procedure and how to monitor their understanding:

- Why am I listening to this message?
- Do I know what _____ means?
- Does this information make sense to me?

FIGURE 8.2

A Cluster Diagram on the Food Groups

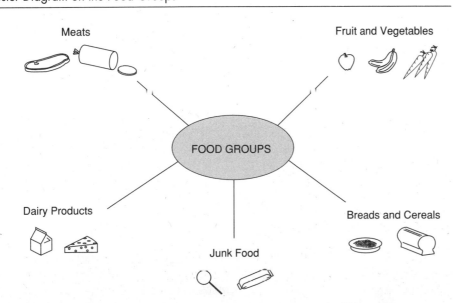

Strategy 4: Discovering the plan. Speakers use one of several types of organization to structure a message. Five common organizational patterns are *description, sequence, comparison, cause and effect,* and *problem and solution.* Students can learn to recognize these patterns and use them to understand and remember a speaker's message more easily. They can develop graphic organizers for each of the five organizational patterns; sample organizers are shown in Figure 8.3. Graphic organizers help students visualize the organization of a message. Excerpts from social studies and science textbooks as well as from informational books can be used in teaching this strategy.

The design of a graphic organizer can be adapted to the information presented. Figure 8.4 shows three possible graphic organizers for the cause-and-effect pattern. Any of the three patterns might be used during a discussion on pollution. In talking about how people's apathy has allowed pollution to occur, the first organizer, single cause leading to single effect, might be used. Or, in explaining that air pollution has affected humans, plants, and the weather, the second pattern might be appropriate. If, instead, you were discussing that recycling and new technological developments are two ways of controlling pollution, the third graphic organizer in Figure 8.4 would be helpful.

Speakers often use certain words to signal the organizational patterns they are following. Signal words include *first, second, third, next, in contrast,* and *in summary.* Students can learn to attend to these signals to identify the organizational pattern the speaker is using as well as to better understand the message.

Strategy 5: Note-taking: Writing down important information. Note-taking helps students become more active listeners. Devine (1981) describes note-taking as "responding-with-pen-in-hand" (p. 156). Students' interest in note-taking begins with the realization that they cannot store unlimited amounts of information in their minds; they need some kind of external storage system. Many of the listening strategies require listeners to make written notes about what they are hearing. *Note-taking* is a general term to describe this strategy. Note-taking is often thought of as a listing or outline, but notes can also be written in clusters.

FIGURE 8.3
Graphic Organizers

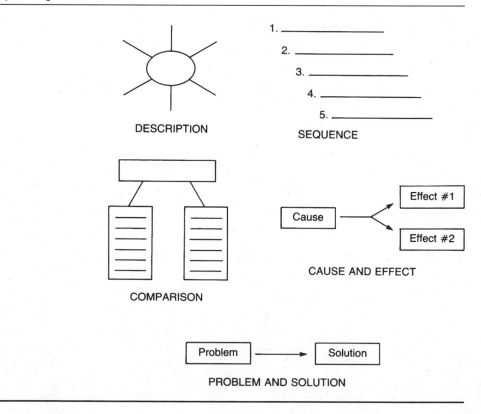

FIGURE 8.4
Possible Graphic Organizers for Cause and Effect

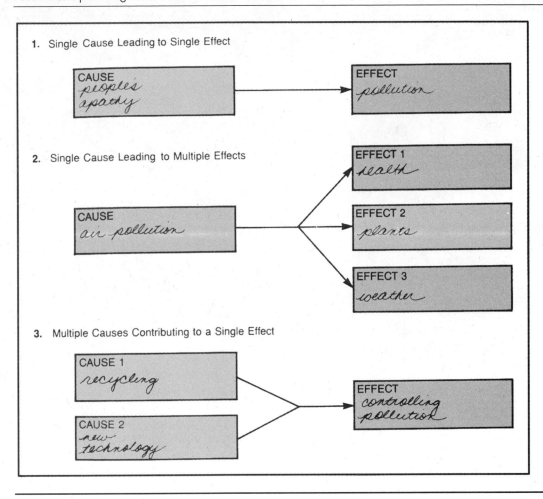

Teachers introduce note-taking by taking notes with the class on the chalkboard. During an oral presentation, the teacher stops periodically, asks students to identify what important information was presented, and lists their responses on the chalkboard. Teachers often begin by writing notes in a list format, but the notes can also be written in outline or cluster formats. Similarly, the teacher can use key words, phrases, or sentences in recording notes. After an introduction to various note-taking strategies, students develop personal note-taking systems in which they write notes in their own words and use a consistent format.

Fourth-grade students might try a special kind of note-taking in which they divide their papers into two columns. They label the left column "note-taking" and the right column "note-making." They take notes in the left column, but more importantly, they think about the notes, make connections, and personalize the notes in the right column, "note-making" (Berthoff, 1981). Students can use this strategy when listening to oral presentations as well as when reading a content area textbook or an informational book. Students need to stop periodically and reflect on the notes they have taken. The "note-making" column should be more extensive than the other column. A sample note-taking and note-making sheet is presented in Figure 8.5. In this figure, a student is taking notes as she reads about illegal drugs.

Children's awareness of note-taking as a strategy "to help you remember what you are listening to" begins in the primary grades. Teachers should demonstrate the usefulness of note-taking on the writing board or on charts with kindergartners and first graders. Second and third graders then begin taking notes in their learning logs as a part of social studies and science classes.

Outlining is a useful note-taking strategy, but it has gained a bad reputation from misuse in secondary and college English classes (Devine, 1981). It may be preferable to use print materials to introduce outlining, because oral presentations are often less structured than print materials,

FIGURE 8.5
Note-Taking and Note-Making Sheet

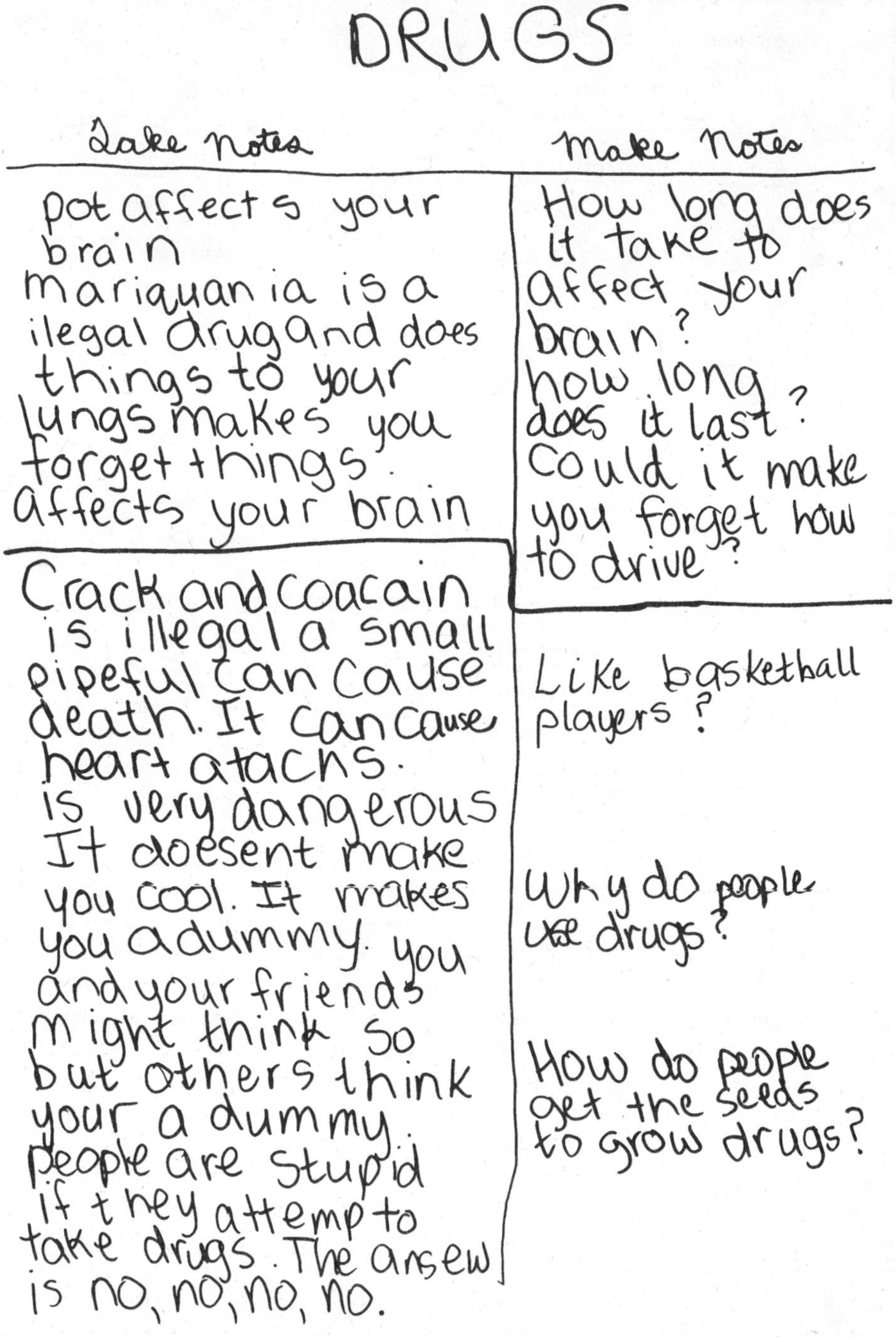

DRUGS

Take notes	Make notes
pot affects your brain mariguania is a ilegal drug and does things to your lungs makes you forget things. affects your brain	How long does it take to affect your brain? how long does it last? Could it make you forget how to drive?
Crack and coacain is illegal a small pipeful can cause death. It can cause heart atacns. Is very dangerous It doesent make you cool. It makes you a dummy. you and your friends might think so but others think your a dummy. People are stupid if they attempt to take drugs. The arsew is no, no, no, no.	Like basketball players? Why do people use drugs? How do people get the seeds to grow drugs?

and students must discover the speaker's plan in order to outline. Teachers who want to teach outlining through oral presentations, however, should begin with a simple organization of perhaps three main ideas with two subordinate ideas for each main idea. Teachers can also give students a partial outline to complete while they give an oral presentation.

The information in the notes students take depends on their purpose for listening. Thus, it is essential that students understand the purpose for listening before they begin to take notes. Some listening tasks require noting main ideas or details; other tasks require noting sequence, cause and effect, or comparisons.

Most language arts textbooks limit instruction in note-taking to taking notes from textbooks and reference materials (Tompkins, Smith, & Friend, 1984). Taking notes from a speaker, however, is an equally important strategy. When they are taking notes from a speaker, students cannot control the speed at which information is presented. They usually cannot relisten to a speaker to complete notes, and the structure of oral presentations is often not as formal as that of print materials. Students need to become aware of these differences so they can adapt their note-taking system to the presentation mode.

 Strategy 6: Getting clues from the speaker. Speakers use both visual and verbal cues to convey their messages and direct their listeners' attention. Visual cues include gesturing, writing or underlining important information on the writing board, and changing facial expressions. Verbal cues include pausing, raising or lowering the voice, slowing down speech to stress key points, and repeating important information. Surprisingly, many students are not aware of these attention-directing behaviors, so teachers must point them out. Once students are aware of these cues, they can use them to increase their understanding of a message.

Teaching Comprehensive Listening

To understand a message they are listening to, students need to learn a strategic approach that involves activities before, during, and after listening. Students must learn to use each of the six listening strategies and apply them in comprehensive as well as critical and appreciative listening activities. You can use the following instructional strategy to teach these listening strategies.

1. *Introduce the strategy.* Explain the listening strategy, how it is used, and the types of listening activities for which it is most effective. Develop a chart listing the characteristics or steps of the strategy; for example, the information about organizational patterns in Figure 8.3 can be listed in a chart for students to refer to.
2. *Demonstrate the strategy.* Demonstrate the strategy as you give an oral presentation or as students listen to a tape-recorded or film presentation. Stop the presentation periodically to talk aloud about what one does as one listens, asks oneself questions, (and takes notes), and point out cues for students. After completing the activity, discuss your use of the strategy with students.
3. *Practice the strategy.* Have students model the strategy during other presentations. Stop the presentation periodically to ask students to describe how they are listening. After several large-group presentations, students can work in small groups and, later, individually practice the strategy.
4. *Review the strategy.* After each listening activity, have students explain the strategy and how they use it.
5. *Teach other strategies.* Present a variety of listening activities and have students experiment to determine if the strategy is effective or if a different strategy might be better. Introduce additional strategies to meet these other listening purposes. After presenting all six strategies and letting students practice them, continue to the next step.
6. *Apply the strategies.* After students develop a repertoire of the six listening strategies, they need to learn to select an appropriate strategy for specific listening purposes. The choice depends both on the listener's and the speaker's purpose. Although students must decide which strategy to use before they begin to listen, they need to continue to monitor their selection during and after listening. Students can generate a list of questions to guide their selection of a strategy and monitor its effectiveness. Asking themselves questions like these before listening will help them select a listening strategy:
   - What is the speaker's purpose?
   - What is my purpose for listening?
   - What am I going to do with what I listen to?
   - Will I need to take notes?
   - Which strategies could I use?
   - Which one will I select?
   These are possible questions to use during listening:
   - Is my strategy still working?
   - Am I putting information into groups?
   - Is the speaker giving me cues about the organization of the message?
   - Is the speaker giving me nonverbal cues, such as gestures and facial expressions?
   - Is the speaker's voice giving me other cues?

These questions are appropriate after listening:

- Do I have questions for the speaker?
- Is any part of the message unclear?
- Are my notes complete?
- Did I make a good choice of strategies? Why or why not? (Tompkins, Friend, & Smith, 1987, p. 39)

Repeat the first five steps of this instructional strategy to teach students how to select an appropriate strategy for various listening activities.

Teachers' actions often determine whether students understand what they are listening to. Using a directed listening strategy with before, during, and after listening components is crucial. Before listening, teachers should make sure students have the necessary background information and then, when they present the new information, they link it to the background information. Teachers explain the purposes of the listening activity and suggest what type of strategy students can use to increase their understanding. While the students listen, teachers can draw graphic organizers on the chalkboard and add key words to help them organize information. This information can also provide the basis for the notes students take either during or after listening. Teachers should use both visual and verbal cues to direct students' attention. Finally, after students listen, teachers should provide opportunities to apply the new information.

C. CRITICAL LISTENING

Children, even primary-grade students, need to develop critical listening (and thinking) skills because they are exposed to many types of persuasion and propaganda. Peer pressure to dress, behave, and talk like their classmates exerts a strong pull on students. Interpreting books and films requires critical thinking and listening. And social studies and science lessons on topics such as pollution, political candidates, and drugs demand that students listen and think critically.

Television commercials are another form of persuasion and propaganda, and because many commercials are directed at children, it is essential that they listen critically and learn to judge the advertising claims. For example, do the jogging shoes actually help you to run faster? Will the breakfast cereal make you a better football player? Will a particular toy make you a more popular child?

Persuasion and Propaganda

There are three basic ways to persuade people. The first is by reason. People seek logical conclusions, whether from absolute facts or from strong possibilities; for example, people can be persuaded to practice more healthful living as the result of medical research. It is necessary, of course, to distinguish between reasonable arguments and unreasonable appeals. To suggest that diet pills will bring about exaggerated weight loss is an unreasonable appeal.

A second means of persuasion is an appeal to character. We can be persuaded by what another person recommends if we trust that person. Trust comes from personal knowledge or the reputation of the person who is trying to persuade. We must always question whether we can believe the persuader. We can believe what scientists say about the dangers of nuclear waste, but can we believe what a sports personality says about the effectiveness of a particular sports shoe?

The third way to persuade people is by appealing to their emotions. Emotional appeals can be as strong as intellectual appeals. We have strong feelings and concern for ourselves and other people and animals. Fear, peer acceptance, and freedom of expression are all strong feelings that influence our opinions and beliefs.

Any of the three types of appeals can be used to try to persuade someone. For example, when a child tries to persuade her parents that her bedtime should be delayed by 30 minutes, she might argue that neighbors allow their children to stay up later—an appeal to character. It is an appeal to reason when the argument focuses on the amount of sleep a 10-year-old needs. And when the child announces that she has the earliest bedtime of anyone in her class and it makes her feel like a baby, the appeal is to emotion. The same three appeals apply to in-school persuasion. To persuade classmates to read a particular book in a book report "commercial," a student might argue that they should read the book because it is short and interesting (reason); because it is hilarious and they'll laugh (emotion); or because it is the most popular book in the second grade and everyone else is reading it (character).

Children need to learn to become critical consumers of advertisements (Rudasill, 1986; Tutolo, 1981). Advertisers use appeals to reason, character, and emotion just as other persuaders do to promote products, ideas, and services; however, advertisers may also use *propaganda* to influence our beliefs and actions. Propaganda suggests something shady or underhanded. Like persuasion, propaganda is designed to influence people's beliefs and actions, but propagandists may use certain techniques to distort, conceal, and exaggerate. Two of these techniques are deceptive language and propaganda devices.

Deceptive language. People seeking to influence us often use words that evoke a variety of responses. They claim something is *improved, more natural,* or *50% better—loaded words* that are deceptive because they are suggestive. When a product is advertised as 50% better, for example, consumers need to ask, "50% better than what?" Advertisements rarely answer that question.

Doublespeak is another type of deceptive language characterized as evasive, euphemistic, confusing, and self-contradictory. Janitors may be called *maintenance engineers,* and repeats of television shows are termed *encore telecasts.* Lutz (1984) cited a number of kinds of doublespeak. Fourth-grade students can easily understand two kinds, euphemisms and inflated language. Other kinds of doublespeak, such as jargon specific to particular groups, overwhelming an audience with words, and language that pretends to communicate but does not, are more appropriate for older students.

Euphemisms are words or phrases (for example, *passed away*) that are used to avoid a harsh or distasteful reality, often out of concern for someone's feelings rather than to deceive. *Inflated language* includes words intended to make the ordinary seem extraordinary—car mechanics become *automotive internists,* and used cars become *pre-owned* or *experienced cars.* Examples of deceptive language are listed in Figure 8.6. Children need to learn that people sometimes use words that only pretend to communicate; sometimes they use words to intentionally misrepresent, as when someone advertises a vinyl wallet as "genuine imitation leather" or a ring with a glass stone as a "faux diamond." Children need to be able to interpret deceptive language and to avoid using it themselves.

Propaganda devices. Advertisers use propaganda devices such as testimonials, the bandwagon effect, and rewards to sell products. Nine devices that elementary students can learn to identify are listed in Figure 8.7. Students in grade 4 and up can listen to commercials to find examples of each propaganda device and discuss the effect the device has on them. They can also investigate to see how the same devices vary in commercials directed toward youngsters, teenagers, and adults. For instance, a snack food commercial with a sticker or toy in the package will appeal to a youngster, and a videotape recorder advertisement offering a factory rebate will appeal to an adult. The propaganda device for both ads is the same: a reward! Propaganda devices can be used to sell ideas as well as products. Public service announcements about smoking or wearing seat belts, as well as political advertisements, endorsements, and speeches, use these devices.

When students locate advertisements and commercials they believe are misleading or deceptive, they can write letters of complaint to the following watchdog agencies:

Action for Children's Television
46 Austin St.
Newton, MA 02160

Federal Trade Commission
Pennsylvania Ave. at Sixth St. NW
Washington, DC 20580

Children's Advertising
Review Unit
Council of Better Business
Bureaus
845 Third Ave.
New York, NY 10022

Zillions Ad Complaints
256 Washington St.
Mt. Vernon, NY 10553

FIGURE 8.6
Examples of Deceptive Language (Lutz, n.d.)

Loaded Words

best buy	longer lasting
better than	lowest
carefree	maximum
discount	more natural
easier	more powerful
extra strong	new/newer
fortified	plus
fresh	stronger
guaranteed	ultra
improved	virtually

Doublespeak / **Translations**

Doublespeak	Translations
bathroom tissue	toilet paper
civil disorder	riot
correctional facility	jail, prison
dentures	false teeth
disadvantaged	poor
encore telecast	re-run
funeral director	undertaker
genuine imitation leather	vinyl
inner city	slum, ghetto
inoperative statement or misspeak	lie
memorial park	cemetery
mobile home	house trailer
nervous wetness	sweat
occasional irregularity	constipation
passed away	died
people expressways	sidewalks
personal preservation flotation device	life preserver
pre-owned or experienced	used
pupil station	student's desk
senior citizen	old person
terminal living	dying
urban transportation specialist	cab driver, bus driver

Students' letters should carefully describe the advertisement and explain what bothers them about it. They should also tell where and when they saw or heard the advertisement or commercial.

Teaching Critical Listening

The following steps in teaching students to be critical listeners are similar to the steps in teaching listening strategies. In this instructional strategy, students view commercials to examine propaganda devices and persuasive language. Later they can create their own commercials and advertisements.

Step 1. Introduce commercials. Talk about commercials and ask students about familiar commercials. Videotape some commercials and view them with students. Discuss the purpose of each commercial. Use these questions about commercials to probe students' thinking about persuasion and propaganda:

- What is the speaker's purpose?
- What are the speaker's credentials?
- Is there evidence of bias?

1. Glittering Generality

Generalities such as "motherhood," "justice," and "The American Way" are used to enhance the quality of a product or the character of a political figure. Propagandists select a generality so attractive that listeners do not challenge the speakers' real point. If a candidate for public office happens to be a mother, for example, the speaker may say, "Our civilization could not survive without mothers." The generalization is true, of course, and listeners may—if they are not careful—accept the candidate without asking these questions: Is she a mother? Is she a good mother? Does being a mother have anything to do with being a good candidate?

2. Testimonial

To convince people to purchase a product, an advertiser associates it with a popular personality such as an athlete or film star. For example, "Bozo Cereal must be good because Joe Footballstar eats it every morning." Similarly, film stars endorse candidates for political office and telethons to raise money for medical research and other causes. Consider these questions: Is the person familiar with the product being advertised? Does the person offering the testimonial have the expertise necessary to judge the quality of the product, event, or candidate?

3. Transfer

In this device, which is similar to the testimonial technique, the persuader tries to transfer the authority and prestige of some person or object to another person or object that will then be accepted. Good examples are found regularly in advertising: A film star is shown using Super Soap, and viewers are supposed to believe that they too may have healthy, youthful skin if they use the same soap. Likewise, politicians like to be seen with famous athletes or entertainers in hopes that the luster of the stars will rub off on them. This technique is also known as guilt or glory by association. Questions to determine the effect of this device are the same as for the testimonial technique.

4. Name-calling

Here advertisers try to pin a bad label on something they want listeners to dislike so that it will automatically be rejected or condemned. In a discussion of health insurance, for example, an opponent may call the sponsor of a bill a socialist. Whether or not the sponsor is a socialist does not matter to the name-caller; the purpose is to have any unpleasant associations of the term rub off on the victim. Listeners should ask themselves whether or not the label has any effect on the product.

5. Plain Folks

Assuming that most listeners favor common, ordinary people (rather than elitish, stuffed shirts), many politicians like to assume the appearance of common folk. One candidate, who really went to Harvard and wore $400 suits, campaigned in clothes from J.C. Penney's and spoke backcountry dialect. "Look at me, folks," the candidate wanted to say, "I'm just a regular country boy like you; I wouldn't sell you a bill of goods!" To determine the effect of this device, listeners should ask these questions: Is the person really the type of person he or she is portraying? Does the person really share the ideas of the people with whom he or she professes to identify?

6. Card Stacking

In presenting complex issues, the unscrupulous persuader often chooses only those items that favor one side of an issue. Any unfavorable facts are suppressed. To consider the argument objectively, listeners must seek additional information about other viewpoints.

7. Bandwagon

This technique appeals to many people's need to be a part of a group. Advertisers claim that everyone is using this product and you should, too. For example, "more physicians recommend this pill than any other." (Notice that the advertisement doesn't specify what "any other" is.) Questions to consider include the following. Does everyone really use this product? What is it better than? Why should I jump on the bandwagon?

8. Snob Appeal

In contrast to the plain folks device, persuaders use snob appeal to try to appeal to the people who want to become part of an elite or exclusive group. Advertisements for expensive clothes, cosmetics, and gourmet foods often use this technique. Listeners should consider these questions in evaluating the commercials and advertisements using this device: Is the product of high quality or does it have an expensive nametag? Is the product of higher quality than other non-snobbish brands?

9. Rewards

Increasingly, advertisers offer rewards for buying their products. For many years, snack food and cereal products offered toys and other gimmicks in their product packages. More often, adults are being lured by this device, too. Free gifts, rebates from manufacturers, low-cost financing, and other rewards are being offered for the purchase of expensive items such as appliances and automobiles. Listeners should consider the value of these rewards and whether they increase the cost of the product.

- Does the speaker use deceptive language?
- Does the speaker make sweeping generalizations or unsupported inferences?
- Do opinions predominate the talk?
- Does the speaker use any propaganda devices?
- Do you accept the message? (Devine, 1982, pp. 41–42)

Step 2. Explain deceptive language. Present the terms *persuasion* and *propaganda*. Introduce the propaganda devices and view the commercials again to look for examples of each device. Introduce loaded words and doublespeak and view the commercials a third time to look for examples of deceptive language.

Step 3. Analyze deceptive language in commercials. Have students work in small groups to critique a commercial as to the type of persuasion, propaganda devices, deceptive language. Students might also want to test the claims made in the commercial.

Step 4. Review concepts. Review the concepts about persuasion, propaganda devices, and deceptive language introduced in the first three steps. It may be helpful for students to make charts about these concepts.

Step 5. Provide practice. Present a new set of videotaped commercials for students to critique. Ask them to identify persuasion, propaganda devices, and deceptive language in the commercials.

Step 6. Create commercials. Have students apply what they have learned about persuasion, propaganda devices, and deceptive language by creating their own products and writing and producing their own commercials to advertise them. Possible products include breakfast cereals, toys, beauty and diet products, and sports equipment, or students might create homework and house-sitting services to advertise. They can also choose community or environmental issues to campaign for or against. The storyboard for a commercial created by a group of students appears in Figure 8.8. As the students present the commercials, classmates act as critical listeners to detect persuasion, propaganda devices, loaded words, and doublespeak.

Using Advertisements. Students can use the same procedures and activities with advertisements they collect from magazines and product packages. Have children collect advertisements and display them on a bulletin board. Written advertisements also use deceptive language and propaganda devices. Students examine advertisements and then decide how the writer is trying to persuade them to purchase the product. They can also compare the amount of text to the amount of pictures. Fox and Allen (1983) reported that children who examined advertisements found that, in contrast to advertisements for toys, cosmetics, and appliances, ads for cigarettes had comparatively little text and used pictures prominently. The students quickly speculated on the reasons for this approach.

D. APPRECIATIVE LISTENING

Students are listening appreciatively when they listen for enjoyment. Appreciative listening includes listening to music, to a comedian tell jokes, to friends when they talk, to a storyteller, and to stories and poems read aloud. We will focus on reading stories aloud to students. When students listen to stories, they develop the ability to visualize, identify the speech rhythm, identify the speaker's style, interpret character from dialogue, recognize tone and mode, understand the effect of the speaker or reader's vocal qualities and physical action, and understand the effect of the audience on the listeners' responses (Wolvin & Coakley, 1979), as well as to gain an understanding of how authors structure stories and how the characters, plot, setting, and other elements are woven together.

Reading Aloud to Students

Sharing books orally is a valuable way to help students enjoy literature. Reading stories to children is an important component in most kindergarten and first-grade classrooms. Unfortunately, teachers often think they need to read to children only until they learn to read for themselves; however, reading aloud and sharing the excitement of books, language, and reading should remain an important part of the language arts program at all grade levels. The common complaint is that there is not enough time in the school day to read to chil-

FIGURE 8.8
Storyboard for a "Dream Date" Commercial

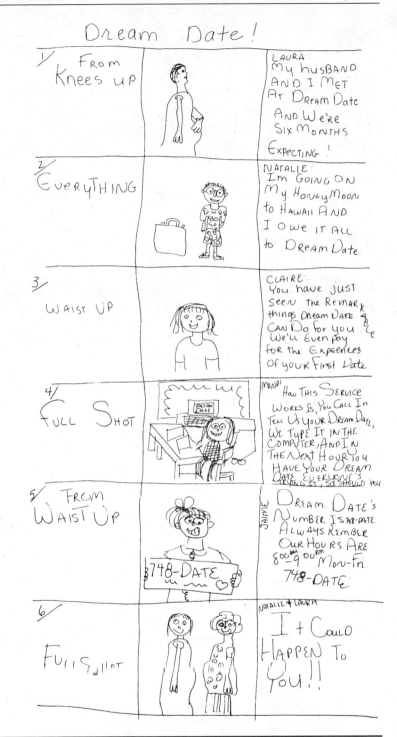

dren, but reading a story or a chapter of a longer story aloud can take as little as 10 or 15 minutes a day. Many educators (Kimmel & Segel, 1983; Sims, 1977; Trelease, 1989) point out the necessity of finding time to read aloud so as to take advantage of the many benefits:

Stimulating children's interest in books and reading
Broadening children's reading interests and developing their taste for quality literature
Introducing children to the sounds of written language and expanding their vocabulary and sentence patterns

Sharing with children books that are "too good to miss"

Allowing children to listen to books that would be too difficult for them to read on their own or books that are "hard to get into"

Expanding children's background of experiences

Introducing children to concepts about written language, different genres of literature, poetry, and elements of story structure

Providing a pleasurable, shared experience

Modeling to children that adults read and enjoy reading to increase the likelihood that children will become lifelong readers

By reading aloud to students daily, you can introduce them to all types of literature and the enjoyment of reading. The guidelines for choosing books to read aloud are simple: choose books you like and that you think will appeal to your students. Trelease (1989) suggests four additional criteria of good read-aloud books: They should be fast-paced to hook children's interest as quickly as possible; contain well-developed characters; include easy-to-read dialogue; and keep long descriptive passages to a minimum. A number of annotated guidebooks can help teachers select books for reading aloud as well as for independent reading. Figure 8.9 lists these guides.

Books that have received awards or other acclaim from teachers, librarians, and children make good choices. Two of the most prestigious awards are the Caldecott and Newbery Awards, found in the libraries in the children's book section. Other lists of outstanding books are prepared annually by professional groups such as the National Council of Teachers of English and the National Council of Teachers of Social Studies. In many states, children read and vote on books to receive recognition, such as the Buckeye Book Award in Ohio and the Sequoia Book Award in Oklahoma. The International Reading Association sponsors a Children's Choices competition in which children read and select their favorite books; a list is published annually.

FIGURE 8.9
Guides for Choosing Read-Aloud Books

Guides for Choosing Books

Bauer, C. F. (1983). *This way to books.* New York: Wilson.

Carroll, F. L., & Mecham, M. (Eds.). (1984). *Exciting, funny, scary, short, different, and sad books kids like about animals, science, sports, families, songs, and other things.* Chicago: American Library Association.

Christensen, J. (Ed.). (1983). *Your reading: A booklist for junior high and middle school students.* Urbana, IL: National Council of Teachers of English.

Freeman, J. (1984). *Books kids will sit still for.* Hagerstown, MD: Alleyside Press.

Kimmel, M. M., & Segel, E. (1983). *For reading out loud! A guide for sharing books with children.* New York: Delacorte.

Lipson, E. R. (1988). *The New York Times parents' guide to the best books for children.* New York: Random House.

McMullan, K. H. (1984). *How to choose good books for kids.* Reading, MA: Addison-Wesley.

Monson, D. L. (Ed.). (1985). *Adventuring with books: A booklist for pre-K–grade 6 (New ed.).* Urbana, IL: National Council of Teachers of English.

Roser, N., & Frith, M. (Eds.). (1983). *Children's choices: Teaching with books children like.* Newark, DE: International Reading Association.

Stensland, A. L. (1979). *Literature by and about the American Indian: An annotated bibliography* (2nd ed.). Urbana, IL: National Council of Teachers of English.

Trelease, J. (1989). *The new read-aloud handbook.* New York: Penguin.

Tway, E. (Ed.). (1981). *Reading ladders for human relations* (6th ed.). Urbana, IL: National Council of Teachers of English.

Journals and Newsletters

CBC Features, The Children's Book Council, 67 Irving Place, New York, NY 10003.

The Horn Book, Park Square Building, 31 St. James Avenue, Boston, MA 02116.

Language Arts, National Council of Teachers of English, 1111 Kenyon Road, Urbana, IL 61801.

The New Advocate, Christopher-Gordon Publishers, P.O. Box 809, Needham Heights, MA 02194.

The Reading Teacher, International Reading Association, P.O. Box 8139, Newark, DE 19711.

Teachers in many primary-grade classrooms read one story aloud as part of a literature or author unit and later during the day read informational books aloud as part of social studies units. Poems, too, are read aloud in connection with content area classes. It is not unusual for primary-grade students to listen to their teacher read aloud three or more stories and other books during the school day. If children are read to only once a day, they will listen to fewer than 200 books during the school year, and this is simply not enough! More than 40,000 books are available for children, and reading stories and other books aloud is an important way to share more of this literature with children.

Repeated Readings. Children, especially preschoolers and kindergartners, often beg to have a familiar book reread. Although it is important to share a wide variety of books with children, researchers have found that children benefit in specific ways from repeated readings (Yaden, 1988). Through repetition, students gain control over the parts of a story and are better able to synthesize the story parts into a whole. The quality of children's responses to a repeated story changes (Beaver, 1982), and children become more independent users of the classroom library center (Martinez & Teale, 1988).

Martinez and Roser (1985) examined young children's responses to stories and found that as stories become increasingly familiar, students' responses indicate a greater depth of understanding. They found that children talked almost twice as much about familiar books that had been reread many times as about unfamiliar books that had been read only once or twice. The form and focus of children's talk changed, too. While children tended to ask questions about unfamiliar stories, they made comments about familiar stories. Children's talk about unfamiliar stories focused on characters; the focus changed to details and word meanings when they talked about familiar stories. The researchers also found that children's comments after repeated readings were more probing and more specific, suggesting that they had greater insight into the story. Researchers investigating the value of repeated readings have focused mainly on pre-school and primary-grade students, but rereading favorite stories may have similar benefits for older students as well.

Other Oral Presentation Modes. Stories can be shared with students through storytelling, readers' theater, and plays. Students can also benefit from other forms of oral presentations, such as tape recordings of stories and filmstrip and film versions of stories. Audiovisual story presentations are available from Weston Woods (Weston, CT 06883), Random House/Miller Brody (400 Hahn Road, Westminster, MD 21157), Pied Piper (P.O. Box 320, Verdugo City, CA 91046), and other distributors.

Teaching Appreciative Listening

Teaching appreciative listening differs from teaching other kinds of listening because enjoyment is the goal. Rather than use the six-step teaching strategy, the directed reading lesson can be adapted for appreciative listening. Activities in this strategy are divided into three steps: before reading, during reading, and after reading.

Before Reading. Teachers activate students' prior knowledge, provide necessary new information related to the story or the author, and interest students in the story. Teachers might discuss the topic or theme, show pictures, or share objects related to the story to draw on prior knowledge or to create new experiences. For example, teachers might talk about students' favorite games before reading Van Allsburg's jungle adventure game, *Jumanji* (1981).

Before beginning to read, teachers set the purpose for reading so that students have a reason for listening to the story.

During Reading. Teachers read the story aloud, during which students should be actively involved with the story. One way to encourage active participation is to use the *Directed Reading Thinking Activity (DRTA),* a procedure developed by Russell Stauffer (1975) in which students make predictions about a story and then read or listen to the story to confirm or reject the predictions. DRTA involves three steps.

Step 1. Predicting. After showing students the cover of the book and reading the title, the teacher begins by asking students to make a prediction about the story using questions like these:

What do you think a story with a title like this might be about?
What do you think might happen in this story?
Does this picture give you any ideas about what might happen in this story?

If necessary, the teacher reads the first paragraph or two to provide more information for students to use in making their predictions. After a brief discussion in which all students commit themselves to one or another of the alternatives presented, the teacher asks these questions:

Which of these ideas do you think would be the likely one?
Why do you think that idea is a good one?

Step 2. Reasoning and predicting from succeeding pages. After students set their purposes for listening, the teacher reads part of the story, and then students begin to confirm or reject their predictions by answering questions such as the following:

What do you think now?
What do you think will happen next?
What would happen if . . . ?
Why do you think that idea is a good one?

The teacher continues reading the story aloud, stopping at key points to repeat this step.

Step 3. Proving. Students give reasons to support their predictions by answering further questions:

What in the story makes you think that?
Where in the story do you get information to support that idea?

The teacher can ask these "proving" questions during the reading or afterward. Note that this strategy can be used both when students are listening to the teacher read a story aloud or when they are reading the story themselves. Use the strategy only when students are reading or listening to an unfamiliar story so that the prediction actively involves them in the story.

Students keep a *reading log* in which they respond after the whole story or after each chapter is read aloud. Primary-grade students keep a reading log by writing the title and author of the story and drawing a picture related to the story. They can also add a few words or a sentence. During an author unit on Tomie de Paola, for instance, second graders, after hearing each de Paola story, record the title on a page in their notebooks, draw a picture related to the story, and write a sentence or two telling what they liked about the story, what it made them think of, or to summarize it. Fourth-grade students write a response after each chapter, and they may add illustrations as well. As an alternative to reading logs, students can discuss the events in the story, retell the story, or write a retelling of the story, either as a class or in small groups.

After Reading. Students share their reading log entries and, through discussion, relate the story to their lives and to other stories they have read. Discussion can be valuable when it leads students to think critically about the story; the focus of discussions should always be on higher-level thinking skills, not factual recall questions.

Enjoyment is reason enough to read aloud to children; however, several kinds of activities extend children's interest in a story after reading. These activities, called *response to literature,* can be spontaneous expressions of interest and delight in a book as well as teacher-planned activities. Hickman (1980) cites the example of a kindergartner named Ben who spontaneously responded to a favorite story when his teacher shared Leo Lionni's *Pezzetino* (1975):

> Ben says, "I like *Pezzetino* because of all the colors 'n stuff, and the way it repeats. He keeps saying it. And there's marbelizing—see here? And this very last page. . ." Then Ben turns to the end of the book and holds up a picture for the group to see. "He cut paper. How many think he's a good cutter?" Ben conducts a vote, counting the raised hands that show a majority of the group believes Leo Lionni to be "a good cutter."(p. 525)

Ben's knowledge of the text and illustrations as well as his enjoyment are obvious. Through his comments and the class vote, Ben is involving his classmates in the story, and it seems likely that *Pezzetino* will be passed from student to student in the class. Spontaneous responses to literature, like Ben's, occur at all grade levels in supportive classrooms where students are invited to share their ideas and feelings.

Teacher-planned response activities include having students make puppets to use in retelling a favorite story, writing letters to authors, creating a mobile for a favorite story, and reading other books by the same author or on a similar theme, to name only a few possibilities. Figure 8.10 lists response to literature activities. These activities are equally useful with books students have listened to read aloud and with books they have read themselves.

The purpose of response to literature activities is for students to personalize and extend their reading. Having them enjoy reading and want to read is another goal. Traditional activities such as having students write a book report or answer factual recall test questions should not be an automatic follow-up to reading aloud because they may discourage interest in reading and literature. Instead, students should engage in activities that grow out of their enjoyment of a particular book.

Figure 8.11 illustrates how to use this teaching strategy with two stories, *Where the Wild Things Are* (Sendak, 1963) and *The Pied Piper of Hamelin* (Mayer, 1987). Sometimes teachers read a story aloud without going through all six steps. At times it is appropriate to just read the story aloud, but most of the time, students should be involved with activities related to the story before and after reading so they have the opportunity to understand and appreciate it.

E. CLASSROOM ACTIVITIES*

Listening for Different Purposes—Why and How   ACTIVITY 8.1

Purpose

1. To realize that we listen for different purposes
2. To identify purposes for listening
3. To describe personal requirements and responsibilities for different listening experiences

Materials

A radio for passive listening; directions or announcements for attentive listening; a paragraph for directed listening; a commercial for critical evaluative listening; a story or record for appreciative listening.

Grade level

All grades; examples for the different types of listening should correspond with the students' ability and interest levels.

Procedures

1. While students are involved in another activity such as finishing art work or another assignment, turn on a radio at low volume. Do not attract the students' attention to the radio. After the radio has played for a few minutes and the other assignment is completed, ask the students if they can tell you what was on the radio broadcast. Ask them to describe the content of the radio program as specifically as possible. Discuss why some students could report what was on the radio while others could not. (Most of the students will not be able to relate very much information unless a favorite personality or subject attracts their attention.) Ask the students to describe this type of listening. When they "tune out" sounds for part of the time, are they able to remember a portion of what they hear? Tell the students that passive listening occurs when a person is not actively involved in the act of listening and does not have a purpose for listening. Have the students list circumstances under which they listen passively. When is passive listening acceptable or advantageous? When is passive listening inappropriate? When could passive listening even get them into trouble?
2. Explain to students that several other kinds of listening are important and ask them if they can identify any other types of listening. Tell them they will experience several different types of listening, describe the listening experience, and suggest purposes for each type of listening.

---

*Activities in this section are adapted from Donna E. Norton & Saundra Norton, *Language Arts Activities for Children*, 3rd ed. (Englewood Cliffs, NJ: Merrill/Prentice Hall, 1993), pp. 66–70, 80–81, 106–107. By permission of the authors and Prentice Hall.

FIGURE 8.10
Types of Response Activities

Art Activities

Create a series of illustrations for a favorite book or story episode and compile the illustrations to form a wordless picture book.

Practice the illustration techniques (e.g., collage, styrofoam prints, watercolors, line drawing) used in a favorite book. Also, examine other books that use the same technique.

Create a collage to represent the theme of a favorite book.

Design a book jacket for a favorite book, laminate it, and place it on the book.

Construct a shoebox or other miniature scene of an episode from a favorite story.

Create a filmstrip to illustrate a favorite story.

Create a game based on a favorite story or series of stories. Possible game formats include card games, board games, word finds, crossword puzzles, and computer games.

Draw a map or make a relief map of a book's setting. Some stories, such as Lasky's *Beyond the Divide* (1983), include a map, usually on the book's end papers.

Create a mobile illustrating a favorite book.

Make a movie of a favorite book by drawing a series of pictures on a long strip of paper. Attach ends to rollers and place in a cardboard box.

Writing Activities

Assume the role of a book character and keep a simulated journal from that character's viewpoint.

Write a book review of a favorite book for the class newspaper.

Write a letter to a pen pal about a favorite book.

Create a poster to advertise a favorite book.

Write another episode for the characters in a favorite story.

Create a newspaper with news stories and advertisements based on characters and episodes from a favorite book.

Write a letter to the author of a favorite book. Check the guidelines for writing to children's authors presented in Chapter 6.

Write a simulated letter from one book character to another.

Select five "quotable quotes" from a favorite book and list them on a poster or in copybooks.

Reading Activities

Research a favorite author and compile the information in a brief report to insert in the author's book.

Read other stories by the same author.

Read other stories with a similar theme.

Tape-record a favorite book or excerpts from a longer story to place in a listening center.

Read a favorite story to children in the primary grades.

Compare different versions of the same story.

Talk and Drama Activities

Give a readers theater presentation of a favorite story.

Write a script and produce a play or puppet show about a favorite book.

Dress as a favorite book character and answer questions from classmates about the character and the story.

Retell a favorite story or episode from a longer story using puppets or other props.

Give a chalk talk by sketching pictures on the writing board or on a large sheet of paper as the story is retold.

Discuss a favorite book informally with several classmates.

Tape-record a review of a favorite book using background music and sound effects.

Videotape a commercial for a favorite book.

Interview classmates about a favorite book.

Other Activities

Plan a special day to honor a favorite author with posters, publicity information from the author's publishers, letters to and from the author, a display of the author's books, and products from other activities listed above.

If possible, arrange to place a conference telephone call to the author or have the author visit the school on that day.

Conduct a class or school vote to determine students' 10 most popular books. Also, many states sponsor annual book awards for outstanding children's books such as Ohio's Buckeye Book Award and Oklahoma's Sequoia Book Award. Encourage students to read the books nominated for their state's award and to vote for their favorite books.

Cook a food described in a favorite book, such as gingerbread cookies after reading Galdone's *The gingerbread boy* (1975) or spaghetti after reading de Paola's *Strega Nona* (1975).

FIGURE 8.11
Using the Teaching Strategy

STEP	WHERE THE WILD THINGS ARE (Sendak, 1963)	THE PIED PIPER OF HAMELIN (Mayer, 1987)
Before Reading		
Initiating	Ask children if they have ever been sent to their rooms for misbehaving. What happens while you are in your room?	Ask students if they have heard the saying "A promise is a promise." What does it mean? Ask them if they keep all promises. When is it not necessary?
Structuring	Hang three large sheets of paper and label them *beginning, middle,* and *end.* Explain that the story is divided into three parts—beginning, middle, and end. After reading, students divide into groups to draw pictures of the three parts.	Explain that this story is a legend that may have some basis in fact. Review the characteristics of a legend and identify other familiar legends. Locate Hamelin (West Germany) on a world map.
During Reading		
Conceptualizing	Read the story aloud using DRTA.	Read the story aloud using DRTA, but have students write their predictions before sharing them orally.
After Reading		
Summarizing	Have students retell the story as a class collaboration with each child choosing one page to draw and dictate (or write) a retelling for. Compile the pages to make a book.	Discuss the story, focusing on the mayor's promise and the piper's retaliation when the promise was not kept.
Generalizing	Read the story *Hey, Al* (Yorinks, 1986) and compare the three parts and the fantasy in the middle part of the two stories.	Ask students to write in response to "A promise is a promise" or "The piper must be paid," What do these sayings mean in the story and today?
Applying	Dramatize the story after making costumes of the wild things from grocery sacks. Divide the dramatization into three acts—Act 1, The Beginning; Act 2, The Middle; and Act 3, The End.	Invite students to choose from these response activities: investigate the Pied Piper legend and its origin; read other legends; create a diorama about the story; in a small group, create a puppet show based on the legend and perform it for a second grade class; compile and illustrate a booklet of well-known sayings.

Examples:

a. *Comprehensive Listening—K–4*

Give the students oral directions for drawing something (perhaps related to a social studies topic) without telling them the finished product. For example:

"Put a piece of paper and a pencil on your desk. Draw a circle the size of an orange in the middle of your paper. Draw a smaller circle above the first circle so the bottom of the smaller circle touches the top of the larger circle. Draw a small triangle on the left side of the top circle; make the narrow point going away from the circle. Draw a round eye on the top circle. Draw a rectangular-shaped tail on the right side of the bottom circle."

Ask the children to tell you what they have drawn. How did they listen to the directions? Why did they need to listen carefully? What was the purpose for this kind of listening? When would they need to do this kind of listening? Why is this kind of listening important to them?

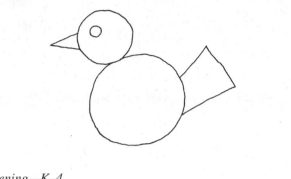

b. *Critical Listening—K–4*

For a critical listening experience, tape-record a commercial used on a children's television show. Before you play the tape, ask the children to listen to identify the source of the tape and why the producer of the material wants them to listen to it. Have them listen to the tape and discuss: Who is trying to persuade us? What are they trying to persuade us to do? Should we believe everything we are told? Why or why not? How should we listen to this type of material? Why? How can we improve our listening when we listen to advertisements?

c. *Appreciative Listening—K–4*

Select a story to read to the students or a record to play for them. Before reading the story or playing the record, tell the students they will have an opportunity to share their favorite parts of the story or record with the group after they have listened to it. After the listening experience, have them describe what they enjoyed most and why they enjoyed it. Discuss this type of listening with the group; have them list the characteristics of appreciative listening and ask them to identify when they would use this type of listening. Have students suggest ways they could improve appreciative listening.

3. Review the different types of listening, the purposes for listening, and the personal requirements and responsibilities for each type of listening. (This activity can be used as an introductory activity to instruction in listening improvement.)

ACTIVITY 8.2   **The Class Crier**

Purpose

1. To develop and improve comprehensive listening ability
2. To repeat class announcements, assignments, and special news concerning the class
3. To perform tasks required by the class announcements, assignments, and special news
4. To learn how people got the news in Colonial times

Materials

Sheet of paper with announcements or assignments for the day; a bell for special news, announcements, or assignments; pictures of a town crier.

Grade level   2–4

Procedures

1. Background information: In Colonial times, there were very few newspapers; consequently, most towns had a town crier. The town crier walked through the streets calling out

the news of the day. If the town crier had special news to tell, he rang a bell or banged on a drum. When the people heard the bell or the drum, they ran to the street to hear the news.

2. Show the class a picture of a town crier during Colonial times. Ask them if they know what the town crier is doing. If they do not know the job of the town crier, explain the town crier's duties and how he attracts attention.

3. Ask the students what the town crier might announce if he visited their class. Discuss suggestions with the class. Tell the students that you are going to use a "Class Crier" to inform them about special announcements, news, and class or group assignments.

4. Put the special announcements or assignments on a sheet of paper similar to one used by a town crier. Read the announcements or assignments to the class as if you were a Colonial town crier. You may also use a bell to announce very important assignments or announcements. Ask individual members of the class to repeat the special announcements or assignments.

5. Have the students evaluate their comprehensive listening ability. Can they repeat announcements and assignments presented by the class crier? Can they perform the assignments announced by the class crier? Do they accomplish whatever is asked of them in the announcements? Do they believe their attentive listening is improving?

6. Students can take turns as a class crier who reads special announcements or news to the class. Develop a bulletin board of the town crier's announcements, assignments, and class news.

Radio's Days of Old   **ACTIVITY 8.3**

1. To develop appreciative listening skills   **Purpose**
2. To develop visual imagery
3. To illustrate characters and settings described in old radio broadcasts
4. To evaluate the use of sound effects and background music on a story
5. To define the climax of a story and describe the techniques used to build excitement

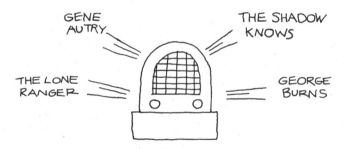

Recordings or tapes of popular radio shows of the past; available shows include those of George   **Materials**
Burns, Jack Benny, The Lone Ranger, Gene Autry, Hopalong Cassidy, Mr. Keen, Tracer of Lost Persons, The Shadow, Escape, Two Thousand Plus, My Friend Irma, Superman, The Green Hornet, and Sherlock Holmes's Adventures. (Sunburst Communications, Pleasantville, NY, publishes *Tune-In,* a series of radio tapes and instructional materials for teaching listening and literature skills with radio broadcasts.)

Depends on broadcast selection and activities used with the selection; young children can   **Grade level**
react to theme songs on radio shows by painting to music or doing creative movement activities; activities requiring students to listen to longer segments, react to plot, or define climax are more appropriate for middle and upper elementary students. Records of old radio shows may be used with large groups, small groups, or individual students who wish to investigate a subject.

1. Ask students if they have ever heard of some of the radio broadcasts from the 1940s   **Procedures**
   and 1950s. (These broadcasts are often played over educational radio stations, or students may have recordings of them.) Ask the students why they believe radio was so popular 50 years ago. Explain that they will have an opportunity to listen to some of

these radio broadcasts. You may wish to suggest that after they have listened to several radio broadcasts, they will also have an opportunity to produce their own radio show complete with sound effects and background music.

2. The listening activities depend on the contents of the radio broadcast. Be sure you listen to the record or tape before you use it with the students. Introduce the broadcast and prepare the students for the listening experience. These activities lend themselves to listening to radio broadcasts:

   a. Because students cannot see the characters in the story, ask them to listen to all the clues that suggest the physical appearance of the main characters or one of the main characters. Have them draw a picture of the character and tell why they drew the character that way. Discuss with them the clues they heard and how they interpreted these clues. (This activity does not have a right or wrong answer unless obvious clues would call for the same interpretation by all listeners.)

   b. The setting for a radio show must also be imagined by each listener. Have students listen for clues about the location and time period of the story. If they do not have enough background experience with that time period, have them research the time period and illustrate the setting. They might illustrate the major setting of the story with dioramas or drawings. For a more extensive setting activity, divide the class into small groups and have them depict the setting on a roll of paper. They can place this roll setting in a box with a window opening and show it as the radio broadcast is replayed. "The Lone Ranger" stories may have several settings, such as a frontier town, an Indian village, a ranch, an old mine, an early railroad, etc. Students may also retell the story without using the radio broadcast.

After students illustrate the setting, allow them to discuss whether or not they would like to live in such a setting.

   c. Sound effects and music add to the radio listener's appreciation. Have the students listen to the sound effects; then allow them to discuss how the sound effects influence their appreciation of the show. Compare the sound effects of a detective show with the sound effects of a western or comedy broadcast. Could the student identify the type of program by merely listening to the sound effects? Have students list the sound effects they hear when they listen to different types of programs.

F. PROBLEM-SOLVING EXPERIENCES INVOLVING LANGUAGE ARTS SKILLS: BUZZ SESSION*

Purpose

1. To interact orally with a group and find workable answers to a problem
2. To develop creative thinking skills
3. To identify the responsibilities of each member of a discussion group
4. To develop respect for other students' opinions

Materials

Suggested topics for discussion and problem solving; newspaper articles that suggest problems requiring solutions.

Grade level

2–4

---

*Experiences in this section are adapted from Donna E. Norton & Saundra Norton, *Language Arts Activities for Children,* 3rd ed. (Englewood Cliffs, NJ: Merrill/Prentice Hall, 1993), pp. 25–26, 27–28. By permission of the authors and Merrill/Prentice Hall.

1. Explain to the students that groups often need a number of ideas or must solve problems in creative ways. One way to gather a lot of ideas before groups try to solve a problem is a "buzz session." During a buzz session, everyone quickly presents ideas and suggestions. All ideas are written down; none are criticized or judged appropriate or inappropriate. After several ideas have been chosen for investigation as workable solutions to the problem, each idea will be discussed in greater detail. The whole class may form a large buzz session with the teacher acting as secretary and moderator, or the class may be divided into smaller groups that are allowed a limited time to generate ideas and suggestions before reporting back to the larger group. (The choice depends on the children's experience and ability.) The class is divided into groups of 6 and allowed to generate ideas rapidly for 6 minutes. If the teacher is not the secretary for the whole group, each group should appoint someone to write down the ideas.

2. Present a problem to the groups that will stimulate their thinking. The problem should be important to the group so the children can empathize with it. The problem should also be phrased in such a way that the solution is not limited by the wording of the problem. Students may suggest problems they feel strongly about, or the teacher can use some of the following problems:

   How can we eliminate the long time spent in the school cafeteria?

   How can we earn money to go on a class trip at the end of the year?

   How can we make our school grounds more attractive?

   How can we make the playground more useable and fun at recess?

   How can we make the streets safer when we walk or ride our bikes to school?

   How can we improve our school newspaper?

   How can we show our parents what we've learned when they come to open house?

   How can we get the "mini-courses" we want and how can we get the teachers for them?

3. After children's ideas have been stimulated in the buzz session, tell them they will have an opportunity to try to really solve the problem through a longer problem-solving discussion session. Tell them that every person in the discussion group has a responsibility to solve the problem. Ask the students to suggest responsibilities they believe would be necessary for solving the problem. List these responsibilities; for example:

In a Problem-Solving Discussion Group, Every Member Has Responsibilities

1. Identify the problem.
2. Collect the facts you need to know so you can contribute to the discussion.
3. Understand the causes of the problem and any characteristics the solution must have.
4. Participate in the discussion.
5. Be a good listener to other peoples' ideas.
6. Keep your mind open for other peoples' viewpoints.
7. Show respect for all ideas.
8. Keep in mind that your main purpose is to find the best solution to the problem, not to sell your idea.

---

4. Give students an opportunity to gather facts on the problem; then divide the class into smaller discussion groups. Choose a chairperson or discussion leader for each group. Prepare the discussion leaders for their responsibilities:

   a. Study the problem.

   b. Prepare a series of questions that stimulate thinking: what, why, who, how?

   c. Open the discussion by explaining the purpose of the group.

   d. Guide the thinking of the group by asking questions and summarizing points.

   e. Ask for examples and support for ideas and suggestions.

   f. Get everyone involved in the discussion.

   g. Summarize ideas.

   Allow the groups to meet and provide guidance when necessary.

5. Provide an opportunity for all discussion groups to share their solutions with the whole class. Discuss the recommendations and try to reach a joint agreement.

6. The newspaper is another source of topics for problem-solving discussion groups. Find examples of stories related to local, state, national, or world problems and have discussion groups tackle the problems. Advice columns also provide topics for problem-solving discussions.

G. ASSESSMENT STRATEGY

As you provide opportunities in the classroom for the children to listen for different purposes and fully develop a wide range of skills, you will want to keep a record of what is going on so you can assess ways the students are developing their specific listening skills and indeed, older students can self-evaluate as they consider where they are strong and what they want to work on. Assessing students' progress can verify how their language arts skills are developing, and several alternative approaches are useful: anecdotal records, classroom observations, checklists, conferences, interviews, language samples, and across the curriculum use (Tompkins & Hoskisson, 1995).

Anecdotal Records

To record anecdotal notes about the students, some teachers write anecdotes on adhesive-backed notes and affix them in a binder that has sections for each student. Thus, after the teacher walks around the room, meets with small groups, and has individual conferences, the teacher can reach into a pocket, withdraw the pad of notes, write an anecdote, and return the completed note to another pocket. Later, the teacher will place the anecdotes on sheets of paper in the binder section for the appropriate student. Anecdotes include what topics a student reserves for individual inquiry, what connections the student makes to other sources, what journal writing is done, what energy the student has in working on the task, notes about individual conferences, remarks about the complexity of word clusters a student has made, notes about writing progress related to writing a draft, suggestions for revisions in writing, proofreading activity with a peer, what happened during an editing conference, and ways the student shared his or her work with the group.

Classroom Observations

Related to analytical listening, Tompkins and Hoskisson (1991) recommend that teachers also view this as comprehensive listening and check the students' understanding and use of various listening strategies by asking students to think about the strategies they used. Then the teacher should ask students what they did when they received information through a listening situation. Students can be encouraged to tell what they did before, during, and after listening. In what ways did the students:

1. Form pictures in their minds?
2. Put information into groups?
3. Ask questions?
4. Recognize the organization (description, sequence, comparison, cause and effect, problem-solution) of the message?
5. Record important information?
6. Get nonverbal clues from the speaker?

Checklists

Consider the overall checklist in Figure 8.12 that can be used by a teacher; it refers to the types of listening skills discussed in this chapter.

Conferences

Conferences with students can be brief and held on the spot or can continue for a set period of time at the teacher's desk, at the student's desk, or at a table that has been designated as a conference area. Some teachers wear a hat or ball cap with the word *conference* on the crown to send a signal to students that important conversation is going on and to wait until the hat is re-

FIGURE 8.12
Checklist of Listening Skills for Grades K–4

The student engages in: Comprehensive Listening	Always	Sometimes	Seldom

1. Recognizes main ideas and details with a visual stimulus
2. Recalls main ideas
3. Recalls details
4. Follows directions
5. Notes key points
6. Summarizes information
7. Responds to information heard

Critical Listening

8. Identifies a speaker's point of view
9. Identifies a speaker's feelings
10. Identifies opinion from facts
11. Compares and contrasts points
12. Categorizes ideas
13. Generalizes from given material
14. Considers effects
15. Predicts outcomes from what was said
16. Applies ideas to other situations
17. Gives examples

Appreciative Listening

18. Shows pleasure and enjoyment while listening to materials
19. Shows appreciation for language sounds
20. Shows appreciation for sounds in the world.

Other

moved before disturbing what is going on. Other teachers place a pennant on a stick in a container to show that a conference is going on. The pennant is moved from the teacher's desk to the student's desk to a conference table depending on where the conversation takes place. Some teachers will make plans with individual students in conferences before reading or writing or meet with small groups to discuss a story or book they have read. Other teachers will meet with individuals to discuss proofreading and editing and help with the mechanics (spelling, punctuation, and capitalization) or meet with a small group to suggest revisions in writing their compositions. Still other teachers will meet with individuals to give instruction that focuses on a particular skill or area that causes difficulty or meet with students who have completed a project to assess their progress as a writer, as a reader, as a listener, as a speaker, and so on. Student input and self-evaluation are welcomed, and the student is asked to make plans for the next project after reflecting about his or her strengths, project preferences, and goals.

Interviews

Holding interviews with students is a valuable way to collect information about their understanding of language arts skills and to elaborate and clarify any misperceptions. A teacher can ask carefully planned questions to determine how students use their language arts skills. Related to developing listening skills, a teacher can ask such questions as:

1. Would you select music for the background for a story set in Australia with a people-affect-the-environment theme (Jeannie Baker's *Window*) that is the same as the music you would select for the background for a story with a fast-paced copycat theme (Peggy Rathman's *Ruby the Copycat*, 1991)? Why or why not? (appreciative listening)
2. What did you hear that helped you think of examples? (critical listening)
3. What do you do when you want to remember the sequence of the story (or the information)? (comprehenseive listening)
4. Do you listen the same way to words that tell the speaker's point of view and feelings as you do to a poem? Why or why not? (critical listening)

5. What do you do when you are trying to tell the difference between opinion and facts? (critical listening)
6. How do you listen when you want to compare information? Contrast information? Categorize ideas? (critical listening)
7. What do you do when you want to tell the main idea? (critical listening)
8. How do you listen if you know that you can predict outcomes from what was said? (critical listening)
9. What helps you apply the ideas you heard in a listening situation to other situations? (critical listening)

Language Samples

Teachers often collect samples of students' language skills during the first month of the school year and then again at the end of the school year. Sometimes, teachers tape-record students' oral language and keep samples of students' writing. These samples allow a teacher to compare the students' contributions and identify the areas of language growth as well as areas in which students still need guidance, assistance, and instruction. The information, written or sketched out in scenes by the students themselves, can be added to the collection of samples. As an example, information the students sketch or write about suitable music that they selected for the background of a particular story could help verify growth in their appreciative listening skills. The students might also give examples of times when they were able to do "two things at once," meaning they were able to listen while doing something else, which could verify a student's use of marginal listening skills. Other information written by students to tell what they do when they want to remember the sequence of the story (or the information) could verify the use of their attentive listening skills. Still other information recorded by individual students about the different ways they listen to different types of material could verify how they are using analytical listening skills. Additionally, if the language samples are to be placed in the students' portfolios for Open House or Back-to-School event or parent conferences, suggest that the students select one-third of the ones to include, that the parents or guardians select one-third, and that the teacher select the remaining third. If any of the samples are to be used for grading purposes, suggest that students select the samples that they want to be assessed.

Across the Curriculum Use

A pre-post instructional approach is to see how well students use their listening skills (and other language skills) in various areas of the curriculum. After instruction, the teacher can take note of how well the students apply any knowledge they have gained about listening skills. For example, when students are discussing the information they gained from a filmstrip about the Pilgrims at Plymouth, the teacher can identify the students who indicate in some way that they had arranged information into groups, recorded information they deemed important, and asked questions about what they wanted to know.

Cautions

The first caution relates to the use of objective tests and test items to assess comprehensive listening skills. Sometimes, teachers use objective tests and test items to measure students' comprehensive listening (see Chapter 5 and section about Preparing Test Items). If you have provided information about how to dial 911 for an emergency or the role of the town crier in America's early colonies, you can check students' understanding of the information and the extent to which students listened. Additionally, you should also assess students' listening more directly. To do this, you can check their understanding of each of the six listening strategies discussed earlier in this chapter and how they apply the strategies in listening activities. As an example, you can ask students to reflect on and talk about the strategies they use and what they do before, during, and after listening; this will give you insights into their thinking in a way that objective tests and test items cannot.

The second caution relates to the use of only one unit of study or one topic to assess students' critical listening skills instead of assessing on an ongoing basis. One way you can assess critical listening on an ongoing basis is to have students view and critique commercials and oral presentations after teaching them about persuasion, propaganda, and deceptive language. Another way to assess students' understanding and critiquing skills is to have them develop their own commercials, advertisements, and oral presentations. Indeed, critical listening that involves these activities and others goes beyond one lesson or unit and involves skills that teachers should return to again and again during the academic year.

H. LANGUAGE ARTS SKILLS LESSON PLAN: LISTENING FOR DETAILS

1. Descriptive Course Data

Teacher:_____   Date: _____

Grade level: All grades K–4, depending on the amount of details developed in the description.

Room number: _____

Unit: Changes (i.e., changing geography of cities; Social Studies context)

Lesson Topic: Listening for Details (Language Arts Skills)

2. Lesson Goals and Objectives

Instructional goals (General objectives).

1. To develop a detailed description of an illustration.
2. To listen attentively to descriptive details and to identify the correct picture.
3. To relate a listening activity to geography.

Specific (performance) objectives.
Cognitive.

1. With others, the student will develop a detailed description of one of the illustrations showing change from Jeannie Baker's book, *Window* (1991).
2. When presented with a detailed oral description of an illustration, the student will be able to listen attentively to identify the appropriate illustration.
3. The student will be able to justify his or her decision.

Affective.

1. The student may show pleasure and enjoyment while listening to one or more of the descriptions of others.

Psychomotor.

1. Using crayons, markers, or paints, the student will be able to create his or her own depiction of the town or city during a different time period.

3. Rationale

The concept of change is prevalent in social studies content as evidenced by recommendations of the National Council for the Social Studies (NCSS) Task Force. State departments of education, school districts, and local schools have also included this concept in their curriculum materials.

4. Plan and Procedures

Introduction. With an opaque projector, show children the illustrations from Jeannie Baker's *Window* (1991) and discuss the idea that the same settings are seen during different periods of time. The book presents detailed collage illustrations showing the same Australian setting over time.

Modeling. Demonstrate for the children a way to compose a brief description of one of the illustrations in *Window*. Write it on the board or on chart paper and include details that the children can easily identify. Invite the children to listen carefully to your description and then identify the appropriate illustration. Ask them to justify their decision, i.e., the features that helped them identify the correct illustration.

Guided (coached) practice. Divide the class into groups. Have one group compose a detailed description of one of the illustrations they saw in *Window*. Copies of the book can be distributed among members of the group. Ask another group to listen attentively to the description, identify the appropriate illustration, and give reasons for their decision. After the initial description, ask children to discuss why they could (or could not) identify the correct illustration. This can lead to them to suggest guidelines that will help them provide accurate descriptions and listen for details.

Assignments. Students may create their own depiction of their town or city and how it has changed in some way. The depictions could include either photographs borrowed from someone at home or in the neighborhood or drawings.

Closure: Relate the activity to the main idea of the book: People affect the environment.

5. Materials Needed

Audiovisual. None.

Other. Illustrations from a book showing the same settings during different time periods: Jeannie Baker's *Window* (1991).

6. Assessment and Revision

Assessment of learning. Careful descriptions and listening carefully for details will be necessary as students try to identify the correct illustrations. Teacher observations and anecdotal notes will document the students who develop a detailed description, who listen attentively to identify the appropriate illustration, and are able to justify their decisions. Teacher observations will note which students enjoy listening to the descriptions of others and create their own depiction of the town or city during a different time period.

Plan for revision. The students require additional opportunities for descriptions and identifications though they are quickly learning to listen attentively. The activity can be continued with *Everything from a Nail to a Coffin* (1991) by Iris Van Rynbach and *New Providence: A Changing Cityscape* (1987) by Renata Von Tscharmer and Ronald Lee Fleming.

SUMMARY

Listening is the most basic and most used of the language modes. Despite its importance, listening instruction has been neglected in elementary classrooms; practice activities have often been substituted for instruction. The process of listening involves receiving, attending, and assigning meaning. Listening and hearing are not synonymous; rather, hearing is part of the listening process.

Students' need to attend to the speaker's message varies with the listening purpose.

- Comprehensive listening is the type of listening required in many instructional activities.
- Critical listening involves learning to detect propaganda devices and persuasive language.
- Appreciative listening is listening for enjoyment.
- Reading aloud is one important way to share literature with students.

QUESTIONS AND ACTIVITIES FOR DISCUSSION

1. Keep a record of how much time you spend listening, talking, reading, and writing for a day or two. Also, record how much time students spend using each of the four language modes while you observe in an K–4 classroom.

2. Visit a classroom and observe how listening is taught or practiced. Consider how practice activities might be changed into instructional activities.

3. Interview primary students about strategies they use while listening. Ask questions such as these:

- What is listening?
- What is the difference between hearing and listening, or are they the same?
- Why do people listen? Why else?
- What do you do while you are listening?
- What do you do to help you remember what you are listening to?
- Do you always listen in the same way, or are there different ways to listen?
- How do you know what is important in the message you are listening to?
- What is the hardest thing about listening?
- Are you a good listener? Why? Why not?

Compare students' responses across grade levels. Are older students in grade 4 more aware of the listening process than younger students are? Can older students identify a greater variety of listening strategies than younger students can?

4. Plan and teach a lesson on one of the comprehensive listening strategies discussed in this chapter.

5. Read one or more stories aloud to a group of students and involve them in several of the response activities listed in Figure 8.10. Also, use the Directed Listening Thinking Activity for students to make and confirm predictions for one of the stories.

6. Become a pen pal with several students and correspond about books their teacher is reading aloud to them.

7. After reading a story aloud to a small group of students, direct a reflective discussion. Be sure to choose a book that will stimulate discussion.

8. Describe any prior concepts you had about teaching listening skills that changed as a result of your experience with this chapter. Describe the changes.

CHILDREN'S BOOKS

Andrews, J. (1990). *The auction.* Ill. by Karen Reczuch. New York: Macmillan.

Baker, J. (1991). *Window.* New York: Greenwillow.

de Paola, T. (1975). *Strega nona.* Englewood Cliffs, NJ: Prentice-Hall.

Galdone, P. (1975). *The gingerbread boy.* New York: Seabury.

Hest, A. (1986). *The purple coat.* Ill. by Amy Schwartz. New York: Macmillan.

Lasky, K. (1983). *Beyond the divide.* New York: Macmillan.

Lionni, L. (1975). *Pezzetino.* New York: Pantheon.

Mayer, M. (1987). *The pied piper of Hamelin.* New York: Macmillan.

Nodset, J. L. (1963). *Who took the farmer's hat?* New York: Harper & Row.

Rathman, P. (1991). *Ruby the copycat.* New York: Scholastic.

Sendak, M. (1963). *Where the wild things are.* New York: Harper & Row.

Van Allsburg, C. (1981). *Jumanji.* Boston: Houghton Mifflin.

Van Rynbach, I. (1991). *Everything from a nail to a coffin.* New York: Orchard Books.

Von Tscharmer, R., & Fleming, R. L. (1987). *New Providence: A changing cityscape.* San Diego: Harcourt, Brace, Jovanovich.

Yorinks, A. (1986). *Hey, Al.* New York: Farrar, Straus and Giroux.

REFERENCES AND SUGGESTED READINGS

Anderson, H. (1949). Teaching the art of listening. *School Review, 57,* 63–67.

Beaver, J. M. (1982). *Say it!* over and over. *Language Arts, 59,* 143–148.

Berthoff, A. E. (1981). *The making of meaning.* Montclair, NJ: Boynton/Cook.

Devine, T. G. (1978). Listening: What do we know after fifty years of theorizing? *Journal of Reading, 21,* 296–304.

Devine, T. G. (1981). *Teaching study skills: A guide for teachers.* Boston: Allyn & Bacon.

Devine, T. G. (1982). *Listening skills schoolwide: Activities and programs.* Urbana, IL: ERIC Clearinghouse on Reading and Communication Skills and the National Council of Teachers of English.

Erickson, A. (1985). Listening leads to reading. *Reading Today, 2,* 13.

Foulke, E. (1968). Listening comprehension as a function of word rate. *Journal of Communication, 18,* 198–206.

Fox, S. E., & Allen, V. G. (1983). *The language arts: An integrated approach.* New York: Holt, Rinehart & Winston.

Hansen, J. (1987). *When writers read.* Portsmouth, NH: Heinemann.

Hickman, J. (1980). Children's response to literature: What happens in the classroom. *Language Arts, 57,* 524–529.

Kimmel, M. M., & Segel, E. (1983). *For reading aloud! A guide for sharing books with children.* New York: Delacorte.

Landry, D. (1969). The neglect of listening. *Elementary English, 46,* 599–605.

Lundsteen, S. W. (1979). *Listening: Its impact on reading and the other language arts* (rev. ed.). Urbana, IL: National Council of Teachers of English.

Lutz, W. (1984). Notes toward a description of doublespeak. *Quarterly Review of Doublespeak, 10,* 1–2.

Lutz, W. (n.d.). *Some examples of doublespeak.* Unpublished manuscript, National Council of Teachers of English.

Martinez, M., & Roser, N. (1985). Read it again: The value of repeated readings during storytime. *The Reading Teacher, 38,* 782–786.

Martinez, M., & Teale, W. H. (1988). Reading in a kindergarten classroom library. *The Reading Teacher, 41,* 568–572.

Pearson, P. D., & Fielding, L. (1982). Research update: Listening comprehension. *Language Arts, 59,* 617–629.

Rankin, P. R. (1928). The importance of listening ability. *English Journal, 17,* 623–640.

Rudasill, L. (1986). Advertising gimmicks: Teaching critical thinking. In J. Golub (Ed.), *Activities to promote critical thinking* (Classroom practices in teaching English, 1986), pp. 127–129. Urbana, IL: National Council of Teachers of English.

Sims, R. (1977). Reading literature aloud. In B. E. Cullinan & C. W. Carmichael (Eds.), *Literature and young children* (pp. 108–119). Urbana, IL: National Council of Teachers of English.

Smith, L. B. (1982). Sixth graders write about reading literature. *Language Arts, 59,* 357–363.

Stauffer, R. G. (1975). *Directing the reading-thinking process.* New York: Harper & Row.

Sticht, T. G., & James, J. H. (1984). Listening and reading. In P. D. Pearson (Ed.), *Handbook of reading research,* pp. 293–318. New York: Longman.

Tompkins, G. E., Friend, M. & Smith, P. L. (1984). Children's metacognitive knowledge about listening. Presentation at the American Educational Research Association Convention, New Orleans, LA.

Tompkins, G. E., Friend, M., & Smith, P. L. (1987). Strategies for more effective listening. In C. R. Personke & D. D. Johnson (Eds.), *Language arts and the beginning teacher* (Chapter 3). Englewood Cliffs, NJ: Prentice-Hall.

Tompkins, G. E., & Hoskisson, K. (1995). *Language Arts: Content and Teaching Strategies* (3rd ed.). Englewood Cliffs, NJ: Merrill/Prentice Hall.

Tompkins, G. E., Smith, P. L., & Friend, M. (1984). Three dimensions of listening and listening instruction in the elementary school. Paper presented at the Southwestern Educational Research Association Annual Meeting, Dallas, TX.

Trelease, J. (1989). *The new read-aloud handbook.* New York: Penguin.

Tutolo, D. (1981). Critical listening/reading of advertisements. *Language Arts, 58,* 679–683.

Werner, E. K. (1975). A study of communication time. Unpublished master's thesis, University of Maryland, College Park.

Wiesendanger, K. D., & Bader, L. (1989). Children's view of motivation. *The Reading Teaeher, 42,* 345–347.

Wilt, M. E. (1950). A study of teacher awareness of listening as a factor in elementary education. *Journal of Educational Research, 43,* 626–636.

Wolvin, A. D., & Coakley, C. G. (1979). *Listening instruction* (TRIP Booklet). Urbana, IL: ERIC Clearinghouse on Reading and Communication Skills and the Speech Communication Association.

Yaden, D. (1988). Understanding stories through repeated read-alouds: How many does it take? *The Reading Teacher, 41,* 556–560.

CHAPTER 9

Speaking: Talk in the Classroom

Talk is the primary expressive language mode (Stewig, 1983a). Both children and adults use it more frequently than writing, and children learn to talk before they learn to read and write. Talk is also the communication mode that all peoples around the world develop. Stewig reports that of the 2,796 languages spoken today, only a fraction of them—approximately 153—have developed written forms.

When they come to school, most children are fluent in oral language. They have had four or five years of extensive practice talking and listening. Because students have acquired basic oral language competencies, teachers often assume they do not need to emphasize talk in the elementary school curriculum. Research shows, however, that students benefit from participating in both informal and formal talk activities throughout the school day and that language is necessary for learning (Cazden, 1986; Golub, 1988; Heath, 1983). Students converse in peer groups when they work on projects, tell and discuss stories with classmates, participate in role-play activities, give reports for social studies and science units, and debate current events. Many of these talk activities are integrated with other language modes and content area subjects. For instance, to give an oral report related to a science unit, students research the topic by reading informational books and interviewing persons in the community with expertise on the topic. Students take notes and write key information on clusters or notecards in preparation for giving the report. They may also construct charts, models, and other visuals to use with their reports.

Heath (1983) questioned whether talk in elementary classrooms is "talk about nothing" and concluded that children's talk is an essential part of the language arts curriculum and is necessary for academic success in all content areas. Quiet classrooms are often considered the most conducive to learning even though research shows that talk is a necessary ingredient for learning. Klein (1979) argues that "talk opportunities must be consciously structured into [the language arts] curriculum and done so in the most likely manner to encourage children to use talk in a wide variety of contexts and for a variety of purposes" (p. 656).

Halliday (1973) stresses that elementary students need to learn to control language functions to become competent language users. In her research, however, Pinnell (1975) found that some of the language functions did not occur as frequently as might be expected in many classrooms. In this chapter, we will discuss the three types of talk activities that represent the language functions. The three types are informal conversations and discussions; more formal debates, oral reports, and interviews; and drama, including dramatic play, role-playing, and storytelling. These talk activities have several benefits: they expand children's oral language skills; they develop students' abilities to use talk for a variety of language functions; and they work to dispel the fear most adults have about speaking before a group.

Informal talk, formal talk, and dramatic activities are powerful tools for learning and are discussed in the following sections. The discussions are specifically designed to help you understand:

1. The importance of talk in learning
2. Types of talk activities in which students, K–4, can participate
3. Ways talk activities can be integrated into literature and content area units of study
4. Examples of problem-solving experiences involving language arts skills
5. Assessment strategy.

A. INFORMAL TALK ACTIVITIES

Conversation and discussion are social activities involving exchange of ideas, information, opinions, and feelings about people, places, things, and events. They are the most basic forms of talk and should be more than incidental activities. Conversations take place in the classroom, on the playground, in the media center, during lunch—anywhere, anytime. Discussions, in contrast, are more planned and often deal with specific topics. Reading Stanley's *The Conversation Club* (1983) is a good way to introduce conversation activities. The book emphasizes the need for participants to listen to each other and to take turns talking. Students may want to organize their own conversation club after listening to the story.

Conversations

Teachers can hold conversations with students at odd moments during the day and may need to plan some special times to talk with quiet children or children who need extra attention. Teachers may find it helpful to have a list of topics to which they can refer when they want to plan a special time for conversations. These are possible topics:

What do you do in your free time?
What books do you like best?
Do you have a hobby?
What sports do you play (or would like to play)?
What games are your favorites?
Do you have a pet? Tell me about it.
What kind of work do you think you will do when you finish school?
If you could live anywhere in the world, where would it be?
What do you like to do on the weekends?
Have you been to any museums?
Do you like to travel? Where have you been?
What do you like to do with your brothers or sisters?
What makes you happy (or unhappy)?

Holding conversations with their students enables teachers to make them feel important, find out about their interests, likes and dislikes, and become their friend. Shuy (1987) says conversation is often thwarted in elementary classrooms because of large class size and the mistaken assumption that silence facilitates learning. Teachers must make an extra effort to provide opportunities for socialization and talk.

Teachers often group students in pairs and small groups to work on reading and math assignments and for projects in other content areas. As they work collaboratively, students naturally converse with their classmates whether they were encouraged to talk or not. Golub (1988) explains that "students are *supposed* to talk with each other as they work together on various classroom projects and activities" (p. 1). Wilkinson (1984) makes several observations about children's language use in small-group situations. She found that in their conversations, students use language representing several different language functions. They ask and answer questions using informative language, make requests to satisfy their own needs using instrumental language, and use regulatory language to control classmates' behavior. Students also use interactional and personal language as they talk informally.

Wilkinson identifies three characteristics of effective speakers in peer group conversations. Although she focuses on students' use of one language function, instrumental language, her findings may be generalized to the wider context of peer group conversations. Wilkinson found that effective speakers' comments were (1) directly and clearly stated to particular students, (2) related to the task at hand, and (3) interpreted as being sincere by classmates.

Wilkinson recommends that teachers "listen in" on students' conversations to learn about students' language competencies and their understanding of an assignment as well as their ability to work in peer groups. Teachers can identify students who are not effective speakers and plan additional group activities to develop their conversational skills.

Show-and-Tell

A daily sharing time is a familiar ritual in many kindergarten and primary-grade classrooms. Children bring favorite objects to school and talk about them. This is a nice bridge between home and school, and the value of show-and-tell is that children have something familiar to talk about.

If sharing time becomes repetitive, children lose interest, so teachers must play an active role to make it a worthwhile activity. Teachers can, for example, discuss the roles and responsibilities of both speakers and listeners. A second-grade class developed the list of responsibilities for speakers and listeners shown in Figure 9.1. This list, with minor variations, has been used with students in upper grades as well.

Some children need prompting even if they have been advised to plan in advance two or three things to say about the object they have brought to school. It is tempting for teachers to speed things up by asking questions and, without realizing it, to answer their own questions, especially for a very quiet child. Show-and-tell could go like this:

TEACHER:	Jerry, what did you bring today?
JERRY:	(Holds up a stuffed bear.)
TEACHER:	Is that a teddy bear?
JERRY:	Yeah.
TEACHER:	Is it new?
JERRY:	(Shakes head yes.)
TEACHER:	Can you tell us about your bear?
JERRY:	(Silence.)
TEACHER:	Jerry, why don't you walk around and show your bear to everyone?

FIGURE 9.1
Responsibilities of Speakers and Listeners

Rules for Show-and-Tell

What a speaker does
    Brings something interesting to talk about.
    Brings the same thing *only* one time.
    Thinks of three things to say about it.
    Speaks loudly so everyone can hear.
    Passes what he/she brought around so everyone can see it.

What listeners do
    Be interested.
    Pay attention.
    Listen.
    Ask the "5 Ws plus one" *who, what, where, when, why,* and *how.*
    Say something nice.

Jerry needed prompting, but the teacher in this example clearly dominated the conversation, and Jerry said only one word—"yeah." Two strategies may help. First, talk with children like Jerry and help them plan something to say. Second, invite listeners to ask the speakers the "5 Ws plus one" questions, also referred to as reporters' or journalists' questions: *who, what, when, where, why,* and *how.* It is crucial that the conversation be among the students!

Classmates should be the audience for show-and-tell activities, but often teachers become the focus (Cazden, 1988). To avoid this, teachers need to join the audience rather than direct the activity. They should also limit their comments and allow the student who is sharing to assume responsibility for the activity and the discussion that follows sharing. Student-sharers can ask three or four classmates for comments before choosing which student will share next. It is often difficult for teachers to share control of their classrooms, but students—even in kindergarten—are capable of handling the activity themselves.

Show-and-tell or sharing activities should continue throughout the elementary grades, because informal talk is a necessary part of classroom life (Camp & Tompkins, 1990). Many middle-grade teachers find the first few minutes of the day an appropriate time for sharing; often, the class becomes a more cohesive and caring group through sharing. Teachers of upper-grade students who change classes every 50 minutes must plan more carefully for sharing activities because of time constraints. Nonetheless, spending two or three minutes at the beginning of each class period in informal sharing, or planning a 50-minute, more formal sharing time every other week, will provide these needed opportunities.

Middle- and upper-grade students participate in sharing activities in much the same way as primary students do. Together students and teachers need to establish guidelines for sharing and discuss how students will prepare and present their show-and-tell. A brief oral presentation involves a process much like listening, reading, and writing do; a process of planning, presenting, and critiquing is recommended (Camp & Tompkins, 1990). Teachers should model a show-and-tell presentation for students by sharing hobbies or other interests.

Students first choose an object, experience, or current events topic and then plan what information they will share about it. To encourage students to choose a meaningful topic for sharing, teachers can read *The Show-and-Tell War* (Smith, 1988). Students plan their presentation by deciding what they want to say and clustering an effective planning strategy. In clustering, students draw a schematic diagram on a sheet of paper and list main ideas and details. They begin by writing the name of the topic in the center of the paper and drawing a circle around the word. Next, students draw lines or rays from the circle and list three, four, or five main ideas about the topic. They circle these words, then draw more lines from the circles and add details related to the main ideas. A sample cluster on porcelain dolls is presented in Figure 9.2. The main ideas and details are drawn out from the center. These clusters are used for gathering and organizing ideas during planning and as notes to refer to during the presentations.

Students' presentations are brief, usually lasting only a minute or two. They share their objects and experiences using the ideas gathered and organized during planning. Students concentrate on speaking clearly and standing appropriately so as to not distract listeners. Older students who have not participated in sharing activities often find talking in front of their classmates intimidating. The planning step is crucial to a successful presentation. Other students should listen effectively by paying attention, asking pertinent questions, and responding to the speaker nonverbally. After the talk, listeners may ask questions to clarify and expand the speaker's comments.

The third component of show-and-tell is critiquing, when teachers and students discuss and critique the presentations using the guidelines in Figure 9.1. These guidelines can be converted into a checklist that both speakers and listeners can complete for each presentation. Through the checklists and discussion, students learn how to give interesting presentations and gain confidence in their ability to speak in front of a group.

Show-and-tell can evolve into an informal type of oral report for middle-grade students. When used effectively, older students gain valuable practice talking in an informal and non-threatening situation. Beginning as a sharing activity, students' talk about a collection of shark's teeth, a program from an Ice Capades Show, a recently found snakeskin, or snapshots of a vacation at Yellowstone National Park can lead to informal dramatics, reading,

FIGURE 9.2
Cluster for a Sharing Presentation

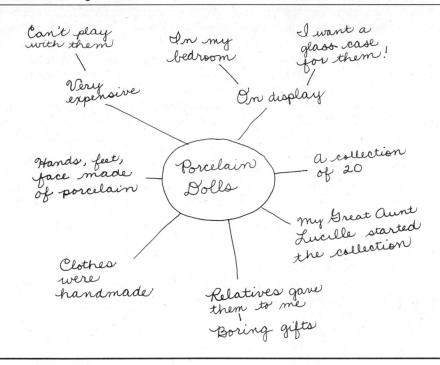

and writing activities. One student may act out dances recalled from the Ice Capades Show; another student may point out the location of Yellowstone National Park on a map or check an almanac for more information about the park. A third student may write about the prized collection of shark's teeth and how they were collected. Experience plus oral rehearsal help students gear up for other language activities.

Discussions

Discussions are an effective means of helping students learn to express themselves in small groups or in whole-class settings. They are usually more purposeful than conversations, and teachers often play an important role by asking questions and moderating the discussion. Dillon (1983) recommends that teachers ask questions "only when you are personally perplexed and you need the information in answer" (p. 21). This recommendation flies in the face of conventional practice in elementary classrooms. Most of the time, teachers ask questions at a rote-memory level for which they know the answer, to assess students' understanding.

Wilen (1986) reviewed the research about questioning strategies and offers these suggestions:

Ask carefully planned questions to organize and direct the lesson.
Ask single questions that are clearly phrased, rather than vaguely worded or multiple questions.
Ask questions in a planned sequence.
Ask factual questions to check basic understanding, but focus on higher-level questions that give students opportunities to think critically and creatively.
Ask questions to follow up students' responses.
Give students sufficient time to think about questions and plan their responses.
Encourage wide participation through interaction among students, drawing in nonvolunteers, and seating students in a circle.
Promote student involvement by having students create questions to ask, lead the discussion, and follow up ideas developed during the discussion.

Researchers have classified questions into cognitive levels. Bloom (1956) developed a scheme of six hierarchical classes, ranging from simple to complex intellectual abilities: knowledge, comprehension, application, analysis, synthesis, and evaluation. Similarly, Guilford (1956) identified five major groups of mental operations: cognition, memory, convergent thinking, divergent thinking, and evaluation. Gallagher and Aschner (1963) developed a four-point category system based on Guilford's model to investigate the interaction between teachers and students. The four categories can be used to classify questions as well: (1) cognitive memory, in which students recite facts or information remembered through rote; (2) convergent thinking, in which students analyze and integrate remembered information; (3) divergent thinking, in which students independently generate information or take a new direction; and (4) evaluative thinking, in which students choose among alternatives and make judgments. In the first two of these categories, there is one expected or "right" answer, and in the third and fourth categories, students' responses are more open-ended. Teachers can compare the questions they prepare for classroom discussions against these categories to gauge the level of mental operations they require of their students.

Discussions about literature. Discussions often accompany reading aloud to students or having them read silently. There are many books that stimulate discussions and talk activities for young children; for instance, Burningham's *Would You Rather . . .* (1979) invites primary-grade students to consider and talk about silly and absurd possibilities; older students are challenged to create stories for Van Allsburg's *The Mysteries of Harris Burdick* (1984). A list of books that encourage talk appears in Figure 9.3.

Middle- and upper-grade students often participate in discussions about the chapter-length books they are reading. Books such as *Tuck Everlasting* (Babbitt, 1975), *How to Eat Fried Worms* (Rockwell, 1975), and *The One-Eyed Cat* (Fox, 1984) are conducive to lively discus-

FIGURE 9.3
Books that Encourage Talk

Ahlberg, J., & Ahlberg, A. (1978). *Each peach pear plum: An "I spy" story.* New York: Scholastic. (P)
Anno, M. (1970). *Topsy turvies: Pictures to stretch the imagination.* New York: Walker. (P–M)
Baylor, B. (1974). *Everybody needs a rock.* New York: Atheneum. (M)
Baylor, B. (1977). *Guess who my favorite person is.* New York: Atheneum. (M)
Blume, J. (1974). *The pain and the great one.* New York: Bradbury Press. (M)
Brown, M. (1983). *Perfect pigs: An introduction to manners.* Boston: Little, Brown. (P)
Burningham, J. (1977). *Come away from the water, Shirley.* New York: Harper & Row. (M)
Burningham, J. (1979). *Would you rather . . .* New York: Crowell. (P)
Conrad, P. (1994). *The tub grandfather.* (Ill. by R. Egielski). New York: HarperCollins. (P)
Degan, B. (1983). *Jamberry.* New York: Harper & Row. (P)
Fleming, D. (1993). *In the small, small pond.* New York: Holt. (P–M)
Gardner, B. (1984). *The look again . . . and again, and again, and again book.* New York: Lothrop. (P)
Hoguet, S. R. (1983). *I unpacked my grandmother's trunk: A picture book game.* New York: Dutton. (P–M)
Kendall, R. (1994). *Russian girl: Life in an old Russian town.* New York: Scholastic. (M)
Kimmel, E. A. (Reteller). (1944). *Anansi and the talking melon.* (Ill. by J. Stevens). New York: Holiday House. (P)
Kroll, S. (1976). *The tyrannosaurus game.* New York: Holiday House. (P–M)
Martin, B. Jr., & Archambault, J. (1988). *Listen to the rain.* New York: Henry Holt. (P–M)
Martin, B. Jr., & Archambault, J. (1990). *Chicka chicka boom boom.* New York: Henry Holt. (P)
Numeroff, L. J. (1985). *If you give a mouse a cookie.* New York: Harper & Row. (P–M)
Scott, A. H. (1993). *Cowboy country.* (Ill. by T. Lewis). New York: Clarion. (M)
Strauss, J. (1984). *Imagine that!!! Exploring make-believe.* Chicago: Human Sciences Press. (P–M)
Van Allsburg, C. (1981). *Jumanji.* Boston: Houghton Mifflin. (P–M)
Van Allsburg, C. (1984). *The mysteries of Harris Burdick.* Boston: Houghton Mifflin. (M)
Wood, A. (1982). *Quick as a cricket.* London: Child's Play. (P–M)
P = primary grades (K–2)
M = middle grades (3–4)

sions. Too often, however, the teacher takes the role of leader rather than participant in discussions. Rather than asking questions to stimulate a deeper understanding of the text and students' responses to it, teachers often ask questions to assess comprehension. Higgins (quoted in Eeds & Wells, 1989) describes typical discussion groups this way: "What you most often get are gentle inquisitions, when what you really want are grand conversations" (p. 4).

To have "grand conversations," teachers must participate in discussions to learn rather than to judge. There are no right answers to most of the questions teachers and students ask; rather, participants use relevant personal experiences to reflect on their reading both critically and creatively. Students keep copies of the books they are reading handy to check specific incidents, ask questions, and support their comments. The group becomes a community of learners in these discussions, in which participants share personal responses to literature and create a social response.

The teacher can develop questions for discussion groups, or students can develop their own according to the guidelines mentioned earlier. Reardon (1988) reports that her third graders write their own questions, and the discussion group spends the first few minutes of group time considering the questions and deciding which ones to actually use. A fifth grader developed these questions for a discussion of *Do Bananas Chew Gum?* (Gilson, 1980):

> I wonder if Sam ever learned how to read. How could he learn?
> I wonder why Sam had a reading problem. What do you think? Why did people hate Alicia?
> I wonder why they called the book *Do Bananas Chew Gum?*
> What would you have called the book? Why?
> Do you think Alicia gets braces? Would you want braces?
> Do you think Sam has other friends besides Alicia and Wally? Who?
> I wonder if Sam ever gets fired from baby-sitting. Do you?
> Would you fire him? Why or why not? (Fiderer, 1988, pp. 60–61)

As the student developed the questions, she checked that they could not be answered with "yes" or "no" and that they required her classmates to give a personal opinion.

From their observational study of fifth and sixth graders conducting "grand conversations" about literature, Eeds and Wells (1989) found that, through talk, students extend their individual interpretations of their reading and even create a better understanding of it. They talk about their understanding of the story and can change their opinions after listening to classmates' alternative views. Students share personal stories related to their reading in poignant ways that trigger other students to identify with them. They are active readers who use prediction as they read. The students also gain insights about how authors use the elements of story structure to develop their message.

Content area discussions. Other discussions grow out of content area study. Issues such as pollution, nuclear weapons, and apartheid are interesting, compelling topics for discussion. Students gather information for the discussion through reading textbooks, informational books, and newspapers and watching television news reports and films. As they participate in discussions—offering information, considering other points of view, searching for additional information to support opinions, and listening to alternative viewpoints—students learn social skills as well as content area information.

B. INTERPRETIVE TALK ACTIVITIES

In interpretive talk activities, teachers and students do not create the material; rather, they interpret others' ideas and words (Busching, 1981). Two types of interpretive drama that involve students in interpreting literature are storytelling and readers theater.

Storytelling

Storytelling is an ancient art that is a valuable instructional tool. Not only should teachers share literature with their students using storytelling techniques, but students can and should tell stories, too. Storytelling is entertaining and stimulates children's imaginations. It expands their language abilities and helps them internalize the characteristics of stories

(Morrow, 1985). Storytelling involves four steps: choosing a story, preparing to tell it, adding props, and telling the story.

Traditional stories, such as folktales, are often chosen for storytelling activities; however, any type of literature can be used. The most important consideration in choosing a story is to select a story you like and want to tell. Morrow (1979) lists other considerations:

The story has a simple, well-rounded plot.
The story has a clear beginning, middle, and end.
The story has an underlying theme.
The story has a small number of well-defined characters.
The story contains dialogue.
The story uses repetition.
The story uses colorful language or "catch phrases."

Figure 9.4 lists stories that contain many of these characteristics. Children can also create and tell stories to accompany wordless picture books. For example, Tomie de Paola's *Pancakes for Breakfast* (1978) is the charming story of a little old woman who tries to cook pancakes for breakfast but runs into a series of problems as she tries to assemble the ingredients. In the end, her neighbors invite her to their home for pancakes. The repetition of events in this story makes it easy for primary grade children to tell. For additional sources of stories, check Caroline Bauer's *Handbook for Storytellers* (1977).

It is not necessary to memorize a story to tell it effectively. Kingore (1982) lists the following six steps as preparation for storytelling:

1. Choose a story you really like.
2. Memorizing is not necessary. Just read the story a few times to get a "feel" for the sequence and major events in the story.
3. Plan interesting phrases or repeated phrases to enliven the language of your story.

FIGURE 9.4
Stories for Elementary Students to Tell

Aardema, V. (1975). *Why mosquitoes buzz in people's ears.* New York: Dial. (M–U)
Andersen, H. C. (1965). *The nightingale.* New York: Harper. (U)
Brown, M. (1947). *Stone soup.* New York: Scribner. (P–M–U)
Brown, M. (1972). *The runaway bunny.* New York: Harper. (P)
Carle, E. (1970). *The very hungry caterpillar.* Cleveland: Collins-World. (P)
Flack, M. (1932). *Ask Mr. Bear.* New York: Macmillan. (P)
Gag, W. (1956). *Millions of cats.* New York: Coward McCann. (P)
Galdone, P. (1973). *The three billy goats Gruff.* Boston: Houghton Mifflin. (P)
Gipson, M. (1975). *Rip Van Winkle.* New York: Doubleday. (M–U)
Grimm, The Brothers. (1971). *The Bremen town musicians.* New York: Greenwillow. (M–U)
Hague, K., & Hague, M. (1980). *East of the sun and west of the moon.* New York: Harcourt. (U)
Hastings, S. (1985). *Sir Gawain and the loathly lady.* New York: Mulberry. (U)
Hyman, T. S. (1983). *Little red riding hood.* New York: Holiday House. (P–M–U)
Kellogg, S. (1973). *The island of the skog.* New York: Dial. (M)
Lionni, L. (1969). *Alexander and the wind-up mouse.* New York: Pantheon. (M)
Lobel, A. (1977). *How the rooster saved the day.* New York: Greenwillow. (M)
Low, J. (1980). *Mice twice.* New York: Atheneum. (M)
Martin, B., Jr., & Archambault, J. (1985). *The ghost-eye tree.* New York: Holt. (M–U)
Mayer, M. (1978). *Beauty and the beast.* New York: Macmillan. (U)
Numeroff, L. J. (1985). *If you give a mouse a cookie.* New York: Harper. (P–M–U)
Slobodkina, E. (1947). *Caps for sale.* New York: Scott. (P)
Steig, W. (1982). *Doctor DeSoto.* New York: Farrar. (M)
Still, J. (1977). *Jack and the wonder beans.* New York: Putnam. (M)
Thurber, J. (1974). *Many moons.* New York: Harcourt. (P–M–U)
Zemach, H., & Zemach, M. (1973). *Duffy and the devil.* New York: Farrar. (M–U)
Zemach, M. (1976). *It could always be worse.* New York: Farrar (P–M–U)

4. Plan simple props or gestures to increase your audience's interest.
5. Prepare a brief introduction that relates the story to your audience's experiences.
6. Practice telling your story in front of a mirror. (p. 29)

This process can be abbreviated when very young children tell stories. They may choose a story they already know well and make props to guide the telling. (Try a set of puppets representing the main characters or a series of drawings.) They are then ready to tell their stories.

Several techniques can make the story come alive as it is told. Morrow (1979) describes three types of props that add variety and interest to stories:

Flannel board. Place drawings or pictures cut from books and backed with flannel on the flannel board as the story is told.
Puppets. Use puppets representing the main characters to tell a story with dialogue. (For ideas on how to construct puppets, check the section in this chapter on puppets.)
Objects. Use stuffed animals to represent animal characters or other small objects to represent important things in the story being told. Try, for instance, using a pile of caps in telling Slobodkina's *Caps for Sale* (1947) or a small gold ball for Thurber's *Many Moons* (1974).

Students tell the stories they have prepared to small groups of their classmates or to younger children. Try dividing the audience into small groups so that more students can tell stories at one time.

Readers Theater

Readers theater is "a formalized dramatic presentation of a script by a group of readers" (Busching, 1981, p. 330). Students each assume a role and read the character's lines in the script. The reader's responsibility is to interpret a story without using much action. Students may stand or sit, but must carry the whole communication of the plot, characterization, mood, and theme by using their voices, gestures, and facial expressions.

Readers theater avoids many of the restrictions inherent in theatrical productions. Students do not memorize their parts; elaborate props, costumes, and backdrops are not needed; and long, tedious hours are not spent rehearsing. Three steps in developing readers theater presentations are selecting a script, rehearsing the play, and staging the play.

Quality play scripts exhibit the same characteristics as do other types of fine literature. Manna (1984) lists five essential characteristics: an interesting story, a well-paced plot, recognizable and believable characters, plausible language, and a distinct style. The arrangement of the text on the page is also an important consideration when selecting a script. There should be a clear distinction between stage directions and dialogue through adequate spacing and by varying the print types and colors. This distinction is especially important for primary-grade students and for older students who are not familiar with the script format.

Readers theater is a relatively new idea, and the number of quality scripts available is limited, although more are being published each year. Play scripts in basal reading textbooks are another source of material for readers theater presentations. Some of the scripts currently available are Gackenback's *Hattie, Tom and the Chicken Witch* (1980), Dahl's *Charlie and the Chocolate Factory* (George, 1976), *Plays from African Folktales* (Korty, 1975), and Laurie's *Children's Plays from Beatrix Potter* (1980).

Students can also prepare their own scripts for readers theater from books of children's literature. Laughlin and Latrobe (1989) suggest that students begin by reading the entire book and thinking about its theme, characters, and plot. Next they choose a scene or scenes to script. Students make copies of the scene and use felt-tip pens to highlight the dialogue. They then adapt the scene by adding narrator's lines to bridge gaps, set the scene, and summarize. Students assume roles and read the script aloud, revising and experimenting with new text until they are satisfied with the script. The final version is typed, duplicated, and stapled into pamphlets. Some of the stories that Laughlin and Latrobe recommend are presented in Figure 9.5.

Begin by assigning readers for each character and a narrator, if the script calls for one. Read through the play once or twice; then stop to discuss the story. Busching (1981) rec-

FIGURE 9.5
Stories that Can Be Scripted for Readers Theater

Atwater, R., & Atwater, F. (1938). *Mr. Popper's penguins.* Boston: Little, Brown. (M)
Burch, R. (1980). *Ida Early comes over the mountain.* New York: Viking. (M)
Cleary, B. (1975). *Ramona and her father.* New York: Morrow. (M)
MacLachlan, P. (1985). *Sarah, plain and tall.* New York: Harper. (M)
Milne, A. A. (1974). *Winnie-the-Pooh.* New York: Dutton. (P–M)
Rockwell, T. (1973). *How to eat fried worms.* New York: Watts. (M)
Stolz, M. (1960). *A dog on Barkham Street.* New York: Harper. (M)
Wallace, B. (1980). *A dog called Kitty.* New York: Holiday House. (M)
Wolff, A. (1993). *Stella & Roy.* New York: Dutton. (P)
Yep, L. (Reteller). (1993). *The man who tricked a ghost.* (Ill. by I. Seltzer). Seattle, WA: Bridgewater Books. (M)

ommends using the "5 Ws plus one" questions—*who, what, where, when, why,* and *how*—to probe students' understanding. Through this discussion, students gain a clearer understanding of the story and decide how to interpret their characters.

After students decide how to use their voice, gestures, and facial expressions to interpret the characters, they should read the script one or two more times, striving for accurate pronunciation, voice projection, and appropriate inflections. Obviously, less rehearsal is needed for an informal, in-class presentation than for a more formal production; nevertheless, interpretations should always be developed as fully as possible.

Readers theater can be presented on a stage or in a corner of the classroom. Students stand or sit in a row and read their lines in the script. They must stay in position through the presentation or enter and leave according to the characters' appearances "on stage." If readers are sitting, they may stand to read their lines; if they are standing, they may step forward to read. The emphasis is not on production quality; rather, it is on the interpretive quality of the readers' voices and expressions. Costumes and props are unnecessary; however, they do enhance interest and enjoyment, as long as they do not interfere with the interpretive quality of the reading.

C. MORE FORMAL TALK ACTIVITIES

For more formal talk activities, children use a process approach in which they prepare and organize their talks before giving them. These more formal, planned occasions grow out of informal talk. Three types are oral reports, interviews, and debates.

Oral Reports

Learning how to prepare and present an oral report is an important language skill for middle- and upper-grade students. But students are often simply assigned to give an oral report without any classroom preparation. Without guidance, they simply copy the report verbatim from an encyclopedia and then read it aloud. The result is that students learn to fear speaking in front of a group instead of building confidence in their oral language abilities.

We will focus on the steps in teaching students how to prepare and present two types of oral reports. The first type includes research reports on social studies or science topics, such as Native Americans, the solar system, or Canada. The second type includes book reviews, television shows, and movies. These oral reports have genuine language functions—to inform or to persuade.

Research reports. Students can prepare and give research reports about topics they are studying in social studies, science, and other content areas. Giving a report orally helps students to learn about topics in specific content areas as well as to develop their communication abilities. Students need more than just an assignment to prepare a report for presentation on a particular date; they need to learn how to prepare and present research re-

FIGURE 9.6
Cluster and Data Chart

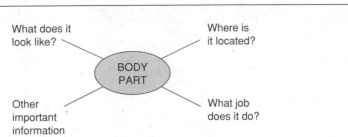

HUMAN BODY REPORT DATA CHART				
Source of information	What does it look like?	Where is it located?	What job does it do?	Other important information

ports. The four steps in preparing reports are choosing a topic, gathering information, organizing information, and making the presentation.

The class begins by choosing a topic for the reports. For example, if a second-grade class is studying the human body, then each student might select a different part of the body for a report. After students have chosen their topics, they need to inventory, or think over, what they know about the topic and decide what they need to learn about it. Students can learn to focus on the key points for their reports in several ways. One strategy is to create a cluster with the topic written and circled in the center of a piece of paper. They key points are drawn out from the topic like rays from the sun. Then students write the details on rays drawn from each main idea, as we mentioned in Chapter 1 in section, "Concept Mapping." Another strategy is a data chart, wherein the teacher provides a chart listing three or more key points to guide students as they gather information for their reports (McKenzie, 1979). Figure 9.6 shows a cluster and data chart for a report on a part of the human body. A third strategy is brainstorming ideas for possible key points by asking questions about the topic prefaced with the "5 Ws plus one": *who, what, where, when, why,* and *how.* The number and complexity of the key points depend on students' age or level of experience.

Students gather information using a variety of reference materials, including, but not limited to, informational books, magazines, newspapers, encyclopedias, almanacs, and atlases. Encyclopedias are a valuable resource, but they are only one possible source, and other reference materials must be available. In addition to print sources, students can view filmstrips, films, and videotapes and can interview people in the community who have special expertise on the topic. For students who have had limited experience locating information in a library, a class trip to the school and public libraries to collect reference materials is useful.

Elementary students are not too young to understand what *plagiarism* is and why it is wrong. Even primary-grade students understand that they should not "borrow" items belonging to classmates and pretend they are theirs. Similarly, students should not "borrow" or "steal" someone's words, especially without asking permission or giving credit in the composition. Writing key words and phrases on clusters or data charts helps students learn to take notes without copying entire sentences and paragraphs from reference books.

The preliminary organization—deciding on the key points—completed in the first step gives direction for gathering the information. Now students review the information they have gathered and decide how best to present it so that the report will be both interesting and well organized. Students can transfer the "notes" they want to use for their reports from

FIGURE 9.7
Using the Teaching Strategy for Oral Reports

Initiating	Students choose specific topics for their reports. Topics should be narrow and specific; the *heart* is a better topic than the *human body*, *tigers* better than *cats*, and *Alexander Graham Bell* better than *inventors*.
Structuring	As a class, decide on key points students will cover in their reports. (If students choose very different topics, they may need to develop their own key points.) Students will use these points as main ideas in their clusters or data charts.
Conceptualizing	Students gather information for their reports by consulting a variety of reference materials, including nonprint sources. They make and use a cluster or data chart to record information.
Summarizing	Students organize the main ideas and the information they have gathered. They decide the sequence for the presentation and choose a particularly interesting piece of information for the introduction. They make visuals (e.g., charts, maps, diagrams) or perhaps design a costume to wear. Also some students will want to record important information on note cards to refer to during the presentation, but they should not write a speech and read it verbatim.
Generalizing	Students rehearse their presentations several times, with a friend or in front of a mirror, if possible. Teachers might also review some elements of a good presentation—speaking loudly enough to be heard, starting with an interesting bit of information, keeping to the key points, having a visual, and making eye contact with the audience.
Applying	Students give their presentations, then get feedback from classmates and the teacher on how effectively they have communicated, either through a discussion or using a checklist or other assessment form.

the cluster or data chart onto note cards. Only key words—not sentences or paragraphs—should be written on the cards.

Students may also develop visuals such as charts, diagrams, maps, pictures, models, and timelines. For example, the second graders who gave reports on parts of the body made drawings and clay models of the parts and used a large skeleton hanging in the classroom to show the location of the organ in the body. Visuals provide a "crutch" for the speaker and add an element of interest for the listeners.

The final step is to rehearse and then give the presentation. Students can rehearse several times by reviewing key points and reading over their note cards. They should not, however, read the report verbatim from the note cards. Students might want to choose a particularly interesting fact to begin the presentation.

Before the presentations begin, discuss the important things speakers should remember. For instance, speakers should talk loudly enough for all to hear, keep to the key points, refer to their note cards for important facts, and use the visuals they have prepared.

Through these four steps, elementary students can learn to prepare and present well-organized and interesting reports. The steps are summarized in Figure 9.7.

Book talks. Students give oral reports to review books they have read or television shows and films they have viewed. Remember, however, that oral reports are only one way to respond to literature; other ideas for sharing and responding include informal dramatics, storytelling, art, and writing activities. The steps in preparing and presenting reviews are similar to those for informational reports:

1. Read or view the selection.
2. Select information for the report, including a brief summary of the selection and bibliographic information; comparisons to other selections (e.g., with similar themes, written by the same author, starring the same actor); strengths and weaknesses; and opinions and conclusions.
3. Record and organize the information on a cluster and then copy key words onto note cards.
4. Briefly rehearse the review.
5. Give the presentation, referring to the note cards but not reading them verbatim.

Interviews

Almost all children see interviews on television news programs and are familiar with the interviewing techniques reporters use. Interviewing is an exciting, real-life communication activity that helps students refine questioning skills and practice all four language modes—listening, talking, reading, and writing (Haley-James & Hobson, 1980).

Interviewing is an important language tool that can be integrated effectively with almost any area of the curriculum. Primary-grade students, for instance, can interview community helpers as part of a social studies unit on the community, and older students can interview long-time area residents about local history. Students can also interview people who live far away, such as a favorite author, legislator, or Olympic athlete, using a long-distance telephone conference call.

One way to introduce interviewing is to watch interviews conducted on a television newscast and discuss the purpose of the interview, what a reporter does before and after an interview, and what types of questions are asked. Interviewers use a variety of questions, some to elicit facts and others to probe for feelings and opinions, but all questions are open-ended. Rarely do they ask questions that require only a *yes* or *no* answer.

Interviewing involves far more than the actual interview. There are three steps in the interview process: planning the interview, conducting it, and sharing the results. The first step, planning, requires arranging for the interview and developing a list of questions to ask. The second step is the interview itself. Students conduct the interview by asking questions they have prepared in advance and taking notes or tape-recording the answers. In the third step, sharing the results, the interviewer prepares a report based on the information he or she has learned. The report can take many different forms, ranging from oral reports to class newspapers to published booklets. The activities in each of the three steps are outlined in Figure 9.8.

Teaching students to interview. Students need to practice developing and asking questions before they interview people outside the classroom. One way to get this practice is to

FIGURE 9.8
Steps in the Interview Process

Planning the Interview
Make arrangements for the interview.
Brainstorm a list of questions to ask the person being interviewed.
Write the questions on note cards, using one card for each question. Be sure the questions are open-ended, not *yes* or *no* questions.
Organize the note cards so you can ask related questions together.
Read over the questions, making sure they will elicit the information you are seeking.

Conducting the Interview
After a friendly greeting, explain the reason for the interview and begin asking the questions.
Allow the person you are interviewing to answer each question fully before you ask another question.
Ask follow-up questions about points that are not clear.
If the answer to one question brings up another question that has not been written down, do not hesitate to ask it.
Be polite and respectful of the answers and opinions of the person you are interviewing.
Take notes on the note cards or take notes and tape-record the interview.
Limit the time for the interview.
Thank the person for participating in the interview.

Sharing the Results
Read over the notes or listen to the tape recording of the interview.
Organize the information collected during the interview.
Share the results of the interview through an oral or written report, a newspaper article, or another type of presentation.

interview classmates. The proverbial "How I Spent My Summer Vacation" report that teachers have students give during the first few days of school can be turned into an interviewing opportunity. Have the class, as a group, brainstorm a list of possible questions; then pair students to interview each other about their summer activities. They can then report their interviews to the class. Other topics for class interviews include favorite films, hobbies, or games.

Next, invite someone, such as a police officer, the manager of a local fast-food restaurant, or a television news reporter, to visit the classroom and be interviewed. Have students follow the three-step interview process. Instruct them to prepare in advance for the interview by developing a list of questions and deciding who will greet the visitor and how the questions will be asked. After the interview, work together to prepare a class collaboration or group report about the interview to publish in the class or community newspaper.

A class interview is a useful practice activity for all students, but it is an especially valuable introduction to interviewing for kindergartners and first graders. After studying interviewing skills, for example, a class of first graders invited the local high school principal to visit their class to be interviewed. The principal, who had been blinded several years earlier, brought his guide dog with him. The children asked him questions about how visually impaired people manage everyday tasks as well as how he performed his job as a principal. They also asked questions about his guide dog. After the interview, students drew pictures and wrote summaries of the interview. One first grader's report is shown in Figure 9.9.

FIGURE 9.9
A First Grader's Interview Summary
Tomara, age 7

Mr. Kirtley came down.
We asked him questions. He
answered them. He is
blind. His dog's name is
Milo.

To follow up an interview, children discuss what they have learned through the interview or dictate a report for the teacher to print on the writing board. Later, the report can be written on chart paper, or photocopies of it can be made to which each child adds drawings.

Students can conduct interviews with family members and other members of the community on a variety of topics. Cooper's *Who Put the Cannon in the Courthouse Square? A Guide to Uncovering the Past* (1985) and Weitzman's *My Backyard History Book* (1975) are excellent books to use with students in planning a community history project. Other stories to use are shown in Figure 9.10. Students work individually or in small groups to interview long-time residents about the community's history, growth and changes, modes of dress, transportation, communication, types of work, and ways to have fun.

Books to use with students in planning a family history project are shown in Figure 9.11. After gathering information through interviews, they write reports that are published in a class or community newspaper or in a book.

Debates

Debates are useful when the whole class is excited about an issue and most or all of the students have taken supporting or opposing positions. The class decides what the issue is, clarifies it, and identifies positions that support or oppose the issue. Students who wish to speak in favor of the issue move to a side of the room designated for supporters, and students who wish to speak against the issue move to the other side. Class members who have not formulated a position sit in the middle of the room. When anyone wishes to participate, he or she goes to the side of the room for the position he or she supports. After hearing arguments, students may change their minds and move to the opposite side of the room; if they are no longer certain what side they are on, they may take a seat in the middle. The teacher initiates the debate by asking someone from the supporting side of the issue to state that side. After the opening statement, the opposing side makes a statement. From then on, each side takes turns making statements. It is permissible to ask someone who has just made a statement a question before a side makes a return statement. Sixth graders who used this informal debate procedure in their social studies class enjoyed the experience and furthered their abilities to express themselves effectively.

A more formal type of debate is appropriate for students in the fourth grade and up. Debates take the form of arguments between opposing sides of a proposition. A *proposition* is a debate subject that can be discussed from opposing points of view; for example:

> Resolved, that students should have a role in setting standards of behavior in classes and in disciplining those students who disrupt classes.

FIGURE 9.10
Books for a Community History Project

Community History

Burton, V. L. (1942). *The little house.* (Ill. by the author). Boston: Houghton Mifflin. (M)

Carlstrom, N. W. (1990). *Blow me a kiss, Miss Lilly.* (Ill. by A. Schwartz). New York: Harper & Row. (M)

Grifalconi, A. (1986). *The village of round and square houses.* (Ill. by the reteller). New York: Little, Brown. (M)

Hamilton, V. (1968). *The house of Dies Drear.* (Ill. by E. Keith). New York: Macmillan. (M)

Hoyt-Goldsmith, D. (1990). *Totem pole.* (Ill. by L. Migdale). New York: Holiday House. (M)

Lisle, J. T. (1987). *The great Dimpole oak.* (Ill. by S. Gammell). A Richard Jackson Book. New York: Orchard Books/Franklin Watts. (M)

Provensen, A., & Provensen, M. (1987). *Shaker Lane.* (Ill. by the authors). New York: Viking. (M)

Pryor, B. (1987). *The house on Maple Street.* (Ill. by B. Peck). New York: Morrow. (M)

Schwartz, A. (1978). *When I grew up long ago: Older people talk about the days when they were young.* (Ill. by H. Berson). New York: Lippincott. (M)

Schweitzer, B. B. (1965). *One small blue bead.* (Ill. by S. Shimin). New York: Macmillan. (M)

Trimble, S. (1990). *The village of blue stone.* (Ill. by J. O. Dewey & D. Reade). New York: Macmillan. (M)

FIGURE 9.11
Books for a Family History Project

Family History

Ackerman, K. (1988). *Song and dance man.* (Ill. by S. Gammell). New York: Knopf. (P)

Adler, D. A. (1976). *A little at a time.* (Ill. by N. M. Bodecker). New York: Random House. (P)

Bryan, A. (Reteller). (1989). *Turtle knows your name.* (Ill. by the reteller). New York: Atheneum. (P)

Bunting, E. (1989). *The Wednesday surprise.* (Ill. by D. Carrick). New York: Clarion. (P)

Cooney, B. (1988). *Island boy.* (Ill. by the author). New York: Viking/Kestrel. (M)

Daly, N. (1988). *Not so fast, Songololo.* (Ill. by the author). New York: Atheneum. (P)

Flournoy, V. (1985). *The patchwork quilt.* (Ill. by J. Pinkney). New York: Dial. (P)

Fox, M. (1989). *Night noises.* San Diego: Gulliver/Harcourt Brace Jovanovich. (P)

Friedman, I. R. (1984). *How my parents learned to eat.* (Ill. by A. Say). Boston: Houghton Mifflin. (P)

Galbraith, K. (1990). *Laura Charlotte.* (Ill. by F. Cooper). New York: Philomet. (P)

Goble, P. (1989). *Beyond the ridge.* (Ill. by the author). New York: Bradbury Press. (M)

Gould, D. (1987). *Grandpa's slide show.* (Ill. by C. Harness). New York: Lothrop, Lee & Shepard. (P)

Grifalconi, A. (1990). *Osa's pride.* (Ill. by the reteller). New York: Little, Brown. (M)

Griffith, H. V. (1988). *Georgia music.* (Ill. by J. Stevenson). New York: Greenwillow. (M)

Griffith, H. V. (1988). *Grandaddy's place.* (Ill. by J. Stevenson). New York: Greenwillow. (M)

Harvey, B. (1986). *My prairie year: Based on the diary of Elenore Plaisted.* (Ill. by D. K. Ray). New York: Holiday. (P)

Heist, A. (1989). *The midnight eaters.* (Ill. by K. Gundersheimer). New York: Four Winds. (P)

Hendershot, J. (1987). *In coal country.* (Ill. by T. B. Allen). New York: Knopf. (M)

Kinsey-Warnock, N. (1989). *The Canada geese quilt.* (Ill. by L. W. Bowman. New York: Cobblehill/Dutton. (M)

Lawson, R. (1940). *They were strong and good.* (Ill. by the author). New York: Viking Publishing Company. (P)

Patent, D. H. (1989). *Grandfather's nose: Why we look alike or different.* (Ill. by D. Palmisciano). New York: Franklin Watts. (P)

Polacco, P. (1988). *The keeping quilt.* (Ill. by the author). New York: Simon and Schuster. (P)

Pomerantz, C. (1989). *The chalk doll.* (Ill. by F. Lessac). New York: Lippincott. (P)

Shecter, B. (1989). *Grandma remembers.* (Ill. by the author). New York: Harper & Row. (P)

Zolotow, C. (1974). *My grandson Lew.* (Ill. by W. P. du Bois). New York: Harper & Row. (P)

After determining the proposition, teams of two to four students each are designated to support the proposition (the affirmative team) or oppose it (the negative team).

Depending on the number of members on each team, this is the order of debate:

1. The first and third statements support the proposition.
2. The second and fourth statements reject the proposition.
3. The first and third rebuttal statements are made by the affirmative team.
4. The second and fourth rebuttal statements are made by the negative team.

Each member makes both a statement about the proposition and a rebuttal statement to the opposite team. Normally there are as many rebuttal statements as there are statements about the proposition. Teachers may vary the procedure to fit the class and their purposes. Students can also choose judges to determine the winning team.

If judges evaluate the debates, let students decide the criteria for judging. Have them brainstorm questions that will form the basis for their criteria. Questions similar to the following might initiate the brainstorming sessions:

Did the speakers communicate their ideas to listeners?

Was a mastery of information evident in the presentations and rebuttals?

Was there evidence that the speakers knew the topic well?

Was the team courteous?

Did the team work cooperatively?

Did the second speaker on each team pick up and extend the statement of the first team member?

Students may want to interview the high school debating team for ideas on judging and presenting their topics. They might also enjoy attending a high school debate.

D. DRAMATIC ACTIVITIES

Drama provides a medium for students to use language, both verbal and nonverbal, in a meaningful context. Drama is not only a powerful form of communication, but also a valuable way of knowing. When children participate in dramatic activities, they interact with classmates, share experiences, and explore their own understanding. According to Dorothy Heathcote, a highly acclaimed British drama teacher, drama "cracks the code" so the message can be understood (Wagner, 1976). Drama has this power because it involves both logical, left-brain and creative, right-brain thinking; it requires active experience (the basic, first way of learning); and integrates the four language modes. Recent research confirms that drama has a positive effect both on elementary students' oral language development and their literacy learning (Kardash & Wright, 1987; Wagner, 1988). Drama is often neglected, however, because some consider it a nonessential part of the language arts curriculum.

Dramatic activities range from young children's dramatic play to scripted plays that students produce. Students create imaginary worlds through their drama, and they increase their understanding of themselves and the world in which they live (Booth, 1985; Kukla, 1987). These activities can be grouped into four categories that are distinguishable from one another in three significant ways: spontaneity, process versus product orientation, and level of formality. The four categories are dramatic play, informal drama, interpretive drama, and theatrical productions.

Young children's natural, make-believe play activities are called *dramatic play.* This kind of drama is spontaneous, unrehearsed, process-oriented, and extremely informal.

Informal drama is the natural outgrowth of dramatic play. Like dramatic play, it is spontaneous, unrehearsed, process-oriented, and informal. Informal drama activities include dramatizing stories and role playing.

Interpretive dramatic activities are those in which students interpret literature using voice, facial features, and gestures. Interpretive drama involves some rehearsal and is somewhat formal. It is a transition between informal drama and theatrical productions; examples include storytelling and readers theater. Participating in these activities refines students' concepts of "story," helps them learn the elements of story structure (e.g., characters, plot, and setting), and introduces them to script conventions.

Theatrical productions are polished performances of a play produced on a stage and before an audience. They require extensive rehearsal, are product-oriented, and are quite formal. Because the purpose of theatrical productions is the polished presentation, they are audience-centered rather than child-centered. They also require that students memorize lines rather than encourage them to be spontaneous and improvisational. They are not recommended for students in elementary grades unless students write the scripts themselves.

Again and again, educators caution that drama activities should be informal during the elementary years (Stewig, 1983a; Wagner, 1976). The one exception is when students write their own play and puppet show scripts and want to perform them.

Dramatic Play

Playing in the housekeeping corner and putting on dress-up clothes—a bridal veil or a police officer's coat and hat—are familiar activities in preschool and kindergarten classrooms. Young children use these activities to reenact familiar, everyday activities and to pretend to be someone or something else. These *dramatic play* activities represent children's first attempt at drama (McCaslin, 1984).

A housekeeping corner is only one possible dramatic play center. Prop kits, which contain collections of materials for dramatic play, can be set out for children to experiment with. For example, a detective prop kit, with a Sherlock Holmes hat, raincoat, flashlight, magnifying glass, notepad, and pencil, becomes a popular center after children read Sharmat's *Nate the Great* series of easy-to-read mystery stories. Even middle-grade students are drawn to prop kit materials after reading Sobol's *Encyclopedia Brown* detective stories and writing their own mystery stories. A variety of prop kit ideas is offered in Figure 9.12.

FIGURE 9.12
Materials for Prop Kits

Post Office Kit

mailboxes (use shoeboxes)	wrapping paper	package seals
	tape	address labels
envelopes	packages	cash register
stamps (use Christmas seals)	scale	money
pens		
string		

Hairdresser Kit

hair rollers	posters of hair styles	ribbons, barrets, clips
brush and comb	wig and wig stand	appointment book
mirror	hairdryer (with cord cut off)	open/closed sign
empty shampoo bottle		
towel	curling iron (with cord cut off)	

Office Kit

typewriter	hole punch	telephone
calculator	file folders	message pad
paper	in/out boxes	rubber stamps
notepads	pens and pencils	stamp pad
transparent tape	envelopes	
stapler	stamps	

Medical Kit (doctor, nurse, paramedic)

white shirt/jacket	thermometer	prescription bottles and labels
medical bag	tweezers	
stethoscope	bandages	walkie-talkie (for paramedics)
hypodermic syringe (play)	prescription pad	

Grocery Store Kit

grocery cart	cash register
food packages	money
plastic fruit and artificial foods	grocery bags
price stickers	marking pen

Many of the prop kits involve reading and writing materials, such as the notepad and pencil in the detective kit, menus in the restaurant kit, and a typewriter in the office kit. Thus, through dramatic play with these materials, young children are introduced to some of the functions of reading and writing.

Props for the kits can be collected, stored in boxes, and then used in social studies, science, math, or literature activities. They can also be used in conjunction with field trips and class visitors; for example, for a unit on community helpers, teachers could arrange a field trip to the post office and invite a mail carrier to the classroom to be interviewed. Then a mail carrier prop kit can be set up. With the information they have learned from the field trip, the in-class interview, and through books, children have many experiences to draw on when they experiment with the props.

Dramatic play has all the values of other types of informal drama (Schickedanz, 1978). Children have the opportunity to use talk in a meaningful context as well as to learn new vocabulary words. As with other talk activities, dramatic play helps children develop socialization skills. The children are integrating all the language modes—listening, talking, reading, and writing—through their play activities, and are also learning content area material.

FIGURE 9.12
Continued

Restaurant Kit

tablecloth	napkins	apron for waitress
dishes	menus	vest for waiter
glasses	tray	hat and apron for chef
silverware	order pad and pencil	

Travel Agency Kit

travel posters	wallet with money and
travel brochures	credit cards
maps	cash register
airplane, train tickets	suitcases

Veterinarian Kit

white shirt/jacket	empty medicine bottles
stuffed animals	prescription labels
cages (cardboard	bandages
boxes)	popsicle stick splints
medical bag	hypodermic syringe
stethoscope	(play)

Library Kit

children's books and	book return box
magazines (with card	sign for book fines
pockets and date due slips)	cash register
date stamp and stamp pad	money
library cards	

Bank Kit

teller window (use a	roll papers for coins
puppet stage)	deposit slips
passbooks	money bags
checks	
money	

Role Playing

Students assume the role of another person as they act out stories or reenact historical events. Through role playing, children have the opportunity to step into someone else's shoes and view the world from another perspective.

From their first experiences in dramatic play, students move into acting out stories, in which they combine retelling with drama. Choose familiar stories—folktales and fables— for students to act out using both dialogue and body movements. The stories listed in Figure 9.13 can be used for role playing activities. Cumulative tales such as *The Three Little Pigs* (Galdone, 1970) and *The Gingerbread Boy* (Galdone, 1975) are good for younger children to dramatize because they are repetitious (and predictable) in sequence, plot, and dialogue. Middle- and upper-grade students can act out favorite scenes from longer stories such as *The Wind in the Willows* (Grahame, 1961) and *Mrs. Frisby and the Rats of NIHM* (O'Brien, 1971). Fourth-grade students can also read biographies and dramatize events from these people's lives. *Columbus* (d'Aulaire & d'Aulaire, 1955) and *And Then What Happened, Paul Revere?* (Fritz, 1973) are two biographies that fourth graders can dramatize.

Booth (Kukla, 1987) has developed an approach he calls *story-drama,* which expands story dramatizing into role playing. After reading and discussing a story, students explore its issues, themes, and deeper meanings through drama.

In role playing, students take the role of another person—not roles in a story, but rather the roles people play in society. Role playing is an educational experience designed to help students gain insights about how to handle real-life problems and understand historical and

FIGURE 9.13
Stories for Role-Playing Activities

Brown, M. (1947). *Stone soup*. New York: Scribner. (P–M)
Brown, M. W. (1972). *The runaway bunny*. New York: Harper & Row. (P)
Carle, E. (1970). *The very hungry caterpillar*. Cleveland: Collins-World. (P)
Flack, M. (1932). *Ask Mr. Bear*. New York; Macmillan. (P)
Gag, W. (1956). *Millions of cats*. New York: Coward McCann. (P)
Galdone, P. (1973). *The three billy goats Gruff*. Boston: Houghton Mifflin. (P)
Galdone, P. (1975). *The gingerbread boy*. New York: Seabury. (P)
Grimm, The Brothers. (1971). *The Bremen town musicians*. New York: Greenwillow. (P–M)
Johnson, O. (1955). *Harold and the purple crayon*. New York: Harper & Row. (See also other books in this series.) (P)
Kellogg, S. (1973). *The island of the skog*. New York: Dial. (P)
Low, J. (1980) *Mice twice*. New York: Atheneum. (P–M)
Slobodkina, E. (1947). *Caps for sale*. New York: Scott. (P)
Steig, W. (1982). *Doctor DeSoto*. New York: Farrar. (P)
Still, J. (1977). *Jack and the wonder beans*. New York: Putnam. (M)
Thurber, J. (1974). *Many moons*. New York: Harcourt. (P–M)
Turkle, B. (1976). *Deep in the forest*. New York: Dutton. (P–M)
Wildsmith, B. (1972). *The owl and the woodpecker*. New York: Watts. (P–M)
Zemach, H., & Zemach, M. (1973). *Duffy and the devil*. New York: Farrar. (P–M)
Zemach, M. (1976). *It could always be worse*. New York: Farrar. (P–M–U)

current events (Nelson, 1988). Heathcote has developed an innovative approach to role playing to help students experience and better understand historical events (Wagner, 1976). Through a process she calls *funneling,* Heathcote chooses a dramatic focus from a general topic (e.g., Ancient Rome, the Civil War, the Pilgrims). She begins by thinking of all the aspects of the general topic and then decides on a dramatic focus—a particular critical moment. For example, using the topic of the Pilgrims, one possible focus is the night of December 20, 1620, eleven weeks after the Pilgrims set sail from England on the *Mayflower* and the night before the ship reached Plymouth.

The improvisation begins when students assume roles; the teacher becomes a character, too. As they begin to role-play the event, questions draw students' attention to certain features and probe their understanding. Questions about the Pilgrims might include:

Where are you?
After 11 weeks sailing the Atlantic Ocean, what will happen?
How are you feeling?
Why did you leave England?
What kind of life do you dream of in the new land?
Can you survive in this cold winter weather?

These questions also provide information by reminding students of the time of year, the problems they are having, and the length of the voyage.

Sometimes Heathcote stops students in the middle of role playing and asks them to write what they are thinking and feeling. As part of the Pilgrim improvisation, students might be asked to write an entry in their simulated journals for December 20, 1620. An example of a simulated journal entry written by a fourth-grade "Pilgrim" is shown in Figure 9.14. After the writing activity, students continue role playing.

Heathcote uses drama to begin study on a topic rather than as a culminating activity in which students apply all they have learned, because she believes role-playing experiences stimulate children's curiosity and make them want to read books and learn more about a historical or current event. Whether you use role playing as an introduction or as a conclusion, it is a valuable activity because students become immersed in the event. By reliving it, they are learning far more than mere facts.

FIGURE 9.14
A Fourth-Grade Pilgrim's Simulated Journal Entry for December 20, 1620
Stephanie, age 10

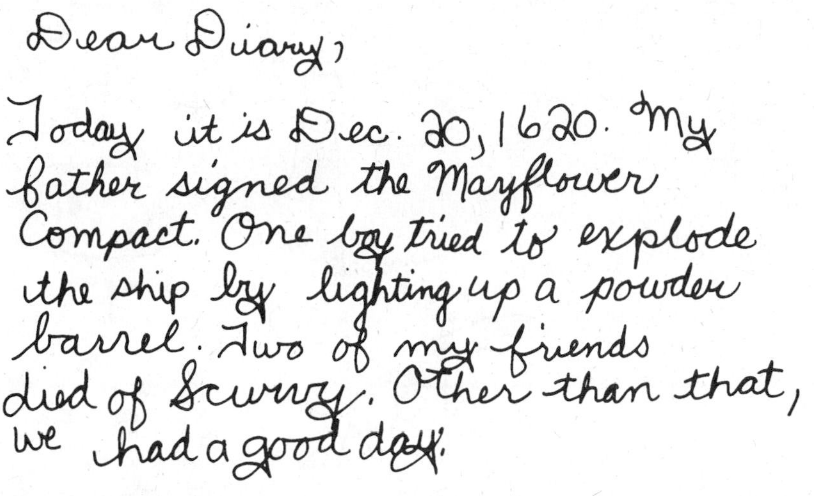

Dear Diary,

Today it is Dec. 20, 1620. My father signed the Mayflower Compact. One boy tried to explode the ship by lighting up a powder barrel. Two of my friends died of Scurvy. Other than that, we had a good day.

Puppets and Other Props

Puppets have long been favorites of children. The delightful combinations of colorful language, novel body constructions, fantasy, and imaginative characters fascinate children. Children can create puppet shows with commercially manufactured puppets, or they can construct their own. When children create their own puppets, the only limitations are students' imaginations, their ability to construct things, and the materials at hand. Puppets can be especially useful with shy students. Puppets can be used not only in all types of drama activities, but also as a novel way to introduce a language skill, such as quotation marks. Teachers can use puppets to improvise a dialogue, and then record it using quotation marks.

Simple puppets provide children with the opportunity to develop both creative and dramatic ability. The simpler the puppet, the more is left to the imagination of the audience and the puppeteer. Constructing elaborate puppets is beyond the resources of both teachers and students. The type of puppets the students make, however, depends on how they will be used. Students can construct puppets using all sorts of scrap materials. We will describe how to make eight types of hand and finger puppets; the eight types are illustrated in Figure 9.15.

Stick puppets. Stick puppets are versatile and perhaps the easiest to make. Sticks, tongue depressors, dowels, and straws can be used. The rest of the puppet that is attached to the stick can be constructed from papier-mâché, Styrofoam balls, pictures students have drawn, or pictures cut from magazines and mounted on cardboard. Students draw or paint the features on the materials they have selected for the head and body. Some puppets may need only a head; others may also need a body. Making stick puppets provides an opportunity to combine art and drama.

Paper bag puppets. This is another simple puppet to make. The paper bags should be the right size to fit students' hands. Paper lunch bags are a convenient size, although smaller bags are better for kindergartners. What characters they portray and what emphasis the students give the size of the character are the determining factors, however. The puppet's mouth can be placed at the fold of the paper bag. Paint on faces and clothes, add yarn for hair, and attach arms and legs. Students should choose ways to decorate their bag puppets to match the characters they develop.

FIGURE 9.15
Types of Puppets

Stick Puppet   Paper Bag Puppet   Cylinder Puppet

Sock Puppet   Styrofoam Puppet   Paper Plate Puppet

Finger Puppet
(with tabs)

Finger puppet
(from glove finger)

Cloth Puppet

Cylinder puppets. Cylinder puppets are made from cardboard tubes from bathroom tissue, paper towels, and aluminum foil. The diameter and length of the cylinder determine the size of the puppet. The cylinders can be painted and various appendages and clothing can be attached. Again, the character's role should determine how the puppet is costumed. Students insert their fingers in the bottom of the cylinder to manipulate the puppet.

Sock puppets. Sock puppets are quite versatile. A sock can be used as is, with button eyes, yarn hair, pipe cleaner antennae, and other features added. The sock can also be cut at the toe to create a mouth and whatever else is needed to give the impression of the character can be added.

Cup puppets. Even primary-grade students can make puppets from Styrofoam cups. They glue facial features, hair, wings, and other decorations on the cup. Pipe cleaners, toothpicks, and Q-tips tipped with glitter can easily be attached to Styrofoam cups. Then sticks or heavy-duty straws are attached to the inside of the cup as the handle.

Paper plate puppets. Paper plates can be used for face puppets as well as for masks. Students add junk materials to decorate teaching puppets and then tape sticks or rulers to the back of the plates as handles.

Finger puppets. Students can make several different types of finger puppets. For one type, students can draw, color, cut out small figures, and then add tabs to either side of the figure and tape the tabs together to fit around the finger. Larger puppets can be taped to fit around the hand. For a second type of finger puppet, students can cut the finger section from a glove and add decoration. The pointed part that separates the compartments of an egg carton can also be used for a finger puppet.

Cloth puppets. If parents are available to assist with the sewing, students can make cloth puppets. Two pieces of cloth are sewn together on all sides except the bottom, then students personalize the puppets using scraps of fabric, lace, yarn, and other materials.

After students have created their puppets, they can perform the puppet show almost any place. They can make a stage from an empty appliance packing crate or an empty television cabinet. They can also drape blankets or cloths in front of classroom tables and desks. They might also turn a table on its side. There may be other classroom objects your students can use as makeshift stages.

Scriptwriting and Theatrical Productions

Scripts are a unique written language form that elementary students need opportunities to explore. Scriptwriting often grows out of role playing and storytelling. Soon students recognize the need to write notes when they prepare for plays, puppet shows, readers theater, and other dramatic productions. This need provides the impetus for introducing students to the unique dramatic conventions and for encouraging them to write scripts to present as theatrical productions.

Play scripts. Once students want to write scripts, they will recognize the need to add the structures unique to dramatic writing to their repertoire of written language conventions. Students begin by examining scripts. It is especially effective to have students compare narrative and script versions of the same story; for example, Richard George has adapted two of Roald Dahl's fantastic stories, *Charlie and the Chocolate Factory* (1976) and *James and the Giant Peach* (1982) into scripts. Then students discuss their observations and compile a list of the unique characteristics of scripts. An upper-grade class compiled the list of unique dramatic conventions presented in Figure 9.16.

The next step is to have students apply what they have learned about scripts by writing a class collaboration or group script. With the whole class, develop a script by adapting a familiar story. As the script is being written, refer to the chart of dramatic conventions and ask students to check that they are using these conventions. Collaborative writing affords unique teaching opportunities and needed practice for students before they must write in-

FIGURE 9.16
Dramatic Conventions Used in Scripts

Important Characteristics of Scripts

1. Scripts are divided into acts and scenes.
2. Scripts have these parts: (a) a list of characters (or cast); (b) the setting (at the beginning of each act or scene); (c) stage directions (written in parentheses); and (d) dialogue.
3. The dialogue carries the action.
4. Description and other information are set apart in the setting or in stage directions.
5. Stage directions give actors important information about how to act and how to feel.
6. The dialogue is written in a special way:

CHARACTER'S NAME: Dialogue

7. Sometimes a narrator is used to quickly fill in parts of the story.

dividually. After the script is completed, have students read it using readers theater procedures, or produce it as a puppet show or play.

Once students are aware of the dramatic conventions and have participated in writing a class collaboration script, they can write scripts individually or in small groups. Students often adapt familiar stories for their first scripts; later, they will want to create original scripts.

Film/video scripts. Students use a similar approach in writing scripts that will be filmed or videotaped, but they must now consider the visual component of the film as well as the written script. They often compose their scripts on storyboards, which focus their attention on how the story they are creating will be filmed (Cox, 1983, 1985). *Storyboards,* or sheets of paper divided into three sections, are used to sketch in scenes. Students place a series of three or four large squares in a row down the center of the paper, with space for dialogue and narration on the left and shooting directions on the right. Cox compares storyboards to road maps because they provide directions for filming the script. The scene renderings and the shooting directions help students tie the dialogue to the visual images that will appear on the film or videotape. Figure 9.17 shows a sample storyboard form with an excerpt from a fourth-grade class collaboration script.

The script can be produced several different ways—as a live-action play, as a puppet show, or through animation. After writing the script on the storyboards or transferring a previously written script to storyboards, students collect or construct the properties they will need to produce the script. As with other types of drama, the properties do not need to be extensive or elaborate—a simple backdrop and costumes will suffice. Students should also print the title and credits on large posters to appear at the beginning of the film. After several rehearsals, the script is filmed using a movie or video camera.

As video cameras and VCR playback systems become common equipment in elementary schools, we anticipate that they will be chosen more often than movie cameras for filming student scripts. Video cameras and tapes are easier and less expensive to use than movie cameras and film, videotapes do not need to be developed as film does and can be reused, and the audio component can be recorded at the same time as the video. Many teachers prefer videotapes to movie films because they can tape rehearsals, which allows students to review their performances and make necessary changes before the final taping.

FIGURE 9.17
Excerpt from a Fourth-Grade Class Collaboration Storyboard Script

DIALOGUE	SCENE	SHOOTING DIRECTIONS
Paula: Hurry up, Parker. You'll miss the bus. Parker: Coming! Paula: Here's what we'll do. We'll go to the library and find a book on how to kill witches.	CITY LIBRARY	They ride the bus to the library. Follow them up the stairs into the library.
Parker: I found the book, Paula! Paula: Let's see, here it is! How to kill a witch. Parker: Here's what we'll do. Psst. Psst. Psst. (whispering)	How to Kill Witches	They find the book. Hold book up. Close up. Check index to find out how to kill her.

E. CLASSROOM ACTIVITIES*

The Telephone	ACTIVITY 9.1

Purpose

1. To make a play telephone and have a conversation with someone
2. To practice conversational skills

Materials

Two paper cups, long strings, nail, two buttons for each child-made phone; toy phones or walkie-talkies.

Grade level

K–4

Procedures

1. Ask the children whether they enjoy talking on the telephone. Discuss the purpose of the telephone and have them list reasons for talking on the telephone. Tell the children that they are going to make their own phones and that they will have a chance to talk to their friends on their phones.
2. You may make one phone for the group to share, a phone for every two children, or have each child make his own phone so each will have one to take home. Directions for making the phones are as follows:

    Carefully poke a hole in the bottom of each paper cup. Put a long piece of string through the hole and tie a button onto the end of the string inside the cup. Attach the string in the same way to the second cup. Stretch the two cups apart so the string is tight. Have one partner hold the cup to his ear, while the other speaks into her cup. Use the child-made phones for conversations.

3. Provide toy telephones and allow children to practice talking on the phone. Some suggested roles include:
   Talking to a friend about things that happened in school
   Calling your mother or father to ask for a ride home because it's raining
   Calling a friend to ask if the friend may stay overnight
   Calling a friend to ask if the friend may accompany your family to the zoo, a museum, or other outing
   Calling the police in an emergency
   Calling the fire department in an emergency
   Calling mother's or father's office or home to ask one of them to pick you up from school because you are sick

Storytelling from Lost-and-Found Advertisements	ACTIVITY 9.2

Purpose

1. To participate in an oral discussion
2. To tell a creative story motivated by humorous or unusual lost-and-found advertisements

Materials

Collection of humorous or unusual lost-and-found advertisements; newspapers containing lost-and-found advertisements.

Grade level

K–4; lost-and-found advertisements can be read to younger children

Procedures

1. Search the lost-and-found advertisements and select thought-provoking ads.
2. Introduce lost-and-found ads to the children by discussing the kinds of things people might lose and how they might try to get the items back. Ask the group if any of them has ever lost anything, why the items were lost, and how they tried to find them.

*Adapted from Donna E. Norton & Saunda Norton, *Language Arts Activities for Children*, 3rd ed. (Englewood Cliffs, NJ: Merrill/Prentice Hall, 1994), pp. 20, 21, 40. By permission of the authors and Prentice Hall.

FIGURE 9.18
Creative Story From Lost-and-Found Ad

Lost: Two male Dobermans in vicinity of the University campus. Answer to the names of Ringo and Savage.	*Lost:* Northgate Cinema, man's wedding ring. Gold with 3 small diamonds. Sentimental value, substantial reward.
Found: Black cat, about 12 months old, wearing flea collar, front paw in cast.	*Lost:* Boy's 20″ Sears motocross bike, black and yellow. Reward from unhappy boy.
$500 REWARD For return of information on 20-ft camper last seen in Westgate Mall Shopping Center.	

FIGURE 9.19
Lost and Found Bulletin Board

3. Talk about the newspaper's lost-and-found section. Show it to the group and explain that people often lose items. Read some of the ads aloud and allow students to speculate about how the item was lost, what happened when it was lost, who found the item, whether there was a reward offered, how the owner would try to find the item, and what the students would do with a reward if they earned it.
4. Allow children to select a specific lost-and-found ad and develop a creative story related to that ad. Some examples include those shown in Figure 9.18.
5. Divide class into smaller groups and allow students to tell their stories to their own groups.
6. Design a "Lost-and-Found" bulletin board. Put the lost-and-found ads and the illustrations of the stories on the bulletin board (see Figure 9.19).
7. Lost-and-found ads may easily be used to motivate creative writing.

ACTIVITY 9.3   **Yankee Doodle**

Purpose

1. To refine speaking, reading, interpreting, and listening skills
2. To promote cooperation through a group activity
3. To increase enjoyment in reading, speaking, and listening through an antiphonal choral arrangement
4. To interpret a piece of folk music written in the 1700s that describes the Revolutionary War

Copies of the folksong "Yankee Doodle."   **Materials**

1–4   **Grade level**

                                                                                             Procedures

1. Background information to share with students: The British brought the song "Yankee Doodle" to America. During the Revolutionary War, however, colonial soldiers adopted the song as one of the symbols for the American struggle for independence.
2. Discuss the significance of the folksong "Yankee Doodle." Allow children to share their knowledge of the Revolutionary War period. Clarify any misconceptions. Have the students read the words to the song. Discuss the meaning of *hasty pudding, Yankee Doodle Dandy, Captain Washington, slapping stallion, swamping gun, horn of powder, a nation louder, little keg,* and *stabbing iron.*
3. Divide the students into two groups. Boy and girl groupings work well for this, since the verses may pertain more to a boy's version of the war, while the chorus sounds as if it is a response to a masculine experience. Other groupings, such as high voices and low voices, however, are equally effective. This folksong may be divided in the following manner:

Boys, or Group 1:	Father and I went down to camp,
	Along with Captain Gooding;
	And there we saw the men and boys
	As thick as hasty pudding.
Girls, or Group 2: (chorus)	Yankee Doodle keep it up,
	Yankee Doodle Dandy,
	Mind the music and the step,
	And with the girls be handy.
Boys, or Group 1:	And there we saw a thousand men,
	As rich as Squire David;
	And what they wasted every day,
	I wish it could be saved.
Girls, or Group 2:	*Repeat chorus*
Boys, or Group 1:	And there was Captain Washington
	Upon a slapping stallion,
	A giving orders to his men;
	I guess there was a million.
Girls, or Group 2:	*Repeat chorus*
Boys, or Group 1:	And then the feathers on his hat,
	They looked so very fine, ah!
	I wanted peskily to get
	To give to my Jermima.
Girls, or Group 2:	*Repeat chorus*
Boys, or Group 1:	And there I see a swamping gun,
	Large as a bag of maple,
	Upon a mighty little cart;
	A load for father's cattle.
Girls, or Group 2:	*Repeat chorus*
Boys, or Group 1:	And evertime they fired it off,
	It took a horn of powder;
	It made a noise like father's gun,
	Only a nation louder.
Girls, or Group 2:	*Repeat chorus*
Boys, or Group 1:	And there I saw a little keg.
	It's head all made of leather,
	They knocked upon it with little sticks,
	To call the folks together.
Girls, or Group 2:	*Repeat chorus*

Boys, or Group 1:	The troopers too, would gallop up
	And fire right in our faces;
	It scared me almost half to death
	To see them run such races.
Girls, or Group 2:	*Repeat chorus*
Boys, or Group 1:	It scared me so I hoofed it off,
	Nor stopped, as I remember,
	Nor turned about till I got home,
	Locked up in Mother's Chamber.
Girls, or Group 2:	*Repeat chorus*

F. PROBLEM-SOLVING EXPERIENCES INVOLVING LANGUAGE ARTS SKILLS

Conflicts that are important to the group can be the focus of problem-solving experiences that develop oral communication and reading and listening skills. After reading *The King's Fountain* (Alexander, 1971), the students, whose families were experiencing a drought in their area because of a lack of rainfall during a very warm spring, discussed the story of the king who took away the water from the villagers so he could build a grand fountain. This led them to explore related issues about surviving without water, ways the villagers would react, and about the power of kings. In small groups, the students role-played some of the drama by dramatizing the problem of the villagers as they pleaded with the king not to redirect the water (Kukla, 1987). After the role play, the groups met to discuss their experiences and ways the drama made the story more memorable.

G. ASSESSMENT STRATEGY

For Conversations

Children can become effective participants in conversations when their comments are effective. Effective speaker's comments have been identified (Wilkinson, 1984):

1. Comments are clearly stated and directed to particular students.
2. Comments are related to the task at hand.
3. Comments are interpreted as sincere by peers.

Using Wilkinson's research, teachers can develop the students' insights into effective speaking by inviting them to self-evaluate on a simple checklist based on the previous findings (see Figure 9.20).

FIGURE 9.20
Self-Evaluation for Effective Speaking

Being a Star Speaker	Always	Sometimes	Never
1. I speak clearly to others.			
2. I speak directly to others.			
3. I talk about what is going on.			
4. I feel sincere about what I say.			
Other:			

Student name:_____   Date:_____

For Show-and-Tell

Students can participate in a class meeting to develop guidelines for preparing and presenting their topic for a show-and-tell time. Once the guidelines are established, students can plan what they want to share, rehearse and present, and invite feedback about the presentation. In the whole group, the students can transform the guidelines into a checklist that they complete after each presentation. Additionally, the teacher can develop a checklist for each presentation and record anecdotal notes about the ensuing feedback to verify the extent to which students are giving interesting presentations and developing the confidence to speak in front of others.

For Debates, Oral Reports, and Interviews

Debates. With students, develop a list of criteria that reflects the performance of each student during a debate. The criteria can be related to the student's delivery, factual information that was used, ways the student kept to the point, the persuasiveness of the student, and so on. Similar lists can be prepared for the Pro group and the Con group. Later, when the students feel comfortable with the idea of having judges (older students, parents, or community members) for their debates, they can suggest that the criteria be used for assessing each student's participation (see Figure 9.21).

For Dramatic Play, Role Playing, and Storytelling

Dramatic Play. Teachers can record the students' interactions about dramatic play with the props from a prop kit by writing a simple anecdote about the activity related to any or all of the following:

1. The student reenacts a familiar activity.
2. The comments are clearly stated and directed to the particular reenactment.
3. The comments are related to the meaningful context.
4. The student uses the functions of listening, speaking, reading, and writing.
5. The student demonstrates that he or she has experiences to draw from when interacting with the props in a prop kit and can use the props for a dramatic play activity.

Role Playing. The group, along with the teacher, can evaluate their role-playing experience. The teacher can ask questions to clarify and elaborate on the ideas and the solutions. In what way was the problem solved? In what way would the solution cause another problem? What are some other ways to solve the problem? Additionally, teachers can record the students' role-playing interactions by writing a simple anecdote about the activity related to any or all of the following:
    The student

1. Assumes the role of another person
2. Views the situation from another perspective
3. Uses dialogue
4. Uses appropriate body movements
5. Can focus on the problem in the story.

FIGURE 9.21
Debate Criteria

	Pro Group		
	James	Muriel	Patricia
1. Delivery			
2. Factual information			
3. Kept to the point			
4. Persuasiveness etc.			

Storytelling. Students can participate in a class meeting to develop guidelines for preparing and telling stories. Once the guidelines are established, students can plan what stories they want to tell, then rehearse and present, and invite feedback about the presentation. In the whole group, the guidelines can be transformed into a checklist for students to complete after each presentation. Additionally, the teacher can develop a checklist for each presentation and record anecdotal notes about the ensuing feedback to verify the extent to which the students are growing and developing in storytelling skills. Some guidelines for storytelling are shown in Figure 9.22.

Readers' theater. Teachers can record the students' interactions in readers' theater by writing a simple anecdote about the activity related to any or all of the following:

1. The student read the selected poem, short story, or excerpt from a story silently first and then orally with the group.
2. The student selected a part or compromised when he or she discovered that not all could have the part(s) desired.
3. The student read the selection orally and added actions—lively face, body, and voice gestures.
4. The student made suggestions for improving the performance.
5. The student rehearsed the selection orally and went through the actions until he or she was familiar with the presentation.

H. LANGUAGE ARTS SKILLS LESSON: INTERVIEWING

1. Descriptive Course Data

Teacher: _____ *Date:* _____
Grade level: All grades; primary grade students, K–3, can interview teachers, parents, and siblings. Fourth-grade students can interview various professional people as they practice interviewing skills that will benefit them throughout their lives.
Room number: _____
Unit: Division of Labor (i.e., the World of Work; Social Studies context)
Lesson Topic: Interviewing (Language Arts Skills)

2. Lesson Goals and Objectives

Instructional goals (General objectives).

1. To identify the purpose and audience for an oral interview.
2. To develop and practice interviewing skills through role playing.
3. To obtain information from another person using interviewing techniques.
4. To use literary characters and plots as motivation for interviewing.

FIGURE 9.22
Guidelines for Storytelling

I like the way _____.
                                   (Teller's name)
1. Was familiar with the sequence and events
2. Used interesting phrases, alliteration, or rhyme, rhythm, and repetition, to enliven the language of the story
3. Gave an introduction
4. Used gestures or simple props
5. Attracted the attention of the listeners.
Signed: _____
                      (Listener's name)

Specific (performance) objectives.
  Cognitive.

1. With others, the student will develop a definition of an *interview*.
2. When presented with examples, the student will participate in developing a list of purposes or needs for interviewing.
3. The student will be able to explain why interviewing skills are important to both the interviewer and the interviewee.

  Affective.

1. The student may show pleasure and enjoyment while role-playing an interview with peers.

  Psychomotor.

1. Using an audiotape recorder, the student will be able to record, play back, and erase.

3. Rationale

The concept of the World of Work is prevalent in Social Studies content as evidenced by recommendations of the National Council for the Social Studies (NCSS) Task Force. State departments of education, school districts, and local schools have also included this concept in their curriculum materials.

4. Plan and Procedures

Introduction. Show the words *conversation* and *interview* to the students. Suggest that both are a means of oral communication. The purposes and methods of these two types of communication, however, are quite different. Ask students if they can suggest some of the differences between having a conversation with someone and having an interview. Lead students to draw the conclusion that a conversation is an informal talk or exchange of ideas in which the topics can include anything that interests the people talking. In contrast, an interview has a predetermined goal, that is, the interviewer asks for specific information and avoids many topics he may consider unimportant.

Modeling. Demonstrate for the children a brief conversation and a brief interview with some of the students. Develop a list of purposes or needs for interviewing. For example, consider Figure 9.23.

FIGURE 9.23
Purposes for Interviewing

People Interview

1. Doctors interview patients to find out why the patients are sick.
2. Managers interview job applicants to decide whom they will hire.
3. Reporters interview people to gather information for a newspaper story.
4. Authors interview people to acquire information for a book or story.
5. Teachers interview students about problems in school.
6. Teachers interview parents about students' problems or work at home.
7. Parents interview teachers about their children's work at school.
8. Lawyers interview clients to learn how to help the clients.
9. College admission people interview high school students to decide if they should be admitted or receive a scholarship.
10. Police interview suspected criminals to learn about their actions.
11. Detectives interview people to learn facts for an investigation.
12. Television news reporters interview people for the TV news.
13. Talk-show hosts interview famous people to learn about their lives.
14. High school students interview different professionals to learn about careers.
15. Company managers interview employees to learn about problems or to decide if the employee should be promoted.

Discuss the different purposes for interviewing and the goals of the interviews as suggested by the purpose. Ask students if they believe interviewing skills are important to both the interviewer and the interviewee. Have them explain why.

Develop a list of "Do's and Don'ts" (such as those shown in Figure 9.24) for interviewing. Fourth-grade students may refer to business reference books to get some tips suggested by people who interview others.

Guided (coached) practice. Divide the class into small groups so they can role-play different interviewing circumstances. Have the groups suggest questions they would like to have answered or name the topics covered for some of the purposes identified for interviewing. For instance, a newspaper reporter interviewing the winner of a gold medal at the Olympics might ask:

1. Why did you decide to enter the Olympics?
2. What kind of training did you do to become a winner?
3. How did you feel when you knew you had won?
4. What other athletic events do you participate in?
5. Do you eat any special foods? If you do, what do you eat?
6. What advice could you give others who also want to be winners in sports?
7. What do you want to do when you get back home?

Have the students in small groups role-play different interviews and record the interviews with an audiotape recorder. Have other students in the group observe the effectiveness of the interview and ask them to suggest changes. Allow all students in each small group to play the part of both the interviewer and the interviewee. Then have them discuss their experiences in both roles. Did they feel differently when they were being interviewed than when they were doing the interviewing? If so, why was there a difference?

Assignments.

Option #1. Ask students to watch a TV talk show, to identify the interviewing techniques they see, and to plan a TV talk show of their own. Ask them to choose the guests they wish to interview and the kinds of information they would like to know. Have them do research to find out about the guests. This activity can focus on themes and be related to subjects studied in content areas. For example:

FIGURE 9.24
Do's and Don'ts for Interviewing

Interviewing

Do	Don't
1. Prepare for the interview, know what you want to ask or anticipate what you'll be asked.	1. Ramble off the topic.
2. Encourage the interviewee to talk.	2. Criticize the interviewer or interviewee.
3. Have a friendly facial expression.	3. Argue with the interviewer or interviewee.
4. Be a careful listener.	4. Show nervousness or discourtesy by tapping the table or chewing gum.
5. Keep the interview on the subject.	5. Ask closed questions that have a single yes or no answer.
6. Ask open questions that allow the interviewee to respond with sufficient information.	6. Dress sloppily.
7. Be polite.	
8. Keep the interview within the preset time limits.	
9. Dress attractively.	

Phil Phox Presents the Greatest Scientists of Our Time
Mike Monroe Interviews the First Astronauts on the Moon
Walter Wallace Talks to Lewis and Clark
Diana Dufflebag Brings You Cinderella, Snow White, Huck Finn, and Jack and the
   Beanstalk

Option #2. After students have role-played several situations, allow them to try their interviewing skills in real situations. A school newspaper, a study of occupations, a study of the school personnel, or a story of the neighborhood could all stimulate the need for an oral interview followed by a report to the class. After the general subject for the interviewing has been selected, have the students list the people they would like to interview and the questions they would like to ask each person. One interview topic might be People Who Run Our School. Students might interview the principal, teachers, secretaries, coaches, librarians, janitors, cooks, the nurse, or bus drivers. Another topic might be Foods Liked and Disliked in the Cafeteria and Why, for which the students could interview other students, teachers, cooks, and anyone who eats in the cafeteria. The interviewers can compile charts showing what they have learned (see Figure 9.25).

Closure. Relate the activity to what they learned about interviewing from the role playing.

5. Materials Needed

Audiovisual. None.

Other. Audiotape recorders and blank tapes; lists of role-playing suggestions for interviewing; newspaper help-wanted ads that can be used to motivate an interviewing session. References containing directions for interviewing may be included for fourth-grade children. Books that can motivate interviewing: modern fiction such as Lois Lowry's *Anastasia's Chosen Career* (1987); nonfiction informational books such as William Jaspersohn's *Magazine: Behind the Scenes at Sports Illustrated* (1983); and biographies that could motivate role-playing interviews such as Robert Quackenbush's *Don't You Dare Shoot That Bear!* (1984) and Wendy Towle's *The Real McCoy: The Life of an African-American Inventor* (1993).

6. Assessment and Revision

Assessment of learning. Teacher observations and anecdotal notes of the interviews in group work and the students' charts showing what they have learned from their interviews will document the progress of students who have practiced interviewing techniques.

Plan for revision. Some students will require additional opportunities to motivate interviewing or role-playing interviewing. Literature selections may be used to motivate interviewing or role-playing interviewing that is stimulated by information provided in a text. For example, after reading *Anastasia's Chosen Career,* students could choose their own career and interview people to decide if that career is one that they would really like. After reading *Magazine: Behind the Scenes at Sports Illustrated* (Jaspersohn, 1983), students can discuss the importance of interviewing when developing magazine stories. Students can discuss such quotes as the following:

> "Getting the interesting quotes and offbeat details for a story is part of every *Sports Illustrated* writer's job, and it often requires a great deal of traveling and interviewing. For a long piece on the Boston Red Sox, for example, staff writer Steve Wulf and reporter Bob Sullivan traveled off and on for two weeks with the team, interviewing everyone from manager Ralph Houk to former catcher Carlton Fisk to the grounds-crewmen who operate the left-field scoreboard. 'In any piece I write,' says Steve Wulf, 'I'm after perspective.' " (p. 22).

After discussing the complicated process for getting interviews and writing the story, students can choose their own stories, conduct interviews, and write the magazine or newspaper entry. After reading *Franklin Delano Roosevelt* or *The Wright Brothers: How They Invented the Airplane,* students can choose interesting instances in the people's lives and role-play interviews that might have taken place.

FIGURE 9.25
Results of Student Interviews

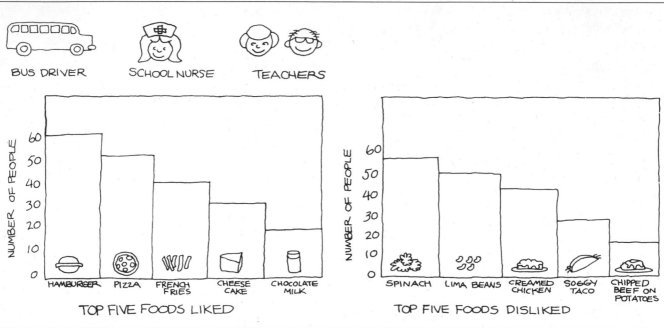

SUMMARY

In the classroom, children should be given opportunities to participate in informal and formal talk activities and to relate to informational content—such as that from the social studies area—in unusual, unique, and creative ways. Oral communication can be the result of study and research when students search for data and make decisions about ways to tell what they found. Scheduled and unscheduled times of talk in the classroom can help students share their findings and present information in different ways.

- Children should be given opportunities to engage in talk activities that include informal conversations and discussions, formal structured debates, oral reports, and interviews as well as dramatic play, role playing, and storytelling.
- Talk activities such as those previously mentioned benefit students when they expand their oral language skills, develop the students' abilities to use talk activities suitable for different language functions, and when the activities develop students' feelings of competence and confidence as they become familiar with speaking before a group.

QUESTIONS AND ACTIVITIES FOR DISCUSSION

1. Using a resource of your choice, locate guidelines for students about preparing and presenting a topic that would be suitable for a show-and-tell time in a grade of your choice. Transform the guidelines into a student checklist for participating students to complete after each presentation. Show it to another person in your group and elicit feedback for revisions. In what ways could the checklist and a follow-up discussion help students give interesting presentations and develop their confidence to speak in front of a whole class?

2. Interview an inservice teacher about which activities he or she is using with special students in regular classrooms or in supplemental pull-out programs. Describe for others how the students benefit from the activity.

3. Interview an inservice teacher about an oral communication activity the teacher uses and how the teacher adapts the activity.

4. In an elementary classroom, observe what types of oral language activities students participate in and what language functions they use. Report back to others.

5. Observe a show-and-tell activity in a primary-grade classroom. What are the characteristics of students who are effective speakers? What questions could the teacher use to generate conversation from less verbal or shy students?

6. Plan and conduct a debate with a group of fourth-grade students. Help them choose a topic from current events, school and community issues, or social studies units.

7. Stock a dramatic play center in a kindergarten or first-grade classroom with one of the prop kits listed in Figure 9.12. Observe children over several days as they interact in the center and keep a log of the activities they participate in and how they use language in their play.

8. Plan and direct a role-playing activity with a group of students in conjunction with a social studies unit. Follow the guidelines in this chapter and integrate a writing activity with the role playing (e.g., by having students keep a journal or writing a letter).

9. Assist a small group of third- or fourth-grade students as they prepare to tell stories to a class of first-grade students. Help students use the six-step procedure discussed in this chapter.

10. Introduce scriptwriting to a group of fourth-grade students by having them compile a list of the unique dramatic conventions used in scriptwriting, and then write a class collaboration script by adapting a familiar folktale.

11. Describe any prior concepts you had about talk in the classroom and teaching speaking skills that changed as a result of your experience with this chapter. Describe the changes.

CHILDREN'S BOOKS

Alexander, L. (1971). *The king's fountain*. New York: Dutton.

Babbitt, N. (1975). *Tuck everlasting*. New York: Farrar, Straus, & Giroux.

Brown, M., & Brown, L. K. (1984). *The bionic bunny show*. Boston: Little, Brown.

Burningham, J. (1979). *Would you rather. . . .* New York: Crowell.

Cooper, K. (1985). *Who put the cannon in the courthouse square? A guide to uncovering the past*. New York: Walker.

Dahl, R. (1961). *James and the giant peach*. New York: Knopf.

Dahl, R. (1964). *Charlie and the chocolate factory*. New York: Knopf.

d'Aulaire, I., & d'Aulaire, E. P. (1955). *Columbus*. New York: Doubleday.

de Paola, Tomie. (1978). *Pancakes for breakfast*. New York: Harcourt Brace Jovanovich.

Fox, P. (1984). *One-eyed cat*. New York: Bradbury.

Fritz, J. (1973). *And then what happened, Paul Revere?* New York: Coward.

Gackenback, D. (1980). *Hattie, Tom and the chicken witch*. New York: Harper & Row.

Galdone, P. (1970). *The three little pigs*. New York: Seabury.

Galdone, P. (1975). *The gingerbread boy*. New York: Seabury.

George, R. E. (1976). *Roald Dahl's Charlie and the chocolate factory*. New York: Knopf.

George, R. E. (1982). *Roald Dahl's James and the giant peach*. New York: Knopf.

Gilson, J. (1980). *Do bananas chew gum?* New York: Lothrop, Lee & Shepard.

Grahame, K. (1961). *The wind in the willows*. New York: Scribner.

Jaspersohn, W. (1983). *Magazine: Behind the scenes at Sports Illustrated*. Boston: Little, Brown.

Lionni, L. (1977). *A flea story*. New York: Pantheon.

Lowry, L. (1987). *Anastasia's chosen career*. Boston: Houghton Mifflin.

O'Brien, R. C. (1971). *Mrs. Frisby and the rats of NIHM*. New York: Atheneum.

Quackenbush, R. (1984). *Don't you shoot that bear!* New York: Simon & Schuster.

Rockwell, T. (1975). *How to eat fried worms*. New York: Franklin Watts.

Sharmat, M. W. (1977). *Nate the great and the phony clue*. New York: Coward.

Slobodkina, E. (1947). *Caps for sale*. New York: Scott.

Smith, J. (1988). *The show-and-tell war*. New York: Harper & Row.

Sobol, D. J. (1980). *Encyclopedia Brown carries on*. New York: Scholastic.

Stanley, D. (1983). *The conversation club*. New York: Macmillan.

Thurber, J. (1974). *Many moons*. New York: Harcourt.

Towle, W. (1993). *The real McCoy: The life of an African-American inventory*. New York: Scholastic.

Van Allsburg, C. (1984). *The mysteries of Harris Burdick*. Boston: Houghton Mifflin.

Weitzman, D. (1975). *My backyard history book*. Boston: Little, Brown.

REFERENCES AND SUGGESTED READINGS

Bauer, C. F. (1977). *Handbook for storytellers*. Chicago: American Library Association.

Bloom, B. S. (1956). *Taxonomy of educational objectives, handbook I: Cognitive domain*. New York: McKay.

Booth, D. (1985). 'Imaginary gardens with real toads?': Reading and drama in education. *Theory into Practice, 24,* 193–198.

Busching, B. A. (1981). Readers theatre: An education for language and life. *Language Arts, 58,* 330–338.

Camp, D. J., & Tompkins, G. E. (1990). Show-and-tell in middle school? *Middle School Journal, 21,* 18–20.

Cazden, C. B. (1986). Classroom discourse. In M. C. Wittrock (Ed.), *Handbook of research on teaching* (3rd ed.), pp. 432–463. New York: Macmillan.

Cazden, C. D. (1988). *Classroom discourse: The language of teaching and learning.* Portsmouth, NH: Heinemann.

Cohen, L. M. (1987). Thirteen tips for teaching gifted students. *Teaching Exceptional Children, 20,* 34–38.

Cox, C. (1983). Young filmmakers speak the language of film. *Language Arts, 60,* 296–304, 372.

Cox, C. (1985). Filmmaking as a composing process. *Language Arts, 62,* 60–69.

Dillon, J. T. (1983). *Teaching and the art of questioning* (Fastback No. 194). Bloomington, IN: Phi Delta Kappa.

Eeds, M., & Wells, D. (1989). Grand conversations: An exploration of meaning construction in literature study groups. *Research in the Teaching of English, 23,* 4–29.

Fiderer, A. (1988). Talking about books: Readers need readers. In J. Golub (Ed.), *Focus on collaborative learning* (Classroom Practices in Teaching English, 1988), pp. 59–65. Urbana, IL: National Council of Teachers of English.

Gallagher, J. J., & Aschner, M. J. (1963). A preliminary report on analyses of classroom interaction. *Merrill-Palmer Quarterly, 9,* 183–194.

Golub, J. (1988). Introduction. In J. Golub (Ed.), *Focus on collaborative learning* (Classroom Practices in Teaching English, 1988), pp. 1–2. Urbana, IL: National Council of Teachers of English.

Guilford, J. P. (1956). The structure of intellect. *Psychological Bulletin, 53,* 267–293.

Haley-James, S. M., & Hobson, C. D. (1980). Interviewing: A means of encouraging the drive to communicate. *Language Arts, 57,* 497–502.

Halliday, M. A. K. (1973). *Explorations in the functions of language.* London: Arnold.

Heath, S. B. (1983). Research currents: A lot of talk about nothing. *Language Arts, 60,* 999–1007.

Joint Committee on the Role of Drama in the Classroom. (1983). *Informal classroom drama.* Urbana, IL: NCTE.

Kardash, C. A. M., & Wright, L. (1987, Winter). Does creative drama benefit elementary school students: A meta-analysis. *Youth Theater Journal,* 11–18.

Kingore, B. W. (1982). Storytelling: A bridge from the university to the elementary school to the home. *Language Arts, 59,* 28–32.

Klein, M. L. (1979). Designing a talk environment for the classroom. *Language Arts, 56,* 647–656.

Korty, C. (1975). *Plays from African folktales.* New York: Scribner.

Kukla, K. (1987). David Booth: Drama as a way of knowing. *Language Arts, 64,* 73–78.

Laughlin, M. K., & Latrobe, K. H. (1989). *Readers theatre for children: Scripts and script development.* Englewood, CO: Libraries Unlimited.

Laurie, R. (1980). *Children's plays from Beatrix Potter.* New York: Warne.

Manna, A. L. (1984). Making language come alive through reading plays. *The Reading Teacher, 37,* 712–717.

McCaslin, N. (1984). *Creative dramatics in the classroom* (4th ed.). New York: Longman.

McKenzie, G. R. (1979). Data charts: A crutch for helping pupils organize reports. *Language Arts, 56,* 784–788.

Morrow, L. M. (1979). Exciting children about literature through creative storytelling techniques. *Language Arts, 56,* 236–243.

Morrow, L. M. (1985). Reading and retelling stories: Strategies for emergent readers. *The Reading Teacher, 38,* 870–875.

Nelson, P. A. (1988). Drama, doorway to the past. *Language Arts, 65,* 20–25.

Norton, D. E., and Norton, S. *Language Arts Activities for Children,* Third Edition. New York: Merrill/Macmillan, 1993.

Pinnell, G. S. (1975). Language in primary classrooms. *Theory into Practice, 14,* 318–327.

Reardon, S. J. (1988). The development of critical readers: A look into the classroom. *The New Advocate, 1,* 52–61.

Roth, R. (1986). Practical use of language in school. *Language Arts, 63,* 134–142.

Schickedanz, J. (1978). 'You be the doctor and I'll be sick': Preschoolers learn the language arts through play. *Language Arts, 55,* 713–718.

Shuy, R. W. (1987). Research currents: Dialogue as the heart of learning. *Language Arts, 64,* 890–897.

Stewig, J. W. (1983). *Exploring language arts in the elementary classroom.* New York: Holt, Rinehart, & Winston.

Stewig, J. W. (1983). *Informal drama in the elementary language arts program.* New York: Teachers College Press.

Wagner, B. J. (1976). *Dorothy Heathcote: Drama as a learning medium.* Washington, DC: National Education Association.

Wagner, B. J. (1988). Research currents: Does classroom drama affect the arts of language? *Language Arts, 65,* 46–55.

Wilen, W. W. (1986). *Questioning skills for teachers* (2nd ed.). Washington, DC: National Education Association.

Wilkinson, L. C. (1984). Research currents: Peer group talk in elementary school. *Language Arts, 61,* 164–169.

CHAPTER 10

The Writing Process

Most writing activities in the elementary grades fall under the rubric *creative writing*. Teachers select a creative topic, such as "If I were a leprechaun . . . ," write it on the chalkboard, and direct students to write a story about being a leprechaun. They allow students 30 minutes to write a single-draft story, then collect the papers to grade—and are often disappointed with the results. Perhaps three or four students have written clever and creative stories; these papers are fun to read, and teachers feel gratified. Two or three students turn in papers of only several words or a single sentence. This is not surprising because these students never complete assignments. The teachers' biggest disappointment, however, is in the remaining 20 mediocre papers. These compositions include a few descriptive sentences, but overall, they lack interesting ideas and cannot be classified as stories.

Unsuccessful experiences with writing often lead teachers to believe their students cannot write, but the problem is not with the students; rather, it is with the traditional approach to writing. These students are not learning how to write, but are simply trying to perform their best on a difficult task that is unclear to them.

In recent years, because of the research about writing, the emphasis in writing instruction has shifted from product to process, and the teacher's role has shifted from merely assigning and assessing the product to working with students throughout the writing process. Table 10.1 summarizes contrasts between the traditional and process approaches to teaching writing.

The writing process includes five stages: prewriting, drafting, revising, editing, and sharing. The key features of each stage are shown in Figure 10.1. The labeling and numbering of the stages should not be construed to suggest that this writing process is a linear series of neatly packaged categories. Research shows that the process is cyclical, involving recurring cycles, and labeling is only an aid to identifying and discussing the activities that represent each stage. In the classroom, the stages merge and cycle. Moreover, students personalize the process to meet their needs and vary the process according to the writing assignment.

This chapter presents an alternative approach to teaching writing through the writing process. It is the same process that adult writers use. By using the writing process, students learn how to write, not how to dislike writing. The discussions are specifically designed to help you understand

1. The steps in the writing process
2. Ways in which students, K–4, learn to use the writing process

TABLE 10.1
The Traditional and Process Approaches to Writing

	THE TRADITIONAL APPROACH	**THE PROCESS APPROACH**
TOPIC SELECTION	A specific creative writing assignment is made by the teacher.	Students choose their own topics, or topics are drawn from content-area study.
INSTRUCTION	Teachers provide little or no instruction. Students are expected to write as best they can.	Teachers teach students about the writing process and about writing forms.
FOCUS	The focus is on the finished product.	The focus is on the process that students use when they write.
OWNERSHIP	Students write for the teacher and feel little ownership of their writing.	Students assume ownership of their writing.
AUDIENCE	The teacher is the primary audience.	Students write for genuine audiences.
COLLABORATION	There is little or no collaboration.	Students write collaboratively and share writing in groups.
DRAFTS	Students write single-draft compositions in which they must focus on content and mechanics at the same time.	Students write rough drafts to pour out ideas and then revise and edit these drafts before making final copies.
MECHANICAL ERRORS	Students are required to produce error-free compositions.	Students correct as many errors as possible during editing but a greater emphasis is on content than on mechanics.
TEACHER'S ROLE	The teacher assigns the composition and grades it after it is completed.	The teacher teaches about writing and provides feedback during revising and editing.
TIME	Students complete most compositions in less than an hour.	Students may spend one, two, or three weeks working on a composition.
ASSESSMENT	The teacher assesses the quality of the composition after it is completed.	The teacher provides feedback while students are writing so they can use it to improve their writing. Assessment focuses on the process that writers use and the finished product.

3. The teacher's role
4. Examples of when students should use the writing process
5. Assessment strategy.

A. PREWRITING

Prewriting is the getting-ready-to-write stage. The traditional notion that writers have a topic completely thought-out and ready to flow onto the page is ridiculous. If writers wait for ideas to fully develop, they may wait forever. Instead, writers begin tentatively—talking, reading, writing—to see what they know and what direction they want to go.

FIGURE 10.1
Overview of the Writing Process Stages

Stage 1: Prewriting
Students write on topics based on their own experiences.
Students engage in rehearsal activities before writing.
Students identify the audience to whom they will write.
Students identify the purpose of the writing activity.
Students choose an appropriate form for their compositions based on audience and purpose.

Stage 2: Drafting
Students write a rough draft.
Students emphasize content rather than mechanics.

Stage 3: Revising
Students share their writing in writing groups.
Students participate constructively in discussions about classmates' writing.
Students make changes in their compositions to reflect the reactions and comments of both teacher and classmates.
Between the first and final drafts, students make substantive rather than only minor changes.

Stage 4: Editing
Students proofread their own compositions.
Students help proofread classmates' compositions.
Students increasingly identify and correct their own mechanical errors.

Stage 5: Sharing
Students publish their writing in an appropriate form.
Students share their finished writing with an appropriate audience.

Prewriting has probably been the most neglected stage in the writing process; however, it is as crucial to writers as a warm-up is to athletes. Murray (1982) believes that 70 percent or more of writing time should be spent in prewriting. During the prewriting stage, students

- Choose a topic
- Consider purpose, form, and audience
- Use informal writing strategies to generate and organize ideas
- Write a collaborative composition.

Choosing a Topic

Choosing a topic for writing can be a stumbling block for students who have become dependent on teachers to supply topics. Traditionally, teachers supplied topics by suggesting gimmicky story starters and relieving students of the "burden" of topic selection. Often, these "creative" topics stymied students, who were forced to write on topics they knew little about or were not interested in. Graves (1976) calls the traditional approach of supplying topics for students "writing welfare." Instead, students need to take responsibility for choosing their own writing topics.

At first, dependent students will argue that they do not know what to write about; however, teachers can help them brainstorm a list of three, four, or five topics, and then identify the one topic they are most interested in and know the most about. Students who feel they cannot generate any writing topics are often surprised that they have so many options available. Then, through prewriting activities, students talk, draw, read, and even write to develop information about their topics.

Asking students to choose their own topics for writing does not mean that teachers never give writing assignments; teachers do provide general guidelines. They may specify the writing form (journals, stories, poems, reports, and so on), and at other times, they may establish the function (for example, to share what students have learned about life in ancient

Egypt), but students should choose their own specific content. For instance, students can demonstrate what they have learned about life in ancient Egypt by writing a report on how people were mummified, a biography of Queen Nefertiti, an acrostic poem on the word *pyramid,* or a story set in ancient Egypt.

Considering Function

As students prepare to write, they need to think about their function or purpose for writing. Are they writing to entertain? To inform? To persuade? Halliday's (1973, 1975) seven language functions apply to written as well as oral language; for example:

Instrumental language	Writing to satisfy needs, as in business letters
Regulatory language	Writing to control the behavior of others, as in directions and rules
Interactional language	Writing to establish and maintain social relationships, as in pen pal letters and dialogue journals
Personal language	Writing to express personal opinions, as in learning logs and letters to the editor
Imaginative language	Writing to express imagination and creativity, as in stories, poems, and scripts
Heuristic language	Writing to seek information and to find out about things, as in learning logs and interviews
Information language	Writing to convey information, as in reports and biographies

Understanding the function of a piece of writing is important because function influences other decisions students make about audience and form.

Considering Audience

Students may write primarily for themselves, to express and clarify ideas and feelings, or they may write for others. Possible audiences include classmates, younger children, parents, foster grandparents, children's authors, and pen pals. Other audiences are more distant and less well known; for example, students write letters to businesses to request information, articles for the local newspaper, or stories and poems for publication in literary magazines.

Children's writing is influenced by their sense of audience. Britton, Burgess, Martin, McLeod, and Rosen (1975) define *sense of audience* as "the manner in which the writer expresses a relationship with the reader in respect to the writer's understanding" (pp. 65–66). When writing for others, students adapt to fit their audience just as they vary their speech to fit an audience. Students must be aware of their audience while writing to choose appropriately. Writing that students do simply to complete assignments often lacks a sense of audience because the student doesn't consider that factor.

Considering Form

One of the most important considerations is the form the writing will take: story? letter? poem? journal entry? A writing assignment could be handled in any one of these ways. As part of a science unit on hermit crabs, for instance, students could write a story about a hermit crab, draw a picture and label body parts, explain how hermit crabs obtain shells to live in, or keep a log of observations about the pet hermit crabs in the classroom. There is an almost endless variety of forms that children's writing may take. Too often students' writing is limited to writing stories, poems, and reports; instead, they need to experiment with a wide variety of writing forms and explore the functions and formats.

Through reading and writing, students develop a strong sense of these forms and how they are structured. Langer (1985) found that by third grade, students responded in distinctly different ways to story and report writing assignments; they organized the writing differently and included varied kinds of information and elaboration. Similarly, Hidi and Hildyard (1983) found that elementary students could differentiate between stories and persuasive essays. Because children are clarifying the distinctions between various writing forms during the elementary grades, it is important that teachers use the correct terminology and not label all children's writing "stories."

Most writing forms look like the text on this page—block form, written from left to right and top to bottom, but some writing forms require a special arrangement on a page and others require special language patterns. Scripts, recipes, poems, and letters are four writing forms that have recognizable formats. Also, some writing forms use special language patterns. Many stories begin with "Once upon a time . . ."; letters require "Dear . . ." and "Sincerely." As children are introduced to these writing forms and have opportunities to experiment with them, they will learn about the unique requirements of the formats.

Teaching children about these three considerations—function, audience, and form—is an important component of writing instruction. Children need to learn to make decisions about the three considerations and to know the range of options available to writers.

Decisions about function, audience, and form influence each other. For example, if the function is to entertain, an appropriate form might be a story, poem, or script—and these three forms look very different on a piece of paper. Whereas a story is written in the traditional block format, scripts and poems have unique page arrangements. Scripts are written with the character's name and a colon, and the dialogue is set off. Action and dialogue, rather than description, carry the story line in a script. In contrast, poems have unique formatting considerations, and words are used judiciously. Each word and phrase is chosen to convey a maximum amount of information. Audience also plays an important role. Audiences for stories, scripts, and poems are often unknown or large, whereas audiences for letters are very specialized. A letter is usually written to a particular person, and although the function of a letter may be to request information or share personal information, it is customized according to audience. Children might share the same information with their pen pal and with their grandparents, but would present the information differently according to degree of familiarity or formality. Although these decisions may change as students write and revise, writers must begin with at least a tentative concept of function, audience, and form as they move into the drafting stage.

Prewriting Activities

Students engage in activities to gather and organize ideas for writing. These activities, which Graves (1983) calls "rehearsal," help students prepare for writing. There are two types of prewriting activities: background activities and informal writing strategies. Background activities are the experiences that provide the knowledge students need for writing, because it is impossible to write well about a topic you don't know well. Rehearsal activities take many forms, including drawing, talking, reading, interviewing, informal drama, field trips, and other content-area experiences.

Drawing. Drawing is the way young children gather and organize ideas for writing. Kindergarten and first-grade teachers often notice that students draw before they write and, thinking that they are eating dessert before meat and vegetables, insist that they write first. But many young children cannot; when asked to write before drawing, they explain that they can't write yet because they don't know what to write until they see what they draw. Young children use drawing and other symbol systems as they grapple with the uniqueness of writing (Dyson, 1982, 1983, 1986).

Talking. Talk in the classroom is necessary to writing. Students talk with their classmates to share ideas about possible writing topics, try out ways to express an idea, and ask questions. They read and react to each other's writing. They also participate in class discussions about writing forms, elements of story structure, and other writing-related issues. Talk continues throughout the writing process as students discuss their compositions in conferences and proofread each other's writing.

Reading. Reading and writing are *symbiotic*—mutually beneficial processes. Through reading, children gather ideas for writing and investigate the structure of various written forms. Reading is a type of experience, and writers need a variety of experiences to draw on. Students often retell a favorite story in writing, write new adventures for favorite story characters, or experiment with repetition, onomatopoeia, or another poetic device used in a book they have read.

Informational books also provide raw material for writing. For example, if students are studying polar bears, they need to gather background information about the animal, its habitat, and predators that they may use in writing a report. If they are interested in Olympic athletes, they may read biographies of Jesse Owens, Nadia Comaneci, Ray Leonard, Mary Lou Retton, and others, and then share what they learn by writing a collection of biographical sketches.

Interviews. Students can interview community members who have special knowledge about the topic they plan to write about. Interviewing involves three steps: planning the interview, conducting it, and sharing the results. In the first step, students arrange for the interview and develop a list of questions to ask during the interview. Next, students conduct the interview by asking questions they have prepared in advance and taking notes or tape-recording answers. Last, students share their information. Sharing can take many different forms, ranging from newspaper articles to reports to books.

Informal Drama. Children discover and shape ideas they will use in their writing through informal drama (Wagner, 1988). According to Mills (1983), having students role-play an experience gives energy and purpose to writing. Writing often grows out of dramatic play and role-playing stories. Children can learn to write directions by writing them for an obvious activity, such as making a peanut butter sandwich. Typically, children omit crucial steps, such as opening the jar; however, if they write the directions after dramatizing the activity, the directions are better organized and more complete. Students can also assess the effectiveness of their written directions by having a classmate try to follow them; they can thus see what steps they have omitted.

Similarly, in social studies units and after reading stories, students can reenact events to bring an experience to life. Heathcote (Wagner, 1976, 1983) advocates an approach in which teachers choose a dramatic focus or a particular critical moment for students to reenact. The improvisation begins with students' assuming roles, and the teacher becomes a character, too. As they role-play the event, the teacher uses questions to draw students' attention to certain features and to prove their understanding. For example, after reading *Sarah, Plain and Tall* (1985) by Patricia MacLachlan, children might reenact the day Sarah took the wagon to town. This is the critical moment in the story: Does Sarah like them and their prairie home well enough to stay? Through role-playing, students become immersed in the event, and by reliving it, they learn far more than mere facts.

Informal Writing Strategies. The second type of prewriting activities is informal writing strategies. Students use the informal writing strategies—brainstorming, clustering, freewriting—to gather and organize information they learn through background experiences. They brainstorm lists of words and ideas, cluster main ideas and details, freewrite to discover what they know about a topic and what direction their writing might take, and cube a complex topic to consider it from several different dimensions. Many young children (and some older students) use drawing to gather and organize ideas for writing.

Collaborative Compositions

Another prewriting activity is to compose a collaborative or group composition. Writing a composition together with the teacher gives students an opportunity to rehearse before writing a similar composition independently. The teacher reviews concepts and clarifies misconceptions during the group composition, and students offer ideas for writing as well as suggestions for tackling common writing problems. The teacher also models or demonstrates the writing process and provides an opportunity for students to practice the process approach to writing in a supportive environment.

First, the teacher introduces the idea of writing a group composition and reviews the assignment. Students compose the class collaboration composition, moving through drafting, revising, editing, and sharing stages of the writing process. The teacher records students' dictation, noting any misunderstandings about the writing assignment or process. When necessary, the teacher reviews concepts and offers suggestions. Students first dictate a rough draft, which the teacher records on the chalkboard or on chart paper. Then teacher and students read the composition and identify ways to revise it. Some parts of the composition will need reworking, and other parts may be deleted or moved. More specific words will be substituted for less specific ones, and redundant words and sentences will be deleted. Students may also want to add new parts to the composition. After making the necessary content changes, students proofread the composition, checking for mechanical errors, paragraph breaks, and for sentences to combine. They correct errors and make changes. Then the teacher or a student copies the completed composition on chart paper or on a sheet of notebook paper. Copies can be duplicated and given to each student.

Collaborative compositions are an essential part of many writing experiences, especially when students are learning to use the writing process or a new writing form. Group compositions serve as a "dry run," during which students' questions and misconceptions can be clarified.

B. DRAFTING

In the process approach to writing, students write and refine their compositions through a series of drafts. During the drafting stage, students focus on getting their ideas down on paper. Because writers do not begin writing with their compositions already composed in their minds, students begin with tentative ideas developed through prewriting activities. The drafting stage is the time to pour out ideas, with little concern about spelling, punctuation, and other mechanical errors.

The Rough Draft

Students should skip every other line when they write their rough draft so they will have space to make revisions. They should learn to use arrows to move sections of text, cross-outs to delete sections, and scissors and tape to cut apart and rearrange text just as adult writers do. They should write on only one side of a sheet of paper so they can cut it apart or rearrange it. As word processors become more accessible in elementary classrooms, revising, shifting, and deleting test will become much easier, but for the time being wide spacing is crucial. (Make small x's on every other line of children's papers as a reminder to skip lines when they draft their compositions.)

Students label their drafts by writing *Rough Draft* in ink at the top of the paper or by stamping them with a ROUGH DRAFT stamp. This label indicates to the writer, other students, parents, and administrators that the composition is a draft, in which the emphasis is on content, not mechanics, and explains why the teacher has not graded the paper or marked mechanical errors. Some students who are just learning the writing process and have been writing single-draft compositions secretly plan to continue to write this way and plan to make this rough draft their final draft if they write carefully. Stamping *Rough Draft* at the top of the paper obviates that possibility and emphasizes that writing involves more than one stage.

When drafting their compositions, students may need to modify earlier decisions about function, audience, and, especially, form; for example, a composition that began as a story may be transformed into a report, letter, or a poem because the new format allows the student to communicate more effectively. The process of modifying earlier decisions continues into the revising stage.

Writing Leads

The lead or opening sentence or two of a composition is crucial. Think about the last time you went to a library to choose a novel to read. Several titles or book jackets may have caught your eye, but to make your selection, you opened the book and read the first paragraph or two. Which book did you choose? You chose the one that "hooked" you or "grabbed" your attention. The same is true for children's writing. Students who consider audience will want to grab that audience. Nothing is such a failure as a piece of writing that no one wants to read! Children use a variety of techniques to appeal to their audience, such as questions, facts, dialogue, brief stories, and problems.

Graves (1983) and Calkins (1986) recommend that students create several leads and try them out on classmates before choosing one. Writing leads gives students valuable knowledge about how to manipulate language and how to vary viewpoint or sequence.

Emphasis on Content

It is important in the rough draft stage not to emphasize correct spelling and neatness; in fact, pointing out mechanical errors during the drafting stage sends students a false message that mechanical correctness is more important than content (Sommers, 1982). Later, during editing, students can clean up mechanical errors and put their composition into a neat, final form.

C. REVISING

During the revising stage, writers refine ideas in their compositions. Students often break the writing process cycle as soon as they complete a rough draft, believing that once they have jotted down their ideas, the writing task is complete. Experienced writers, however, know they must turn to others for reactions and revise on the basis of these comments. Revision is not just polishing; it is meeting the needs of readers by adding, substituting, deleting, and rearranging material. By definition, *revision* means *seeing again,* and in this stage writers see their compositions again with the help of classmates and teacher. Activities in the revising stage are

- Rereading the rough draft
- Sharing the rough draft in a writing group
- Revising on the basis of feedback from the writing group

Rereading the Rough Draft

Writers are the first to revise their compositions. Some revision occurs during drafting, when writers make choices and changes. After finishing the rough draft, writers need to distance themselves from the draft for a day or two, then reread the draft from a fresh perspective, as a reader might—not as a writer who knows what he or she intended to say. As they reread, students make changes—adding, substituting, deleting, and moving—and place question marks by sections they need help with, so they bring them up in their writing group.

Writing Groups

Students meet in writing groups* to share their compositions with small groups of classmates. Because writing cannot occur in a vacuum and must meet the needs of readers, feedback is crucial. Mohr (1984) identifies four general functions of writing groups: (1) to offer the writer choices; (2) to give the writer's responses, feelings, and thoughts; (3) to show different possibilities in revising; and (4) to speed up revising. Writing groups provide a "scaffold," or supportive environment, in which teachers and classmates talk about plans and strategies for writing and revising (Applebee & Langer, 1983; Calkins, 1983).

Writing groups can form spontaneously when several students have completed drafts and are ready to share their compositions, or can be formal groupings with identified leaders. Writing groups in a primary-grade classroom might form spontaneously when students finish writing and go to the reading rug and sit in a chair designated the "author's chair" (Graves & Hansen, 1983). As soon as a child with writing to share is sitting in the chair, others who are available to listen and respond go to sit in front of the author's chair. When

---

*Adapted from G. Tompkins & M. Friend (1988). After Your Students Write: What's Next? *Teaching Exceptional Children, 20,* 4–9.

three or four children have arrived for the writing group, the writer reads the writing and the other children listen and respond to it, offering compliments and relating this piece of writing to their own experiences and writing. Sometimes the teacher joins the listeners on the rug to participate in the writing group; if the teacher is involved in another activity, the children work independently. Writing groups in another primary-grade classroom might be more formal; reading groups may become writing groups when children have completed a rough draft and are ready to share their writing with classmates and teacher. The teacher participates in these groups, providing feedback along with the students.

After writing group arrangements are established, students meet to share their writing through these activities:

- The writer reads the composition aloud to the group.
- Listeners respond with compliments about the composition.
- The writer asks listeners for assistance with trouble spots.
- Listeners offer comments and suggestions for improving the composition.
- Each writer in the group repeats the process.
- Writers identify two or three revisions they will make to improve their compositions.

The writer reads. Students take turns reading their compositions aloud to the group. Everyone listens politely, thinking about the compliments and suggestions they will make after the writer finishes reading. Only the writer should look at the composition, because when classmates and the teacher look at it, they quickly notice and comment on mechanical errors, even though the emphasis during revising is on content. Listening to the writing without looking at it keeps the focus on content.

Listeners offer compliments. After the reading, group members offer compliments, stating what they liked about the writing. These positive comments should be specific and focus on strengths. General remarks such as "I like it" or "It was good," even though positive, are not effective feedback. When teachers first introduce revision, they should model appropriate responses, because students will not know how to offer specific and meaningful comments. Working together, teacher and students brainstorm a list of acceptable comments and post it in the classroom for reference. Acceptable comments may focus on organization, leads, word choice, voice, sequence, dialogue, theme, and so on. Figure 10.2 lists sample compliments.

The writer asks questions. After a round of positive comments, writers ask for assistance with trouble spots they have identified earlier when rereading their writing, or they may ask questions that reflect more general concerns about how well they are communicating. Admitting that they need help from their classmates is a major step in learning to revise. Sample questions to classmates also appear in Figure 10.2. The teacher can model some of these questions, prefacing them with "If I were the writer, I might ask . . . "; when students understand what is expected of them, they can brainstorm a list of questions to add to their list of compliments. Many students find it difficult to ask questions about their writing, but when they work with their writing to the extent that they ask questions, as in the examples above, they have become writers who look to their classmates for assistance.

Listeners offer suggestions. Members of the writing group next ask questions about things that were unclear to them and make suggestions about how to revise the composition. Almost any writer resists constructive criticism, and it is especially difficult for elementary students to appreciate comments and suggestions. This approach is far more constructive than the traditional approach, however, in which the teacher grades the paper and covers it with comments and corrections. Students ask the same types of questions that adult writers ask. Figure 10.3 also lists sample questions that writing group members can use to make comments and suggestions. Again, the teacher should model some of the questions, and when students understand what is expected of them, they can brainstorm a list of comments and suggestions. It is important to take time to teach students what kinds of com-

FIGURE 10.2
Page: Writing Group Responses
SOURCE: Adapted from Tompkins & Friend, 1988.

Listeners' Compliments

I like the part where . . .
I'd like to know more about . . .
I think your main idea is . . .
You used some powerful words, like . . .
I like the way you described . . .
I like the way you explained . . .
I like the way you wrote . . .
Your writing made me feel . . .
I like the order you used in your writing because . . .
I think your dialogue was realistic, the way (character) said . . .
Your writing reminded me of . . .

Writer's Questions

What do you think the best or strongest part is in my writing?
What did you learn from my writing?
What do you want to know more about?
What part doesn't make sense?
Is there a part that I should throw away?
Can you tell what my main idea is?
How can I make my writing clearer?
What details can I add?
Did I use some tired words that I need to change?
Are there some sentences I should combine?

Listeners' Comments and Suggestions

What is your favorite part?
What part are you having trouble with?
Could you write a lead sentence to "grab" your readers?
Do you need a closing?
I got confused in the part about . . .
Could you add more to this part because . . .
Could you leave this part out because . . .
Could you use a different word for _____ because . . .
Is this paragraph on one topic?
Do your paragraphs seem to be in the right order?
Could you combine some sentences?
What do you plan to do next?

---

ments and suggestions are acceptable so that they will word what they say in a helpful rather than hurtful way.

Repeat the process. The feedback process is repeated for each student's composition. This is the appropriate time for teachers to provide input as well. They should react to the piece of writing as any other listener would—not error-hunting with red pen in hand (Sommers, 1982). In fact, most teachers prefer to listen to students read their compositions aloud rather than read them themselves and become frustrated by the numerous misspelled words and nearly illegible handwriting common in rough drafts.

Writers plan for revision. At the end of the writing group, students each make a commitment to revise their writing based on the comments and suggestions of the group members. The final decisions on what to revise always rest with the writers themselves, but with the understanding that their rough drafts are not perfect comes the realization that some revision will be necessary. When students verbalize their planned revisions, they are more likely to complete the revision stage. Some students also make notes for themselves about their revision plans. After the group disbands, students make the revisions.

FIGURE 10.3
A Revision Hierarchy

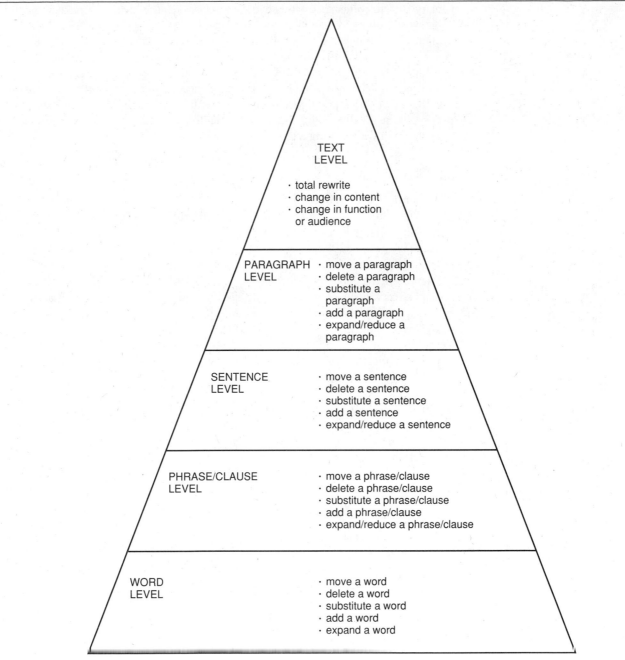

Students' Revisions

In revising, students add words, substitute sentences, delete paragraphs, and move phrases. They cross out, draw arrows, and write in the space left between the double-spaced lines of their rough drafts. Students move back and forth into prewriting to gather additional information, into drafting to write a new paragraph, and back into revising to substitute an overused word. Messiness is inevitable, but despite the scribbles, students are usually able to decipher what they have written.

Students' changes can be classified as additions, substitutions, deletions, and movements, and the level of changes as a word, a phrase/clause, a sentence, a paragraph, or the entire text (Faigley & Witte, 1981). There is a hierarchy of complexity both in the four types of revisions and in the levels of revision, as illustrated in Figure 10.3. The least complex change is the addition of a word, and the most complex change is at the text level. Elementary students often focus at the word and phrase/clause level and make more additions and substitutions than deletions and movements.

Teachers can examine the types and levels of revisions students are making by examining their revised rough drafts; the revisions are another gauge of students' growth as writers. Teachers may want to share this hierarchy with students in fourth grade and older, so they know the available revision options and encourage them to keep a record of their revisions. Even though some revisions may be considered more sophisticated than others, students should make the change that is most effective for their writing—they should not move a paragraph when adding a sentence is the more effective revision.

D. EDITING

Editing is putting the piece of writing into its final form. Until this stage, the focus has been on content; now the focus changes to mechanics, and students polish their writing by correcting spelling and other mechanical errors. The goal here is to make the writing "optimally readable" (Smith, 1982). Writers understand that if their compositions are not readable, they have written in vain, because their ideas will never be read.

Mechanics are the commonly accepted conventions of written Standard English. They include capitalization, punctuation, spelling, sentence structure, usage, and formatting considerations specific to poems, scripts, letters, and other writing forms. The use of these commonly accepted conventions is a courtesy to those who will read the composition.

The optimal time to teach mechanical skills is during the editing stage of the writing process, not by means of workbook exercises. When editing a composition that will be shared with a genuine audience, students are more interested in using mechanical skills correctly so they can communicate effectively.

In a study of two third-grade classes, Calkins (1980) found that the students in the class who learned punctuation marks as a part of editing could define or explain more marks than the students in the other class who were taught punctuation skills in a traditional manner, with instruction and practice exercises on each punctuation mark. In other words, the results of this research, as well as other studies (Bissex, 1980; Elley, Barham, Lamb, Wyllie, 1976; Graves, 1983), suggest that a functional approach to teaching the mechanics of writing is more effective than practice exercises.

Students move through three activities in the editing stage: getting distance from the composition; proofreading to locate errors; and correcting errors.

Proofreading

Students are more efficient editors if they set the composition aside for a few days before beginning to edit. After working so closely with a piece of writing during drafting and revising, they are too familiar with it to be able to locate many mechanical errors. With the distance gained by waiting a few days, children are better able to approach editing with a fresh perspective and gather the enthusiasm necessary to finish the writing process by making the paper optimally readable.

Students proofread their compositions to locate and mark possible errors. Proofreading is a unique type of reading in which students read slowly, word by word, hunting for errors rather than reading quickly for meaning (King, 1985). Concentrating on mechanics is difficult because of our natural inclination to read for meaning. Even experienced proofreaders often find themselves reading for meaning and thus overlooking errors that do not inhibit meaning. It is important, therefore, to take time to explain proofreading and demonstrate how it differs from regular reading.

To demonstrate proofreading, teachers take a piece of student writing and copy it on the chalkboard or display it on an overhead projector. The teacher reads it several times, each time hunting for a particular type of error. During each reading, the teacher reads the composition slowly, softly pronouncing each word and touching the word with a pencil or pen to focus attention on it. The teacher marks possible errors as they are located.

Errors are marked or corrected with special proofreader's marks. Students enjoy using these marks, the same ones that adult authors and editors use. Proofreader's marks that elementary students can learn to use in editing their writing are presented in Figure 10.4.

Editing checklists help students focus on particular categories of error. Teachers can develop checklists with two to six items appropriate for the grade level. A first-grade checklist, for example, might include only two items—perhaps one about capital letters at the beginning of sentences and a second about periods at the end of sentences. In contrast, a middle-grade checklist might include items such as using commas in a series, paragraph indention, capitalizing proper nouns and adjectives, and spelling homonyms correctly. During the school year, teachers revise the checklist to focus attention on skills that have recently been taught. A sample third-grade editing checklist is presented in Figure 10.5; the writer and classmate work together as partners to edit their compositions. First, students proofread their own compositions, searching for errors in each category on the checklist and, after proofreading, check off each item. After completing the checklist, students sign their names and trade checklists and compositions. Now they become editors and complete each other's checklist. Having writer and editor sign the checklist helps to impress on them the seriousness of the activity.

Correcting Errors

After students proofread their compositions and locate as many errors as possible, they correct the errors individually or with their editor's assistance. Some errors are easy to correct; some require use of a dictionary; others involve instruction from the teacher. It is unrealistic to expect students to locate and correct every mechanical error in their compositions—not even published books are error-free! Once in a while, students may even change a correct spelling or punctuation mark and make it incorrect, but overall they correct far more errors than they create.

Editing can end after students and their editors correct as many mechanical errors as possible, or after students meet with the teacher in a conference for a final editing. When mechanical correctness is crucial, this conference is important. Teachers proofread the composition with the student, and they identify and make the remaining corrections together, or

FIGURE 10.4
Proofreader's Marks

Delete	ℓ	Most whales are ~~big and~~ ℓ huge creatures.
Insert	∧	A baby whale is ∧ a calf. (called)
Indent paragraph	⊓	⊓ Whales look a lot like fish, but the two are quite different.
Capitalize	≡	In the United states it is illegal to hunt whales.
Change to lower case	/	Why do beached /Whales die?
Add period	⊙	Baleen whales do not have any teeth⊙
Add comma	∧	Some baleen whales are blue whales∧ gray whales and humpback whales.
Add apostrophe	⌄	People are the whale⌄s only enemy.

FIGURE 10.5
A Third-Grade Editing Checklist

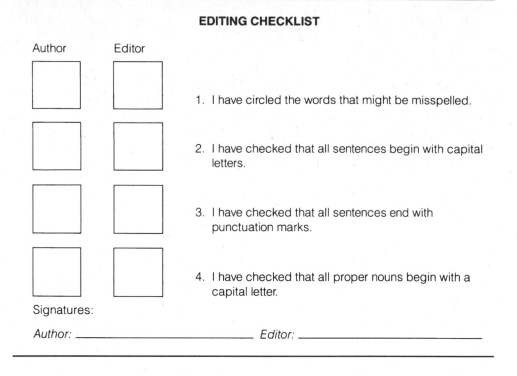

the teacher makes checkmarks in the margin to note errors for the student to correct independently.

Minilessons. Many teachers use the editing stage as a time to informally assess students' mechanical and spelling skills and to give minilessons on a skill that a child or several children are having trouble with. The teacher notes which students are having difficulty with a particular skill—paragraphing, capitalizing proper nouns, or using the apostrophe in possessives—and conducts a brief minilesson using the students' writing instead of a language textbook. In this brief, five- to ten-minute lesson, the teacher reviews the particular skill and students practice the skill as they help to correct their classmates' writing. Then they may practice the skill a few more times on sentences they create or using text from their journals or another writing project. If additional work is needed, they might develop a lesson on it to teach to their classmates or students in another class. This procedure individualizes instruction and teaches the skill when learning it matters to students.

E. SHARING

In the final stage of the writing process, *sharing,* students bring the composition to life by publishing their writing or sharing it orally with an appropriate audience. When they share their writing with real audiences of classmates, other students, parents, and the community, students come to think of themselves as authors.

Concept of Author

Most of the time children assume the role of "student" in school; however, they take more interest in a subject and learn more about it when they assume a more active role. The real-life role for writing is "author." Authors write for real purposes and for genuine audiences. In contrast, students often write so the teacher will have something to grade. Explaining that the writing process they are using is similar to what authors use is one way to help students think of themselves as authors.

Another way children move from the "student" to the "author" role is by developing the concept of an author. Graves and Hansen (1983) believe primary classrooms should have a special chair, designated the "author's chair," where whoever sits there—either teacher or child—is reading a book. At the beginning of the year, most of the books read from that chair are picture books; however, when children begin to write and construct their own books, they sit in that chair to share them. Sitting in the special author's chair and sharing their books makes children gradually realize that they are authors! Graves and Hansen describe children's transition from student to author in three steps:

1. *Replication: Authors write books.* After hearing many books read to them and reading books themselves, students develop the concept that authors are the people who write books.
2. *Transition: I am an author.* Sharing the books they have written with classmates from the author's chair helps students view themselves as authors.
3. *Option-awareness: If I wrote this published book now, I wouldn't write it this way.* Students learn that they have options when they write, and this awareness grows after experimenting with various writing functions, forms, and audiences.

In classrooms where reading, writing, and sharing writing are valued activities, students become authors. Often they recopy a story or other piece of writing into a stapled booklet or hardcover book, and these published books are added to the classroom or school library. Sometimes students form a classroom publishing company and add the name of the company and the year the book was made on the title page. In addition, students can add an "All About the Author" page with a photograph at the end of their books, just as information about the author is often included on book jackets of adult authors.

Ways to Share Writing

Students read their writing to classmates or share it with larger audiences through hardcover books placed in the class or school library, class anthologies, letters, newspaper articles, plays, filmstrips and videotapes, or puppet shows. These and other ways to share children's writing are listed in Figure 10.6. Sharing enables students to communicate with genuine audiences who respond to their writing in meaningful ways. Sharing writing is a social activity that helps children develop sensitivity to an audience and confidence in themselves as authors. When students share writing, Dyson (1985) advises that teachers consider the social interpretations—students' behavior, teacher's behavior, and interaction between students and teacher—within the classroom context. Individual students will naturally interpret the sharing event differently. More than just providing the opportunity for students to share writing, teachers need to teach students how to respond to their classmates. Teachers themselves serve as a model for responding to students' writing without dominating the sharing.

FIGURE 10.6
Twenty-five Ways to Share Writing

Read writing aloud in class	Display poetry on a "poet-tree"
Submit to writing contests	Send to a pen pal
Display as a mobile	Make a hardbound book
Contribute to class anthology	Produce a roller movie
Contribute to the local newspaper	Display on a bulletin board
Place in the school library	Make a filmstrip
Make a shape book	Make a big book
Read the writing on a cassette tape	Design a poster
Submit to a literary magazine	Read to foster grandparents
Read at a school assembly	Share as a puppet show
Share in writing groups	Display at a public event
Share with parents and siblings	Read to children in other classes
Produce a videotape	

Bookmaking. One of the most popular ways for children to share their writing is by making and binding books. Simple booklets can be made by folding a sheet of paper into quarters, like a greeting card. Students write the title on the front and use the three remaining sides for their compositions. They can also construct booklets by stapling sheets of writing paper together and adding construction paper covers. Sheets of wallpaper cut from old sample books also make good, sturdy covers. These stapled booklets can be cut into various shapes, too. Students can make more sophisticated books by covering cardboard covers with contact paper, wallpaper samples, or cloth. Pages are sewn or stapled together, and the first and last pages (endpapers) are glued to the cardboard covers to hold the book together. Directions for making one type of hardcover book are shown in Figure 10.7.

Publishing student writing. Students can also submit stories, poems, and other pieces of writing to magazines that publish children's writing. Some magazines also accept artwork to accompany the compositions. Students should check a recent issue of the magazine or write to the editor for specific guidelines before submitting a contribution. These are general guidelines for submitting students' writing:

> Read the information in the magazine about the types of contributions the editor wants to receive. Send the contribution to magazines that publish that type of writing.
> Follow the information in the magazine in submitting the contribution.
> Write a cover letter to send with the contribution, giving the author's name, address, telephone number, and age. Also state in the letter that the contribution is original.
> Send a self-addressed, stamped envelope so the editor can return the contribution if it will not be published.
> Keep a copy of the contribution in your files.
> Expect to wait three months or more before learning whether the contribution has been accepted for publication.

Children should be warned that competition is stiff in many publications and that their contributions may not be accepted even though they are well written. Children should not expect to receive monetary compensation for their writing; the honor is in seeing their name in print!

Responding to Student Writing

The teacher's role should not be restricted to that of evaluator. Again and again researchers report that, although teachers are the most common audience for student writing, they are also one of the worst audiences because they read with a red pen in their hands (Lundsteen, 1976). Teachers should instead read their students' writing for information, for enjoyment, and for all the other purposes that other readers do. Much of students' writing does not need to be assessed; it should simply be shared with the teacher as a "trusted adult" (Martin, D'Arcy, Newton, & Parker, 1976).

If children use a process approach to writing, there is less chance they will plagiarize, because they will have developed their compositions, step by step, from prewriting and drafting to revising and editing. Nonetheless, at some time or other, most teachers fear that a composition they are reading is not the student's own work. Jackson, Tway, and Frager (1987) cite several reasons that children might plagiarize. First, some students may simply internalize a piece of writing through repeated readings so that, months or years later, they do not realize it is not their own work. Second, some students may plagiarize because of competition to succeed. Third, some students plagiarize by accident, not realizing the consequences of their actions. A final reason some students plagiarize is that they have not been taught to write by means of a process approach, so they may not know how to synthesize information for a report from published sources. The two best ways to avert having students copy work from another source and pass it off as their own are (1) to teach them the writing process and (2) to have students write at school rather than at home. Students who work at school and move through the various writing process activities know how to complete the writing project.

FIGURE 10.7
Directions for Making Hardcover Books

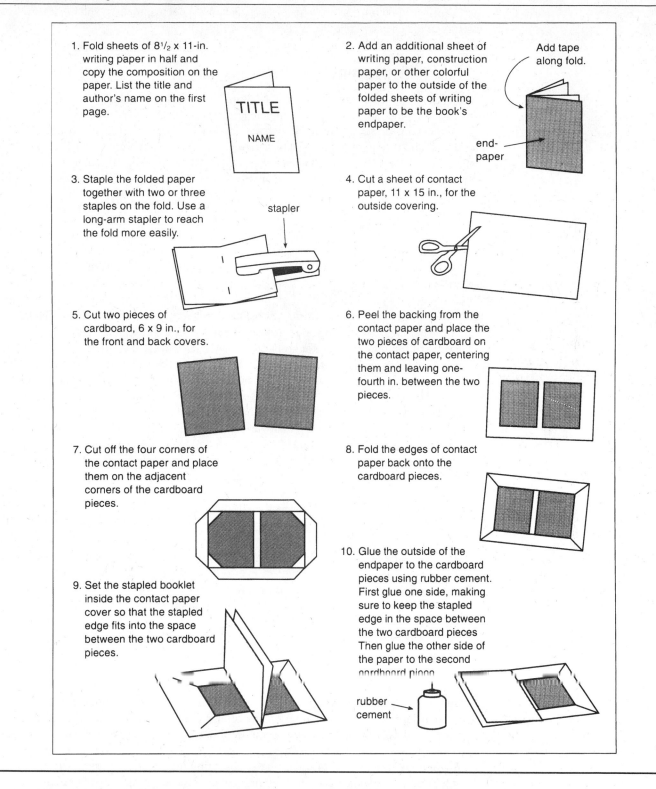

1. Fold sheets of 8½ x 11-in. writing paper in half and copy the composition on the paper. List the title and author's name on the first page.

2. Add an additional sheet of writing paper, construction paper, or other colorful paper to the outside of the folded sheets of writing paper to be the book's endpaper.

Add tape along fold.

end-paper

3. Staple the folded paper together with two or three staples on the fold. Use a long-arm stapler to reach the fold more easily.

stapler

4. Cut a sheet of contact paper, 11 x 15 in., for the outside covering.

5. Cut two pieces of cardboard, 6 x 9 in., for the front and back covers.

6. Peel the backing from the contact paper and place the two pieces of cardboard on the contact paper, centering them and leaving one-fourth in. between the two pieces.

7. Cut off the four corners of the contact paper and place them on the adjacent corners of the cardboard pieces.

8. Fold the edges of contact paper back onto the cardboard pieces.

9. Set the stapled booklet inside the contact paper cover so that the stapled edge fits into the space between the two cardboard pieces.

10. Glue the outside of the endpaper to the cardboard pieces using rubber cement. First glue one side, making sure to keep the stapled edge in the space between the two cardboard pieces Then glue the other side of the paper to the second cardboard piece.

rubber cement

To measure students' growth in writing, it is not always necessary to assess finished products (Tway, 1980). Teachers make judgments about students' progress in other ways. One of the best ways is to observe students while they write and note whether they engage in prewriting activities, whether they focus on content rather than mechanics in their rough drafts, and whether they participate in writing groups.

When it is necessary to assess students' writing, teachers can judge whether students have completed all components of the writing project as well as the quality of the final product. (You will find information about assessing stories, poems, reports, and other forms of writing in the chapters that discuss these forms.)

F. THE WRITING PROCESS IN ACTION

Although it may seem that the stages of the writing process are five separate ingredients that must be combined in sequence to complete a recipe, this is an oversimplification. In practice, writers move back and forth through the stages to develop, refine, and polish their compositions, and they participate in some activities, such as revising and editing, throughout the writing process (Hayes & Flower, 1980). Not all writing must go through all the stages. A journal entry, for example, may be abandoned after drafting, and editing receives less attention if a story will be shared orally as a puppet show.

Introducing the Writing Process

Introducing students to the writing process and helping them learn the activities involved in each stage are crucial. The teacher explains the stages and has students develop a short composition as they practice each stage. The following guidelines may be useful.

1. *Teach the informal writing strategies before introducing the writing process.* There are so many things to explain about the writing process that students can get bogged down the first time they move through the five stages. One way to shorten the first writing process experience is to first teach students the informal writing strategies.
2. *Use the writing process terminology.* When introducing the process approach, teachers should use the names of the stages and the other terminology in this chapter. Even young children learn to use the terminology quickly and easily.
3. *Write class collaborations.* Too many teachers ignore the class collaboration step of the prewriting stage. Although students do not need to write class collaborations for every writing project, it is an important step here because the teacher models all the activities students will soon be doing individually. Teachers sometimes omit this step because they worry they can't lead a class collaboration; this is a needless fear, as many students have good ideas and will be eager to share them.
4. *Keep first writings short.* Students' first process writings should be short pieces— only one or two paragraphs—so they can move through the writing process rather quickly. A seven-page biography of Amelia Earhart is not a good first process writing because of the time and effort involved in gathering information, writing the rough draft, sharing it in writing groups, locating and correcting mechanical errors, and recopying the final draft. Personal narratives in which students write about an event in their own lives work well for the first writings.
5. *Practice critiquing compositions as a class.* Working in writing groups teaches children new activities—giving compliments, asking writer-questions, and offering suggestions. Because these activities are unfamiliar to most students, introduce the activities and practice them as a class before having students work in writing groups. Read aloud a sample (and anonymous) composition and critique the composition together as a class. After listening to it read aloud, students offer compliments, the teacher role-plays the author and asks a question or two about trouble spots, and then students make suggestions for improvement.
6. *Begin with compliments in writing groups.* During the first two or three writing group sessions, teachers may have students shortcut the procedure and stop after complimenting the writer. When students feel comfortable giving compliments, you can add the next step, having the writer ask questions. Finally the remaining steps are added. Introducing writing group activities in a step-by-step approach gives students the opportunity to learn each activity.
7. *Keep writing folders.* Keep students' writing in manila folders. They can put prewriting activities, informal writings, rough drafts, writing group notes, and editing checklists

into this file. When a writing project is completed, all materials are organized, stapled together, and clipped to the final copy. Students prepare a new folder for the next writing project.

Learning the writing process takes time. Students need to work through the entire process again and again until the stages and activities become automatic. Then students can manipulate the activities to meet the different demands of particular writing projects and modify the process to accommodate their personal writing style.

Using the Writing Process

After students learn the stages of the writing process and some of the activities in each stage, they use this knowledge to write stories, poems, and many other forms of writing. It would be convenient if this five-stage model equated to prewriting on Monday, drafting on Tuesday, revising on Wednesday, editing on Thursday, and sharing on Friday, but it does not. In fact, it is difficult to predict how long a writing project will take because of the variations in how students write.

Students are engaged in various activities during each writing process stage. The activities vary according to the function, audience, and form of the writing. Activities in writing myths, animal reports, color poems, and business letters are outlined in Table 10.2. When students write myths, for example, they read myths and analyze what constitutes a myth. They record what they have learned in a list of characteristics and refer to the list to write a class collaboration myth. These activities represent the prewriting stage of gathering ideas. During the drafting stage, students write a rough draft of their myth. In revising, they meet in writing groups to share their myths and get feedback on how to improve them. Then students make revisions based on the feedback they receive. Students may move on to the editing stage or may do more prewriting, drafting, or meet again in a writing group for additional feedback. When they move into editing, students proofread their myths with a classmate and correct as many mechanical errors as possible before meeting with the teacher for a final editing. Students complete the writing process by recopying the myth into a hardbound book and reading the myth to students in another class. As an alternative, a small group of students might prepare and videotape a dramatic presentation of the myth and show it to students in other classes.

Similar activities are shown in Table 10.2 for three other writing projects. Students may use brainstorming for one writing project, clustering in another, or, in yet another project, review the format of a business letter, but all are prewriting activities because they prepare students to write. Variation in each stage results from differences in the function, audience, and form of the project.

The Teacher's Role

The teacher's role in the writing process varies according to the stage. Simpson (1986) describes teachers' roles as forming a partnership with students, instructing, listening, encouraging, challenging, and responding. Figure 10.8 features a list of tasks teachers can use to monitor their behavior as their roles shift during the writing process; we will examine those roles in each stage of the process.

Prewriting. During prewriting, teachers make plans for the writing project, provide necessary background experiences, and arrange for rehearsal activities. They also teach students about informal writing strategies or about the writing form (e.g., biographies) that students will write. Teachers also provide a scaffold for students through class collaborations.

Drafting. Teachers provide support and encouragement as students pour out their ideas during drafting. They confer with students as they search for words to express themselves, to clarify their thinking, and to search for voice. It is important in this stage not to emphasize correct spelling and neatness. In fact, when teachers point out mechanical errors during the drafting stage, they send a false message that mechanical correctness is more important than content.

TABLE 10.2
An Analysis of Four Writing Projects

	WRITE A MYTH	WRITE AN ANIMAL REPORT	WRITE A COLOR POEM	WRITE A BUSINESS LETTER
Function: **Form:** **Audience:**	Imaginative Story Classmates	Informative Report Younger children (books to be replaced in school library)	Imaginative Poem Classmates and family	Instrumental Business letter Unknown
Stage 1 Prewriting	Read myths. Analyze characteristics of myths. Brainstorm a list of characteristics. Write a collaborative myth.	Design research questions. Gather and organize information on a cluster. Interview an expert and add information to cluster.	Review the form of a color poem. Read examples of color poems written by students. Write a collaborative color poem.	Review the form of a business letter. Brainstorm a list of the information to include in the letter.
Stage 2 Drafting	Write a rough draft of the myth.	Write a rough draft of the report.	Write a rough draft of the color poem, beginning each line or stanza with a color.	Write a rough draft of the letter.
Stage 3 Revising	Share the rough draft in a writing group. Listeners offer compliments and suggestions. Ask questions about the content and form of the myth. Make revisions based on classmates' suggestions.	Share the rough draft in a writing group. Listeners offer compliments and suggestions. Ask questions about the completeness of the information in the report. Make revisions based on classmates' suggestions.	Share the rough draft in a writing group. Listeners offer compliments and suggestions. Ask questions about the content and form of the poem. Make revisions based on classmates' suggestions.	Share the rough draft in a writing group. Listeners offer compliments and suggestions. Ask questions about the completeness of the information in the letter and appropriateness of language. Make revisions based on classmates' suggestions.
Stage 4 Editing	Proofread with a classmate and the teacher to locate and correct errors.	Proofread with a classmate and the teacher to locate and correct errors. Add a bibliography.	Proofread with a classmate and the teacher to locate and correct errors.	Proofread with a classmate and the teacher to locate and correct mechanical and formatting errors.
Stage 5 Sharing	Recopy the myth and share with classmates. Alternative: Videotape a dramatic presentation of the myth.	Construct a hardbound book. Recopy the report in the book. Share the book with younger children and add to the school library.	Recopy the poem and add to a personal anthology. Share with classmates.	Recopy the letter. Address the envelope. Mail the letter.

Revising. During the revising stage, the teacher is a reader and reactor just as students are, responding, as Sommers suggests, "as any reader would, registering questions, reflecting befuddlement, and noting places where we are puzzled about the meaning" (1982, p. 155). Teachers participate in writing groups and conferences and model appropriate responses, admiring students' efforts and seeing potential as well as providing feedback about how to improve writing. Teachers offer suggestions in this stage rather than at the end of the process because students still have the opportunity to benefit from the suggestions and incorporate changes into their writing.

Editing. It is unrealistic to expect students to locate and correct every mechanical error in their compositions during editing, so many teachers find it more practical to focus on particular categories of error in each composition. In a conference, they can quickly review a particular problem area, such as quotation marks, and help the student make the necessary

FIGURE 10.8
The Teacher's Role in the Writing Process

Prewriting

The teacher:

Provides background experiences so students will have the prerequisite knowledge to write about the
    topic

Allows students to participate in decisions about topic, function, audience, and form

Defines the writing project clearly and specifies how it will be assessed

Teaches information about the writing form

Provides opportunities for students to participate in idea gathering and organizing activities

Writes a class collaboration with students

Drafting

The teacher:

Provides support, encouragement, and feedback

Emphasizes content over mechanics

Teaches students how to draft

Encourages students to cycle back to prewriting to gather more ideas or ahead to revise when needed

Revising

The teacher:

Organizes writing groups

Teaches students how to function in writing groups

Participates in a writing group as any listener and reactor would

Provides feedback about the content of the writing and makes suggestions for revision

Insists that students make some revisions

Encourages students to cycle back to prewriting or drafting when necessary

Editing

The teacher:

Teaches students how to edit with partners

Prepares editing checklists for students

Assists students in locating and correcting mechanical errors

Diagnoses students' errors and provides appropriate instruction

Corrects any remaining errors that students cannot correct

Sharing

The teacher:

Arranges for genuine audiences for student writing

Does not serve only as a judge when receiving student writing

---

corrections. This mini-lesson procedure individualizes instruction, and during the school year, teachers review the mechanical skills each student needs. If correctness is crucial, teachers can make the corrections or put checkmarks in the margin to note remaining errors so that students can complete the correcting.

Sharing. Teachers need to make sure students have genuine audiences to share their writing with. Sending letters to pen pals, reading student-written picture books to a kindergarten class, compiling a class anthology, and submitting a newspaper article to the local newspaper all require behind-the-scenes work by the teacher. Most importantly, teachers should enjoy students' writing as other audiences do, not simply serve as an evaluator.

G. CLASSROOM ACTIVITIES*

Myself and My Family   ACTIVITY 10.1

1. To develop creative writing skills through artistic interpretations of the family   **Purpose**
2. To refine oral expression by talking about something close to the family

---

*Adapted from D. E. Norton & S. Norton, *Language Arts Activities for Children*, 3rd ed. (Englewood Cliffs, NJ: Merrill/Prentice Hall, 1993), pp. 146, 152, 158. By permission of the authors and Prentice Hall.

Materials

An accordion-pleated book with a page for each member of the family and family pets (construct an accordion-pleated book by folding large sheets of heavy drawing paper in half; connect several sheets with tape to make a book large enough to accommodate pictures of the child's family and a story about each picture).

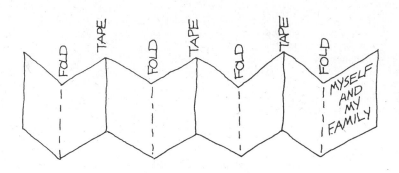

Grade level

Kindergarten, lower elementary grades 1–2.

Procedures

1. Show children an accordion-pleated book with your picture on the front and the title "Myself and My Family." Read the title to the children or allow them to read it. Ask the children what they think would be inside this special book. Allow them to make suggestions; show them your book. (Young children enjoy learning more about their teacher so this activity stimulates oral discussion and questions.) Your book may contain photographs and illustrations and should include a separate page for each member of your family and a short story describing each family member. After you discuss your book, tell the children they will have an opportunity to make their own books about themselves and their families. Allow them to suggest subjects they would like to include in their own books.

2. Help children make their accordion-pleated books. Have them illustrate their covers and print the title of the book.

3. On subsequent days, have children illustrate a page for each member of their families including pets. (Photographs may be used, if every child has access to pictures of their family members.) After they have drawn each picture, have them write or dictate a story about that person. Interact with each child as he is writing. Ask questions about the member of the family to help children develop their stories. (The length of each story will depend on the level of each child. Kindergarten children may dictate short labels for their pictures while second-grade children may write lengthy stories.)

4. Allow children opportunities to share their family books with the class and talk about their own families. Provide opportunities for other children to ask questions about each child's family.

My First 100 Years

ACTIVITY 10.2

Purpose

1. To refine creative writing skills by writing about an old doll, old toy, or picture of an old doll or toy
2. To participate in a discussion about the experiences and adventures of a toy and its owner

Materials

An old or antique doll that has obviously been played with, an old toy soldier, etc., or a picture of an antique toy that looks as if it has been used by children. This activity could be used to motivate the reading of Rachel Field's *Hitty: Her First Hundred Years* (1929, 1957) or Holling Clancy Holling's *Paddle to the Sea* (1941).

Grade level

Grades 2–4.

Book summaries

Hitty: Her First Hundred Years develops the memoirs of a doll who began her life in Maine and had many adventures including sailing on a whaler. *Paddle to the Sea* is a story of a "Paddle Person" and his small canoe, which was carved by a Native American boy and placed into Lake Superior. On the bottom of the canoe is carved, "Please put me back in the water. I am Paddle to the Sea." The story and illustrations follow Paddle to the Sea as he goes from Lake Superior to the Grand Banks off the coast of Newfoundland.

Procedures

1. Show the toy to the students. Ask them if the toy looks like one they could buy in a toy store today. What is different about this toy? How do they know the toy is old? Who do they think might have owned this toy? Did the girl or boy love the toy?

    Continue a discussion about the historic time during which this toy was popular and ask the students to speculate about adventures the doll or toy may have had with one or more owners. For example, did the toy go west on a covered wagon? Did the toy go down the Mississippi on a riverboat?
2. Ask the children to write a story about the adventures of the toy and its owner or owners. Interact with the children as they write their stories.
3. Allow students to share their adventure stories with the class or with a small group.
4. Another time, you might introduce an old toy by telling where you found or bought the toy; then let children speculate about the child who left, owned, or lost the toy. For example:

    I have been trying to solve a mystery about this old doll and the girl who owned and played with her. Maybe if you hear about how I got the doll, you can help me with this mystery.

    There once was a big, old deserted house on a farm in Iowa. A man who builds houses saw the farm and decided he wanted to tear down the old house and build a new house on the same spot. It was a beautiful site for a house. There were gnarled apple trees in the backyard, and a huge, green, grassy space covered with wild flowers in front.

    This builder decided to check the house to make sure there was nothing in it before he sent for the wrecking crew to tear it down. As he was going through the old house, he came to a second-floor bedroom that looked as if it had belonged to a child. The walls were covered with faded wallpaper with pink roses, and a child's drawings could be seen on the walls. The room had a large closet that probably held the child's clothes and other possessions. The builder opened the closet door to make sure nothing was inside. Something attracted his attention when he looked up at a high shelf. He put his hand up on the shelf and found this old doll tucked away there.

    Will you help me solve this mystery? Who do you think left this doll? Why do you think it was left? The doll looks as if it was played with a great deal. What adventures do you think the girl and her doll had? How do you think the girl felt when she discovered she didn't have her doll? How do you think the doll felt when it was left behind?

5. This writing activity may be used to motivate reading or listening to *Hitty: Her First Hundred Years* or *Paddle to the Sea*. Both of these award-winning books follow the adventures of toys or miniatures as they face the unknown. Explain to students that they have written stories about possible adventures of old toys. Tell the students that professional authors may be motivated about the "what ifs" associated with toys that have lived long lives or are placed in settings in which they are on their own. Read and discuss each of the books. Allow students to respond to the plots and compare the types of adventures developed by the authors with those developed by the students. Before reading *Paddle to the Sea,* the students will benefit from looking at maps that show the Great Lakes and the St. Lawrence River. They should realize just what type of challenge that Paddle to the Sea faced.

ACTIVITY 10.3   My Own Totem Pole

Purpose

1. To refine creative writing skills through artistic interpretation and oral discussion
2. To develop reference skills, interpret a famous person through a totem pole representation and write an accompanying story that interprets that person's life
3. To develop oral interviewing skills, draw totem poles of family members and write an accompanying story
4. To interpret a totem pole legend of family members and write a creative story describing the totem pole legend

Materials

Cardboard cylinder and construction paper for making totem symbols; writing materials; references and pictures of totem poles; Diane Hoyt-Goldsmith's *Totem Pole* (1990); reference books, biographies, and other nonfiction books chosen by the students.

Grade levels

Purposes 3 and 4 can be achieved at any level because the story can be written or dictated. Purpose 2, however, requires the ability to read references or other sources to learn about the background of a famous person.

Book summary

Totem Pole presents, in text and illustrations, background information about the totem pole and the carving of one particular totem pole for the Klallam Indians who live on the Port Gamble Reservation on the Northwest Coast of North America. The text includes the importance of songs, stories, and dances in connection with the totem pole.

Procedures

1. Background: Totem poles are found along the North Pacific coast from southern Canada to Alaska. The Northwest Indians carved and painted large tree trunks that sometimes rose to a height of fifty or sixty feet. The totem poles were erected in front of the house of the clan chief as symbols of the owner's prestige. The figures might tell the story of the clan legend or of the great deeds of the totem-pole owner. Strange figures, faces, whales, fish, bears, ravens, and birds with outstretched wings told the story of the family ancestors or other events that were significant for the family. The story began at the top of the totem and continued down from the distant and mystic past to the figure of the owner carved at the base of the totem. The Indian totems usually contained a representation of the owner's guardian totemic animal, which is why the poles are called totem poles.
2. Show pictures of totem poles, read references about totem poles, and discuss what they symbolize. Read and discuss Diane Hoyt-Goldsmith's *Totem Pole*. Be sure that students understand the importance of the totem pole in revealing the history and beliefs of the tribe.
3. Ask each child to select a famous person whom they would like to learn more about. Have them read a reference, biography, or other literature selection to increase their knowledge about the person. Ask them to think about how they could depict the person's life through figures similar to those used by the Indians. Have them draw a totem de-

picting the person's life; then ask them to write a story about it, explaining why they chose the specific incidents for the totem. This totem might be the story of a sports hero, a famous man or woman in history, or a character in literature. For example, totem poles could be developed for folk heroes such as Paul Bunyan, Mike Fink, Captain Stormalong, Daniel Boone, Davy Crockett, Johnny Appleseed, Windwagon Smith, or Pecos Bill. A Pecos Bill Totem Pole might include the following incidents:

4. For another totem-writing activity, suggest that students make totems that describe their own family histories or portray members of their families. Before they do this activity, ask them to interview their parents or other relatives to learn more about their own backgrounds. After they draw the totems, have them write a story explaining the characters on the totem and why they chose those symbols.

5. Another totem-writing activity allows children to fantasize about their own legends or to develop a totem about their own experiences. Tell the students that Indian totems usually contained a representation of the owner's guardian totemic animal. Ask the children to think about the animal they would choose as their guardian; have them include the animal on the totem. Allow them to develop a fantasy totem or a real-life totem. Ask them to illustrate the totem and write a story abut the representations on the totem.

6. To relate this writing activity to social studies, ask students in grades 3–4 to do research on a Native American tribe, draw a totem for the tribe, and write a story about the representations on the totem.

H. PROBLEM-SOLVING EXPERIENCE INVOLVING LANGUAGE ARTS SKILLS: ORGANIZATION USING A PROBLEM, CAUSE, AND SOLUTION FORMAT*

Purpose

1. To identify the organizational pattern of a paragraph or multiparagraph selection using a problem, cause, and solution of problem format
2. To brainstorm ideas for problem investigations
3. To write a paragraph or multiparagraph selection using a problem, cause, and solution of problem format

Materials

Examples of paragraphs or multiparagraph selections using this format (social studies, science writing).

Grade level

Grades 3–4 and older.

Procedures

1. Show and discuss several paragraphs written in a problem, cause, and solution of problem format. Read the paragraphs with the children and help them discover the organization. For example, the problem of an argument on the playground might be written about in the following way:

The Basketball and Marble Feud

Every day this week, our third-grade class has had an argument at the beginning of recess. Some of the students want to use the blacktop on the school yard to play basketball. Other students want to play marbles on that same space. Both groups get in each others' way and shout at each other. We are trying to solve this problem. We could take turns. The basketball players could use the blacktop during morning recess. The marble players could use the blacktop during afternoon recess. We are also looking for other good places to play marbles. If we find a good spot, we will all be happy during both recesses.

Help students discover the organization of the paragraph. You could draw the order of this paragraph in the following way:

Problem   *An argument at recess*

↓ Cause of Problem   ↓ Some students want to play basketball and
                                         some want to play marbles in the same space.

↓ Possible Solutions to Problem   ↓ Taking turns on blacktop.
                                         Another place to play marbles.

2. Provide a variety of one-paragraph or multiparagraph selections using this form. Encourage students to think of materials that are organized in this format including social studies texts and newspaper articles.
3. Provide opportunities for students to write their own paragraphs or longer articles. Brainstorm with the class and list a number of problems they could investigate. Some problems might be closely related to the school and community and would require investigation by observation and interviewing. Other problems may be related to content subjects or national concerns and require library research. (This will also depend on the students' grade level.)

---

*Adapted from D. E. Norton & S. Norton, *Language Arts Activities for Children,* 3rd ed. (Englewood Cliffs, NJ: Merrill/Prentice Hall, 1993), pp. 193–194. By permission of the authors and Prentice Hall.

Problems We Could Investigate

The taste and appearance of the spinach served in the school cafeteria
Discovering that your bicycle is missing
The pollution of the river near our school
A forest fire in our state park
The electricity was off for four hours this morning
A small percentage of people voted in the last election

I. ASSESSMENT STRATEGY
Assessing Students' Writing

By observing students while they are writing, teachers can note how students move through the writing process stages, from gathering and organizing ideas during prewriting, to pouring out and shaping ideas during drafting, to meeting in writing groups to get feedback and making substantive changes during revising, to proofreading and correcting mechanical errors in editing, and to publishing and sharing their writing in the last stage (McKenzie & Tompkins, 1984). Figure 10.9 lists several characteristic activities in each stage of the writing process. Teachers can observe students while they write and participate in other writing process-related activities and place checkmarks and add comments as necessary for each observed activity. Students can also use the checklist for self-assessment to help make them aware of the activities in the writing process.

The writing process checklist can also be adapted for various types of writing projects. If students are writing autobiographies, for example, the checklist can include items in the prewriting stage about developing a lifeline and clustering ideas for each chapter topic. The sharing stage can include items such as adding a table of contents, an illustration for each chapter, and sharing the complete autobiography with at least two other people.

J. LANGUAGE ARTS SKILLS LESSON PLAN: LETTER WRITING*
1. Descriptive Course Data

Teacher: _____   *Date*: _____

Grade level: All grades; a personal letter is an appropriate subject for all children, and older children may also write a business letter.
Room number: _____
Unit: Communication (in Family Life and Business World; Social Studies context)
Lesson Topic: Letter Writing (Language Arts Skills)

2. Lesson Goals and Objectives

Instructional goals (general objectives).
1. To understand that personal letters have a different purpose and audience than business letters.
2. To write a personal letter to a friend or relative.
3. To develop a purpose for writing a business letter.
4. To relate children's literature to letter writing and to motivate letter writing using literature.

Specific (performance) objectives.
Cognitive.
1. With others, the student will develop their own definitions of an *interview*.
2. When presented with examples, the student will explain the purpose and the audience of the letter(s).

---

*Adapted from D. E. Norton & S. Norton, *Language Arts Activities for Children*, 3rd ed., (Englewood Cliffs, NJ: Merrill/Prentice Hall, 1993), pp. 178–180. By permission of the authors and Prentice Hall.

FIGURE 10.9
A Writing Process Checklist

Student _____	Dates					
Prewriting Can the student identify the specific audience to whom he/she will write?						
Does this awareness affect the choices the student makes as he/she writes?						
Can the student identify the purpose of the writing activity?						
Does the student write on a topic that grows out of his/her own experience?						
Does the student engage in rehearsal activities before writing?						
Drafting Does the student write rough drafts?						
Does the student place a greater emphasis on content than on mechanics in the rough drafts?						
Revising Does the student share his/her writing in conferences?						
Does the student participate in discussions about classmates' writing?						
In revising, does the student make changes to reflect the reactions and comments of both teacher and classmates?						
Between first and final drafts, does the student make substantive or only minor changes?						
Editing Does the student proofread his/her own papers?						
Does the student help proofread classmates' papers?						
Does the student increasingly identify his/her mechanical errors?						
Sharing Does the student publish his/her writing in an appropriate form?						
Does the student share this finished writing with an appropriate audience?						

3. The student will participate in contrasting a personal letter and a business letter by discussing some of the differences.

Affective.

1. The student may show pleasure and enjoyment while writing a personal (business) letter.

Psychomotor.

1. Using a pen or pencil, the student will write a business letter or a personal letter to a friend or relative.

3. Rationale

The concept of ways people communicate is prevalent in social studies content as evidenced by recommendations of the National Council for the Social Studies (NCSS) Task Force through topics of family life and the world of work. A perusal of curriculum materials will indicate where the topic of communication has been included by local schools, districts, and state departments of education.

4. Plan and Procedures

Introduction. Show the children an envelope with a personal letter enclosed. Ask them if they would like to receive letters written just for them. If this letter was addressed to them, who would they wish the sender to be? What would they like to read in the letter? Who would be the audience for the letter? What would be the purpose of the letter?

Modeling. Read examples of two letters; one should be an interesting personal letter to someone the writer knows and the other should be a business letter requesting information from someone the writer does not know. Ask the children to listen to each letter and identify the purpose and audience for each. For example, consider Figure 10.10 and 10.11.

Have the children contrast the differences between the purposes and audiences for a personal letter and a business letter. The children may suggest any of the points in Table 10.3:

With the children, discuss the contents of the personal and business letters. What is the subject matter of each one? Are there any special requirements for each letter? Suggest that the personal letter is an informal, friendly exchange between two people who know each other well. It is like having a conversation. The business letter is more formally written. The letter usually asks for or gives information to a busy company or business that does not know the writer. The request for information needs to be stated clearly so the correct information or product will be received. Write a brief personal letter on an overhead transparency so the children can watch as you write. Think "out loud" as you write so the children will "hear" your thought processes as you develop the friendly letter.

Guided (coached) practice. Introduce one or two books based on letter writing to the children. Ask them to notice how each author writes the story around a series of letters or postcards. The following books are suitable for this purpose:

FIGURE 10.10
Personal Letter

July 23, 19_____

Dear Sally,

This is the most exciting time I have ever had at camp. Do you remember that I wanted to ride horseback every day? You just wouldn't believe the beautiful horse they gave me. His name is Cinnamon. He is brown and has a black mane and tail. He is real spicy, too. I feel just great when we run across the meadows. I'd like to ride on forever or, at least, till I get hungry again.

Speaking of food—do you remember what happened last year when we found a worm in the salad? You wouldn't believe what I found in my chili burger yesterday! A real grasshopper was sitting there staring at me! I screamed, and everyone stopped talking. Our table decided to protest this new food. The camp cooks say it will never happen again. They gave me an extra brownie. I think it was to keep me quiet so I wouldn't complain any more.

Say hello to everyone for me. Don't have that slumber party you talked about until I get home. I'll tell you about it when I see you next week.

Your best friend,

Jean

FIGURE 10.11
Business Letter

> 13 Rosewood Circle
> Turnersville, NJ 08012
> October 14, 19__
>
> Alaska State Division of Tourism
> Pouch E—907
> Juneau, Alaska 99811
>
> Dear Sirs:
>
> The fourth-grade class at Jefferson Elementary School is studying festivals in Alaska. Several free brochures for festivals are listed in the State of Alaska Visitor Guide. We would like to order the following brochures:
>
> L—001 Alaska Festival of Music
> L—002 Anchorage Fur Rendezvous
> L—003 Iceworm Festival
> L—004 Muskeg Stomp
> L—005 Equinox Marathon
> L—012 Cry of the Wild Ram
> L—024 Alaska State Sled Dog Championship
> Thank you for sending us the brochures.
>
> Sincerely
>
> Jerry Johnson
> 4th-grade class
> Jefferson Elementary School

TABLE 10.3
Purposes and Audiences for Personal and Business Letters

	PURPOSE	AUDIENCE
PERSONAL LETTER	1. To exchange interesting personal information	1. Friend 2. Relative
BUSINESS LETTER	1. To request information 2. To give information about a business or product 3. To influence a policy maker.	1. Business person who does not know me 2. Government official who does not know me

Grades 1–3.

Caseley, J. (1991). *Dear Annie.* New York: Greenwillow. This book is based on a series of letters written by Annie and Annie's grandfather. The letters span a number of years between Annie's birth and her years in the early elementary grades.

James, S. (1991). *Dear Mr. Blueberry.* New York: Macmillan. This book features the correspondence between a child and her teacher. The child is convinced that a whale lives in her pond. Mr. Blueberry's letters provide factual information about whales and suggest that a whale could not live in a small pond.

Williams, V. B., & Williams, J. (1988). *Stringbean's Trip to the Shining Sea.* New York: Greenwillow. This story is based on a series of postcards and snapshots sent home by a boy as he travels across the United States.

Grade 4.

Cleary, B. (1983). *Dear Mr. Henshaw.* New York: Morrow. The correspondence develops as 10-year-old Leigh Botts writes letters to his favorite author.

While reading aloud *Dear Annie,* encourage the children (grades 1–3) to notice that the writing is based on personal letters between a grandfather and his granddaughter. The content of the letters is based on everyday experiences that interest both the writers. In contrast, *Dear Mr. Blueberry* includes factual information about whales provided by the girl's teacher. Both of these books include exchanges between two people, although the purposes for the letters are quite different. *Stringbean's Trip* focuses on postcards, photographs, and travel experiences that allow the sender to give information to his family at home. Stringbean Coe and his brother Fred send home some photographs and daily postcards during the summer they travel from Kansas to the Pacific in Fred's truck. Through his writing, Stringbean reacts to the trip and his flare-ups with his brother, tells how it felt to be homesick, and records some of the ways he takes care of Potato, the dog who went along on the trip. There are no exchanges of ideas with those at home but the postcards are written to a family audience.

If reading *Dear Mr. Henshaw* to fourth-grade students, encourage them to notice that the letters written by the 10-year-old boy to his favorite author reveal information about the boy and the changes that occur to him during the plot of the story.

Use these books to motivate the children to write their own stories based on letters or postcards. Their stories can be based on exchanges of letters between friends or family members, exchanges of letters to gain information, or postcards that might be sent if the children were on a vacation.

Next, have the children write a personal letter to a friend or relative. Help them during the writing process. Have them mail the letters.

Assignments. With third- and fourth-grade students, provide a purpose for composing a business letter such as the request for information from the Alaska Travel Bureau. Ask the students to write and mail the letters.

Closure. Relate the lesson to what children learned about letter writing from modeling, listening to literature, and composing their own letters.

5. Materials Needed

Audiovisual. None

Other.

Caseley, J. (1991). *Dear Annie.* New York: Greenwillow.

Cleary, B. (1983). *Dear Mr. Henshaw.* New York: Morrow.

James, S. (1991). *Dear Mr. Blueberry.* New York: Macmillan.

Williams, V. B., & Williams, J. (1988). *Stringbean's Trip to the Shining Sea.* New York: Greenwillow.

6. Assessment and Revision

Assessment of learning. Teacher observations and anecdotal notes will document the learning and participation of students who have practiced letter writing techniques. The anecdotal notes will reflect which students are able to explain the purpose and the audience of the letters(s); to contrast a personal letter with a business letter by discussing some of the differences; to show interest, pleasure, and enjoyment while writing a personal (business) letter; and to complete a letter to a friend or relative and a business letter.

Plan for revision. Some students will require additional opportunities for letter writing and writing their own stories based on letters and postcards. Letter writing and related story writing can be motivated with literature selections such as those listed in Figure 10.12 and

FIGURE 10.12
Books That Reveal the Significance of Letters

Austin, J. (1986). *The jolly postman or other people's letters.* Boston: Little Brown. The book contains real letters inside, and a teacher may take out the letters, each from its own envelope, and read aloud what well-known fairy tale characters have written to each other. (grades 1–4)

Everett, G. (1992). *L'il Sis and Uncle Willie.* New York: Rizzoli. Corresponding through letters begins for L'il Sis after her Uncle Willie visits her in her home in South Carolina. Her uncle is William H. Johnson, an African American painter, whose work is shown in the National Museum of American Art in Washington, DC. (grades 2–4)

Kellogg, S. (1986). *Best Friends.* New York: Dial. Kathy and Louise, two best friends, find that their plans for a summer of "togetherness" are spoiled when Louise goes to visit her aunt and uncle in the mountains. To keep in touch, Louise writes postcards to Kathy about her new friends. (grades K–3)

O'Connor, J. (1979). *Yours till Niagara Falls, Abby.* New York: Hastings. This is a humorous look at camping through the actions of spunky Abby Kimmel, who writes and is always wise-cracking as she meets her bunk mates, the counselors, and Aunt Tilly, the camp director. (grade 4)

Smith, J. L. (1992). *Nelson in love: An Adam Joshua Valentine's Day story.* HarperCollins. Adam Joshua joins others in making valentines, writing notes, and making marker-heart tattoos with initials. (grades 1–3)

---

the students can be asked to discuss the purposes of the letters in each of the books that reveal the significance of letters.

SUMMARY

The writing process involves five interrelated stages that both students and adult authors work through:

- In prewriting, students consider function, audience, and form, and they participate in activities to gather and organize ideas.
- In drafting, students write a rough draft, with emphasis on content rather than mechanics.
- Next, in the revising stage, students share their writing and make substantive content changes.
- Students edit to identify and correct spelling, capitalization, and punctuation errors.
- In the last stage, students publish and share their writing.

In contrast to the traditional approach to writing, the emphasis in the writing process is on the *process* students use when they write, not on the finished product. After students learn about each stage of the writing process, they use it to write stories, reports, poems, and other forms of writing. Teachers become facilitators or partners, and their role varies according to the stage of the process.

QUESTIONS AND ACTIVITIES FOR DISCUSSION

1. Observe students using the writing process in an elementary classroom, K–4. In what types of prewriting, drafting, revising, editing, and sharing activities are they involved?

2. Interview students who use a process approach to writing and other students who use a traditional approach. Ask questions similar to the following and compare the students' answers:

   - How do you choose a topic for writing?
   - How do you get started writing?
   - Do you ask your classmates or the teacher to read your writing?
   - What do you do when you are having a problem while writing?
   - What is easiest about writing for you?
   - What is hardest about writing for you?
   - What is the most important thing to remember when you are writing?
   - What happens to your writing after you finish it?
   - What kinds of writing (e.g., stories, poems, reports) do you like best?

3. Sit in on a writing conference in which students share their writing and ask classmates for feedback in revising their compositions. Make a list of the students' questions and comments. What conclusions can you draw about their interactions with each other? You might want to compare your findings with those reported in "Talking about writing: The language of writing groups" (Gere & Abbott, 1985).

4. Examine language arts textbooks to see how they approach writing. Do they use the process approach? Do some steps in the writing process lend themselves to the textbook format better than others?

5. Reflect on your own writing process. Do you write single-draft papers, or do you write a series of drafts and refine them? Do you ask friends to read and react to your writing or to help you proofread your writing? Write a two- to three-page paper comparing your writing process to the process described in this chapter. How might you modify your own writing process in light of the information in this chapter?

6. Describe any prior concepts you had about writing in the classroom and teaching writing that changed as a result of your experience with this chapter. Describe the changes.

CHILDREN'S BOOKS

Austin, J. (1986). *The jolly postman or other people's letters*. Boston: Little Brown.

Caseley, J. (1991). *Dear Annie*. New York: Greenwillow.

Cleary, B. (1983). *Dear Mr. Henshaw*. New York: Morrow.

Everett, G. (1992). *L'il Sis and Uncle Willie*. New York: Rizzoli.

Field, R. (1929, 1957). *Hitty: Her first hundred years*. Ill. by D. P. Lathrop. New York: Macmillan.

Holling, C. H. (1941). *Paddle to the sea*. Boston: Houghton Mifflin.

Hoyt-Goldsmith, D. (1990). *Totem Pole*. Photographs by L. Migdale. New York: Holiday.

James, S. (1991). *Dear Mr. Blueberry*. New York: Macmillan.

Kellogg, S. (1986). *Best Friends*. New York: Dial.

MacLachlan, P. (1985). *Sarah, Plain and Tall*. New York: Harper & Row.

O'Connor, J. (1979). *Yours till Niagara Falls, Abby*. New York: Hastings.

Smith, J. L. (1992). Nelson in love: An Adam Joshua Valentine's Day story. HarperCollins.

Williams, V. B., & Williams, J. (1988). *Stringbean's trip to the shining sea*. New York: Greenwillow.

REFERENCES AND SUGGESTED READINGS

Applebee, A. L., & Langer, J. A. (1983). Instructional scaffolding: Reading and writing and natural language activities. *Language Arts, 60,* 168–175.

Bissex, G. L. (1980). *Gyns at wrk: A child learns to write and read.* Cambridge, MA: Harvard University Press.

Britton, J., Burgess, T., Martin, N., McLeod, A., & Rosen, H. (1975). *The development of writing abilities (11–18)*. London: Schools Council Publications.

Calkins, L. M. (1980). When children want to punctuate: Basic skills belong in context. *Language Arts, 57,* 567–573.

Calkins, L. M. (1983). *Lessons from a child: On the teaching and learning of writing*. Portsmouth, NH: Heinemann.

Calkins, L. M. (1986). *The art of teaching writing*. Portsmouth, NH: Heinemann.

Dyson, A. H. (1982). The emergence of visible language: Interrelationships between drawing and early writing. *Visible Language, 6,* 360–381.

Dyson, A. H. (1983). Early writing as drawing: The developmental gap between speaking and writing. Presentation at the Annual Meeting of the American Educational Research Association, Montreal, CA.

Dyson, A. H. (1985). Second graders sharing writing: The multiple social realities of a literacy event. *Written Communication, 2,* 189–215.

Dyson, A. H. (1986). The imaginary worlds of childhood: A multimedia presentation. *Language Arts, 63,* 799–808.

Elley, W. B., Barham, I. H., Lamb, H., & Wyllie, M. (1976). The role of grammar in a secondary school English curriculum. *Research in the Teaching of English, 10,* 5–21.

Faigley, L., & Witte, S. (1981). Analyzing revision. *College Composition and Communication, 32,* 400–410.

Fine, E. S. (1987). Marbles lost, marbles found. Collaborative production of text. *Language Arts, 64,* 474–487.

Gere, A. R., & Abbott, R. D. (1985). Talking about writing: The language of writing groups. *Research in the Teaching of English, 19,* 362–381.

Graves, D. H. (1976). Let's get rid of the welfare mess in the teaching of writing. *Language Arts, 53,* 645–651.

Graves, D. H. (1983). *Writing: Teachers and children at work.* Exeter, NH: Heinemann.

Graves, D. H., & Hansen, J. (1983). The author's chair. *Language Arts, 60,* 176–183.

Halliday, M. A. K. (1973). *Explorations in the functions of language.* London: Edward Arnold.

Halliday, M. A. K. (1975). *Learning how to mean: Explorations in the development of language.* London: Edward Arnold.

Hayes, J. R., & Flower, L. S. (1980). Identifying the organization of writing processes. In L. W. Gregg & E. R. Steinberg (Eds.),

Cognitive processes in writing, pp. 3–30. Hillsdale, NJ: Erlbaum.

Hidi, S., & Hildyard, A. (1983). The comparison of oral and written productions in two discourse modes. *Discourse Processes, 6,* 91–105.

Jackson, L. A., Tway, E., & Frager, A. (1987). Dear teacher, Johnny copied. *The Reading Teacher, 41,* 22–25.

King, M. (1985). Proofreading is not reading. *Teaching English in the two-year college, 12,* 108–112.

Langer, J. A. (1985). Children's sense of genre. *Written Communication, 2,* 157–187.

Lundsteen, S. W. (Ed.). (1976). *Help for the teacher of written composition: New directions in research.* Urbana, IL: National Conference on Research in English and ERIC Clearinghouse on Reading and Communication Skills.

Martin, N., D'Arcy, P., Newton, B., & Parker, R. (1976). *Writing and learning across the curriculum (11–16).* London: Schools Council Publications.

McKenzie, L., & Tompkins, G. E. (1984). Evaluating students' writing: A process approach. *Journal of Teaching Writing, 3,* 201–212.

Mills, B. S. (1983). Imagination: The connection between writing and play. *Educational Leadership 41,* 50–53.

Mohr, M. M. (1984). *Revision: The rhythm of meaning.* Upper Montclair, NJ: Boynton/Cook.

Murray, D. H. (1982). *Learning by teaching.* Montclair, NJ: Boynton/Cook.

Simpson, M. K. (1986). What am I supposed to do while they're writing? *Language Arts, 63,* 680–684.

Smith, F. (1982). *Writing and the writer.* New York: Holt, Rinehart & Winston.

Sommers, N. (1982). Responding to student writing. *College Composition and Communication, 33,* 148–156.

Tompkins, G. E., & Friend, M. (1988). After your students write: What's next? *Teaching Exceptional Children, 20,* 4–9.

Tway, E. (1980). Teacher responses to children's writing. *Language Arts, 57,* 763–772.

Wagner, B. J. (1976). *Dorothy Heathcote: Drama as a learning medium.* Washington, DC: National Education Association.

Wagner, B. J. (1983). The expanding circle of informal classroom drama. In B. A. Busching and J. I. Schwartz (Eds.), *Integrating the language arts in the elementary school,* pp. 155–163. Urbana, IL: National Council of Teachers of English.

Wagner, B. J. (1988). Does classroom drama affect the arts of language? *Language Arts, 65,* 46–55.

CHAPTER 11

The Writers' Tools: Spelling, Handwriting, Grammar, Punctuation and Capitalization

Spelling, handwriting, grammar, punctuation, and capitalization are all empowering vehicles to which young children can be introduced. As young children begin to write, they can create unique spellings based on their knowledge of English orthography. Handwriting is a developmental motor skill that has a functional purpose for children. Teachers can introduce grammar through sentence-combining activities with the study of patterns that authors of children's books use for their audience. Additionally, punctuation and capitalization can be taught in conjunction with meaningful writing activities.

Spelling as a writer's tool. Charles Read (1971, 1975), one of the first researchers to study preschoolers' efforts to spell words, discovered that they used their knowledge of phonology to invent spellings. Based on Read's work, other researchers began to systematically study the development of children's spelling abilities. Henderson and his colleagues (1977) have studied the manner in which children proceed developmentally from invented spelling to correct spelling. This research puts spelling into a developmental framework that is closely related to the psycho- and sociolinguistic view of language learning, which emphasizes that children construct their own knowledge of language systems—including the orthographic (writing) system. This chapter describes spelling as a tool that writers need for communicating with their readers. The discussions related to spelling are specifically designed to help you understand

1. How young children, K–4, learn to spell
2. Examples of ways teachers teach spelling
3. Assessment strategy for spelling.

Handwriting as a writer's tool. Writing for genuine audiences is a way to convey to children the importance of legibility. They will want the addresses on letters, postcards, and packages to be decipherable so they will be delivered by the post office, and they will want their published prose and poetry to be read because their handwriting is legible. This chapter describes handwriting as a tool that writers need for communicating with their readers. The discussions related to handwriting are specifically designed to help you understand

1. The handwriting forms that young children learn to use
2. Examples of ways teachers teach handwriting
3. Diagnosis, correction, and assessment strategies for handwriting.

Grammar as a writer's tool. Grammarians have described the structure of English in three different ways, which influence how grammar is taught in today's elementary schools. *Traditional grammar,* the first approach, is prescriptive and includes the teaching of parts of speech, parts of sentences, and types of sentences. *Structural grammar,* the second approach, is an attempt to describe how language is really used and includes the teaching of seven basic sentence patterns with nouns, verbs, complements (to verbs), modifiers, and connectives. *Transformational grammar* is the third approach, and it attempts to describe the ways language works and the cognitive processes used to produce language. To use this approach in the classroom, educators have introduced sentence combining in which children focus on the construction of sentence(s) as they analyze, combine, select, rearrange, elaborate on, organize, refocus, and edit their writing. Teachers can incorporate sentence-combining activities by having children study the syntactic patterns that authors use. To do this, the author's sentences need to be analyzed so that the writing readily demonstrates sentence combining. The discussions related to grammar are specifically designed to help you understand

1. The teaching of grammar
2. Examples of ways teachers connect grammar instruction to literature and writing
3. Assessment strategies for grammar.

Mechanics of punctuation and capitalization as writers' tools. The mechanics of writing include punctuation and capitalization and are most effectively taught in conjunction with meaningful writing activities. The discussions related to the mechanics of writing are specifically designed to help you understand

1. Punctuation taught in grades K–4
2. Capitalization taught in grades K–4
3. Assessment strategy for the mechanics of writing.

A. HOW YOUNG CHILDREN LEARN TO SPELL

Based on observations of children's spellings, researchers have identified five stages that children move through on their way to becoming conventional spellers, and at each stage they use different types of strategies (Bean & Bouffler, 1987). The stages are precommunicative spelling, semiphonetic spelling, phonetic spelling, transitional spelling, and correct spelling (Gentry, 1978, 1981, 1982a, 1982b, 1987).

Stage 1: Precommunicative Spelling (Ages 3–5)

In this stage, children string scribbles, letters, and letterlike forms together, but they do not associate the marks they make with any specific phonemes. Precommunicative spelling represents a natural, early expression of the alphabet and other concepts about writing. Children may write from left to right, right to left, top to bottom, or randomly across the page. Some precommunicative spellers have a large repertoire of letter forms to use in writing, and others repeat a small number of letters over and over. Children may use both upper- and lowercase letters, but they show a distinct preference for uppercase letters. At this stage, children have not discovered how spelling works or the alphabetic principle that letters represent sounds in words.

Stage 2: Semiphonetic Spelling (Ages 5–6)

At this stage, children begin to represent phonemes in words with letters, indicating that they have a rudimentary understanding of the alphabetic principle, that a link exists between letters and sounds. Spellings are quite abbreviated, and children use only one, two, or three letters to represent an entire word. Examples of Stage 2 spelling are DA (*day*), KLZ (*closed*), and SM (*swimming*).

Stage 3: Phonetic Spelling

In this third stage, children's understanding of the alphabetic principle is further refined. They continue to use letter names to represent sounds, but they also use consonant and vowel sounds at this stage. Examples of Stage 3 spelling are LIV (*live*), DRAS (*dress*), and PEKT (*peeked*). As these examples show, children choose letters on the basis of sound alone, without considering acceptable English letter sequences (e.g., using -*t* rather than -*ed* as a past tense marker in *peeked*) or other spelling conventions. These spellings do not resemble English words, and although spelling does not look like adult spelling, it can be deciphered. The major achievement of this stage is that, for the first time, children represent *all* essential sound features in the words they are spelling. Henderson (1980b) explains that words are "bewilderingly homographic" at this stage because children spell on the basis of sound alone; for example, *bat, bet,* and *bait* might all be spelled BAT (Read, 1971).

Stage 4: Transitional Spelling (Ages 7–8)

Transitional spellers come close to the correct spellings of English words. They spell many words correctly, but continue to misspell words with irregular spellings. Examples of Stage 4 spelling are HUOSE (*house*), TRUBAL (*trouble*), EAGUL (*eagle*), and AFTERNEWN (*afternoon*). This stage is characterized by children's growing ability to represent the features of English orthography. First, they include a vowel in every syllable (as the *trouble* and *eagle* spellings show). Next, they demonstrate knowledge of vowel patterns even though they might make a faulty decision about which marker to use. For example, *toad* is often spelled TODE when children choose the wrong vowel marker, or TAOD when the two vowels are reversed. Also, transitional spellers use common letter patterns in their spelling, such as YOUNIGHTED for *united* and HIGHCKED for *hiked*. In this stage, children use conventional alternatives for representing sounds, and although they continue to misspell words according to adult standards, transitional spelling resembles English orthography and can easily be read. As the examples show, children stop relying entirely on phonological information and begin to use visual clues and morphological information as well.

Stage 5: Correct Spelling (Age 9 and older)

As the name implies, children spell many, many words correctly at this stage, but not all. They have mastered the basic principles of English orthography, and this achievement indicates that children are ready for formal spelling instruction (Gentry 1981; 1982a). Children typically reach Stage 5 and are ready for formal spelling instruction by the age of 8 or 9. During the next four or five years, children learn to control homonyms (e.g., *road-rode*), contractions, consonant doubling and adding affixes (e.g., *runing/running*), and vowel and consonant alternations. They also learn to spell most common irregularly spelled words. Spellers also learn about spelling alternatives—different ways to spell the same sound. The characteristics of each of the five stages of invented spelling are summarized in Figure 11.1

In a short period of three or four years, young children move from precommunicative spelling to correct spelling. This learning happens informally rather than through direct instruction; when formal spelling instruction begins before children have reached the fifth stage, their natural development is interrupted. Typically, children are advised to sound out words or to memorize spellings. Sounding out is a stage children naturally progress through in the developmental sequence. If instruction interrupts their progress at that point, they are less likely to generalize the morphemic component of spelling. Similarly, the fourth and fifth stages are cut short when children memorize words.

B. TEACHING YOUNG CHILDREN HOW TO SPELL

After students have reached the correct stage of spelling development and spell 90 to 95 percent of words correctly, they are ready for formal spelling instruction. Providing opportunities for students to read and write each day is prerequisite to any spelling program. Spelling is a writer's tool best learned through writing (Bean & Bouffler, 1987). Students who write daily and use invented spellings will move naturally toward correct spelling.

FIGURE 11.1
Characteristics of the Invented Spelling Stages
SOURCE: Adapted from Gentry, 1982, pp. 192–200.

Stage 1: Precommunicative Spelling

Child uses scribbles, letterlike forms, letters, and sometimes numbers to represent a message.
Child may write from left-to-right, right-to-left, top-to-bottom, or randomly on the page.
Child shows no understanding of phoneme-grapheme correspondences.
Child may repeat a few letters again and again or use most of the letters of the alphabet.
Child frequently mixes upper- and lowercase letters but shows a preference for uppercase letters.

Stage 2: Semiphonetic Spelling

Child becomes aware of the alphabetic principle that letters are used to represent sounds.
Child uses abbreviated one-, two-, or three-letter spelling to represent an entire word.
Child uses letter-name strategy to spell words.

Stage 3: Phonetic Spelling

Child represents all essential sound features of a word in spelling.
Child develops particular spellings for long and short vowels, plural and past tense markers and other aspects of spelling.
Child chooses letters on the basis of sound without regard for English letter sequences or other conventions.

Stage 4: Transitional Spelling

Child adheres to basic conventions of English orthography.
Child begins to use morphological and visual information in addition to phonetic information.
Child may include all appropriate letters in a word but reverse some of them.
Child uses alternate spellings for the same sound in different words, but only partially understands the conditions governing their use.
Child uses a high percentage of correctly spelled words.

Stage 5: Correct Spelling

Child applies the basic rules of the English orthographic system.
Child extends knowledge of word structure including the spelling of affixes, contractions, compound words, and homonyms.
Child demonstrates growing accuracy in using silent consonants and doubling consonants before adding suffixes.
Child recognizes when a word doesn't "look right" and can consider alternate spellings for the same sound.
Child learns irregular spelling patterns.
Child learns consonant and vowel alternations and other morphological structures.
Child knows how to spell a large number of words.

When they write, children guess at spellings using their knowledge of letter names and sounds. They gradually recognize that the words they are reading and writing are spelled the same way each time. When students recognize that words have consistent spellings, they are ready to be helped in a direct way. Teachers can then begin to point out conventions of the spelling system.

Emphasis on correct spelling, like handwriting and other mechanics, belongs in the editing stage of the writing process. As children write and revise their rough drafts, they should be encouraged not to worry about correct spelling and to invent spelling as needed. Stopping to ask a classmate or the teacher how to spell a word, or checking a spelling in a dictionary while pouring out ideas in a rough draft, interrupts the writer's train of thought. Through the process approach, children recognize spelling for what it is—a courtesy to the reader. As they write, revise, edit, and share their writing with genuine audiences, students will begin to learn that they need to spell correctly so that their audience will be able to read their compositions.

Reading also plays an enormous role in learning to spell. During reading, students store the words that they can recall on sight. The ability to recall how words look helps students decide when a spelling is or is not correct. If a word does not look right, they must check the spelling. When they decide a word does not look right, they can either rewrite the word several different ways until it does look right, or they can ask the teacher or a classmate who knows the spelling.

There are two basic approaches to teaching spelling. One is *contract spelling;* students choose which words they want to learn to spell according to the words they need for their writing and for content area study. The second approach is based on spelling *textbooks,* and the methods of teaching emphasize phoneme-grapheme correspondences. Some textbooks also emphasize morphology, and students study words in terms of root words, prefixes, and suffixes.

The Contract Spelling Approach

Research on children's invented spelling suggests that spelling is best learned through writing and that spelling instruction should be individualized so that children can learn to spell the words they need for their writing. In the contract approach, students choose words from their writing to learn to spell, and, because they are using the words in their writing and want to learn them, they remember how to spell them more easily. Students develop individual contracts with the teacher to learn specific words during the week. Contract spelling places more responsibility on students for their own learning, and when students have responsibility, they tend to perform better.

Developing the word list. Contract spelling begins with the development of a weekly word list from which teachers and students select. Words for the master list are drawn from all the words students needed in their writing activities during the previous week and words related to content area units or seasonal words. To accumulate words for the list, students can keep a sheet of paper taped to their desks, and teachers can record the words students need help with on the slips of paper. Or, teachers can write the needed words on slips of paper, which students return to a box on the teacher's desk after they are used. The list may include 30, 40, or even 50 words at the middle and upper grades.

The master word list also provides an opportunity to point out aspects of orthography. Students can look for phoneme-grapheme correspondences and develop lists of words to discover which letters most frequently represent each phoneme and whether the letters are in the initial, medial, or final positions. Students can also examine inflectional endings and the rules that operate on them as the words occur in sentences. In addition, students can examine the words for applications of the spelling rules with few exceptions.

Pretest. The master list of words serves as the pretest at the beginning of the week, and students try to spell as many of the master words as they can. From the words that each student misspells, he or she chooses words to study during the week, and these words become each student's spelling contract. After students have corrected their own pretests, they complete a spelling contract similar to the form shown in Figure 11.2. Students circle the words they spelled correctly on the pretest and transfer this information to the word list by circling the number of each correctly spelled word. Then they draw a box around the number of each word they plan to learn that week. If the word list and spelling contract are on the same form, students have less trouble keeping track of their work.

The master word list offers the opportunity to include words at several levels of difficulty because of the students' different spelling needs. Because of the range of words on the master word list, students will be able to select words at their own level for their spelling contracts. They will need to experiment to determine the appropriate difficulty level for them and the number of words they can learn each week. Good spellers will be able to learn both more difficult words and a greater number of words each week than poor spellers will. Five words a week will be an achievement for some students, whereas others may be able to learn 10 or 15 words.

Negotiating the spelling contract. Students negotiate with the teacher for the number of words they believe they can learn in one week. This number includes the words they spelled correctly plus additional words they misspelled on the pretest that they think they can learn. The negotiations help students learn to be realistic about their spelling ability.

FIGURE 11.2
Spelling Contract and Word List

Name: _____
Week: _____

Spelling Contract

Number of words spelled correctly on the pretest: _____
Number of words to be learned: _____
Total number of words contracted: _____

1.* _____	16. _____
2. _____	17. _____
3. _____	18. _____
4. _____	19. _____
5. _____	20. _____
6. _____	21. _____
. . .	. . .
15. _____	30. _____

Instructions

1. Circle the number of each word you spelled correctly on the preset.
2. Draw a box around the number of each word you plan to learn. Use a pencil so that you can make changes if necessary.
*The teacher writes the master list on these lines before duplicating the form.

Word study. Students spend approximately 5 to 10 minutes studying the words each day during the week. Instead of busywork activities such as using their spelling words in sentences or gluing yarn in the shape of the words, research shows it is more effective for students to learn and use a systematic strategy for practicing spelling words. The strategy should focus on the whole word rather than breaking it apart into sounds or syllables, and it should include visual, auditory, and kinesthetic components. An eight-step strategy that meets these two criteria is as follows.

1. Look at the word and say it.
2. Read each letter in the word.
3. Close your eyes and spell the word to yourself.
4. Look at the word. Did you spell it correctly?
5. Copy the word from your list.
6. Cover the word and write it again.
7. Look at the word. Did you write it correctly?
8. If you made any mistakes, repeat the steps. (Cook et al., 1984, p. 1)

Weekly final test. A final test is administered at the end of the week on the words the students have contracted to learn. The teacher reads the master list, and students write only those words they have contracted to learn. To make it easier to administer the test, students first list the numbers of the words they have contracted to spell on their test papers; they can locate the numbers of their contracted spelling words on their spelling contracts.

Follow-up. Any words that students misspell should be included on their lists for the following week. Students should also list these problem words in a special spelling log notebook and try to determine why the words are difficult for them.

The Spelling Textbook Approach

The spelling textbook approach is the traditional way to help students learn to spell. There is little variation in the content of the textbooks and in the methods suggested for teaching the words. Typically, the textbook is arranged in week-long units, with lists of 10 to 20 words around which a variety of practice activities are planned. Researchers have made five recommendations regarding use of the textbook approach. The recommendations deal with study and testing procedures, unit arrangements, the word list, instructional strategy, and time allocation.

Study and testing procedures. Most spelling textbooks use a variation of the *test-study-test* plan, in which students are given a pretest on Monday, encouraged to study during the week the words they missed, and are retested on Friday. Some teachers omit the pretest and use a study-test plan in which students study all words, even those they already know; other teachers add a midweek trial test (test-study-test-study-test plan). Researchers have found that the pretest is a critical component in the study procedure. The pretest helps to identify words that students already know how to spell. By eliminating those words, students can direct their study toward the words that are difficult for them. Students need immediate feedback about their efforts to learn to spell. According to T. D. Horn (1947), the best way to improve students' spelling is to have them correct their own pretests and trial tests to receive immediate feedback.

Unit arrangement. Spelling textbooks use a weekly plan that includes lessons for each of the five days. On Monday, the words in the new unit are introduced, and, typically, students copy the word list and sometimes use the words to write sentences or to fill in blanks to complete a paragraph. On Tuesday, spellers usually have a set of exercises that provides practice for an aspect of word structure, such as phoneme-grapheme correspondences, spelling patterns, or root words and affixes. In many programs, Wednesday is the day for the trial test, and some programs also include additional word study activities. Spelling textbooks provide a variety of activities for Thursday, ranging from grammar, dictionary, and handwriting activities to enrichment word activities. Friday is reserved for the final spelling test. A sample textbook unit appears in Figure 11.3.

The word list. Spelling lists usually include the most frequently used words. Spelling textbooks for the elementary grades present at least 3,000 words, and researchers have found that these 3,000 most frequently used words account for more than 97 percent of all the words children and adults use in writing. Even more interesting, the three most frequently used words—*I, and, the*—account for 10 percent of all words written, and the 100 most frequently used words represent more than 50 percent of all the words written (E. Horn, 1926). Thus, a relatively small number of words accounts for an amazingly large percentage of words students use in their writing. Figure 11.4, lists the 100 most frequently used words.

The words in each unit are often grouped according to spelling patterns or phonetic generalizations; that is, all the words in one spelling list may follow a vowel rule (e.g., *i-e*) or a spelling pattern (e.g., *-igh*). Researchers question this approach; Johnson, Langford, and Quorn (1981) found that "the effectiveness of teaching spelling via phonic generalizations is highly questionable" (p. 586). Students often memorize the rule or spelling pattern and score perfectly on the spelling test, but later are unable to choose among spelling options in their writing. For example, after learning the *i-e* vowel rule and the *-igh* spelling pattern in isolation, students are often stumped about how to spell a word such as *light*. They have learned two spelling options for /ay/, *i-e* and *-igh*, and *lite* is an option, one they often see in their environment. Instead of organizing words according to phonetic generalizations and spelling rules, many educators recommend that teachers simply point out the rules whenever they occur.

The Instructional Strategy. Students need a systematic and efficient strategy for learning to spell words. The strategy should focus on the whole word rather than breaking it apart into sounds or syllables, and it should include visual, auditory, and kinesthetic components, as does the strategy outlined for contract spelling. Similar strategies are presented in most spelling textbooks. Research indicates that a whole-word approach to spelling instruction is more successful than phonetic or syllable approaches (T. Horn, 1969).

Time Allocation. Assignments in spelling textbooks often require at least 30 minutes per day to complete, totaling two hours per week of spelling instruction. Research indicates that

FIGURE 11.3
Sample Unit from a Third-Grade Spelling Textbook
Cook, Esposito, Gabrielson, & Turner, 1984, pp. 90–93.

23

OUR WORDS

sport	pour	score
order	or	poor
storm	corner	sore
forget	snow	course
horn	fort	fourth

PATTERN POWER

Say each spelling word.

1. Write the three spelling words in which /ôr/ as in **born** is spelled **ore**.

2. Write the eight spelling words in which /ôr/ is spelled **or**.

3. Write the three spelling words in which /ôr/ is spelled **our**.

4. Write the spelling word in which /ôr/ is spelled **oor**.

> In most words, /ôr/ as in **born** is spelled **or**, **ore**, or **our**.

90

MEANING MASTERY

Mr. Gibben has a very unusual store.
Use the spelling words below to complete
this paragraph about his strange shop.

sore   order   sport   corner   storm   horn

Mr. Gibben owns an odd store just around the (1) _____. He has
everything you can think of. If you like to play music, you can buy a
_____. If your back is (3) _____, you can buy
(2) _____
something to make it feel better. You can buy equipment for any kind of
_____ you want to play. You can even buy a coat to keep you
(4) _____
warm in a snow (5) _____. If you want something he does not

have, Mr. Gibben will (6) _____ it for you.

DICTIONARY SKILLS

Pretend *forget* and *snore* are guide words on a dictionary page. Write in
alphabetical order the ten spelling words that would appear on this page.
Be sure to include the guide words. The first one is done for you.

1. *forget*   6. _____
2. _____   7. _____
3. _____   8. _____
4. _____   9. _____
5. _____   10. _____

FIGURE 11.3 cont'd.

WORD BUILDING

You can make new words by adding **-ly** at the end of some base words. Add the suffix **-ly** to each base word below. Write the new words. The first one is done for you.

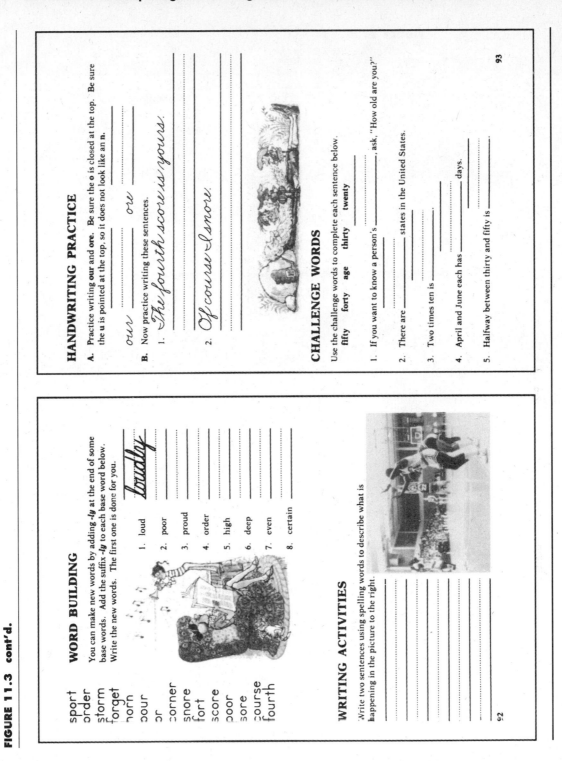

sport
order
storm
forget
horn
pour
or
corner
snore
fort
score
poor
sore
course
fourth

1. loud   _loudly_
2. poor   _____
3. proud   _____
4. order   _____
5. high   _____
6. deep   _____
7. even   _____
8. certain _____

WRITING ACTIVITIES

Write two sentences using spelling words to describe what is happening in the picture to the right.

_____

_____

_____

_____

92

HANDWRITING PRACTICE

A. Practice writing **our** and **ore**. Be sure the **o** is closed at the top. Be sure the **u** is pointed at the top, so it does not look like an **n**.

our _____   ore _____

B. Now practice writing these sentences.

1. _The fourth score is yours._

_____

2. _Of course I snore._

_____

CHALLENGE WORDS

Use the challenge words to complete each sentence below.

fifty   forty   age   thirty   twenty

1. If you want to know a person's _____, ask, "How old are you?"

2. There are _____ states in the United States.

3. Two times ten is _____.

4. April and June each has _____ days.

5. Halfway between thirty and fifty is _____.

93

FIGURE 11.4
The 100 Most Frequently Used Words
Hillerich, 1978, p. xiii.

I	there	how	around
and	with	do	see
the	one	about	think
a	be	some	down
to	so	her	over
was	all	him	by
in	said	could	did
it	were	as	mother
of	then	get	our
my	like	got	don't
he	went	came	school
is	them	time	little
you	she	back	into
that	out	will	who
we	at	can	after
when	are	people	no
they	just	from	am
on	because	saw	well
would	what	now	two
me	if	or	put
for	day	know	man
but	his	your	didn't
have	this	home	us
up	not	house	things
had	very	an	too

only 60 to 75 minutes per week should be spent on spelling instruction, however, and greater periods of time do not result in increased spelling ability (Johnson et al., 1981). Many of the activities in spelling textbooks involve language arts skills that are not directly related to learning to spell (Graves, 1977). If these activities, which often duplicate other language arts activities, were eliminated and students were to focus for 15 minutes each day on practicing their spelling words using the instructional strategy, they could learn to spell more quickly and more easily.

A checklist for assessing spelling textbooks according to these five criteria and researchers' recommendations is presented in Figure 11.5.

Learning to Use a Dictionary

Students need to learn to locate the spellings for unknown words in the dictionary. Of the approximately 450,000 entry words in an unabridged dictionary, students typically learn to spell 3,000 by the end of eighth grade—leaving 447,000 words unaccounted for! Obviously, students must learn how to locate the spellings of many of these additional words. Whereas it is relatively easy to find a "known" word in the dictionary, it is much harder to locate an unfamiliar word, and students need to learn what to do when they do not know how to spell a word. One approach is to consider spelling options and predict possible spellings for unknown words, then check the predicted spelling by consulting a dictionary. This strategy involves six steps:

1. Identify root words and affixes.
2. Consider related words (e.g., *medicine-medical*).
3. Determine the sounds in the word.
4. Generate a list of spelling options.
5. Select the most likely alternatives.
6. Consult a dictionary to check the correct spelling.

The fourth step is undoubtedly the most difficult. Using knowledge of both phonology and morphology, students develop a list of possible spellings. Phoneme-grapheme relationships

FIGURE 11.5
Checklist for Assessing Spelling Textbooks

Spelling Textbook Assessment

Textbook _____

Publisher _____

Grade Level _____   Reviewer _____

Study and Testing Procedures

_____ Does the textbook use a test-study-test plan (or a variation of that plan)?

_____ Do students take a pretest before studying the list of spelling words?

_____ Do students correct their own pretests and trial tests?

_____ Do students study all words in the list or only those that they do not know how to spell?

Unit Arrangement

_____ Does the textbook use a five-day approach?

_____ Do the activities focus on learning to spell the words or on related activities such as grammar, dictionary skills, or handwriting?

Spelling Words

_____ How are the spelling words selected?

_____ Are the spelling words grouped according to spelling patterns or phonetic generalizations?

Instructional Strategy

_____ Does the textbook present a systematic and efficient strategy for learning to spell words?

_____ Does the strategy focus on whole words rather than breaking words apart into sounds or syllables?

_____ Does the strategy include visual, auditory, and kinesthetic components?

Time

_____ How much time is required for students to complete the assignments in the textbook?

---

may rate primary consideration in generating spelling options for some words; root words and affixes or related words may be more important in determining how other words are spelled.

C. HANDWRITING FORMS

Two forms of handwriting are currently used in elementary schools: *manuscript,* or printing, and *cursive,* or connected writing, illustrated in Figure 11.6. Typically, students in the primary grades learn and use the manuscript form and switch to cursive handwriting in the middle grades, usually in second or third grade (Koenke, 1986).

Manuscript Handwriting

Manuscript handwriting is considered superior to the cursive form for young children because they seem to lack the necessary fine motor control and eye-hand coordination for cursive handwriting. In addition, manuscript handwriting is similar to the type style in primary-level reading textbooks. Only two lower case letters, *a* and *g,* are different in typed and handwritten forms. The similarity is assumed to facilitate young children's introduction to reading and writing.

Barbe and Milone (1980) suggested several additional reasons that students in the primary grades should learn manuscript before cursive handwriting. First, manuscript handwriting is easier to learn. Studies show that young children can copy letters and words written in the manuscript form more easily than when they are written in the cursive form. Also, young children can form the vertical and horizontal lines and circles of manuscript handwriting more easily than the cursive strokes. Furthermore, manuscript handwriting is more legible than cursive handwriting. Because it is easier to read, signs and advertisements are printed in letter forms closely approximating manuscript handwriting. Finally, people are often requested to print when completing applications and other forms. For these reasons,

FIGURE 11.6
Manuscript and Cursive Handwriting Forms
Barbe et al., 1984.

manuscript handwriting has become the preferred handwriting form for young children as well as a necessary handwriting skill for older children and adults.

Cursive Handwriting

When most people think of handwriting, the cursive or connected form comes to mind. The letters in cursive handwriting are joined together to form a word with one continuous movement. Children often view cursive handwriting as the "grown-up" type. Primary-grade students often attempt to imitate this form by connecting the manuscript letters in their names and other words before they are taught how to form and join the letters. Awareness of cursive handwriting and interest in imitating it are indicators that students are ready for instruction.

D. WAYS TEACHERS TEACH HANDWRITING

Young children enter kindergarten with different backgrounds of handwriting experience. Some 5-year-olds have never held a pencil, and many others have written cursivelike scribbles or manuscript letterlike forms. Some preschoolers have learned to print their names and some other letters. Handwriting in kindergarten typically includes three types of activities: stimulating children's interest in writing, developing their ability to hold writing instruments, and refining their fine motor control.

Developing the Ability to Hold Writing Instruments

Students develop the ability to hold a pencil or other writing instrument by modeling parents and teachers and through numerous opportunities to experiment with pencils, pens, paint brushes, crayons, and other writing instruments.

Refining Motor Skills

Young children develop and refine their fine motor skills through a variety of motor activities and experiences with manipulative materials. Possible activities include building with blocks, stringing beads, completing parquetry designs and puzzles, drawing, cutting, pasting, and other art activities.

Handwriting instruction in kindergarten usually focuses on teaching children to form upper- and lowercase letters and to print their names. Many kindergarten teachers use a multisensory approach: students trace letters in shaving cream, sand, and fingerpaint; glue popcorn in the shape of letters; and arrange blocks or pipe cleaners to form letters. Children learn to print their names through similar multisensory activities and through daily practice writing their names on attendance sheets, experience stories, paintings, and other papers.

Handwriting must be linked with writing at all grade levels, even in kindergarten. Young children write labels, draw and write stories, keep journals, and write other messages (Klein & Schickedanz, 1980). The more they write, the greater their need becomes for instruction in handwriting. Writers need to know how to grip a pencil, how to form letters, and how to space between letters and words. Instruction is necessary so students will not learn bad habits that later must be broken. Students often devise their own rather bizarre way to form a letter, and these bad habits will cause problems when they need to develop greater writing speed.

Handwriting in the Primary Grades

Formal handwriting instruction begins in first grade. Students learn how to form manuscript letters, how to space between them, and to develop skills related to the six elements of legibility. Researchers have found that primary-grade students have more difficulty forming the lowercase than the uppercase letters, and by third grade, some students still have difficulty forming *r, u, h,* and *t* (Stennett, Smithe, & Hardy, 1972).

A common handwriting activity requires students to copy short writing samples from the chalkboard, but this type of activity is not recommended. For one thing, young children have great difficulty with far-to-near copying (Lamme, 1979), a piece of writing should be placed close to the child for copying. Children can recopy their own compositions, language experience stories, and self-selected writing samples; other types of copying should be avoided. It is far better for children to create their own writing than to copy words and sentences they may not even be able to read!

Writing Instruments and Paper.   Special pencils and handwriting paper are often provided for handwriting instruction. Kindergartners and first graders commonly use "fat" beginner pencils because it has been assumed that these pencils are easier for young children to hold; however, most children prefer to use regular-sized pencils that older students and adults use. Moreover, regular pencils have erasers! Research now indicates that beginner pencils are not better than regular-sized pencils for young children (Lamme & Ayris, 1983). Likewise, there is no evidence that specially shaped pencils and little writing aids that slip onto pencils to improve children's grip are effective.

Many types of paper, both lined and unlined, are used in elementary classrooms. Paper companies manufacture paper lined in a range of sizes. Typically, paper is lined at two-inch intervals for kindergartners, $\frac{7}{8}$-inch intervals for first graders, $\frac{3}{4}$-inch intervals for second graders, $\frac{1}{2}$-inch intervals for third graders, and $\frac{3}{8}$-inch intervals for older students. Lined paper for first and second graders has an added midline, often dotted, to guide students in forming lowercase letters. Sometimes a line appears below the baseline to guide placement of letters such as lowercase, *g, p, q,* and *y* that have "tails" that drop below the baseline. The few research studies that have examined the value of lined paper in general and paper lined at these specific intervals offer conflicting results. One recent study suggests that younger children's handwriting is more legible when they use unlined paper and older children's is better when they use lined paper (Lindsay & McLennan, 1983). Most teachers seem to prefer that students use lined paper for handwriting activities, but students easily adjust to whichever type of writing paper is available. Children often use rulers to line their paper when they are given unlined paper, and, likewise, they ignore the lines on lined paper if they interfere with their drawing or writing.

Left-Handed Writers

Approximately 10 percent of the American population is left-handed, and there may be two or three left-handed students in most classrooms. Until recently, teachers insisted that left-handed students use their right hands for handwriting because left-handed writers were thought to have inferior handwriting skills. Parents and teachers are more realistic now and accept children's natural tendencies for left- or right-handedness. In fact, research has shown that there is no significant difference in the quality or speed of left- or right-handed students' writing (Groff, 1963).

Teaching left-handed students. Teaching handwriting to left-handed students is not simply the reverse of teaching handwriting to right-handed students (Howell, 1978). Left-handed students have unique handwriting problems, and special adaptations of procedures for teaching right-handed students are necessary. In fact, many of the problems that left-handed students have can be made worse by using the procedures designed for right-handed writers (Harrison, 1981). The special adjustments are necessary to allow left-handed students to write legibly, fluently, and with less fatigue.

The basic difference between right- and left-handed writers is physical orientation. Right-handed students pull their hands and arms toward their bodies as they write, whereas left-handed writers must push away. As left-handed students write, they move their left hands across what they have just written, often covering it. Many children adopt a "hook" position to avoid covering and smudging what they have written.

Because of their different physical orientation, left-handed writers need to make three major types of adjustments: how they grip their pens or pencils, how they position the writing paper on their desks, and how they slant their writing (Howell, 1978).

Special adaptations are summarized in Figure 11.7.

Teaching Strategy

Handwriting is best taught in separate periods of direct instruction and teacher-supervised practice. As soon as skills are taught, they should be applied in real-life writing activities. Busywork assignments, such as copying lists of words and sentences from the chalkboard, lack educational significance. Moreover, students may develop poor handwriting habits or learn to form letters incorrectly if they practice without direct supervision. It is much more

FIGURE 11.7
Special Adaptations for Left-Handed Writers

1. Group left-handed students together for handwriting instruction.
2. Provide a left-handed person to serve as the model if you are not left-handed. Perhaps another teacher, parent, or an older student could come to the classroom to assist left-handed students.
3. Direct students to hold their pencils farther back from the point than right-handed students do.
4. Encourage students to practice handwriting skills at the chalkboard.
5. Have students tilt their papers to the right, rather than to the left, as right-handed students do.
6. Encourage students to slant their cursive letters slightly to the right, but allow them to form them vertically or even with a slight backhand slant.
7. Encourage students to eliminate excessive loops and flourishes from their writing to increase handwriting speed.

difficult to correct bad habits and errors in letter formation than to teach handwriting correctly in the first place.

Handwriting instruction and practice periods should be brief; 15- to 20-minute periods of instruction several times a week are more effective than a single lengthy period weekly or monthly. Regular periods of handwriting instruction are necessary when teaching the manuscript form in kindergarten and first grade and the cursive form in second or third grade.

The strategy that follows can be adapted to teach the manuscript and cursive handwriting forms. The adaptation is multisensory, with visual, auditory, and kinesthetic components, and is based on research in the field of handwriting (Askov & Greff, 1975; Furner, 1969; Hirsch & Niedermeyer, 1973). The five steps of the strategy follow.

1. The teacher demonstrates a specific handwriting skill while students observe. During the demonstration, the teacher describes the steps involved in executing it.
2. Students describe the skill and the steps for executing it as the teacher or a classmate demonstrates the skill again.
3. The teacher reviews the specific handwriting skill, summarizing the steps involved in executing the skill.
4. Students practice the skill using pencils, pens, or other writing instruments. As they practice the skill, students softly repeat the steps involved in executing it, and the teacher circulates, providing assistance as needed.
5. Students apply the skill they have learned in their writing. To check that they have learned the specific skill, students can review their writing over a period of several days and mark examples of correct use.

An example of applying this strategy in teaching manuscript letter formation is shown in Figure 11.8.

The Teacher's Role

As in most language arts activities, the teacher plays a crucial role in handwriting instruction. The teacher *teaches* the handwriting skill and then *supervises* as students practice it. Research has shown the importance of the teacher's active involvement in handwriting instruction and practice.

One aspect of the teacher's role is particularly interesting. To save time, teachers often print or write handwriting samples in advance on practice sheets. Then they distribute the sheets and ask students to practice a handwriting skill by copying the model they have written. Researchers have found, however, that *moving* models, that is observing the teacher write the handwriting sample, are of far greater value than copying models that have already been written (Wright & Wright, 1980). Moving models are possible when the teacher circulates around the classroom, stopping to demonstrate a skill for one student and moving to assist another.

E. TEACHING GRAMMAR

The traditional way to teach grammar is to use language arts textbooks. Students read rules and definitions, copy words and sentences, and mark them to apply the concepts presented in the text. This type of activity often seems meaningless to students. Instead, the teacher should use literature and the students' own writing; the study of words and their arrangement into sentences allows students to manipulate language (Cullinan, Jaggar, & Strickland, 1974; Tompkins & McGee, 1983).

Teachers have two ways to determine which grammatical concepts they will teach: they can identify the concepts they are supposed to teach from a list in a language arts textbook, or they can identify concepts they need to teach by assessing students' writing and noting what types of grammar and usage errors they are making. The concepts can be taught to the whole class or to small groups of students, but they should be taught only to students who don't already know them—it is a waste of time to teach something to a student who already

FIGURE 11.8
Using the Teaching Strategy to Teach Letter Formation

---

1. Initiating

Demonstrate the formation of a single letter or family of letters (e.g., the manuscript circle letters—*O, o, C, c, a, e, Q*) on the chalkboard while explaining how the letter is formed.

2. Structuring and Conceptualizing

Have students describe how the letter is formed while you or a student forms the letter on the chalkboard. At first you may need to ask questions to direct students' descriptions. Possible questions include:

> How many strokes are used in making the letter?
> Which stroke comes first?
> Where do you begin the stroke?
> In which direction do you go?
> What size will the letter be?
> Where does the stroke stop?
> Which stroke comes next?
> Students will quickly learn the appropriate terminology such as *baseline, left-right, slant line, counterclockwise,* and so on to describe how the letters are formed.

3. Summarizing

Review the formation of the letter or letter family with students while demonstrating how to form the letter on the chalkboard.

4. Generalizing

Have the students print the letter at the chalkboard, in sand, and with a variety of other materials such as clay, shaving cream, fingerpaint, pudding, and pipecleaners. As students form the letter, they should softly describe the formation process to themselves.
> Have students practice writing the letter on paper with the accompanying verbal descriptions.
> Circulate among students providing assistance and encouragement.
> Demonstrate and describe the correct formation of the letter as the students observe.

5. Applying

After practicing the letter or family of letters, have students apply what they have learned in authentic writing activities. This is the crucial step!

---

knows it. Atwell (1987) suggests using "mini-lessons" that are brief, to the point, and meaningful because of their immediate connections to reading and writing.

Teaching Strategy

The following six-step strategy for mini-lessons can be used for teaching traditional, structural, or transformational grammar concepts to small groups of students or to the whole class. (Steps 4, 5, and 6 are on p. 331.) You will notice that no worksheets are recommended; instead, plan to use excerpts from books students are reading or from students' own writing.

1. Introduce the concept, using words and sentences from children's literature or students' writing.
2. Provide additional information about the grammatical concept and more examples from children's literature or students' writing.
3. Provide activities to help students establish relationships between the information presented in the first and second steps. Five activities to use in this strategy are word hunts, concept books, sentence slotting, sentence expansion, and moving language around.

Word hunts. Students can identify words representing one part of speech or each of the eight parts of speech from books they are reading or from their own writing. A group of fifth graders identified words representing each part of speech from Van Allsburg's *The Polar Express* (1985):

> *nouns:* train, children, Santa Claus, elves, pajamas, roller coaster, conductor, sleigh, hug, clock, Sarah

pronouns: we, they, he, it, us, you, his, I, me
verbs: filled, ate, flickered, raced, were, cheered, marched, asked, pranced, stood, shouted
adjectives: melted, white-tailed, quiet, no, first, magical, cold, dark, polar, Santa's
adverbs: soon, faster, wildly, apart, closer, alone
prepositions: in, through, over, with, of, in front of, behind, at, for, across, into
conjunctions: and, but
interjections: oh, well, now

Similarly, students can hunt for parts of sentences or sentence types in books of children's literature.

F. LEARNING GRAMMAR THROUGH LITERATURE
Concept Books

Students can examine concept books that focus on one part of speech or another grammatical concept. For example, Barrett describes the essential characteristics of a variety of animals in *A Snake Is Totally Tail* (1983), and most of the descriptions include an adverb. After students read the book and identify the adverbs, they can write their own sentences, following the same pattern, and illustrate the sentences on posters, mobiles, a mural, or in a class book. Useful books for teaching traditional grammar concepts are listed in Figure 11.9.

Sentence Slotting

Students can experiment with words and phrases to see how they function in sentences by filling in sentences that have slots, or blanks. Sentence slotting teaches students about sev-

FIGURE 11.9
Books that Illustrate Traditional Grammar Concepts

Nouns	Heller, R. (1987). *A cache of jewels and other collective nouns.* New York: Grosset & Dunlap.
	Hoban, T. (1981). *More than one.* New York: Greenwillow.
	Terban, M. (1986). *Your foot's on my feet! and other tricky nouns.* New York: Clarion.
	Wildsmith, B. (1968). *Fishes.* New York: Franklin Watts.
Verbs	Beller, J. (1984). *A-B-Cing: An action alphabet.* New York: Crown.
	Burningham, J. (1986). *Cluck baa, jangle twang, slam bang, skip trip, sniff shout, wobble pop.* New York: Viking.
	Heller, R. (1988). *Kites sail high: A book about verbs.* New York: Grosset & Dunlap.
	Hoban, T. (1975). *Dig, drill, dump, fill.* New York: Greenwillow.
	McMillan, B. (1984). *Kitten can . . . A concept book.* New York: Lothrop.
	Maestro, B., & Maestro, G. (1985). *Camping out.* New York: Crown.
	Neumeier, M., & Glasser, B. (1985). *Action alphabet.* New York: Greenwillow.
	Shiefman, V. (1981). *M is for move.* New York: Dutton.
	Terban, M. (1984). *I think I thought and other tricky verbs.* New York: Clarion.
Adjectives	Boynton, S. (1983). *A is for angry: An animal and adjective alphabet.* New York: Workman.
	Duke, K. (1983). *Guinea pig ABC.* New York: Dutton.
	Hoban, T. (1981). *A children's zoo.* New York: Greenwillow.
	Maestro, B., & Maestro, G. (1979). *On the go: A book of adjectives.* New York: Crown.
	McMillan, B. (1989). *Super, super, superwords.* New York: Lothrop.
Adverbs	Barrett, J. (1983). *A snake is totally tail.* New York: Atheneum.
Prepositions	Bancheck, L. (1978). *Snake in, snake out.* New York: Crowell.
	Berenstain, S., & Berenstain, J. (1968). *Inside, outside, upside, down.* New York: Random House.
	Berenstain, S., & Berenstain, J. (1971). *Bears in the night.* New York: Random House.
	Hoban, T. (1973). *Over, under, and through and other spatial concepts.* New York: Macmillan.

eral different grammatical concepts. They can first experiment with parts of speech using a sentence like this:

The snake slithered _____ the rock.

> over
> around
> under
> to

Students can brainstorm a number of words to fill in the slot, all of which will be prepositions; adjectives, nouns, verbs, and adverbs will not make sense. This activity can be repeated to introduce or review any part of speech.

Sentence slotting also demonstrates to students that parts of speech can substitute for each other. In the following sentence, common and proper nouns as well as pronouns can be used in the slot:

_____ asked his secretary to get him a cup of coffee.

> The man
> Mr. Jones
> He

A similar sentence-slotting example demonstrates how phrases can function as an adverb:

The dog growled _____.

> ferociously
> with his teeth bared
> daring us to reach for his bone

In this example, the adverb *ferociously* can be used in the slot, as well as prepositional and participial phrases. Sentences with an adjective slot can be used to demonstrate that phrases function as adjectives. The goal of this activity is to demonstrate the function of words in sentences. Many sentence-slotting activities, such as the last example, also illustrate that sentences become more specific with the addition of a word or phrase. Through these activities, students experiment with the grammatical options they have been learning. Remember, however, that the purpose of these activities is to experiment with language; they should be done with small groups of students or the whole class, not as individual worksheets.

Sentence Expansion

Students can expand simple, or kernel, sentences, such as *A frog leaps* or *The car raced,* by adding modifiers. The words and phrases with which they expand the basic sentence can add qualities and attributes, details, and comparisons. The "5 Ws plus one" help students focus on expanding particular aspects of the sentence; for example:

Basic sentence	A frog leaps.
What kind?	green, speckled
How?	high into the air
Where?	from a half-submerged log and lands in the water with a splash
Why?	to avoid the noisy boys playing nearby
Expanded sentence	To avoid the noisy boys playing nearby, *a green, speckled frog leaps* high into the air from a half-submerged log and lands in the water with a splash.

Depending on what questions one asks and the answers students give, many other expanded sentences are possible from the same basic sentence. Students enjoy working in small groups to expand a basic sentence so they can compare their expanded versions with the other groups. Instead of the "5 Ws plus one" questions to expand sentences, the teacher can ask older students to supply a specific part of speech or modifier at each step of expansion.

The students or the teacher can create basic sentences for expansion or take them from children's literature. Very few basic sentences appear in stories, but one can identify and use the basic sentence within an expanded sentence. Students enjoy comparing their expanded versions of the basic sentence with the author's. When students are familiar with the story the sentence was taken from, they can try to approximate the author's meaning. Even so, it is likely that they will go in a variety of directions, and because students' expanded sentences may vary greatly from the author's, they come to realize the power of modifiers to transform a sentence.

Moving Language Around

Hudson (1980) suggests "moving language around" to help students learn about the structure of English and how to manipulate language. Students begin with a sentence and then apply four operations to it: they add, delete, substitute, and rearrange. With the sentence "Children play games," these manipulations are possible:

Add	Children play games at home.
	Children like to play games.
Delete	Children play.
Substitute	Adults play games.
	Children like games.
	Children play Nintendo.
Rearrangement	Games are played by children.
	Games play children.

The last sentence is nonsensical, but thought-provoking, nonetheless.

These activities help students learn more about the relationship between changes in form and changes in meaning. After practicing the concepts with these activities, the teacher completes the final steps of the strategy:

4. Review the major points related to the grammatical concept. Students can freewrite about the concept to summarize and clarify their thinking or make notes in their learning logs.
5. Ask students to locate examples of the concept in books they are reading or in their writing as a comprehension check. They should also share the examples they locate with classmates.
6. Students apply the newly learned grammatical concept in their writing. In writing groups, students can focus on how the writer used the grammatical concept. They can compliment the writer for using the concept or make suggestions as to how the writer can revise the writing to incorporate the concept. As teachers grade students' writing, they can award points to students who have used the grammatical concept in their writing.

This teaching strategy can be used to teach any grammatical concept. A language arts textbook can supplement the steps, but it is not necessary.

G. LEARNING GRAMMAR THROUGH WRITING

Because children's knowledge of grammar and usage depends on the language spoken in their homes and neighborhoods, some primary- and middle-grade students do not recognize a difference between *me and him* and *he and I*. When the error is brought to their attention, they do not understand, because semantically—at a meaning level—the two versions are identical. Moreover, *me and him* sounds "right" to these students because they hear this construction at home. When other corrections are pointed out to middle- and upper-grade students, they repeat the correct form, shake their heads, and say that it doesn't sound right. *Real* sounds better to some than *really* because it is more familiar. An explanation that adverbs rather than adjectives modify adjectives is not useful either, even if students have had traditional grammar instruction. Correction of nonstandard English errors is perceived as a repudiation of the language spoken in children's homes rather than an explanation that written language requires a more formal language register or dialect. Jaggar (1980) recommends that teachers allow for language differences, acknowledging that everyone speaks a dialect and one is not better or more correct than another.

A better way to deal with grammar and usage errors is to use a problem-solving approach during the editing stage of the writing process. Locating and correcting errors in students' writing is not as threatening as correcting their talk, because it is not as personal. Also, students can more easily accept that "book language" is a different kind of English. During editing, students are error-hunting, trying to make their papers "optimally readable" (Smith, 1982). They recognize that it is a courtesy to readers to make their papers as correct as possible. Through revising and editing, classmates note errors and correct each other and teachers point out other errors. Sometimes teachers explain the correction (e.g., the past tense of bring is *brought,* not *brung*), and at other times they simply mark the correction, saying that "we usually write it this way." Some errors should be ignored, especially young children's errors; correcting too many errors only teaches students that their language is inferior or inadequate. Guidelines for correcting students' grammar and usage errors are summarized in Figure 11.10.

The goal in dealing with nonstandard English speakers is not to replace their dialects, but to add standard English to students' language options.

H. THE MECHANICS OF WRITING

Hodges (1991) emphasizes the need for writers to be familiar with graphic features, such as punctuation, segmentation, and capitalization: "Punctuation sets apart syntactic units, and provides intonational cues and semantic information. Segmentation (the spaces between words in print) identifies word boundaries. In conjunction with periods, capital letters have both semantic and syntactic uses in indicating proper names and sentence boundaries" (p. 779).

Punctuation

Punctuation is important because it clarifies meaning. During oral interchanges listeners hear signals—pauses, speech stops, rising and falling voice tones—that help them comprehend meaning. Writers replace these vocal signals with punctuation. The early activities in which children dictate short stories or sentences to place under pictures provide readiness for and instruction in punctuation.

Studies show that punctuation—particularly with commas and periods—is frequently a problem for elementary-age children (Hazlett, 1972; Porter, 1974). The punctuation usually taught in the elementary grades is listed in Table 11.1.

FIGURE 11.10
Guidelines for Correcting Students' Grammar and Usage Errors in Compositions

HOW TO DEAL WITH STUDENTS' GRAMMAR AND USAGE ERRORS

- Use a problem-solving approach to correct grammar and usage errors.
- Correct errors during the editing stage of the writing process.
- Consider the function, audience, and form of the composition when determining whether to correct errors or which errors to correct.
- Let students know that correcting grammatical and usage errors is a courtesy to readers.
- Keep explanations for corrections brief.
- Sometimes, simply make the change and say that in writing it is done this way.
- Don't ask students if the correction makes the writing "sound better."
- Use sentence-slotting and sentence-combining activities to rid the composition of lackluster and repetitious words and short, choppy sentences.
- Ignore some errors, especially young children's.
- Respect the language of children's home and community, and introduce standard written English as "book language."

TABLE 11.1
Punctuation Taught in Elementary Grades

PUNCTUATION RULE	EXAMPLE
1. A period is used at the end of a sentence.	1. We went to the zoo.
2. A period is used after numbers on a list.	2. 1. Show and Tell 2. Reading
3. A period is used after abbreviations.	3. Sun. Mon. Tues. Mr. Mrs.
4. A question mark is used after a sentence that asks a question.	4. What was the name of Billy's dog?
5. A comma is placed between the day of the month and the year.	5. Today is October 1, 1980.
6. A comma is used between the names of a city and a state.	6. We live in Ithaca, New York.
7. A comma is used after the salutation in a letter.	7. Dear Sandy,
8. A comma is used after the closing of a letter.	8. Your friend, Jimmy
9. Commas divide items in a list.	9. Susan brought an acorn, a colored maple leaf, and an ear of Indian corn.
10. A comma is used before a coordinating conjunction (upper elementary).	10. He wanted to eat the whole pie, but he knew he would be sick.
11. A comma is used to signal the subject of the sentence (upper elementary).	11. Even though the day was hot, we all decided to go on a picnic.
12. A comma is used when a slight interruption offers additional information (upper elementary).	12. Jim Black, our basketball coach, is a very nice man.
13. A comma is used between two equal adjectives that modify the noun (upper elementary).	13. That swimmer is a strong, healthy athlete.
14. An exclamation mark follows a statement of excitement.	14. Help! Help! Jimmy is chasing me with a snake!
15. An apostrophe shows that letters have been omitted in a contraction.	15. I will = I'll
16. An apostrophe is used to show possession.	16. This is Judy's basketball.

Capitalization

Capitalization is another signal that clarifies meaning. Writers signal the beginning of a sentence with a capital letter and the end of a sentence with a period, question mark, or exclamation mark. Writers also signal important titles and names by capitalization. If a writer capitalizes *Northeast,* he or she is referring to a specific section of the country; if the writer does not capitalize *northeast,* the reference is to a direction.

Most children seem to have fewer problems applying capitalization rules than applying punctuation rules. The National Assessment of Educational Progress concluded: "Capitalization errors tended to appear less frequently in the 9-year-old papers than most of the other kinds of errors" (Hazlett, 1972, p. 12). The National Assessment found that most high-quality papers were free of capitalization errors; this was also true of middle-quality papers. The low-quality papers were, however, inconsistent; the first word in a sentence was often left uncapitalized, and many common nouns, such as *deer* and *tree,* were capitalized. The judges concluded that children who wrote the low-quality papers had some idea of when to use capitals and when not to, but their ideas were incomplete. It thus appears that most children learn about and apply appropriate capitalization in their writing, while a few will require more concentrated assistance.

Introduce children to capitalization in their early, dictated stories. A teacher who writes a sentence on the board or chart can point out the capital letter at the beginning of each sentence. When writing names of people, cities, states, or holidays teachers can again indicate the importance of the capital letter. Capitalization rules usually taught in the elementary grades are listed in Table 11.2.

Teaching Strategy

Both punctuation and capitalization clarify written communication. Children need to understand why mechanical skills are necessary, but they must also be aware that writing is primarily concerned with the development of content and ideas. In this context, punctuation and capitalization are very important during the editing process.

How can you maintain balance without overemphasizing one aspect of writing to the detriment of the other? Kean and Personke (1976) offer three general guidelines for instruction in mechanics.

1. Several of the mechanics of written language are learned as children write, read, and observe, making formal classroom presentations unnecessary in many cases. Students who did not naturally learn them may require individual help.
2. Individual variation in readiness makes it likely that learning will be most efficient when instruction is conducted among small groups of children who are at similar stages of readiness. [This means small-group instruction of children who demonstrate similar needs, rather than whole-class instruction.]
3. Instruction in mechanics needs to begin and culminate in a real writing situation; if isolated practice is necessary, it should be in the intermediate learning stage.

If you follow these guidelines, you will call the children's attention to various punctuation and capitalization items as they encounter them in reading or in dictating charts and

TABLE 11.2
Capitalization Taught in Elementary Grades

CAPITALIZATION RULE	EXAMPLE
1. Capitalize the first word in a sentence.	1. The first grade is planning a puppet show.
2. Capitalize the first and last names of people.	2. Sandy Smith
3. Capitalize the pronoun "I".	3. I do not think I will go.
4. Capitalize the name of a street.	4. Our school is on Southwest Parkway.
5. Capitalize the name of the city and state.	5. We live in San Francisco, California.
6. Capitalize the names of months, days, holidays.	6. Today is Monday, June 1. Christmas Hanukkah
7. Capitalize the first word and other important words in titles.	7. We are reading A Snowy Day.
8. Capitalize a title such as Mr., Mrs., Miss, or Ms.	8. Our teacher is Mrs. Chandler.
9. Capitalize the greeting in a letter.	9. Dear Martin,
10. Capitalize the first word in the closing of a letter.	10. Your friend,
11. Capitalize the titles of persons (upper elementary).	11. Doctor Erickson General Washington
12. Capitalize all cities, states, countries, continents, and oceans (upper elementary).	12. United States North America Pacific Ocean
13. Capitalize proper adjectives (upper elementary).	13. French
14. Capitalize the names of organizations (upper elementary).	14. Girl Scouts Boy Scouts
15. Capitalize the names of sections of the country but not directions (upper elementary).	15. The Northeast has many large cities. Lake Superior is northeast of Minneapolis.
16. Capitalize words referring to the Bible and the Deity (upper elementary).	16. The Bible God

stories. This provides readiness for a skill they will need in writing and may enable some children to apply the skill accurately in their own writing.

I. CLASSROOM ACTIVITIES*

Building Sentence Patterns	ACTIVITY 11.1

1. To develop an understanding of sentence form
2. To identify words and types of words that fit a specific pattern in a sentence

Purpose

Examples of model sentences.

Materials

Lower elementary (sentences may be read aloud to children who cannot read)

Grade level

1. Show students sentences using the cloze technique that follows. Have students suggest words that might fit the position. In each case, talk about the types of appropriate words. For example:

Procedures

Julie _____.
| ran | jumped | laughed |
| hopped | sang | skipped |

The _____ jumped.
| girl | boy | cat | cricket | dog |
| rabbit | lion | man | woman | |

The _____ clown laughed.
| funny | clumsy | small | fat | skinny |
| tall | tiny | silly | red | |

Suzie walked _____ down the street.
| slowly | rapidly | hurriedly |
| clumsily | happily | quietly |

2. These sentences can be finished with a pantomime activity; for example, a child chooses an action word to complete a sentence and pantomimes the action so the rest of the group can identify the action and complete the sentence.

Tic-Tac-Toe	ACTIVITY 11.2

1. To strengthen spelling skills
2. To write spelling words during an enjoyable game activity

Purpose

Lists of spelling words; tic-tac-toe game boards drawn on cardboard or on the chalkboard.

Materials

All grades

Grade level

1. Several procedures may be used for spelling reinforcement with a tic-tac-toe format. Some possibilities include the following:
   a. Divide the spelling group into two teams. Pronounce a spelling word for the first person on one team. Have the person write the word. If she writes the word correctly, the team member places an *x* or an *o* on the tic-tac-toe board. Next, pronounce a word for the first person on the opposing team. Continue pronouncing words to members of each team until a team has won horizontally, diagonally, or vertically.

Procedures

---

*Adapted from D. E. Norton & S. Norton, *Language Arts Activities for Children*, 3rd ed. (Englewood Cliffs, NJ: Merrill/Prentice Hall, 1993), pp. 222, 231, 236. By permission of the authors and Prentice Hall.

b. Divide the spelling group into two teams. Pronounce the spelling word for team one. Have each person on the team write the word. If all team members write the word correctly, the team places an *x* or *o* on the tic-tac-toe board. (This approach allows every team member to participate in the spelling activity. However, team members should be matched according to spelling ability.)

c. Divide the spelling group into two teams or divide the spelling groups into two individual players per game. Place spelling words on individual cards. Shuffle the spelling-word cards and place them face down on a tic-tac-toe board. The first team chooses a square, the caller pronounces the word, and the first team member or the whole team writes the word. If the word is spelled correctly, the team places its *x* or *o* on the appropriate square. If the team cannot spell the word correctly, the second team or individual can try to spell the word. Continue playing until a team or individual wins the game.

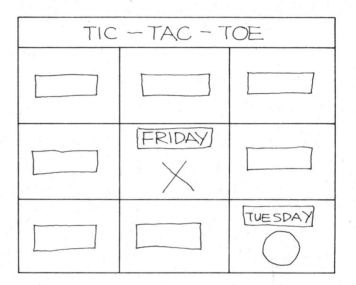

ACTIVITY 11.3   **Personal Learning Centers for The Writer's Tools**

Purpose

1. To develop a useful personal learning center for spelling, handwriting, punctuation, capitalization, and letter writing
2. To reinforce spelling, handwriting, punctuation, capitalization, and letter-writing skills

Materials

Cardboard box (about the size of a desk top) for each child; lists of spelling words; manuscript or cursive writing forms; punctuation chart; capitalization chart; letter-writing forms.

Grade level

All grades

Procedures

1. Provide directions so each student can make his or her personal learning center. Cut the bottom, top, and front out of a cardboard box; this leaves the left side, back, and right side:

BACK

LEFT   RIGHT

2. Tape large pockets onto the inside of the left, back, and right sides of the cardboard frame. (Construction paper or used file folders can be taped on three sides to form these pockets.)

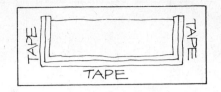

3. Next, discuss the kinds of information that would be helpful to the students while they write a story, a content area assignment, or a letter. (This information can change and should be designed according to the needs of the individual children.) The following is suggestive of the types of information many students find valuable:

   a. Alphabetical lists of basic spelling words. Words from the spelling series used by the school and Dolch or Thorndike lists of utilitarian words can be compiled and placed in a pocket marked "spelling." This basic list can be supplemented with words each child uses frequently in writing.

Words Often Confused in Writing

affect	to influence
effect	outcome
capital	city where government is located; a capital letter (A)
capitol	building where the legislature meets
desert	dry, barren region
dessert	a sweet served at the end of a meal
hear	to listen to
here	to this place
lose	to misplace
loose	not fastened
principal	something of importance; the administrator of a school
principle	a truth or belief
stationary	unmoving
stationery	paper used for writing letters
there	in that place
their	belonging to them
they're	contraction of "they are"
to	in the direction of
too	also
two	the number 2
weather	condition of the atmosphere
whether	choice or alternative

---

   c. A copy of the appropriate manuscript or cursive alphabet. Lower elementary students usually use a manuscript style of writing, while middle and upper elementary students usually use cursive writing.

   d. A punctuation chart. The items included will again depend on the student's needs. Such a chart might include the following information:

Punctuation Chart

Punctuation Period .	Example
1. Use periods at the end of sentences.	This is Monday morning.
2. Use periods after abbreviations.	U.S.A., Fri., Aug., Mr.
3. Use periods after numbers in a list.	1. Seeds 2. Soil

continued

Question Mark ?

1. Use a question mark after a sentence that asks a question. — When are you going to the movie?

Exclamation Mark !

1. Use an exclamation mark after a statement of excitement. — Great! We'll win!

Comma ,

1. Use a comma to separate a series of three or more items. — We had hot dogs, corn, milk, and cake for lunch.
2. Use a comma between the name of a city and state. — We visited San Francisco, California.
3. Use a comma between the month and the year. — Our Independence Day was July 4, 1776.
4. Use a comma after the salutation of a letter. — Dear Mom,
5. Use a comma after the closing of a letter. — Sincerely,
6. Use a comma before a coordinating conjunction that separates two independent clauses. — She wanted to buy a new coat, but she couldn't find one she liked.

Apostrophe '

1. Use an apostrophe to show possession of a singular noun. — This is Toby's bicycle.
2. Use an apostrophe to show possession of a plural noun. — We saw the boys' basketball team play this afternoon.
3. Use an apostrophe to show that letters have been left out in a contraction. — You're, can't, isn't, I'll

e. A sample of the form and punctuation for a letter. For example:

```
                              Name of Street _____
                              City, State, Zip _____
                              Month, Date, Year _____

Greeting, _____

                        Message
_____
_____
_____
_____

                              Closing, _____
                              Signature _____
```

f. Guidelines for capitalization. For example:

Use Capital Letters

1. Sentences begin with capital letters. — The dog was lost for one week.
2. Names begin with capital letters. — George Washington
3. Names of cities, states, countries, and rivers begin with capital letters. — Seattle, New Jersey, Canada, Mississippi

continued

4. Names of days, months, and   Monday, January, Memorial Day
   holidays begin with capital letters.
5. Titles of books begin with capital letters.   Across Five Aprils
6. Titles such as Miss and Mr. begin   Miss, Mr., Mrs., Ms., Dr.
   with capital letters.
7. Greeting of a letter begins with   Dear Jackie,
   a capital letter.
8. The closing of a letter begins with   Your friend,
   a capital letter.   Sincerely,

4. Any other useful equipment can be included in the personal learning center such as the child's personal writing folder, proofreading suggestions, or a dictionary and reference guide.
5. When the personal writing center is complete, the students can fold it flat for easy storage. They can use the center whenever they need it.

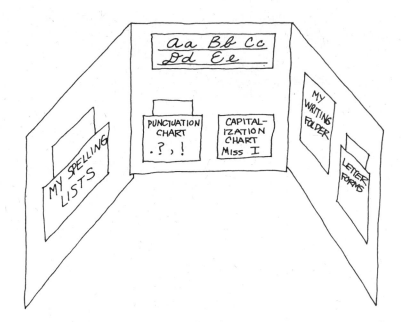

J. PROBLEM-SOLVING EXPERIENCES INVOLVING LANGUAGE ARTS SKILLS*

Experience: What Major Influences Changed the English Language in the United States?

ACTIVITY 11.4

1. To investigate the development of the English language in the United States
2. To investigate the major influences for change in the English language in the United States
3. To understand that the English language is constantly changing

Purpose

Tapes of English speakers from England and the United States; references such as dictionaries that describe the history of American English; maps of the United States and Europe.

Materials

Upper elementary, middle school

Grade level

*Adapted from Norton & Norton, 1993, 219–221. By permission of the authors and Prentice Hall.

Procedures

1. Ask students if they believe that a person speaking English in England and a person speaking English in the United States would sound alike or if all their words would mean the same thing. This would be a good opportunity to play a tape of a speaker from England or to have a visitor from England talk to the students. Have the students listen for words that are used differently than in the United States and for differences in dialect.

   The following story was written by Jacki Thomas, a graduate student from Bristol, England. She is illustrating some differences between English and American usage:

   > Lavinia Prendergast was awoken one day by a telephone call. It was her mother-in-law phoning to ask if she could come to stay with her and her husband for a fortnight. "Gosh!" she thought when she put the phone down, "this flat is a mess, I'd better start tidying up!"
   >
   > But first she weighed herself on the scales—"Oh, that's good, still only 9 stone 3," she said with relief. Then she started rushing around to get the flat cleaned up.
   >
   > She thought she would do the curtains while she was doing the washing, but she couldn't get the tap to the washing machine on, so she started washing up . . . no washing-up liquid left! So she had to get dressed to nip down to the corner shop, and she threw her dressing gown on the bed. "It's gonna be one of those days!" she exclaimed. Even as she said it, she noticed the moths had got to the jumper her mother-in-law had knitted for her last Christmas, and she knew she'd lost the spare darning wool she had sent with it.
   >
   > Lavinia put the baby in the pram and put her purse in her handbag, when the phone went again. It was her friend, asking if she could come round for a chat and a cup of tea, but Lavinia thought she'd be too busy to stop for elevenses today.
   >
   > She wasn't long getting the washing-up liquid and started washing the dishes as soon as she got back—she dried up the cutlery and crockery but left the frying pan and saucepans to drain. She washed out a few smalls and hung them out on the line with her new plastic pegs. She vacuumed the carpets, tidied up the living room, mopped the floors in the toilet and kitchen, then laid the table for lunch.
   >
   > She just had time to get a couple of biscuits and get a glass of milk out of the fridge and was going to turn on the telly when she heard a cardoor slam outside the flat; she looked out and recognized her mother-in-law's estate car—she was just getting her case out of the boot.

fortnight	two weeks
flat	apartment
curtains	drapes
do the washing	do laundry
washing-up liquid	detergent
nip	hurry
corner shop	small all-purpose store
dressing gown	housecoat
jumper	pullover sweater
darning wool	repair yarn
pram	baby buggy where baby lies down
purse	billfold, wallet
handbag	purse
come round	come over
elevenses	cup of tea, or coffee and cookies
cutlery	silverware
crockery	dishes
smalls	underwear
pegs	clothespins
9 stone 3	141 pounds
tap	faucet
boot	trunk
estate car	station wagon
biscuits	cookies

2. Discuss—"We have learned that the English language was greatly influenced by people from other European countries when these people invaded England, came to live in England, or traded with the English." Since the English language spoken in England is somewhat different from the English language spoken in the United States, ask the students to suggest possible situations that might have influenced and changed the English language spoken in the United States.

3. Allow students to form groups to investigate a specific period of history and its influence on our language. Historically accurate fiction offers many examples of speech that is authentic for both time and place. Historical dictionaries are also useful. Some suggested study groupings include:

SKILLET

SPIDER

The Colonists brought English to America

Pioneer America added colorful language (e.g., to go on the warpath, to take to the woods)

European immigrants brought their language to America (e.g., a frying pan is called a *skillet* by some and a *spider* by others; a pail and faucet may be called a *bucket* and *spigot*)

Technology and new inventions add to language (e.g., television is new to this century; acronyms, like *radar,* are created from the first letters of words: *radio detecting and ranging*)

Slang expressions add color to language and change meanings of common words (e.g., a term like *turkey* does not necessarily refer to the bird served for Thanksgiving dinner)

Have the research groups present their findings aloud to the class, using the speech patterns of the period. Suggest creative methods for sharing the language of the periods such as an original play, or a scene from authentic literature.

4. One way to study the influence of a nationality or a period in history on the United States is to investigate cities, towns, and areas that have names signifying foreign, Native American, or historical influence. Have students locate names in the area, state, or nation that demonstrate the influence of a group or period in history. Among many other locations, Native American place names show up in Menomonie and Winnebago, Wisconsin; Cheyenne and Ten Sleep, Wyoming; Ketchikan, Alaska; and Pontiac, Michigan. Spanish influence appears in El Cajon and Escondido, California, and La Junta, Colorado. German influence is felt in New Braunfels, Texas, and French influence in New Orleans and Lafayette, Louisiana, and in Ste. Anne de Beaupre, Quebec.

K. ASSESSMENT STRATEGY
Assessing Students' Progress in Spelling

Analyzing children's stage of spelling development. Teachers can analyze spelling errors in children's compositions by classifying the errors according to the five stages of spelling development. Knowing the stage of a child's spelling development will suggest an appropriate type of spelling instruction. Children who are not yet at the correct stage of spelling development (that is, who do not spell approximately 90 to 95 percent of words correctly) do not benefit from formal spelling instruction. Instead, early instruction may interfere with spelling development because children move from phonetic spelling to memorizing spelling words without learning any visual and morphological strategies. Spelling can be categorized by means of a chart, such as that in Table 11.3, to gauge the children's stage of spelling development and to anticipate upcoming changes in their spelling

TABLE 11.3
Categories of Spelling Errors Made by Correct Stage Spellers
SOURCE: Hitchcock, 1989, pp. 100–101

CATEGORY	DESCRIPTION	SAMPLE
Phonetic	Students spell the word as it sounds.	*doter* for *daughter*
Omission of pronounced letter	Students omit a letter that is pronounced.	*aross* for *across*
Vowel pattern rule	Students use wrong vowel digraph or misuse silent *e*.	*speach* for *speech*
Reversal of a letter	Students reverse letters in words.	*croner* for *corner*
Vowel substitution	Students substitute one vowel for another, use incorrect vowel to represent the schwa sound, or substitute a vowel for a consonant.	*jab* for *job* *anemals* for *animals* *firet* for *first*
Homonym	Students use wrong homonym for the meaning intended.	*peace* for *piece*
Pronunciation	Students shorten or lengthen words, substitute graphemes, or shorten suffixes.	*spose* for *suppose*
Insertion of a letter	Students insert a letter that is not needed.	*ulgly* for *ugly*
Semiphonetic	Students use several letters chosen phonetically to represent a word.	*peda* for *party*
Double consonants	Students double a consonant when it is not needed or fail to double a consonant when needed.	*untill* for *until* *peper* for *pepper*
Consonant substitution	Students substitute one consonant for another or substitute a consonant for a vowel.	*swin* for *swim* *fell* for *feel*
Compounding	Students separate compound words or combine words that are not compound words.	*a way* for *away* *alot* for *a lot*
Plurals, possessives, and contractions	Students omit an apostrophe in possessives and contractions and add an apostrophe in plurals.	*moms* for *mom's* *make's* for *makes* *wont* for *won't*
Affixes	Students use the wrong prefix or suffix.	*sking* for *skiing* *dissappeared* for *disappeared*
Omission of a silent letter	Students omit silent letters that are not heard in the pronunciation of the word.	*bome* for *bomb*

strategies. To do this, write the stages of spelling development across the top of the chart, and list each word in the child's composition under one of the categories, ignoring proper nouns, capitalization errors, and poorly formed (or reversed) letters.

Grades on weekly spelling tests are the traditional measure of progress in spelling. Both contract spelling and the textbook approach provide teachers with a convenient way to assess students, based on the number of words they spell correctly on weekly tests. This method of assessing student progress is somewhat deceptive, however, because the goal of spelling instruction is not simply to spell words correctly on weekly tests but to use the words, correctly spelled, in writing. Grades on weekly spelling tests are meaningless unless students can use the words in their writing. Samples of student writing should be collected periodically to determine whether words that were spelled correctly on tests are being spelled correctly in writing assignments. If students are not applying in their writing what they have learned through the weekly spelling instruction, they may not have learned to spell the words after all. Students sometimes memorize the words or the spelling pattern for the tests without really learning to spell the words.

When students perform poorly on spelling tests, consider whether faulty pronunciation or poor handwriting is to blame. Ask students to pronounce words they habitually misspell to see if pronunciation or dialect differences may be contributing to spelling problems. Students need to recognize when pronunciation does not always predict spelling. In some parts of the U.S., people pronounce the words *pin* and *pen* as though they were spelled with the same vowel. Sometimes we pronounce *better* as though it were spelled *bedder* and *going* as though it were spelled *goin'*. Ask students to spell orally the words they spell incorrectly in their writing to see whether handwriting difficulties are contributing to spelling problems. Sometimes a lesson on how to connect two cursive letters (e.g., *br*) or a reminder about the importance of legible handwriting will solve the problem.

In addition to the grades on weekly spelling tests, it is essential that teachers keep anecdotal information and samples of children's writing to monitor their overall progress in learning to spell. Teachers need to examine error patterns and spelling strategies in these samples. Checking to see if students have spelled their spelling words correctly in writing samples provides one type of information, and examining writing samples for error patterns and spelling strategies provides an additional type of information. Fewer misspellings do not necessarily indicate progress, because to learn to spell, students must experiment with spellings of unfamiliar words, which will result in errors from time to time. Students often misspell a word by misapplying a newly learned spelling pattern. The word *extension* is a good example. Fourth-grade students spell the word *extenshun*, then change their spelling to *extention* after they learn the suffix *-tion*. Although they are still misspelling the word, they have moved from using sound-symbol correspondences to using a spelling pattern— from a less sophisticated to a more sophisticated spelling strategy.

Students' behavior as they proofread and edit their compositions also provides evidence of progress in spelling. They should become increasingly able to spot misspelled words in their compositions and to locate the spelling of unknown words in a dictionary. It is easy for teachers to calculate the number of spelling errors students have identified in proofreading their compositions and to chart students' progress in learning to spot errors. Locating errors is the first step in proofreading; correcting the errors is the second step. It is fairly easy for students to correct the spelling of known words, but to correct unknown words, they must consider spelling options and predict possible spellings before they can locate the words in a dictionary. Teachers can also document students' growth in locating unfamiliar words in a dictionary by observing their behavior when they edit their compositions.

Teachers should collect writing samples to document children's spelling competence. Teachers can note primary-grade students' progression through the stages of invented spelling by analyzing writing samples against the checklist in Table 11.3 to determine a general stage of development. A sample checklist is presented in Figure 11.11. Teachers and students can use this checklist to analyze students' spelling errors and plan for instruction.

Assessing Students' Handwriting

The goal of handwriting instruction is for students to develop legible handwriting. To reach this goal, students must first understand what qualities or elements determine legibility and then analyze their own handwriting according to these elements.

Elements of legibility. The six elements of legible and fluent handwriting are letter formation, size and proportion, spacing, slant, alignment, and line quality (Barbe, Lucas, Wasylyk, Hackney, & Braun, 1984).

FIGURE 11.11
Assessing Students' Spelling Errors

SPELLING ERROR ANALYSIS

Name _____   Total words _____
Paper _____   Errors _____
Date _____   Percentage _____

List mispelled words according to category.

1. Phonetic
2. Omission of pronounced letter
3. Vowel pattern rule
4. Reversal of a letter
5. Vowel substitution
6. Homonym
7. Pronunciation
8. Insertion of a letter
9. Semiphonetic
10. Double consonants
11. Consonant substitution
12. Compounding
13. Plurals, possessives, and contractions
14. Affixes
15. Omission of a silent letter

Letter formation. Letters are formed with specific strokes. Letters in manuscript handwriting are composed of vertical, horizontal, and slanted lines plus circles or parts of circles. The letter *b,* for example, is composed of a vertical line and a circle, and *M* is composed of vertical and slanted lines. The cursive letters are composed of slanted lines, loops, and curved lines. The lowercase cursive letters *e* and *ℓ,* for instance, are composed of a slant stroke, a loop, and an undercurve stroke. An additional component in cursive handwriting is the connecting strokes used to join letters. Samples of both manuscript and cursive writing are shown in Figure 11.12.

Size and proportion. Through the elementary grades, students' handwriting becomes smaller, and the proportional size of upper- to lowercase letters increases. Uppercase manuscript letters are twice the size of lowercase letters. When second- and third-grade students first begin cursive handwriting, the proportional size of letters remains 2:1; later, the proportion of uppercase to lowercase cursive letters increases to 3:1 for middle- and upper-grade students. The three sizes are illustrated in Figure 11.13.

Spacing. Students must leave adequate space between letters in words and between words in sentences if their handwriting is to be read easily. Spacing between words in man-

FIGURE 11.12
Entries from Students' Copybooks from Galdone's *The Three Bears* (1972) and Sterne's *Tyrannosaurus Wrecks: A Book of Dinosaur Riddles* (1979)

Someone has been sleeping in my bed,

said Baby Bear,

in his biggest teeny-tiny voice,

"and she is still there!"

Jennifer, age 6

What kind of cookies do little dinosaurs like? Ani-mammal crackers.

Aaron, age 9

FIGURE 11.13
Size and Proportion of Elementary Students' Handwriting

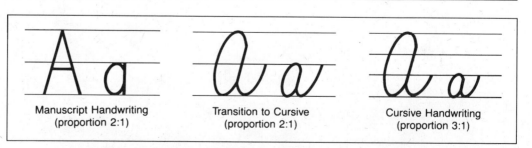

Manuscript Handwriting
(proportion 2:1)

Transition to Cursive
(proportion 2:1)

Cursive Handwriting
(proportion 3:1)

uscript handwriting should equal one lowercase letter *o*, and spacing between sentences should equal two lowercase *o's*. The most important aspect of spacing within words in cursive handwriting is consistency. To correctly space between words, the writer should make the beginning stroke of the new word directly below the end stroke of the preceding word. Spacing between sentences should equal one uppercase letter *O*, and spacing between paragraphs should equal two uppercase letter *O's*.

Slant.   Letters should be consistently parallel. Letters in manuscript handwriting are vertical, and in the cursive form, letters slant slightly to the right. To ensure the correct slant, right-handed students tilt their papers to the left, and left-handed students tilt their papers to the right.

Alignment.   For proper alignment in both manuscript and cursive handwriting, all letters are uniform in size and consistently touch the baseline.

Line quality.   Students should write at a consistent speed and hold their writing instruments correctly and in a relaxed manner to make steady, unwavering lines of even thickness.

Correct letter formation and spacing receive the major focus in handwriting instruction during the elementary grades. Although the other four elements usually receive less attention, they, too, are important in developing legible and fluent handwriting.

Diagnosing and correcting handwriting problems.   Students can refer to the characteristics of the six elements of legibility to diagnose their handwriting problems. Primary-grade students, for example, can check to see if they have formed a particular letter correctly, if the round parts of letters are joined neatly, or if slanted letters are joined in sharp points. Older students can examine a piece of handwriting to see if their letters are consistently parallel or if the letters touch the baseline consistently. A sample checklist for evaluating manuscript handwriting is shown in Figure 11.14. Checklists can also be developed for cursive handwriting. It is important to involve students in developing the checklists so they can appreciate the need to make their handwriting more legible.

Another reason students need to diagnose and correct their handwriting problems is because handwriting quality influences teacher evaluation and grading. Markham (1976) found that both student teachers and experienced classroom teachers consistently graded papers with better handwriting higher than papers with poor handwriting, regardless of the quality of the content. Students in the elementary grades are not too young to learn that poor quality or illegible handwriting may lead to lower grades.

Assessing Students' Knowledge About Grammar

The traditional way to assess knowledge about grammar is by giving students a written test that asks them to identify parts of speech or to write sentences that are simple,

---

FIGURE 11.14
A Checklist for Manuscript Handwriting

HANDWRITING CHECKLIST

Name _____

Writing Project _____

Date _____

_____ 1. Did I form my letters correctly?

    Did I start my line letters at the top?

    Did I start my circle letters at 1:00?

    Did I join the round parts of the letters neatly?

    Did I join the slanted strokes in sharp points?

_____ 2. Did my lines touch the midline or top line neatly?

_____ 3. Did I space evenly between letters?

_____ 4. Did I leave enough space between words?

_____ 5. Did I make my letters straight up and down?

_____ 6. Did I make all my letters sit on the baseline?

compound, or complex. As we discussed regarding spelling and handwriting, however, a better gauge of students' understanding of writers' tools is to observe how they use them in their writing.

Teachers can develop checklists of grammar and usage skills (such as Figure 11.15) to teach at a particular grade level or list errors they observe in students' writing. Then teachers observe students as they write and examine their compositions to note errors, plan and teach mini-lessons based on students' needs, note further errors and plan and teach other mini-lessons, and so on. As teachers identify grammar and usage problems, they should plan mini-lessons to call students' attention to the problems that make a bigger difference in writing (Pooley, 1974). For example, in the sentences *Mom leave me go outside* and *I fell off of my bike,* the use of *leave* for *let* is a more important problem than the redundant use of *of.*

Assessing Students' Use of Punctuation and Capitalization: The Mechanics of Writing

Many children are able to begin sentences with capital letters and end them with periods after a teacher has pointed out these mechanics during frequent language experience activities. Some children, however, require additional direct teaching of these skills before they can apply them consistently. When direct teaching is necessary, it should take place in

FIGURE 11.15
Using the Teaching Strategy

TEACHING MIDDLE-GRADE STUDENTS TO IDENTIFY SUBJECTS AND PREDICATES

1. **Introduce the concept.**

   Explain, using 10 sentences written on sentence strips, that a sentence is made up of a subject and a predicate. Choose sentences from *Sarah, Plain and Tall* (MacLachlan, 1985), which the class is reading as part of a unit on pioneers. Have students take turns highlighting the subject of each sentence with a yellow highlighter pen and the predicate with a blue highlighter pen.

2. **Provide additional information about the grammatical concept.**

   Review information presented earlier (that sentences are made up of a subject and a predicate) and reread the sentences on sentence strips. Then ask students to work in small groups to write a sentence about *Sarah, Plain and Tall* on a sentence strip. Have the groups present their sentences to the class and highlight the subject and predicate. Next, ask students to examine the subjects of the sentences to determine what goes into the subject and what goes into the predicate.

3. **Provide activities.**

   Have students work in small groups to write two sentences on sentence strips about pioneers. Next, students cut their sentences into two pieces, separating the subjects and the predicates. Then students can experiment with the sentence parts and combine the pieces to form both sensible and nonsense sentences.

4. **Review major points.**

   As a class, develop a bulletin board display to review that sentences are composed of subjects and predicates. Use some of the sentence pieces from the previous activity.

5. **Locate examples in literature.**

   Have students copy two sentences from informational books on pioneers available in the classroom and highlight the subject and the predicate. Then have students share their work in small groups.

6. **Apply in writing.**

   Students work on mobiles, charts, dioramas, displays, and other projects related to the pioneer unit. Students write at least five sentences to describe their projects and meet in writing groups to review the sentences and, specifically, to check that each sentence includes a subject and a predicate. Part of the assessment for the project will focus on whether their project descriptions are complete sentences with subjects and predicates.

groups, with children who show the same readiness or need for a new or reviewed skill. Table 11.4 shows one method for teaching the separation of words in series with a comma.

L. LANGUAGE ARTS SKILLS LESSON PLAN: RELATING MEANING AND SPELLING*

1. Descriptive Course Data

Teacher: _____   *Date:* _____

Grade level: 4th grade

Room number: _____

Unit: Written Communication (in Family Life and Business World; Social Studies context)

Lesson Topic: Relating Meaning and Spelling (Language Arts Skills)

2. Lesson Goals and Objectives

Instructional goals (general objectives).

1. To identify the relationship between spelling and meaning.

Specific (performance) objectives.

Cognitive.

1. With others, the student will discuss the idea that many words give clues to spelling.
2. When presented with examples, the student will use words in sentences and compare meanings so the similarities in spelling can be identified.

Affective.

1. The student may show interest in becoming a word detective as he or she looks for examples of word families that share similar meanings and spellings (e.g., *major* and *majority* or *culture* and *cultural*).
2. The student may share a word detective book with other members of the group.

Psychomotor.

1. Using a pen or pencil, the student will develop booklets of spelling word pairs (or families) that show a relationship between meaning and spelling.

TABLE 11.4

Steps in Instruction for "A comma separates words in series"

GUIDELINE	EXAMPLE
1. Call attention to the rule in reading or dictated stories.	1. Find sentences that contain words in series in reading. Point them out in language experience. Example: Oranges, grapefruit, and lemons grow in Florida.
2. Observe a mechanical need in an actual writing situation.	2. Students are writing series of words without using the appropriate punctuation.
3. Develop individual or small-group instruction designed to eliminate the problem.	3. Have the students read four or five sentences with words in series. Ask the students to inductively state the rule. Write new sentences on chalkboard without commas. Have the students put in the commas, using colored chalk. Reinforce the principle with games.
4. Assign a real writing task that requires application of the skill.	4. "Write a sentence telling us what you had for breakfast." "Write a sentence listing the members of your family."
5. Observe to see if the mechanical problem has been eliminated.	5. Observe future writing. Are the students using the skill? If not, provide further direct teaching.

*Adapted from D. E. Norton & S. Norton, *Language Arts Activities for Children,* 3rd ed. (Englewood Cliffs, NJ: Merrill/Prentice Hall, 1993), pp. 234–235. By permission of the authors and Prentice Hall.

3. Rationale

The concept of ways people communicate is prevalent in social studies content as evidenced by recommendations of the National Council for the Social Studies (NCSS) Task Force through topics of family life and the world of work. Curriculum materials indicate where the topic of communication has been included by local schools, districts, and state departments of education. Further, Carol Chomsky's work (1970) suggests that many spellings relate to semantic function in the language rather than to phonetic representation. Lexical spellings thus represent meaning and can lead the speller and reader directly to a word's meaning. The research suggests that instruction should emphasize regularities in meaning between related words, an approach that may be used not only for spelling but also for vocabulary development and reading.

4. Plan and Procedures

Introduction.   Discuss with children the fact that many words give clues to spelling, and if we understand the meanings of two similar words, we can improve spelling. Ask the children to pronounce and identify the relationships between *nature* and *natural*. Point out that even though the two words are pronounced differently, they are closely related in meaning. Ask the children to use the two words in sentences and have them compare the meanings to identify the similarities in spelling.

Modeling.   Show children how to study other words in the same way, such as *library* and *librarian.*

Guided (coached) practice.   Introduce other words, such as *govern* and *governor.* Follow the same procedure as described under "modeling." Then ask the children to become word detectives and have them study other words such as these:

gymnasium	gymnastics
photograph	photography
microscope	microscopic
history	historical

They can also look for their own examples of word families that share similar meanings and spellings.

Assignments.   With the children develop booklets of spelling-word pairs or families that show a relationship between meaning and spelling. Have them use their words in sentences and ask them to share their word detective books with other members of the class.

Closure.   Relate the lesson to what the children learned about the relationship between spelling and meaning, to the idea that many words give clues to spelling, and to the idea that if we understand the meanings of two similar words, we can improve spelling.

5. Materials Needed

Audiovisual.   None

Other.   Lists of pairs of words that demonstrate the relationship between spelling and meaning.

6. Assessment and Revision

Assessment of learning.   The teacher observes and makes anecdotal notes of the spelling skills demonstrated and the students' contracts to show which words they are interested in spelling correctly. The children staple their contracts inside their folders so the teacher can keep track of each student and note how they are keeping track of themselves. Sometimes, the children will confer with the teacher during scheduled conferences (three mornings a week).

Plan for revision.   As the teacher, I have been pleased at how well the students work at their spelling skills and how responsible they have become. They are learning spelling from each other and support each other as they learn. In addition to conferences with the students, I want to use classroom conferences when students want help on spelling, teach basic spelling skills in mini-lessons, and discuss further the relationship between spelling and word meaning.

SUMMARY

Concerning spelling, the alphabetic principle suggests a one-to-one correspondence between phonemes and graphemes, but English does not have this correspondence. English is a historic rather than a phonetic language, and events in the development of the language and borrowing of words from other languages explain many of the seeming inconsistencies. When young children begin to write, they

- Create invented spellings based on their knowledge of English orthography
- Move, according to research, through a sequence of five stages in learning to spell during elementary school
- May reach the fifth stage, correct spelling, in which they spell at least 90 percent of the words in their compositions correctly, an indication that they are ready for formal spelling instruction
- May choose their spelling words from the words they need to spell in their writing projects and for content area study (this approach is called contract spelling and is recommended)
- May be involved in the textbook approach to spelling, a formal program; students in a formal spelling program, however, should read widely, write daily, and connect their spelling words to a content area study.

Two forms of handwriting are taught in grades K–4—manuscript handwriting (the print form) and cursive writing (a connected flowing form). Young children

- Usually learn the manuscript form first and are introduced to cursive handwriting in second or third grade
- May show their lefthandedness and teachers can make adaptions for them
- Can focus on the elements of legible handwriting, which are letter formation, size, proportion, spacing, slant, alignment, and line quality
- Can apply their writing skills in genuine writing activities
- Can assess their own handwriting, especially through the use of checklists based on the elements of legibility.

Concerning grammar and the controversy that exists today about teaching the traditional type, the structural type, or the transformational type, teachers should see grammar as a writer's tool and teach it through children's literature or as part of the editing stage of the writing process.

Instruction in punctuation and capitalization fosters the understanding of language and grammar. Both capitalization and punctuation are signals that help readers understand written communication.

QUESTIONS AND ACTIVITIES FOR DISCUSSION

Spelling

1. Examine several spelling textbooks at the grade level you teach or expect to teach and evaluate them using the checklist in Figure 11.5. How well do the textbooks adhere to the research findings about how spelling should be taught?

2. Observe how spelling is taught in a classroom where the textbook approach is used and in another class in which contract spelling is used. Compare the two approaches. If possible, assist in teaching a lesson in each classroom.

3. Collect samples of a student's writing and analyze the spelling as shown in Table 11.3 and Figure 11.11.

4. Interview a fourth-grade student about spelling. Ask questions such as these:

   - Who do you know who is a good speller? Why is he/she a good speller?
   - Are you a good speller? Why? Why not?
   - What do you do when you do not know how to spell a word? What else do you do?
   - How would you help a classmate who did not know how to spell a word?

- Are some words harder for you to spell than other words? Which words?
- What rules about how to spell words have you learned?
- Do you think that "sound it out" is a good way to try to figure out the spelling of a word you do not know? Why or why not?
- Do you use a dictionary to look up the spelling of words you do not know how to spell?
- Do you have a list of words to learn to spell each week?
- How do you study these words?

5. Help students proofread their writing and identify possible misspelled words. Watch what strategies students use to identify and correct misspelled words.

6. Students ask many questions about the seeming inconsistencies of English words and their spellings. For example, first graders often ask why there are silent *e*'s. Consult *Answering Students' Questions About Words* (Tompkins & Yaden, 1986) to find answers to students' questions. Use the answers and activities suggested in the book to prepare and teach a spelling lesson to a small group of students.

Handwriting

7. Practice forming the manuscript and cursive letters shown in Figure 11.6 until your handwriting approximates the models. Practicing these handwriting forms will prepare you for working with elementary students. Be sure, though, to take note of the manuscript or cursive handwriting forms displayed in the classroom before beginning to work with students, because schools use several different handwriting programs. The programs are similar, but some students, especially younger children, are quick to point out when you are not forming a letter correctly!

8. Practice manuscript and cursive handwriting skills with a small group of middle- or upper-grade students using copybooks. Supply students with small notebooks and have them copy favorite poems, quotations, excerpts from stories they are reading, and other short pieces of writing. Meet with students weekly for several weeks as they work in their copybooks.

9. Practice manuscript handwriting skills with a small group of kindergartners or first graders using the "Let's Go on a Bear Hunt" activity in Appendix E.

Grammar

10. Examine your feelings about whether grammar should be taught in elementary schools. If you decide it should be, how should it be taught? Compare your opinions with the arguments you find for and against teaching grammar in Davis's "In Defense of Grammar" (1984) and Small's "Why I'll Never Teach Grammar Again" (1985) or in "Grammar Should Be Taught and Learned in Our Schools" (Goba & Brown, 1982).

11. Examine language arts textbooks to see how they present grammar. What percentage of the textbook pages is devoted to grammar instruction? What types of activities are included? Is grammar instruction tied to literature and writing activities?

12. Interview students about their knowledge of grammar and how they apply it in their writing. Use questions such as these:

    Do you study grammar in school?
    What kinds of grammar activities does your teacher assign?
    What have you learned about grammar?
    Do you think it's important to learn about grammar? Why or why not?
    Do authors need to know about grammar? Why or why not?
    Do you use what you know about grammar when you write? Why or why not?

13. Plan and teach a lesson using one of the activities suggested in the chapter.

14. Examine your feelings about how mechanics of writing should be taught in elementary schools. If you decide it should be, how should it be taught?

15. Examine language arts textbooks to see how they present mechanics. What percentage of the textbook pages is devoted to this instruction? What types of activities are included?

16. Plan and teach a lesson about the mechanics using one of the activities suggested in the chapter.

17. Describe any prior concepts you had about the writers' tools in the classroom and teaching them that have changed as a result of your experience with this chapter. Describe the changes.

CHILDREN'S BOOKS

Barrett, J. (1983). *A snake is totally tail*. New York: Atheneum.

Bunting, E. (1984). *The man who could call down owls*. Illustrated by Charles Mikolaycak. New York: Macmillan Co.

——. (1986). *The Mother's Day Mice*. Illustrated by Jan Brett. New York: Clarion.

Durell, A., and Sachs, M. (Ed.). (1990). *The big book for peace*. New York: Dutton.

Ernst, L. C. (1990). *Ginger jumps*. New York: Bradbury.

Flournoy, V. (1985). *The patchwork quilt*. Illustrated by Jerry Pinkney. New York: Dial Press.

Gág, W. (1928, 1956). *Millions of cats*. New York: Coward-McCann.

Galdone, P. (1972). *The three bears*. New York: Houghton Mifflin.

Heide, F. P., and Gilliland, J. H. (1990). *The day of Ahmed's secret*. Illustrated by Ted Lewin. New York: Lothrop, Lee & Shepard.

Hutchins, P. (1990). *What game shall we play?* New York: Greenwillow.

Lauber, P. (1986). *Volcano: The eruption and healing of Mount St. Helens*. New York: Bradbury.

McCully, E. A. (1990). *The evil spell*. New York: Harper & Row.

Rylant, C. (1990). *Henry and Mudge and the happy cat*. Illustrated by Sucie Stevenson. New York: Bradbury.

Sterne, N. (1979). *Tyrannosaurus wrecks: A book of dinosaur riddles*. New York: Crowell.

Van Allsburg, C. (1985). *The polar express*. Boston: Houghton Mifflin.

Van Leeuwen, J. (1990). *Oliver pig at school*. Illustrated by Ann Schweninger. New York: Dial.

Wexler, J. (1985). *From spore to spore: Ferns and how they grow*. New York: Dodd, Mead & Co.

White, E. B. (1952). *Charlotte's web*. New York: Harper & Row.

REFERENCES AND SUGGESTED READINGS

SPELLING

Allred, R. A. (1977). *Spelling: An application of research findings*. Washington, DC: National Education Association.

Anderson, K. F. (1985). The development of spelling ability and linguistic strategies. *The Reading Teacher, 39,* 140–147.

Applebee, A. N., Langer, J. A., & Mullis, I. V. S. (1987). *Grammar, punctuation, and spelling: Controlling the conventions of written English at ages 9, 13, and 17* (Report No. 15-W-03). Princeton, NJ: Educational Testing Service.

Barron, R. W. (1980). Visual and phonological strategies in reading and spelling. In U. Frith (Ed.), *Cognitive processes in learning to spell*. London: Academic Press.

Bean, W., & Bouffler, C. (1987). *Spell by writing*. Rozelle, New South Wales (Australia): Primary English Teaching Association.

Beers, J. W., & Henderson, E. H. (1977). A study of developing orthographic concepts among first graders. *Research in the Teaching of English, 11,* 133–148.

Chomsky, C. (1970). Reading, writing, and phonology. *Harvard Educational Review, 40,* 287–309.

Chomsky, N. (1965). *Aspects of the theory of syntax*. Cambridge, MA: M.I.T. Press.

Chomsky, N., & Halle, M. (1968). *The sound pattern of English*. New York: Harper & Row.

Cook, G. E., Esposito, M., Gabrielson, T., & Turner, G. (1984). *Spelling for word mastery*. Columbus, OH: Merrill.

Dale, E., & O'Rourke, J. (1971). *Techniques of teaching vocabulary*. Palo Alto, CA: Field Educational Publications.

Frith, U. (1980). Unexpected spelling problems. In U. Frith (Ed.), *Cognitive processes in learning to spell*. London: Academic Press.

Gentry, J. R. (1978). Early spelling strategies. *Elementary School Journal, 79,* 88–92.

Gentry, J. R. (1981). Learning to spell developmentally. *The Reading Teacher, 34,* 378–381.

Gentry, J. R. (1982a). An analysis of developmental spellings in *Gnys at wrk*. *The Reading Teacher, 36,* 192–200.

Gentry J. R. (1982b). Developmental spelling: Assessment, *Diagnostique, 8,* 52–61.

Gentry, J. R. (1987). *Spel . . . is a four-letter word*. Portsmouth, NH: Heinemann.

Graves, D. H. (1977). Research update: Spelling texts and structural analysis methods. *Language Arts, 54,* 86–90.

Graves, D. H. (1983). *Writing: Teachers and students at work*. Portsmouth, NH: Heinemann.

Grief, I. P. (1981). "When two vowels go walking," they should get lost. *The Reading Teacher, 34,* 460–461.

Henderson, E. H. (1980a). Developmental concepts of word. In E. H. Henderson & J. W. Beers (Eds.), *Developmental and cognitive aspects of learning to spell: A reflection of word knowledge*, pp. 1–14. Newark, DE: International Reading Association.

Henderson, E. H. (1980b). Word knowledge and reading disability. In E. H. Henderson & J. W. Beers (Eds.), *Developmental and cognitive aspects of learning to spell: A reflection of word knowledge*, pp. 138–148. Newark, DE: International Reading Association.

Hillerich, R. L. (1977). Let's teach spelling—Not phonetic misspelling. *Language Arts, 54,* 301–307.

Hillerich, R. L. (1978). *A writing vocabulary for elementary children*. Springfield, IL: Thomas.

Hitchcock, M. E. (1989). *Elementary students' invented spellings at the correct stage of spelling development*. Unpublished doctoral dissertation, Norman, OK: University of Oklahoma.

Hodges, R. E. (1982). Research update: On the development of spelling ability. *Language Arts, 59,* 284–290.

Horn, E. (1926). *A basic writing vocabulary*. Iowa City: University of Iowa Press.

Horn, E. (1957). Phonetics and spelling. *Elementary School Journal, 57,* 233–235, 246.

Horn, E. (1960). Spelling. In C. W. Harris (Ed.), *Encyclopedia of educational research* (3rd ed.), pp. 1337–1354. New York: Macmillan.

Horn, T. D. (1947). The effect of the corrected test on learning to spell. *Elementary School Journal, 47,* 277–285.

Horn, T. D. (1969). Spelling. In R. L. Ebel (Ed.), *Encyclopedia of educational research* (4th ed.), pp. 1282–1299. New York: Macmillan.

Johnson, T. D., Langford, K. G., & Quorn, K. C. (1981). Characteristics of an effective spelling program. *Language Arts, 58,* 581–588.

Marsh, G., Friedman, M., Desberg, P., & Welsh, V. (1981). The development of strategies in spelling. In U. Frith (Ed.), *Cognitive processes in learning to spell.* London: Academic Press.

Paterson, K. (1977). *Bridge to Terabithia.* New York: Crowell.

Read, C. (1971). Pre-school children's knowledge of English phonology. *Harvard Educational Review, 41,* 1–34.

Read, C. (1975). *Children's categorization of speech sounds in English* (NCTE Research Report No. 17). Urbana, IL: National Council of Teachers of English.

Read, C. (1986). *Children's creative spelling.* London: Routledge & Kegan Paul.

Stewig, J. W. (1987). Students' spelling errors. *Clearing House, 61,* 34–37.

Taylor, K. K., & Kidder, E. B. (1988). The development of spelling skills: From first grade through eighth grade. *Written Communication, 5,* 222–244.

Templeton, S. (1979). Spelling first, sound later: The relationships between orthography and higher order phonological knowledge in older students. *Research in the Teaching of English, 13,* 255–265.

Tompkins, G. E., & Yaden, D. B. (1986). *Answering students' questions about words.* Urbana, IL: ERIC Clearinghouse on Reading and Communication Skills and National Council of Teachers of English.

Zutell, J. (1979). Spelling strategies of primary school children and their relationship to Piaget's concept of decentration. *Research in the Teaching of English, 13,* 69–79.

HANDWRITING

Askov, E., & Greff, K. N. (1975). Handwriting: Copying versus tracing as the most effective type of practice. *Journal of Educational Research, 69,* 96–98.

Barbe, W. B., Lucas, V. H., Wasylyk, T. M., Hackney, C. S., & Braun, L. A. (1984). *Zaner-Bloser creative growth in handwriting* (Grades K–8). Columbus, OH: Zaner-Bloser.

Barbe, W. B., & Milone, M. N., Jr. (1980). *Why manuscript writing should come before cursive writing* (Zaner-Bloser Professional Pamphlet No. 11). Columbus, OH: Zaner-Bloser.

Furner, B. A. (1969). Recommended instructional procedures in a method emphasizing the perceptual-motor nature of learning in handwriting. *Elementary English, 46,* 1021–1030.

Galdone, P. (1972). *The three bears.* New York: Houghton Mifflin.

Graves, D. H. (1983). *Writing: Teachers and children at work.* Exeter, NH: Heinemann.

Groff, P. J. (1963). Who writes faster? *Education, 83,* 367–369.

Harrison, S. (1981). Open letter from a left-handed teacher: Some sinistral ideas on the teaching of handwriting. *Teaching Exceptional Children, 13,* 116–120.

Hildreth, G. (1960). Manuscript writing after sixty years. *Elementary English, 37,* 3–13.

Hirsch, E., & Niedermeyer, F. C. (1973). The effects of tracing prompts and discrimination training on kindergarten handwriting performance. *Journal of Educational Research, 67,* 81–83.

Horton, L. W. (1970). Illegibilities in the cursive handwriting of sixth graders. *Elementary School Journal, 70,* 446–450.

Howell, H. (1978). Write on, you sinistrals! *Language Arts, 55,* 852–856.

Jackson, A. D. (1971). A comparison of speed of legibility of manuscript and cursive handwriting of intermediate grade pupils. Unpublished doctoral dissertation, University of Arizona. *Dissertation Abstracts, 31* (1971), 4384A.

Klein, A., & Schickedanz, J. (1980). Preschoolers write messages and receive their favorite books. *Language Arts, 57,* 742–749.

Koenke, K. (1986). Handwriting instruction: What do we know? *The Reading Teacher, 40,* 214–216.

Lamme, L. L. (1979). Handwriting in an early childhood curriculum. *Young Children, 35,* 20–27.

Lamme, L. L., & Ayris, B. M. (1983). Is the handwriting of beginning writers influenced by writing tools? *Journal of Research and Development in Education, 17,* 32–38.

Lindsay, G. A., & McLennan, D. (1983). Lined paper: Its effects on the legibility and creativity of young children's writing. *British Journal of Educational Psychology, 53,* 364–368.

Markham, L. R. (1976). Influences of handwriting quality on teacher evaluation of written work. *American Educational Research Journal, 13,* 277–283.

Stennett, R. G., Smithe, P. C., & Hardy, M. (1972). Developmental trends in letter-printing skill. *Perceptual and Motor Skills, 34,* 183–186.

Sterne, N. (1979). *Tyrannosaurus wrecks: A book of dinosaur riddles.* New York: Crowell.

Thurber, D. N. (1981). *D'Nealian handwriting* (Grades K–8). Glenview, IL: Scott, Foresman.

Tompkins, G. E. (1980). Let's go on a bear hunt! A fresh approach to penmanship drill. *Language Arts, 57,* 782–786.

Wright, C. D., & Wright, J. P. (1980). Handwriting: The effectiveness of copying from moving versus still models. *Journal of Educational Research, 74,* 95–98.

GRAMMAR

Applebee, A. N., Langer, J. A., & Mullis, I. V. S. (1987). *Grammar, punctuation, and spelling: Controlling the conventions of written English at ages 9, 13, and 17.* Princeton, NJ: Educational Testing Service.

Atwell, N. (1987). *In the middle: Writing, reading, and learning with adolescents.* Upper Montclair, NJ: Boynton/Cook.

Barrett, J. (1983). *A snake is totally tail.* New York: Atheneum.

Braddock, R., Lloyd-Jones, R., & Schoer, L. (1963). *Research in written composition.* Champaign, IL: National Council of Teachers of English.

Cullinan, B., Jaggar, A., & Strickland, D. (1974). Oral language expansion in the primary grades. In B. Cullinan (Ed.), *Black dialects and reading.* Urbana, IL: National Council of Teachers of English.

Davis, F. (1984). In defense of grammar. *English Education, 16,* 151–164.

Edelsky, C. (1989). Putting language variation to work for you. In P. Rigg & V. G. Allen (Eds.), *When they don't all speak English: Integrating the ESL student into the regular classroom,* pp. 96–107. Urbana, IL: National Council of Teachers of English.

Elbow, P. (1973). *Writing without teachers.* New York: Oxford University Press.

Elley, W. B., Barham, I. H., Lamb, H., & Wyllie, M. (1976). The role of grammar in a secondary school English curriculum. *Research in the Teaching of English, 10,* 5–21.

Fraser, I. S., & Hodson, L. M. (1978). Twenty-one kicks at the grammar horse. *English Journal, 67,* 49–53.

Goba, R. I., & Brown, P. A. (1982). Grammar should be taught and learned in our schools. *English Journal, 73,* 20–23.

Haley-James, S. (Ed.). (1981). *Perspectives on writing in grades 1–8.* Urbana, IL: National Council of Teachers of English.

Hillocks, G., Jr. (1987). *Research on written composition: New directions for teaching.* Urbana, IL: National Conference on Research in English and the ERIC Clearinghouse on Reading and Communication Skills.

Hudson, B. A. (1980). Moving language around: Helping students become aware of language structure. *Language Arts, 57,* 614–620.

Hunt, K. W., & O'Donnell, R. C. (1970). *An elementary school curriculum to develop better writing skills.* Washington, DC: U.S. Government Printing Office.

Jaggar, A. (1980). Allowing for language differences. In G. S. Pinnell (Ed.), *Discovering language with children,* pp. 25–28. Urbana, IL: National Council of Teachers of English.

Malmstrom, J. (1977). *Understanding language: A primer for the language arts teacher.* New York: St. Martin's Press.

Mellon, J. C. (1969). *Transformational sentence combining: A method for enhancing the development of syntactic fluency in English composition* (NCTE Research Report No. 10). Urbana, IL: National Council of Teachers of English.

Noyce, R. M., & Christie, J. F. (1983). Effects of an integrated approach to grammar instruction on third graders' reading and writing. *Elementary School Journal, 84,* 63–69.

O'Hare, F. (1973). *Sentence combining: Improving student writing without formal grammar instruction* (NCTE Research Report No. 15). Urbana, IL: National Council of Teachers of English.

Pooley, R. C. (1974). *The teaching of English usage.* Urbana, IL: National Council of Teachers of English.

Small, R. (1985). Why I'll never teach grammar again. *English Education, 17,* 174–178.

Smith, F. (1982). *Writing and the writer.* New York: Holt, Rinehart & Winston.

Strong, W. (1986). *Creative approaches to sentence combining.* Urbana, IL: ERIC Clearinghouse on Reading and Communication Skills and the National Council of Teachers of English.

Suhor, C. (1987). Orthodoxies in language arts education. *Language Arts, 64,* 416–419.

Tompkins, G. E., & McGee, L. M. (1983). Launching nonstandard speakers into standard English. *Language Arts, 60,* 463–469.

Weaver, C. (1979). *Grammar for teachers: Perspectives and definitions.* Urbana, IL: National Council of Teachers of English.

White, E. B. (1952). *Charlotte's web.* New York: Harper & Row.

THE MECHANICS OF WRITING: PUNCTUATION AND CAPITALIZATION

Baele, E. R. (1968). *The effect of primary reading programs emphasizing language structure as related to meaning upon children's written language achievement at third grade level.* Doctoral dissertation, University of California, Berkeley.

Baker, C. L. (1989). *English syntax.* Cambridge, MA: MIT Press.

Bauman, J., and Stevenson, J. (1986). Teaching students to comprehend anaphoric relations. In J. W. Irwin (Ed.), *Understanding and teaching cohesion comprehension.* Newark, DE: International Reading Association.

Cartelli, L. M. (1980, March). Reading comprehension: A matter of referents. *Academic Therapy, 15,* 421–430.

Chomsky, N. (1957). *Syntactic structures.* The Hague: Mouton & Co.

Cohen, S. B., & Plaskon, S. P. (1980). *Language arts for the mildly handicapped.* Columbus, OH: Merrill Publishing Co.

Cox, B. E., Shanahan, T., & Sulzby, E. (1990). Good and poor readers' use of cohesion in writing. *Reading Research Quarterly 25,* 47–65.

DeHaven, E. P. (1983). *Teaching and learning the language arts.* Boston: Little Brown.

Fay, G., Trupin, E., & Townes, B. D. (1981, January). The young disabled reader: Acquisition strategies and associated deficits. *Journal of Learning Disabilities, 14,* 32–35.

Francis, W. N. Revolution in grammar. In W. Allen (Ed.), *Readings in applied English linguistics* (2nd ed.). New York: Appleton-Century-Crofts.

Gearheart, B. R., Weishahn, M., & Gearheart, C. J. (1992). *The exceptional student in the regular classroom.* (5th ed.). New York: Merrill/Macmillan.

Goodman, R. (1965). Transformational grammar. In N. Stageburg (Ed.), *An introductory English grammar.* New York: Holt, Rinehart & Winston.

Hartwell, P. (1985). Grammar, grammars, and the teaching of grammar. *College English, 47,* 105–127.

Hazlett, J. A. (1972). *A national assessment of educational progress. Report 8, Writing: National results.* Washington, DC: U.S. Government Printing Office.

Henderson, A. J., & Shores, R. E. (1982, March). How learning disabled students' failure to attend to suffixes affects their oral reading performance. *Journal of Learning Disabilities, 15,* 178–182.

Hillocks, G., Jr. (1986). *Research on written composition: New directions for teaching.* Urbana, IL: ERIC Clearinghouse on Reading and Communication Skills and the National Conference on Research in English.

——, & Smith, M. W. (1991). Grammar and usage. In J. Flood, J. Jensen, D. Lapp, & J. Squire (Eds.), *Handbook of research on teaching the English language arts.* New York: Macmillan.

Hirsch, E. D. (1982). Some principles of composition from grade school to grad school. In G. Hillocks (Ed.), *The English curriculum under fire: What are the real basics?* Urbana, IL: National Council of Teachers of English, pp. 39–52.

Hodges, R. (1991). The conventions of writing. In J. Flood, J. Jensen, D. Lapp, & J. Squire (Eds.), *Handbook of research on teaching the English language* (pp. 775–786). Hew York: Macmillan.

Hunt, K., & O'Donnell, R. (1970). *An elementary school curriculum to develop better writing skills.* Washington, DC: U.S. Department of Health, Education, and Welfare, Bureau of Research.

Kean, J. M., & Personke, C. (1976). *The language arts, teaching and learning in the elementary school.* New York: St. Martin's Press.

Knott, G. P. (1979, Winter). Developing reading potential in black remedial high school freshmen. *Reading Improvement, 16,* 262–269.

Krashen, S. D. (1984). *Writing: Research, theory, and applications.* Oxford: Pergamon Press.

Lamb, P. (1977). *Linguistics in proper perspective* (2nd ed.). Columbus, OH: Merrill.

Lerner, J. (1976). *Children with learning disabilities* (2nd ed.). Boston: Houghton Mifflin.

Lodge, H. C., & Trett, G. L. (1968). *New ways in English.* Englewood Cliffs, NJ: Prentice-Hall.

Mackie, B. C. (1982). *The effects of a sentence-combining program on the reading comprehension and written composition of fourth-grade students.* Doctoral Dissertation, Hofstra University. (University Microfilms No. DA 8207744).

McClure, J., Kalk, M., & Keenan, V. (1980, May). Use of grammatical morphemes by beginning readers. *Journal of Learning Disabilities, 13,* 34–49.

Mellon, J. (1964). *The basic sentence types and their simple transforms.* Culver, IN: Culver Military Academy.

——. (1969). *Transformational sentence combining: A method for enhancing the development of syntactic fluency in English composition.* Champaign, IL: National Conference of Teachers of English.

Moe, A. J., & Irwin, J. W. (1986). Cohesion, coherence, and comprehension. In J. W. Irwin (Ed.), *Understanding and teaching cohesion.* Newark, DE: International Reading Association.

National Council of Teachers of English. (1983). *Ideas for teachers from teachers: Elementary language arts.* Urbana, IL: National Council of Teachers of English.

O'Hare, F. (1973). *Sentence combining: Improving student writing without formal grammatical instruction.* Urbana, IL: National Council of Teachers of English.

Otto, W., & Smith, R. J. (1980). *Corrective and remedial teaching.* Boston: Houghton Mifflin.

Pooley, R. (1960, March). Dare schools set a standard in English usage? *English Journal, 49,* 176–181.

Porter, J. (1974, January). Research report. *Elementary English, 51,* 144–151.

Roberts, P. (1962). *English sentences.* New York: Harcourt Brace Jovanovich.

Savage, J. F. (1977). *Effective communication.* Chicago: Science Research Associates.

Stoddard, E. P. (1982). The combined effect of creative thinking and sentence-combining activities on the writing ability of above average ability fifth and sixth grade students. Doctoral Dissertation University of Connecticut. *Dissertation Abstracts International.* (University Microfilms No. DA 821 3235)

Stotsky, S. L. (1983). Research on reading/writing relationships: A synthesis and suggested directions. *Language Arts, 60,* 627–642.

Strong, W. (1986). *Creative approaches to sentence combining.* Urbana, IL: National Council of Teachers of English.

Tiedt, I., & Tiedt, S. (1975). *Contemporary English in the elementary school.* Englewood Cliffs, NJ: Prentice-Hall.

CHAPTER 12

Reading and Connections With Writing

I n an integrated language arts curriculum, you will be particularly interested in the reading skills of the children as they engage their study in a content context such as literature and social studies. The discussions related to reading and connections with writing in this chapter are specifically designed to help you understand

1. The reading process and instructional guidelines
2. The similarity between the reading and writing processes
3. Examples of ways teachers help young children make the connection between reading and writing
4. Examples of ways teachers integrate reading and writing
5. Assessment strategy for reading-writing connections, such as writing stories, research reports, newspaper articles, letters, life-stories, and poems.

A. READING

In the past decade there has been a significant shift in thinking about reading and writing. Reading and writing were once thought of as the flip sides of a coin—they were opposites; a reader decoded or deciphered written language and a writer encoded or produced written language. Then researchers began to note similarities between the two processes and talked of reading and writing as parallel processes. Reading was described as a process much like the writing process, and readers and writers used strategies for making meaning from the text. The important connection was that the goal of both reading and writing is to make meaning. Teachers were encouraged to have students write about their reading and read their own writing. Reading and writing should be taught together, teachers were told, not reading in the morning and writing in the afternoon (Anderson et al., 1985). We now know that interrelationships or interactions between the two language processes exist, and reading and writing can be described as essentially similar processes of meaning construction.

B. INSTRUCTIONAL GUIDELINES

Specific guidelines follow for teaching in an integrated language arts approach:

1. *Strengthen a young child's language skills to benefit reading progress.* The language and reading connection is supported by research studies that show how language skills ben-

efit a child's reading achievement. Superior language ability correlates with advanced reading ability (Borkowski et al., 1983; Snow, 1983). Positive influences on reading derive from young children's listening to stories (Cochran-Smith, 1983). Improving the oral language skills of Mexican-American children who were beginning readers was found to lead to an improvement in their reading skills (Perez, 1981).

2. *Strengthen a young child's metalinguistic awareness as it relates to reading to benefit the child's understanding of how language works.* In metalinguistics (thinking about language) awareness, there are three understandings that are related to beginning reading: (1) the functions of print, (2) the forms and structure of print, and (3) the conventions of print. Some children are confused about these concepts that are related to reading. They often do not know what a word is or what the parameters of written words are. Some overgeneralize the ideas the printed symbols stand for; for example, a child may say the word *kitty* for the printed word *cat.*

3. *Strengthen a young child's knowledge of the alphabet.* There is a relationship between knowing letter names and success in beginning reading: the students who know the names of letters on entering school may also be those who have the necessary visual perceptions, attention spans, and other skills needed in beginning reading. While it would be an error to think that all children should be taught the names of the letters before learning to read, it seems that young children from various backgrounds come to kindergarten knowing the names of more than half the letters of the alphabet (Johnson & Baumann, 1984). Children who know most or all of the letters are higher achievers (Mason, 1980).

4. *Plan reading readiness programs.* For children in preschool and in kindergarten, plan a reading readiness program for all, but focus on those who have little or no knowledge about letters, words, and books. Focus on the interests and abilities of these children during instruction, and they will progress in learning to read (McCormick & Mason, 1984).

5. *Teach phonics to students; those who are taught phonic skills become better readers than those who only memorize sight words* (Chall, 1967). Systematic instruction in skills in recognizing words leads to better achievement (Bond & Dykstra, 1967). Beginning readers who learn the sound and symbol associations for consonants first (rather than those for vowels) score significantly higher in reading achievement than students who receive instruction in vowel sounds first (Hillerich, 1967).

6. *Teach context clues in context.* This is an aid to word identification, since the clues assist identification of words necessary in reading comprehension. According to Hudson and Haworth (1983), introducing words in a context helps students to learn the words and also helps them with oral reading since they can evaluate their oral reading scores by referring to the context clues (Pflaum & Ianis, 1982).

7. *Teach a decoding strategy.* When teaching decoding, consider the pattern of development through which children move as they learn to decode. First, children seem to overuse context clues and underuse phonics. Second, they seem to overuse phonics and underuse meaning. Third, children (sometimes as late as grade 6) seem to develop the skill of using phonics and context clues together (Biemiller, 1970). Teaching second-grade children with a context-and-phonics approach was found to lead to an instructional level of one-half grade higher for the experimental group than for the control group students who simply read sentences several times (Spiegel et al., 1983).

8. *Teach skills of fast, efficient word identification.* Research studies indicate that one basic difference between good and poor readers is that good readers identify words rapidly and use visual recognition or sound-symbols associations (Stanovich, 1980). Students should be encouraged to reread material, and oral rereading should be demonstrated (Kahn, 1980).

9. *Teach reading comprehension.* Teach reading comprehension directly so students can monitor their own comprehension and think about their own thinking (encourage students to use their metacognitive abilities to summarize their understanding of what is learned) (Borkowski et al., 1983).

10. *Give instruction in word meanings.* Realize that text difficulty (which includes vocabulary) affects the ability of students to comprehend and retain information; thus, stud-

ies show that students who receive instruction in word meanings have greater mastery of those meanings than those who receive no instruction (Beck et al., 1982). Teach meaning for some of the difficult words in the selections the students are reading before the students read the selection: this increases comprehension of that selection (Kaneenui et al., 1982).

11. *Plan activities before reading a selection.* Prereading activities can activate a student's background knowledge. The relationship between background knowledge and comprehension is positive; the greater the reader's background knowledge that is related to the text, the greater the comprehension of the text material (Baldwin et al., 1985).

12. *Teach the ways that authors arrange stories and informational texts.* This teaching will aid student comprehension of narrative and expository writing styles. When students receive instruction in the structure of texts, their comprehension improves. Understanding of the structure of texts is supported by asking students to predict outcomes, to retell stories, and to discuss causal relationships (Rand, 1984). Studies of students in grades 4 through 6 showed that students who had instruction in story grammar improved their comprehension and recall of stories (Whaley, 1981).

13. *Give direct instruction to help students distinguish main ideas in text material.* Direct instruction is needed to help students distinguish main ideas in text material where the ideas appear in different places in the paragraphs, and to help students infer main ideas when the ideas are not stated directly or clearly. In grades 5 and 6, it seems that some students can select main ideas from paragraphs on worksheets but are not able to transfer this skill to finding main ideas in text materials (Taylor et al., 1985). To encourage transfer of this skill, consider asking students in cooperative learning groups to work at one of the following tasks suitable for their abilities: to select the topic for a paragraph that is taken from an actual text the students are using in one of their content areas; to select the main idea from several choices given; to select the main idea that is located at the beginning, middle, or end of a paragraph taken from a text, or determine that the main idea is not stated and should be inferred from selected paragraphs; or to determine which details from a paragraph support information about the main idea by writing the details on a graphic web, with the main idea recorded in the center and the details recorded on strands that radiate from the center.

In grades 1 and 2, it appears that students can select a stated main idea when it is in the first or the last sentence of a paragraph, but they have difficulty inferring main ideas (Moore et al., 1983).

14. *Demonstrate the process of making inferences.* Model the process of inferring in materials on the students' instructional reading levels. The ability to make inferences is one of the skills that differentiate good from poor readers. As part of your direct instruction, you will want to integrate a student's prior knowledge with the text before reading the material and ask questions that call for information inferred by the student (Holmes, 1983).

15. *Teach critical reading skills to all.* Teach critical reading skills to all students, including disadvantaged and below-grade-level readers. Intermediate-grade remedial reading students who were taught critical thinking abilities through listening became significantly better at critical listening and critical reading than a control group (Boodt, 1984). Further, Clark and Palmer (1982) found that disadvantaged students in grades 4 and 6 and in middle schools who were given instruction in critical reading were just as capable of reading critically as their advantaged peers.

16. *Encourage the students to make mental images before they read.* Several studies show that visualization training does increase the comprehension of some students. Studies of students in grades 3 through 6 point out that careful daily instruction in the use of visualization improved student learning from the text (Tierney & Cunningham, 1984).

17. *Ask sequenced questions about the story.* To improve understanding of the story, ask questions in an order that follows the pattern of the story structure and that mention the setting, the initiating event, the reaction of the character, the action, and the consequence of the action (Sadow, 1982).

18. *Teach students to use the survey, question, read, recite, and review approach to study content in materials.* Research synthesis by Estes and Richards (1985) indicates that these are study habits found in high-achieving students. Questioning before reading (a step in this approach) also aids comprehension (Baker & Brown, 1984). And students using the

approach score higher on recall of content material and make gains in content areas (Adams et al., 1981).

19. *Plan instruction in outlining and in note taking.* To increase a student's mastery over content material, demonstrate outlining and note taking. Students who outline increase their learning (Slater, 1985), and those who take notes increase their comprehension and recall of materials (Estes & Richards, 1985).

20. *Give instruction on taking tests.* Take time to teach how to take tests to improve students' performances on tests and to ensure that the results more accurately reflect their learning (Dreisbach & Keogh, 1982; McPhail, 1981; Uttero, 1988). Both low and high achievers can benefit. In one study of both groups by Bob Lange (1981), the students who received instruction in test taking increased their grade equivalent scores from three to eight months over a control group.

21. *Demonstrate fluent oral reading.* Instruction in fluent oral reading can be helpful for readers who read with poor expression or phrasing (Allington, 1983). Read aloud to your students. A program of reading aloud combined with direct teaching was shown to support large gains in academic achievement for third-grade students (Lopez, 1986). Reading aloud facilitates the students' ability to compose stories and improves their narrative writing. Further, children's literature is an important part of the writing context, because it provides authentic experiences for student writers as they borrow and improvise from the literature to create their own texts.

22. *Plan listening instruction.* There is a relationship between reading and listening. One study of fourth-grade students who were reading two and one-half years below grade level were provided 20-minute listening periods daily for 30 days. When compared with the control group, those who had received the listening training performed significantly better on a standardized reading achievement test (Lemons & Moore, 1982). In a study of fifth-grade students, the experimental group received instruction with a listening activity and then transferred what had been learned to reading. The control group received instruction in a traditional way. The experimental group made greater gains on a standardized reading achievement test in relationships, interpretation, and appreciation (Seaton & Wielan, 1981).

23. *Promote a writing and reading interaction in the classroom.* Writing and reading are processes that complement each other. The reading comprehension of good writers is better than that of average writers, and better writers do more free reading than those with lesser abilities (Shanahan, 1980). Students in grades 5, 6, and 7, who receive training in writing summaries, have greater comprehension and retention when they apply that skill as they read (Bromley, 1985). Sentence manipulation activities have positive effects on students and their reading and writing ability.

24. *Tell students what they are going to learn, the reasons for learning it, and how the new learning is related to previous learning.* Your direct instruction should include an introduction that tells the students what they are going to learn, the reason for learning it, and how the new learning relates to what they have previously learned. Next, explain the skill and show students exactly how to use the skill. Then, give some time for guided practice during which you ask the students to use the skill. You may change the context in which the skill is being used and ask students to use it in the new context. Then ask the students to tell what they have learned. More independent practice is suggested as the students use this skill in still another context, perhaps for a homework activity.

C. THE READING AND WRITING PROCESSES

Reading and writing are both transactive processes (Harste, Woodward, & Burke, 1984; Rosenblatt, 1978). In Chapter 11, we described the writing process as a recursive process involving a variety of activities as students gather and organize ideas, draft their compositions, revise and edit the drafts, and, finally, publish and share their writings. Reading involves a similar process of several steps during which readers construct meaning through their interaction with text or reading materials. The term *text* includes all reading materials—stories, maps, newspapers, cereal boxes, textbooks, and so on; it is not limited to basal reader textbooks.

The Reading Process

Reading is a sociopsycholinguistic process like writing. It can be described as a *transaction,* or interaction between the mind of the reader and the language of the text in a particular situational and social context. Meaning is constructed when the reader transacts with the text. Comprehension does not go from the page to the reader; instead, it is a complex negotiation between text and reader that is shaped by the immediate situational context and broader sociolinguistic contexts. The immediate situational context includes the reader's knowledge about the topic, purpose for reading, and other factors related to the immediate environment. Broader sociolinguistic contexts include the language community the reader belongs to and how closely it matches the language used in the text, the reader's culturally based expectations about reading, and the reader's own expectations about reading based on previous experiences. This description of reading is presented schematically in Figure 12.1.

Readers begin the reading process by activating their prior knowledge or schemata about the text. The title, an illustration, something someone says about the text, the topic, or something else may trigger this activation, but for the reader to make meaning from the text, a schema in the mind must be activated. Then readers sample the text, recognizing some words and decoding others using phonics and context cues. (It is not necessary for readers to recognize every word or to look at every letter in a word to decode it.) From this sampling, readers construct personal meaning using the text as a blueprint. This is the transaction between the text and the reader's mind. As readers construct meaning, they continue reading, and as long as what they are reading fits the meaning they are constructing, the transaction continues. When something doesn't make sense, readers slow down, back up,

FIGURE 12.1
The Reading Process
SOURCE: Weaver, 1988, p. 30.

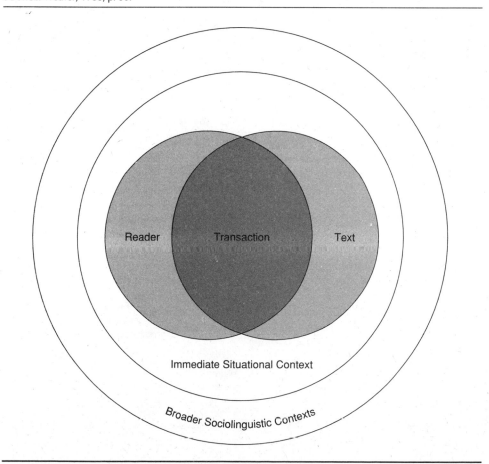

and reread until they are making meaning again. After reading, the construction of meaning from the text is extended. Readers compare, interpret, and evaluate their understanding through talk, writing, reading, and projects. Rosenblatt (1978) explains that as students write about reading, they unravel their thinking so that we can see how they understand and, at the same time, help them elaborate and clarify their responses.

Comparing the Two Processes

The reading and writing processes have comparable *before, during,* and *after* activities. As shown in Figure 12.2, reading and writing activities at each of the three stages are similar, and in both reading and writing, the goal is to construct meaning. Notice the activities listed for rereading and revising in the *during* stage, for example. Fitzgerald (1989) analyzed these two activities and concluded that they draw on similar processes of author-reader-text interactions. Similar analyses can be made for other activities, as well.

Tierney (1983) explains that reading and writing are multidimensional and involve concurrent, complex transactions between writers, between writers as readers, between readers, and between readers as writers. Writers participate in several types of reading activities. They read other authors' works for ideas and to learn about the structure of stories, but they also read and reread their own work—to problem-solve, discover, monitor, and clarify. The quality of these reading experiences seems closely tied to success in writing. "Readers as writers" is a newer idea, but readers are involved in many of the same activi-

FIGURE 12.2
A Comparison of the Reading and Writing Processes
Adapted from Tompkins & Hoskisson, 1995.

WHAT READERS DO	WHAT WRITERS DO
Before	
Readers use knowledge about • the topic • syntax • phonology	Writers use knowledge about • the topic • syntax • phonology
Readers bring expectations cued by • previous reading experiences • format of the text • purpose for reading • audience for reading	Writers bring expectations cued by • previous writing experiences • previous reading experiences • purpose for writing • audience for writing
During	
Readers read to • predict outcomes • monitor predictions • create meaning	Writers prewrite and draft to • gather ideas • organize ideas • write a rough draft
Readers reread to • discuss text • interpret meaning • clarify meaning • examine the impact of words, sentences, and paragraphs to the whole text • make notes	Writers revise and edit to • discuss text • interpret meaning • clarify meaning • examine the impact of words, sentences, and paragraphs to the whole text • identify and correct mechanical errors
After	
Readers • respond in many ways • reflect on the reading • feel success • want to read again	Writers • get response from readers • give response to readers • feel success • want to write again

ties that writers use. They generate ideas, organize, monitor, problem-solve, and revise. Smith (1983) believes that reading influences writing skills because readers unconsciously "read like writers":

> To read like a writer we engage with the author in what the author is writing. We can anticipate what the author will say, so that the author is in effect writing on our behalf, not showing how something is done but doing it with us. . . . Bit by bit, one thing at a time, but enormous numbers of things over the passage of time, the learner learns through reading like a writer to write like a writer. (pp. 563–564)

Also, both reading and writing are recursive, cycling back through various parts of the process, and, just as writers compose text, readers compose their meaning.

Teachers can help students appreciate the similarities between reading and writing in many ways. Tierney (1983) explains: "What we need are reading teachers who act as if their students were developing writers and writing teachers who act as if their students were readers" (p. 151). These are some ways to point out the relationships between reading and writing:

Help writers assume alternative points of view as potential readers.
Help readers consider the writer's purpose and viewpoint.
Point out that reading is much like composing, so that students will view reading as a process, much like the writing process.
Talk with students about the reading and writing processes.
Talk with students about reading and writing strategies.

Readers and writers use a number of strategies for constructing meaning as they interact with print. As readers, we use a variety of problem-solving strategies to make decisions about an author's meaning and to construct meaning for ourselves. As writers we also use problem-solving strategies to decide what our readers need as we construct meaning for them and for ourselves. Comparing reading to writing, Tierney and Pearson (1983) described reading as a composing process because readers compose and refine meaning through reading much as writers do.

Langer (1986) followed this line of thinking in identifying four strategies that both readers and writers use to interact with text. The first strategy is generating ideas: both readers and writers generate ideas as they get started, as they become aware of important ideas and experiences, and as they begin to plan and organize the information. Formulating meaning is the second strategy—the essence of both reading and writing. Readers and writers formulate meaning by developing the message, considering audience, drawing on personal experience, choosing language, linking concepts, summarizing, and paraphrasing. Assessing is the next strategy. In both reading and writing, students review, react, and monitor their understanding of the message and the text itself. The fourth strategy is revising, wherein both readers and writers reconsider and restructure the message, recognize when meaning has broken down, and take appropriate action to change the text to improve understanding.

Langer's research will have a great impact on reading and writing instruction because she has documented that readers and writers use the same four major groups of literacy strategies. Through Langer's work we see how readers use a strategy, such as revision, that is often thought of as part of the writing process. Readers use revision, but they use it differently than writers do.

Benefits of Connecting Reading and Writing

Researchers have linked reading and writing, but what about the practical benefits of connecting reading and writing? Tierney and Leys (1986) analyzed research on the reading-writing connection and found these benefits:

Some reading experiences contribute to students' writing performance.
Some writing experiences contribute to student's reading performance.
Writers acquire values and behaviors from reading and readers acquire values and behaviors from writing.
Successful writers integrate reading into their writing experience and successful readers integrate writing into their reading experience.

D. MAKING THE CONNECTION WITH YOUNG CHILDREN

Young children's introduction to reading and writing begins before they come to school. Parents and other caregivers read to young children, and they observe adults reading. They learn to read signs in their community. Children experiment with writing and have parents write for them. They also observe adults writing. When young children come to kindergarten, their understandings about reading and writing expand quickly through the language-rich classroom environment and teacher-led demonstrations of reading and writing (Noyce & Christie, 1989). Three types of teacher-led demonstrations of literacy are assisted reading, the language experience approach, and big books.

Assisted Reading

Assisted reading is a technique that parents and teachers can use to introduce young children to reading (Hoskisson, 1974, 1975a, 1975b, 1977; Hoskisson & Krohm, 1974; Hoskisson, Sherman, & Smith, 1974). Adults read to young children and allow them to handle books. Children learn that books have front and back parts and top and bottom dimensions, and they discover that readers begin at the front of the book and turn pages toward the back. They learn this by holding books while listening to stories, by playing with books, and by trying out the behaviors they have experienced while being read to.

Pictures also play an important role in books read to young children because they provide contextual situations that bridge the gap between children's actual experiences and the abstract language presented by authors. Pictures provide the context, the visual images that help children relate what they know to what is presented in the story. Eventually children will be able to supply their own context to the stories they read, but in the beginning, pictures bridge the gap from the abstract to the real.

As children learn that pictures relate the meaning of the story to their own experiences, they begin to attend to the words they hear and consider the meaning again. Before long they can "read" a book by using the pictures as prompts in retelling the story. Most parents have succumbed to the temptation to skip pages of a story they have read innumerable times, only to have children correct them. Although parents tend to call this memorization, children store the meaning of the story rather than memorize exact words; skipping any part disrupts this meaning and results in the corrective feedback they give their errant parents.

1. *Reading to children.* The first stage in assisted reading is to read to children and have them repeat each phrase or sentence. At first most children's attention will not be on the lines of print as they repeat the words. They may be looking around the room, at the pictures in the book, or at other parts of the book. To direct their attention to the lines of print, the reader points to the words on each line as they are read. This allows children to see that lines of print are read from left to right, not randomly. Many different books are read and reread during this stage. Rereading is important because the visual images of the words must be seen and read many times to ensure their recognition in other stories. Later, one repetition of a word may be sufficient for subsequent recognition of the word in context.

2. *Repeated reading.* When children begin to notice that some words occur repeatedly, from story to story, they enter the second stage of assisted reading. In this stage, the reader reads and children repeat or echo the words; however, the reader does not read the words the children seem to recognize. The reader omits those words, and children fill them in. The fluency, or flow, of the reading should not be interrupted. If fluency is not maintained during this stage, children will not grasp the meaning of the passage, because the syntactic and semantic cues that come from a smooth flow of language will not be evident to them.

3. *Shared reading.* The transition to stage three occurs when children begin to ask the reader to let them read the words themselves. Stage three may be initiated in this manner by the child, or it may be introduced by the person assisting the child. When children know enough words to do the initial reading themselves, they read and the person assisting supplies any unknown words. It is important to assist children so that the fluency of the reading is not disrupted. In stage three, children do the major portion of the reading, but they tire more easily because they are struggling to use all the information they have acquired about written language. Children at this stage need constant encouragement; they must not feel a sense of frustration or failure. Moving to independent reading is a gradual process.

Language Experience Approach

The *language experience approach* (LEA) to beginning reading instruction is based on children's language and experiences (Ashton-Warner, 1965; Lee & Allen, 1963; Stauffer, 1970). According to this method, students dictate about their experiences, either as a group or individually, the teacher does the writing, and the text they develop becomes the reading material. Because the language comes from the children themselves and the content is based on their experiences, students are usually able to read the text easily. Reading and writing are connected as students are actively involved in reading what they have written.

STEP 1: Provide the experience. A meaningful experience is identified to serve as the stimulus for the writing. For group writing, it can be an experience shared in school, a book read aloud, a field trip, or some other experience, such as having a pet or playing in the snow, that all students are familiar with. For individual writing, the stimulus can be any experience that is important for the particular student.

STEP 2: Discuss the experience. Students and teacher discuss the experience prior to writing. The purpose of discussion is to review the experience so that students' dictation will be more interesting and complete. Teachers might begin the discussion with an open-ended question, such as "What are you going to write about?" As students talk about their experiences, they clarify and organize ideas, use more specific vocabulary, and extend their understanding.

STEP 3: Record the dictation. Teachers write down the student's dictation. Texts for individual students are written on sheets of writing paper or in small booklets, and group texts are written on chart paper. Teachers print neatly, spell words correctly, and preserve students' language as much as possible. It is a great temptation to change the student's language to the teachers' own, in either word choice or grammar, but editing should be kept to a minimum so that students do not get the impression that their language is inferior or inadequate.

For individual texts, teachers continue to take the student's dictation and write until the student finishes or hesitates. If the student hesitates, the teacher rereads what has been written and encourages the student to continue. For group texts, students take turns dictating sentences, and after writing each sentence, the teacher rereads it.

It is interesting that, as students become familiar with dictating to the teacher, they learn to pace their dictation to the teacher's writing speed. At first, students dictate as they think of ideas, but with experience, they watch as the teacher writes and supply the text word by word.

STEP 4: Read the text. After the text has been dictated, the teacher reads it aloud, pointing to each word. This reading reminds the student of the content of the text and demonstrates how to read it aloud with appropriate intonation. Then students join in the reading. After reading group texts together, individual students can take turns rereading. Group texts can also be copied so each student has a copy to read independently.

STEP 5: Extend the text. After dictating, reading, and rereading their texts, students can extend the experience in several ways; these are possibilities:

- Add illustrations to their writing.
- Read their texts to classmates from the author's chair.
- Take their texts home to share with family members.
- Add this text to a collection of their writings.
- Pick out words from their texts that they would like to learn to read.

The language experience approach is an effective beginning reading method. Even students who have not been successful with other types of reading activities can read what they have dictated. There is a drawback, however; teachers provide a "perfect" model when they take children's dictation—they write neatly and spell words correctly. After language experience activities, some young children are not eager to do their own writing. They prefer their teacher's "perfect" writing to their own childlike writing. To avoid this problem, young children should be doing their own writing in personal journals and responding to literature activities at the same time they are participating in language experience activities so they will learn that sometimes they do their own writing and at other times the teacher takes their dictation.

Despite the differences, the language experience approach and process writing are compatible and can be used together to help kindergartners experiment with print. Karnowski (1989) points out that the two approaches are alike in several ways. Students are actively involved in creating their own text in both LEA and process writing. Reading and writing are presented as meaningful, functional, and genuine in both, and the two approaches stress the meaning-making nature of communication. Karnowski suggests that LEA can be modified to make it more like process writing:

1. *Prewriting*. Students gather ideas for writing through experiences, talk, and art.
2. *Drafting*. Students dictate the LEA text, which the teacher records. This writing is a first draft.
3. *Revising*. Students and teacher read and reread the LEA text. They talk about the writing and make one or more changes.
4. *Editing*. Student and teacher reread the revised text and check that spelling, punctuation, capital letters, and other mechanical considerations are correct. Then students recopy the text in a book format.
5. *Sharing*. Students share the text with classmates from the author's chair, and the text can be used for other reading activities. With these modifications, students can learn that reading and writing are whole processes.

Big Books

Big books are greatly enlarged picture books that teachers use in shared reading, most commonly with primary-grade students. According to this technique, developed in New Zealand, teachers enlarge a picture book, place it on an easel or chart rack where all the students can see it, and read it with small groups of students or the whole class (Holdaway, 1979). Any type of picture book may be turned into a big book, but predictable books, nursery rhymes, songs, and poems are most popular. Teachers can purchase these books from educational publishers (such as Scholastic or the Wright Group), and some publishers of basal reading textbooks have developed big books to supplement their programs. Teachers can also make big books themselves by printing the text of a picture book on large sheets of posterboard and adding illustrations. The steps in making a big book are listed in Figure 12.3. Heald-Taylor (1987) lists these types of big books that teachers can make:

Replica book. An exact copy of a picture book
Newly illustrated book. A familiar book with new illustrations
Adapted book. A new version of a familiar picture book
Original book. An original book composed by students or the teacher

FIGURE 12.3
Steps in Making a Big Book

1. Choose a picture book, short story, nursery rhyme, song, or poem to enlarge.
2. Collect materials, including sheets of posterboard or chart paper, pens, crayons, paints, or other art materials.
3. Print the text of the story, nursery rhyme, song, or poem on the sheets of paper, dividing the text evenly across the pages of the book and leaving at least half the page for the illustration.
4. Add illustrations, which can be done freehand or by children. Teachers can also use opaque projectors to reproduce the illustrations.
5. Add a title page with names of authors, illustrations, and copyright. When students adapt books, that should also be stated on the title page.
6. Design a cover.
7. Put the pages into sequence.
8. Bind the book together with metal rings, yarn, or other clips.

With the big book on a chart stand or easel, the teacher reads it aloud, pointing to every word. Before long, students are joining in the reading. Then the teacher rereads the story, inviting students to help with the reading. The next time the book is read, the teacher reads to the point that the text becomes predictable, such as the last word of a sentence or the beginning of a refrain, and the students supply the missing text. Having students supply missing text is important because it leads to independent reading. When students have become familiar with the text, they are invited to read the big book independently (Slaughter, 1983).

Students can also make big books of familiar stories to retell and of original stories that they compose. First, students choose a familiar story and write a retelling of it, or they write an original story. Next, they divide the text page by page and prepare illustrations. Then they write the text on large sheets of posterboard and add the illustrations. They make the title page and cover and compile the pages, and teachers can use the book with young children just as they would use commercially produced big books and big books they made themselves.

Teachers can use big books for a variety of reading and writing activities. Students identify individual letters and words, and the teacher uses words from the stories to analyze phonetic principles. Students can predict vocabulary words and events from the story and develop comprehension skills. Elley (1989) used two experiments with classroom teachers in New Zealand who read stories aloud to elementary school children (7- and 8-year olds) and gave pre- and posttests to measure the extent of the new vocabulary the children gained from the reading. Results showed that oral story reading is a significant source of vocabulary acquisition, whether or not the reading is accompanied by teacher explanation of word meanings.

E. MAKING THE CONNECTION WITH AUTHORS

In reading stories, poems, and informational books, students become curious about the people who write and illustrate books. Units that focus on particular authors and illustrators will further their interest. One way that students learn about authors and illustrators is by reading about them. A number of biographies and autobiographies of well-known authors and illustrators, including Beatrix Potter (Aldis, 1969), Jean Fritz (1982), and Tomie de Paola (1989) are available for elementary students. Students can also read profiles of favorite authors in books such as Hopkins's *Books Are by People* (1969) and *More Books Are by More People* (1974). Filmstrips, videotapes, and other audiovisual materials about authors and illustrators are becoming increasingly available. Figure 12.4 lists books and audiovisual materials about authors. In addition, students can read journal articles to learn about favorite writers. Many articles profiling authors and illustrators have been published in *Language Arts, Horn Book,* and other journals, which teachers can clip and file. A last source of information is the publicity brochures that teachers or students can request from publishers and that are usually free of charge.

A second way to learn about authors and illustrators is by writing them letters. Students can share their ideas and feelings about the books they are reading, ask how a particular character was developed, or why the illustrator used a particular art medium.

A third way children can learn about authors is by meeting them in person. Authors and illustrators often make public appearances at libraries, bookstores, and schools. Students also meet authors at young authors' conferences, often held in schools as the culminating event for a year's work in writing.

F. MAKING THE CONNECTION WITH STORIES

Teachers are increasingly using trade books either in conjunction with or instead of basal readers. Recently, there has been a trend toward using predictable books for beginning reading instruction, a practice that is supported by research (Heald-Taylor, 1987; Lawrence & Harris, 1986).

Directed Reading-Thinking Activity

In the *Directed Reading-Thinking Activity* (DRTA) (Stauffer, 1975), students make predictions about a story and then read to confirm or reject their predictions. The procedure in-

FIGURE 12.4
Books and Audiovisual Materials About Children's Authors and Illustrators

Books

Aldis, D. (1969). *Nothing is impossible: The story of Beatrix Potter.* New York: Atheneum. (M)

Blair, G. (1981). *Laura Ingalls Wilder.* New York: Putnam. (P–M)

Blegvad, E. (1979). *Self-portrait: Erik Blegvad.* Reading, MA: Addison-Wesley. (P–M)

Cleary, B. (1988). *A girl from Yamhill: A memoir.* New York: Morrow. (M)

Dahl, R. (1984). *Boy: Tales of childhood.* New York: Farrar. (M)

de Paola, T. (1989). *The art lesson.* New York: Putnam. (P)

Fritz, J. (1982). *Homesick: My own story.* New York: Putnam. (M)

Goodall, J. S. (1981). *Before the war, 1908–1939. An autobiography in pictures.* New York: Atheneum. (wordless picture book) (M)

Henry, M. (1980). *The illustrated Marguerite Henry.* Chicago: Rand McNally. (M)

Lewis, C. S. (1985). *Letters to children.* New York: Macmillan. (M)

Hyman, T. S. (1981). *Self-portrait: Trina Schart Hyman.* Reading, MA: Addison-Wesley. (P–M)

Peet, B (1989). *Bill Peet: An Autobiography.* Houghton Mifflin. (M)

Yates, E. (1981). *My diary—My world.* New York: Westminister. (M)

Zemach, M. (1978). *Self-portrait: Margot Zemach.* Reading, MA: Addison-Wesley. (P–M)

Collections of Profile Articles

Commire, A. (1971–1985). *Something about the author* (38 volumes). Chicago: Gale Research. (M)

Hoffman, M., & Samuels, E. (Eds.). (1972). *Authors and illustrators of children's books.* New York: Bowker. (M)

Hopkins, L. B. (1969). *Books are by people: Interviews with 104 authors and illustrators of books for young children.* New York: Citation. (M)

Hopkins, L. B. (1974). *More books by more people: Interviews with 65 authors of books for children.* New York: Citation. (M)

Jones C., & Way, O. R. (1976). *British children's authors: Interviews at home.* Chicago: American Library Association. (M)

Wintle, J., & Fischer, E. (1975). *The pied pipers: Interviews with the influential creators of children's literature.* London: Paddington Press. (M)

Audiovisual Materials

"Bill Peet in his studio," Houghton Mifflin (videotape).

"The case of a Model-A Ford and the man in the snorkel under the hood. Donald J. Sobol," Random House (sound filmstrip).

"Charlotte Zolotow: The grower," Random House (sound filmstrip).

"David Macaulay in his studio," Houghton Mifflin (videotape).

"Edward Ardizzone," Weston Woods (film).

"Ezra Jack Keats," Weston Woods (film).

"First choice: Authors and books," set of nine sound filmstrips from Pied Piper featuring Judy Blume, Clyde Bulla, Beverly Cleary, John D. Fitzgerald, Sid Fleischman, Virginia Hamilton, Marguerite Henry, E. L. Konigsburg, and Theodore Taylor.

"First choice: Poets and poetry," set of five sound filmstrips from Pied Piper featuring Nikki Giovanni, Karla Kuskin, Myra Cohn Livingston, David McCord, and Eve Merriam.

"Gail E. Haley: Wood and linoleum illustration." Weston Woods (sound filmstrip).

"James Daugherty," Weston Woods (film).

"Laurant de Brunhoff: Daydreamer," Random House (sound filmstrip).

"Maurice Sendak," Weston Woods (film).

"Meet Stan and Jan Berenstain," Random House (sound filmstrip).

"Meet the Author," a collection of 12 sound filmstrips or videotapes from Random House featuring well-known authors such as L. Frank Baum, Dr. Seuss, and Charlotte Zolotow.

"Meet the Newbery author," collection of 22 individual sound filmstrips from Random House featuring Lloyd Alexander, William H. Armstrong, Natalie Babbitt, Carol Ryrie Brink, Betsy Byars, Beverly Cleary, James Lincoln and Christopher Collier, Susan Cooper, Eleanor Estes, Jean Craighead George, Bette Green, Virginia Hamilton, Marguerite Henry, Jamake Highwater, Madeleine L'Engle, Arnold Lobel, Scott O'Dell, Katherine Paterson, Isaac Bashevis Singer, Laura Ingalls Wilder, Elizabeth Yates, and Laurence Yep.

"Mr. Shepard and Mr. Milne," Weston Woods (film).

"Poetry explained by Karla Kuskin," Weston Woods (sound filmstrip).

"Robert McCloskey," Weston Woods (film).

"Steven Kellogg: How a picture book is made," Weston Woods (sound filmstrip).

"Tomi Ungerer: Storyteller," Weston Woods (film).

"A visit with Scott O'Dell," Houghton Mifflin (videotape).

"Who's Dr. Seuss? Meet Ted Geisel," Random House (sound filmstrip).

FIGURE 12.4 cont'd
P = grades (K–2)
M = grades (3–4)

Addresses for Audiovisual Manufacturers

Houghton Mifflin Co.
2 Park Street
Boston, MA 02108

Random House
School Division
400 Hahn Road
Westminister, MD 21157

Weston Woods
Weston, CT 06883

Pied Piper
P.O. Box 320
Verdugo City, CA 91046

FIGURE 12.5
Steps in the Directed Reading-Thinking Activity

Step 1: Predicting

After showing students the cover of the book and reading the title, the teacher begins by asking students to make a prediction about the story, using questions such as:

- What do you think a story with a title like this might be about?
- What do you think might happen in this story?
- Does this picture give you any ideas about what might happen in this story?

The teacher or students may read the first paragraph or two of the story, if necessary, to provide more information to use in making predictions. Then students write a brief response and read their responses aloud. After sharing their responses, the teacher asks these questions:

- Which of these ideas do you think would be the likely one?
- Why do you think that idea is a good one?

Step 2: Reasoning and Predicting from Succeeding Pages

After setting their purpose for reading or listening, the students or teacher read part of the story, and students begin to confirm or reject their predictions. At crucial points in the story, the teacher asks questions such as:

- What do you think now?
- What do you think will happen next?
- What would happen if. . . ?
- Why do you think that idea is a good one?

Students write brief responses and read them aloud. Then the students or the teacher continue reading the story.

Step 3: Proving

Students give reasons to support their predictions by writing answers to questions such as:

- What in the story makes you think that?
- Where in the story do you get information to support that idea?

The teacher can ask these "proving" questions during the story or after it has been read.

---

volves three steps, presented in Figure 12.5, and works best with stories in which characters must make difficult choices or solve complex problems. There is little point in making predictions in response to questions with obvious answers.

This procedure can be easily adapted for writing by having students write their predictions before sharing them orally (Tompkins, 1990). A group of fourth and fifth graders in a reading lab class listened to Lionni's *Tico and the Golden Wings* (1964), a fable about a bird named Tico who was born without wings. He was, however, a happy bird, because he had friends who took care of him. One day a wishingbird granted Tico's wish for wings, and he received wings covered with golden feathers. After his jealous friends abandoned him, Tico traveled around the world, giving away his golden feathers to people who needed help.

Black feathers grew on his wings in place of the golden feathers, and when he was all black again, Tico's friends welcomed him.

The teacher began by reading the title and showing the cover of the picture book. She asked, "What do you think the story will be about?" and the students wrote the following responses:

Tico will probably have them at the first of the story and then lose them at the end.
Tico might have regular wings at first and then something drastic might happen and he would get gold wings.
He'll have them at the beginning and he keeps them forever.
Tico was just a normal bird and then one day his wings turned to gold.

Soon Tico is given the opportunity to make a wish, and the teacher asked, "What do you think Tico will wish for?" Students predicted:

Tico wants wings so he can fly like the other birds.
Tico wishes for golden wings and to be able to fly from tree to tree and soar through the sky like other birds.

Later, after Tico gets the golden wings, he meets a poor man with a sick daughter, and the teacher asked, "How do you think Tico will help the poor man and his sick daughter?" Students answered:

Tico would fly to town and get the medicine.
He would call for that wishingbird and ask her.
Tico will pick one of his golden feathers off and give it to the man.

After Tico gives away all of his golden feathers, the teacher asked, "Will Tico's friends welcome him back now?" and students wrote:

Yes, because he don't have golden wings no more.
Yes, because he is just like the other birds now.
Yes, because his friends won't think he's trying to be better than them.
Yes, they will because he is different on the outside but still the same on the inside.

After reading the end of the story, students were asked, "Did you like the story? Why or why not?" Before beginning an oral discussion of the story, they reflected:

Yes, because it told about Tico's ups and his downs.
Yes, I did because it was interesting.
Yes, because it was a very exciting book.
Yes, because Tico was a smart bird to give his golden wings to the poor people so he can be the same as the other birds.
I liked it because Tico was a likable bird.

After students wrote each response, they read them aloud to the group before the teacher continued reading. Then students had a purpose for listening: to learn if their predictions were correct. Through this activity, students engaged with the text, anticipated story events, and constructed meaning and an emotional response.

A warning is in order: teachers should not interrupt a story too often, because this procedure can become tedious for students who are comprehending and making their own predictions (Corcoran, 1987). The process is more useful with less capable readers who need help making connections or for students who are reading a complex piece of literature. For the remedial readers who used DRTA with *Tico and the Golden Wings,* the procedure encouraged them to probe their thoughts more deeply than if they had simply listened to the story read aloud.

Predictable Books

Predicting is a strategy we use in all aspects of our lives. In reading, we predict what the author will say next and how he or she will say it. Readers globally predict the next event in a story at the same time they make a more local prediction about the next sentence. They may also predict how the author will use language in the rest of a sentence and what letters are likely to be in the rest of a word. Prediction is an important reading strategy for all kinds of books, but some books are especially easy to predict because they contain repetitive phrases or sentences, repetitive sentences in a cumulative structure, or sequential events that make them easier to read. These *predictable books* are a valuable tool for beginning readers because the repetitive patterns enable children to predict the next sentence or episode in the story (Bridge, 1979, Heald-Taylor, 1987; Rhodes, 1981; Tompkins & Webeler, 1983).

A list of predictable books appropriate for beginning readers, arranged in three categories, is presented in Figure 12.6. Books in the first category, repetitive sentences, include phrases or sentences that are repeated throughout the story. An example is Gag's *Millions of Cats* (1956), in which the refrain "Cats here, Cats there, Cats and kittens everywhere, Hundreds of cats, Thousands of cats, Millions and billions and trillions of cats" is repeated again and again. The second category, repetitive sentences in a cumulative structure, in-

FIGURE 12.6
Predictable Books for Primary-Grade Students

Repetitive Sentences
Ahlberg, A. (1990). *The Black Cat.* Ill. by A. Amstutz. New York: Greenwillow.
Ahlberg, A. (1990). *The pet shop.* Ill. by A. Amstutz. New York: Greenwillow.
Aylesworth, J. (1989). *Mother Halverson's new cat.* Ill. by T. Goffe. New York: Atheneum.
Carlstrom, N. W. (1990). *Moose in the garden.* Ill. by L. Desimini. New York: HarperCollins Children's Books.
Deming, A. G. (1988). *Who is tapping at my window?* Ill. by M. Wellington. New York: E. P. Dutton.
Farjeon, E. (1990). *Cats sleep anywhere.* Ill. by M. Price Jenkins. New York: HarperCollins Children's Books.
Herson, K. & D. (1989). *The copycat.* Ill. by C. Stock. New York: Atheneum.
Hilton, N. (1990). *The long red scarf.* Ill. by M. Power. New York: Carolrhoda.
Hood, T. (1990). *Before I go to sleep.* Ill. by M. Begin-Callanan. New York: G. P. Putnam's Sons.
Kasza, K. (1990). *When the elephant walks.* Ill. by author. New York: G. P. Putnam's Sons.
Komaiko, L. (1990). *My perfect neighborhood.* Ill. by B. Westman. New York: Harper & Row.
Martinez, R. (1990). *Mrs. McDockerty's knitting.* Ill. by C. O'Neill. Boston: Houghton Mifflin.
Stott, D. (1990). *Too much.* Ill. by author. New York: E. P. Dutton.
Thomas, P. (1990). *"Stand back," said the elephant, "I'm going to sneeze!"* Ill. by W. Tripp. New York: Lothrop, Lee & Shepard.
Van Laan, N. (1990). *A mouse in my house.* Ill. by M. Priceman. New York: Knopf.

Repetitive Sentences in a Cumulative Structure
Armstrong, J. (1992). *Hugh can do.* Ill. by K. B. Root. New York: Crown.
Aylesworth, J. (1989). *Mr. McGill goes to town.* Ill. by T. Graham. New York: Holt.
Baker, K. (1990). *Who is the beast?* San Diego, CA: Harcourt Brace Jovanovich.
Carlstrom, N. W. (1992). *Baby-O.* Ill. by S. Stevenson. Boston: Little, Brown.
Dragonwagon, C. (1989). *This is the bread I baked for Ned.* Ill. by I. Seltzer. New York: Macmillan.
Fox, M. (1990). *Shoes from Grandpa.* Ill. by P. Mullins. New York: Orchard Books/Watts.
Kherdian, D., & Hogrogian, N. (1990). *The cat's midsummer jamboree.* New York: Philomel.
MacDonald, E. (1990). *Mike's kite.* Ill. by R. Kendall. New York: Orchard.
Neitzel, S. (1989). *The jacket I wear in the snow.* Ill. by N. W. Parker. New York: Greenwillow.
Robart, R. (1987). *The cake that Mack ate.* Ill. by M. Kovalski. New York: Joy Street.
Saunders, D. & J. (1990). *Dibble and dabble.* New York: Bradbury.
Zacharius, T. (1990). *But where is the green parrot?* Ill. by W. Zacharius. New York: Delaocrte.

Sequential Patterns
Alain. (1964). *One, two, three, going to sea.* New York: Scholastic.
Baskin, L. (1972). *Hosie's alphabet.* New York: Viking.
Carle, E. (1969). *The very hungry caterpillar.* Cleveland: Collins-World.
Carle, E. (1977). *The grouchy ladybug.* New York: Crowell.
Carle, E. (1987). *A house for a hermit crab.* Saxonville, MA: Picture Book Studio.
Domanska, J. (1985). *Busy Monday morning.* New York: Greenwillow.
Keats, E. J. (1973). *Over in the meadow.* New York: Scholastic.
Mack, S. (1974). *10 bears in my bed.* New York: Pantheon.
Martin, B. (1970). *Monday, Monday, I like Monday.* New York: Holt, Rinehart & Winston.
Schulevitz, U. (1967). *One Monday morning.* New York: Scribner.
Sendak, M. (1975). *Seven little monsters.* New York: Harper & Row.

cludes books in which phrases or sentences are repeated and expanded in each episode. In *The Gingerbread Boy* (Galdone, 1975), for instance, the gingerbread boy repeats and expands his boast as he meets each character. Books in the third category, sequential patterns, use cultural sequences, such as letters of the alphabet, numbers, and days of the week, to structure the story; for example, *The Very Hungry Caterpillar* (Carle, 1969) combines the number and day of the week sequences. Children may also use rhyme to anticipate events in reading; many of the Dr. Seuss stories use rhyme extensively to make them predictable.

Predictable books are excellent reading materials for young children because they are able to gain reading "independence" quickly. In related studies, Bridge and her colleagues (1982) and Chandler and Baghban (1980) found that primary-grade children learn sight words more easily with predictable picture books than with traditional basal readers. Bridge and others found that first graders were likely to use both phonics and context clues to identify unfamiliar words while children reading in basal readers depended on phonics alone. Chandler and Baghban found that students in grades 1, 2, and 3 who used the predictable books as a supplement improved significantly in reading over a control group as measured by the Metropolitan Achievement Tests.

Teachers often choose predictable books to make into big books for shared reading because of their repetitions (Heald-Taylor, 1987). Teachers read the selection aloud to students, then reread it many times, with teacher or a student tracking the text with a pointer. One of several procedures can be used to share the text:

Unison. Teacher and students read the story together as a group, in unison.
Repetition. The teacher reads the story one sentence at a time, and students repeat the sentence in unison.
Refrain. The teacher reads the story, but students read the refrain or repeated text.
Cloze. The teacher reads most of text, but pauses for students to fill in missing words or phrases that are highly predictable (Heald-Taylor, 1987).

Connecting to writing. Not only are predictable books useful as reading material for young children, but they also provide patterns for their writing. Children often create their own books following the repetitive sentence patterns, cumulative story episode structures, and other sequential patterns they have learned.

Wordless Books

Another way to connect reading and writing is with *wordless books* in which the story or information is told through the illustrations. Teachers typically use these books with young children because even nonreaders can enjoy and understand many of them. Children can tell a story from the pictures, talk about it, and begin to recognize some of the elements in stories. They can identify familiar objects and follow along as the teacher demonstrates how to "read" the story. Children also can tell the story for a small group, role-play events in the story, and dictate or write their own versions. Many wordless books, however, have sophisticated story lines and several levels of understanding that make them appropriate for students in grade 4 and older.

The writing connection. Wordless picture books can be used for a variety of writing activities (Roberts, 1990). Children can write dialogue for the characters that they name and use cartoonlike balloons affixed with adhesive-backed paper or write their own versions of an event. These books are especially useful for teaching point of view because there is no text to influence the reader. Thus, the children can tell, dictate, or write the story from different views more easily. Additionally, these books offer connections between illustrations and writing. Just as there are connections between books and writing expository text to make something known, so are there similarities between the visual presentations in wordless books and the characteristics of different types (modes) of writing (Roberts, 1990). With wordless books, children can begin to recognize story structures such as comparing and contrasting, problem-solution, or explanation, which are shown in the illustrations. Children can learn to use the structures in the pictures in their prewriting activities. With repeated exposure to wordless books, they will learn that messages that are sent visually,

i.e., this is a narrative (a procedure, a sequence, a topic presentation). Thus, wordless books are valuable because they give children the opportunity to learn to link visual messages to words that they can then use in an oral discussion of the message sent—for example, that the story is a narrative, a procedure, a sequence, or a topic presentation. For children in grades 3 and 4 and older, many wordless books incorporate story structures that are linked to several writing modes—the narrative mode, procedural mode, time-order sequence mode, and topic exposition mode. Thus, wordless books can be linked to writing in several ways:

- Wordless books that can be connected to a narrative mode of writing tell stories in pictures, stimulate the use of descriptive words, offer opportunities to name the characters, to tell the plots, and sometimes, include possibilities for comparing and contrasting. (A list of such books is shown in Figure 12.7.)
- Wordless books that can be connected to a procedural mode of writing show a procedure or a process in identified steps (see Figure 12.8).
- Wordless books that can be connected to a time-order sequence mode of writing tell selected events in a sequence. Sometimes, the characters solve a problem or there are cause-and-effect situations within the illustrations (see Figure 12.9).
- Wordless books that can be connected to a topic exposition mode of writing are presentations that show a clear topic with a main idea and supporting details in the illustrations (see Figure 12.10).

The observed connections from the visual presentation in a wordless book to a writing mode can be a signal to the teacher to introduce some of the words related to the particular

FIGURE 12.7
Wordless Books With Connections to Narrative Writing

Narrative Presentations in Wordless Books*

Collington, P. (1987). *The angel and the soldier boy.* Ill. by author. New York: Knopf.
Drescher, H. (1987). *The yellow umbrella.* Ill. by author. New York: Bradbury.
Goodall, J. S. reteller. (1988). *Little Red Riding Hood.* Ill. by the reteller. New York: Macmillan.
McCully, E. A. (1984). *Picnic: A wordless picture book.* Ill. by author. New York: Harper & Row.
McCully, E. A. (1985). *First snow: A wordless picture book.* Ill. by author. New York: Harper & Row.
McCully, E. A. (1987). *School: A wordless picture book.* Ill. by author. New York: Harper & Row.
McCully, E. A. (1988). *The Christmas gift: A wordless picture book.* Ill. by author. New York: Harper Junior Books.
McCully, E. A. (1988). *New baby: A wordless picture book.* Ill. by author. New York: Harper Junior Books.
Wiesner, D. (1988). *Free fall.* Ill. by author. New York: Lothrop, Lee & Shepard.
Winter, P. (1980). *Sir Andrew.* Ill. by author. New York: Crown.

*Words to introduce for oral discussion and writing connection: *on the contrary, likewise, in spite of, or, on the other hand, although, nevertheless, through, notwithstanding, conversely, otherwise, less, similarly, many,* and *yet.*

FIGURE 12.8
Wordless Books With Connections to Procedural Writing

Procedural Presentations in Wordless Books*

Burningham, J. (1983). *Five down: Numbers as sizes; Count up, learning sets.* Ill. by author. New York: Viking.
Burningham, J. (1983). *Just cats: Learning groups.* Ill. by author. New York: Viking.
Burningham, J. (1983). *Pigs plus: Learning addition.* Ill. by author. New York: Viking.
Burningham, J. (1983). *Read One: Numbers as words.* Ill. by author. New York: Viking.

*Words to introduce for oral discussion and writing connection: *first, second, third, in addition, next, also, then,* and *last.*

FIGURE 12.9
Wordless Books and Connections to Time-Order Writing

Time-Order Presentations in Wordless Books*

Ernst, L. C. (1986). *Up to ten and down again.* Ill. by author. New York: McEldererry/Macmillan.
Goodall, J. S. (1986). *The story of a castle.* Ill. by author. New York: McEldererry/Macmillan.
Mari, I. & E. (1970). *The apple and the moth.* Ill. by authors. New York: Pantheon.
Mari, I. & E. (1970). *The chicken and the egg.* Ill. by authors. New York: Pantheon.

*Words to introduce for oral discussion and writing connection: Time-Order: *yesterday, one day, tomorrow, first, immediately, once, meanwhile, soon, in the meantime, after, afterward,* and *next;* Time-Sequence: *at the same time, first, second, soon, finally, while, when, then,* and *next.*

FIGURE 12.10
Wordless Books and Connections to Topic Exposition Writing

Topic Exposition Presentations in Wordless Books*

Anno, M. (1980). *Anno's Italy.* Ill. by author. New York: Collins.
Anno, M. (1982). *Anno's Britain.* Ill. by author. New York: Philomel.
Anno, M. (1983). *Anno's USA.* Ill. by author. New York: Philomel.
Anno, M. (1984). *Anno's Flea Market.* Ill. by author. New York: Philomel.
Crews, D. (1980). *Truck.* Ill. by author. New York: Greenwillow.
Crews, D. (1982). *Carousel.* Ill. by author. New York: Greenwillow.
Crews, D. (1982). *Harbor.* Ill. by author. New York: Greenwillow.
Cristini, E., & Puricelli, L. (1981). *In my garden.* Ill. by authors. Boston: Alphabet Press/Neuebauer Press.
Cristini, E., & Puricelli, L. (1981). *In the pond.* Ill. by authors. Boston: Alphabet Press/Neuebauer Press.
Cristini, E., & Puricelli, L. (1981). *In the woods.* Ill. by authors. Boston: Alphabet Press/Neuebauer Press.
Munro, R. (1985). *The inside-outside book of New York City.* Ill. by author. New York: Dutton.
Munro, R. (1987). *The inside-outside book of Washington, D. C.* Ill. by author. New York: Dutton.
Munro, R. (1989). *The inside-outside book of London.* Ill. by author. New York: Dutton.

*Words to introduce for oral discussion and writing connection: *consequently, therefore, accordingly, thus, as a result, finally,* and *in conclusion.*

writing mode through an oral discussion about the book's presentation. Children will begin to incorporate the words as they have repeated opportunities in written discourse activities.

Pattern Books

Many children's books have a pattern or format that children can adapt for their own writing. For example, one type of pattern book is the genre of alphabet books. The patterns in alphabet books, and other books, too, help children make sense of what they hear, read, talk about, see, and write. When the patterns are recognized, they can become models for certain uses and features of language. Among these models and features, patterns can be introduced to children that present:

- Creative uses of language
- Words, meanings, and actions of language
- Ways of playing with language
- A foundation for oral responses, reading, and writing
- A base for additional learning skills. (Roberts, 1987, 1994)

As a choice, children may be interested in writing about what animals they have seen during their outings to a local zoo, park, or nature area after listening to *As I Was Crossing Boston Common* (1975) written by Norma Farber and illustrated by Arnold Lobel. Farber's book is designed to introduce 26 unfamiliar animals to children as the main character, a turtle, meets them on the Common. Children can dictate or write original sentences, use the pattern in their stories, or suggest endings for the book's sentence pattern—"As I was crossing _____ (name of place), not very fast, not very slow; I met someone with a _____ (name of animal) in tow." The descriptions for the animals are on the final pages in a list beginning with an angwantibo, a small West African lemur, and ending with an East Indian civet cat—a Zibet. The children can use the writing process (see Chapter 11) as they draft and refine their writing. They can use the pattern as a feature of their own stories but adapt the format as they wish. Alphabet books that children can use as models for dictating and writing are listed in Figure 12.11.

Basal Reader Stories

Instead of doing workbook pages before and after reading a selection in a basal reader, students can keep a reading log and write about the stories they read. They can brainstorm lists of words or cluster the main ideas from the story. They can also respond to the reading through a variety of talk, drama, reading, and writing activities (Buckley, 1986). What is important is that students connect the basal reader stories to real-world reading and writing so they see a reason to learn language skills. These are some activities through which students can respond to reading:

> *Brainstorming.* Students brainstorm a list of words related to the topic or theme of a story, then use the words in a freewrite.
>
> *Writing class collaboration stories.* Students choose a favorite story and retell it; each student retells one page, and after the pages are completed, they compile them to form a book that can be placed in the class library.

FIGURE 12.11
Alphabet Books With Patterns for Dictating and Writing

Accumulation

Berenstain, S., & J. (1972). *C is for clown: A circus of C words.* Ill. by authors. New York: Random House.

Hoguet, S. R. (1983). *I unpacked my grandmother's trunk: A picture book game.* Ill. by author. New York: E. P. Dutton.

Yolen, J. (1975). *All in the woodland early: An ABC book.* Ill. by J. B. Zalben. New York: Philomel/Putnam Group.

Alliteration

Chouinard, R., & M. (1988). *The amazing animal alphabet book.* Ill. by R. Chouinard. New York: Doubleday.

de Brunhoff, L. (1983). *Babar's ABC.* Ill. by author. New York: Random House.

Kellogg, S. (1987). *Aster aardvark's alphabet adventures.* New York: Morrow.

Onomotopeia

Cleary, B. (1964). *The hullabaloo ABC.* Ill. by E. Thollander. Berkeley: Parnassus.

Whitehead, P. (1985). *Let's go to the farm.* Ill. by E. Gold. Mahwah, NJ: Troll.

Repetition

Boynton, S. (1983). *A Is for angry: An animal and adjective alphabet.* Ill. by author. New York: Workman.

Eichenberg, F. (1952). *Ape in a cape: An alphabet of odd animals.* New York: Harcourt Brace Jovanovich.

Purvis, M. E. (1985). *Animal alphabet: Wild animals.* Ill. by author. Bonita: Children's Center Publications of California.

Rhyme

Anglund, J. W. (1960). *In a pumpkin shell: A Mother Goose ABC.* Ill. by author. New York: Harcourt Brace Jovanovich.

Hague, K. (1984). *Alphabears: An ABC book.* New York: Holt.

Lalicki, B. (Compiler). (1984). *If there were dreams to sell.* Ill. by Margot Tomes. New York: Lothrop, Lee & Shepard.

Writing simulated journals. After reading a story, students assume the persona of a story character and write a journal from that person's viewpoint.

Comparing a story to other versions of a story. After reading a basal reader version of a well-known story, students read other versions of the story in trade books and compare the different versions. There are many versions available, for example, of "The Hare and the Tortoise," "Cinderella," and other folktales.

Drawing a wordless picture book. Students choose a favorite story, draw a series of pictures to illustrate it, and compile the pictures to make a wordless picture book.

Writing dialogue. Students rewrite an excerpt from a script in narrative form.

Retelling stories from different viewpoints. Students retell stories from the viewpoint of another character; the retellings can be oral, tape-recorded, or written.

Research and informational writing. Students choose a subject (e.g., Alaska, rabbits) from one of the informational selections in the textbook, research the topic, and write a concept book or brief report on it.

Writing simulated letters. Students write simulated letters from one character to another; then classmates who have also read the story answer the letters.

Developing timelines. Students choose a person profiled in a biographical or autobiographical selection in the textbook and develop a timeline of the person's life; they also highlight the part of the timeline discussed in the selection.

G. MAKING THE CONNECTION WITH INFORMATIONAL BOOKS

Many forms of writing are organized or structured in particular ways. Many students are familiar with elements of story structure, such as characters and plot, through telling and reading stories as well as watching them on television. They write poems such as haiku and cinquain, which follow syllable-counting formulas, and read and write biographies, which usually follow a chronological sequence.

Informational books are trade books that deal with careers, animals, countries, planets, human body, Indians, and other nonfiction topics, social studies and other content area textbooks, and encyclopedias. They are also called *expository texts*. Reading educators have examined content area materials for elementary and high school levels to devise ways to help students comprehend the materials more easily. They have identified a number of patterns or structures used in these texts, called *expository text structures*.

Expository Text Structures

Five of the most common organizational patterns are description, sequence, comparison, cause and effect, and problem and solution (Meyer & Freedle, 1984; Niles, 1974). The following section describes these patterns and presents sample passages and cue words that signal use of each pattern. (See Figures 12.7 through 12.10 for examples of wordless books that can introduce these patterns visually.)

Description. In this organizational pattern, the writer describes a topic by listing characteristics, features, and examples. Phrases such as *for example* and *characteristics are* cue this structure. When students delineate any topic, such as the Mississippi River, eagles, or Alaska, they use description.

Sequence. The writer lists items or events in numerical or chronological order. Cue words include *first, second, third, next, then,* and *finally.* Directions for completing a math problem, stages in an animal's life cycle, and events in a biography are often written in the sequence pattern.

Comparison. The writer explains how two or more things are alike or different. *Different, in contrast, alike, same as,* and *on the other hand* are cue words and phrases that signal this structure. When students compare and contrast book and movie versions of a story, reptiles and amphibians, or life in ancient Greece with life in ancient Egypt, they use this organizational pattern.

Cause and effect. The writer explains one or more causes and the resulting effect or effects. *Reasons why, if . . . then, as a result, therefore,* and *because* are words and phrases that cue this structure. Explanations of why dinosaurs became extinct, the effects of pollution on the environment, or the causes of the Civil War are written using the cause and effect pattern.

Problem and solution. In this expository structure, the writer states a problem and offers one or more solutions. A variation is the question and answer format, in which the writer poses a question and then answers it. Cue words and phrases include *the problem is, the puzzle is, solve,* and *question . . . answer.* Students use this structure when they write about why money was invented, saving endangered animals, and building dams to stop flooding. They often use the problem-solution pattern in writing advertisements and other persuasive writing as well.

These organizational patterns correspond to the traditional organization of main ideas (or topic sentences) and details within paragraphs. The main idea is embodied in the organizational pattern and the details are the elaboration; for example, in the following passage, the main idea is that the modern Olympic games are very different from the ancient Olympic games. The details are the specific comparisons and contrasts. We can diagram the main idea and details for the comparison as follows:

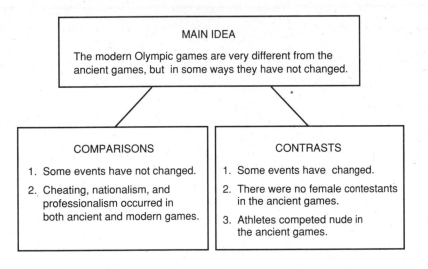

Diagrams called *graphic organizers* can help students organize ideas for the other four organizational patterns as well.

Most of the research on expository text structures has focused on older students' use of these patterns in reading; however, elementary students also use the patterns and cue words in their writing. A class of second graders examined the five expository text structures and learned that authors use cue words as a secret code to signal the structures. Then they read informational books that used each of the expository text structures, and wrote paragraphs to use the patterns themselves. Working in small groups, they developed organizational patterns. For example, information about igloos might be written as a description, as a comparison to Indian teepees, or as a solution to a housing problem in the Arctic.

KWL Strategy

Another way to help students take an active role in reading and writing informational books is the *KWL strategy* (Ogle, 1986, 1989)–*KWL* stands for Know, Want to Know, and Learned. Teachers use this three-step strategy to help students prepare to read, read, and understand informational texts.

1. *Before reading.* To begin, the teacher asks students to brainstorm what they know about a topic and records the information in the "K" or "What We Know" column on a class chart, as shown in Figure 12.12. As students suggest information and as conflicts and con-

FIGURE 12.12
K-W-L Chart
Ogle, 1986, p. 565

K What We Know	W What We Want to Find Out	L What We Learned

Categories of information we expect to use:

A.
B.
C.
D.

fusions arise, the teacher adds questions in the "W" or "What We Want to Find Out" column. Then students complete the "K" and "W" columns on individual charts like the one in Figure 12.12. (Teachers can omit individual charts when working with young children.) Brainstorming information in the "K" column helps students activate prior knowledge, and developing questions in the "W" column provides students with specific purposes for reading. Next, teachers ask students to look for ways to chunk or categorize the information they brainstormed and for information they expect to find in the text they will read. For example, second graders making a KWL chart on penguins might identify these categories: what they look like, where they live, how they move, and what their families are like. Older students might use categories such as appearance, habitat, enemies, and classification.

2. *During reading*. Students read actively, looking for new information and for answers to questions in the "W" column. Depending on the length and complexity of the material,

students can read the complete piece, or it can be broken into parts. As students read, they can take notes about what they are learning on their KWL charts, or they can recall the information after reading.

3. *After reading.* Students reflect on what they have learned and complete the "L" or "What We Learned" column of the class chart. Then they complete the "L" column on their individual charts. Students can also add additional information to the categories section of the charts to reflect the types of information the author included in the informational text.

The KWL strategy is useful for helping students gain more from an individual reading assignment, such as if a second-grade class were reading a book about penguins. It can also be used during a unit of study in social studies, science, or another content area. Students begin by completing the "K" and "W" columns and the categories sections at the beginning of the unit, then add to the chart throughout the two, three, or four weeks of the unit. At the end of the unit, students complete the chart and share what they have learned. Students are thus better prepared to learn, to organize their learning, to clarify misconceptions, and to appreciate their learning.

H. CLASSROOM ACTIVITIES

Teaching Children to Write Stories

ACTIVITY 12.1

During the preschool years, children develop a concept of story by listening to stories read aloud and telling stories. With this introduction, elementary students are ready to learn more about how stories are organized and how authors use the elements of story structure. Students use this knowledge to compose the stories they write as well as to comprehend stories they read.

Our teaching strategy builds on students' concept of story by examining the elements of story structure in connection with a literature program and then having students apply the elements in writing stories. The reader-writer connection is crucial: as readers, students consider how the author used a particular structure and its impact on themselves as readers; then, as writers, they experiment with structure and consider the impact on their classmates who read the stories.

This teaching strategy has two components: preparing to teach and teaching students about the elements of story structure. Before introducing an element, teachers prepare by learning about the element, collecting stories that exemplify the element, and developing a set of instructional materials. In the second component, teachers introduce students to an element of story structure. Students read stories and analyze how authors use the element in the story. Next, they participate in activities, such as retelling stories and drawing clusters, in which they investigate how authors used the element in particular stories. With this background of experiences, students write collaborative and individual stories applying what they have learned about the element. Elements of the story structure are plot, setting, characters, theme, point of view, repetition, conflict, and the beginning, middle, and end of stories.

Teaching Children to Write Research Reports

ACTIVITY 12.2

To write a research report, either as a class collaboration or individually, students use a process approach. They search for answers to questions about a topic, then compose a report to share what they have learned. Designing questions and gathering information is the prewriting stage; they complete the stages by drafting, revising, editing, and publishing their reports.

Writing an individual report is similar to writing a collaborative report. Students design research questions, gather information to answer the questions, and compile what they have learned in a report. Writing individually demands two significant changes, however:

(1) students must narrow their topics and (2) must assume the entire responsibility for writing the report.

1. *Choose and narrow a topic.* Students choose topics for research reports from a content area, hobbies, or other interests. After choosing a general topic, such as cats or the human body, they need to narrow the topic so that it is manageable. The broad topic of cats might be narrowed to pet cats or tigers, and the human body to one organ or system.

2. *Design research questions.* Students design research questions by brainstorming a list of questions in a learning log. They review the list, combine some questions, delete others, and finally arrive at four to six questions that are worthy of answering. When they begin their research, they may add new questions and delete others if they reach a dead end.

3. *Gather and organize information.* As in collaborative reports, students use clusters or data charts to gather and organize information. Data charts, with their rectangular spaces for writing information, serve as a transition for upper-grade students between clusters and note cards.

4. *Draft the report.* Students write a rough draft from the information they have gathered. Each research question can become a paragraph, a section, or a chapter in the report.

5. *Revise and edit the report.* Students meet in writing groups to share their rough drafts and make revisions based on the feedback they receive from their classmates. After they revise, students use an editing checklist to proofread their reports and identify and correct mechanical errors.

6. *Publish the report.* Student recopy their reports in books and add bibliographic information. Research reports can also be published in several other ways; for example, as a filmstrip or video presentation, as a series of illustrated charts or dioramas, or as a dramatization.

ACTIVITY 12.3   Teaching Children to Write Newspapers

Students learn to write newspaper articles using a process approach. They learn about the format of newspaper articles and then apply what they have learned by writing a class newspaper or simulated newspapers.

1. *Read to learn about the format of newspaper articles.* Students learn about the types of newspaper articles by reading and examining newspapers. Have students bring in newspapers or order a class set of your local newspaper or *USA Today.* Working in pairs or small groups, students investigate the parts of a newspaper that would appeal to their audience. They also decided to include a letter the class had received from Patricia Lee Gauch, an author of children's books who had recently visited the class. Then the teacher and another group of students decided on the arrangement of articles and glued them to sheets of paper. The teacher had the newspaper duplicated, and the distribution staff collated and stapled the copies and distributed them to each student in the class and to the other classes in the school. Although it is nice to have the articles typed, it is not necessary. Students can recopy their own articles neatly.

Kindergarten teachers often ask students to dictate accounts of the week's events to form a one-page class newspaper that students take home to inform their parents about what is going on in the classroom. The teacher and the children decide together what important events to write about, and the teacher records the children's dictation on the chalkboard. Next, the teacher reads the rough draft with the children and encourages them to suggest changes, additions, and deletions to improve the article. After the children are satisfied with their articles, the teacher copies them onto paper and duplicates it for the children to take home. A class newspaper is an excellent way to keep parents informed about what is happening in the classroom, introduces young children to another form and function of written language, and helps them learn to use the writing process to communicate effectively.

Simulated Newspapers

Students can write simulated newspapers in connection with units in other content areas, applying what they have learned about historical events and personalities. Simulated newspapers contain the same categories of articles as real newspapers—current events, weather, advertisements, editorials, and sports news; the change is that they reflect the era in which they are supposed to have been written. Students have to consider, for example, whether a Revolutionary War newspaper might include football game scores or a satellite weather map.

1. *List categories and examples.* Students list the categories they discover on a chart, and cite examples of each category to add to the chart. Fourth-grade students might cite editorials, letters to the editor, syndicated columns, and editorial cartoons as examples of opinion articles. After they learn about the structure of newspaper articles, students are ready to write their own.

2. *Plan the newspaper and the articles each student will write.* Certain decisions must be made before starting to write the newspaper. For example, students need to choose a name for the newspaper, decide what categories of articles to include, identify the audience, and develop a timeline for its production.

After making these decisions, students write articles for the various categories they will include in the newspaper. All students act as reporters. Students can be assigned to write specific articles, but it is often more effective to have them sign up for the articles they wish to contribute.

3. *Gather and organize information for the articles.* Students use informal writing strategies, such as brainstorming and clustering, to gather and organize information for their articles. The "5 Ws Plus One" activity is the most effective approach to news articles. Students write the topic of the article in the center circle and then draw out *who, what, when, where, why* and *how* rays to complete the cluster.

4. *Write articles using the writing process.* Students use the process approach to write their articles; after completing their rough drafts, they meet in writing groups to revise and edit. After the articles have been completed, they can be typed or recopied neatly by hand. Word processing programs can help simplify formatting the newspaper.

5. *Compile the newspaper from articles and illustrations.* The editorial staff meets to make final decisions about which articles to include in this issue of the newspaper and what additional work needs to be done. After the articles are selected, they must be arranged on sheets of paper, using either traditional cut-and-paste layouts or a word-processing program. Then the newspaper is duplicated and distributed.

Teaching Children to Write Letters   ACTIVITY 12.4

Students use the process approach (see Chapter 11) to write both friendly and business letters.

1. *Gather and organize information for the letter.* Students participate in prewriting activities, such as brainstorming or clustering, to decide what information to include in their letters. If they are writing friendly letters, particularly to pen pals, they also identify several questions to include.

2. *Review the friendly or business letter form.* Before writing the rough drafts of their letters, students review the friendly or business letter form.

3. *Write the letters using a process approach.* Students write a rough draft, incorporating the information developed during prewriting and following either the friendly or business letter style. Next, students meet in a writing group to share their rough drafts, receive compliments, and get feedback. They make changes based on the feedback and edit their letters with a partner, proofreading to identify errors and correcting as many as possible. They also make sure they have used the appropriate letter format. After making all the me-

chanical corrections, students recopy their letters and address envelopes. The crucial last step is to mail the letters.

| ACTIVITY 12.5 | **Teaching Children to Write Life-Stories** |

Students learn to write life-stories through a process approach. The instructional strategy is similar for writing autobiographies and biographies, but the two forms are different and should be taught separately.

1. *Read to learn about the format and unique conventions.* Others' autobiographies and biographies can serve as models for the life-stories students write. Many autobiographies of scientists, entertainers, sports figures, and others are available for upper-grade students, but, unfortunately, only a few autobiographies have been written for younger children. A list of suggested biographies appears in Figure 12.13, some are entire-life and others are shorter-event types. When students read autobiographies, they should note which events the narrator focuses on, how the narrator presents information and feelings, and what the narrator's viewpoint is.

Biographies of well-known people such as explorers, kings and queens, scientists, sports figures, artists, and movie stars, as well as "common" people who have endured hardship and shown exceptional courage, are available for elementary students to read. Biographers Jean Fritz and the D'Aulaires have written many excellent biographies for primary and middle-grade students, some of which are noted in the list.

Students' autobiographies and biographies from previous years are another source of books for your class to read. Students can often be persuaded to bring their prized life-stories back the following year to share with your students.

2. *Gather information for the life-story.* Students gather information about themselves or about the person they will write about in several different ways. Students are the best source of information about their own life, but they may need to get information from parents and other family members. Parents often share information from baby books and photo albums, and older brothers and sisters can share their remembrances. Another strategy stu-

FIGURE 12.13
Biographies

Biographies

Adler, D. A. (1989). *A picture book of Martin Luther King.* New York: Holiday House. (See other biographies by the same author.) (P–M)

Aliki. (1988). *The many lives of Benjamin Franklin.* New York: Simon & Schuster. (See other biographies by the same author.) (M)

Blassingame, W. (1979). *Thor Heyerdahl: Viking scientist.* New York: Elsevier/Nelson. (M)

D'Aulaire, I., & D'Aulaire, E. P. (1936). *George Washington.* New York: Doubleday. (See other biographies by the same authors.) (P–M)

Dobrin, A. (1975). *I am a stranger on Earth: The story of Vincent Van Gogh.* New York: Warne. (M)

Felton, H. W. (1976). *Deborah Sampson: Soldier of the revolution.* New York: Dodd, Mead. (M)

Freedman, R. (1987). *Lincoln: A photobiography.* New York: Clarion. (M)

Fritz, J. (1973). *And then what happened, Paul Revere?* New York: Coward-McCann. (See other biographies by the same author.) (P–M)

Giff, P. R. (1987). *Laura Ingalls Wilder.* New York: Viking. (M)

Greenberg, K. E. (1986). *Michael J. Fox.* Minneapolis: Lerner. (M)

Greenfield, E. (1977). *Mary McLeod Bethune.* New York: Crowell. (P–M)

Jakes, J. (1986). *Susanna of the Alamo: A true story.* New York: Harcourt Brace Jovanovich. (M)

Mitchell, B. (1986). *Click: A story about George Eastman.* Minneapolis: Carolrhoda Books. (M)

Peterson, H. S. (1967). *Abigail Adams: "Dear partner."* Champaign, IL: Garrard. (M)

Provensen, A., & Provensen, M. (1984). *Leonardo da Vinci.* New York: Viking. (A moveable book) (M)

Quackenbush, R. (1981). *Ahoy! Ahoy! are you there? A story of Alexander Graham Bell.* Englewood Cliffs, NJ: Prentice-Hall. (See other biographies by the same author.) (P–M)

Stanley, D. (1986). *Peter the great.* New York: Four Winds. (P–M)

dents can use to gather information for an autobiography is to collect objects that symbolize their life and hang them on a "lifeline" clothesline or put them in a life-box made from a shoebox (Fleming, 1985). They can then write briefly about each object, explaining what it is and how it relates to their lives. They can also decorate the box with words and pictures clipped from magazines to create an autobiographical collage.

For biographical writing, students can interview their subject, either in person or by telephone and letter. To write a historical biography, students read books to learn about the person and the time period in which he or she lived. Other sources of information are films, videotapes, and newspaper and magazine articles. Students also need to keep a record of their sources for the bibliography they will include with their biographies.

Lifelines. Students sequence the information they gather, either about their life or someone else's, on a lifeline or timeline. This activity helps students identify and sequence milestones and other events. They can use the information on the lifeline to identify topics for the life-story.

3. *Organize the information for the life-story.* Students select from their lifelines the topics they will write about and develop a cluster with each topic as a main idea. They add details from the information they have gathered; if they do not have four or five details for each topic, they can search for additional information. When students aren't sure if they have enough information, they can cluster the topic using the "5Ws Plus One" questions (*who, what, when, where, why,* and *how*) and try to answer the six questions. If they can complete the cluster, they are ready to write; if they cannot, they need to gather additional information. After developing the cluster, students decide on the sequence of topics and add an introduction and conclusion.

4. *Write the life-story using the writing process.* Students use their clusters to write their rough drafts. The main ideas become topic sentences for paragraphs, and details are expanded into sentences. After they write the rough draft, students meet in writing groups to get feedback on their writing, then make revisions. Next, they edit and recopy. They add drawings, photographs, or other memorabilia. Students also add a bibliography to a biography, listing their sources of information. Besides making the final copy of their life-stories, students can share what they have learned in other ways. They might dress up as the subject of their biography and tell the person's story or let classmates interview them.

Teaching Children to Write Poems   ACTIVITY 12.6

Before students write poems, teachers need to provide them with an "enlightened" view of poetry. Children often have misconceptions that interfere with their ability to write poems. Many students think poems must rhyme and, in their search for rhymes, create inane verse.

Introducing Students to Poetry

Children need to have a concept of poetry before writing poems. One way to expand students' knowledge about poetry is to share a variety of poems written by children and adults.

Another way to introduce poetry is to read excerpts from the first chapter of *Anastasia Krupnik* (Lowry, 1979), in which 10-year-old Anastasia, the main character, is excited when her teacher, Mrs. Westvessel, announces that the class will write poems. Anastasia works at home for eight nights to write a poem. Lowry does an excellent job of describing how writers search long and hard for words to express meaning and the delight that comes when they realize their poems are finished. Then Anastasia and her classmates bring their poems to class to read aloud; one student reads his four-line rhymed verse.

I have a dog whose name is Spot.

He likes to eat and drink a lot.

When I put water in his dish,

He laps it up just like a fish. (p. 10)

Anastasia is not impressed. She knows the child who wrote the poem has a dog named Sputnik, not Spot! But Mrs. Westvessel gives it an A and hangs it on the bulletin board. Soon it is Anastasia's turn, and she is nervous because her poem is very different. She reads her poem about tiny creatures that move about in tidepools at night:

hush   hush   the sea-soft night is aswim
with wrinklesquirm creatures
                                    listen(!)
to them   move   smooth   in the moistly dark
    here in the   whisperwarm wet. (pp. 11–12)

In this free-form poem without rhyme or capital letters, Anastasia has created a marvelous picture with invented words. Regrettably, Mrs. Westvessel has an antiquated view that poems should only be about serious subjects, be composed of rhyming sentences, and use conventional capitalization and punctuation. She doesn't understand Anastasia's poem, and gives Anastasia an F because she didn't follow directions.

Although this first chapter presents a depressing picture of elementary teachers and their lack of knowledge about poetry, it is a dramatic introduction about what poetry is and what it is not. After reading excerpts from the chapter, develop a chart with your students comparing what poetry is in Mrs. Westvessel's class and what poetry is in your class. Figure 12.14 lists some rules students might follow in writing poetry.

Teaching Students to Write Poems Following a Poetic Form

After the teacher introduces students to an "enlightened" view of poetry, they are ready to write. Beginning with formula poems (e.g., "I wish . . ." poems and color poems) will probably make the writing easier for young children or for students who have had little or no experience with poetry. Steps for writing any type of poetry are as follows.

1. *Explain the poetic form.* The teacher describes the poetic form and explains what is included in each line or stanza. Displaying a chart that describes the form or having students write a brief description of the poetic form in their writers' notebooks helps them remember it.

2. *Share examples written by children.* The teacher reads other children's poems that adhere to the form. You can share poems from this chapter along with additional poems written by your students. Point out how the writer of each poem used the form. Then you can share examples written by adults.

3. *Review the poetic form.* After explaining the poetic form and sharing poems, review the form and read one or two more poems that follow it. Have students explain how the poems fit the form, or have them freewrite about the poetic form to check their understanding.

FIGURE 12.14
Notebook Page Guidelines for Writing Poems

RULE ABOUT WRITING POETRY

Mrs. Westvessel's Rules	Our Rules
1. Poems must rhyme.	1. Poems do not have to rhyme.
2. The first letter in each line must be capitalized.	2. The first letter in each line does not have to be capitalized.
3. Each line must start at the left margin.	3. Poems can take different shapes and be anywhere on a page.
4. Poems must have a certain rhythm.	4. You hear the writer's voice in a poem—with or without rhythm.
5. Poems should be written about serious things.	5. Poems can be about anything—serious or silly things.
6. Poems should be punctuated like other types of writing.	6. Poems can be punctuated in different ways or not be punctuated at all.
7. Poems are failures if they don't follow these rules.	7. There are no real rules for poems and no poem is a failure.

4. *Write class collaboration poems.* Students write a class collaboration poem before writing individual poems. Each contributes a line for a class collaboration "I wish . . ." poem or a couplet for an "I used to/But now" poem. To write other types of poems, such as concrete poems, students can work together by suggesting ideas and words. They dictate the poem to the teacher, who records it on the chalkboard or on chart paper. Older students work in small groups to create poems. Through collaborative poems, students review the form and gather ideas to use later in writing their own poems. The teacher should compliment students when they play with words or use poetic devices. Students also need information about how to arrange the poem on the page, how to decide about capital letters and punctuation marks, and why it may be necessary to "unwrite" and delete some words.

5. *Write individual poems using the writing process.* The first four steps are prewriting experiences that prepare students to write their own poems following the poetic form they have been taught. Students write rough drafts, meet in writing groups to receive feedback, make revisions based on this feedback, and then edit their poems with a classmate and with the teacher. Students then share their poems.

I. PROBLEM-SOLVING EXPERIENCE THROUGH LANGUAGE ARTS SKILLS: WHAT IS THE IMPORTANCE OF SELECTED NATIVE AMERICAN SYMBOLS AS THE SYMBOLS RELATE TO THE CULTURE?*

1. To develop an appreciation for illustrations
2. To discover that illustrations may reinforce various Native American symbols
3. To develop observational abilities
4. To develop understanding of the Native American culture by discussing the importance of these symbols as the symbols relate to the culture

Purpose

Various books illustrated by Paul Goble, including *Dream Wolf* (1990), *The Girl Who Loved Wild Horses* (1978), *The Gift of the Sacred Dog* (1980), *Star Boy* (1983), *Buffalo Woman* (1984), and *Beyond the Ridge* (1989); a list of common Native American symbols.

Materials

Dream Wolf tells the story of two lost children who are helped to return to safety by a wolf. *The Girl Who Loved Wild Horses* tells about a Native American girl's attachment to horses. The *Gift of the Sacred Dog* reveals how horses were given to the Native American people. *Star Boy* is a story about an Native American who proves his bravery. *Buffalo Woman* reveals why the Native peoples and the buffalo are closely related. *Beyond the Ridge* follows an older Native American woman after she dies and goes to a new land.

Book summaries

All grades

Grade level

1. Introduce the idea of visual symbols by showing and discussing several symbols that are familiar to the students. For example, show an American flag and ask the students to share the meanings, feelings, and emotions that are associated with the flag. Continue this introduction by sharing and discussing illustrations of symbols such as doves representing peace, valentines representing love, and eagles representing the American spirit.
2. Explain to the students that various cultures have symbols that mean a great deal to those cultures. Present a list of important symbols that are common in Native American traditional literature. Explain to the students that they will be searching illustrated books that depict the Native American culture to identify if illustrators also use those symbols. Introduce and discuss the importance of the symbols shown in the following chart. As the students search for the symbols they should consider what the symbols represent in that illustration and within the story.

Procedures

*Adapted from D.E. Norton & S. Norton, *Language Arts Activities for Children,* 3rd ed. (Englewood Cliffs, NJ: Merrill/Prentice Hall, 1993), pp. 375–376. By permission of the authors and Prentice Hall.

3. The following chart lists common Native American symbols and their usual meanings, and provides space for students to give examples from texts in which that symbol is shown in the illustration:

SYMBOLS	MEANINGS	LITERATURE EXAMPLES
Beaver:	Tenacity, Dependability	
Braids:	Experience	
Butterfly:	Life, Child's toy	
Circle:	Wholeness	
Coyote:	Gentle trickster, Teacher	
Evening:	Rest, Dreams	
Eyes:	Perception	
Fire:	Spirit of the people, Children	
Fox and Kits:	Peers	
Grandmother or Grandfather:	Teacher	
Hawk:	One who has no enemies	
Lake:	Mirror or wholeness	
Prairie:	Everyday life	
Rainbow:	Myths, Strengths, Connection of spirit and physical	
River:	Spirit of life	
Stone:	Power	
Sweetgrass:	Earth's purification	
Thunderbird:	Thunder and lightning, Part of creation story	
Touching Ground:	Being in contact with nature, Laws of Mother Earth	
Turtle:	Traditions, Old symbol	

4. As a class activity, you may choose to identify and discuss the symbols located in one book before the students search independently for symbols. For example, ask students to listen to the story and view the illustrations in *The Girl Who Loved Wild Horses*. The text includes illustrations that show butterflies, braids, lake as a mirror reflection, girl lying on the ground, turtles, prairie, stone, rainbow, and circles.

5. After the students have observed and discussed the symbols and illustrations in one book, ask them to search for possible symbols in other illustrated books. Divide the class into groups and ask them to identify and discuss possible symbols found in other illustrations. Ask the students to discuss the possible meanings and the appropriateness for these symbols in the illustrations.

6. Students may draw their own illustrations in which they use these symbols. They can write stories that include the symbols.

J. ASSESSMENT STRATEGY

Assessing Children's Stories

Assessing the stories students write involves far more than simply judging the quality of the finished stories. Any assessment should also take into account students' activities and learning as they study the element of story structure as well as the activities they engage in while writing and refining their stories. Teachers should consider four components in assessing students' stories: (1) students' study of the element of story structure; (2) their knowledge about and application of the element in writing; (3) their use of the writing process; and (4) the quality of the finished stories.

These are ways to assess the first component, students' participation in the study of the element:

1. *Review the element.* Review the characteristics of the element under study, using the charts introduced in the first step. Ask students to restate the definition and characteristics of the element in their own words, using one book they have read to illustrate the characteristics.

2. *Write a class collaboration story.* Have students apply what they have learned about the element of story structure by writing a class (or group) collaboration story. A collaborative story provides students with a rehearsal before they write stories independently. Review the element of story structure and refer to the chart presented in the first step as the story is being written. Encourage students to offer ideas for the story and explain how to incorporate the element into the story. Follow the writing process stages by writing a rough draft on the chalkboard, chart paper, or using an overhead projector. Then students revise the story, working both to improve the content as well as to check that the particular element of story structure has been incorporated. Next, edit the story and make a final copy to be shared with all class members.

3. *Write individual stories.* Have students write individual stories incorporating the element and other elements of story structure they have already learned. Students use the process approach, in which they move through the drafting, revising, editing, and publishing stages of the writing process. The activities in the first five steps of this instructional strategy constitute the prewriting stage; now, students complete the remaining stages of the writing process. First, they write rough drafts of their stories and meet in writing groups to share their writing. Writing group members focus their comments on both the content of the story and how effectively the writer has used the story structure element. Next, they revise, using the feedback they receive. Before completing the revising stage, students can complete a "Revision Checklist" in which they doublecheck their story to be sure they have applied the element. A sample revision checklist for plot is presented in Figure 12.15. The first two questions in the checklist require students to focus on the conflict situation in their story and their overall development, the two most important components of plot. The third question focuses on a trouble-spot for many students—roadblocks that complicate the plot—and asks students to count their roadblocks and add more if they don't have at least three. After editing their stories and correcting as many mechanical errors as possible, students recopy the stories and share them with an appropriate audience.

Assessing Children's Research Reports

Students need to know the requirements for the research project and how they will be assessed or graded. Many teachers distribute a checklist of requirements for the project before students begin working, so they know what is expected of them and can assume

FIGURE 12.15
A Revision Checklist

REVISION CHECKLIST ON PLOT

Name _____

Story _____

1. Which type of conflict did you use in your story?

2. Draw a plot diagram of your story.

3. How many roadblocks are in your story? _____

Circle each of the roadblocks on your plot diagram with a colored pencil.

REMEMBER!
YOU MUST HAVE AT LEAST 3 ROADBLOCKS IN YOUR STORY.

---

responsibility for completing each step of the assignment. The checklist for an individual research report might include these observation behaviors and products:

- Choose a narrow topic.
- Identify four or five research questions.
- Use a cluster to gather information to answer the questions.
- Write a rough draft with a section or chapter to answer each question.
- Meet in writing groups to share your report.
- Make at least three changes in your rough draft.
- Complete an editing checklist with a partner.

A checklist enables students to monitor their own work and learn that writing is a process, not just a final product.

After completing the project, students submit their folders to the teacher for assessment. The teacher considers all the requirements on the checklist in determining the student's grade. If the checklist has 10 requirements, each requirement might be worth 10 points, and the grading can be done objectively on a 100-point scale. Thus, if the student's project is complete with all required materials, the student scores 100, or a grade of A. Points can be subtracted for work that is sloppy or incomplete.

Assessing Children's Newspaper Articles

As with other types of projects, students need to know the requirements for the newspaper project and how they will be assessed before beginning to work. Again, a checklist approach. The checklist might require the following components:

- Cut out samples of five kinds of newspaper articles and paste them in your learning log.
- Make a "5Ws Plus One" cluster for your article.
- Write one article for the newspaper.
- Participate in a writing group to revise your article.
- Make at least two revisions.
- Edit your article with a classmate.
- Draw an illustration to go with your article.
- Write three possible titles for your article.
- Type or recopy your article for the newspaper.

Students keep the checklist in their project folders and check off each item as they complete it. At the end of the project, students submit their folders to be assessed or graded.

Assessing Students' Letters

Traditionally, students wrote letters and turned them in for the teacher to grade. The letters were returned to the students after they were graded, but they were never mailed. Educators now recognize the importance of having an audience for student writing, and research suggests that students write better when they know their writing will be read by someone other than the teacher. Whereas it is often necessary to assess student writing, it would be inappropriate for the teacher to put a grade on the letter if it is going to be mailed to someone. Teachers can instead develop a checklist for evaluating students' letters without marking on them.

A primary-grade teacher developed the checklist in Figure 12.16, which identifies specific behaviors and measurable products. The teacher shares the checklist with students before they begin to write so they know what is expected of them and how they will be graded. At an evaluation conference before the letters were mailed, the teacher reviewed the checklist with each student. The letters were mailed without evaluative comments or grades written on them, but the completed checklist went into students' writing folders. A grading scale can be developed from the checklist; for example, points can be awarded for each checkmark in the *yes* column or five checkmarks can be determined to equal a grade of A, four checkmarks a B, and so on.

FIGURE 12.16
A Checklist for Assessing Students' Letters

LETTER CHECKLIST

Name _____

	Yes	No
1. Did you include questions in your letter?	☐	☐
2. Did you put your letter in the friendly letter form?	☐	☐
_____ return address		
_____ greeting		
_____ 3 or more paragraphs in the body		
_____ closing		
_____ salutation and name		
3. Did you write a rough draft of your letter?	☐	☐
4. Did you revise your letter with suggestions from people in your writing group?	☐	☐
5. Did you proofread your letter and correct as many errors as possible?	☐	☐

Assessing Students' Life-Stories

Students need to know the requirements for their autobiography or biography project and how they will be assessed or graded. A checklist for an autobiography might include the following components:

- Make a lifeline showing at least one important event for each year of your life.
- List at least three main-idea topics and at least five details for each topic.
- Write a rough draft with an introduction, three or more chapters, and a conclusion.
- Meet in a writing group to share your autobiography.
- Make at least three changes in your rough draft.
- Complete an editing checklist with a partner.
- Write a final copy with photos or drawings as illustrations.
- Add an "All about the Author" page.
- Compile your autobiography as a book.
- Decorate the cover.

The checklist for a biography might list the following requirements:

- Learn about the person's life from at least three sources (and no more than one encyclopedia).
- Make a lifeline listing at least 10 important events.
- Write at least 10 simulated journal entries as the person you are studying.
- List at least three main-idea topics and at least five details for each topic.
- Write a rough draft with at least three chapters and a bibliography.
- Meet in a writing group to share your biography.
- Make at least three changes in your rough draft.
- Complete an editing checklist with a partner.
- Recopy the biography.
- Add an "All about the Author" page.

Students keep the checklist in their project folders and check off each item as it is completed; at the end of the project, they submit the folders to be assessed or graded. Teachers can award credit for each item on the checklist, as we discussed regarding research reports. This approach helps students assume greater responsibility for their own learning and gives them a better understanding of why they receive a particular grade.

Assessing Students' Poems

Poems provide options for students as they experiment with ways to express their thoughts. Although children experiment with a variety of forms during the elementary grades, it is not necessary to test their knowledge of particular forms. Knowing that a haiku is a Japanese poetic form composed of 17 syllables arranged in three lines will not make a child a poet. Descriptions of the forms should instead be posted in the classroom or added to writers' notebooks for students to refer to as they write.

Assessing the quality of students' poems is especially difficult, because poems are creative combinations of wordplay, poetic forms, and poetic devices. Instead of trying to give a grade for quality, students may be assessed on other criteria:

- Has the student used the formula presented in class?
- Has the student used the process approach in writing, revising, and editing the poem?
- Has the student used wordplay or a poetic device in the poem?

Teachers might also ask students to assess their own progress in writing poems. Students keep copies of their poems in their writing folders or poetry booklets so they can review and assess their own work. If a grade for quality is absolutely necessary, students should choose several of the poems in their writing folders for the teacher to evaluate.

K. LANGUAGE ARTS SKILLS LESSON PLAN: GAINING MEANING FROM READING*

1. Descriptive Course Data

Teacher: _____   *Date:* _____
Grade level: 4th grade.
Room number: _____
Unit: Reading (Literature)
Lesson Topic: Introducing the text *The Pied Piper of Hamelin (Mayer, 1987)*

2. Lesson Goals and Objectives

Instructional goal.
1. To gain meaning from reading.

Specific (performance) objectives.
Cognitive.
1. With others, the student will compare the story to other legends with which students are familiar.
2. When presented with the illustrations on the cover of the book, the student will predict what might happen in the story.

Affective.
1. The student will be invited to talk about the story.

Psychomotor.
1. Using a pen or pencil, the student will brainstorm and write a list of words related to the story and create an extended response to the story.

3. Rationale

The concept of reading as a way people communicate is prevalent in literacy studies. Curriculum materials indicate where reading (i.e., teacher-led demonstrations of literacy) has been included by local schools, districts and state departments of education.

4. Plan and Procedures

Introduction. Discuss with children who are familiar with the story to talk about it. Have children compare the story to other legends with which they are familiar. Write their com-

---

*Adapted from G. Tompkins & K. Hoskisson, *Language Arts: Content and Teaching Strategies,* 3rd ed. (Englewood Cliffs, NJ: Merrill/Prentice Hall, 1995), pp. 268–269. By permission of the authors and Prentice Hall.

parisions on the board. Show the illustration on the cover of the book and ask the children to predict what might happen in the story. Write their predictions on the board.

Modeling. Show children how to read aloud. Invite them to listen to you read the text aloud.

Guided (coached) practice. The children may read the text silently with guidance. The teacher may meet with small groups in guided reading or the entire class may read together.

To explore the text, the children make comments immediately after reading either by talking about the story or writing in a reading log. According to Davala (1987), when logs become a regular part of classroom activities, students take an active part in their own learning, and they "tune in to the curriculum when they explore it personally." As students make connections between their own experiences and events in the story, they create mental images, anticipate what will happen next, construct a reaction, and value the story.

To focus on vocabulary, ask children to brainstorm a list of words related to the story and to sort the words into categories. For example, the words *burrowing, mimicking, vermin,* and *filthy* all relate to the rats.

To focus on construction of a reaction, have children freewrite a response to these lines from the story: "A promise is a promise" and "the piper must be paid."

Assignment. Have the children build on the responses they made earlier and reread the story to create a more extended response. The response can take one of several forms:

Compare the version they are reading to other versions of the story.
Compare the Pied Piper to another legendary character.
Create puppets or flannel board figures and retell the story.
Dramatize the story.
Dress a doll as the Piper.
Interview a public health official to learn why rats are harmful or to learn how pests
  are controlled in a contemporary environment.
Make a diorama of an event in the story.
Paint a mural of the story.
Research the legend of the Pied Piper.
Write a retelling of the story.

Closure. Relate the lesson to what the children learned about the messages ("A promise is a promise" and "the piper must be paid") in the story. Return to the board to restate the earlier predictions the children made after seeing the illustration on the cover of the book. Have them determine how many of their predictions came true.

5. Materials Needed

Audiovisual.
None

Other. Copies of *The Pied Piper of Hamelin* (Mayer, 1987).

6. Assessment and Revision

Assessment of learning. The teacher observes and makes anecdotal notes of the reading skills demonstrated and the students' contracts to show their participation in comparing the story to other legends, making predictions, and talking about the story. The assessment also includes the students' participation in writing in their reading logs, brainstorming and writing a list of words related to the story, and creating an extended response to the story. At times, they will confer with the teacher when the teacher schedules time for reading conferences (three mornings a week).

Plan for revision. As the teacher, I have been pleased at how well the students read the text independently. They are learning to read independently through Uninterrupted

Sustained Silent Reading (USSSR) and Drop Everything and Read (DEAR) time. They each read silently without interruption for a specified time period (approximately 20 minutes a day in grade 4 and up) (Berglund & Johns, 1983). I feel that this activity gives the students an opportunity to transfer and apply isolated skills in a pleasurable, independent reading experience.

SUMMARY

Research provides instructional guidelines and shows that children learn to read and write better when the two processes are connected.

- Shanahan (1988) has developed instructional principles for relating reading and writing so that children develop a clear conception of literacy. These principles include (1) Instruction should include reading and writing in meaningful contexts daily, and reading and writing should be introduced in kindergarten. (2) Instruction should reflect the developmental nature of the reading-writing relationship; the reading-writing connection should be made clear to children. (3) Instruction should emphasize both process and product as well as the communicative functions of reading and writing.
- Children can be introduced to the elements of story structure—such as beginning, middle, and end of stories, repetition, plot, setting, characters, theme, and point of view—as they read different types of stories such as folktales, fables, fantasies, hero stories, and myths. They can apply what they have learned about story structure when they write stories using the process approach.
- Children can interact with information books related to social studies and other content areas and apply what they have learned collaboratively and individually in writing "All About _____" reports and other research reports.
- Children can read news articles and write their own newspapers, contemporary and simulated.
- Children can write friendly letters to friends and business letters when they want to request information, to pass along a compliment to a worker, to complain about a problem, or to order an item through the mail or to transact other business.
- Children can read autobiographies and biographies (life-stories) and get acquainted with this form of writing before they write their own stories.
- Children's concept of poetry can be expanded beyond just rhymed lines through the oral reading of a variety of poems written by children and adults. Further, children can write formula poems and other types successfully when the poetic form is explained, read aloud, written collaboratively, and then composed individually.
- Importantly, children use the writing process in their types of writing as they draft, refine, and polish their work. After writing, it is crucial for children to share their writing with genuine audiences.

QUESTIONS AND ACTIVITIES FOR DISCUSSION

1. Compile a list of at least seven books (folktales, fables, fantasies, hero stories, and myths) to use in teaching stories at the grade level you teach or plan to teach. Annotate each story briefly and add comments about the element of story structure—beginning, middle, and end of stories; repetition; plot; setting; characters; theme; and point of view—that the story exemplifies.

2. Interview a student about his or her concept of story and how the student writes a story. Report on the interview to your group. Ask such questions as these:
   - Tell me why you like (or do not like) to write stories.
   - What things do authors put in stories to make them good?
   - Tell me about one of the stories you have written.
   - What are some of the things you think about when you write a story?
   - What do you put in your stories to make them good?
   - What would you like to learn more about to write better stories?
   - What have your teachers taught you about writing stories?

3. Some specialists say that using predictable literature has merits such as serving as a temporary support for beginning readers and writers and offering repeating story events, sentence structures, and cumulative patterns. Other specialists point out that there are limitations to using such material. Some of the limitations that have been cited include the presumptions that children cannot write independently and that the teacher should be the dominant figure in the classroom, who models the pattern and has the children repeat the pattern. Other limitations emphasize that using patterns in literature lack a research base to support vocabulary and syntactic development.

Review more of the pros and cons of using predictable materials by reading this source: Linda Watson-Ellam. (1988, March). Using literary patterns: Who's in control of the authorship? *Language Arts, 65*, 291–301. Report on the article to your group and state the points with which you agree or disagree.

4. Read aloud a predictable book to kindergarten or first-grade children. Then make a big book and retell the story through a language experience approach.

5. Examine 20 wordless books and develop a card file that includes information about the visual presentation in each book and how the illustrations can connect to a possible text structure if words were written about them—narrative, procedural, time order, and topic exposition.

6. Use the KWL strategy to teach a social studies lesson.

7. Write and publish a simulated newspaper related to a social studies unit.

8. Engage children in interviewing a community leader and then writing a collaborative biography (life-story) or in writing a biography about a historical figure.

9. Engage children in writing "business" letters to request a "pen pal" arrangement with a teacher in another school and continue through the year by having them write friendly letters to their new friends.

10. Read aloud poems with children and encourage them to respond through choral reading, dramatizing, compiling a picture book version of the poem, or creating an art work.

11. Locate favorite poems, write them on index cards, and compile a collection of at least 10 poems appropriate for the grade level you teach or plan to teach.

12. Describe any prior concepts you had about teaching reading in the classroom and connections to writing that changed as a result of your experience with this chapter. Describe the changes.

CHILDREN'S BOOKS

Adler, D. A. (1989). *A picture book of Martin Luther King*. New York: Holiday House. (See other biographies by the same author.)

Ahlberg, A. (1990). *The black cat*. Ill. by A. Amstutz. New York: Greenwillow.

Ahlberg, A. (1990). *The pet shop*. Ill. by A. Amstutz. New York: Greenwillow.

Anno, M. (1980). *Anno's Italy*. Ill. by author. New York: Collins.

Anno, M. (1982). *Anno's Britain*. Ill. by author. New York: Philomel.

Anno, M. (1982). *Anno's flea market*. Ill. by author. New York: Philomel.

Anno, M. (1983). *Anno's USA*. Ill. by author. New York: Philomel.

Armstrong, J. (1992). *Hugh can do*. Ill. by K. B. Root. New York: Crown.

Aylesworth, J. (1989). *Mr. McGill goes to town*. Ill. by T. Graham. New York: Holt.

Aylesworth, J. (1989). *Mother Halverson's new cat*. Ill. by T. Goffe. New York: Atheneum.

Baker, K. (1990). *Who is the beast?* San Diego, CA: Harcourt Brace Jovanovich.

Berenstain, S., & J. (1972). *C Is for clown: A circus of C words*. Ill. by authors. New York: Random House.

Burningham, J. (1983). *Five down: Numbers as sizes; Count up, Learning Sets*. Ill. by author. New York: Viking.

Burningham, J. (1983). *Just cats: Learning groups*. Ill. by author. New York: Viking.

Burningham, J. (1983). *Pigs plus: Learning addition*. Ill. by author. New York: Viking.

Burningham, J. (1983). *Read one: Numbers as words*. Ill. by author. New York: Viking.

Carle, E. (1969). *The very hungry caterpillar*. Cleveland: Collins-World.

Carle, E. (1977). *The grouchy ladybug*. New York: Crowell.

Carle, E. (1987). *A house for a hermit crab*. Saxonville, MA: Picture Book Studio.

Carlstrom, N. W. (1990). *Moose in the garden*. Ill. by L. Desimini. New York: HarperCollins Children's Books.

Chouinard, R., & M. (1988). *The amazing animal alphabet book*. Ill. by R. Chouinard. New York: Doubleday.

Collington, P. (1987). *The angel and the soldier boy*. Ill. by author. New York: Knopf.

Crews, D. (1982). *Truck*. Ill. by author. New York: Greenwillow.

Crews, D. (1982). *Carousel*. Ill. by author. New York: Greenwillow.

Crews, D. (1982). *Harbor*. Ill. by author. New York: Greenwillow.

Cristini, E., & Puricelli, L. (1981). *In my garden*. Ill. by authors. Boston: Alphabet Press/Neuebauer Press.

Cristini, E., & Puricelli, L. (1981). *In the pond*. Ill. by authors. Boston: Alphabet Press/Neuebauer Press.

Cristini, E., & Puricelli, L. (1981). *In the woods*. Ill. by authors. Boston: Alphabet Press/Neuebauer Press.

D'Aulaire, I., & D'Aulaire, E. P. (1936). *George Washington*. New York: Doubleday. (See other biographies by the same authors.)

de Brunhoff, L. (1983). *Babar's ABC*. Ill. by author. New York: Random House.

de Paola, T. (1989). *The art lesson*. New York: Putnam.

Deming, A. G. (1988). *Who is tapping at my window?* Ill. by M. Wellington. New York: E. P. Dutton.

Domanska, J. (1985). *Busy Monday morning*. New York: Greenwillow.

Dragonwagon, C. (1989). *This is the bread I baked for Ned*. Ill. by I. Seltzer. New York: Macmillan.

Drescher, H. (1987). *The yellow umbrella*. Ill. by author. New York: Bradbury.

Ernst, L, C. (1986). *Up to ten and down again.* Ill. by author. New York: McEldererry/Macmillan.

Farber, N. (1975). *As I was crossing Boston Common.* New York: Dutton.

Farjeon, E. (1990). *Cats sleep anywhere.* Ill. by M. Price Jenkins. New York: HarperCollins Children's Books.

Felton, H. W. (1976). *Deborah Sampson: Soldier of the revolution.* New York: Dodd, Mead.

Fox, M. (1990). *Shoes from grandpa.* Ill. by P. Mullins. New York: Orchard Books/Watts.

Freedman, R. (1987). *Lincoln: A photobiography.* New York: Clarion.

Fritz, J. (1973). *And then what happened, Paul Revere?* New York: Coward-McCann. (See other biographies by the same author.)

Fritz, J. (1982). *Homesick: My own story.* New York: Putnam.

Gag, W. (1956). *Millions of cats.* New York: Coward-McCann.

Galdone, P. (1960). *The gingerbread boy.* New York: McGraw Hill.

Giff, P. R. (1987). *Laura Ingalls Wilder.* New York: Viking.

Goble, P. (1978). *The girl who loved wild horses.* New York: Bradbury.

Goble, P. (1980). *The gift of the sacred dog.* New York: Bradbury.

Goble, P. (1983). *Star boy.* New York: Bradbury.

Goble, P. (1984). *Buffalo woman.* New York: Bradbury.

Goble, P. (1989). *Beyond the ridge.* New York: Bradbury.

Goble, P. (1990). *Dream wolf.* New York: Bradbury.

Goodall, J. S. (1986). *The story of a castle.* Ill. by author. New York: McEldererry/Macmillan.

Goodall, J. S. (Reteller). (1988). *Little Red Riding Hood.* Ill. by the reteller. New York: Macmillan.

Greenberg, K. E. (1986). *Michael J. Fox.* Minneapolis: Lerner.

Greenfield, E. (1977). *Mary McLeod Bethune.* New York: Crowell.

Herson, K., & D. (1989). *The copycat.* Ill. by C. Stock. New York: Atheneum.

Hilton, N. (1990). *The long red scarf.* Ill. by M. Power. New York: Carolrhoda.

Hoguet, S. R. (1983). *I Unpacked my grandmother's trunk: A picture book game.* Ill. by author. New York: E. P. Dutton.

Hood, T. (1990). Before I go to sleep. Ill. by M. Begin-Callanan. New York: G. P. Putnam's Sons.

Hopkins, L. B. (1969). *Books are by people.* New York: Citation.

Hopkins, L. B. (1974). *More books are by more people.* New York: Citation.

Jakes, J. (1986). *Susanna of the Alamo: A true story.* New York: Harcourt Brace Jovanovich.

Kasza, K. (1990). *When the elephant walks.* Ill. by author. New York: G. P. Putnam's Sons.

Keats, E. J. (1973). *Over in the meadow.* New York: Scholastic.

Kherdian, D., & Hogrogian, N. (1990). *The cat's midsummer jamboree.* New York: Philomel.

Komaiko, L. (1990). *My perfect neighborhood.* Ill. by B. Westman. New York: Harper & Row.

Lionni, L. (1964). *Tico and the golden wings.* New York: Pantheon.

Lowry, L. (1979). *Anastasia Krupnik.* Boston: Houghton Mifflin.

McCully, E. A. (1984). *Picnic: A wordless picture book.* Ill. by author. New York: Harper & Row.

McCully, E. A. (1985). *First snow: A wordless picture book.* Ill. by author. New York: Harper & Row.

McCully, E. A. (1987). *School: A wordless picture book.* Ill. by author. New York: Harper & Row.

McCully, E. A. (1988). *The Christmas gift: A wordless picture book.* Ill. by author. New York: Harper Junior Books.

McCully, E. A. (1988). *New baby: A wordless picture book.* Ill. by author. New York: Harper Junior Books.

MacDonald, E. (1990). *Mike's kite.* Ill. by R. Kendall. New York: Orchard.

Mack, S. (1974). *10 bears in my bed.* New York: Pantheon.

Mari, I., & E. (1970). *The apple and the moth.* Ill. by authors. New York: Pantheon.

Mari, I., & E. (1970). *The chicken and the egg.* Ill. by authors. New York: Pantheon.

Martin, B. (1970). *Monday, Monday, I like Monday.* New York: Holt, Rinehart & Winston.

Martinez, R. (1990). *Mrs. McDockerty's knitting.* Ill. by C. O'Neill. Boston: Houghton Mifflin.

Mayer, M. (1987). *The Pied Piper of Hamelin.* New York: Macmillan.

Mitchell, B. (1986). *Click: A story about George Eastman.* Minneapolis: Carolrhoda Books.

Munro, R. (1985). *The inside-outside book of New York City.* Ill. by author. New York: Dutton.

Munro, R. (1987). *The inside-outside book of Washington , D. C.* Ill. by author. New York: Dutton.

Munro, R. (1989). *The inside-outside book of London.* Ill. by author. New York: Dutton.

Neitzel, S. (1989). *The jacket I wear in the snow.* Ill. by N. W. Parker. New York: Greenwillow.

Peterson, H. S. (1967). *Abigail Adams.* "Dear partner." Champaign, IL: Garrard.

Provensen, A., & Provensen, M. (1984). *Leonardo da Vinci.* New York: Viking. (A moveable book)

Quackenbush, R. (1981). *Ahoy! Ahoy! are you there? A story of Alexander Graham Bell.* Englewood Cliffs, NJ: Prentice-Hall. (See other biographies by the same author.)

Robart, R. (1987). *The cake that Mack ate.* Ill. by M. Kovalski. New York: Joy Street.

Stanley, D. (1986). *Peter the great.* New York: Four Winds.

Stott, D. (1990). *Too much.* Ill. by author. New York: E. P. Dutton.

Thomas, P. (1990). *"Stand back," said the elephant, "I'm going to sneeze!"* Ill. by W. Tripp. New York: Lothrop, Lee & Shepard.

Van Laan, N. (1990). *A mouse in my house.* Ill. by M. Priceman. New York: Knopf.

Wiesner, D. (1988). *Free fall.* Ill. by author. New York: Lothrop, Lee & Shepard.

Winter, P. (1980). *Sir Andrew.* Ill. by author. New York: Crown. (cause-and-effect within a story)

Yolen, J. (1975). *All in the woodland early: An ABC book.* Ill. by J. B. Zalben. New York: Philomel/Putnam Group.

Zacharius, T. (1990). *But where is the green parrot?* Ill. by W. Zacharius. New York: Delacrote.

REFERENCES AND SUGGESTED READINGS

Abrahamson, R. F. (1981). An update on wordless picture books with an annotated bibliography. *The Reading Teacher, 32,* 417–421.

Adams, A., et al. (1981, Fall). Instructional strategies for studying content area texts in the intermedate grades. *Reading Research Quarterly, 18*(1), 27–55.

Aldis, D. (1969). *Nothing is impossible: The story of Beatrix Potter.* New York: Atheneum.

Allington, R. (1983, February). Fluency: The neglected reading goal. *The Reading Teacher, 36*(6), 556–561.

Anderson, R. C., Hiebert, E. C., Scott, J. A., & Wilkinson, I. A. G. (1985). *Becoming a nation of readers: The report of the Commission on Reading.* Washington, DC: National Institute of Education.

Ashton-Warner, S. (1965). *Teacher.* New York: Simon & Schuster.

Baker, L., & Brown, A. L. (1984). Metacognitive skills in reading. In D. Pearson (Ed.), *Handbook of Reading Research.* New York: Longman.

Baldwin, R. S. (1985, Spring). Effects of topic interest and prior knowledge on reading comprehension. *Reading Research Quarterly, 20*(4), 497–508.

Beck, I. L., et al. (1982, Spring). Effects of long-term vocabulary instruction on lexical access and reading comprehension. *Journal of Educational Psychology, 74*(3), 506–521.

Berglund, R. L., & Johns, J. L. (1983). A primer on uninterrupted sustained silent reading. *The Reading Teacher, 36,* 534–539.

Biemiller, A. (1970). The development of the use of graphic and contextual information as children learn to read. *Reading Research Quarterly, 1*(1), 75–96.

Bond, G. L., & Dykstra, R. (1976, Fall). The cooperative research program in first grade reading instruction. *Reading Research Quarterly, 2*(1), 10–138.

Boodt, G. M. (1984, January). Critical listeners become critical readers in remedial reading class. *The Reading Teacher, 37*(4), 390–394.

Borkowski, J. et al. (1983, Winter). Metamemory and metalinguistic development: Correlates for children's intelligence and achievement. *Bulletin of the Psychonomic Society, 21*(2), 393–396.

Bridge, C.A. (1979). Predictable materials for beginning readers. *Language Arts, 56,* 503–507.

Bridge, C. A., & Burton, B. (1982). Teaching sight vocabulary through patterned language materials. In J. A. Niles & L. A. Harris (Eds.), *New inquiries in reading research and instruction* (Thirty-first yearbook of the National Reading Conference), pp. 119–123. Rochester, NY: National Reading Conference.

Bridge, C. A., Winograd, P. N., & Haley, D. (1983). Using predictable materials vs. preprimers to teach beginning sight words. *The Reading Teacher, 36,* 884–891.

Bromley, K. D. (1985, January). Precise writing and outlining enhance content learning. *The Reading Teacher, 38*(4), 406–411.

Buckley, M. H. (1986). When teachers decide to integrate the language arts. *Language Arts, 63,* 369–377.

Chall, J. (1967). *Learning to read: The great debate.* New York: McGraw-Hill.

Chandler, J., & Baghban, M. (1980, April). Predictable books guarantee success. *Reading Horizons, 26,* 167–173.

Clark, B. K., & Palmer, B. C. (1982). Reading and the disadvantaged: Some myths and facts. *Reading World, 21*(1), 208–212.

Cochran-Smith, M. (1983). *The making of a reader.* Norwood, NJ: Ablex.

Corcoran, B. (1987). Teachers creating readers. In B. Corcoran & E. Evans (Eds.), *Readers, texts, teachers,* pp. 41–74. Upper Montclair, NJ: Boynton/Cook.

D'Angelo, K., (1979). Wordless picture books: Also for the writer. *Language Arts, 56,* 813–814.

Davala, V. (1987). Respecting opinions: Learning logs in middle school. In T. Fulwiler (Ed.), *The Journal Book,* pp. 179–186. Portsmouth, NH: Boynton-Cook.

Degler, L. S. (1979). Putting words into wordless books. *The Reading Teacher, 30,* 399–402.

Dreisbach, M., & Keogh, B. K. (1982, December). Testwiseness as a factor in readiness test performance of young Mexican-American children. *Journal of Educational Psychology, 74*(3), 224–229.

Elley, W. B. (1989, Spring). Vocabulary acquisition from listening to stories. *Reading Research Quarterly, 24*(2), 174–187.

Estes, T. H., & Richards, H. C. (1985, Fall). Habits of study and test performance. *Journal of Reading Behavior, 17*(1), 1–13.

Fitzgerald, J. (1990). Effects of group conferences on first graders' revision in writing. *Written Communication, 7,* 96–135.

Fleming, M. (1985). Writing assignments focusing on autobiographical and biographical topics. In M. Fleming, & J. McGinnis (Eds.), *Portraits: Biography and autobiography in the secondary school,* pp. 95–97. Urbana, IL: National Council of Teachers of English.

Fleming, M., & McGinnis, J. (Eds.) (1985). *Portraits: Biography and autobiography in the secondary school.* Urbana, IL: National Council of Teachers of English.

Harste, J. C., Woodward, V. A., & Burke, C. L. (1984). Examining our assumptions: A transactional view of literacy and learning. *Research in the Teaching of English, 18,* 84–108.

Heald-Taylor, G. (1987). How to use predictable books for K–2 language arts instruction. *The Reading Teacher, 40,* 656–661.

Hillerich, R. L. (1967, Fall). Vowel generalizations in first grade reading achievement. *The Elementary School Journal, 68*(2), 246–251.

Holdaway, D. (1979). *The foundations of literacy.* Sydney, Australia: Ashton Scholastic.

Holmes, B. C. (1983, October). A confirmation strategy for improving poor readers' ability to answer inferential questions. *The Reading Teacher, 37*(1), 144-148.

Hoskisson, K. (1974). Should parents teach their children to read? *Elementary English, 51,* 295-299.

Hoskisson, K. (1975a). The many facets of assisted reading. *Elementary English, 52,* 312–315.

Hoskisson, K. (1975b). Successive approximation and beginning reading. *Elementary School Journal, 75,* 442–451.

Hoskisson, K. (1977). Reading readiness: Three viewpoints. *Elementary School Journal, 78,* 44–52.

Hoskisson, K., & Krohm, B. (1974). Reading by immersion: Assisted reading. *Elementary English, 51,* 832–836.

Hoskisson, K., Sherman, T., & Smith, L. (1974). Assisted reading and parent involvement. *The Reading Teacher, 27,* 710–714.

Hudson, J., & Haworth, J. (1983, Fall). Dimensions of word recognition. *Reading, 17*(2), 87–94.

Johnson, D., & Baumann, J. F. (1984). Word identification. In P. D. Pearson (Ed.), *Handbook of reading research.* New York: Longman, 1984.

Kahn, R. (1980, Winter). The method of repeated readings: Expanding the neurological impress method for use with disabled readers. *Journal of Reading Disabilities, 2*(2), 90–92.

Kaneenui, E. K., et al. (1982, Winter). Effects of text construction and instructional procedures for teaching word meanings on comprehension and recall. *Reading Research Quarterly, 17*(2), 367–388.

Karnowski, L. (1989). Using LEA with process writing. *The Reading Teacher, 42,* 462–465.

Kellough, R. D., & Roberts, P.L. (1994). *A resource guide for elementary school teaching: Planning for competence* (3rd Ed.) New York: Macmillan.

Lange, B. Promoting text wiseness. *Journal of Reading, 24*(8), 740–743.

Langer, J. (1986). Reading, writing, and understanding: An analysis of the construction of meaning. *Written Communication, 3,* 219–267.

Lawrence, P., & Harris, V. (1986, May). A strategy for using predictable books (based on *Drummer Hoff* by Barbara Emberly). *Early Years, 16,* 345.

Lee, D. M., & Allen, R. V. (1963). *Learning to read through experience* (2nd ed.). New York: Meredith.

Lemons, R. L., & Moore, S. C. (1982, Fall). The effects of training in listening on the development of reading skills. *Reading Improvement, 19*(2), 212–216.

Lopez, J. G. (1986). The relative impact of oral reading combined with direct teaching methodology on reading comprehension, listening, and vocabulary achievement of third-grade students. *Dissertation Abstracts International, 47*:3974A.

Mason, J. M. (1980, Fall). When do children begin to read: An exploration of four-year-old children's letter and word reading competencies. *Reading Research Quarterly, 15*(1), 203–227.

McCormick, C., & Mason, J. (1984). *Intervention procedure for increasing preschool children's interest in and knowledge about reading.* Cambridge, MA: Bolt, Beranek, & Newman.

McPhail, I. P. (1981). Why teach test wiseness? *Journal of Reading, 25*(1), 22–28.

Meyer, B. J., & Freedle, R. O. (1984). Effects of discourse type on recall. *American Educational Research Journal, 21,* 121–143.

Moore, D., et al. (1983). Reader's conceptions of the main idea. In I. A. Niles & L. A. Harris (Eds.), *Searches for meaning in reading language processing and instruction.* Rochester, NY: National Reading Conference.

Niles, O. S. (1974). Organization perceived. In H. L. Herber (Ed.), *Perspectives in reading: Developing study skills in secondary schools.* Newark, DE: International Reading Association.

Norton, D. E., & Norton, S. (1993). *Language arts activities for children* (3rd ed.) New York: Merrill/Macmillan.

Noyce, R. M., & Christie, J. F. (1989). *Integrating reading and writing instruction in grades K–8.* Boston: Allyn & Bacon.

Ogle, D. M. (1986), K-W-L: A teaching model that develops active reading of expository text. *The Reading Teacher, 39,* 564–570.

Ogle, D. M. (1989). The know, want to know, learn strategy. In K. D. Muth (Ed.), *Children's comprehension of text: Research into practice,* pp. 205–223. Newark, DE: International Reading Association.

Perez, E. (1981, October). Oral language competence improves reading skills of Mexican-American third graders. *The Reading Teacher, 35*(1), 24–29.

Pflaum, S., & Ianis, B. (1982, Fall). Oral reading research and learning disabled children. *Topics in Learning and Learning Disabilities, 1*(1), 33–42.

Pickert, S. M. (1978, January). Repetitive sentence patterns in children's books. *Language Arts, 55,* 16–18.

Rand, M. K. (1984, January). Story schema: Theory, research, and practice. *The Reading Teacher, 37*(4), 377–383.

Rhodes, L. K. (1981). I can read! Predictable books as resources for reading and writing instructions. *The Reading Teacher, 34,* 511–518.

Roberts, P. L. (1987). *Alphabet books as a key to language patterns: An annotated action bibliography.* Hamden, CT: Library Professional Publications.

Roberts, P. L. (1990, Fall). Learning about text structure through the wordless book-writing connection. *The California Reader, 24,* 9–11, 24.

Roberts, P. L. (1994). *Alphabet: A handbook of ABC books and book extensions for the elementary classroom* (2nd ed.). School Library Media Series No. 3. Metuchen, NJ: The Scarecrow Press.

Rosenblatt, L. (1978). *The reader, the text, the poem: The transactional theory of literary work.* Carbondale: Southern Illinois University Press.

Sadow, M. W. (1982, February). The use of story grammar in the design of questions. *The Reading Teacher, 35*(5), 518–522.

Seaton, H. W., & Wielan, O. P. (1981). A study of the effects of listening/reading transfer on four measures of reading comprehension. In G. H. McNinch (Ed.), *Comprehension: Process and product.* Athens, GA: The American Reading Forum.

Shanahan, T. (1980, Spring). The impact of writing instruction on learning to read. *Reading World, 19*(3), 357–368.

Shanahan, T. (1988). The reading-writing relationship: Seven instructional principles. *The Reading Teacher, 41,* 636–647.

Slater, W. H. (1985, May). Teaching expository text structure with structural organizers. *Journal of Reading, 28*(8), 712–718.

Slaughter, J. P. (1983). Big books for little kids: Another fad or a new approach for teaching beginning reading? *The Reading Teacher, 36,* 758–762.

Smith, F. (1983). Reading like a writer. *Language Arts, 60,* 553–564.

Smith, F. (1988). *Joining the literacy club: Further essays into education.* Portsmouth, NH: Heinemann.

Smith, P. L., & Tompkins, G. E. (1988). Structured notetaking: A new strategy for content area readers. *The Journal of Reading, 32,* 46–53.

Snow, C. (1983, Fall). Literacy and language relationships during the preschool years. *Harvard Educational Review, 53*(1), 165–189.

Spiegel, D. L., et al. (1983). An investigation of a context-plus-phonics strategy for increasing second-grade students' use of context to aid word recognition. In J. A. Niles & L. A. Harris (Eds.), *Searches for meaning in reading/language processing and instruction*. Rochester, NY: National Reading Conference.

Stanovich, K. (1980, Fall). Toward an interactive compensatory model of individual differences in the development of reading fluency. *Reading Research Quarterly, 16*(1), 32–71.

Stauffer, R. G. (1970). *The language experience approach to the teaching of reading*. New York: Harper.

Stauffer, R. G. (1975). *Directing the reading-thinking process*. New York: Harper.

Taylor, B., et al. (1985, Fall). A comparison of students' ability to read for main ideas in social studies textbooks and to complete main idea worksheets. *Reading World, 24*(2), 10–15.

Tierney, R. J. (1983). Writer-reader transactions: Defining the dimensions of negotiation. In P. L. Stock (Ed.), *Forum: Essays on theory and practice in the teaching of writing*, pp. 147–151. Upper Montclair, NJ: Boynton/Cook.

Tierney, R. J., & Cunningham, L. W. (1984). Research on teaching reading comprehension. In D. Pearson (Ed.), *Handbook of reading research*. New York: Longman.

Tierney, R. J., & Leys, M. (1986). What is the value of connecting reading and writing? In P. L. Stock (Ed.), *Convergences:*

Transactions in reading and writing, pp. 15–29. Urbana, IL: National Council of Teachers of English.

Tierney, R. J., & Pearson, P. D. (1983). Toward a composing model of reading. *Language Arts, 60,* 568–580.

Tompkins, G. E. (1990). *Teaching writing: Balancing process and product*. Columbus, OH: Merrill.

Tompkins, G. E., & Hoskisson, K. (1995). *Language arts: Content and teaching strategies* (3rd ed.). Englewood Cliffs, NJ: Merrill/Prentice Hall.

Tompkins, G. E., & McGee, L. M. (1989). In K. D. Muth-Glynn (Ed.), *Children's comprehension of narrative and expository text: Research into practice*. Newark, DE: International Reading Association.

Tompkins, G. E., & Webeler, M. B. (1983). What will happen next? Using predictable books with young children. *The Reading Teacher, 36,* 498–502.

Uttero, D. A. (1988, January). Activating comprehension through cooperative learning. *The Reading Teacher, 41*(4), 390–395.

Weaver, C. (1988). *Reading process and practice: From socio-psycholinguistics to whole language*. Portsmouth, NH: Heinemann.

Whaley, J. F. (1981, April). Story grammars and reading instruction. *The Reading Teacher, 34*(7), 762–771.

Methods and Activities for Social Studies

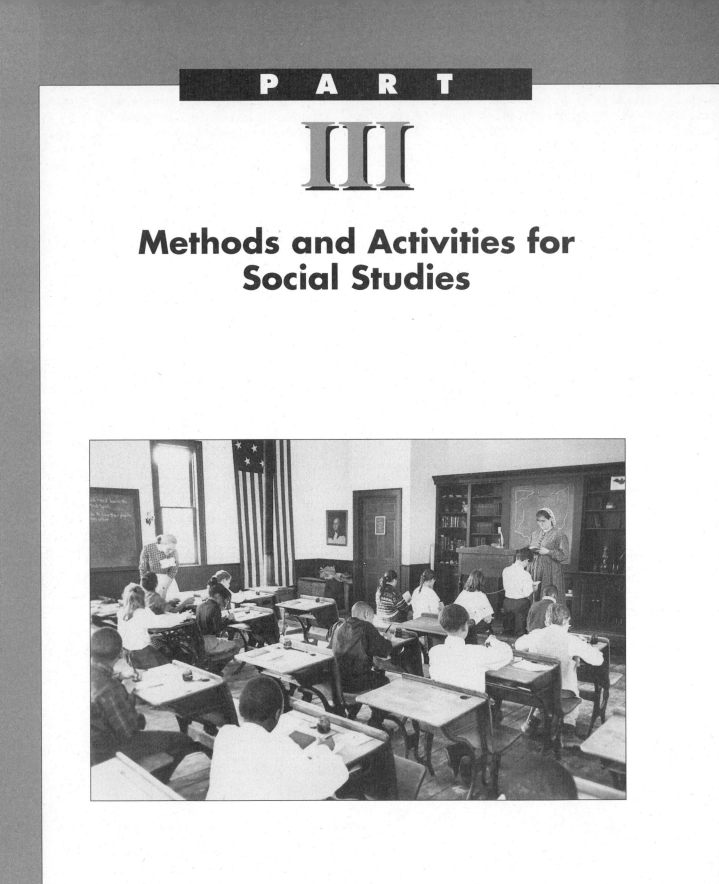

During this final decade of the twentieth century, there has been a rejuvenation of national and local emphasis on the importance of children having early, continued, and meaningfully connected experiences in social studies. As indicated by *Charting a Course: Social Studies for the 21st Century,* the 1989 publication of the National Council of Social Studies, "the study of political, economic, cultural, and environmental aspects of societies in the past, present, and future . . . the social studies equip children with the knowledge and understanding of the past necessary for coping with the present and planning for the future, enabling them to understand and participate effectively in their world, and explain their relationships to other people and to social, economic, and political institutions" (p. xi).

As you have learned, for higher levels of thinking and for learning that is connected and most meaningful, research supports the use of an integrated curriculum and instructional techniques for social interaction. As a classroom teacher, your instructional task is two-fold: (1) to plan for and provide developmentally appropriate hands-on experiences, with useful materials and the supportive environment necessary for children's meaningful exploration and discovery; (2) to know how to facilitate the most meaningful and longest lasting learning possible once the child's mind has been activated by the hands-on experience. Part III will present instructional techniques that are designed to help you complete those tasks. The emphasis in Part III of this text is on the teaching of social studies and will reflect the current best thinking about the field of social studies teaching.

While the goals and vision of the social studies are to prepare young people for citizenships and leadership in the next century, the National Commission on Social Studies in the Schools (1989) has recommended that the social studies curriculum revolve around the following:

1. The history and culture of the people of the United States
2. The history and culture of other people in the world
3. Geographic knowledge, national and worldwide, to provide a sense of place and relationship in time to historical and current events
4. U.S. democratic traditions and political institutions, ideals, and values and a comparison and contrast of them with other political systems
5. The U.S. economic system and a comparison and contrast of it with other economic systems
6. Knowledge of other social sciences, such as anthropology, sociology, and psychology, where feasible and appropriate
7. Humane values and human achievements in religion, literature, philosophy, and the arts
8. A social studies curriculum for the elementary schools based on a core curriculum
9. The ability to think critically and to speak and write clearly and intelligently. (p. 1)

CHAPTER 13
Early Social Studies Learning
Adapted from Carol Seefeldt & Nita Barbour, Early Childhood Education: An Introduction, *3rd ed. (Englewood Cliffs, NJ: Merrill/Prentice Hall), pp. 556–589. By permission of Carol Seefeldt, Nita Barbour, and Prentice Hall*

CHAPTER 14
Integrating Social Studies Across the Curriculum
Adapted from John Jarolimek & Walter C. Parker, Social Studies in Elementary Education, *9th ed. (Englewood Cliffs, NJ: Merrill/Prentice Hall), pp. 327–364. By permission of the authors and Prentice Hall.*

CHAPTER 15
Reaching Students With Special Needs
Adapted from Gail Tompkins & Kenneth Hoskisson, Language Arts: Content and Teaching Strategies, *3rd ed. (Englewood Cliffs, NJ: Merrill/Prentice Hall, 1995). By permission of the authors and Prentice Hall.*

In *Social Studies for Early Childhood and Elementary School Children: Preparing for the 21st Century* (1989), the National Council for the Social Studies identified three strands for social studies teaching: knowledge, attitude, and skills. The council also listed the disciplines of history, geography, economics, sociology, political science, and anthropology as the areas of study and in support, the California State Department of Education published a History-Social Science Framework that indicated that the "knowledge of the history-social science disciplines . . . and the humanities is essential in developing individual and social intelligence; preparing students for responsible citizenship; comprehending global interrelationships; and understanding the vital connections among, past, present, and future (p. 3).

Chapter 13 focuses on fostering children's social studies knowledge, skills, and attitudes. Chapter 14 focuses your attention on ways of integrating social studies with other subjects of the curriculum for grades K–4. It presents ways to engage students in the active exploration of problems and issues that they have identified and encountered, helping them to make the important connections between social studies and human affairs.

Continuing with an emphasis on student-centered instruction and project-centered methodology, those topics are especially emphasized in Chapter 15, which gives suggestions for individualizing your instruction to reach the wide range of learning abilities and diverse backgrounds of your students. ■

CHAPTER 13

Early Social Studies Learning

I n this chapter we discuss the processes of thinking and concept formation related to social studies, the products and processes involved, and the goals of social studies education in early childhood through primary grades. Specifically, this chapter is designed to help you understand

1. The ways children's knowledge of self forms a foundation for learning about others and the world
2. The ways children gain knowledge of social studies as they live, grow, and experience
3. The ways teachers can foster self-esteem and understanding of other cultures
4. The ways field trips foster knowledge and concepts of social studies.

All of education has the goal of preparing children to become members of a society, yet the social studies are uniquely suited to fostering the knowledge, skills, and attitudes necessary for participation in a democracy. The knowledge, skills, and attitudes that make up the field of social studies enable children to participate in the small democracy of their classroom today and prepare them to take their place as fully functioning citizens of a democracy when they are adults.

A. GOALS FOR THE SOCIAL STUDIES

The National Council for the Social Studies (NCSS) and the National Commission on Social Studies in the Schools (NCSSS) have suggested goals for the social studies. They include:

1. *Knowledge*. Embracing all of the disciplines of the social sciences, everything concerning the nature of people and their world, the heritage of the past, and all of contemporary social living.

The National Council for the Social Studies suggests that children learn:
- A sense of history
- Concepts of geography
- Concepts of economics

2. *Attitudes and Values*. Social studies for children are more than a collection of separate though related understandings of the social sciences. For a society to perpetuate itself, its young must clearly understand the values and attitudes of that society (NCSS, 1989; National Commission on Social Studies in the Schools, 1989). The democratic beliefs

drawn from the Constitution and the Declaration of Independence, such as due process, freedom of speech and expression, equal protection, and civil participation, are rooted in the concepts of respect for self and others and for the equality of others.

3. *Skills.* The survival of a democratic society is possible only when its members are able to think and make decisions. The social studies teach the social skills of cooperating and relating with others and participation in a democratic society.

B. KNOWLEDGE

Children's social world expands beyond that of the classroom and teachers of young children have the responsibility of helping children develop knowledge of the wider world. Children who have knowledge of their complex world feel more secure and can reach out to others, those near to them and those far away.

Field Trips

Through trips into the community to see and observe the adult world, children can become aware of and explore their immediate world. Trips provide children with firsthand opportunities to learn about their world. Through trips children:

- Have contact with adult models in the world of work
- Observe social systems, such as banking, garbage collection, traffic control, fire and police protection, and other systems
- Use the methods of the scientist as they gain skills in observing, collecting information, inferring, and drawing conclusions
- Use the methods of the historian as they examine traces of the past
- Have a mutual experience that can later be recreated in dramatic play or expressed through music, dance, art, or literature
- Are stimulated to gain new ideas and motivated to further learning.

Almost every social studies concept can be fostered through the field trip, either within the school or in the immediate community. For the key concepts from geography, field trips could be taken to observe weather conditions or changes that occur with the seasons, as well as the earth's surfaces—lake, grassy field, or sandy beach. As you take the trip, children organize themselves in space, locate various places, and use maps.

Other trips might be taken to foster history concepts, such as a walk through the neighborhood to note any changes. You might watch as people build or tear down a house, build a road, or fill in a pond. You may take a walk to a historic marker in the community, a museum, or a very old building to study traces of the past. Visiting an older person in the community can foster concepts of the past and of the continuity of human life. Children could find out how the older person lived when he or she was the same age as they are now.

Concepts from economics might be fostered through field trips to stores to make purchases, introducing the idea of being a consumer, or to someplace where goods are being produced. A trip to the supermarket or airport can introduce the idea of diversity of jobs as children list and observe the variety of positions people hold.

Be certain to visit service providers in the community, such as physicians and dentists, the library, and the county clerk, to foster the idea that we consume services as well as goods. A trip to a farm might be taken to find out more about how a farmer balances consumers' wants and needs.

Figure 13–1 summarizes the places to which field trips can be taken.

Before the trip. Field trips are a serious commitment of time and money for you, the children, the parents, and the community. Before planning any trip, evaluate it in terms of your goals for children's learning. Then establish specific objectives for the trip. You might select any of the key concepts from the social sciences as objectives or focus on concepts from another area of the curriculum.

Assess the children's experiences. Find out which places they've been to many times, which they'd like to learn more about, and which their parents would like them to visit.

Remember, however, that just because children have been someplace many times doesn't rule it out as an excellent field trip. Returning to a familiar place gives children a common interest to foster dramatic play or another creative enterprise. Also, you may as a group be able to go "behind the scenes" and see things denied to the general public. Also very young children feel a sense of comfort when they are familiar with a place and can focus their attention on the goals of the trip.

Check with your school or program to determine the rules and regulations concerning field trips. Insurance coverage for drivers, safety restraints for children, and permission slips may be required. Also note that permission slips inform parents of your plans, but they may not legally protect you or the school from liability.

Permission may also be required from the principal or director or, in some cases, the parent advisory board. If you're planning a number of trips during the year, you might get permission for all of them at one time.

First, take the trip without the children so that you can plan how you will get there with the children and so you will be acquainted with the place. Talk with the people, informing them of the goals of the trip and the children's nature and interests. After you've seen the place, you'll be in a better position to determine what learning will result from the visit.

Walking field trips are the most valuable for young children. They are short, matching children's attention span. Also because children are at least partially familiar with the places they are walking to, the trips offer them more opportunities for learning. Walking trips are inexpensive, and can be taken more frequently than those requiring a bus or other form of transportation. Yet even a walking trip demands careful planning. What streets will you cross? How many adults will be needed to make the trip safely? Will the children need a rest stop, and where would this be?

Prepare the children. Once you are ready for the trip, prepare the children. Children need some background information about the place they'll visit and some indication of what to look for once there. Have them list the questions they have or what they want to find out about, either dictating them to you or writing them. Have them think about the kind of behavior that will be expected both on the way to the place and during the visit. If there are restrictions on their behavior, perhaps touching equipment or talking during certain parts of the trip, you'll want to talk about these restrictions and perhaps even role play the situation. Preparation may take several days, as children role-play going to the site, decide on the questions they'll ask when there, and read books or look at pictures about the place before going.

Prepare the adults. Adults who will go with you also need careful instructions and preparation. They need to know the behavior expected of them, how the children are supposed to behave before and during the trip, where and how you'll reassemble when they arrive at the site, and other procedures for the trip. Children assigned to each adult should be carefully identified. Name tags with a type of identification for each accompanying adult are helpful.

Because you can't be with all the children at all times during the trip, share with the parents some of the points of interest you expect children to observe. Suggest questions they might ask to help children to focus their attention or give them a list of questions the children have prepared.

Prepare the people at the site. They need to know the goals of your trip and the children's interests. Let them know how long the children's attention spans are and how great their ability to understand different concepts.

Taking the trip. Even though you've made careful plans for the trip and you, the children, and the assistants are well prepared, you must be flexible. One class on a walking field trip to the post office became so interested in observing a cherry picker and workers fixing telephone wires that they never made it to the post office. One of the parents went to the post office to inform the postal workers of the change in plans, and the trip was rescheduled.

FIGURE 13.1
Summary of Field Trips

Walking Field Trips

Don't overlook the interesting things right in the school or neighborhood. Walking field trips are popular with children.

Within the school

Many possibilities exist within the school for field trips. Children can:
- Visit the nurse's, principal's or director's, or custodian's offices within the school.
- Trace the route the contents of the trashcan take when they leave their room.
- First find all of the signs without words in the school, and then those with words.
- Record all of the different materials in the school building: the tile in the bathroom, wood flooring, tile on the floor or walls, plaster and wood, glass and metal.
- Count the number of doors on a given floor.
- Listen to the footsteps of people going downstairs.
- Identify all of the machines in the office, kitchen, and engineer's room.
- Observe repairpersons at work.
- Record the colors they find in school materials.
- Go to different sides of the school building, look out the windows, and record what they see from the four sides of the building.
- Count the number of people who work in the school, and record the diversity of jobs.
- Trace the pipes from the bathroom to the basement.
- Record every sound they hear in the office, hallway, or lunchroom.
- Wait for the letter carrier.

Outside the school building

Go outside and staying within the play yard focus children's attention on:
- The shapes they see on the building.
- Locating their room from the outside.
- The wind in the trees.
- Counting the number of surfaces on the play yard.
- Locating and recording the address of the school.
- Recording the sounds they hear.
- Identifying the materials on the outside of the school building.
- Finding out what they see from the different sides of the building.
- Watching the traffic, counting the number of trucks, cars, buses, and other vehicles passing by.
- Identifying the trees on the play yard.
- Locating the principal's or director's office from different spots on the play yard.
- Finding out how their feet feel on different surfaces of the play yard.
- Recording all of the colors they see on the building.
- Observing deliveries to the school, perhaps milk, food, or supplies.

Flexibility is necessary when using bus transportation as well. More than one trip has ended unsuccessfully because the bus driver wasn't there when expected. Have materials available to keep children productively involved if there are unexpected delays. Crayons and paper are good standbys, as are finger plays and songs.

Always consider toileting and providing for drinks of water when planning any field trip. Be sure children have used the bathroom before leaving on the trip, and check out bathroom facilities at your destination. Allowing time for toileting and drinks should be part of your plan. Carry a canteen of water and paper cups with you, as well as moist towelettes, tissue, and first-aid supplies. If at all possible, take a camera or ask a parent to bring one. Photos of the children while on the trip help children recall their experiences later.

On the trip, share the questions the children want answered with your hosts. You can help enrich the trip by giving the host a printed list of questions and things the children want to find out about.

After the trip. Have plans ready for your arrival back at the school. Children are likely to be tired, so low-key activities are best. Allow time for children to relax and wind down before trying to talk about the trip.

Follow-up activities help children to clarify their experiences. Add appropriate equipment to the play areas that will encourage children to role play their experiences. Additional

FIGURE 13.1 cont'd.

Around the block

A number of valuable trips can be taken by walking around the block or within a few blocks of the school. These include:

- Observing a neighbor's flower or vegetable garden.
- Identifying street signs and traffic signals.
- Observing different clothing people walking on the street are wearing.
- Counting the number of red lights.
- Seeing how many different types of flags they can find.
- Locating signs without words, and then those with words.
- Imagining the whereabouts of the people whose cars are parked along the road.
- Counting the number of houses on a hill.
- Visiting local shops or stores, the gas station, firehouse, library, shoe repair store, or other places nearby.
- Going to the nearby park to have a picnic.
- Watching electrical wires being repaired.

Places to Visit

Your home

Children are amazed to find out you have a home other than the school. You actually have a TV, a bathroom, and a bed!

Places their parents work

If at all possible, arrange for individual children to visit their parents at work. This is especially important for children in an all-day child-care program.

Behind the counter trips

Threes and fours, just as older children, enjoy seeing what goes on behind the scenes at stores, gas stations, bakeries, hamburger stands, or camera, paint, or photographer's studios.

A field

Open fields for running, picking wild flowers, resting under a tree, or having a picnic make excellent places to visit.

The homes of neighbors

When your school or center borders on the homes and yards of neighbors, ask if you can bring the children to the yard to visit with them and ask them about their life.

The principal's, director's, or religious leader's office

Visit the office of the person who is viewed as the authority by the children. If your center is located in a religious facility, visit the sanctuary and have the religious leader describe what happens during the services.

---

colors of paint and crayons as well as other art materials may be useful in helping children recreate their experiences. A trip to a chicken hatchery, for instance, might call for addition of yellow paints and papers, and perhaps even soft, yellow materials to the art supplies. A trip to the post office might be followed by the addition of a table with envelopes, rubber stamps, pencils, papers, and stamps, fostering post office play.

One kindergarten group requested "a really whole lot of boxes" following a trip to the hospital. From these boxes they built a miniature hospital. Their hospital rooms were well equipped and even included the physical therapy room and operating rooms.

Thank-you letters to the host are a must. Not only do these promote cooperation in the community, but also they give children experience in functional writing and reading. Include information about the trip in the newsletter to the parents, letting them know how the children are using this experience in their learning.

A Reverse Field Trip

A well-planned trip into the community gives children a more in-depth understanding of their world. However, it can also be advantageous to bring community resources into the classroom. Children can take nature walks, but you can also bring in specimens for them to examine more closely. The acorns from a tree, an abandoned bird's nest or beehive, and plant life from a nearby pond all make learning within the classroom reality-based.

You can ask community representatives to visit the school as well. Fire and police departments commonly have trained representatives who will discuss safety with you and the children in the school. Plumbers might be willing to bring tools and demonstrate fixing a leaky faucet. Or a local puppeteer or theater group can recreate their art in the classroom.

Printed materials, audiovisual materials, and special models or exhibits prepared by industries or businesses in the area can also be used effectively. A local television station may have taped a special program on the community and let you play it in your school.

Prepare children for these visitors in much the same way you plan for a field trip. Provide them with background information, have them draw up questions to ask the visitor, and be sure they understand the kind of behavior they should extend to the guest who will make the visit rewarding for all. Some teachers appoint a host or hostess to greet the visitors and thank them as they leave. Role-playing the situation gives children greater confidence when the time comes.

The guest also needs to be prepared in terms of understanding the children's level of interest, maturity, and excitability. One amateur archeologist visited a first-grade class with specimens of dinosaur bones found in the area. He put them on a table to display, but was horrified when the children went to handle them and began to play "dinosaurs" with them.

Bringing visitors and resources to the classroom fosters children's understanding of their world just as the field trip does. Both expand the children's world and introduce them to social science concepts. So that the trip and the resource visit promote children's thinking skills and are of the highest value, find ways for children to relate the experiences from one trip to another. You might do this through questioning, providing props in the dramatic play areas, or through the use of audiovisual aids, books, or other materials. Ask the children to describe their experiences, categorize and classify them, and communicate them through drawing, painting, dancing, dictating, writing, or some other form of expression.

History

As children explore their immediate environment, key concepts from the study of history can be fostered. Through field trips, you can introduce children to the concepts of the past, change, and the continuity of life.

Change occurs right within the school. As children walk through the school, their attention can be focused on the things that change and on the immediate past. Room arrangements, decorations, art displays, and the building itself change. You can help children to recall the immediate past and to discuss the changes that occur.

Walking through the neighborhood, children can observe signs of change with the seasons or changes that people make. With each change—a house being painted, roads built, buildings renovated—you and the children can discuss what is happening, why, and how things change.

Visits to historic markers in the community, to museums, older homes, or other places of interest may be possible. Some museums will send traveling exhibits to the school.

Visiting an older person in the neighborhood can foster concepts of the past, change, and the continuity of human life. Kindergarten or primary children could interview the older person to find out the games they played and toys they liked best when they were young. Because these often are similar to the ones children enjoy today, you can help children to see that although things change, many human things—feelings, likes, dislikes—stay the same. There is a continuity to human life that children experience as they visit older people. Children might speculate on the changes that will occur as they grow.

Economics

The concepts of scarcity and plenty, the meaning of producers and consumers, and the advantages of division of labor have been identified in the field of economics education (see Minneapolis Public Schools, 1967). Field trips into the community will offer children an opportunity to become aware of and explore these economic concepts.

Although they will not have developed a complete understanding of producer and consumer until after age 12 or so (Bent & Bombi, 1988), children become aware of the meaning of being a consumer by going to stores to make purchases. If children are producing something together, perhaps a playhouse or police car, a trip can be taken to a hardware store to purchase needed supplies. Groups of children will be given responsibility for one purchase. One group can purchase nails, another the wood siding. In this way, children become aware of the relationship between consumer and producer because they play both roles.

Other trips can be taken to doctors, dentists, or to the library so children become aware of the fact that people produce services as well as goods. With primary age children, you can discuss how people pay for the doctor, dentist, librarian, or teacher. It's difficult for children to conceive of service providers as receiving a salary.

When children are consumers, they must make choices. Knowing what things they want and which they need helps them to make wise decisions. Many times during the school day, as children are given choices, teachers might remind the children to ask themselves if this is something they want or really need. "Which things are necessary?" "Is this something you really must have or just want?"

Geography

Location is one of the major concepts identified by the Joint Committee on Geographic Education and the National Council for Geographic Education for study by young children (Fromboluti, 1991). Concepts of location go hand in hand with concepts of direction. Children will use directions to locate themselves in space and to locate their homes and school. Beginning with trips taken within the school building, ask children to do the following:

- Walk to the cafeteria or office and tell how they would locate their room from this point in the school.
- Take a walk around the school building to find the signs and numbers that tell where things are located. Have them look for signs and symbols on streets and buildings.
- Go outside, cross the street, or walk far enough from the school so children can view the entire building. Ask children to locate their room from this viewpoint. Or have them point out the office, director's office, or other parts of the building.
- Locate stores and other landmarks in the neighborhood in relation to the school. Take a walk to the park, or any nearby place of interest. Draw a simple map to follow and have children note the signs and landmarks that tell them where they are as they walk along.

Maps are one tool people use to locate themselves and others on the earth. Maps, however, are an abstraction of reality and constitute an extremely complex idea for children. Nevertheless, by using maps in connection with field trips, children's awareness of maps and their use can be fostered.

C. ATTITUDES AND VALUES

The democracy of an early childhood program supports and fosters the attitudes and values of equality and respect for others. It seems that, for the egocentric young child, the fostering of these attitudes and values begins with a focus on development of the attitude of respect for self. Without first respecting oneself, it seems unlikely that one can respect others.

The idea that respect and love for others begins with first learning to love yourself stems from the Bible and the Talmud. The biblical command to love your neighbor as yourself suggests that in order to love your neighbor, one must first develop love of self. The Talmudic sage Hillel questions, "If I am not for myself, who is for me; and being for my own self, what am I? If not now, when?"

A child's self-concept, or self-image, is the foundation on which she or he will build all future relationships with others and the world. The more adequate children feel about themselves, the better able they are to reach out and relate to others and to feel a sense of oneness with people and the things in their world. Permeating the entire early childhood program will be concern for fostering a sense of self-worth, dignity, and a healthy self-concept in each child. From this base, children learn to relate with others and gain knowledge of their world.

Fostering a Good Self-Concept

The enhancement of *self-concept* is a valued goal of education. Although the words are not strictly synonymous, *self-esteem, self-concept,* and *self-image* can be broadly defined as a person's perceptions of self. It is formed by experiences with and interpretations of one's environment. It is something that is greatly influenced by others (Shavelson & Bolus, 1982). Although definitions of self-concept vary, Shavelson and Bolus describe it as:

1. *Complex and structured construct.* Consists of both a descriptive component (I have green eyes) and an evaluative one (I believe in loyalty). This complexity is different from constructions such as cognition, intelligence, and creativity.
2. *Multifaceted.* Consists of particular facets that reflect the category system adopted by a particular child or that shared by a group.
3. *Hierarchical.* Consists of moving from the development of a perception of behavior to inferences about one's self. The self can become situation specific (in school, I'm a good writer; at home, I'm the older brother who takes care of my younger one).

The Physical Self

Self-awareness is thought to have its origin when infants begin to discover themselves as physical beings, separate from the rest of the environment. The seemingly aimless flinging about of babies' arms and hands is believed to be attempts to determine the boundaries of physical self and the environment. Sensations of cold, hunger, and warmth all work together to help infants learn about body and self. During the entire sensorimotor period, children use their bodies to learn more about the physical self. Recognizing the importance of children's perceptions of their physical self for the development of a good self-concept, a teacher can turn to:

- *Photos.* Take photos of children for scrapbooks, bulletin boards, or gifts.
- *Mirrors.* Provide full-length, magnifying, and hand mirrors for children to see themselves. Give them feedback as they observe themselves: "You have black hair and eyes," "Look at your shoulders," or "You're growing each day, look how tall you are."
- *Games.* Play games that emphasize body parts, such as "Looby Loo" or "Simon Says" as well as using movement exploration activities.
- *Booklets and charts.* Make booklets or charts of activities children can do. A booklet called "I Can" could begin with the main sentence, "I can run . . ." that serves as a base for other pages, such as "I can run quickly," "I can run on tiptoe," or "I can run with my hands in the air." Children dictate the text and illustrate the pages.

Understanding, accepting, and having a clear sense of self include gender identity, gender role, and sexual orientation. Gender identity is believed to be necessary for children to make sense of their world. Once children construct a stable gender identity, they develop gender-appropriate values and standards.

Gender identity seems a necessary stage of development. Stereotyping on the basis of sex, however, is inappropriate. Teachers are powerful reinforcers of stereotypes. They have been found to interact with girls in ways that differ from their interactions with boys, which leads to the perpetuation of stereotyping and negates development of a positive self-image for both sexes (Sheldon, 1990).

Observing nursery school teachers, Serbin and O'Leary (1975) found that boys were valued for what they would be and girls for what they would give. Girls seemed to be aware of their lower status and tried harder to please and to be attentive and well behaved; boys, however, were rewarded more for their potential than their good behavior. Serbin and O'Leary (1975) also observed that teachers interact with boys and girls differently. They found that teachers rewarded girls for dependent behaviors, repeatedly paying attention to girls who clung to them, stood near them, or waited for directions. At the same time, the teachers praised boys for the tasks they did on their own and for being independent.

Teachers have also been found to challenge boys to try harder and to repeat tasks to achieve mastery. Perhaps this is because boys weren't as neat in their work or too obedient. Girls, on the other hand, were never challenged toward greater achievement. This challenge differential may be related to women in our society having achieved far less than men in many fields. Girls, because of this type of differential treatment, may become alienated from themselves and distrustful of their own intuitions and affirmations. They learn to fit themselves into the mold of society, and as adults, may know something is wrong, but will continue their anxieties by continuing to settle for the security of society's prevailing patterns (Riley, 1984, p. 16).

The Psychological Self

We know ourselves as physical beings, but self-esteem involves more than recognition of the physical body. It also deals with self-knowledge, self-perception, and our attitudes and emotions.

Emotions. As children grow and mature, their emotions grow. Emotions proceed through a series of stages from the infant's relatively undifferentiated emotional responses to what is termed emotional maturity. By the age of 3 months, infants seem to be able to differentiate between distress and delight, and by 2 years of age a child can express a full range of emotions, including fear, disgust, anger, jealousy, distress, delight, elation, and affection.

Children, like adults, have ways of handling emotions and expressing feelings. In an early childhood setting, children learn new ways of expressing emotions and feelings that are socially accepted and will not interfere with their own or others' learning. Help children develop an understanding of their emotions by:

1. Recognizing and naming their feelings
2. Understanding and accepting them
3. Helping them to find wholesome outlets for their feelings.

Attitudes. Attitudes and values are another part of the psychological self. Our attitudes are believed to influence how we feel about something and to affect the way we respond, behave, and act. An opinion is simply a verbal expression of belief, but attitudes imply an emotional liking or disliking of something.

Everything in an early childhood program is bound up in and influenced by attitudes and values. Even the very act of attending school reflects our attitude toward education. Because attitudes and values are a part of the school situation, you have the responsibility to help children understand and clarify their attitudes and beliefs. Asking children the following questions is believed helpful in promoting self-understanding (Raths, 1962, p. 35).

- Are you glad you feel that way?
- Have you thought of any other ways of doing that?
- Have you felt this way for some time?
- What are some examples of what you have in mind?
- What are some things that are good about the way you feel?
- Is this idea so good that everyone should feel the same way?
- Who else do you know that feels that way?

Children's names are very much a part of the psychological self. Allport (1958) believes "the sense of self depends on more than the bodily me" and that self-concepts depend heavily on labels for self and others. By the second year of life, children are beginning to use their name in reference to themselves and their possessions.

The most important linguistic aid of all is the child's own name. He hears it constantly. "Where is Johnny's nose? Where are Johnny's eyes? Good Johnny." By hearing his name repeatedly, the child gradually sees himself as a distinct and recurrent point of reference. (Goodman, 1976, p. 26)

Each child entering a school group needs to feel the sense of self that comes when others use his or her name. Teachers who call children by name are helping them to differentiate self from group, as well as to integrate individuals into the group. The name lets children sense their distinctiveness, helping them establish their independent status within the group and at the same time permitting entry into it.

Some teachers make a class booklet at the beginning of school. They take a photo of each child, paste it in the scrapbook, and label the picture with the child's name. Five- and 6-year-olds can be given ditto masters and asked to draw a picture of themselves on the sheet. Depending on the children's skills, the teachers or the children can write their names under the picture. The ditto masters are then run off and stapled together to form booklets that each child gets.

Other teachers make a mural of children's photos and names titled "We Are in Room 1." Experience stories about each child in the class can be written. Place a photo of the child along with a story dictated or written by the child on a wall chart. The charts decorate the hallway or the room.

Fostering Respect for Others

When children are valued and respected within the democracy of an early childhood program, they are able to respect others, both those who are similar to themselves and those who differ. We need to teach children to embrace and value the many cultures that make up our nation not only for their beauty, but also because "we can't afford the cost in terms of human potential that any other course would demand" (Hornbeck, 1984).

The general goals of multicultural education are to develop an understanding of and appreciation for all racial, ethnic, and cultural groups. Specific goals are to provide information on:

- The history and culture of racial, ethnic, and cultural groups in the community, the nation, and the world
- Historical events, situations, and conflicts—interpretations of these from diverse ethnic perspectives
- The contributions that racial, ethnic, and cultural groups have made to the development of American civilization
- The social and economic conditions that racial, ethnic, and cultural groups have experienced and continue to experience in the United States
- The nature of racism, bias, and prejudice as these affect the behavior and experience of racial, ethnic, and cultural groups. (Maryland State Department of Education, 1980, p. 5)

Multicultural education, with its broad and specific goals, "requires that the total school environment be changed so that students from diverse ethnic and racial groups will experience educational equality" (Banks, 1982, p. 592). At the same time, children learn specific information about other groups and begin to value diversity. Because such learning cannot be accomplished with a separate subject-matter curriculum, an infusion model has been suggested. These goals are consciously incorporated, or infused, into the total curriculum.

Education that is multicultural should be

an on-going, ever-present attempt to promote among our students a recognition and understanding of the similarities and differences among people. A sense of self-esteem and a genuine respect for other individuals and groups are encouraged at all times. (Curriculum and Instruction/ Charles County Public Schools, 1984)

Developmental Stages

An understanding of how children develop concepts of other cultural, ethnic, and racial groups is necessary to infuse a multicultural curriculum into the total program. Children form concepts of others in the same way they form concepts of their own group. Lambert and Klineberg's study (1967) provides the most complete explanation of how children learn about others. From their study of children in a number of different nations, Lambert and Klineberg concluded that the manner in which the concept of "own group" is taught has important consequences. The process of establishing this concept apparently produces an exaggerated and caricatured view of one's own nation and people. The stereotyping process appears to start in the early concepts children develop of their own group; children do not begin stereotyping foreign peoples until age 10.

Early training in national contrasts appears to:

- Make certain foreign groups outstanding examples of peoples who are different.
- Give children the impression that foreign people are different, strange, and unfriendly. Children stressed the differences of foreigners, which suggests an overall orientation of suspicion.
- Affect children's self-concepts. Children in some nations think of themselves in racial, religious, or national terms. Self-concepts of certain groups of children reflect what Lambert and Klineberg (1967) presume to be the culturally significant criteria used in their training to make distinctions between their own group and others.

The study made clear that parents and other significant people in the child's environment transfer their own emotionally colored view of others to the child. Significant others seem to assign specific attributes to members of particular groups during the period of cognitive development when the child has not fully differentiated one group from another or his own group from others.

Children's self-concepts, the way they are taught about others, and their parents and significant others who do the teaching are all important factors in children's gaining international understanding. In planning to teach young children, it is critical to know that the child will naturally recognize the focus on people's differences more easily than on their similarities.

Significant Others

Teachers, as well as children, bring to their classrooms a decided set of values, attitudes, and understandings. Before attempting to teach multicultural education, you must first examine your own understandings, feelings, and attitudes.

Many Americans believe, rather chauvinistically, that our country is superior to all others. Perhaps children have picked up these attitudes before they enter the classroom. You must try to show children why this attitude is not necessarily accurate. Ask yourself:

- What have I read from each country? Did this reading present an accurate point of view? Was it current? Was it written by someone of that nationality?
- Am I familiar with any of the country's films? What do I know of the art of the country? Have I read a current novel?
- What do I know of the religious customs of the country? The government? The economy? Is my current information up-to-date? Is it free from stereotypes?
- Are my background materials relevant to the culture as a whole, or do they represent just one portion of the people?

Focus on Similarities

You should always try to focus on similarities rather than differences among people. Very young children are able to identify differences and begin to stereotype others by focusing on them. Therefore it seems feasible to begin by focusing on the similarities among people everywhere, regardless of culture.

People the world over are alike in many ways. Children who understand the similarities among people are able to move to recognizing the uniqueness of each cultural group without fear, distrust, or stereotyping. In all cultures, people have the following features, although the specifics vary:

- Art forms
- Group rules

- Social organization
- Needs for food, shelter, clothing, and other materials
- Language

Art forms. Children who are encouraged to create their own poetry, paintings, dance, literature, or crafts can readily understand and appreciate the art of others. Art from all nations helps children discover people's common heritage. Children can:

- Visit museums and display art from all over the world
- Begin an exchange of their paintings, drawings, or creative writing with a school in another country
- Invite visitors to tell folktales from their nations and compare the tales with those of the United States
- Listen to poetry from other lands—perhaps some haiku from Japan—and dictate or write their own

The visual arts and music allow for personal expression, communication, and tangible achievement without depending on words. They provide a comfortable means for valuing similarities among peoples, as well as for recognizing the uniqueness of groups. As you study the art of other nations, compare it with the art of the children, artworks of others, and art products unique to cultures of America.

Group rules. As children begin to realize that rules are necessary to live together effectively, they can understand how groups function more successfully when the rights of each group member are recognized. Children who can establish their own rules for using playground equipment or for behaviors in the classroom are beginning to learn that people everywhere use a system of rules.

The school has rules as well. Children in the primary grades may relate the rules of their school to those of their classroom, home, and community. Perhaps the rules of the city, state, and nation can be identified and related to children's experiences with school rules. The fact that all people everywhere have rules can be pointed out.

Social organizations. Although family and social group composition changes dramatically from place to place, all human beings live in some type of group or social organization. To comprehend similarities among social groups, children in the primary grades can:

- Graph their families' composition to show how many different kinds of family units are represented in their classroom. You'll want to point out how all units are, at the same time, similar and different.
- Exchange letters with a family in some other nation to learn how the family is the same as their own family.
- Invite some visitors from other countries to tell about their own families, the activities family members do together, and how they share work or celebrate holidays.

Similar needs. People have similar needs. The universal needs for food, shelter, clothing, and other materials can be introduced. Explore the things children in the kindergarten or primary grades need to live.

- Have them draw a picture of the house they live in. Classify the pictures by type of home. Discuss the need for homes. Find pictures of homes in other places. Avoid stereotyping by making certain these homes represent current living conditions as well as the variety of homes found in any given country.
- Make booklets titled "Things My Family Needs." Compare children's booklets. Relate these needs and wants to those of people in other countries.
- Discuss the foods children like to eat, why they eat, and find out what foods children would like to try. What foods do they eat on special occasions? Chart them and trace these preferences to the children's cultural, ethnic, or racial background.

- Everyone needs clothing. Discuss clothing children need and clothing they would like to have. Find out how people dress in different parts of our nation, such as Florida, Alaska, or in the Southwest. Find out how people dress in other nations and why. Again, be certain not to stereotype groups. Present current, factual representations of clothing, not only clothing worn in the past, such as wooden shoes from Holland or kimonos from Japan.

Language. People everywhere communicate verbally and nonverbally. Children can learn that both verbal and nonverbal communication skills are involved as they express feelings, ideas, attitudes, and knowledge. Verbal communication may involve many different languages; nonverbal communication is useful when you do not understand the verbal communication of others. Children can be given many opportunities to communicate in the classroom on a one-to-one basis or in large or small groups. Methods might include using a telephone or tape recorder or dictating to you. Draw children's attention to the use of nonverbal communication and extend the concept by introducing sign language, role playing, and dramatizations.

Listen to someone speaking another language. You, a visitor, or one of the children might teach a few phrases of the language. The children might learn a simple folk song using the language or listen to songs sung in another language.

By emphasizing the things that bind people together and helping children see the similarities that exist among all people regardless of culture, you introduce them to the multicultural nature of the world. As children learn about their own country, they also learn about other countries and cultures. A child's self-concept, as well as the attitudes and values of significant others, plays an important role in developing multicultural understandings.

D. SKILLS

The entire early childhood program and curriculum is designed to foster children's social skills and ability to participate in a democratic society. With a strong self-concept, children are ready to develop the skills of communicating, sharing, cooperating, and participating in a social group.

Social Skills

Children who have a strong sense of self are ready to learn to live with others. The ability to communicate is basic to living and working with others. In *Democracy and Education*, Dewey (1944) pointed out that

> . . . communication is the way in which they come to possess things in common. Without communication to ensure the participation in a common understanding to secure similar emotional and intellectual dispositions, there could be no community, no group with which to relate. (p. 7)

Communicating

Not all communication is verbal. Children are quick to read one another's emotions, feelings, and attitudes through nonverbal means of communication. One kindergartner was overheard telling another, "Don't be scared, I've been there before. It's O.K., it just smells funny" as they walked through the hall on the way to visit the engineer's room. No one had said a word about being frightened, but as the children descended into the dark basement, surrounded by strange smells and sounds, one child sensed another was afraid of the unknown.

Communication demands the ability to put oneself into the role of another. Social communication is based on this ability and requires:

- An understanding that there is a perspective other than one's own, and that not everyone sees, feels, or thinks alike
- A realization that an analysis of another's perspective would be useful
- The ability to carry out the analysis as necessary
- Knowledge of how to translate the results of analysis into effective social behavior; that is, in terms of getting along better with persons whose viewpoints are under consideration (Flavell, 1979)

These abilities grow and develop with time, maturity, and practice. Dramatic play offers children experiences with taking on the role of another. In it, children act as if they were the mother, baby, father, or teacher. Other experiences can be arranged to give children the idea that successful communication requires knowledge of other's viewpoints:

- Help children connect their own feelings with the actions and things they're involved in. When opportunities arise, you can ask them, "How did you feel then?" "What made you so angry?" "What made you so happy?"
- Communicate to children your understanding of the context of their experiences. "You feel angry now, because . . ." "You're happy because . . ." "I think Booketee is sad because . . ."
- Suggest problems for children that they can solve through role play: "What if you're waiting for your turn on the slide, and . . ."

Sharing

Learning to communicate is, in part, learning to share. Children communicate by sharing ideas, taking turns listening and speaking, and sharing their time and interests. Learning to share is an important goal of the preschool and primary classroom because children begin to realize that the welfare of society depends on the willingness of its members to share.

Most sharing occurs when there are small groups of children and high teacher- or adult-child ratios. Small groups allow for:

- Increased teacher-child interaction, which appears to let children know they are valued and respected and helps to eliminate unnecessary frustrations.
- Increased recognition. Children can share their ideas and feelings more readily in smaller groups. They have more opportunities to participate in activities such as taking the lunch money to the office, carrying the flag, or having the teacher read their story.
- Increased feelings of social adequacy. When children are just learning to relate with others, large groups may produce feelings of inadequacy. But children will usually find it easy to handle small numbers of others and will feel more adequate and competent (Ladd, 1990).

Models. As early as 1937, Murphy observed that in preschool groups where teachers are noticeably spontaneous, warm, and responsive, children show more sympathy and understanding toward one another. Prescott, Jones, and Kritchevsky (1967) found that teachers who deliberately try to respond to children's needs serve as models for behavior. Further evidence suggests that more sharing takes place in groups where the teachers make the effort to work closely with individuals and to help individual children enter into social groups.

Direct teaching. At times, direct instruction in sharing might be used. Some teachers have children practice sharing by using dolls in role-playing situations that may arise in the group. Giving children a doll, you might say, "Pretend both of the dolls want the car. What will they do?" Information on how to go about taking turns and informing another of your intentions and desires can be communicated as the children play with their dolls.

Cooperating

Cooperating is another skill that means becoming less egocentric, so that you give something of yourself and become less concerned about yourself and more about the welfare of the group. Guidance and support in learning to cooperate are necessary as children balance the task of developing a strong sense of self with learning to become a member of the group. Not all cooperation is democratic. When individuals lose too much of themselves to follow the will of the group, democracy isn't the result. Democratic cooperation means that an individual's desire to be with others and belong to a group is integrated with the desire to retain individuality. Reinforcement, lessening competition, and planning group activities all work to foster the behaviors associated with cooperation (Kemple, 1991).

Reinforcement. Children will be more cooperative when they are rewarded. Weingold and Webster (1964) asked two groups of children to work on a mural. In one group, each child was rewarded for the group product. In the other, children were told that only the child doing the best job would receive the reward. In the first group there was an increase in friendly, cooperative behaviors and peer interactions; in the other group, less attention was given to the product, and boasting and other depreciating behaviors increased.

Eliminating competition. Competition is the opposite of cooperation. In many classrooms, competition is fostered because of the belief that it's good for children and consistent with the values of our society. Competition, however, can destroy cooperation, and it is especially damaging to children's self-identity in a group. To encourage cooperative behaviors, you can reduce competition:

- Play games without winners or losers.
- Continue to recognize and reinforce children for their individuality.
- Ask each child to take part in special tasks.
- Compliment and reward children for cooperative actions.
- Model cooperative behaviors.

Participating in a Democracy

From the base of social interactions in the classroom, children learn to value participation in a democratic society. The ability to be responsible for oneself and to participate fully in the welfare of a group is an asset in any society, but in a democratic society, it is a requirement for citizenship. The disposition to work for the common good and to participate in joint efforts begins early.

For young children, under the age of 7 or 8, participation begins as they assume responsibility for themselves. Rooms for 3- and 4-year-olds are arranged not only to permit but also to promote children to take responsibility for their own dressing, toileting, and washing. These very young children may begin to assume responsibility for others and the group by joining in small groups for brief discussions, to dictate thank you notes or other letters, or to listen to stories and sing songs together. With adult assistance, 3- and 4-year-olds can participate in setting tables, serving food, clearing up after play and work, or caring for plants and animals that belong to the group.

Early on, children without disabilities learn to participate in enabling children with special needs to function fully in the group. In one group of 4-year-olds, Kathy, a girl with spina bifida, received regular and casual help from her classmates who did not have special needs. They handed her crutches to her, helped her on with her coat, carried things for her, and waited patiently for her as they played together.

Over the age of 5 or 6, children participate in other group activities. They can plan together and divide up responsibilities. Sharing ideas, children in the primary grades are able to solve problems and make plans for their own learning. Children who are given responsibilities they can fulfill within the group are learning to participate in a democratic society. Experiences with voting and following the will of the majority give children opportunities to experience democracy in action.

With very young children, everyone can have her or his own way. For example, children can vote to make either gelatin or pudding, with each group being allowed to make and then eat what they choose. Or the class may be divided for games, those voting for "Simon Says" playing in one area of the room, and those for "Looby Loo" in another area. After a number of experiences with voting, the entire class may follow the will of the majority.

Learning to live and participate within the group means setting rules and following them. Children should take part in establishing rules in the class. They can contribute to the rules for woodworking, block building, use of the bathroom and water tables, and so forth.

Other rules are made for children, and children learn to value them as well. Everyone must participate in a fire drill, for example. Because there is little opportunity for them to contribute to the rules of the drill, the children can use this occasion to discuss why it is important to follow certain rules, why rules are made, who makes them, and how they are made. Children can also become aware of other rules they must follow: the traffic laws, rules for riding the bus, and rules for home. These questions might be discussed: "What would happen if no one followed the rules?" "Do you think everyone should obey traffic rules?" "Why?"

Experiencing rules and discussing the purposes for them can help children realize that rules are made to protect them and others. Children should also realize that they have the responsibility to follow the rules, to make rules that are needed for living within a group, to change rules that no longer function to protect them or others, and to adjust the rules to fit changing situations.

Children's ideas should continually be moving toward conventional knowledge:

- Knowing that rules and laws are established by people
- Realizing that rules and laws are always changing
- Understanding that they have control over their own lives
- Being empathic, socially responsible, and considerate of others.

Valuing Democracy

The knowledge, attitudes, and skills of the social studies prepare children to take their place as productive citizens of a democratic society. In an early childhood program, however, children are not just preparing to become members of a democracy, but they also are citizens of the democratic society of the classroom and school. Within the democratic environment of the early childhood program, children practice principles of democracy. Daily they contribute to building and fostering a democratic society, and daily they receive the benefits of belonging to this society.

Through every experience in the program, young children learn that they are worthy, valued, and respected. They know that their individual needs and wants will be met and that their rights to freedom of speech and pursuit of happiness and other rights will be protected. At the same time, they are learning to expand their concerns and give up some of their egocentrism for the good of others and the group. As members of a democratic community, children develop a sense of shared concern, recognizing that their interests overlap with the interests of others and that their welfare is inextricably entwined with the welfare of others.

It is the teacher who establishes and maintains the basic principles of democracy in the classroom. The way the teacher establishes control, deals with individual children and their interactions with one another, and teaches sends a powerful message to children about the values of a democracy. Although there is no one right or wrong way for a teacher to do this, when observing in a democratic classroom, one immediately becomes aware of how teachers actively support individual worth and dignity while at the same time protect and nurture the welfare of the total group. In a democratic group, certain tenets are consistently followed:

1. *Teachers share control.* Teachers do not give orders and expect children to follow their directions blindly. Rather than emphasizing the task or skill to be learned, teachers focus on how children are feeling, reacting, and interacting with one another.
2. *Children make choices.* Instead of the teacher prescribing work to be done, how, and under what time constraints, children make choices about what they will learn, how, and with whom. Cookbook approaches, filling in the blanks, and following prescribed lesson plans are replaced with centers of interest, learning stations, and other materials for children to explore and use as tools for learning. Rather than solo learning, group work and projects are fostered.
3. *Discipline is firm and consistent, but does not revolve around force, coercion, or threat.* Already believing that rules come from authority and that being good means following orders, children need to participate in setting and following rules and begin the long process of being able to separate intent from action.
4. *Freedom of thought and speech are fostered.* Children are expected to have opinions and express them. This expectation governs every area of the curriculum. Instead of giving children duplicated sheets to color or patterns to trace around for art, children are asked to express their own ideas, thoughts, and feelings in drawings, paintings, or their con-

structions. In language arts, they are asked to discuss, write, and express what they know and feel and how to make choices about how they will learn math and science skills.

5. *Children are never overwhelmed by the power of others.* Teachers are not power figures in the classroom, nor do they permit individual children to govern through power assertions, bullying, or threats.

6. *A sense of community is built.* A classroom is a group of individuals. The teacher develops this group into a community by helping children share goals. Even young children can begin to see that they are a part of, and share in, the common goals of their family, their own group of friends, the class, and the school. Not only are children encouraged to see themselves within the context of the total group, but small groups within the total group are fostered.

7. *Teachers model respect for others.* A teacher who cares about and respects each child in the group and each adult who works with the children serves as a model for the children. Teachers model and encourage mutual respect. They let children know in a number of very explicit ways that each person is respected and cared for.

8. *Teachers elicit respectful, caring behaviors from the children.* Teachers model respect and caring for other children but they also teach children how to care for and respect others.

SUMMARY

The social studies, that part of the curriculum concerned with the study of people and their interactions with others and the environment, transmits a way of life to the young. Through social studies:

- Children gain knowledge of social studies as they live, grow, and experience. Developmentally, learning about one's self, about others, and the world, go hand in hand. Children's interactions with others provide knowledge of self and these interactions promote knowledge of the world and one's place in it.
- Children gain knowledge about self-image and self-concept that is the foundation on which they will build all future relationships with others and the world. The more adequate children feel about themselves, the better able they are to reach out and relate to others and to feel a sense of oneness with people and the things in their world.
- Children use a sense of self-worth, dignity, and healthy self-concept as a base from which they learn to relate to others and to gain knowledge of the world.

QUESTIONS AND ACTIVITIES FOR DISCUSSION

1. Interview someone from a culture other than yours. Ask what elements of the culture the interviewee would like children to understand and how this could best be presented to children. Report on your interview to others in your group.

2. Start a file of children's games from around the world. Teach one game to a small group of children and explain the origin of the game.

3. Plan a social studies lesson to develop knowledge or attitudes or skills for children in a grade of your choice. If possible, try your lesson out with a group of children. After the lesson, reflect on what you would change or not change in the lesson.

4. Analyze some materials to use with children to ascertain whether the materials reflect the many groups in our country in a balanced way. For example, if girls and women are presented as mainly passive in a story, balance this with a story of girls or women who are assertive and forceful. Report your findings to your group.

5. Locate children's books that accurately represent minorities and the multiethnic composition of our country and others of your choice. Remember that minorities make up many different cultures that can be found in books. For example, a study of the Caribbean can reflect at least eight different countries and various dialects that developed in each particular island as a result of the blending of native African languages and the colonial languages. Grace Nichols expresses this in her poem "Tapestry" from *The Heinemann Book of Caribbean Poetry* (1992) edited by Ian MacDonald and Steward Brown, selectors. Nichols says the Caribbean tapestry is richer for the "African countenance," the "European countenance," the "Amerindian cast of cheek," the "Asianic turn of eye" and the "tongue's salty accommodation."

6. Write to your state department of education or local school district for guidelines for teaching social studies, multicultural education, and eliminating sex discrimination. For general information, write to one of the following:

    Connecticut Project on Global Perspectives, 218 E. 18th St., New York, NY 10003

    Resource Center on Sex Equity, Council of Chief State School Officers, 400 North Capital Str., NW, # 379, Washington, DC 20001

    Social Science Education Consortium, Inc., ERIC Clearinghouse for Social Studies/Social Science Education, Boulder, CO 80302

    Women's Educational Equity Act, Publishing Center, 55 Chapel St., Newton, MA 02150

7. Describe any prior concepts you held that changed as a result of your experiences with this chapter. Describe the changes.

CHILDREN'S BOOKS

Books that reflect the pluralistic nature of our culture and the world:

HISTORICAL

Anno, M. (1978). *Anno's journey*. New York: Philomel.

Brenner, B. (1978). *Wagon wheels*. Ill. by Don Bolognese. New York: Harper & Row.

Clifton, L. (1973). *All of us come across the water*. Ill. by John Steptoe. New York: Harper & Row.

Fritz, J. (1973). *And then what happened, Paul Revere?* Ill. by Margot Tomas. New York: Coward-McCann.

Fritz, J. (1980). *Where do you think you're going, Christopher Columbus?* Ill. by Margot Tomas. New York: Putnam.

Goodall, J. (1979). *The story of an English village*. New York: Atheneum.

Gray, G. (1978). *How far Felipe?* Ill. by Ann Grifalconi. New York: Harper & Row.

Haley, G. E. (1973). *Jack Jourett's ride*. New York: Viking.

Hall, D. (1983). *Ox cart man*. Ill. by Barbara Cooney. New York: Viking.

Houston, G. (1992). *My Great-Aunt Arizona*. Ill. by S. C. Lamb. New York: HarperCollins.

Lankford, M. D. (1992). *Hopscotch around the world*. Ill. by K. Milone. New York: Morrow.

Lobel, A. (1971). *On the day Peter Stuyvesant sailed into town*. New York: Harper & Row.

Povensen, A., & Provensen, M. (1983). *The glorious flight: Across the channel with Louis Berliot*. New York: Viking.

Rylant, C. (1982). *When I was young in the mountains*. Ill. by Diane Goode. New York: Dutton.

Sandin, J. (1981). *The long way to a new land*. New York: Harper & Row.

Spier, P. (1973). *The Star-Spangled Banner*. New York: Doubleday.

Spier, P. (1981). *The legend of New Amsterdam*. New York: Harper & Row.

AFRICAN AMERICAN

Bang, M. (1983). *Ten, nine, eight*. New York: Greenwillow.

Carew, J. (1980). *Children of the sun*. Ill. by Leo Dillon & Diane Dillon. Boston: Little, Brown.

Clifton, L. (1979). *The lucky stone*. Ill. by Dale Payson. New York: Delacorte.

Everett, G. (1991). *Li'l Sis and Uncle Willie*. Ill. by W. H. Johnson. New York: Rizzoli.

Jaquith, P. (1981). *Bo Rabbit smart for true: Folktales from the Gullah*. Ill. by Ed Young. New York: Philomel.

Jordon, J. (1975). *New life: New room*. Ill. by Ray Cruz. New York: Crowell.

Mathias, S. B. (1975). *The hundred penny box*. Ill. by Leo Dillon & Diane Dillon. New York: Viking.

Musgrove, M. (1976). *Ashanti to Zulu*. Ill. by Leo Dillon & Diane Dillon. New York: Dial.

Scott, A. (1967). *Sam*. Ill. by Symeon Shimin. New York: McGraw.

Steptoe, J. (1966). *Stevie*. New York: Harper & Row.

Ward, L. (1978). *I am Eyes Ni Macho*. Ill. by Nonny Hogrogian. New York: Greenwillow.

ASIAN

Estes, E. (1978). *The lost umbrella of Kim Chu*. Ill. by Jacqueline Ayer. New York: Atheneum.

Hoyt-Goldsmith, D. (1992). *Hoang Anh, a Vietnamese-American Boy*. Ill. by L. Migdale. New York: Holiday.

Mosel, A. (1976). *The funny little woman*. Ill. by Blair Lent. New York: Scribner's.

Pattison, D. (1991). *The river dragon*. Ill. by Jean & Mou-sien Tseng. New York: Lothrop.

Uchida, Y. (1976). *The rooster who understood Japanese*. Ill. by Charles Robinson. New York: Scribner's.

Yagawa, S. (1981). *The crane wife*. Ill. by Suekichi Akaba. (Trans. Katherine Patterson). New York: Morrow.

Yashima, T. (1953). *The village tree*. New York: Viking.

Yashima, T. (1955). *Crow boy*. New York: Viking.

Yolen, J. (1977). *The seeing stick*. Ill. by Remy Charlip & Demetra Maraslis. New York: Crowell.

LATINO/HISPANIC

Aardema, V. (1979). *The riddle of the drum: A tale from Tizapan, Mexico.* Ill. by Tony Chen. New York: Four Winds.

Behrens, J. (1978). *Fiesta!* Photographs by Scott Taylor. Chicago: Children's.

de Paola, T. (1980). *The lady of Guadalupe.* New York: Holiday.

MacDonald, I., & Brown, S. (Eds.). *The Heinemann book of Caribbean poetry.* New York: Heinemann.

INTERRACIAL

Bang, M. (1983). *Dawn.* New York: Morrow.

Isadora, R. (1983). *City seen from A to Z.* New York: Greenwillow.

NATIVE AMERICAN

Baker, O. (1981). *Where the buffaloes began.* Ill. by Stephen Gammell. New York: Frederick Warne.

Baylor, B. (1975). *The desert is theirs.* Ill. by Peter Parnell. New York: Scribner's.

Baylor, B. (1982). *Moonsong.* Ill. by Ronald Himler. New York: Scribner's.

Bulla, R. C., & Syson, M. (1978). *Conquista!* Ill. by Ronald Himler. New York: Crowell.

Mohr, N. (1979). *Felita.* Ill. by Ray Cruz. New York: Dial.

Politi, L. (1978). *The nicest gift.* New York: Scribner's.

Sonneborn, R. (1987). *Friday night is Papa night.* Ill. by Emily McCully. New York: Penguin.

Dodge, N. C. (1975). *Morning arrow.* Ill. by Jeffrey Lunge. New York: Lothrop, Lee & Shepard.

Goble, P. (1978). *The girl who loved wild horses.* Scarsdale, NY: Bradbury.

Jeffers, S. (1991). *Brother Eagle, Sister Sky.* New York: Dial.

Locker, T. (1991). *The land of the gray wolf.* New York: Dial.

REFERENCES AND SUGGESTED READINGS

Allport, G. (1958). *The nature of prejudice.* New York: Anchor.

American Association for the Advancement of Science. (1990). *The liberal art of science: An agenda for action.* Washington, DC: Author.

Banks, J. A. (1982). Multiethnic education and the quest for equality. *Phi Delta Kappan, 12,* 592–685.

Bent, A. E., & Bombi, A. S. (1988). *The child's construction of economics.* New York: Cambridge University Press.

Curriculum and Instruction/Charles County Public Schools. (1984). *Education that is multicultural: A curriculum infusion model.* College Park: University of Maryland.

Dewey, J. (1944). *Democracy and education.* New York: Free Press. (Originally published 1916)

Flavell, J. H. (1979). Metacognitive and cognitive monitoring. *American Psychologist, 34,* 906–911.

Fromboluti, C. S. (1991). *Helping children learn geography.* Washington, DC: Department of Education.

Goodman, M. (1976). *The culture of childhood.* New York: Teachers College Press.

Hornbeck, D. W. (1984). *Guidelines for multicultural education.* Baltimore: Maryland State Board of Education.

Kemple, K. M. (1991). Preschool children's peer acceptance and social interaction. *Young Children, 45*(3), 70–75.

Ladd, G. W. (1990). Having friends, keeping friends, making friends, and being liked by peers in the classroom: Predictors of children's early school adjustment. *Child Development, 61,* 1081–1100.

Lambert, W., & Klineberg, O. (1967). *Children's views of foreign people: A cross-cultural study.* New York: Appleton-Century-Crofts.

Maryland State Department of Education. (1980). *Guidelines for multicultural education.* Baltimore: Author.

Minneapolis Public Schools. (1967). *Economic education.* Minneapolis: Author.

Murphy, L. (1937). *Social behavior and personality.* New York: Columbia University Press.

National Council for the Social Studies. (1989). *Social studies for early childhood and elementary school children: Preparing for the 21st century.* Washington, DC: Author.

National Commission on Social Studies in the Schools. (1989). *Charting a course: Social studies for the 21st century.* New York: Author.

Prescott, E., Jones, E., & Kritchevsky, S. (1967). *Group day care as a child rearing environment.* Pasadena, CA: Pacific Oaks College.

Raths, J. (1962). Clarifying children's values. *National Elementary Principal, 42,* 34–39.

Riley, S. S. (1984). *How to generate values in young children.* Washington, DC: National Association for the Education of Young Children.

Seefeldt, C., & Warman, B. (1990). *Young and old together.* Washington, DC: National Association for the Education of Young Children.

Serbin, L., & O'Leary, D. (1975, December). How nursery schools teach girls to shut up. *Psychology Today,* 57–63.

Shavelson, R. J., & Bolus, R. (1982). Self-concept: The interplay of theory and methods. *Journal of Educational Psychology, 74*(1), 3–17.

Sheldon, A. (1990). "Kings are royaler than queens": Language and socialization. *Young Children, 45*(2), 4–10.

Weingold, H., & Webster, R. (1964). Effects of punishment on cooperative behavior in children. *Child Development, 35,* 1211–1216.

CHAPTER 14

Integrating Social Studies Across the Curriculum

As most teachers will attest, interdisciplinary education and collaborative unit planning are two of the most popular trends in elementary education. But no clear pattern for either has emerged yet. Some teachers are concerned mainly about combining reading and writing instruction with subject-matter instruction. Others are interested primarily in integrating social studies with science, mathematics, and the arts. Still others are eager to find powerful themes around which all curricular areas, from reading to math and music appreciation, can be brought together. In this chapter we will present ideas for integrating social studies in a K–4 curriculum. Specifically, this chapter is designed to help you understand

1. The importance of integrating social studies around a theme and an example of an integrated unit with minds-on/hands-on activities
2. The pitfalls of an integrated curriculum and possible solutions
3. The literacy connection and producing original biographies.

A. EXEMPLARY INTEGRATED UNIT

We begin with some examples, a gallery of exhibits drawn from actual classroom life. We invite readers to use them to develop a concept of interdisciplinary education.

VIGNETTE	EXPLORE

Explore is an integrated social studies/science curriculum developed by teachers and curriculum specialists in a Colorado school district together with the renowned concept learning and thinking skills expert, Sydelle Seiger-Ehrenberg.* This is a K–6 program. Pat Willsey believes deeply in the blending of thinking skills instruction with concept learning. Willsey, a key player in the development of *Explore* and now an elementary school principal in the district, took seriously the admonition of researchers to integrate thinking and knowledge instruction: "There is no choice to be made between a content emphasis and a thinking skills emphasis. No depth in either is possible without the

---

*Explore Curriculum, developed and written jointly by Sydelle Seiger-Ehrenberg and School District no. 12, Adams County, Northglenn, Colorado, 1990. All material in this section is quoted or adapted from *Explore* curriculum documents.

Continued

other" (Resnick & Klopfer, 1989). Note this blend in *Explore's* outcome statement: "As a result of using thinking strategies and other relevant skills, K–6 students will develop an understanding of the orderliness, diversity, relationships, and changes that exist/occur and are created in the natural world and in human experience. Further, they will learn to make intelligent, responsible decisions/choices/judgments/plans in light of each understanding."

The curriculum for grades 3 and 4 concentrates on the first two conceptual themes respectively. Students are to become proficient in the use of thinking strategies for developing deep and flexible understandings of *orderliness* (consistency, pattern) and *diversity* (variety, uniqueness) that exist or are created:

- In living things
- In the natural environment
- In communities of people and other living things.

Further, these third- and fourth-grade children are not expected to develop these understandings only to have them lie dormant in their minds. Rather, they are to learn to *use* them and, through usage, further develop them by making reasoned judgments and plans in light of their understanding. This activity is built directly into the unit plans. Note how this curriculum design, like Mrs. Lindquist's, emphasizes the interdependence of thinking (judging, planning) and knowing (understanding orderliness and diversity in living things, nature, and human communities).

Rounding out the third- and fourth-grade *Explore* curriculum is the study of occupations and avocations in which people use and develop greater understanding of living things, nature, and human communities. Following are four lessons in the first of 12 units. Because our space is limited, we present abridged and slightly revised versions. We begin with the introductory lesson to the grade 3 curriculum.

Introductory Lesson

Intended Learning Outcome: Students will be aware of the general procedures they will be following this year to study science and social studies topics.

Students are told that this year they will be studying science and social studies "as if all of you were scientists." They are then placed in pairs to discuss the question, "From what you know, what does it mean to be a 'scientist?' What does a scientist do?"

As students share their responses, the teacher often asks verification questions, especially the central question of science, *How do you know that's true?* This becomes a common question in *Explore* classrooms. Eventually, the teacher presents the following four-step procedure on a chart.

The Scientific Way of Learning

Step 1—Question

Step 2—Hypothesize, Predict

Step 3—Investigate

Step 4—Analyze/Evaluate Data, Conclude

The teacher then puts the following list on the board:

What plants need to grow
What the stars and planets are made of
How people in communities get along with each other
What the dinosaurs looked like
How people lived long ago
How people live now
What happens when you mix certain chemicals
How we know about weather and climate

After making sure that the class understands each item on the list, the teacher asks students what they know about each topic *as a result of scientists investigating it.*

The teacher then asks the students to go back over the list and name the kind of scientist that investigates some of these things. For example, "What do people call a scientist who investigates stars and planets? life in human communities? how people lived long ago? dinosaurs?" It is not important that students learn all the names of scientists,

Continued

but that they realize, first, that there are different types of scientists and, second, that social studies stems from the work of *social* scientists.

To review, the teacher then says, "As you study science and social studies this year, you will be working just like the scientists we have been talking about. What does that mean? What will you be doing? What are the four things we said all scientists do?"

The teacher displays a list of activities related to airplanes and says to students "Suppose we were going to study airplanes and how they fly, and I told you that you would be working like real scientists. Which of the things on this list would you expect to be doing?"   **Assessment 1**

1. Make up a story about airplanes.
2. Find some facts about airplanes and how they fly.
3. Ask questions about airplanes and how they fly.
4. Draw a picture of an airplane.
5. Describe a trip you took on an airplane.
6. Try to think of possible answers to your questions about airplanes and how they fly.
7. Build a model of an airport.
8. Keep looking for more facts about airplanes to see if the answers to your questions are right.

The teacher reviews the four-step procedure and then shows students a rock, leaf, shell, or similar item, giving them this task: "Suppose you were a scientist and had never seen anything like this before. What would you do to investigate it? Be prepared to tell us what you would do, how, and why."   **Assessment 2**
Homework

Unit 1, Lesson 1

Focus Question: (Each lesson begins with a focus question to direct student/teacher attention.) What is true of all living things that distinguishes them from nonliving things?

Intended Learning Outcome: Students will develop a concept of living things in terms of both the characteristics common to all living things and those that distinguish living things from nonliving things.

The teacher introduces the lesson: "First we are going to study living things and how they are *alike*. Since we're going to work as *scientists*, what is the first thing we need to do to study living things?" The teacher then reviews the chart, The Scientific Way of Learning, now focusing on the topic, Living Things and How They Are Alike.   **Question**

Student attention is focused on the question, "How do we know whether something is or is not alive?" The teacher points to the second step in the four-step procedure and asks students what they need to do after they have asked a question: come up with possible answers. Then the teacher repeats the question, and students hypothesize. The teacher elicits responses, helping students to explain what they mean, and writes them on a chart: **Hypothesis**

We *think* something is alive if it has these characteristics:

_____

_____

_____

_____

_____

_____

The teacher emphasizes that students should give the information they *think* is true. Later they will investigate to find out which of their present ideas are correct. After a few

Continued

characteristics are placed on the chart, students work in pairs to come up with additional responses.

Investigation

The teacher helps children to move into step 3 of the scientific procedure: "As scientists, what is our next step?" Students should respond that they need to *investigate,* that is, find new information to check the accuracy of what they have put on the chart, and find out what else belongs on it. They may ask, "How can we find the kind of information we need?" At this point *Explore* takes students through a detailed introduction to their textbooks and other references where relevant information might be found. This amounts to teaching students how to use their textbooks as an information source.

Once students are familiar with information sources, they are ready to investigate, to test the characteristics they have listed on their charts. *Explore* uses the concept formation strategy, discussed in chapter 2. The teacher says, "To test our ideas, let's investigate several living things and find out whether the things we have listed are true of all of them." Each child is given a data-retrieval chart (see Figure 14.1).

In pairs, using the reference books they just studied, students gather the information each questions requires for each living thing on the chart. Pairs then report their work to the whole class, and the teacher uses a class-size retrieval chart to record their work. A transparency of the student chart placed on an overhead projector works well.

**Analyzing Data
Concluding**

The teacher guides students through the concept-formation strategy as a way of making sense of all the data by drawing it together into a concept. "Let's see what all this information tells us about all living things. First, what do you see is true of some living things but not of others?" Here the teacher is eliciting *differences* among the examples. Then students are directed to focus on *similarities.* "What do you find is true of *all* living things, regardless of what kind?" After this, students are asked to compose a conclusion, or *summary:*

We know something is a living thing if it

_____

_____

FIGURE 14.1
Data-Retrieval Chart

RETRIEVAL CHART
LIVING THINGS

List from chart	bird	tree	fish	cactus	person
Moves? How?					
Grows? For how long?					
Changes? In what ways?					
Reproduces others like self?					
Needs food? What kind? From where?					
Needs air?					
Needs water?					

Continued

Students write an informational (expository) paragraph explaining what living things are, giving examples, and telling how they differ from nonliving things.

Writing a Conclusion

Continuing the fourth step in "The Scientific Way of Learning," students are helped to push their understanding of the concept still further. The teacher has them test their conclusion and at the same time identify the characteristics that distinguish living from nonliving things by having students inspect a nonliving thing—a cloud, an airplane, popcorn, fire, or a balloon.

Classifying

The teacher says, "Let's consider something nonliving, like a cloud. What answers do we get to each of the questions on our chart when we ask it about a cloud?" Later, "Based on the information we now have about a cloud, what about it could make it *seem* like a living thing?" and, "What is true of all living things that is not true of a cloud and proves it is not a living thing even if it moves?"

Students should be introduced to the term scientists use as a synonym for a living thing: organism.

Labeling

Students are helped to review *how* they learned what distinguishes living from nonliving things.

Review

The teacher prepares a bulletin board with two sections, one marked LIVING THINGS, the other NONLIVING THINGS. Students are directed to bring in a magazine picture or drawing of something that belongs in each section. Each student should be prepared to tell the class the characteristics that make each item belong in one category or another.

Assessment

Unit 1, Lessons 2 and 3

We briefly sketch here the other two lessons in the first unit of the third-grade *Explore* curriculum. The focus question of Lesson 2 is this: What do all living things need to survive and develop as they should? Here the intended learning outcome is that students develop a concept of the *needs* of all organisms. The concept they develop, again using a data-retrieval chart and the concept-formation strategy, will include these characteristics:

- Clean air and water
- Nutrition
- Sufficient light and warmth
- Protection from enemies and disease
- Opportunity for the organism to reach its potential

The focus question of Lesson 3 is this: What decisions, choices, judgments, plans, and so on, do people have to make to see to it that living things have what they need to survive and develop? The intended learning outcome is that students develop awareness of and commitment to individual and group *action,* which ensures that living things can meet their needs for survival and development.

This lesson moves children from conceptualizing what living things are, and what they need to thrive, to perceiving reasons for human action on behalf of living things.

living things: attributes ⟶   needs ⟶   action

In this way, this first unit of *Explore* goes to the heart of the most important of the five themes of geography: human-environment interaction.

There are two main learning activities in Lesson 3. The first has students consider cases where threatening conditions are putting living things at risk by making it difficult or impossible for them to get what they need. Students are then helped to suggest courses of action that might improve the situation.

Sample situations:

1. There has been a very heavy snowfall. All the food and water for birds and deer has been covered with snow for several days and the animals can't get to any.

Continued

2. It has not rained for weeks. The farmers are worried because their crops are not getting enough water.
3. People who picnic near the lake have been throwing junk into it for years. Much of this junk is harmful to the fish, insects, birds, and plants that live in or near the lake.

Students discuss these situations in small groups (three or so) and recommend courses of action. Two focus questions guide their work on each case:

1. Which living things would have trouble surviving if no one did anything to change the situation? Explain why they would have trouble surviving.
2. What could people like you and I do so that the living things in this situation could survive? Explain how each suggestion would help the living things survive.

The second learning activity has children gather data on situations in which the needs of living things are threatened *and* in which people took specific actions that helped living things meet their needs. The teacher assembles reading materials about such people or invites them to class from the community. After gathering and recording data about them, students use the concept-formation strategy to compare and contrast these people and their specific actions. Finally, they return to the courses of action they suggested in the first part of the lesson, revising and adding ideas for action based on the information they gathered about real situations.

B. MAKING SENSE OF INTEGRATED EDUCATION

The examples described above suggest just a few of the possibilities available to teachers wanting to integrate social studies education with other disciplines and with instruction on reading, writing, and other skills. These are projects that may be difficult for the student teacher or beginning teacher to undertake. *Explore* is feasible for a beginning teacher, but it assumes the teacher has a well-developed understanding of the concept-formation strategy and considerable experience with blending instruction on content and thinking. There may be simpler ways for a teacher to begin to develop integrated courses of study, and we look at one of these, learning with biographies, in the next section. First, however, we shall define some terms and anticipate some of the pitfalls of planning interdisciplinary units.

Definitions

To understand integrated or interdisciplinary education, one must first understand the idea of academic disciplines. These are fairly distinct bodies of knowledge, each with its own preferred method of study. Anthropology, for example, is concerned with accumulating a body of knowledge (facts, concepts, generalizations, questions) about culture and customs; anthropologists' preferred method of accumulating this knowledge is ethnographic field work. Biology, sociology, political science, literature, history, and archeology are other distinct bodies of knowledge and method. The school subject called "social studies" is itself an interdisciplinary field. It draws on history and the social sciences—geography, political science, economics, anthropology, sociology, and psychology. The school subject called "science" is also interdisciplinary, drawing on biology, chemistry, physics, physiology, and other natural sciences. "Art," too, is interdisciplinary, combining drawing, painting, sculpting, writing, and other skills.

Interdisciplinary education, however, usually refers not to integrated work *within* these school subjects but *between* and *among* them—between and among social studies, science, literature, art, music, math, and so on. As well, it refers to the development of literacy—reading and writing competence—within these school subjects. Compare these definitions (adapted from Jacobs, 1989; Gehrke, 1991):

Discipline: A specific body of teachable knowledge with its own key concepts and generalizations, methods of inquiry, and special interests.
Interdisciplinary: A knowledge view and curriculum approach that purposefully draws knowledge, perspectives, and methods of inquiry from more than one discipline together to examine a central theme, problem, person, or event.

Under this definition, interdisciplinary education brings several categories of knowledge together for the purpose of helping children more fully understand the object of study. Note that the purpose is not to eliminate the individual disciplines but to use them as tools or resources. Wise teachers do not hide the disciplines from children; instead, they call the disciplines by their proper names and help children to examine them. Recall that the *Explore* curriculum teaches children about the different kinds of science and scientists in its introductory lesson. This is to help children develop a more mature understanding of inquiry itself and an appreciation for diverse *ways* of knowing. Anthropology brings a cultural perspective to a topic, while political science brings questions about power and freedom. Biology brings still different concepts, interests, and questions.

Interdisciplinary education's singular strength, then, is its potential for helping children to get beyond superficial knowledge. It can enable them to develop in-depth, multidimensional understandings on topics that are worth the time and effort. There is little sense in the traditional practice of separating American history and American literature, which in some ways are two dimensions of the same topic. The integration will enrich students' knowledge of each and strengthen their grasp of the whole. Reading, discussing, and dramatizing historical fiction of 1776, for example, and Patrick Henry's "Give Me Liberty or Give Me Death" speech—both integral to the study of the American Revolution—deepens the understanding that will come. We present the following simple integrations in the hope that they will inspire readers to invent their own.

> Mr. Atencio reads stories of courageous people to his kindergartners—stories of Harriet Tubman, Lewis and Clark, and Geronimo. Then the children retell these stories, eventually acting them out. They dictate the "script" to Mr. Atencio, who types it and copies it for the children.
>
> Mrs. Hill has her first-grade children grow corn and potatoes in classroom seed boxes, under grow lamps, while they are learning about Columbus's expeditions. This is their introduction to worldwide ecological changes that were the consequence of the initial contacts between Europeans and Americans. Students keep track of their observations in their science journals.
>
> Mr. Coulter teaches reading and writing to his second graders as a common enterprise called *literacy*. The children's work is published in a classroom newsletter that reports current events, rules, elections of class officers, committee business, field trips, games, and the like.
>
> Ms. Kubota's third-grade children write comparative histories of their own community, Mesa Verde, and the Plymouth colony. These histories are then embedded in plays the children write, in which children from the three communities meet. There are no separate writing lessons.

Pitfalls

Skillful teachers manage to avoid most of the pitfalls that inevitably accompany innovations in curriculum and instruction. Interdisciplinary education has its own set of pitfalls and conceptual errors.

Either/or thinking ("putting all the eggs in one basket"). This error involves the assumption that either a discipline-based curriculum or an interdisciplinary curriculum is always the right thing to do. Neither is true. Both are needed at different times and for different purposes. It is important to exercise professional judgment, using each when appropriate. This is the eclectic approach, and for thoughtful teachers, it is usually the best course.

Trivializing learning. While discipline-based education sometimes fragments knowledge, thoughtful teachers recognize that interdisciplinary education can create its own problems. It is particularly susceptible to trivializing the curriculum. This occurs when unimportant content is selected for instruction simply because it easily can be integrated with other content. Meanwhile, important content goes untaught. Just because a learning activity crosses disciplinary boundaries does not make it worthwhile. What makes an activity worthwhile is that students are forming or extending a powerful understanding or skill. As psychologist Jerome Bruner (1960) put it years ago, "The first object of any act of learning, over and beyond the pleasure it may give, is that it should serve us in the future. Learning should not only take us somewhere; it should allow us later to go further more easily" (p. 17). Here is the point: Teachers need to be sure that learning activities are significant and that they contribute to the accomplishment of major curriculum goals (Brophy & Alleman, 1991).

Confusion. Interdisciplinary education needlessly confuses learners when teachers require them to study simultaneously topics that more fruitfully could be examined separately. Imagine students trying to study three cultures' customs, literature, art, and scientific achievements all at the same time. The loss in analytic clarity and the increased difficulty would not justify the gains hoped for by integrating social studies, literature, art, and science. Experts in any field do not attempt to tackle a problem by focusing their attention on all its parts at once. John Dewey (1927) advised, wisely, that we limit a topic for study in such a way as to avoid what he called "the great bad." This is "the mixing of things which need to be kept distinct." Experts limit the problem they are working on; they analyze it, break it into its component parts. They do this to understand the big picture better and, therefore, to know where they most profitably might begin chipping away at the problem.

We should not train students to study a topic by making a jumbled mess of it. Readers may remember the helpful clear plastic illustrations often found in a biology textbook. These made it possible to achieve a sort of layered understanding of the human body. Readers are permitted to focus only on the skeletal system or only on muscle tissue or major organs, and then to lay these systems on top of one another to examine the whole picture and the interaction of parts.

*Dis*integration, then, can be helpful. It also can be needlessly fragmenting. Knowing how and when to separate topics to discern them and make them meaningful and knowing, on the other hand, when to integrate them is a major achievement of skillful teaching.

Confusion also can result when so-called integrated activities require students to do things they are not prepared to do, such as role playing scenes from Mexico when they have learned nothing about Mexico except its location on a map (Brophy & Alleman, 1991). Whether in interdisciplinary or disciplinary contexts, instruction should always build carefully on knowledge children already possess, develop in them an awareness of the knowledge they lack, and strategically introduce them to new knowledge.

A little of this, a little of that. Closely related to the pitfall of trivializing learning is what one expert calls "the potpourri problem" (Jacobs, 1989). This occurs when a unit is composed of bits of information from each discipline. If the subject is the Mayan Civilization, for example, we will find a bit of history, a bit of art, a bit of science, and a bit of math, but not *enough* of any to integrate into a meaningful whole.

Pet solutions. The fifth pitfall—the rush to pet solutions—occurs when a potential solution is embraced before alternatives have been carefully considered (Roby, 1985). Fads often become pet solutions, but so do old habits, as with the teacher who for twenty years has had children choose their own writing topics rather than narrowing their choice for them. Currently a popular pet solution is the idea of "themes" (or phonics or the whole language approach) as the cure-all for elementary school curriculum planning. The essence of any pet solution is that critical thinking is sacrificed to a dearly held belief; professional judgment is replaced with a new habit. There is no substitute for good judgment in teaching. Avoiding each of these pitfalls is a matter of exercising judgment.

C. WHERE TO BEGIN? THE LITERACY CONNECTION

Bruner's advice is perhaps the best: Begin with learning that not only takes students somewhere important, but that also allows them later to go further more easily. Recalling this advice, the most significant place to begin interdisciplinary unit planning probably is with the blending of literacy education and social studies education. Both are strengthened as a consequence of being combined, and the combination permits students later to go further more easily with each. By literacy education we mean reading and writing treated as a common enterprise. Integrating literacy education with social studies education, returning to the idea with which this chapter began, gives literacy education the kind of context it needs. Strong literacy education cannot take place in a vacuum; it is most successful when situated in the collaborative pursuit of content goals. Likewise, it is through reading and writing that children are engaged with the social studies topics.

An example: Fourth-grade children are developing their reading ability as they are helped to read short stories, newspaper accounts, and expository (textbook) material about two remarkable American reformers, Sojourner Truth and Susan B. Anthony. They are developing their writing ability as they write original biographies of these women in cooperative groups. Moreover, they write the script for a winter play called "Profiles of Great Americans," and read and write poetry on the theme *courage*. The principles realized in this example are simple but powerful:

1. Literacy instruction should overlap instruction on important content. The overlap generally robs neither and it strengthens both. As a rule of thumb, the more overlap, the better.
2. Literacy instruction should be embedded in a rich social environment where high expectations are combined with lots of support, coaching, practice, and feedback. In other words, children need to be *apprenticed* into literacy (Resnick, 1990). Cooperative learning can be a good vehicle for such interaction.

With these two principles in hand, we can now present the idea of learning through biography. Drawing on the work of Myra Zarnowski (1990), we detail a strategy for bringing literacy and social studies together in a powerful and exciting way: students writing original biographies of important historical figures.

D. PRODUCING ORIGINAL BIOGRAPHIES

Sojourner Truth was first sold when she was 9 years old, probably in the year 1807. She was born a slave in New York State to a Dutch man named Hardenbergh, so that was her name, too—Belle Hardenbergh. When she was 9, John Neely became Belle's new owner. He paid $50 and got both the Dutch-speaking African girl and 100 sheep. Two years later, after learning some English and suffering beatings at the hands of the Neely family, she was sold again, this time for $105 to Martin Schryver, who had a farm near the Hudson River. In 1810, Belle was sold yet again. Her new master, Mr. Dumont, wrote in his ledger, "For $300, Belle, about 13 years old, six feet tall." Years later, with the help of Quakers, Belle won her freedom and took the name Sojourner Truth. It was a good handle for the life she was about to live: a seeker and speaker of truth.

Her speeches attracted great crowds and are today among schoolchildren's favorites. For example, in May of 1851, she addressed a women's rights convention in Akron, Ohio. Before she or any of the other women could speak, Protestant ministers—all male—dominated the proceedings, deriding the women who wanted social reform. Francis Gage later wrote what happened after the ministers were through:

> Then, slowly from her seat in the corner rose Sojourner Truth, who, till now, had scarcely lifted her head. She moved solemnly to the front, laid her old bonnet at her feet, and turned her great speaking eyes on me.
>
> There was a hissing sound of disapprobation above and below. I rose and announced, "Sojourner Truth," and begged the audience keep silence for a few moments.
>
> The tumult subsided at once, and every eye was fixed on this almost Amazon form, which stood nearly six feet high, head erect and eyes piercing the upper air like one in a dream. At her first word there was a profound hush. She spoke in deep tones, which, though not loud, reached every ear in the house and away through the doors and windows:
>
> "Well, children, where there is so much racket, there must be something out of kilter. That man over there says women need to be helped into carriages and lifted over ditches—and to have the best place everywhere. Nobody ever helps me into carriages or over mud-puddles—or gives me the best place at the table!"

Raising herself to her full height, and lifting her voice to a pitch like rolling thunder, Sojourner asked, "And ain't I a woman? Look at me! Look at my arm!" She bared her right arm to the shoulder, showing her tremendous muscular power. "I have ploughed and planted and gathered into barns, and no man could get ahead of me! And ain't I a woman?

"I could work as much and eat as much as a man—when I could get it—and bear the lash as well! And ain't I a woman?

"My mother bore ten children and saw them sold off to slavery, and when I cried with my mother's grief, none but Jesus heard me! And ain't I a woman?

"Then that little man in black says women can't have as many rights as men. If the first woman God ever made was strong enough to turn the world upside down all alone, these women together" (and she glanced over the platform) "ought to be able to turn it back and get it right side up again! And now that the women are asking to do it, the men better let 'em."

Long cheering greeted this. "I'm obliged to you for hearing me," she concluded, "and now old Sojourner hasn't got nothing more to say." (Clatlin, 1987, pp. 81–82)

Sojourner had much more to say. When she wasn't speaking for women's rights, she was speaking against slavery. And after President Lincoln ended slavery, Sojourner worked in Washington DC—"Mr. Lincoln's city"—to overcome the remnants of slavery: racism and deeply entrenched prejudice. She tried to help freed Africans find work and homes, and she worked for a time as a nurse in Freedman's Hospital. These were chaotic, heartbreaking times. The Civil War, in which her son fought in the famous 54th Massachusetts Regiment, became a slaughter on both sides. And just as it ended, Lincoln, whom she had met and much admired, was killed by an assassin.

Still, she was not defeated. Another biographer, Jeri Ferris (1988), writes of yet another of Sojourner's efforts to right wrongs:

One afternoon as Sojourner walked back to the hospital with an armful of blankets, she was so tired she just couldn't walk any more. Horsedrawn streetcars clanged up and down the road, filled with white folks. Sojourner waited for a car to stop, but none did. Finally, as yet another car passed her, she called out, "I want to ride!" People crowded around, the horses stopped, and Sojourner got on. The conductor was furious and demanded she get off. Sojourner settled back in her seat. "I'm not from the South," she said firmly, "I'm from the Empire State of New York, and I know the law as well as you do."

The next day she tried to ride another streetcar. Again the conductor would not stop. Sojourner ran after the car and caught up with it. When the horses stopped, she jumped on. "What a shame," she panted, "to make a lady run so." The conductor threatened to throw her off. "If you try," she said, "it will cost you more than your car and horses are worth." He didn't.

The third time Sojourner tried to ride a streetcar, she was with a white friend. "Stand back," shouted the conductor to Sojourner, "and let that lady on."

"I am a lady too," said Sojourner, and she stepped aboard with her friend. (pp. 53, 55)

We provide this sketch of the life and times of Sojourner Truth to introduce a strategy for helping children to produce original biographies. The creation of an original biography is a splendid way to invite children to read, write, and discuss their way to an in-depth understanding of great citizens such as Sojourner Truth. The names in the following list are a small sample of other persons whose life and times warrant in-depth study by elementary school children. In the spirit of concept formation, teachers can select three or four people who *together* would help children to form the concept of *democratic citizen*. Thus the class could write three or four biographies during a school year, all the while keeping track of the similarities among these people—similarities that make them all examples of democratic citizens:

- They knew that popular sovereignty is the bedrock of democracy, and that this means taking personal responsibility for the health of civic life.
- They took time from their private lives to be active in civic life.
- They understood the difference between complaining and proposing solutions.
- They understood, within the constraints of their times, that democracy means majority rule *and* minority rights.
- They exhibited courage on behalf of these principles.

Biographies Suitable for Grades 1–4

Greg Louganis	Abraham Lincoln
Benjamin Franklin	Christopher Columbus
Martin Luther King, Jr.	George Washington
Thomas Jefferson	

Democratic citizen of course is not the only concept around which subjects can be selected for biographies, though it is one of the most important. Other central ideas are *explorers, inventors and scientists, champions of the poor, friends of nature, leaders, dictators, revolutionaries,* and *heroes.* A teacher might orchestrate children's biographical studies around one of these themes, having them produce over the year three or four biographies on that theme rather than one each on different themes. This approach should help children to build an in-depth understanding of that theme. On the other hand, teachers might, to cover more ground, mix the kinds of subjects about whom their children write, for example, choosing a hero (Crazy Horse or Harriet Tubman), an inventor (Benjamin Franklin or Eli Whitney), a scientist (Galileo or Newton), and a great citizen (Sojourner Truth or James Madison). Figure 14.2 suggests several themes and related subjects.

Procedure for Writing Biographies

The teacher will need to (1) select the person about whom children will write their biographies, (2) help the children learn about the person and keep track of what they are learning, (3) help children reflect on the person's life and identify key events, and (4) orchestrate the cooperative production of biographies in small groups.

Selecting a subject. Several criteria guide the selection of subjects for children's biographies:

Criteria 1. Most important is that the person chosen bring children into contact with powerful ideas of history, government, geography, economics, or other social studies disciplines. Individuals who can help children build understandings of one or more of the following seven themes will not only bring children to the heart of social studies but also build firm foundations for further learning.

Criteria 2. Another criterion for subject selection is the likelihood that children will be captivated by this life. It may help some children become more interested in the person if information is available on his or her childhood. Ben Franklin's early troubles with his brother James, for example, James Madison's illnesses as a child, and Sojourner Truth's harrowing childhood all seem to fascinate children, broadening them by giving them access to *other* children's lives—lives that are different but reassuringly similar, too. Learning a great deal about a person can itself make that person captivating to the young biographer. As this third-grade student quite wisely reported, one cannot know for certain what makes a subject interesting. He seems to conclude, however, that familiarity breeds interest, not contempt:

Everyone else was real interested in Hiawatha but I wasn't because, well, the things I knew about him just were boring. But the more I found out, the way they learned to hunt and stuff in the long house, and all the magic, well it got real interesting. Now I know him a lot.

Criteria 3. Another criterion is the availability of materials. The "snapshot biography" method we outline here requires students to learn a great deal about the subject (Zarnowski, 1990). If the subject is obscure, chances are good that neither the textbook nor the school library will have ample books, primary documents, narrative biographies, or other materials.

Consider how Mr. Brem, a fourth-grade teacher, selects biographical subjects. He has decided to weave a yearlong study of *leadership* through the state history curriculum his school district requires in that grade. He wants his pupils to study and eventually write biographies of three state leaders. He wants the leaders to be culturally diverse, and he wants

FIGURE 14.2

Examples of Thematic Clusters of Persons of Prominence Suitable for Biographical Study.

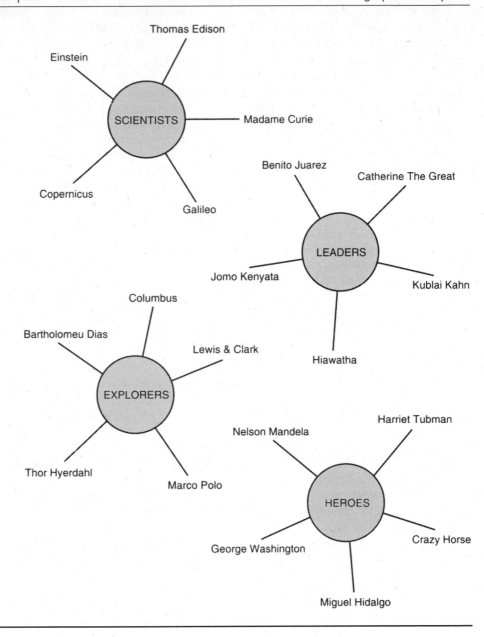

them to expose students to different historical periods and geographical areas of the state. Now Mr. Brem begins his materials search. A booklet he received last year from the state arm of the League of Women Voters provides information on several civic leaders, and he asks a committee of students to select one of these for the class to study. The social studies education office at the state capital publishes material on the state's governors; Mr. Brem selects the states first governor. Now he has selected two of the three subjects he needs. Since they are both European Americans, Mr. Brem wants the third leader to belong to an ethnic minority.

Unaware of who this might be or where materials can be obtained, he appoints another committee of students to go to the school librarian for help. The librarian refers them to information on a civic leader who helped to organize the early Chinese-American community in the state. Now the class has a set of three leaders and is ready for the reading-and-writing approach to biographical study.

Learning about the subject of a biography. Before children can begin to write about a biographical subject, they need to learn something about him or her. Let us be clear, however, that the learning sequence is not read, then write. Rather, it is write a little, drawing on prior experience, then find out a little. Write some, learn a little more, write some more, and so on. One of the major advances in the science of instruction in the past ten years is that teachers do not have to provide all of the facts before asking students to think. The advice instead is to integrate data gathering and reflection. The teacher should concentrate student attention on the higher-order task, in this case production of the biography, which in turn motivates gathering facts about the subject and interpreting his or her life.

So, students begin learning about the subject, let us say Sojourner Truth, by finding out a little something about her. Perhaps the teacher begins by reading aloud for just 20 minutes from Jeri Ferris's book, concentrating on the beginning of the story when Sojourner is taken from her mother and sold to Mr. Neely at the age of nine. Then the teacher asks the children to discuss this passage—the idea of buying and selling persons, in this case a child. She asks them to imagine the feelings of Belle on the auction block and the feelings of her mother and father. She may ask them what they have learned elsewhere about the enslavement of people. Perhaps some of them will talk about the Jews in Egypt in biblical times, maybe some have seen the restored version of the old movie about Spartacus, perhaps some will talk about the Holocaust. Some children may know quite a bit about the capture and subsequent ownership of Africans through books they have read or lessons they have had in prior grades or in church. The discussion will provide the teacher with diagnostic information about children's current knowledge of slavery while activating the students' prior knowledge. The write/learn-write/learn sequence can continue with these steps:

1. Now the teacher can ask students to bring out their journals and begin to write. She may ask them to write about the same things she previously asked them to talk about, which should be the easiest for them. Then she might ask them to predict what will happen to Sojourner in her new master's home. This should make them want to gather more information. Where will they get it?

2. The teacher knows that Sojourner's life with Mr. Neely is documented in the textbook. So, the next day she has children take out their journals to remind themselves of the predictions they wrote yesterday. Then, they are given 20 minutes to read the pertinent section in the text and return to their journal to write what really happened. Next, the teacher turns student attention to the map of the Northeast in the textbook and, based on clues given in the passage read aloud yesterday and the text passage today, helps them to find the state where Sojourner first was bought and sold (New York). In their journals, she has them enter the date and sketch a map of New York under the title, Where Sojourner Truth's Story Begins.

3. Now that they know where the story began (the geographic theme, *location*), students are helped to get a feel for New York (the geographic theme, *place*). Their teacher has them go to their cooperative teams and, working with the textbook, answer these questions:
    a. What states, countries, and bodies of water border New York?
    b. Is the geography of New York all the same, or are there different landforms? If so, what are they?
    c. If Sojourner was able to fly away from the Neely farm, which route would have the fewest mountains to fly over?
   The teacher then tells students to sketch all of this on a blank handout map of New York, including a legend so readers can understand their symbols.

4. The next day, the teacher reads aloud Virginia Hamilton's retelling of the folk tale, *The People Could Fly* (1988). A wonderfully hopeful tale, though at the same time tragic, it tells of African slaves literally flying from bondage to freedom:

> They say the people could fly. Say that long ago in Africa, some of the people knew magic. And they would walk up on the air like climbin' up on a gate. And they flew like blackbirds over the fields.

But when the people were captured for slavery, we learn in the tale, they shed their wings. The slave ships were too crowded for wings. A few, however, kept the power. Toby did, and he used it to help the others to escape. One day Sarah was hoeing and chopping as fast as she could, a hungry baby on her back, but the baby "started up bawling too loud." The Overseer hollered at Sarah to keep the baby quiet, but Sarah fell under the babe's weight and her own weakness. The Overseer began to whip her. "Get up, you black cow," he called. Sarah looked to Toby: "Now, before it's too late," she panted. "Now." Toby raised his arms and whispered the magic words to her. "Kum . . . yali, kum buba tambe."

> Sarah lifted one foot on the air. Then the other. She flew clumsily at first, with the child now held tightly in her arms. Then she felt the magic, the African mystery. Say she rose just as free as a bird. As light as a feather. (pp. 21–26)

Afterward, students return to their journals to reflect on this new material. The teacher now could highlight the themes *freedom, suffering,* and *survival,* and children could be directed to compare this tale to others they have heard on this theme.

5. The teacher continues over the next two or three weeks to read aloud from biographies and other accounts of Sojourner Truth, and from related stories and reference material. Student committees are sent to the library to gather data on people, places, events, and issues raised in the teacher's readings that students want to find out more about. As well, the teacher assembles some material for the students to read themselves—material in the textbook on Lincoln's decision to free the slaves and material on influential abolitionists: Frederick Douglass, who escaped from slavery in the south; William Lloyd Garrison, who published *The Liberator,* an abolitionist newspaper; and the Grimké sisters, Angelina and Sarah, who moved north after having been raised with captive Africans on a South Carolina plantation. This information helps to elaborate the children's understanding of Sojourner's life, as well as her civic missions, and should lead to their producing much stronger, richer biographies.

6. Information on the women's movement of the 1800s needs also to be gathered, such as the Seneca Falls Convention convened by Lucretia Mott and Elizabeth Cady Stanton in 1848. This is the same movement Sojourner jolted with her "Ain't I A Woman" speech, delivered three years later at a second women's rights convention.

7. The setting for all this information needs also to be grasped; consequently, students should study the geography of New York, Ohio, and Michigan—the three states where Sojourner spent much time working, speaking, and living. In this way, students learn about the subject of their biography and gradually piece together in their minds a model of Sojourner's life and times.

Reflection and settling priorities. After several weeks of reading, writing, and mapping their biographical subject's life, children are ready to reflect on this life and its times and places, and to select key events. A few of these events will become the focal points of the chapters in the book students will write together (Zarnowski, 1990).

1. *Opening.* The teacher announces that today is the day the class begins to pull together all that has been learned about the subject, and informs students of what is to come.
2. *Brainstorming.* The teacher asks students to brainstorm all the events in the subject's life that they found interesting, all the events they believe were pivotal in the subject's life, all the events they figure made the subject the most and least proud, and so on. The point here is to get a long list of varied events in the subject's life. Here are just a few of the events in Sojourner's life that students have suggested.
   - The time she was separated from her mother
   - The second time she was sold
   - The third time she was sold
   - Confronting Mr. Dumont
   - Rescued by Quakers
   - Names herself Sojourner Truth
   - "Ain't I A Woman?" speech

- Meeting President Lincoln
- Working as a nurse in Washington, DC
- Confronting the trolley conductor
- Meetings with Garrison and Douglass.

When the brainstorming slows, the teacher has students take a break—go to recess, clean the room, do something physically active. When they return, they open their journals and search for other events to add to the list. They come up with more:

- Being born in captivity
- Speaking out for women's rights
- Becoming an abolitionist
- Living in New York
- Traveling by buggy in Ohio.

3. *Selecting.* Students now are asked to move into cooperative groups of four or five children each. Their first task as a group is to select four or five of the key events brainstormed by the whole class. These might be the four events that interested students the most, or the teacher might direct them to use other criteria. For example, if the teacher previously has worked with children on the meaning of time lines, she or he might have them divide Sojourner's life into four equal segments and choose one event from each segment. Or, the teacher might have them choose one event in each of four categories: meetings with remarkable people, life as a slave, speeches, life as an abolitionist.

Once the key events have been selected, the children in each cooperative group divide the events among themselves, each choosing one event. Dividing the events—and thus the labor—is crucial to the coming task: producing an original biography.

Writing and illustrating. The students are now ready to write and illustrate a biography of their subject. Each cooperative group will produce a biography on the same subject, in this case Sojourner Truth. Some teachers have each group use the same biography title, *The Life and Times of (Sojourner Truth)*. Others let each group create its own variation on this title.

Each person on the team is responsible for one chapter. The chapter's topic is the key event selected before. Groups will have different chapters in their books because each group will choose a different set of four key events. However, if the teacher wishes, he or she can use the cooperative groupwork technique called Jigsaw (Aronson, 1978). In this technique, one member of each small group is working on the same key event as one child on each of the other groups; consequently, these children can meet together to work on their chapter.

The teacher achieves this by *not* allowing groups to select their own four events. Rather, after the large-group brainstorming of key events, the *large group* also selects four events that will become the chapters in the groups' biographies. Thus, the book may shape up like this:

Title: THE COURAGE AND CONVICTION OF SOJOURNER TRUTH

Chapter 1: "Sold for 50 Dollars!"

Chapter 2: "New Name, New Life"

Chapter 3: "Ain't I A Woman?"

Chapter 4: "The Trolley Incident"

The child on the team who is responsible for Chapter 1 joins with other children from other teams also working on "Sold for 50 Dollars!" Meanwhile, the child on each team responsible for Chapter 2 joins with the other "2s," and so on. These are called *expert groups*. Together they discuss what they will write and draw, read one another's drafts, and provide feedback. This is advisable with younger children who are just beginning to write early versions of paragraphs; the group support is helpful, and the teacher can more easily monitor and coach her four expert groups than if every child in the room was writing on a different topic.

Whether the teacher uses the Jigsaw technique or not, the children's work has two parts: They have to write a description of the key event for which they are responsible, and they must draw an accompanying illustration. The least experienced writers may produce only a one- or two-paragraph description, and may fit their illustration on the same page. The teacher may press more experienced writers, however, to produce a two- or three-page description. The illustration is embedded in the text somewhere as in "real" biographies. Skillful teachers are able to boost their children's confidence about both the writing and the drawing by encouraging them to "just get started, get something on paper, pull something together from your journal, whatever; we'll go back and polish it later." (Teachers and children who play the board game, *Pictionary,* understand that illustrating is very different from producing realistic drawings. Virtually anyone can illustrate.)

Each team thus produces the rudiments of a biography: a title page and four chapters. But real biographies have more, and so should these. The following parts of a book make a more complete biography, and they generally can all be done even by the youngest children:

Title page. Title plus complete publication information, for example: The Life and Times of Sojourner Truth (see Figure 14.3).

Foreward. Written by someone other than the four authors, for example, a parent, another teacher, the mayor, a school board member, a bus driver. Instruct the Foreward writer to write no more than one page and to address two matters:

1. Tell readers some ways you feel you can relate personally to the person about whom the biography was written.
2. Tell readers something about the book.

Introduction with time line and map. The introduction should contain a brief message to readers telling them the subject of the book: Who is its subject? Where and when did he or she live? What, in a nutshell, did he or she do? Why? It is also considerate to tell readers the topic of each chapter. A helpful way to portray the *when* is to sketch a time line

FIGURE 14.3
An Example of a Biography Written by Students as a Cooperative Learning Project.

of the subject's life. The *where* statement should be illustrated with a map, either physical or political, or both, with a legend to help readers understand the symbols.

Chapters 1–4. Each chapter needs a title and author name. Its body is a written description of a key event in the subject's life with an illustration that captures the key event.

About the authors page. Ask each child to write a sentence or paragraph about her- or himself. The teacher might ask each group to decide how long the author statement should be. Children can be prompted to tell readers their full name, the name of the city or town where they live, their age, and something they like to do:

> Wing Luke lives in Denver, Colorado, with his family. He is 9 years old and loves to play soccer. He wrote chapter 4, "The Trolley Incident."

Biography writing integrates literacy learning with social studies learning. By embedding literacy instruction in important social studies content *and* collaborative group work, the teacher creates the kind of social context that can support in-depth learning. Reading comprehension and writing instruction become much more than plodding through new vocabulary and learning sentences and paragraphs in a vacuum; literacy comes to mean problem solving, interpretation, competing interpretations, conversation, provocation, writing and rewriting to find out what one thinks is true and what one believes ought to be done, and experimenting with new possibilities that exist now only in the imagination. This is an integrated curriculum.

E. THE CHANGING CONCEPT OF LITERACY

The biography-production method we have been discussing is embedded in a conception that sees reading and writing not as fixed abilities that one either has or lacks. Rather, reading and writing are seen as processes—more precisely, as *crafts*—that evolve through trial, error, and support from those more accomplished.

This emphasis on process is changing the way highly skilled teachers orchestrate language arts/literacy instruction. They understand that an individual's reading and writing skills grow and change over time. One's literacy is not static; it evolves, and its evolution depends on the individual's social context, that is, his or her "literacy community." All of us belong to one sort of discourse community or another, and that membership functions to socialize us into one or more patterns of using our minds—of reading, writing, and talking. On one hand, we might be socialized into a literacy community that expects and rewards no more than minimal language use— say, for reading street signs, a ballot, and directions on a medicine label; for "filling out" job applications, "filling out" worksheets, and "completing" credit card applications.

On the other hand, we might be socialized into a literacy community that expects and encourages something quite different. Here, language is used in the service of higher-order, important tasks, for example, to plan research on civic problems with an eye toward improving social life, as an avenue to satisfying aesthetic experiences in literature and the arts, and as a means of lively conversation and, hence, conflict resolution and mutual understanding.

Students spend a good part of the day integrating reading, writing, and social studies, and other subjects as well. They do this by working on biographies of someone whose life and times carry them imaginatively and deeply into essential content. The biographical approach is, of course, only one vehicle, but it is a powerful and feasible one. Children are expected to do more than "fill out" this or "complete" that; they are expected instead to develop the crafts of reading and writing and, as they do so, to bring them to the service of important social studies (and science and mathematics) understandings. We now take these notions of high literacy and integrated education one step further by considering the importance of *culture* (see Figure 14.4).

Teachers recognize that first, classrooms are multicultural places. Students differ from one another and the teacher in one or more of these categories of culture: ethnicity, race, gender, and social class. Second, topics often need to be studied from more than one cultural perspective. Together, these add up to what is called *multicultural education*. We will examine each in turn.

FIGURE 14.4
Schematic Representation of Integrated Education.

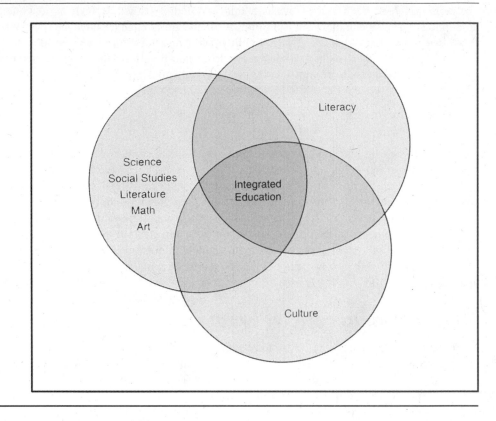

Science
Social Studies
Literature
Math
Art

Literacy

Integrated
Education

Culture

Hospitable Learning Climate

As for the first, skillful teachers create learning communities that genuinely welcome cultural differences among the children gathered there. These teachers are as eager to find out about the cultural backgrounds of their children as they are to discover any other diagnostic information that will help them to individualize learning. Differences are not treated as disadvantages; they are not even perceived that way. Rather, they are perceived and treated as part of the child's experience— his or her prior knowledge—that must be integrated into teaching and learning if desired outcomes are to be reached. This is a tall order. How do these teachers do it?

Perhaps the most helpful thing they do is not implementing a set of techniques but cultivating in themselves an *attitude*. They cultivate in their own professional behavior an anthropologist's perspective on their own cultural roots and those of the children. They recognize that they themselves have been socialized into one or more cultures—that they are not culturally neutral, suspended above ethnicity, race, class, gender, and particular linguistic traditions. Quite the opposite, teachers are thoroughly immersed. Every teacher speaks one or more language and dialect; every teacher belongs to one racial group or another and to one ethnic group, gender, and social class or another.

Skillful teachers do not make much of this fact in overt ways, they don't "advertise" their culture, but they are keenly aware of it and appreciate how profoundly culture influences their point of view and what they do with students. Fundamentally, *this cultural knowledge helps them more clearly to see the cultural tapestry of the classroom—themselves included.* Perceiving clearly the cultural roots of their own speaking, thinking, and behaving helps them to not ignore the classroom tapestry but instead to pay attention to it, study it, develop expertise on it, and use it. This makes it possible for them to provide what we might call "a hospitable learning climate" for all their students, whatever their cultural backgrounds. It is a learning community that honors diversity. Consider the following case:

Mrs. Carey teaches in the third grade, where the social studies theme is "Communities Now and Then." She has always prided herself on being able to tell both short and long versions of America's story. The long version is the one she tells in her third-grade class, and it takes a whole school year. Her children study European and Asian immigrant communities, both now and long ago. They build replicas of the Plymouth and Jamestown colonies but also St. Augustine, Florida, and Santa Fe, New Mexico. And they study the Chinese men who immigrated to work the railroads, reading related stories. Her short version reduces the nine months to a phrase, "We are a nation of immigrants."

This short version, really a title for the yearlong study, indicates the main idea around which Mrs. Carey orchestrates content and instruction. It is the *story line,* to use a metaphor from literature, and functions powerfully to fashion teaching and learning.

After years of telling this story, Mrs. Carey realized that her own immigrant experience, several generations before, along with her own studies in school of the great European immigration around the year 1900, had unknowingly shaped the story line. She looked at her Hispanic and African American students and realized they were not part of the "nation of immigrants" story line. Most of her Hispanic students did not immigrate; rather, the land of their ancestors, once in Mexico, was annexed to the United States after the Mexican-American War. And the ancestors of her black students hardly immigrated; they were forcibly removed from Africa.

She began an effort to change her story. She wanted to do this for the sake of accuracy, but she also felt that the old story line may have kept some of her students from really going after this material. Maybe they felt that the story, like somebody else's shoes, didn't fit them. For the moment, Mrs. Carey is experimenting with two story lines, "We are a nation of many cultures" and "*E pluribus unum*—out of many, one."

Multiple Perspectives

The second aspect of multicultural education emphasizes a compare-and-contrast approach to the content children are to learn. Teachers make it a point to plan units so that a topic is studied from more than one perspective, and the children must wrestle with their similarities and differences. This strategy has important advantages over the single-perspective approach.

First, any one perspective is prevented from being put forward as neutral (as one teacher put it, "This isn't a perspective, this is the truth!"). Second, children are introduced to the

---

VIGNETTE:	**EUROPEAN/NATIVE AMERICAN ENCOUNTERS, GRADE 1**

Speare's *Sign of the Beaver* (1983) and Bulla's *Squanto: Friend of the Pilgrims* (1954)   **Materials**

European colonists arriving on the east coast of North America encountered not a new   **Cultural**
world but a very old one inhabited by millions of people belonging to many different   **Perspectives**
cultures. Children's tendency to stereotype Native Americans—that is, to gloss over the
differences among them—can be countered by presenting the differences straightfor-
wardly, using historical fiction. In this activity, the class contrasts two native men: the legendary *Squanto: Friend of the Pilgrims,* and the Indian at the center of Elizabeth George
Speare's *Sign of the Beaver.* The latter is neither "savage" nor "friendly," and children
learn something of his culture.

The teacher reads these stories aloud, stopping occasionally to have the children retell   **Activity**
what they have heard so far. This lets the teacher diagnose their understanding and
watch for what catches their interest. Eventually, students dramatize meetings between
the two men in which they share stories of their respective cultures.

Consider using both books as springboards for in-depth study on the two Indian cultures   **Note**
presented. Where exactly did they live? What kind of a place was it? How did they interact with the natural environment? Were they different from other Indian groups in the
same geographical regions? What was their language? religion? law? medicine? family structure? shelter? food? education? economy?

heart of historical thinking: making sense of competing accounts. Third, children are provided learning opportunities that involve comparison across multiple cases. This is strong pedagogy. Research suggests that it increases retention and facilitates students' later *use* of this material when they are working on other things.

With the vignette of the multiple-perspective approach to integrated unit planning, we close this chapter with the emphasis on culture.

SUMMARY

The social studies can be an integrating core for literacy, literature, and culture when:

- Teachers integrate social studies education with other disciplines and with instruction in reading, writing, and other skills.
- Teachers initiate an integrated curriculum that combines several categories of knowledge for the purpose of helping children more fully understand the topic of study.
- Teachers use an integrated curriculum to enable children to develop in-depth understandings on topics worthy of their time and effort. As an example, both history and literature can present its two dimensions and enrich a particular topic.
- Teachers emphasize reading and writing as processes to change the way they implement language arts/literacy/social studies instruction. For example, working on biographies of someone whose life carries students into substantive content is one powerful way to emphasize this process.

QUESTIONS AND ACTIVITIES FOR DISCUSSION

1. Review the *Explore* curriculum. Then add a fifth lesson to the four-lesson unit that was described. Select one of the following topics for its focus, then write a *focus question* and an *intended learning outcome* statement.
   - Careers involving the study and/or protection of living things
   - International comparison of living things and their needs
   - An organism's "potential"
   - Biographies of one or more people studied in Lesson 3
   - Community service related to actions suggested in Lesson 3

2. Ask the librarian in two different elementary/middle school libraries to give you a tour of the biography sections. Ask the librarian to identify several of the more popular biographies. As you examine them, consider these questions: (a) What conceptual themes are suggested by these subjects? (b) Could any three or four of them be woven through a school year, all related to a single theme (e.g., leadership)? (c) Which eras of American history are not represented by biographies in either library?

3. Reread the example involving Mr. Atencio's kindergarten class. (See p. 425.) Then, plan a biographical approach with kindergarten children that uses a retelling technique.

4. Design an array of biography "book" formats. What forms could kindergartners' books take? How about fourth graders?

5. In addition to "snapshot" biographies, to what other genres of writing might children be introduced? Plan a lesson that would introduce them to one of these other genres. For example, plan an introduction to *historical fiction,* then plan the lessons for teaching them to write historical fiction, perhaps a story about the meeting of two people from different texts.

6. Select three eras of United States history and locate multiple-perspectives curriculum materials for each for a grade of your choice.

7. Study the diverse cultural identities of a group of children. Use firsthand observation, interviews, and reference books (e.g., ethnic studies textbooks). Take field notes, as an anthropologist would. Pay special attention to the variation within groups. For example, children of European ancestry are not "all alike," nor are children of Asian or African ancestry. Similarly, children whose first language is Spanish differ widely from one another.

8. Describe any prior concepts you held that changed as a result of your experiences with this chapter. Describe the changes.

CHILDREN'S BOOKS

Adler, D. A. (1989). *A picture book of Abraham Lincoln.* Ill. by John and Alexandra Wallner. New York: Holiday.

Adler, D. A. (1989). *A picture book of George Washington.* Ill. by John and Alexandra Wallner. New York: Holiday.

Barrett, M. (1989). *Meet Thomas Jefferson.* Ill. by Pat Fogarty. New York: Random House.

Bulla, C. (1954). *Squanto: Friend of the Pilgrims.* New York: Thomas Crowell.

Cary, B. (1989). *Meet Abraham Lincoln.* Ill. by Stephen Marchesi. New York: Random House.

Clatlin, E.B. (1987). *Sojourner Truth and the struggle for freedom.* New York: Burron.

de Kay, J. T. (1989). *Meet Christopher Columbus.* Ill by John Edens. New York: Random House.

de Kay, J. T. (1989). *Meet Martin Luther King, Jr.* Ill. with photos. New York: Random House.

Ferris, J. (1988). *Walking the road to freedom: A story about Sojourner Truth.* Minneapolis: Carolrhoda Books.

Greene, C. (1988). *Benjamin Franklin: A man with many jobs.* Ill. by Steven Dobson. Chicago: Childrens.

Hamilton, V. (Reteller). (1988, February). *The people could fly. Cricket, 15*(6), 21–26.

Heilbroner, J. (1989). *Meet George Washington.* Ill. by Stephen Marchesi. New York: Random House.

Milton, J. (1989). *Greg Louganis: Diving for gold.* Ill. with photos. New York: Random House.

Scarf, M. (1989). *Meet Benjamin Franklin.* Ill. by Pat Fogarty. New York: Random House.

Speare, E. G. (1983). *The sign of the beaver.* Boston: Houghton Mifflin.

REFERENCES AND SUGGESTED READINGS

Aronson, E. (1978). *The jigsaw classroom.* Beverly Hills, CA: Sage.

Banks, J. A., & McGee Banks, C.A. (1989). *Multicultural education: Issues and perspectives.* Needham Heights, MA: Allyn & Bacon.

Brophy, J., & Alleman, J. (1991, October). A caveat curriculum integration isn't always a good idea. *Educational Leadership, 49* (2), 66.

Brown, R. (1991). *Schools of thought.* San Francisco: Jossey-Bass.

Bruner, J. (1960). *The process of education.* Cambridge, MA: Harvard University Press.

Dewey, J. (1927). *The public and its problems.* Chicago: Swallow.

Gehrke, N. J. (1991, Winter). Explorations of teachers' development of integrative curriculums. *Journal of Curriculum and Supervision, 6*(2), 107–117.

Graves, D. H. (1983). *Writing: Teachers and children at work.* Portsmouth, NH: Heineman.

Heath, S. B. (1983). *Ways with words.* New York: Cambridge University Press.

Jacobs, H. H. (1989). *Interdisciplinary curriculum: Design and development.* Alexandria, VA: Association for Supervision and Curriculum Development.

Langer, J. A., & Applebee, A. N. (1986). Reading and writing instruction: Toward a theory of teaching and learning. In E. Z.

Rothkopf (Ed.), *Review of research in education,* vol. 13, 171–194. Washington, DC: American Educational Research Association.

Paley, V. G. (1981). *Wally's stories.* Cambridge, MA: Harvard University Press.

Resnick, L. B. (1990, Spring). Literacy in school and out. *Daedalus 119*(2), 169–185.

Resnick, L. B., & Klopfer, L. E. (Eds.). (1989). *Toward the thinking curriculum: Current cognitive research.* Alexandria, VA: Association for Supervision and Curriculum Development.

Roberts, P. L., & Kellough, R. D. (1995). *A guide for developing interdisciplinary thematic units.* Englewood Cliffs, NJ: Merrill/Prentice Hall.

Roby, T. (1985). Habits impeding deliberation. *Journal of Curriculum Studies,* 17(1), 17–35.

Rutherford, F. J., & Ahlgren, A. (1990). *Science for all Americans.* New York: Oxford University Press.

Zarnowski, M. (1990). *Learning with biographies: A reading and writing approach.* Washington, DC: National Council for the Social Studies and National Council for Teachers of English, published jointly.

CHAPTER 15

Reaching Students With Special Needs

In this chapter we will discuss how to provide social studies and language arts instruction for students with a wide range of learning abilities and diverse backgrounds. Specifically, this chapter is designed to help you understand how to:

1. Work with special needs students
2. Individualize your teaching
3. Provide instruction for children with physical differences
4. Provide instruction for children who are intellectually different
5. Provide instruction for children of culturally diverse backgrounds.

A. SPECIAL NEEDS CHILDREN IN YOUR CLASSROOM
How Does Mainstreaming Affect Your Social Studies Teaching?

Mainstreaming is the placement of developmentally different students in the least restrictive educational environment. Two federal laws were passed that directly affect teachers and students. In 1975, Congress passed the Education for All Handicapped Children Act in Public Law 94–142. The act requires that children with disabilities be educated to the "maximum extent appropriate" with children who do not have disabilities and that "removal of handicapped children from the regular educational environment occurs only when the nature or severity of the handicap is such that education in regular classes with the use of supplementary aids and services cannot be achieved satisfactorily" (*Federal Register,* August 23, 1977, p. 821). The legislation does not stipulate that every exceptional child will be placed in regular classrooms; it does mean, however, that you may need to modify your teaching to mainstream children with special needs by:

1. Including special needs children in regular class activities and establishing for the class a range of goals that include special needs children
2. Assessing the abilities of the children and considering how each child's abilities affect his or her capacity to participate in an integrated language arts/social studies curriculum
3. Locating and adapting class materials for the particular needs of the children
4. Incorporating a range of experiences to meet the needs of the special children (Reynolds & Birch, 1988; Strickland & Turnbull, 1990).

What Kinds of Special Students Might Be in Your Classroom?

For many developmentally different students, the least restrictive environment may be the regular classroom, sometimes with a supplemental pull-out program, sometimes without. This placement involves more than just the physical integration of developmentally different students into a regular classroom. Exceptional students have educational and social needs that need to be met. Thus, classroom teachers can modify their social studies programs to meet the students' individual needs and to integrate them socially into the class by allowing them to participate as much as possible in classroom activities. Conscientious teachers will keep in mind that exceptional students with special needs will benefit from the same social studies content and teaching strategies that other students do with some modifications. Instructional strategies that allow students to use their abilities in real-life activities tend to facilitate the development of their social and communicative skills. The material in Chapters 1 and 2 emphasized the ways children learn and can foster effective interactions with exceptional students. When we understand how children learn, we realize that no one way to teach students with special needs is significantly different from the ways other students are taught.

B. INDIVIDUALIZED SOCIAL STUDIES INSTRUCTION
Elements of Individualized Social Studies Instruction

When you have in your class children who are mainstreamed by federal law or other students with special needs, you will be challenged to individualize your teaching. Individualizing your teaching will help you respond to children who have impaired health or limited or impaired hearing; to those who have orthopedic impairments; and to those who have intellectual differences or social differences (behavior disorders or emotional impairments). To respond to the needs of these special students, adapt some of the following elements into your teaching:

1. Plan a variety of instructional materials and activities suited to the needs of the students, including activity centers, self-instructional packets, and individualized study guides.
2. Select different media for different students, especially, computers and software, audio-visual aids.
3. Organize ways for students to work on different topics or activities and engage them in designing their own activities.
4. Schedule additional time to interact with individuals and small groups.

Suggestions for Individualizing Social Studies Instruction

Activity centers. In a corner of the classroom, you can offer activities with ideas and materials for students and invite them to engage in simple self-directed activities. Each activity can be presented on an activity card and students can choose one or more that interests them. The activity can include divergent questions to stimulate the student's thinking.

Display areas. Invite the children to display items or collections related to their study of social studies topics that interest them. Arrange for a display area on a desk, countertop, or bookcase and ask students to display their collections—for example, photographs of a historical period, replicas of state flags, state birds, or a "1776" collection. Invite student's to open their own displays by:

1. Putting together their collections—artwork, artifacts, stamps, toys, dolls
2. Displaying the collection in some special arrangement either on a table, a shelf, the floor, or in a box
3. Researching what kind of objects they have and where they got them
4. Making a collection card (a display record) for each item and writing down all they know about it. Have students use index cards to write information for the items in the display and place a card near each item in their exhibits

5. Designing and writing labels for each item so others who see the display will know what it is and why it is important
6. Designing and writing invitations to others to visit the display.

By scheduling the displays for no longer than one week for each student, you can give every student an opportunity to participate during the academic year. Have students indicate their interests or home collections on the first day of school and use the information to schedule students through the year. Have them display their collections as related social studies topics are studied. To collect this information on the first day, put up a narrow strip of mural paper below the writing board and write the social studies topics along the top of the mural. Have students write their names under the topics in which they are interested and use the mural as a reference for scheduling student-created displays throughout the months.

Taped panel discussions. Engage students in designing their own panel discussions and ask for a volunteer to tape-record the discussion. After the discussion, engage them in a group meeting to listen to the tape and discuss their contributions.

Tradebooks. Invite students to read a book of their choice related to the social studies topic and report on it to the group in a creative way. Social studies tradebooks (library books) add interest to a topic for students since they are available on different reading levels. You can schedule a group visit to the school library or to a nearby public library to meet the children's librarian. Ask the librarian to show the children several biographies of people who are related to the social studies topic being studies. Life-stories of minorities, women, and the developmentally different should be included. Arrangements can be made for the children to receive their own library cards, check out books, read them, and work together to present a brief skit to show a particular event in the life-story of the famous person whose biography they read. For other examples, they can give their report in the format of a television commercial, a totem pole, a shoebox diorama, a sketch or drawing, or an audiotape. They can be dressed as the main character, sing a jingle, be a "town crier," show a videotape, present a mural they painted, use an overhead transparency, puppets, or a felt or flannel story board, and so on.

A good resource for locating social studies books is the annual "Notable Children's Trade Books in the Field of Social Studies" published each spring by the Children's Book Council in *Social Education*.

Individualized study guides. Engage students in making their own study guides (educational photo albums) for places to visit for other children to use. Work collaboratively with the children to help them prepare a self-directed study guide for a community place, a social studies topic, or a related children's book. As an example, they can sketch or draw their favorite object they saw during a visit to a site of interest in their area to include in the guide or write informative pages with the heading, "While visiting this place, you can look for . . . ." (a blanket made for dancing—Tlingit blanket of cedar bark and goat wool). Children can prepare self-directed guides about various community places they have visited and give the guide to others to encourage other children to visit some of the interesting or historic sites in the area.

Different media for different students. Incorporate television programs, computers and software, and other audiovisual aids. As an example, have students write for any television listings and related guides from the educational television stations in your area. Engage them in writing a list of any shows related to the social studies topic you are studying. Have them fold a sheet of paper into four columns and write these headings for the columns: "TV Program," "Channel," "Time and Date," and "Related Topic." Have the children review the list and record the information in the columns. Have the children watch a program that you want to assign and ask them to write specific questions on a question sheet about the program to share with the whole group. The question sheet might begin with, "After you see this program, you will know the answer(s) to such question(s) as. . . ."

Additionally, invite the children to watch the programs that interest them and collect social studies materials from newspapers, magazines, and brochures for a social studies scrap book.

Computers and software and other electronic aids can be incorporated successfully. For ways to use this technology in your classroom, refer to Chapter 6.

Different topics with student-designed activities. Engage the children in vital, active topics of study, such as improving the environment of their school campus or conducting a survey of people in their community who could be possible resources for the social studies topic being studied. Some children might be interested in attracting birds to their community by building birdhouses, bird feeders, or birdbaths; others might be interested in designing and constructing a rock and flower garden to attract butterflies native to the area. Still others might want to pledge to be a community of learners and friends during the first month of school and contribute student-created items to bury in a time capsule in the corner of the school campus. During the last month of school, the students can retrieve the capsule and discuss the items they contributed to determine the extent to which they carried out their pledge to be a friendly classroom community.

Regardless of the project, the children can suggest their own activities as they gather information related to the topic. They can organize their activities as they construct, maintain, and care for their project. Still others might want to visit community places such as museums, planetariums, parks, and so on. During these visits, parents or guardians could be invited to go with their children and assist in a student-designed activity such as writing a self-directed guide for other students to use. After the visit, the students can write to ask for information about what, if any, special social studies exhibits (programs) are planned in the future. Invite them to announce the information to the group or to prepare an attractive eye-catching bulletin to display the information on a class bulletin board.

Additional time to interact with individuals and small groups. Increased time can be devoted to individual children and small groups when each child is given a file or portfolio in which the child places journals, diaries, learning logs, and examples of the types of social studies activities that he or she has designed or completed. Turn back to Chapter 5 for more information on the use of portfolios.

C. SOCIAL STUDIES FOR CHILDREN WITH PHYSICAL DIFFERENCES
Experiences for Children With Visual Impairments

To modify your social studies curriculum for visually impaired children, you can:

1. Provide multisensory, concrete activities with real objects at a social studies activity center and have directions on an audiotape. The tape should include verbal descriptions. Emphasize the use of touch as an observation skill. Ask a sighted student to volunteer to be a partner with the visually impaired student and perhaps provide some of the taped verbal descriptions. For example, when the sighted student accompanies the visually impaired student to an activity center to determine "What could these objects be used for?" and "What objects are similar to these today?" the sighted student can record aloud his or her verbal description(s) of the object(s) to be observed—perhaps an old apple corer, a tin washboard, an old green glass medicine bottle, a button hook for ladies' boots. As the visually impaired student listens, the student can ask for any additional information needed for the observation. The tape can be replayed as needed.

2. Include Books on Tape™, large-print materials or Braille reading materials available from a large public library and other sources. If possible, include Braille writer, slate and stylus, large-print typewriter or computer with 18- or 24-point font capability. Ask sighted students to be classroom guides, to read directions, and to help prepare some materials for their visually impaired partners. For instance, small squares of fine-grain sandpaper and course-grain sandpaper can be glued to the inches of a ruler or tape measure to enable a visually impaired partner to "observe" and measure a historic object related to a social studies topic.

Experiences for Children With Hearing Impairments

To modify your social studies curriculum for children with hearing impairments, you can:

1. Invite children to sit near ongoing activities so they can lipread if needed. Let a child with a hearing impairment move away from any distracting noises.
2. Whenever possible, use captioned films and filmstrips. Use visual text whenever tapes are used. Ask a hearing student to volunteer to be a partner with a student with a hearing impairment to act out (model) directions and repeat directions as needed.
3. Provide hands-on activities with visual aids and real objects.

Experiences for Children With Physical Impairments

To modify your social studies curriculum for children with physical impairments, you can:

1. Provide seating and desks that are adjusted for wheelchairs. Ascertain that students have plenty of space for movement, free access to the room, and are seated near an exit for safety during fire drills and other emergency procedures.
2. Ask a student to volunteer to be a partner with a student with a physical impairment to help with manipulation of materials as necessary and to aid in writing responses if needed.
3. Provide hands-on activities with visual aids and real objects.

D. SOCIAL STUDIES FOR INTELLECTUALLY DIFFERENT STUDENTS
Meeting the Needs of Students With Learning Disabilities

Students with learning disabilities (LD) have a disorder in one or more of the basic psychological processes involved in understanding or in using spoken or written language. This may show itself in an imperfect ability to listen, think, speak, read, write, or spell. According to the *Federal Register* (August 23, 1977, p. 786), "The term includes conditions such as perceptual handicaps, brain injury, minimal brain disfunction, dyslexia, and developmental asphasia. To modify your social studies curriculum for these children, you can:

1. Ascertain that they are seated away from distracting noises; change seating for different activities. For example, they can have priority seating during class discussions where you can make eye contact frequently.
2. Provide multisensory, concrete, relevant materials in brief activities; ask a student to volunteer to assist in writing responses.
3. Increase the time you devote to the student and provide immediate feedback and praise; check frequently on the student's progress.
4. When needed, modify the student's reading level and offer oral tests (which can be audiotaped) instead of written ones.

Meeting the Needs of Students With Mild Retardation

To modify your social studies curriculum for these children, you can:

1. Ascertain that they are seated away from distracting noises; change seating for different activities. They can have priority seating during class discussions where you can make eye contact frequently.
2. Provide multisensory, concrete, relevant materials in brief activities; provide active involvement, repetition, and low-level reading materials.
3. Increase practice in a variety of ways, provide cues, immediate feedback, and praise; check frequently on the student's progress.
4. When needed, engage the student in mastery learning and collaborative group work; provide help in writing responses.
5. When needed, modify the student's reading level and offer oral tests (which can be audiotaped) instead of written ones.

6. Make activities concrete, meaningful, and related to personal experience. For example, a walking field trip near the school can generate functional words to read, such as stop signs and names of businesses and services. Use an instant camera to take photographs of words in the environment and place the pictures in a class book after students have dictated their own sentences and used the words in context.

7. Provide peer-tutors for individualized instruction with repetition and practice as needed. Engage peer-tutors in rereading favorite books that have language patterns and repeated phrases or sentences. Use the books to teach oral language patterns. Further, have students dictate/write their own books using the patterns.

8. Engage students in telling and dictating stories using wordless books.

9. Introduce students to the activity of writing a repetitive pattern poem such as the "I Wish" or "If I Were" poem. Although they may not be successful in writing limericks, haiku, and other forms, they can write poems with repetitive patterns.

10. Engage students in dramatic play and informal conversations with others.

Meeting the Needs of Gifted and Talented Students

Gifted and talented students have special needs just as other special learners do. Some of the students, though great in ability, need an individual program. For example, you may consider the extent to which your school and district have a special gifted class or a magnet school that incorporates individual programs. In addition, you can discuss accelerating the instructional program of gifted students by discussing with a school counselor or psychologist the benefit of advancing gifted students to a higher grade level, keeping them mainstreamed in a regular education classroom with self-instructional programs, or enriching their instruction with a special pull-out program. The following suggestions will help you plan instruction for the gifted and talented :

1. Introduce the students to an individualized and noncompetitive classroom environment.
2. Encourage risk taking and learning by trial and error.
3. Engage students in taking greater responsibility and control of their learning with the teacher in the role of "resource organizer."
4. Encourage gifted students to interact with other students.
5. Present high expectations and let students know you expect them to do their best.
6. Provide instruction in research skills, higher-level thinking, and problem solving.
7. Suggest involvement in community projects. (Cohen, 1987)

E. SOCIAL STUDIES FOR CULTURALLY DIVERSE STUDENTS
Bilingual and Non-English-Speaking Students

Some students in your classroom may be bilingual speakers because they speak a native language at home that is different from the language the teachers use at school. They have a special linguistic and social skill of speaking their native language, mixing it with some English and shifting back and forth in the languages—sometimes even within the same sentence.

These guidelines will help you plan instruction:

1. Become knowledgeable about available transitional programs in which instruction in the students' native language can be linked to learning English.
2. Become knowlegeable about maintenance programs where instruction in both English and the students' native language continues through the elementary school years.
3. Demonstrate ways that you understand and appreciate the culture and language of the students and begin teaching "fundamantal" words to help the students feel comfortable in the school and classroom environment. Some of the fundamental words and phrases include greetings such as "Hello" and "My name is . . ." as well as an indication of need, such as "I need to go to the restroom." Invite volunteers to take turns and be peer-tutors and partners for the newcomers.
4. Schedule a "Newcomer" tour of the school campus and the classroom where the students see the location of the fire equipment, bus area, play area, cafeteria, school library, drink-

ing fountains and restrooms, principal's office, first aid kit, and so on. In the classroom, engage the students in drawing maps of the classroom and adding labels for classroom objects in their native language and English. Additionally, they can draw maps of the school campus and the neighborhood and indicate where they live in the area.

5. Arrange for a newcomer to be with a partner to take part in such activities as leading the way to the bus area, play area, drinking fountains, and cafeteria; accompanying the partner to deliver a message to another teacher; helping erase the writing board or put up a mural; and playing a sport or social game.

6. Schedule talking time for students to engage in oral language with partners through discussion, conversations, and informal drama activities. Read to them and engage them in assisted reading.

7. Locate an older child (or adult volunteer aide) who speaks both the child's native language and English to teach English-speaking children words and phrases in the child's native language. A volunteer aide who speaks the child's native language can facilitate the non-English speaker's entry into the classroom.

8. Invite students to write and draw pictures in journals to help them develop writing fluency. Ask them to dictate labels and captions to go with their journal drawings.

Students Who Are Language Delayed

Students are language-delayed when their language development is significantly slower than the rate for others their age. As a teacher, you would note several characteristics of a language-delayed student. They might speak in very childlike phrases, lack the ability to use language in a purposeful way, talk very little at school, lack the ability to produce the sentences that their peers can, and lack some of the concepts that are part of daily life. Guidelines for planning instruction include:

1. Extensive experience with language and systematic instruction through concrete experiences (for example, they can write caption books in which they add word or phrase captions to magazine illustrations).

2. Many experiences with language functions including the use of predictable books to provide exposure to language patterns.

3. Opportunities for speech in the context of interpersonal relationships—conversations, sharing, show-and-tell, group work, and dramatic play, role playing, and puppetry.

4. The use of predictable books and song picture books with particular language patterns (see Figure 15.1).

FIGURE 15.1
Song Picture Books

Adams, P. *Bring a torch, Jeanette Isabella.*
Adams, P. *This old man.*
Aliki, *Go tell Aunt Rhody.*
Bonne, R., & Mills, A. *I know an old lady.*
Emberley, B., & Emberley, E. *One wide river to cross.*
Exelrod, A. *Songs of the wild west.*
Galdone, P. *Over in the meadow: An old nursery counting rhyme.*
Harvey, B. *The zebra riding cowboy: A folk song from the old west.*
Langstaff, J. *Oh, a-hunting we will go.*
Moore, Y. *Freedom songs.*
Nic Leodhaus, S. *Always room for one more.*
O'Malley, K. *Froggy went a-courtin'.*
Rounds, G. *Casey Jones: The story of a brave engineer.*
Quackenbush, R. *Old MacDonald had a farm.*
Quackenbush, R. *She'll be comin' round the mountain.*
Quackenbush, R. *The man on the flying trapeze.*
Spier, P. *The fox went out on a chilly night.*
Spier, P. *Go tell Aunt Rhody.*
Westcott, N. B. *There's a hole in the bucket.*
Zuromskis, D. *The farmer in the dell.*

---

5. Engaging children in cutting out pictures from newspapers, magazines, and brochures, and adding words or phrases as captions. Have them dictate/read their captions, talk about the pictures and reuse the captions in complete sentences.
6. Reread favorite books to them and use assisted reading.

Students Who Are Nonstandard English Speakers

Reflective of our country's cultural pluralism, all English speakers speak one dialect or another with distinguishing features in the pronunciation of words, choice of words, and use of grammatical forms. The English dialect heard in schools, read in the daily newspapers, read in magazine articles, and used by television and radio commentators and reporters is known as standard English. Other ways of speaking with nonstandard speech patterns are generally referred to as nonstandard English.

Guidelines for planning instruction include the following:

1. Show students their language is accepted. Books of children's literature with dialogue written in different dialects can be introduced to help children learn about the rich variety of language.
2. Establish expectations that students are capable of using two (or more) dialects.
3. Engage students in oral language activities (without interrupting them) so they will use the forms of standard English.
4. Read aloud predictable books that have standard English patterns and have students read, role-play, and retell the story through puppetry. Have children dictate or rewrite an event in the story.
5. Have children use a selected English pattern with new content.
6. Conference with a child to compose a story and revise the story with standard English forms.

SUMMARY

The issues related to the instruction of exceptional children are complex. Because many children with special needs often make smaller academic gains than children identified as regular education students, the education of the special needs children is of great concern to teachers. The language arts/social studies program can be modified to meet the needs of these students when they are mainstreamed into regular classrooms. This chapter discussed these topics:

- Students who are mainstreamed can be gifted, linguistically different, and developmentally different. Gifted students are those who are talented but who often need an individualized or enriched program. Some linguistically different students will be bilingual; others will be non-English-speaking children, and still others may be language-delayed. Developmentally different students can be those identified as learning disabled, mentally retarded, or emotionally disturbed.
- Teaching strategies that can be used with many exceptional learners include assisted reading, use of predictable books, and dictating and writing original stories. Further, there is a need for increased opportunities for speech—conversations, sharing, show-and-tell, group work, dramatic play, role playing, and puppetry.

QUESTIONS AND ACTIVITIES FOR DISCUSSION

1. Investigate carefully some available social studies curriculum materials and decide how you could adapt some of the materials to meet the special needs of students in your classroom.

2. Select one special needs student. Prescribe three activities for the student that would enrich the social studies topics you are studying with the student's class.

3. Select a social studies topic to explore with culturally diverse children using real-life problems from their immediate environment that are relevant to their lives.

4. Engage in one of these simulated experiences:

   a. Sit immobile in a chair in the classroom for a brief length of time without getting up. Have someone help you by sharpening your pencil or getting a book for you. What problems did you face? What feelings did you have? What could you do to overcome some of the problems?

b. Place ear plugs in you ears and have a colleague teach you a brief studies lesson. Report to others some of the problems that you faced. What could you do to overcome the problems?

c. Blindfold yourself and try to move around the classroom. Have a colleague lead you through the room first. Then list the information you wanted your colleague to tell you to help you maneuver around the room. File the list and refer to it when you have a student with a visual impairment in the class.

d. Interview an interpreter for the deaf and ask him or her about guidelines for working with students with hearing impairments. Record the suggestions and use as a reference when you have a student with a hearing impairment in the class.

CHILDREN'S BOOKS

Adams, P. (1963). *Bring a torch, Jeanette Isabella*. Boston: Playspace.

Adams, P. (1974). *This old man*. New York: Grosset & Dunlap.

Aliki. (1974). *Go tell Aunt Rhody*. New York: Macmillan.

Bonne, R., & Mills, A. (1961). *I know an old lady*. Skokie, IL: Rand McNally.

Emberley, B., & Emberley, E., (1966). *One wide river to cross*. Englewood Cliffs, NJ: Prentice-Hall.

Exelrod, A. (1991). *Songs of the wild west*. New York: Metropolitan Museum of Art/Simon & Schuster.

Galdone, P. (1986). *Over in the meadow: An old nursery counting rhyme*. Englewood Cliffs, NJ: Prentice-Hall.

Harvey, B. (1988). *The zebra riding cowboy: A folk song from the old west*. New York: Holiday.

Langstaff, J. (1974). *Oh, a-hunting we will go*. New York: Atheneum.

Moore, Y. (1990). *Freedom songs*. New York: Orchard.

Nic Leodhaus, S. (1965). *Always room for one more*. New York: Holt.

O'Malley, K. (1992). *Froggy went A-courtin'*. New York: Stewart, Tabori & Chang.

Rounds, G. (1968). *Casey Jones: The story of a brave engineer*. Chicago: Children's Press.

Quackenbush, R. (1972). *Old MacDonald had a farm*. Philadelphia: Lippincott.

Quackenbush, R. (1973). *She'll be comin' round the mountain*. Philadelphia: Lippincott.

Quackenbush, R. (1975). *The man on the flying trapeze*. Philadelphia: Lippincott.

Spier, P. (1961). *The fox went out on a chilly night*. New York: Doubleday.

Spier, P. (1973). *Go tell Aunt Rhody*. Philadelphia: Lippincott.

Westcott, N. B. (1990). *There's a hole in the bucket*. New York: Harper & Row.

Zuromskis, D. (1978). *The farmer in the dell*. Boston: Little, Brown.

REFERENCES AND SUGGESTED READINGS

Clark, B. (1992). *Growing up gifted: Developing the potential of children at home and at school* (4th ed.). Englewood Cliffs, NJ: Merrill/Prentice Hall.

Cohen, L. M. (1987). Thirteen tips for teaching gifted students. *Teaching Exceptional Children, 20,* 34–38.

Jarolimek, J., & Parker, W. C. (1993). *Social studies in elementary education* (9th ed.). Englewood Cliffs, NJ: Merrill/Prentice Hall.

Lewis, R. B., & Doorlag, D. H. (1991). *Teaching special students in the mainstream* (3rd ed.). Englewood Cliffs, NJ: Merrill/ Prentice Hall.

Morrison, G. S. (1991). *Early childhood education today* (5th ed.). Englewood Cliffs, NJ: Merrill/Prentice Hall.

Reynolds, M. C., & Birch, J. W. (1988). *Adaptive mainstreaming: A primer for teachers and principals* (3rd ed.). White Plains, NY: Longman.

Strickland, B. B., & Turnbull, A. (1990). *Developing and implementing Individualized Education Programs*. Englewood Cliffs, NJ: Merrill/Prentice Hall.

Wolf, J. S. (1990). "The gifted and talented." In N. G. Haring & L. McCormick (Eds.), *Exceptional children and youth* (5th ed.). Englewood Cliffs, NJ: Merrill/Prentice Hall.

Selected Activities for Integrated Language Arts and Social Studies

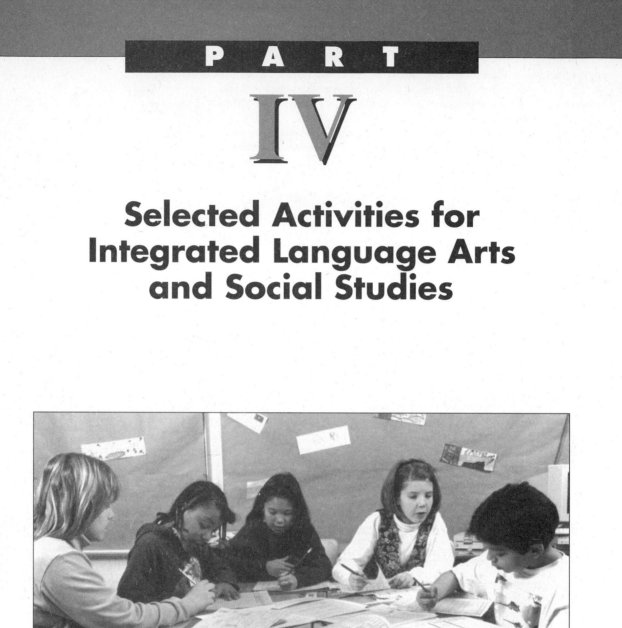

As has been discussed throughout this book, for higher levels of thinking and for learning that is most meaningful and longest lasting for children, it is absolutely necessary to use instructional techniques that encourage interaction and cooperation among all students, that depend on collaborative learning between the students and the teachers, and that integrate the disciplines.

Further, as we have emphasized throughout, as a classroom teacher and as a member of a community of learners, your instructional task is to (1) plan for and provide developmentally appropriate hands-on experiences and to (2) facilitate the most meaningful and longest lasting learning possible once the children's minds have been activated by those experiences. For use in your teaching, Part IV presents activities designed to do just that.

As we said in the opener to Part I, the term *integrated curriculum* (and any of its synonyms) refers to *both a way of teaching and a way of planning and organizing the instructional program so the discrete disciplines of subject matter are related to one another in a design that matches the developmental needs of the learners and that helps to connect their learning in ways that are meaningful to their current and past experiences.* In that respect, integrated curriculum is the antithesis of traditional disparate subject-matter-oriented teaching and curriculum designations.

Today's interest in developing and implementing integrated curriculum and instruction has risen almost simultaneously from a number of sources: (1) the success at curriculum integration enjoyed by elementary schools, (2) the literature-based movement in reading and language arts, and (3) recent research in cognitive science and neuroscience about how children learn.

As is true for traditional curriculum and instruction, an integrated curriculum approach is not without critics. Such an approach may not necessarily be the best approach for every school or the best for all learning for every child. It also is not necessarily the manner by which every teacher should or must always plan and teach. In attempts to connect children's learning with their experiences, efforts fall at various places on a spectrum or continuum of sophistication and complexity.

The activities presented in this final chapter are designed to encourage interaction and cooperation among students, to encourage collaborative learning between students and their teachers, and to integrate in interesting and meaningful ways language arts and social studies, and specific disciplines as well. It is up to you to determine where the use of each falls on the spectrum of integrated learning. When selecting integrated activities for children's active learning, you should ask yourself these questions:

- Does the activity involve more than one subject area?
- Does the activity involve the children in exploring a topic in depth and over an extended period of time?
- Does the activity provide interesting, meaningful, and accurate learning that relates to children's daily lives?

CHAPTER 16
Activities for Integrated Language Arts and Social Studies
Sets of activities (except for unpublished activities) are excerpted from the following: John Jarolimek & Walter C. Parker, *Social Studies in Elementary Education,* 9th ed. (Englewood Cliffs, NJ: Merrill/Prentice Hall, 1990), pp. 68–69, 77, 114, 115, 142, 164, 201, 212, 214–216, 272–274, 319–320, 324; from Carol Seefeldt & Nita Barbour, *Early Childhood Education: An Introduction,* 3rd ed. (Englewood Cliffs, NJ: Merrill/Macmillan, 1994), pp. 35–36, 56, 85–87, 112–116; 119–126, 132, 137–144, 144–152, 155–156, 162, 166–169, 171–176, 179, 182–185, 186–199, 190–191, 194–195, 202–212, 216–217; 220, 235, 237, 249, 252, 254, 261, 285–289, 301, 370–371, 457; from Carol Seefeldt, *Social Studies for the Preschool-Primary Child,* 4th ed. (Englewood Cliffs, NJ: Merrill/Prentice-Hall, 1993), pp. 90–91, 126, 137, 162, 189, 190, 290; from Donna Norton & Saundra Norton, *Language Arts Activities for Children,* 3rd ed. (Englewood Cliffs, NJ: Merrill/Prentice Hall, 1994), pp. 40–41, 80–81, 97–98, 137–138, 146, 152–153, 165–166, 358–359, 375–379, 384–385, 391–392, 358–399; from Donna Norton, *The Effective Teaching of*

Language Arts, 4th ed. (Englewood Cliffs, NJ: Merrill/Prentice Hall, 1993), lpp. 79, 201, 261, 301, 331, 348, 401, 457, 523; and from Gale Tompkins & Kenneth Hoskisson, *Language Arts,* 2nd ed. (Englewood Cliffs, NJ: Merrill/Prentice Hall, 1991), pp. 540, 542, 552.

- Does the activity give the children the opportunity to work collaboratively and co-operatively while making and recording observations and gathering and defending their own evidence?
- Does the activity give children opportunities to express their results in a variety of ways?
- Does the activity accomplish the objective(s) for which it is intended?
- Is the activity within the ability and developmental level of the students?
- Is the activity worth the time and cost needed to do it?
- Within reasonable limits, is the activity safe for children to go?

If, in considering your activity, you could answer "yes" to these questions, your instructional plan is likely to offer active and integrated learning for your children. The activities selected for Chapter 16 also meet these guidelines. ■

CHAPTER 16

Activities for Integrated Language Arts and Social Studies

I n this final chapter we present six sets of learning activities that encourage interaction and cooperation among students, that depend on collaborative learning between the students and the teachers, and that integrate language arts and social studies, and in some instances, specific disciplines in interesting ways.

Each set of activities is presented in a way that should make it immediately usable to you. Some take more class time to do than do others. Except for those activities that are designated for fourth graders, all others are appropriate for any grade, K–4. Study each one to determine its appropriateness for use with your own distinctive group of students. The following symbols are used for some of the activities:

T = Teacher directing discussion or demonstration with whole class
I = Student working individually on task
G = Students working in groups of two, three, or four

LEARNING TO WORK TOGETHER

SET 1:
LEARNING AND WORKING NOW AND LONG AGO

Role-Playing Friendships ACTIVITY 1.1

Engage children in role-playing friendly solutions to selected social situations and suggest alternative ways of resolving conflicts. Use skits, puppets, and group discussions about hypothetical situations. Help children develop friendship skills through (1) discussions about who is a friend and the activities friends play together and (2) group play activities, and (3) by ensuring that children lacking friendship skills work in groups with those who have acquired the skills. For children who have difficulty becoming a member of a group, act as a facilitator with a suggestion, "Barbara, you can . . ." or "Tell him what you want."

Names Column in Class Newspaper ACTIVITY 1.2

To emphasize the uniqueness of each student, let each child dictate "news" that has his or her name in it for a "Names" column in a daily class newspaper written on chart paper. Invite children to dictate their participation in various "naming" activities such as "the time we sang songs (read poems, told stories, played games) and put my name in it" and "the time we put our names on things that belonged to us."

ACTIVITY 1.3   **Friendly Help**

Read aloud children's stories about friendships and helping others. For example, read aloud Molly Cone's *The Great Snake Escape* (HarperCollins, 1994), a story about two friends, Mirabel, a goose, and Maxie, a frog, who share their anxieties when they read about a cobra escaping from the zoo. While reading about the escape in a newspaper, Maxie falls into a trash can and can't get out. Mirabel looks for something to help get her friend out and meets the cobra, who offers to assist Maxie. In return, the two friends help the cobra board a ship for its native country, India. Follow up with a discussion about how the children have made new friends (by helping, sharing, or other ways). Sharing and helping skills also can be taught by directed doll or puppet play, by practice in solving conflicts over toys, or through comments such as, "Take another turn and then it is _____'s turn."

ACTIVITY 1.4   **Sense of the Past**

Learning about the past requires that children develop a sense of the passage of time. Daily, ask the children questions such as the following:

1. Do you remember what we did for _____?
2. What things should we have for our writing time (class newspaper, Valentine's party)?
3. What did you like best about yesterday? What did we have for lunch yesterday? What did you like best about our walk around the school? What did you like best about kindergarten (first grade) this week?
4. How many days has it been since _____ (Monday, Carl's birthday)?
5. How many windy (rainy, snowy, sunny) days did we have last week? How many days has it been since our (Valentine, Thanksgiving) party?
6. What can you do this year that you could not do last year?

ACTIVITY 1.5   **Signs of Friendship**

Read aloud to children some excerpts from the story, *One Small Blue Bead* (Scribner's, 1992, grades 1–3) by Byrd Baylor. The story is about the people who think *they* are the only humans. Have children mention the chores the boy did while his elderly friend searched for other humans and how the two friends were working together to achieve something—a sign of friendship. Ask children to compare and contrast the chores the boy did with the chores they do today. What is similar about the chores? Different?

Discuss the boy's first encounter with the newcomer, a boy from another group—who offered a turquoise bead, a sign of friendship, and material exchanges among people. Have the children offer signs of friendship they offer to newcomers today and do these activities:

- Team up in pairs and play the roles of the young boy and the stranger who gives him the blue bead.
- Develop questions that could be asked by the two boys when they met.
- Discuss what each boy would feel, say, and do in the situation when the bead is offered and accepted.
- Act out ways the two boys could work together. Have the young boy step forward and tell the audience what he is thinking and feeling while he is talking to the stranger. The two continue the role playing.
- Reverse their roles of boy and newcomer and then replay the situation. Have the newcomer step forward and tell the audience what he is thinking and feeling while he is talking to the young boy. The two continue the role playing.
- Transform the role-play situation into an artistic format and draw, paint, or sketch how the encounter with the newcomer might have happened. The drawing can be a simulated

pictograph. Make transparencies of the sketches to project on the overhead projector and use for background scenery for additional role playing.

WORKING TOGETHER TO EXPLORE, CREATE, AND COMMUNICATE

| **Human-Made Objects** | **ACTIVITY 1.6** |

Have the children ask their family members (or friends) about the oldest human-made objects in their homes. It can be anything—clothing, dishes, kitchen utensil, diary entry, a letter, or a photograph. Ask the children to interview the adult and pose the following questions:

- Who owned it first?
- How was it used?
- What does the object tell us about the person and the time period?

Ask the children to sketch the object and, if appropriate, label its parts. When the children bring their sketches to school, let them discuss their drawings in small groups and determine which object is the most unusual, the oldest, and most useful today. Let the groups report to the whole group and tell which object was determined for each category. Follow up by asking the students to invite an antique collector or the owner of an antique store to visit the class and talk about some of the oldest objects he or she brings to class.

| **Environmental Beauty** | **ACTIVITY 1.7** |

Place boxes labeled "Glass," "Cans," and "Paper" in a corner of the room to help children sort classroom trash and, if appropriate, arrange for them to take the boxes to a recycling center. The children can be introduced to the recycling "habit" by recycling some items you bring from home—glass bottles, jars, paper, foil pie plates, TV dinner trays, and so on.

REACHING OUT TO TIMES PAST AND IN THE FUTURE

Invite children to look at an old object that you bring to class. Tell as much as you know about the object—who owned it, its use, and what it tells people about its time period. Ask children to suggest the counterpart for the object today (a wooden butter mold might suggest pre-molded sticks of packaged butter as a contemporary counterpart).

Then ask children to think of something they own today that they think they will keep all their lives. Then have them draw the object. Have children work with partners and predict (give guesses and hunches) what would happen in the future if an archaeologist—a person who studies the life and customs of people of ancient times—found their object(s). Ask them to respond to "What might the archeologist say about you—the object's owner?" Then have them write their thoughts on the back of their drawings before displaying their work in a class almanac entitled, *The Information Please Amateur Archaeologists' Almanac*. On a subsequent day, place sketches of several artifacts on an overhead transparency and ask the students to take the role of archaeologists who have discovered the artifacts. Ask the students to make observations and conclusions about each of the artifacts.

| **Cultural Values** | **ACTIVITY 1.8** |

Cultural values can be transmitted through folktales. For example, folktales can illustrate to African-American children the importance of faith and perseverance, including the body of literature that features heroes, from the mythical John Henry to Jack Johnson and Joe Louis.

Literature that tells the stories of real-life African-American heroes and heroines, such as Jackie Robinson, Marian Anderson, and Booker T. Washington, transmits the message that quicksand and land mines characterize the road to becoming an African-American achiever in America and that it is possible to overcome these. Some examples are:

Abrahams, R. D. (1985). *Afro-American folktales*. New York: Random House.

Adoff, A. (1984). *Black is brown is tan*. New York: Harper.

Dumas, A. (1982). *Golden legacy*. Seattle: Baylor.

Giovanni, N. (1982). *Sing a soft black song*. New York: Hill and Wang.

REACHING OUT TO THE REVOLUTIONARY WAR

ACTIVITY 1.9   Yankee Doodle

T G

Share background information about the folksong "Yankee Doodle" with students about how the British brought the song to America. During the colonies' Revolutionary War, however, colonial soldiers adopted the song as one of the symbols for their struggle for independence. Have students share their knowledge of this period and discuss words or phrases in the song that might be unfamiliar to them, e.g., *hasty pudding, Yankee Doodle Dandy, Captain Washington, slapping stallion, swamping gun, horn of powder, nation louder, littlekeg*, and *stabbing iron*. Reproduce the folksong for the students and divide the class into two groups of high and low voices for a choral reading. Example:

> Group 1:   Father and I went down to camp,
> Along with Captain Gooding;
> And there we saw the men and boys
> As thick as hasty pudding.
>
> Group 2:   Yankee Doodle keep it up,
> Yankee Doodle Dandy,
> Mind the music and the step,
> And with the girls be handy.
>
> Group 1:   And there we saw a thousand men,
> As rich as Squire David,
> And what they wasted every day,
> I wish it could be saved.
>
> Group 2:   Yankee Doodle keep it up,
> Yankee Doodle Dandy,
> Mind the music and the step,
> And with the girls be handy.
> (and so on).

ACTIVITY 1.10   A War Tale

I G

After listening to/reading *Yankee Doodle: A Revolutionary War Tail* (Dorling Kindersley, 1992, grades 1–2) by Gary Chalk, review the illustrations again of the mice and other animals dressed in authentic clothing of the 1700s. Discuss the overview of the song and the colonists' actions toward independence. Leave the book at an activity center so children can look closely at the cartoon-style illustrations and informative side notes or retell the story in a sequence of sketches. In the center, invite children to construct their own mice puppets to re-dramatize the events in the story. Puppets can be made from sticks, paper bags, cylinders, socks, cups, paper plates, cloth, and from cut paper figures or single compartments of egg cartons pasted on paper strips to be used as finger rings. Have the materials ready and available in boxes. Have children turn a table on its side to make a stage for their puppets to perform.

Additionally, at a craft table, children can select clay or play dough to make Liberty Bell replicas or other related items. They can locate materials for assembling individual books about this time period in history; or they can select art supplies to make pictures of historical figures, places, and events for a bulletin board.

The Class Crier   ACTIVITY 1.11

To develop students' awareness of how people got the news in colonial times and to develop attentive listening ability, show the students a picture of a town crier in colonial times. Ask them if they know what the town crier is doing. If they do not know the job of the crier, explain the duties of the town crier and how the crier attracted attention by ringing a bell or beating a drum. Ask the students what the crier might announce if the crier visited their classroom today. Discuss suggestions with the students and write their ideas on the board. Tell the students that there will be a Class Crier to announce special items, the news, and class or group assignments. Put the announcements on a sheet of paper similar to that used by a town crier. Read some announcements or assignments to the class as if you were the town crier. Use a bell to announce the most important words. Ask individual students to repeat the special assignments or announcements as town criers, too. Put the sheets of paper used by the criers on a bulletin board. Have the students evaluate their listening skills using the following questions:

1. Can the students repeat the announcements and assignments presented by the class crier?
2. Can they perform the assignments announced by the crier?
3. Did they accomplish what was asked of them in the announcements?
4. Do they believe their attentive listening skills are improving?

Conflict Resolution   ACTIVITY 1.12

Help children deal with their feelings openly and to understand that all people have feelings. The book *The Pink Party* (Hyperion, 1994) by Maryann MacDonald allows children to discuss their feelings of jealousy, guilt, or fear and to realize that everyone gets jealous and angry. In the story, a best friend wants everything that the other friend has until jealousy strains their relationship. In the end, the two friends realize that their friendship is their most valuable possession. You can express some personal feelings, too: "I was feeling angry when that happened" and "That made me feel good and happy inside." Help children see that everyone has feelings and help them relate openly to one another and to others in their world.

Problem Solving   ACTIVITY 1.13

When a problem arises in the classroom or on the school grounds, help the children identify the problem and suggest the information that they need to study the problem. Just as historians do, children can reach conclusions after analyzing the information they have and drawing conclusions.

**SET 2:
A CHILD'S PLACE
IN TIME AND SPACE**

DEVELOPING SOCIAL SKILLS AND RESPONSIBILITIES

Responsibilities   ACTIVITY 2.1

From a favorite edition of *Aesop's Fables* read "The Ant and the Grasshopper" and discuss the responsibilities of the ant and the grasshopper as well as the lesson that was learned.

Have children get into small groups to practice a short skit of the fable and then perform it for another group. After the performance, invite children to contribute what responsibilities they had during the small-group work and the performance. Ask them to tell what they did to get along together and what they might do differently next time (social skills). For additional performances, engage children in performing skits in rhyme about other fables from *Play Aesop* (Eldridge Pub. Co., 1971) by Gloria Delmar.

ACTIVITY 2.2   **Social Studies Show-and-Tell**

T **G**

Relate the daily show-and-tell time to a social studies unit of study and ask children to suggest a topic, object, or event as the focus for show-and-tell. In a brief class meeting, have children volunteer if they will share and mention what information will be shared. They can also mention ways they can speak so all can hear them and ways, as listeners, they can participate by questioning, listening with respect, providing written feedback, and applauding the speaker(s). Write the children's suggestions on a chart, the board, or an overhead transparency. To prepare for a show-and-tell time, have children gather their ideas about the topic and plan their sharing by browsing and reading through materials and reflecting about what they want to say. Occasionally, two or more students may ask to make a presentation together since they want to present information about a social concern together. As examples, they may want to stage a brief skit where the setting is a public meeting in which the local farmers are protesting the diminishing amount of water they are receiving from the state's nearby water aquaduct. A water resource representative explains that the water is diminished in the farming area to keep the water level high for an endangered species of salmon to spawn in a nearby river. The students, taking different roles, can research what they can say on the topic, and the audience can take roles as farmers in the public meeting in the skit.

ACTIVITY 2.3   **Group Rules**

I **G**

With children, discuss why "rules" are needed to live together in their families and that family members work and play together better when the "rights" of each family member are recognized. Invite them to establish their own rules for using the playground equipment at school (or walking to the cafeteria or working together in collaborative groups). Have them compare their rules with some of the "rules" in their families. On the board, a chart, or overhead transparency, write "Playground Rules" for one column and "Family Rules" for another. Have the children suggest the rules and note the similarities.

Playground Rules	Family Rules
1.	1.

ACTIVITY 2.4   **Building a Sense of Community**

I **G**

Build a sense of community among the students through a field trip. In planning a trip to a community site, children can help decide on group rules for the trip, which questions will be asked and answered, and what will be viewed. After the trip, ask the children to complete a mural that shows their experiences. Allow the children to discuss their interests related to the trip and divide them into interest groups to work together to sketch and paint their section of the mural. When each interest group has completed its section, have children report on their work to the whole group.

The Flag   ACTIVITY 2.5

I G

Ask children in what places they have seen America's flag and have them draw and color illustrations for a class book entitled "I See the Flag." They can write or dictate brief stories of the flags they have seen in their neighborhood and community. As a follow up, invite a member of a patriotic group (American Legion, Veterans of Foreign Wars) to class to demonstrate ways of handling and caring for the flag.

EXPANDING CHILDREN'S GEOGRAPHIC WORLD

Field Trip   ACTIVITY 2.6

T I G

With children, plan a field trip in the community where soil is being excavated for a new house or building. Have children take pencils, small notebooks, and paper cups with them and ask them to sketch what they observe—the excavation equipment, the workers on their jobs, tools used, the roots of plants in the soil, creatures in overturned earth, and rocks found. Have children get soil samples in the paper cups. Then return to the class and label the cups *top soil, sub soil, soil 2 feet deep,* and so on. Engage children in planting bean seeds in the cups and observing the growth of the seeds. Have them observe which of the different levels of soil they obtained produced the best growth. They can take daily measurements of the growth of the seeds and record the information on a chart, announce weekly growth height, and search for information about elements that contribute to fertile soil.

Living/Nonliving Things on Earth   ACTIVITY 2.7

I G

After the children go on a walk outside, organize a section of mural paper into the categories *Living Things* and *Nonliving Things.* Invite the children to sketch things they saw on the walk and paste them in the appropriate sections. If children have collected objects (rocks, sand, pieces of plants and trees) during the walk, have them place the objects on a table that is appropriately labeled. Help them make mini-booklets of the sketches or found objects of living things and nonliving things they saw on the walk.

Mapping the Classroom Furniture   ACTIVITY 2.8

I G

Invite children in groups to develop a plan for rearranging the classroom furniture by using a large sheet of art paper (to represent the classroom) and smaller different-colored shapes to represent desks, bookcases, tables, and so on. A blue paper shape can represent the bookcase, a red paper shape the piano, and so on. Have the children move the paper pieces around until they are satisfied with the classroom arrangement. Ask a volunteer from each group to report to the whole group on their arrangement. If desired, select one of the classroom maps as a guide to place the furniture. As a follow-up, invite the children to make similar maps for a particular room in their homes.

Cardinal Directions   ACTIVITY 2.9

I G

Take the children outside in the morning to observe the position of the sun (in the eastern sky). Return to observe the position of the sun at noon (in the southern sky). Ask children where the sun had been in the morning to help them establish a connection between the direction of east and to observe that the placement of the sun at noon is in a different direction. Return to observe the position of the sun in the late afternoon (the western sky). Ask children where the sun had been in the morning and at noon to help them establish a connection between the directions of east and south and to note that the placement of the sun in the late afternoon is in a different direction. In the room, have students fold a sheet of art paper into three columns and sketch a stick figure representing themselves in each column. Ask them to draw the position of the sun as they saw it in the *morning* in the first column; as they saw it at *noon* in the second column; and as they saw it in the *late afternoon* in the third column. Repeat the activity on other days.

ACTIVITY 2.10   **Distance**

Invite the children to suggest something they could use as a unit of measure, such as a thumb, a shoe, a pencil, a length of string, or a ribbon. Engage them in measurement activities such as the following:

1. Measuring from one side of the room to the other
2. All the way around their desks
3. The height of the piano or bookcase.

Have them report their measurements, for example, that it takes the lengths of 27 pencils to measure the distance around their desks. Give them rulers to measure objects a second time and have them report the measurements to others. Add some measuring tools to the collection of items that children can take to the playground at recess (with the understanding that they use the tools to measure something and tell the whole group what they learned). Include cloth tape measures, trundle wheels, and odometers.

ACTIVITY 2.11   **Mapping Our Classroom**

Review with the children in grades 2 through 4 their knowledge of maps and any map-reading experiences they have had. Mention that a map is an exact diagram of objects or places that really exist. Show the students a map and map legend drawn to depict some place in the classroom—perhaps the top of the teacher's desk or the top of the table in the activity center. Ask them to look closely at the map and have them walk around the room to discover the location of the place drawn on the map. After most of the students have found the location illustrated on the map, discuss the meaning of each item (books, pen, pencils, calendar) on the map legend. Ask students to find different items from the legend. Invite a student to describe the location of an item on the map and have another find that item where it really exists in the room. Invite the students to select a location in the room and draw a map and map legend of that location. For example, they can select a bulletin board, a desk top, a listening center. After they have sketched their own maps, engage them in writing a brief story to describe their map *without naming the exact location on the map* and the activities they can do at their map's location. Have students trade their maps and brief stories so others can read their maps and discover the locations they depict. Place the maps and stories in a class book entitled *Our Classroom Book of Maps* and make it available in the class reading corner, social studies activity center, or map learning station.

ACTIVITY 2.12   **Climate**

Have children keep a daily calendar as you draw their attention to the climate—sunny and warm, rainy and cold, cloudy and cool. Discuss the different clothing worn for different weather conditions and have children sketch articles of the clothing on the square for the date on their calendars. Take the children outside briefly to make comparisons:

1. *On a sunny day.* "Let's stand in the sun and then in the shade. What is different? Leave a wet paper towel outside. How long did it take the paper to dry?"
2. *On a windy day.* "Let's walk facing the wind and then walk with our backs to the wind. What is different? Leave a wet paper towel outside. How long did it take the paper to dry? When does the paper dry more quickly—on a sunny day or windy day?"
3. *On a rainy day.* "Let's walk in the light rain. What is different about the playground in the rain? Leave a wet paper towel outside. How long did it take the paper to dry?"

After experiencing the weather outside, read aloud some poems about the weather to the children. Invite them to act out some of the lines in the poems.

Environment   ACTIVITY 2.13

Help children identify the plants they see on a field trip on the school grounds or in the neighborhood. Encourage them to talk about colors, shapes, and sizes. Have them count the plants they see (perhaps 20 different types of plants growing on the school ground) and look for likenesses and differences. Ask them to recall what types of conditions supported the plant life (soft soil, shady area, or watery area near sprinkler head). Have the children establish their own "classification" system and arrange the plant leaves in groups.

Earth Day   ACTIVITY 2.14

Earth Day can be a time to study how people care for the earth. With the children, brainstorm ways they can do their part by planting something in the playground, cleaning and decorating the classroom, or doing something for the neighborhood or regional picnic areas or parks. Write their suggestions in a graphic web format with "Ways We Can Care for the Earth" in the center of the web. The suggestions can be listed at the ends of lines that radiate from the center.

Suggestions   Suggestions

Ways We Can Care

for the Earth

Suggestions   Suggestions

Have children work in small groups to generate ideas for implementing some of their suggestions. Ask a volunteer from each group to report on the suggested implementations to the whole class. Have the class select one or two of the implementations and make a plan for getting involved in recognizing Earth Day.

Aesthetics   ACTIVITY 2.15

After a nature walk, have children focus on the beauty of the environment and sketch, draw, or paint their impressions of flowers, leaves, trees, birds, insects, and so on. Decorate the classroom with the art work and ask children to contribute to a display of beauty in the environment by bringing the shiniest red apple, a length of driftwood, or unusual rocks and pebbles. Engage the children in handling the objects in the display and observing the items with a magnifying glass. Talk with them about what they see, smell, and feel to emphasize shapes, sizes, smells, textures, and colors in nature.

ACTIVITY 2.16   Interdependency

To foster the concept of interdependency, bring a living thing into the classroom, such as an insect, plant, turtle, or goldfish. Have children discuss what the living thing needs (plants need water, soil, and sun; insects need plants; reptiles need insects) and what care the children can provide for it. Invite volunteers to take care of the living thing daily and ask the children to give a brief report about what they did each day during a "show-and-tell" time. Emphasize the importance of balance in nature and relate this interdependency to the children's dependency on certain plants, animals, air, and water. Have them graphically show this chain of dependency by making paper-chain bracelets with paper links that state, "I depend on plants (animals, air, water) because. . . ."

ACTIVITY 2.17   Changes in the Neighborhood

To observe changes in the neighborhood (streets being repaired, new buildings going up; old buildings being razed), discuss with children about where they are going, what they will do, and what they will see. To further engage them in decision making about the trip, have them list any questions they would like to have answered during the trip and elicit their ideas about safety during the trip. Write their ideas on a chart and ask each one to be a safety monitor on the trip. Follow-up with these activities:

1. Ask them which of their favorite songs they would sing as they walk on the trip and who will volunteer to be the song leader(s).
2. Introduce a teacher-made map to show the route of the walk they will take.
3. Take an audiotape recorder to record what they hear.
4. During the trip, take time for the children to watch actions that are interesting to them, to ask questions, and to talk about what they see.
5. Back in the classroom, debrief children about the trip with activities such as:
   a. Asking them to dictate or write a story about the trip
   b. Listening to the tape recorder
   c. Reviewing the route of the trip on the map and discussing what was seen at different points on the map
   d. Asking children to make up their own riddles about what was seen: "I am thinking of something we saw on the trip. It was _____ and _____ and made of _____. What was it?"
   e. Asking children in small groups to use squares of paper to sketch the changes taking place in houses, stores, and streets that they saw on the trip. Have the children place their sketches in a pile and then sort the sketches into categories.

ACTIVITY 2.18   Regions

To acquaint children with the characteristics of their neighboring community, take them on several field trips with the purpose of having them list all the things they found in their neighborhood. They can carry mini-notebooks in which to write or sketch what they observe. Back in the classroom, have the children tell what they found and list their ideas on the board in categories that are connected to the concept of *regions*:

Physical Properties That   *Physical Properties That Affect*
Affect the Ways People Use Land   *the Ways People Live in Groups*

Other   Other

Geography Themes   ACTIVITY 2.19

To integrate geography and literature and to increase the students' understanding of the Native people before and at the time of Columbus, provide some historical background about the time period and the location of *Encounter* (1992) by Jane Yolen. *Encounter* is a fictional interaction between a Taino Indian boy and Columbus and his men on the island of San Salvador in 1492. The plot indicates that dreams forewarn the boy about the negative consequences of the arrival of the explorers. Explain to the students that this is a story about what might have happened. Point out the location of San Salvador in the West Indies. Write a heading on the board, A Geographer's Chart for *Encounter,* and mention to students that they can take the point of view of geographers and use a procedure developed by geographers that allows them to inquire about places on the earth and to analyze the relationships of the places to the people who live there. Discuss the topics of location, place, relationships within the place, movement, and regions (based on the work of the Committee on Geographic Education in 1983) as features of the geographers' procedure and list them on the chart as the story in *Encounter* is discussed:

A GEOGRAPHER'S CHART FOR *ENCOUNTER*

Location

In the West Indies in 1492; in San Salvador Bay where the ships of Columbus are anchored.

Place

The illustrations in *Encounter* show physical features of the place.

Relationships

The Taino people believed in welcoming newcomers; the printed text and pictures contrast the Taino people and Columbus and his crew; the lifestyle of the Taino people was changed after the arrival of Columbus, and their language, culture, and religion eventually died out.

Movement

There was an exchange of possessions as the Tainos gave cotton thread and spears and the Spaniards gave beads and hats. The ideas of the Spanish prevailed.

Regions

The region was changed because of the Spaniards' acquisition of and effect on the resources including the Tainos themselves. For example, in 50 years, the Taino population decreased from 300,000 people to 500.

Ask students to transform the information on the chart into another format (such as a word web, a before-Columbus and after-Columbus collage, a classroom mural of events, a timeline of events, a story of how they would have acted had they been there, or a role-playing situation of some of the conflicts).

EXPANDING CHILDREN'S ECONOMIC WORLD

Workers in the World of Work   ACTIVITY 2.20

On a length of adding machine tape, have children sketch mini-mural scenes of their daily activities from morning to night. Ask volunteers to show their sketches to the whole group and display them on a bulletin board. As each scene is presented, elicit suggestions from the other children about workers who helped make the scene possible, for example, truck drivers who brought the cereal that was eaten, the store clerk who sold groceries to the family, workers who made the child's clothing, builders who built the apartment or house, bus manufacturers who made the bus that took the child to school, and so on. Write the workers' labels under the appropriate scene on the tape. Ask children to name people they know who work in any of the categories and invite one or more of them to class to tell the class more about their economic contributions. Before the workers arrive, have children determine what questions they want to ask. After the visit, ask them to write thank-you letters to the visitors to tell them what they learned from the class visit.

DEVELOPING AWARENESS OF TODAY'S ECONOMIC WORLD

ACTIVITY 2.21   **Dramatic Play Kit**

After the children have interviewed a worker who visited the classroom, have them collect items for a dramatic play kit for informal drama activities. For example, for a unit on today's economic world and community helpers, arrange a field trip to a nearby store and invite someone from the store to the class to be interviewed. After the visit, items for a store kit can be displayed in the room—the items can include artificial fruits and vegetables, colored dots for price stickers, play money, grocery bags, marking pens, and empty food packages. Larger items in the room can include a table for a checkout counter, another for grocery shelves, a cash register, and a grocery cart. Invite the children to use the information they got from the field trip, the class visitor, and the class books to reenact some of the familiar everyday activities they now know about as they pretend to be someone working or buying in the store.

DEVELOPING AWARENESS OF CULTURAL DIVERSITY, NOW AND LONG AGO

ACTIVITY 2.22   **Rhymes of Cultural Groups**

Read various rhymes to the students before inviting them to dramatize the characteristics of the rhymes. The following books may be used for this purpose:

- *Tortillitas Para Mama, and Other Nursery Rhymes/ Spanish and English* (1981) by Margot Griego
- *Chinese Mother Goose Rhymes* (1982) by Robert Wyndham
- *The Prancing Pony: Nursery Rhymes from Japan* (1967) by Charlotte De Forests
- *It's Raining Said John Twaining* (1973) by N. M. Bodecker
- *De Angeli's Book of Nursery and Mother Goose Rhymes* (1954) by Marguerite De Angeli
- *Dragon Kites and Dragonflies: A Collection of Chinese Nursery Rhymes* (1986) by Demi.

After reading selected rhymes aloud, have students dramatize the language of the nursery rhymes by doing finger plays and the counting rhymes, clapping along with appropriate rhymes, acting out the turning and twirling rhymes, and joining in with nonsense words.

ACTIVITY 2.23   **Cultural Heritage Makes You Proud**

After reading one of the following stories, ask children to meet in small groups to talk about what they learned about culture (family life, food, clothing, shelter, animals) from the story. In the whole group, ask children to contribute their ideas about the meaning of "knowing about one's background and cultural heritage makes you proud." After rereading the story, ask them to assume the role of characters and act out one of the stories in small groups to see the world from a culturally diverse perspective. Encourage them to add gestures, facial expressions, body movements, and dialogue for the following books:

- *African Heritage.* Aardema, V. (1981). *Bringing the rain to Kaiti Plain.* New York: Dial. This is a Kenyan tale with an accumulating style about animals during a long drought. Folk literature.
- *Asian Heritage.* Heyer, M. (1986). *The weaving of a dream: A Chinese folktale.* New York: Viking. In this tale, a poor widow weaves her dreams into a beautiful brocaded fabric. When some fairies steal it, it seems the widow will die of grief if her three sons cannot recover her treasured dreams.
- *European Heritage.* Turner, A. (1987). *Time of the bison.* Ill. by B. Peck. New York: Macmillan. In this story of family life in prehistoric times, Scar Boy wants to earn a new "true" name and is surprised when he is honored for sculpting a horse's image from clay. Fiction.
- *Latino/Hispanic Heritage.* Alexander, E. (1989). *Llama and the great flood: A folktale of Peru.* New York: Crowell. This tale from the Andes is about how a llama leads people to safety and saves them from a flood.
- *Middle Eastern/Mediterranean Heritage.* Al-Saleh, K. (1985). *Fabled cities, princes and Jinn from Arabic myths and legends.* Schocken Press. This collection of stories from Arabia and Persia can be read aloud to (and sometimes reworded for) primary-grade children.
- *Original Native American Heritage.* McDermott, G. (1974). *Arrow to the sun.* New York: Viking. This Pueblo Indian tale portrays the people's reverence for the sun and tells about the Lord of the Sun, who sends a spark to Earth. The spark becomes a boy who searches for his father.

Cross-Cultural Music Appreciation ACTIVITY 2.24

To encourage language development and appreciation for music as part of a literary heritage, have students sing songs and discuss the content of the music that reinforces knowledge of the culture from which the songs originated. Books for this purpose are the following:

- Bryan, A. (1974). *Walk together children: Black American spirituals, Volume One.* New York: Atheneum.
- Bryan, A. (1982). *I'm going to sing: Black American spirituals, Volume Two.* New York: Atheneum.
- Bryan, A. (1991). *All night, all day· A child's first book of African-American spirituals.* New York: Atheneum.
- Bierhorst, J. (1979). *A cry from the earth: Music of North American Indians.* Four Winds.
- Field, E. (1973). *Eskimo songs and stories.* New York: Delacorte.
- Fox, D. (1987). *Go in and out the window: An illustrated songbook for young people.* New York: Metropolitan Museum of Art/Holt.
- Hart, J. (1982). *Singing bee! A collection of favorite children's songs.* Lothrop, Lee & Shepard.
- Hom, D. (1977). *The literature of American music in books and folk music.* Scarecrow Press.

Additionally, students can use the visual arts to interpret the music. For example, opportunities for studying the history of art are included in *Go In and Out the Window* by Dan Fox. Each of the songs in this book is accompanied by a reproduction of a work of art that is on display at the Metropolitan Museum of Art.

ACTIVITY 2.25   **Jafta in South Africa**

To illustrate similes through a setting in the diversity of a boy's day in South Africa, read aloud *Jafta* (1981) by Hugh Lewin. Show the illustrations. The illustrations show animals that are native to South Africa and depict similes as they portray one of Jafta's feelings. As one example, the text reads, "When I'm happy, I purr like a lioncub." The accompanying picture shows Jafta, happy and hugging an equally happy cub.

Discuss the illustrations and the comparison made by the author, talk about the characteristics of similes, and explain how the illustrations help students visualize the comparisons. Elicit comparisons the students recall for times when Jafta is happy and when he is cross. Write their ideas on the board in two webs about feelings:

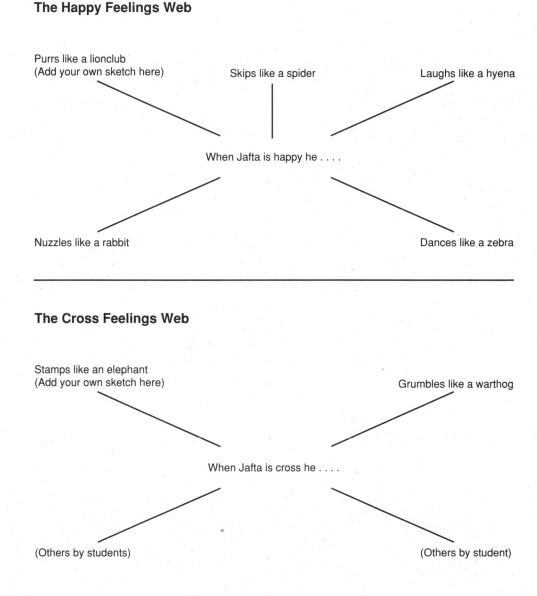

The Happy Feelings Web

Purrs like a lionclub
(Add your own sketch here)   Skips like a spider   Laughs like a hyena

When Jafta is happy he . . . .

Nuzzles like a rabbit   Dances like a zebra

The Cross Feelings Web

Stamps like an elephant
(Add your own sketch here)   Grumbles like a warthog

When Jafta is cross he . . . .

(Others by students)   (Others by student)

Have students identify the similes in the webs and then elaborate by adding their own sketches to illustrate the similes. Have them share their webs with other students in small groups.

People Who Supply Our Needs   ACTIVITY 3.1

Ask children to brainstorm as many different jobs related to their needs of food, clothing, shelter, and health as they can think of in the class. Write the children's suggestions on the board, dry marker chart, or overhead transparency. Have children document the different jobs related to their needs by browsing through the Yellow Pages of the telephone directory and noting any jobs related to food, clothing, shelter, and health. Have them report what they found. What jobs did they find in the Yellow Pages that were not on their list? What jobs were on their list that were not found in the Yellow Pages? Emphasize the need for the wide variety of jobs to supply our needs. Then facilitate a discussion with the following questions:

- What are some of the different jobs in our area that you documented with the ads from the Yellow Pages?
- Why do you think there are so many different jobs in our city? community?
- Why do you think that your family does NOT do these different jobs all by itself?
- Do you think that the people who do these jobs have or do *not* have some special abilities to do the work (doctors, nurses, other health care workers)? Why do you think that way?

Have each child select one job from the list on the board or from the Yellow Pages and give his or her reasons for the importance of the job (how it supplies our needs). Ask children to create drawings to show a worker doing the job they selected and place the drawings in a class book entitled "Different Jobs in Our City (Community)."

Myself and My Family   ACTIVITY 3.2

To refine oral expression and develop writing skills related to the family, invite students to see a teacher-made accordion-pleated book with the title *Myself and My Family*. Read the title and ask children to make suggestions about what they think would be inside this special book. Tell children they will have an opportunity to make their own books about themselves and their families. Ask them to suggest subjects they would like to include in their own books. Assist children as they:

1. Make their own accordion-pleated books. Have them illustrate the covers and print the title of the book.
2. Illustrate a page for each member of the family (including pets) on subsequent days. After students have drawn each picture, have them write or dictate a story about the family member. Ask questions about the family member to help children develop their stories.

3. Allow children opportunities to share their family books with the class and talk about their own families.

ACTIVITY 3.3

T G

The Family's Quilt

Display a quilt made by a grandparent or other ancestor to the children and discuss its place in a family's history. Read aloud one or two intergenerational stories that present the family activity of making a quilt and review the illustrations on an opaque projector with the whole group. Ask the children these questions:

- What do you think is being shown in the illustration(s)?
- What family relationship seems to be shown?
- When do you think the illustration took place (long ago, today)?
- In what way does the illustration show you something that is valued by the family?
- What do the illustrations tell you about the family life of the people? How is the family life in this story similar to your family life? How is it different?
- Overall, would you say that this was a time when quilts and blankets and bedding were easy for a family to buy? Why or why not?
- How could we figure out what a family like this could use to make a quilt?
- Why do you think they spent so much time making a quilt?
- What might happen if your family had to make their own bedding today?
- What are some of the ways that different people can keep warm at night when they sleep?

Invite children to browse in the school library and locate other intergenerational stories for classroom reading. Ask children to consider the selected books as a group and suggest a title (main idea, generalizing) for the group of books. Selections can include some of the following:

- *African heritage—Contemporary setting.* Flournoy, V. (1985). *The patchwork quilt.* New York: Dial. This book shows making a quilt in a contemporary setting, an activity that brings a family together as they recall events related to the fabric remnants. They realize that the completed quilt tells the family's "history" as well as intergenerational caring, love, and respect for the elderly in an African-American family. As the family members help Grandmother sew, they come closer together, remember past experiences that are related to the quilt scraps, and are pleased with the finished quilt that displays so beautifully the memories of many events in their lives.
- *European heritage—Nineteenth century.* Polacco, P. (1988). *The keeping quilt.* New York: Simon & Schuster. This is a true story about a quilt kept by the author's family. It begins with the time when the author's Great-Gramma Anna came to America from Russia during the last century as a Russian immigrant to start life anew in New York. The only things that little Anna had from Russia were some memories and a dress that was getting too small for her. "We will make a quilt to help us always remember home," Anna's mother says. "It will be like having the family in back-home Russia dance around us at night." With the words, she takes the dress and Anna's babushka, Uncle Vladimir's shirt, Aunt Havala's nightdress, an apron from Aunt Natasha, and makes a keeping quilt. Anna's dress becomes part of a bright quilt that later is handed down through four generations. Pulled together by the keeping quilt, the family uses the quilt in different ways—as a Sabbath tablecloth, a wedding canopy, and a blanket to welcome new babies into the world. For a plaything, it is even taken to the park to become an imaginary tent in a steaming Amazon jungle.
- *Native People heritage—Hawaii, contemporary setting.* Guback, G. (1994). *Luka's quilt.* Greenwillow. K-2. This is a story of intergenerational love. Luka and her grandmother have quarreled because the traditional plain Hawaiian quilt that her grandmother was making for her does not have the large beautiful flowers that Luka wanted. On Lei

Day, Luka's grandmother asks that they declare a truce so they can celebrate the festival together. Luka agrees and participates in making flower leis. In return, Luka's grandmother makes a colorful fabric lei to accent the plain quilt and this heals Luka's hurt feelings. Includes words such as *tatami mat, lei,* and *shave ice* that might be unfamiliar to some children.

Interviewing a Parent About an Ancestor of Long Ago   ACTIVITY 3.4

Invite children to use their listening skills and interview a parent or other relative about an ancestor of long ago. Have children brainstorm questions to ask during the interview and write them on the board. There may be questions related to the ancestor's work and recreation, friends, family configuration, children, and family needs that can be shown in a pattern for the interview on the board:

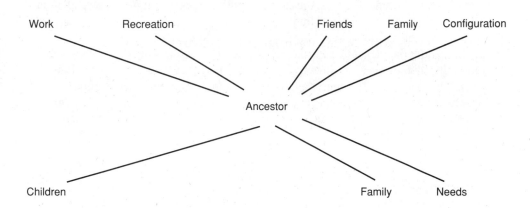

After the interviews, have children who wish to do so report on what they learned from the parent or other relative about the ancestor and different family lifestyles that are represented.

Lifestyles   ACTIVITY 3.5

With children, read stories set in the past as well as contemporary realistic stories to introduce people and families of different cultures to provide basic knowledge about their lifestyles now and long ago. Ask children to listen for the ways the people and families got their food and water, ways they provided shelter, ways they obtained clothing, ways they worked, the tools they used, intergenerational relationships, if any, and how they traveled. On the board, develop a chart *without a title* of these main ideas related to the people's heritages:

	African	Asian	Latino/Hispanic	Native American
Food				
Water				
Shelter				
Clothing				
Work				
Recreation				
Tools				
Intergenerational relationship				
Travel				

Let children work in partnerships to create their own chart similar to the one on the board and list the background information they received from the story. Have each partnership meet with another partnership and read and discuss their information. They can combine information if they wish on another chart they create. After the children have written their information, have them meet together as a whole group and suggest information to place on the chart on the board. Elicit reasons from the children as to why they suggested what they did and have them suggest a title for the chart that could summarize or generalize what they did or what information was gathered.

**SET 4:
CONTINUITY
AND CHANGE**

**OUR LOCAL HISTORY: DISCOVERING
OUR PAST AND OUR TRADITIONS**

ACTIVITY 4.1

Window of Change

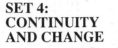

To relate a listening activity to the past, first read aloud *Window* (1991) by Jennie Baker, a story that shows the same setting as the environment changes over time. Show and discuss the illustrations. Divide the students into two groups. Have each group dictate or write a description of one of the illustrations in the book. Ask the other group to listen to the description, identify the matching illustrations, and tell the reasons why they selected the illustration they did. Further, the students can discuss why they could or could not identify the illustration and go on to suggest guidelines to help them provide descriptions that include accurate details. Have students relate the story to what is going on in their community today and have them create their own sketches of their community as it might have looked in different time periods.

ACTIVITY 4.2

One Hundred Years

Show an old doll or picture of an old doll to the students and ask them if the doll looks like one they would see in a toy store today. Have them point out what is different about the doll and how they know the doll is old. Ask them to imagine who they think might have owned the doll. Let students continue to speculate about who owned the doll or lost it and introduce a writing/dictation activity titled "Help Me with the Mystery":

HELP ME WITH THE MYSTERY

I have been trying to solve a mystery about this old doll and the girl who owned and played with her. Maybe if you hear about how I got the doll, you can help me with this mystery.

There was once a big, old, deserted house on a farm in Iowa. A man who builds houses saw the farm and decided he wanted to tear down the old house and build a new one on the same spot. It was a beautiful site for a house. There were gnarled apple trees in the backyard and a huge, green lawn of grass and wild flowers in front.

The builder decided to check the house to make sure there was nothing in it before he sent for the wrecking crew to tear it down. As he was going through the old house, he came to a second-floor bedroom that looked as if it had belonged to a child. The walls were covered with faded wallpaper with pink roses, and a child's drawings could be seen on the walls. The room had a large closet that probably held the child's clothes and other possessions. The builder opened the closet door to make sure nothing was inside. Something attracted his attention when he looked up at a high shelf. He put his hand up on the shelf and found this old doll tucked away there.

Will you help me solve this mystery? Who do you think left this doll? Why do you think it was left? The doll looks as if it was played with a great deal. What adventures do you think the girl and her doll had? How do you think the girl felt when she discovered she didn't have her doll? How do you think the doll felt when it was left behind?"

After the writing or dictation activity, invite students to listen to a story of another lost doll, *Hitty: Her First Hundred Years* (Macmillan, 1957) by Rachael Field, an award-winning book that follows the adventures of a doll as it faces the unknown. Mention to the students that they have written their stories about the possible adventures of an old doll. Tell them that professional authors may be motivated by the "what ifs" associated with dolls and toys that have lived long lives or are placed in settings in which they are on their own. Read and discuss *Hitty* and allow students to respond to the plot and compare the types of adventures Hitty had with the types of adventures they developed in their writing or dictation activity.

Our Home State   ACTIVITY 4.3

Have children participate in one or more of the following activities related to the history of their home state:

- Locate their home state on a map and examine its setting in North America. Ask them to identify mountains, rivers, valleys, and harbors, if any. Ask children which parts of the setting would have attracted people to settle there in the past. Record their ideas on the board.
- Have children use resource material to locate information about the Native Americans who made homes in their home state. Collect information about Native American beliefs, legends, economic activities, social organization. Describe their relationship with the environment or setting in their home state.
- Help children see that today's populated areas are frequently the same areas settled by early Native Americans and discuss the features in the geography that have influenced settling in the areas. Point out that geographical features provide a link or a connection between the early settlements in the past and the present heavily populated cities.
- Read aloud stories related to Native Americans, explorers, and colonists in the students' home state and discuss the motives for colonization. Discuss stories of people from different cultures who settled in the area and their early contributions to the home state. Have children map the routes of explorers and locate settlements of early colonists and native people. Ask children to determine the geographic features of the state that would have helped or hindered access to their home state.
- Help children develop a timeline to show several events that affected the history of their home state. Arrivals of people from different cultures should be noted. Include women and minority groups who helped to build the state.
- Engage children in turning the timeline into a class mural with sketches of the events and people of different cultural groups. Include the contributions of women who helped to build the home state.
- Introduce and discuss the preamble to the constitution of the home state and the government that it created.
- With maps, have children follow the routes in the 1800s that linked the east coast to the west coast and identify events that brought changes to their home state, such as the Pony Express, the Overland Mail Service, and the telegraph. Discuss the newcomers who arrived during this time period and any hostilities toward the newcomers that erupted.
- Have children examine the special significance of water in their home state and ways the state became home to diverse groups of people.
- Engage children in locating materials that document that the culture of their home state now reflects a mixture of influences from various cultures, such as Native American, European, the Far East, and Latino/Hispanic.
- Have children suggest some of the cultural contributions that diverse people brought to their home state in the past. List the suggestions on the board in a column headed "Contributions of Different Cultures in the Past" and have children compare their suggestions with the contributions made by diverse people today. Write the suggestions in a second column labeled "Contributions of Different Cultures Today."
- Have children divide into small groups and select a feature of the development of their present-day home state to research. Groups could select commerce, agriculture, education, communication, trade, industry, transportation and the highway system, or water projects such as dams and power plants.

OUR NATION'S HISTORY: CONFLICT BETWEEN
THE COLONIES AND THE BRITISH PARLIAMENT

ACTIVITY 4.4   **Conflict in the Colonies**

In discussing the conflict in the colonies between the British Parliament and the first Continental Congress in 1774, children in grade 4 and older can listen to selections from speeches made in England by William Pitt or Edmund Burke, who both pleaded for moderation in dealing with the colonies. After listening, children can:

- Work together and develop a timeline of events in the Revolution (such as the battles of Bunker Hill, Lexington, and Concord; the selection of George Washington as commander of the army; the final battle at Yorktown; the role of free black people in the battles; the role of women such as Abigail Adams and Molly Pitcher; and Patrick Henry's famous speech to his fellow legislators to support the fight against Britain).
- Listen to or read biographies of leaders such as George Washington, Thomas Jefferson, and Benjamin Franklin.
- Listen to and orally interpret a choral reading for "Concord Hymn" by Ralph Waldo Emerson and "Paul Revere's Ride" by Henry Wadsworth Longfellow.
- Listen to or read historical fiction such as *I'm Deborah Sampson* by Patricia Clapp.
- Write an entry in a simulated journal of some public figure of the times and an issue that concerned him or her.
- Write a recipe used by colonists and then elaborate on the recipe pattern to write a creative original recipe that shows their understanding of some of the events that were going on during this time period (for example, a recipe for selecting a commander of the army, for ending a battle, for supporting freedom for all, for improving the participation of women in government, for supporting or not supporting the fight against Britain, and for warning colonists about invading troops).

OUR NATION'S HISTORY: MEETING PEOPLE
ORDINARY AND EXTRAORDINARY

ACTIVITY 4.5   **Playing Detective With Famous Americans (grade 4)**

To identify details that are related to a male or female historical figure who is a member of a minority group, students can develop brief paragraphs about famous people in history without naming the person in the description. Have other students listen for details to identify the person. Ask them to recall the point at which they could identify the person and any details that were similar to those of another historical figure. Have students develop their own paragraphs to describe a famous person and trade their papers with others in the class. After the students read or listen to the received paragraphs, ask them to identify the person in history, list the details, and tell why the details supported their identification of the person.

SET 5:
OUR CHANGING STATE (GRADE 4 AND UP)

ACTIVITY 5.1   **The Physical Setting: Our State and Beyond**

With a large state map, have children identify some of the state's physical attributes—mountains, valleys, rivers, harbors—and list them on the board or on an overhead transparency. Have children work in pairs to research these geographic features elsewhere in the world and determine ways people in other areas use similar geographic features. Have children respond to the following in journals where they write words of their choosing about:

- My favorite place in the state
- Things that make me happy (sad) in my state

- Places I have been in my state
- My next vacation in my state
- If I were a mountain (or valley, harbor, desert, etc.), I could affect the way we live. . . . (and homes, clothing, food, transportation).
- If I were a mountain (or river, harbor, desert, etc.), I could affect the jobs—the way we make a living in our state. . . .
- How my state uses the geographic resources we have
- How other people in other states use the geographic resources they have.

Ask children to trade their journal writing with their partners and elicit feedback about the ideas they expressed. When their journal writing is returned to them, have them decide which revisions they will make.

Pre-Columbian Settlements and People   ACTIVITY 5.2

T   I   G

Provide background information about pre-Columbian settlers and explorers by reading aloud excerpts from *Who Discovered America? Settlers and Explorers of the New World Before the Times of Columbus* (Random House, 1970) by Patricia Lauber.

- Tell the children they are going to hear about the people who welcomed Columbus and ask them what ideas they think might be important to listen for in the story. Write their ideas on the board. Read aloud Lauber's nonfiction about the native people living on a Bahamian island in the late 1400s. After the story, ask children if their ideas listed on the board were ones they heard in the story and if there are additional ideas they want to add.
- Have children compare the way the Tainos welcomed Columbus with the way their own family members welcome guests in their home. Have children compare the way Columbus behaved as a guest with the way guests behave in the family's home. Overall, would you say that the Tainos were friendly? Why or why not? How could we figure out why the Tainos would be friendly to people who were strangers? Why do you think they were friendly and not hostile? What might have happened if the Tainos had *not* been friendly and peaceful? What are some of the ways that people can become friends with strangers?
- As further background information, read aloud *Hiawatha: Messenger of Peace* (Margaret K. McElderry/Macmillan, 1992) by David Fradin. It is the story of Hiawatha, an Iroquois Indian, who preached peace and helped unite Iroquois tribes–Seneca, Onondaga, Oneida, Mohawk, Tuscarora, and Cayuga—into the Iroquois Confederacy. Emphasize the way Hiawatha worked for peace with others. Have students meet in small groups to select one event for a script for informal reader's theater. Then add narrator's lines and assign lines for Hiawatha and others. Let them read the script aloud, standing to read their lines, and change their script until they are satisfied with the event they selected. Ask each group to add gestures, facial expressions, voice changes, and perform their script for another group.
- Ask students to organize the information they have gained about pre-Columbian people in different parts of the world by working in partnerships and listing ways the Tainos peacefully welcomed Columbus and the ways Hiawatha worked in a peaceful manner with different tribes. Have each partnership meet with another partnership to read and discuss what each pair has written. The partners can make additions and deletions and select someone to report to the whole group. After the reports are made and the children's ideas recorded on the board, ask the children to tell ways their own families welcome others and work peacefully with others using these headings on the board: "The Tainos," "Hiawatha," "Our Family." Ask the children to each suggest a title for the chart and write their titles on slips of paper. Place the slips in a container, draw one, and read it aloud. Have children in the whole group give reasons why they think the title is an appropriate one for the chart.

ACTIVITY 5.3   **Exploration: Search for Water**

T G

Have children work in small groups to take the roles of explorers who have found a water source for the expedition. Give each group a paper cup filled with water that has been lightly colored with food dye—red, yellow, green, blue, purple. The "explorers" do not know if the water is safe to drink because they have not used this water source before. Indeed, they are not sure if they can drink it safely. In their groups, have children discuss what decisions they could make concerning the water (drink it/not drink it) and what consequence each decision might bring. After the discussion, have small groups reassemble as a total class and report their decisions. Write each group's decision on the board or overhead transparency and have the children predict the consequences. Record the consequences using these headings: "Group Decision(s)" and "Consequences (What Could Happen)." Have children tell what they know about contemporary waterworks and ways water is tested for drinking purposes. Follow-up activities can include the following:

- Invite an employee from the local waterworks to visit the class and explain what goes on daily to provide safe drinking water.
- Schedule a field trip to a nearby waterworks.
- Read aloud *The Magic School Bus at the Waterworks* (Scholastic, 1986) by Joanna Cole and Bruce Degen.

ACTIVITY 5.4   **Franklin**

T G

Give students a sense of the times in the Middle Colonies by reading aloud excerpts from a biography of Benjamin Franklin and discuss the diversity in the Middle Colonies—which included English, Dutch, Swedish, German, Irish, Scottish, Catholic, Jewish settlers—as well as the value and usefulness of an almanac that many colonists used. The almanac is an all-purpose book that contained a calendar, weather predictions, information about the tides and moon changes, and dates of historical events to remember. Sometimes, the almanac also included health hints, proverbs, popular sayings, recipes, and humorous notes. Mention that in 1732, Benjamin Franklin published *Poor Richard's Almanac* and included some of his brief sayings such as "Waste not, want not" and "A stitch in time saves nine." Ask children to suggest contemporary words that they can contrast to Franklin's:

What Franklin Said	*What We Say Today*
1. Waste not, want not	1.
2. A stitch in time saves nine.	2.

Invite children to transform the written lists into a visual format for a room display and illustrate pairs of comic strip-style pictures with a word bubble to show Franklin's saying on the left side of the paper and a word bubble to show contemporary words on the right side. Before they draw, invite children to request and "reserve" the saying of their choice aloud in the group.

To interpret proverbs in Benjamin Franklin's *Poor Richard's Almanac* and to develop critical listening and thinking skills, explain to students the background of *Poor Richard's Almanac*. Franklin published a yearly magazine called *Poor Richard's Almanac* starting in 1732. It had weather reports, news about the tides, cooking lessons, poems and other information for the people. It was popular, useful, and entertaining and the most famous part became the proverbs that emphasized hard work and frugality to help a person become healthy, wealthy, and wise—these were sayings that Franklin wrote or obtained from others.

Discuss this time in history when Franklin lived and wrote the almanac. Books for this purpose include *Poor Richard* (1941) by James Daugherty, a biography that covers Franklin's life and activities, *What's the Big Idea, Ben Franklin* (1978) by Jean Fritz, a portrayal of Franklin as an inventor, ambassador and coauthor of the Declaration of Independence, and *Benjamin Franklin: The New American* (1988) by Milton Meltzer, a carefully documented account of Franklin as an American statesman.

Read some of the proverbs by Franklin to the students and ask them to explain what they think the proverb means. Ask them to tell the reasons for their interpretations. Ask them if they believe the proverb is as worthy today as it was in the 1700s. Why or why not? The following examples of proverbs can be discussed, illustrated, and developed into a bulletin board display or class booklet:

Beware of little expenses; a small leak will sink a great ship.
Content makes poor men rich; discontent makes rich men poor.
Doing an injury puts you below your enemy; revenging one makes you but even with him; forgiving it sets you above him.
Early to bed and early to rise makes a man healthy, wealthy, and wise.
Eat to live, not live to eat.
Keep conscience dear, then never fear.
Lost time is never found again.
Pardoning the bad is injuring the good.
There are lazy minds as well as lazy bodies.
Wealth and content are not always bedfellows.
When you are good to others, you're good to yourself.
Who is strong? He who can conquer his bad habits.
The wise man draws more from his enemies than the fool from his friends.
Words may show a man's wit, but actions show his meaning.

From Franklin's Sayings to Today's Idioms   ACTIVITY 5.5

With children, introduce the idea of idioms as groups of words that have a special meaning—the words say things in a figurative manner. Ask children to sketch posters of idioms after they listen to or read figurative sayings in a selected trade book such as *Chin Music: Tall Talk and Other Talk* (Lippincott, 1979) by Alvin Schwartz. Have them transform their art work into word posters by labeling the objects in their sketches.

T **G**

WESTWARD MOVEMENT

Geography From Pecos Bill   ACTIVITY 5.6

The tall tale of *Pecos Bill* will help introduce children to the geography related to the Westward Movement, to the settlers who followed Daniel Boone's trail over the Cumberland Gap into Kentucky, and to the viewpoint of the Native Americans who occupied these same lands. After you read aloud the book, *Pecos Bill* (Morrow, 1986, grades 2–5) by Steven Kellogg, guide students to the terms in the tall tale that relate to geography. List the words on the board and invite the children to locate the place on a map. For instance, the words, "his kinfolk decided that New England was becoming entirely too crowded, so they piled into covered wagons and headed west," can encourage girls and boys to locate "New England" and "West from New England" on a map of the United States. With blank maps of America, older students can draw symbols or objects for other terms on the map as they listen again to the tall tale. They can research the history of the area with books that offer summaries. Have children listen to the words about Pecos Bill as he tries to corner the wild stallion, Lightning, and ask them to identify additional locales and such places as East Texas, Pecos River, and Hell's Gulch. They can retell the adventure where Bill chases Lightning to the Arctic Circle and the Grand Canyon and returns to Pinnacle Peak. Have children find those places on the maps. Additionally, the map on the book's endpapers can motivate students to sketch and color original small scenes of Pecos Bill and his adventures on their own original maps.

- Read aloud another version of Pecos Bill, *The Legend of Pecos Bill* (Bantam, 1993) by Terry Small, and mention that Sluefoot Sue's mother came from the Chickasaw people, a Woodland tribe from America's southeast, and that the plot takes place in the Washitaw Valley in Oklahoma and then in Texas. With maps, ask children to identify these geographical places. Invite those who are interested further in the topic to study the cultures of the Chickasaw people and other Plains tribes in America's Southwest and determine their points of view about the Westward Movement. Some may be interested in the points of view of the Eastern Apache, Comanche, Kiowa, Osage, Tonakawa, Waco, and Wichita.
- Engage interested children in drawing maps of America's Southwest region that include Oklahoma, Texas, and other states that were the "stomping grounds" of Pecos Bill and Sluefoot Sue. Using the maps, have children discuss why ranchers wanted to raise cattle in the area and ask them to trace routes of trail drives and mark cattle raising areas.

OUR STATE'S GROWTH AND ITS LINK TO THE REST OF THE UNITED STATES

ACTIVITY 5.7   **Our State's Growth**

Engage children in examining the lives of those who helped their home state become part of the United States and to grow under its Constitution. They can consider the influx of newcomers who arrived from Europe and other areas. For example, children in Illinois can listen to a description of Abraham Lincoln's boyhood during this period read aloud from *Abraham Lincoln* by Ingri and Edgar D'Aulaire. Further:

- Have children sing songs of the boatmen and pioneers of the times.
- Have children listen to or read tall tales about Paul Bunyan, Mike Fink, and others.
- Have children listen to or read biographies of Native American leaders such as Chief Tecumseh of the Shawnee, Chief John Ross of the Cherokee tribe, and Chief Osceola of the Seminole tribe.
- Have older children (grade 4 and up) listen to or read about the events now known as the Cherokees' "Trail of Tears."

OUR MODERN STATE

ACTIVITY 5.8   **Newcomers, New Technology, and Cities**

Have children in small groups identify the diverse people who live in their home state by collecting information from resource material. To collect information, have children replicate the following chart on an overhead transparency and record the information they find:

DIVERSE PEOPLE	FAMILY LIFE	OCCUPATIONS	CELEBRATIONS	OTHER
African Heritage				
Asian Heritage				
European Heritage				
Latino/ Hispanic Heritage				
Native American Heritage				
Other				

Have children show their group chart on the overhead projector. Ask children in the whole group to contribute any information they have related to the information written on the chart. Guide children to some generalized points of view with questions such as "When you compare your family life with _____, what can you say about the way your family does things?" and "When you compare your celebrations with _____, what can you say about the way you celebrate events?"

A Research Report   ACTIVITY 5.9

With students, select a topic for research reports related to social studies. If a fourth-grade class is studying their state, for example, then each student may select a different city (area, region, feature such as transportation or crops) for a report. After students have "reserved" their topics, they should think about what they know about it and what they want to learn about it. Ask them to draw a topic web with their topic written in the center and then write questions about what they want to know in circles linked by lines to the topic word in the center. As the student finds information, he or she writes the details on the lines that link the question to the topic word in the center of the web. Have students meet with partners to review the information and talk over ways to present the report in an interesting and organized way—through visuals, charts, diagrams, maps, models, timelines, pictures. Let students rehearse their report and then give their presentations. As an option, schedule a class meeting before the presentations to elicit the students' suggestions for responsibilities of the speakers and audience members. Write their suggestions on a chart or overhead transparency for a reference during class meetings.

SET 6:
THE WAR FOR INDEPENDENCE   **MAKING A NEW NATION (GRADE 4 AND UP)**

Colonists and British   ACTIVITY 6.1

Elicit what the children know about America's War for Independence from Britain. How is the way the colonists welcomed the British different from and similar to the way your neighborhood welcomes newcomers? Overall, would you say that the colonists were accepting of the British and their point of view? Why or why not? How could we figure out why the colonists would be unaccepting to the British? Why do you think they were unaccepting and not friendly? What might have happened if the colonists had been accepting of the British and their point of view? What are some of the ways that people can have different points of view without a resulting war?

AMERICA'S WESTWARD EXPANSION

Newcomers in the West   ACTIVITY 6.2

Have students locate resource materials and document the contributions of the different groups of people who built America. Ask children to identify the newcomers' countries of origin and locate on a map with colored dot stickers the regions of America where they settled. Have them locate the origins of these groups:

- Newcomers who farmed
- Newcomers who contributed to the arts and crafts
- Newcomers who built railroads
- Newcomers who mined
- Newcomers who were industrial workers
- Newcomers who wrote literature and music
- Newcomers who became scientists
- Newcomers who were entertainers

ACTIVITY 6.3   **Documents of the West**

To help bring aspects of settlers in the West alive, have children get acquainted with documents of the west, such as in listening to and retelling folklore, tall tales, lyrics of songs, diaries, biographies, and journals and in writing in simulated journals and diaries. For example:

- Have children sing some of the folk songs and sea chanteys of the time period.
- After reading journals and diaries, have children dramatize the experience of moving west to Oregon by wagon trail. Events in the drama can include how the expeditions were organized, how scouts helped along the trail, where the trails went, and what dangers—including hostile Indians, deserts, rivers, storms, lack of medical assistance—the wagoneers faced.
- Have children locate biographies, journals, and diaries that document the part pioneer women played in the westward expansion. Ask them to report on the women who became farmers, teachers, missionaries, entrepreneurs, and even voters in Wyoming in 1869.
- With maps, ask children to compare and contrast two of the trails, such as the trail to Santa Fe and the trail to Texas. Have children collect background information that relates to the following features on a chart on the board:

FEATURES	TRAIL TO SANTA FE	TRAIL TO TEXAS
1. Purpose of the journal		
2. Where the trail ran		
3. Effect of geography —Climate —Rivers —Vegetation		
4. Life in the settlements at the end of the trail		
5. Reactions of Native Americans to the migration		

Have children offer the background information they have collected about life on the trails and write notes in appropriate spaces on the chart. After discussing the reactions of Native Americans to the migration of travelers along the trails, ask children to give their suggestions about the reasons American Indians had an increasing concern about the migration.

AMERICA IN THE PAST

ACTIVITY 6.4   **Documents of the Past**

Read aloud several phrases from the Declaration of Independence, the Preamble to the Constitution, and the Bill of Rights and have children select two or three of the phrases in each document. Have children give their ideas about the meaning the phrases have for them. Write the children's words on overhead transparencies to show on the projector. Ask children what action they could take now to implement the meaning of the phrases they selected and add their ideas. The following chart shows some possible responses.

Meaning of Phrase	Social Action
"safeguard freedom"	Meet and interview elected officials.
"value diversity"	Develop projects to help others.
"change under law"	Invite judges and officers in the neighborhood to talk about the work they do.
"contribute to welfare of the community"	Beautify the community.

Have children select one of the social actions to implement and ask them to give reasons for their choices. Suggest a class meeting to organize what needs to be done.

AMERICA IN THE PRESENT

Root Words ACTIVITY 6.5

Students can use the study of root words as an integrating language activity for the study of contemporary language in present-day America. With the whole group, invite students to suggest words related to a root word (such as *auto*) to get an idea of other words used today that have been developed from it. Doing this, students can be helped to recognize the root word in other words and get acquainted with word meanings and spellings. For example, the root word *auto* (meaning "self") is the source of several contemporary words, such as *autobiography, automatic,* and *automobile.* On the board, have student volunteers write words in clusters to show the root word in the center and the words that have developed from it. Invite them to illustrate the words with sketches and display them in the classroom.

A Class Magazine ACTIVITY 6.6

Students can use the publication of a class magazine as the integrating activity for the study of their local community. Each student can select an elderly relative or resident in the community as one source of information. They can arrange to interview the person and tape-record the conversation using oral history procedures. The procedures include these:

1. Brainstorm questions to be asked and role-play the first and second interview in advance.
2. Tape-record the first interview and evaluate what was done before role-playing the second one.
3. Have students ask these questions during their interview: How is the way the relative attended school similar to the way you attend school? How is it different? Overall, would you say that the schools were similar? Why or why not? How could we figure out *why* the community has changed over the years? Why do you think the changes occurred? What might have happened if the community had *not* changed? What are some of the ways that communities do not change?

Factual and Futuristic Autobiography ACTIVITY 6.7

To develop and improve writing skills and help students understand the concept of autobiography, real aloud *Bill Peet: An Autobiography* (1989) by Bill Peet. Ask students what they discovered about the author, his experiences, and his life. Discuss the concept of autobiography as an account of a person's life written by the person. It is a record of how a person thinks and feels as he or she experiences life. Engage students in writing their own factual autobiographies up to the present. Have them include information about where they were born, their family members, friends, pets, trips, hobbies, and their likes and dislikes.

When students have finished their factual autobiographies, engage them in writing a futuristic autobiography. Ask them to imagine that they are much older—perhaps 90 years old—and they are now well known in the career they have chosen. They are to imagine that they have been asked to write an autobiography about their accomplishments and experiences. Invite students to brainstorm ideas about what they would like to have accomplished by the time they are 90. Once students have written their futuristic autobiographies, attach their factual autobiographies to the front. Have students share both of their autobiographies in small groups.

SUBJECT INDEX